BASIC CHEMISTRY
for Christian Schools®

BASIC CHEMISTRY FOR CHRISTIAN SCHOOLS®

John S. Wetzel

Bob Jones University Press, Greenville, South Carolina 29614
Textbook Division

NOTE:

The fact that materials produced by other publishers are referred to in this volume does not constitute an endorsement by Bob Jones University Press of the content or theological position of materials produced by such publishers. The position of the Bob Jones University Press, and the University itself, is well known. Any references and ancillary materials are listed as an aid to the student or the teacher and in an attempt to maintain the accepted academic standards of the publishing industry.

BASIC CHEMISTRY for Christian Schools®

John S. Wetzel, M.S.

Produced in cooperation with the Bob Jones University Division of Natural Science of the College of Arts and Science, and Bob Jones Academy.

ISBN 0-89084-285-X

15 14 13 12 11 10 9 8 7 6 5

CONTENTS

Introduction vii
Chapter 1: Science, Chemistry, and You **1**
Science and the Scientific Method 1
The History of Chemistry 4
Chemistry and You 11
Chapter 2: Matter **19**
The Classification of Matter 19
Energy in Matter 26
The Measurement of Matter 30
Chapter 3: Atomic Structure **43**
The Development of Atomic Models 43
The Quantum Model 54
Numbers of Atomic Particles 61
Chapter 4: Elements **71**
The Periodic Table 71
Periodic Trends 78
Descriptive Chemistry 83
Chapter 5: Chemical Bonds **99**
How and Why Atoms Bond 99
The Quantum Model and Bonding 109
Chapter 6: Describing Chemical Composition **127**
Oxidation Numbers 127
Nomenclature 132
The Mole 139
Chapter 7: Describing Chemical Reactions **155**
Writing Equations 156
A Classification Scheme 161
Stoichiometry 165
Chapter 8: Gases **177**
The Nature of Gases 177
Gas Laws 181
Gases and the Mole 193
Chapter 9: Solids and Liquids **209**
Solids 209
Liquids 220

Chapter 10: Water **235**
The Water Molecule 235
The Reactions of Water 244
Water in Compounds 247
Chapter 11: Solutions **253**
The Dissolving Process 253
Measures of Concentration 259
Colligative Properties 264
Colloids 270
Chapter 12: Thermodynamics and Kinetics **277**
Thermodynamics 277
Kinetics 290
Chapter 13: Chemical Equilibrium **305**
Theories of Chemical Equilibrium 305
Applications of Equilibrium Chemistry 315
Chapter 14: Acids, Bases, and Salts **327**
Definitions and Descriptions 327
Equilibria, Acids, and Bases 330
Neutralization 343
Chapter 15: Oxidation-Reduction **353**
Redox Reactions 353
Electrochemical Reactions 366
Chapter 16: Organic Chemistry **379**
Hydrocarbons 379
Substituted Hydrocarbons 396
Chapter 17: Biochemistry **415**
Carbohydrates 416
Proteins 424
Lipids 430
Cellular Processes 433
Chapter 18: Nuclear Chemistry **445**
Natural Radioactivity 445
Induced Reactions 458
Appendixes 469
Glossary 479
Index 490

To the Student

The title *BASIC CHEMISTRY for Christian Schools®* may raise some questions in your mind. First, you might ask, "Why is the word *basic* in the title? Is not chemistry one of those 'killer' courses?" While it is true that chemistry has a reputation for being difficult, the term *basic* applies in several ways. This book is basic in the sense that it contains the central topics of high school chemistry, it explains complicated theories with simple ideas, and it uses an understandable format.

What Is Basic about *BASIC CHEMISTRY*?

Before reading any further, scan over the table of contents on pages v-vi. This year you will study about the make-up of matter, the design of atoms, the periodic table, bonding, formulas, reactions, solutions, acids and bases, and several specialized branches of chemistry. These topics make up a basic, yet comprehensive, high school course.

This chemistry course is basic because simple, fundamental ideas are used to explain concepts. Words, not mathematical equations, are used to describe the content. For example, descriptions of the forces between positive and negative electrical charges help to explain where electrons exist in atoms, why molecules have unique three-dimensional shapes, why some things dissolve in water, and why salt has a very high melting point.

Finally, this book is basic because it is an efficient educational tool. Important terms have been boldfaced in the text and defined in the glossary. Sample problems, with their solutions, are included in the text. Review questions at the end of each chapter give you a chance to practice and solidify what has been learned. These tools can help you to better learn the basic facts of chemistry.

What Is Christian about Chemistry?

A second question that the title *BASIC CHEMISTRY for Christian Schools®* could raise is "What is Christian about chemistry?" Some people have developed the idea that higher mathematics and science have little to do with the Bible or the Christian life. They often think that because chemistry deals with scientific facts, or because it is not pervaded with evolutionary ideas, there is no need to study it from a Christian perspective.

Those with ideas such as these fail to see the many ways that Christianity and chemistry are related. Listed below are several reasons that Christian students should study chemistry.

1. Your knowledge of and faith in God can be increased by a detailed study of creation. When God wished to show Job His wisdom, power, and greatness, He gave Job a tour of the things He had created (Job 38-41). After seeing the intricacies, the grandeur, and the splendor of the universe, Job declared, "I know that thou canst do every thing, and that no thought can be withholden from thee. . . . I have heard of thee by the hearing of the ear: but now mine eye seeth thee" (Job 42:2, 5). Like Job, you can learn new things about God through a study of His creation.
2. Christians can be more effective for the Lord when they combine strong academics with genuine faith in God. Daniel, Moses, Paul, and Luke are examples of men who used their good education to serve the Lord. No matter what career the Lord has planned for you, you should prepare as well as you can. Chemistry is a necessary part of the preparation for many vocations.
3. Chemistry offers unique opportunities for the development of Christian character in your life. Discipline, diligence, accuracy, organization, inquisitiveness, and thoroughness are just a few of the characteristics that you can develop from your study of chemistry.
4. Christian students must be aware of scientific supports for Creation. Often chemistry is involved in the debate on the origin of the universe and life. You should be informed about the laws of thermodynamics, the formation of chemical bonds, and the structure of atoms. While the impressive scientific evidence will not win unsaved men to Christ, it is still important. Christians should be able to show that their faith is sound, reasonable, and superior to any alternative.
5. Spiritual truths must serve as moral guidelines when chemistry is applied in our society. Today's chemists can do many things. They could begin genetic engineering, build many new chemical factories, and make advancements in nuclear power. Yet sometimes the things scientists *could* do are not the things they *should* do. Wisdom, discernment, and sound values—things not learned from academic textbooks—must guide these decisions. The world needs dedicated Christians who are qualified to speak out about these important topics.
6. Christians have been instructed to subdue and care for God's creation. A knowledge of chemistry will help you know how to use, yet not abuse, what God has provided. Even if you

are not a scientist, you are a member of a society that is grappling with the issues of acid rain, nuclear waste, clean air, noise pollution, energy sources, and water purification. You should become informed and take part in the decisions that affect the way in which God's creation will be taken care of.

A Plan of Attack

Tough nuts can be cracked open by a combination of force and strategy. One without the other will not work. Succeeding in chemistry is much like cracking open a nut: it takes a combination of diligent study and an intelligent approach. Nothing takes the place of study, but this plan of attack can make your work more efficient. If chemistry seems like a tough nut to crack, follow these suggestions.

1. Relate new material to previously learned concepts. By doing this, you will avoid becoming swamped with many isolated facts. Only a few concepts will be totally new to you. You will have seen most of the material in your physical science and biology courses.
2. Look for basic explanations of complicated ideas. What seems complicated becomes simple when you understand "why."
3. Develop an appreciation for God's creation. Seeing how marvelous it is will whet your appetite for more.
4. Expose yourself to the industrial applications of chemistry. Many of the review questions illustrate how the theory in the text is applied in the real world.
5. Use the mathematical skills you have learned in the past. Most problems in chemistry rely on the math you learned in algebra. Organize your work, and do it neatly.
6. Keep an open mind about enjoying what you are learning. Small children often miss out on enjoying many delicious foods because they make up their minds ahead of time that they will not like them. Do not deny yourself the fascination of chemistry because you think you will not like it.

May your study of chemistry bring you an increased understanding of the world around you, a solid preparation for future studies, and a heightened interest in science. More importantly, may your studies this year help you to honor Christ and to do His will.

"That in all things He might have the preeminence."
Colossians 1:18

ONE

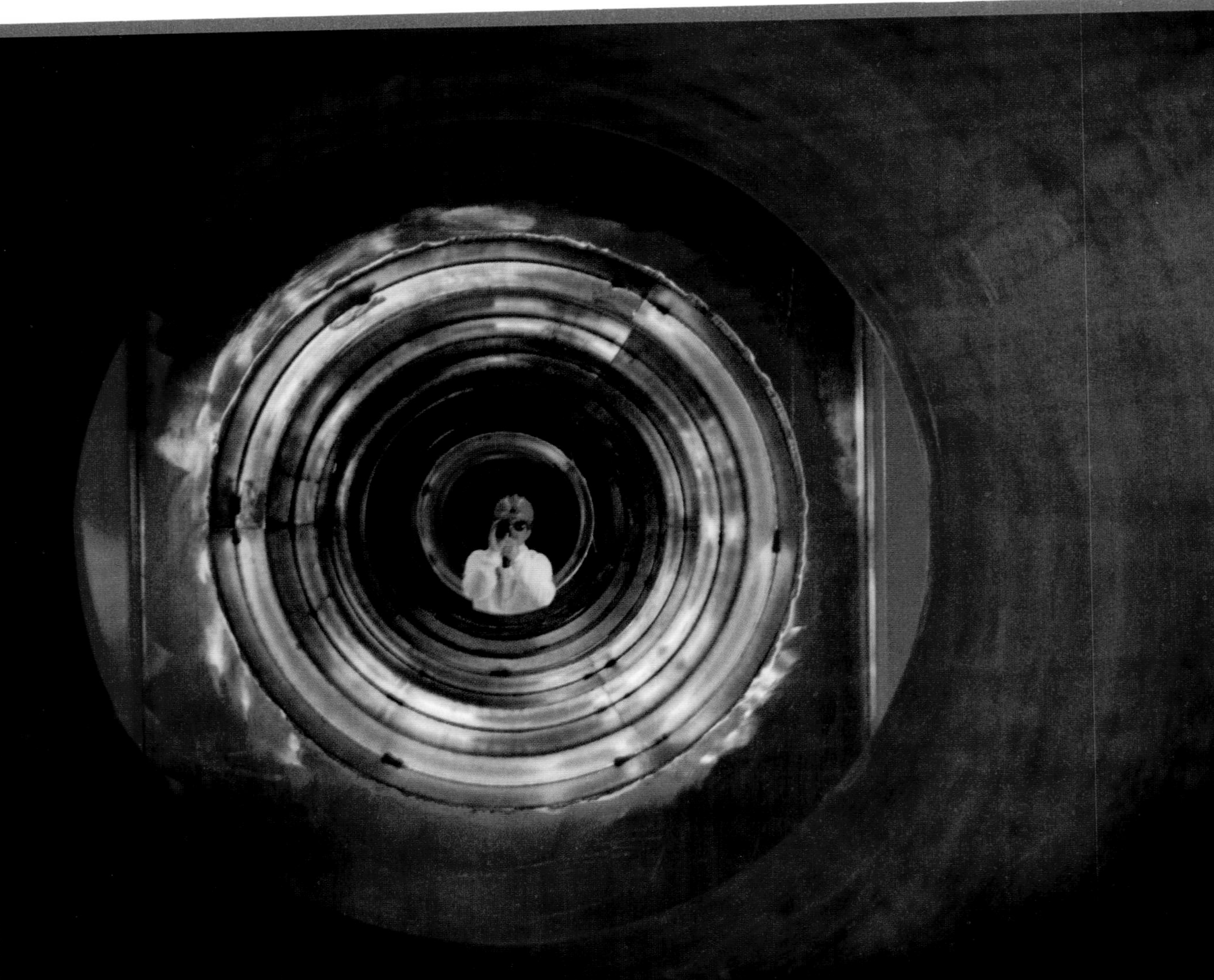

SCIENCE, CHEMISTRY, & YOU

WHAT'S THE CONNECTION?

WHAT is science? For centuries science was a branch of philosophy, and scientists were more like debaters than researchers. Scholars reasoned and argued about the nature of truth and the universe. In the late 1500s science drastically changed. Pure reasoning and argumentation gave way to observation and experimentation. This new way of examining the universe developed into modern science. As scientists studied the creation through observation and experimentation, chemistry emerged as a distinct discipline. With the rich legacy provided by Old Testament craftsmen, Greek philosophers, and medieval alchemists, the science of chemistry soon flourished. Chemistry now touches so many areas of our lives that every person should have some knowledge of this subject.

Science and the Scientific Method

1–1 Inductive Reasoning: Starting with the Facts

Science had remained a stagnant body of knowledge for nearly two thousand years before a certain stout young man received a professorship at the University of Pisa. Within a few months Galileo asked questions that revolutionized the scientific community. Instead of relying on ancient philosophies, he made observations and collected data on his own. He argued that inductive reasoning, not deductive reasoning, was the proper and logical method of approaching a problem. While **deductive reasoning** starts with general statements and works toward specifics, **inductive reasoning** starts with specifics and works toward general conclusions.

This idea of inductive reasoning was vastly different from the prevailing belief that logic always leads to truth. In the past, men rejected observations that went against accepted philosophies. They thought that although the senses could be deceived, rational thought could not. Galileo's experiments brought the conflict between logic and physical evidence to a climax. Just how strong was this controversy? Consider the fate of a fifteenth-century student who dared to suggest that he could determine the number of teeth in a horse's mouth by actually counting them. His enraged professor expelled him from class for his "unscholarly" approach to science.

1-1 Inductive reasoning was not well received in the 1400s.

1–2 The Scientific Method: Not a Formula, but a Process

Inductive reasoning starts with observations. After making observations, scientists often see a problem worth investigating. From their observations they propose general, unproven statements called **hypotheses.** To determine whether their hypotheses are true, the scientists must gather more information, usually from carefully controlled experiments and surveys. If the research proves or disproves the hypotheses, scientists can then frame theories. A theory that is backed by many additional observations and studies is sometimes called a scientific law.

Scientists have modified and expanded the inductive approach to fit their needs. The approach that resulted is called the scientific method. The **scientific method** of inquiry is a general, inductive approach to discovering information about our universe. This general process can be broken down into several steps: recognizing a problem, making observations, proposing a hypothesis, organizing and analyzing data, framing a theory, and verifying the theory. Is this list different from one you have seen before? If so, do not be surprised. There are almost as many versions of the scientific method as there are scientists. Most of these versions can be considered correct, since they merely describe the same process with different words.

The inductive approach is fundamental to the study of the universe. Researchers use it to investigate the mysteries of God's creation and to learn how to use natural laws for man's benefit. **Science** is the systematic study of nature based on observations. Although science is a large number of previously established facts, it is also an on-going activity, a process.

1–3 Theories: Not an End, Just a Beginning

When hypotheses seem workable and are supported by observations, they are called **theories.** Theories play a double role in scientific research. While they usually serve to solve scientific problems, they often introduce new ones! Theories help scientists to organize a body of data, and they also suggest new avenues of research. A theory proposed by William Wollaston in the early 1800s served these two purposes. It helped Wollaston solve a short-range problem and also led him to an unexpected, but major, scientific discovery.

Wollaston was searching for some material that he could use as the reaction vessel when he produced sulfuric acid. After carefully studying platinum, he concluded that its inertness would make it an ideal material. Unfortunately, the platinum metal produced in the 1800s was too brittle to be shaped into the desired forms. Wollaston theorized that impurities caused the brittleness. He ordered laboratory analyses of his platinum, but the reports said that his platinum was pure. Dissatisfied, Wollaston meticulously reanalyzed the metal and found some impurities that had been overlooked. He carefully isolated two substances and identified their properties. When he found no record of substances with these properties, he concluded that he had discovered two new elements. These elements, now called palladium and rhodium, have become important ingredients in high-temperature alloys. Wollaston's fortune resulted from his production of malleable platinum, but his fame came from his discovery of two elements. His theory about impurities in platinum solved one problem, but it also led to a new avenue of research.

When you as a student examine chemical theories, keep in mind that they are not above question. Theories should be examined, not blindly accepted. If you think through the theories used in this text, you will have a more thorough understanding of them. Like Wollaston, you may even hit on a new idea.

1–4 Scientific Laws: Descriptions, Not Rules

The scientific method relies on observations, but observations have limitations. Observations are subjective; therefore, the scientific method cannot make value judgments. Observations can be in error; thus the scientific method can also be in error. Consequently, the scientific method cannot determine truth with absolute certainty. This is an important point, for many students confuse scientific laws with "truth." Simply labeling an idea as a scientific "law" does not make that idea infallible. Many so-called "laws of science" have met a hasty end when confronted with new evidence. Nonetheless, tested, workable **laws** do correctly describe the behavior of matter in God's universe and form the foundations of true science.

If you feel that the ideas of science are a bit unstable, you are right! But this instability is both a limitation and a strength of science. The constant examination of laws and theories allows scientists to upgrade their ideas with each new discovery. Laws and theories can and should be continually verified by new observations. While man's descriptions of creation may change, the God who established the foundational truths of the universe will not change. As Psalm 102:25-27 states, "Of old hast thou laid the foundation of the earth: and the heavens are the work of thy hands. They shall perish, but thou shalt endure: yea, all of them shall wax old like a garment; as a vesture shalt thou change them, and they shall be changed: But thou art the same, and thy years shall have no end."

The History of Chemistry

Chemistry is the study of matter and the observable changes in matter brought about by interactions with energy. This simple definition summarizes the broad scope of chemistry. In the past, however, the scope of chemistry has not been as broad. During ancient times, for example, chemistry had primarily a practical application. As time passed and theory and reasoning became important, chemistry became more philosophical. The emphasis eventually changed again as experimentation replaced reason. Today theory, experimentation, and practical application are all important parts of chemistry.

1–5 The Age of Practical Skills: Old Testament Times

Chemistry developed as a practical skill during Old Testament times. As the descendants of Adam gained the necessary skills to make weapons, tools, and other utensils, they laid the early foundations of chemistry. By the time of Abraham, man had already reached a surprising degree of chemical technology. The Sumerians, for example, were well skilled in **metallurgy,** the science of obtaining metals from their ores. Some of the first metals to be smelted were gold, silver, and copper. These soft metals were easily shaped into jewelry and coins. Old Testament men also manufactured bronze, an alloy made from molten tin and molten copper. The production of bronze provided the right material for making strong metal weapons.

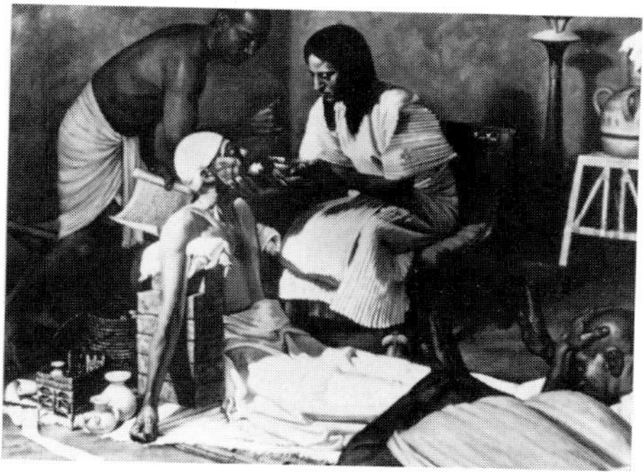

1-2 Early apothecary shops sold many goods, but they focused on the chemicals used for medicinal purposes **(left).** Through trial and error, Egyptian doctors discovered many useful chemicals **(right).**

The Sumerians were not the only civilization developing their chemical technology at this time. The Egyptians were also making great progress, especially in medicine. By the time Joseph was sold into slavery, **apothecaries** were an important part of Egyptian culture. These early pharmacists prepared and sold a wide variety of chemicals and herbs. Surprisingly, several of these substances were effective medicines. A quick search through an apothecary's stockroom would reveal such "prescriptions" as copper salts—used as an antiseptic, magnesia—used as a laxative, opium—used as a sedative, and various herbs—used to treat diseases.

A clay tablet that dates from about the same period as the exodus gives detailed recipes for ceramic finishes on pottery and tiles. The Phoenicians, who are credited with being the first to make soap, used snails to make a dye that served as the basis of a thriving textile business. Their purple cloth was a prized commodity in King Solomon's time.

The development of processed iron had a great military impact on the ancient world. Marauding tribes armed with iron swords swept through the Middle East and even into the Greek peninsula. Until then, the best armament had been the bronze sword. Yet bronze swords splintered into pieces under a heavy blow from the stronger iron weapons. When the Philistines occupied Canaan during the days of Saul, they did not allow the Israelites to make iron weapons (I Sam. 13:19-22). Ironically, the Lord used a young boy's stone instead of an iron sword to defeat the Philistine army.

1–6 The Age of Critical Thought: Greek Influences

From 600 B.C. through the time of the early church, Greek philosophers debated their ideas about matter. Unlike their predecessors, the Greeks desired knowledge rather than practical skills. Luke noted this fact in Acts 17:21: "For all the Athenians and strangers which were there spent their time in nothing else, but either to tell, or to hear some new thing." The Greeks were the first to introduce a systematic approach to chemistry. This use of critical thinking was important to the Greeks, for they prided themselves in their disciplined minds and bodies. Just as the Olympic competitions tested physical strength, logical arguments tested the mind.

The theories developed by the Greek philosophers were so logical that they dominated science for the next two thousand years. In some ways, however, this domination hindered the development of chemistry. The Greeks' high regard for logic and their lack of equipment prevented them from making observations and doing experiments. Because the Greeks did not test their ideas, their theories contained several major errors. For instance, they thought that the universe was made of four elements: earth, wind, fire, and water.

1–7 The Age of Applied Experimentation: The Alchemists

During the time of Christ, a large scientific community formed in Alexandria, Egypt. Greeks who traveled to this center of learning blended their deductive logic with the ancient skills of the apothecaries. It was in ancient writings from this Greco-Egyptian city that the word *chemia,* from which the word *chemistry* is derived, first appeared. Although some claim that *chemia* comes from the name of a legendary apothecary, the word probably comes from the Egyptian word for "black." Either way, the label "black" fits well, for the strange skills practiced in Alexandria were much like black arts.

As the influence of the Roman empire shrunk, the Arabs took control of Alexandria. Fascinated by the black arts, Arab scholars learned all they could. As "chemia" became a part of their culture, they added the Arabic *al* (the) and called it **alchemy.** Alchemy spread into Europe with the Arab conquest of Spain. One of the first major alchemists in Europe was Jabir ibn-Hayyan. Geber (the English version of his name) wrote many books about chemical techniques. He distilled acetic acid from vinegar, prepared nitric acid, and studied the transmutation of metals.

The alchemists gradually forsook practical studies to pursue the secret of converting ordinary metals into gold. Many royal courts financed such searches for an unlimited source of gold. Not surprisingly, many charlatans sought royal funds, so they resorted to trickery. False bottoms in kettles, hollow stirring rods, and other similar devices were used to deceive noblemen and to keep the royal funds flowing. Alchemists also believed that magical powders could cure diseases and extend lifespans. These false hopes fueled the legends of "elixirs of life" and "fountains of youth" that lured Ponce de Leon to the New World.

1-4 While alchemists are usually thought of as frauds or deluded fools, they made important contributions to the field of chemistry.

Despite their failures, alchemists did provide modern chemistry with a rich legacy of techniques and laboratory equipment. Alchemists developed techniques such as distillation, sublimation, precipitation, and crystallization. They also were master designers of glassware and porcelain. But the most important contribution of the alchemists was their experimental approach. Francis Bacon noted this contribution when he wrote:

> Alchemy was like the man who told his sons he had left them gold buried somewhere in his vineyard; where they by digging found no gold, but by turning up the [dirt] about the roots procured a plentiful vintage.

1-5 An early pharmacy.

Alchemy made its first steps toward modern chemistry under the guidance of the Swiss alchemist Philippus Paracelsus. In the early 1500s Paracelsus promoted the use of chemicals to treat disease. Convinced that this was the future direction of alchemy, he influenced his fellow alchemists to supply compounds for physicians. This application of chemistry to medicine became the forerunner of modern pharmacology.

1–8 The Rise of Modern Chemistry: The Transition

Not until the middle of the 1600s did chemists dispute the Greek idea of the four basic elements. Robert Boyle proposed a completely new definition of elements. He said that elements are substances that cannot be chemically decomposed into simpler substances.

1-6 Chemists of the 1700s used glassware like this as they identified the elements.

Earth, air, fire, and water could not be called elements by this new definition. Chemists were on the verge of discovering the basic units of matter.

One of the most significant elements to be discovered was oxygen. In 1774 Joseph Priestley heated mercuric calx—mercury(II) oxide—and obtained a gas in which substances easily burned. Shortly thereafter, the French chemist Antoine Lavoisier observed that several substances *gained* rather than lost weight after combustion. After a series of carefully controlled experiments, Lavoisier concluded that Priestley's gas was a common substance in the air that combined with other substances in combustion. Lavoisier named Priestley's discovery oxygen. Lavoisier's use of the scientific method and his reliance on careful measurements served as a model for many other chemists. His work earned him a spot among the founders of modern chemistry.

1–9 Chemistry Today

By 1800 chemistry had become an academic discipline. In the New World several colleges made chemistry a part of their curriculum. Benjamin Rush was the first professor of chemistry in the United States. His lectures at the Philadelphia Medical School

FACETS OF CHEMISTRY

The Scientific Method of Antoine Lavoisier

Substances lose weight when they burn, right? After all, a hefty log turns into a small pile of ashes after a night in a campfire! Observations like this led many scientists to assume that burning always decreased the mass of a substance. Early scientists thought that burning allowed a mysterious substance called phlogiston to escape. The loss of phlogiston supposedly accounted for the decrease in weight during burning. Yet one observant scientist saw something that threatened the widely accepted phlogiston theory. On November 1, 1772, the French chemist Antoine Lavoisier delivered a sealed note to the secretary of the French Academy of Sciences.

"About eight days ago I discovered that sulfur in burning, far from losing weight, on the contrary, gains it; it is the same with phosphorus. This increase in weight arises from a prodigious quantity of air that is consumed during combustion. . . . The discovery, which I have established by experiments which I regard as decisive, has led me to think that what is observed in the combustion of sulfur and phosphorus may well take place in the case of all substances that gain weight by combustion."

Lavoisier had observed a significant gain in weight when phosphorus and sulfur burned. This contradicted the prevailing idea that all substances lost weight when they burned. Lavoisier recognized that this set the foundation stone of chemical education in the new nation. At Princeton, professors attacked the old Greek ideas and used demonstrations and experiments in their teaching. These early professors foreshadowed the importance the United States would achieve in chemistry within the next two centuries.

As chemical knowledge expanded throughout the world, specialized branches of chemistry developed. Scientists were soon forced to concentrate in one area. The branch of **organic chemistry** developed as a result of investigations by Friedrich Wohler. Until 1826 it was commonly believed that organic compounds could be produced only by living organisms. Wohler amazed the scientific community by synthesizing urea (a waste product from animals) from two "inorganic" compounds. This discovery provided the foundation for a new branch of chemistry: the study and synthesis of organic compounds.

Soon other branches of chemistry developed. **Inorganic chemistry, analytical chemistry, physical chemistry, nuclear chemistry,** and **biochemistry** soon developed into separate fields. Today these branches overlap considerably. For example, a chemist who studies the rate at which aspirin (an organic compound) forms could be called a physical organic chemist.

1-7 A modern chemical laboratory.

contradiction posed a problem well worth investigating. Were sulfur and phosphorus isolated exceptions to the phlogiston theory, or was the entire theory faulty? After careful study of the matter, Lavoisier proposed a daring hypothesis: Substances *gain* something from the atmosphere when they burn. This idea went against the accepted theory and would not be listened to without experimental proof. To prove that his hypothesis was correct, Lavoisier knew he must first identify the "something" from the atmosphere that substances gain when they burn.

At first Lavoisier suspected that carbon dioxide caused the increase in mass. Several experiments soon proved that carbon dioxide would not support combustion of any type. The discovery of oxygen by fellow chemist Joseph Priestley gave several valuable clues. When heated, mercuric calx (a compound of oxygen and mercury) releases large quantities of oxygen gas and leaves silvery, elemental mercury behind. Lavoisier duplicated Priestley's procedure with this blood-red compound. The results of this experiment gave Lavoisier necessary insight into his problem. Perhaps oxygen was the component of air that combined with burning substances and increased their masses. To test this idea, Lavoisier developed a controlled experimental procedure to produce mercuric calx from mercury and ordinary air and then from mercury and pure oxygen. Both procedures produced the same compound. Oxygen was the substance in the air that combined with substances as they burned!

Lavoisier began with a problem, made observations, researched and defined the problem, and then developed a hypothesis. He then conducted experiments in which he gathered more observations, chose his solution, and then verified it. His consistent use of the scientific method in his chemical investigation did not guarantee success, but it did keep him on the right path. With the help of other researchers and a keen mind, Lavoisier made a discovery that changed the theoretical framework of chemistry.

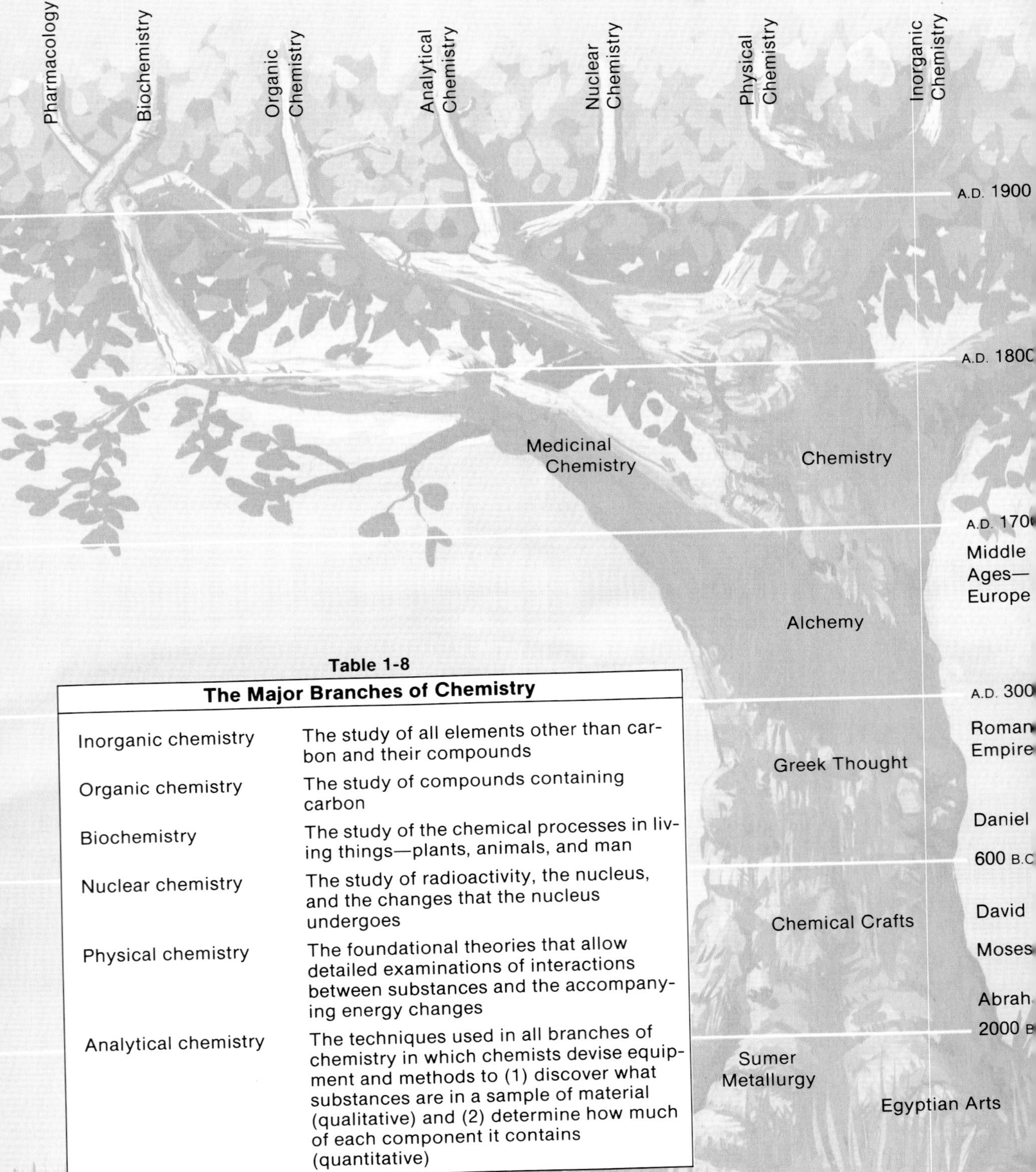

Table 1-8

The Major Branches of Chemistry	
Inorganic chemistry	The study of all elements other than carbon and their compounds
Organic chemistry	The study of compounds containing carbon
Biochemistry	The study of the chemical processes in living things—plants, animals, and man
Nuclear chemistry	The study of radioactivity, the nucleus, and the changes that the nucleus undergoes
Physical chemistry	The foundational theories that allow detailed examinations of interactions between substances and the accompanying energy changes
Analytical chemistry	The techniques used in all branches of chemistry in which chemists devise equipment and methods to (1) discover what substances are in a sample of material (qualitative) and (2) determine how much of each component it contains (quantitative)

"In the beginning God created the heaven and the earth."

Just as the branches of chemistry overlap with each other, the entire subject of chemistry overlaps with other subjects. For example, the production of new elements and the study of subatomic particles blends physics with nuclear chemistry. Likewise, studies of protein structure combine biology and biochemistry. Today chemistry contains so many important topics that it is now the largest scientific discipline in the world.

Chemistry and You

At this moment you have a set of preconceived ideas about what chemistry is, what this course holds in store for you, and how chemistry will affect your life. Take a minute to focus on your attitudes toward chemistry. You may be already interested in the marvels of God's creation, and you may be looking forward to learning more about its composition. You may be thinking about chemistry's reputation for being a difficult course. You may see it as just another requirement for graduation and admission to some college program. You might be asking, "How can chemistry benefit me in the future?" That is a fair question, and it deserves a straightforward answer.

1–10 Character Development

A chemistry course provides a unique opportunity for you to develop academic and personal character. Learning about electrons, periodic tables, and acids is important because of the scientific ideas involved. But the study of chemistry also promotes self-discipline by requiring diligence and organization. As challenging material comes your way, you have the opportunity to respond with effort and a determination to do your best.

1-9 Successful laboratory work requires organization, skill, attention to details, and accurate observations.

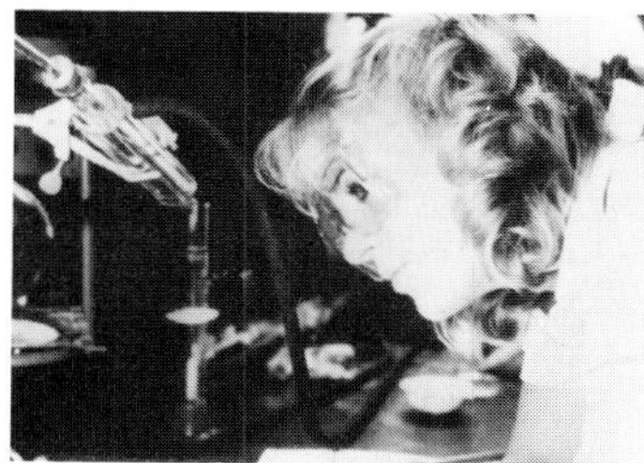

This book is designed to help you understand the major concepts in chemistry, not to supply you with thousands of facts. Facts are necessary, but they do not stand independently. Concepts and principles must relate facts to each other and provide an organized framework. Do not be satisfied with memorizing facts. Instead, force yourself to see relationships between facts and to understand the concepts and the principles.

The process of investigating chemistry in the laboratory also allows you to develop your character. Before you begin an experiment, you must organize and schedule your work. While carrying out an experiment, you must use precise physical skills such as measuring and filtering. You must also report observations accurately and honestly. At the end of each experiment, you must analyze your work, identify errors, and develop logical conclusions based on experimental results. Habits of carefulness and industriousness developed in the laboratory will serve you well in the future.

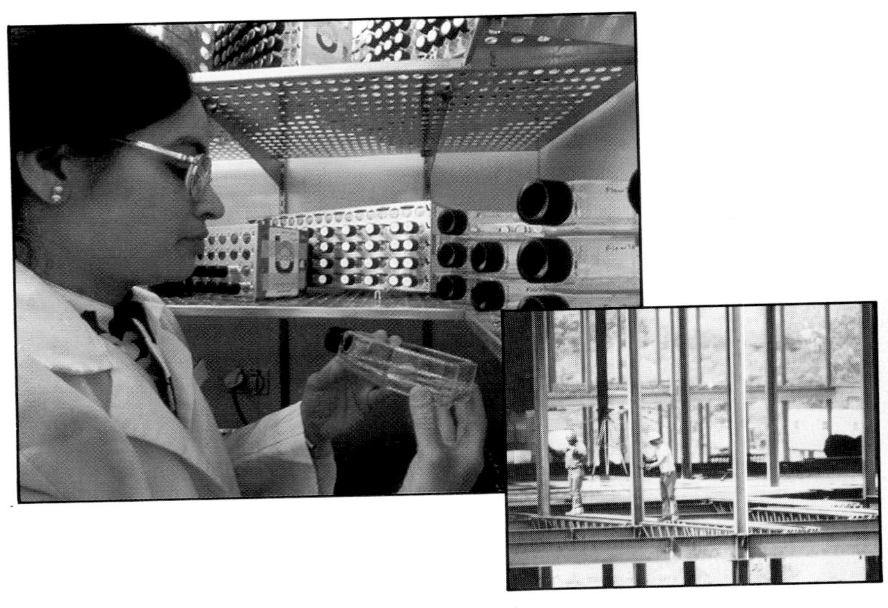

1-10 A knowledge of chemistry can be useful in almost every vocation.

1–11 Vocational Preparation

Why study chemistry? Because it will prepare you for your life's work. A knowledge of chemistry helps those who will work in both technical and nontechnical jobs. No matter what occupation you foresee for yourself, a chemistry course can help you reach your potential in that field.

Obviously, chemical researchers need a strong background in chemistry. Some research chemists work in the area of pure science. They seek to extend scientific knowledge for the sake of finding out new facts about matter. Although the main intent of these researchers is not to develop new commercial products, practical applications often result from their work. Most chemists, however, work in the area of applied science. They seek to use scientific knowledge to create useful products. Chemists in many industries are constantly developing new fabrics, cosmetics, plastics, fuels, paints, foods, pesticides, drugs, and fertilizers. All chemists, whether they are working with pure or with applied science, need a strong foundation of chemical knowledge. High school chemistry serves as the cornerstone of this foundation and as a stepping stone to new ideas.

Photographers, architects, farmers, cosmetologists, nurses, dental hygienists, meteorologists, pharmacists, and x-ray technicians are not what you would call practicing chemists. Nevertheless, they rely on chemistry to do their jobs. A knowledge of chemical principles is recommended, if not required, for jobs such as these.

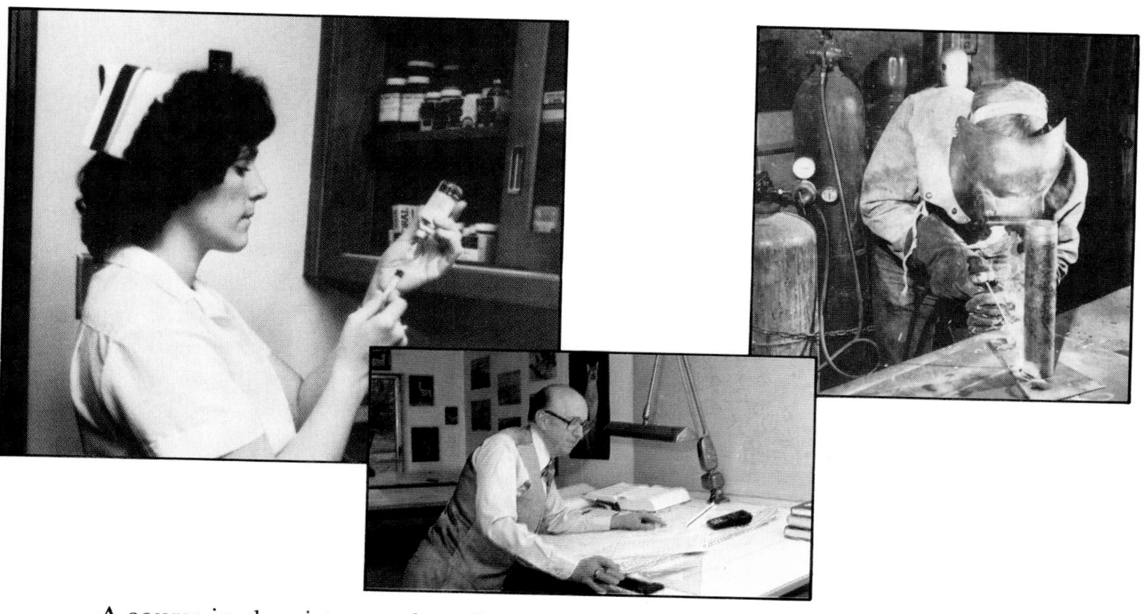

A course in chemistry can benefit you even if you do not foresee a career in chemistry or some other technical field. What help is chemistry to housewives, mechanics, and businessmen? More than you might think. Housewives who provide nutritious meals want to substitute polyunsaturated fats for saturated fats. Chemistry can help these housewives to choose the best foods and to understand the reasons for their choices. Mechanics should know about octane numbers, leaded gasoline, and nitrous oxide pollutants to be knowledgeable in their field. Future businessmen can also benefit from chemistry. Today's society is becoming more technical every day. To be a knowledgeable consumer, you need an understanding of the materials that you buy for your own use and sell in your business. No matter what your future vocation may be, a knowledge of the basic principles of chemistry can help you function better in our society.

1–12 Expanded Christian Witness

Those who have accepted Jesus Christ as their personal Saviour have an additional, compelling reason to learn about chemistry. Christians are in this world to tell others about Christ and His redeeming work. In many cases they can witness for Christ more effectively if they have prepared themselves in a wide variety of fields, including chemistry.

As diplomats for Christ and His Kingdom, Christians must do all they can to present the gospel clearly to as many people as possible. Good political diplomats not only refrain from bad behavior, but they also try to relate to the people of their host country. They follow local traditions, dress well, and do their best to learn the people's language. Diplomats for Christ also have this two-fold task of refraining from bad behavior and relating to the people of this world. They must develop their personalities, educate themselves, meet people, and express the gospel well. It would be a tragedy if a Christian neglected to develop himself and became a hindrance to the spread of the gospel.

God puts no premium on ignorance. Christians can be more effective for God if they seize opportunities to learn. Although God does use sincere but unschooled people, He does not approve of people's wasting opportunities to develop their minds. Scripture tells of many men who were used by God to do great things after they had diligently prepared themselves. The apostle Paul commanded respect across the world because of his formal schooling, his fluency in several languages, and his knowledge of literature. These abilities opened many doors to Paul and gave him an expanded witness. Luke, the author of Acts, was a medical doctor and an eloquent writer. He was privileged to use both these skills during the days of the early church. Moses, most noted for his spiritual leadership, was also learned in the medicinal and chemical knowledge of the Egyptians. This knowledge and the respect it commanded very likely helped him to gain access to Pharaoh's court and equipped him to lead the Israelites. Daniel had a tremendous influence on the Babylonian and the Medo-Persian empires because of his great character and wisdom. He gained these qualities by studying diligently as a teenager. Each of these men had a great impact for the Lord because of the way they prepared themselves for His service. None of these spiritual heroes could have been as effective as they were had they neglected their opportunities to learn.

1–13 Enhanced Appreciation of God

> By the word of the Lord were the heavens made; and all the host of them by the breath of his mouth. He gathereth the waters of the sea together as an heap: he layeth up the depth in storehouses. Let all the earth fear the Lord: let all the inhabitants of the world stand in awe of him. For he spake, and it was done; he commanded, and it stood fast (Ps. 33:6-9).

God's voice spoke into existence a universe that is wondrous to behold. Stars, some so large that they would reach out to Mars if they replaced the sun, are scattered across galaxies. Our earth hangs in space with nothing but carefully balanced forces holding it in place. The beauty of a sunset, a forest, and the Grand Canyon deserve a reverent respect. Even the casual observer can see proofs of God's existence and His awesome power. Romans 1:20 says that "the invisible things of him from the creation of the world are clearly seen, being understood by the things that are made, even his eternal power and Godhead."

Like everyone else, chemistry students see evidences of God's power and existence. They also have the opportunity to observe many additional attributes of God in His creation. Orderliness and logic can be seen in the structure of crystals. A concern for details is evident in the architecture of atoms. Natural laws such as the laws of thermodynamics reveal God's sovereignty. God's goodness is obvious when we consider the abundant provisions He has given to sustain life. The intricate structure of a DNA molecule generates a sense of beauty and creativity. Yes, nature shows God's omnipotence, but it also displays many of His other attributes. A careful study of the universe will enhance your appreciation of its Author.

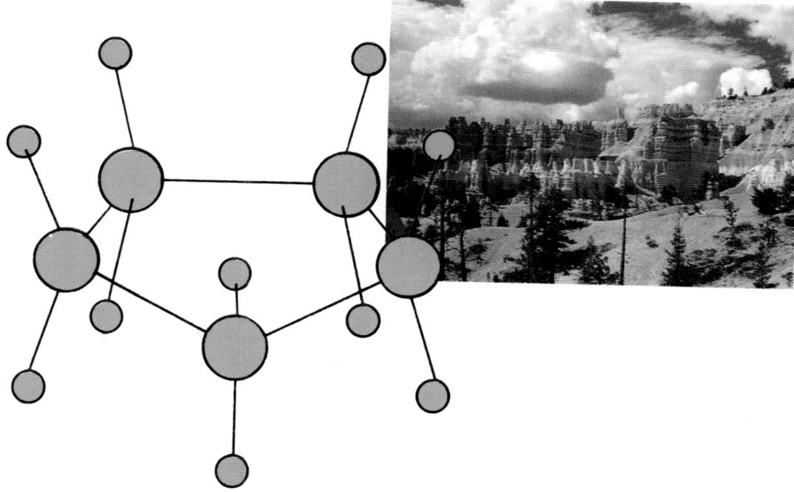

1-11 The closer we study creation, the more we learn about the Creator.

Coming to Terms

deductive reasoning
inductive reasoning
hypothesis
scientific method
science
theory
law
chemistry
metallurgy
apothecary
alchemy
organic chemistry
inorganic chemistry
analytical chemistry
physical chemistry
nuclear chemistry
biochemistry

Review Questions

1. What is the difference between inductive and deductive reasoning? Which type of reasoning do scientists use to develop theories?
2. By what criteria did the Greeks judge their scientific ideas? What criteria do modern scientists use?
3. What crucial difference separates the Greek philosophers from modern chemists?
4. List one version of the scientific method.
5. Can scientific laws be proved to be wrong? Why or why not?
6. Describe how men in Old Testament times practiced chemistry. Why did the Greeks pursue science? the alchemists?
7. Although alchemists are sometimes criticized, they developed several things that benefit modern chemists. What are they?
8. What is the difference between organic chemistry and inorganic chemistry?
9. Tell which type of chemistry is being performed (organic, inorganic, analytical, physical, nuclear, or biochemistry). Give more than one answer when appropriate.
   a. A representative of the Food and Drug Administration (FDA) determines what kinds of vitamins are present in a box of cereal.
   b. A NASA (National Aeronautical and Space Administration) chemist studies the amount of energy that is released when a shuttle is launched.
   c. A chemist studies how DNA (deoxyribonucleic acid) controls the growth of a certain type of cancer. DNA is a molecule that controls the transfer of genetic information.
   d. A chemist determines how much energy a jogger uses in one hour.
   e. Wollaston searches for impurities in platinum.

f. A chemist develops a method to synthesize octane, which is composed of carbon and hydrogen.
g. A chemist studies methods for plating zinc onto a new steel alloy consisting of iron, chrome, and molybdenum.

10. Name four ways in which a knowledge of chemistry can benefit Christians.
11. Classify each of the following activities as pure chemistry, applied chemistry, or both.
    a. Determining how much energy is released when iron forms rust
    b. Determining how the size of silver grains on photographic film affects the resolution of the finished print
    c. Isolating a chemical compound from the leaves of a newly discovered tropical plant
    d. Developing a method of purifying the polluted well-water of Woburn, Massachusetts
    e. Determining what elements exist on a distant star
12. Which of the following people are performing tasks or using items based on knowledge acquired by chemists?
    a. A beautician removing fingernail polish with liquid fingernail-polish remover
    b. A housewife using bleach to remove stains from a shirt
    c. A fireman using a carbon dioxide fire extinguisher to put out a fire
    d. A lawyer trying to prove someone's guilt based on the fact that a certain poison was found in the victim's body
    e. A student washing bicycle grease off his hands with turpentine instead of water
    f. A carpenter choosing whether to buy aluminum or iron nails
    g. A motorist adding a fuel treatment to his car's gas tank to remove water from the gasoline
    h. An artist painting with acrylic polymer paint
    i. A doctor trying to diagnose a patient's problems with the aid of a blood analysis
    j. A pastor describing the properties of fire and brimstone
    k. A church board deciding on the type of roof to put on a new church building
    l. A secretary using a copying machine that produces two-color copies
13. The text mentioned how knowledge and training enabled Moses, Daniel, Paul, and Luke to serve the Lord more effectively. Can you name several other biblical characters who used their intellects and training to serve God?

TWO

MATTER

WHAT CHEMISTRY IS ALL ABOUT

THE materials that make up the physical universe were created out of nothing (*ex nihilo*) by God. There is no conclusive proof for or against this statement. It is a statement of faith and the foundational truth in a Christian perspective of chemistry.

"Through faith we understand that the worlds were framed by the word of God, so that things which are seen were not made of things which do appear" (Heb. 11:3).

What is matter? *Matter* is difficult to define because it encompasses practically everything. To establish a meaning for this basic term, scientists define matter by the way it is measured. Since the measurable properties common to all matter are volume and mass, **matter** is operationally defined as "anything that takes up space and has mass."

The Classification of Matter

The world that God spoke into existence contains a variety of materials. Cars, electrons, people, sand, uranium, trees, and sulfuric acid are just a few of the many types of matter. A study of all this matter needs the organization that a good classification scheme can provide. Although there are many possible classification systems, this text will use one that divides matter into two major categories: pure substances and mixtures. Distinctions will be made between the two categories on the basis of the physical and chemical properties of matter.

2–1 Chemical and Physical Properties

Properties are the distinguishing characteristics of matter. Scientists divide these characteristics into two classes: physical and chemical. The **physical properties** of a material are related to the physical relationships among the particles in that material. How many particles are there? How do they move? How closely are they packed together? Many times physical properties of matter are defined as properties that a person can measure without changing the material. Scientists can measure color, shape, texture, odor, taste, electrical conductivity, and density without changing the material.

Chemists use several physical properties to describe matter. **Density** describes how the particles are "packed" into a material. Dense objects have many particles packed into a relatively small space. Less dense objects have fewer particles in the same space. Materials that are **malleable** can be easily hammered into shapes. Some materials can be drawn into thin wires. This property is called **ductility. Conductivity** measures the ability of a material to transfer heat or electricity between its particles.

2-1 The processing of steel involves both chemical and physical changes. A powerful press causes a steel part to undergo a physical change **(top).** Impurities can be removed from molten steel because they react chemically with oxygen **(bottom).**

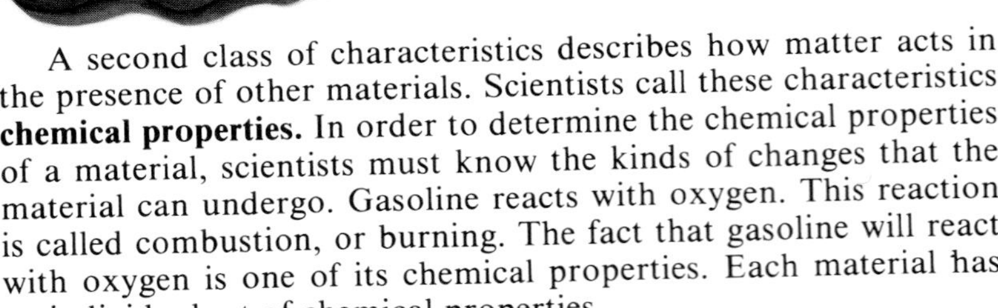

A second class of characteristics describes how matter acts in the presence of other materials. Scientists call these characteristics **chemical properties.** In order to determine the chemical properties of a material, scientists must know the kinds of changes that the material can undergo. Gasoline reacts with oxygen. This reaction is called combustion, or burning. The fact that gasoline will react with oxygen is one of its chemical properties. Each material has an individual set of chemical properties.

The terms *physical change* and *chemical change* are closely associated with the two sets of properties. Changes that occur in a material without changing the identity of the material are **physical changes.** Physical changes cause changes in both state and shape. Boiling is a physical change in which a material changes from its liquid state to its gaseous state. The identity of the material is not altered.

Chemical changes, or **chemical reactions,** are changes in the identity of a material. When iron rusts, it undergoes a chemical change. The iron particles combine with oxygen particles to form rust. These new particles are totally different from oxygen or iron particles. The chart below contains a comparison of physical and chemical changes.

Table 2-2

	Physical Changes	Chemical Changes
Definition	A change in state or shape that does not alter the identity of the material	A change in the composition of the particles of a material that alters the identity of the material
Particle changes	The positions of the particles may change.	The composition of the particles will change.
Results	Chemical properties are not altered.	New particles are formed that have different chemical and physical properties.
Examples	Ice melting, flour ground from wheat, sugar dissolved in water	Metal rusting, oil burning, wood rotting, food digesting

2–2 Pure Substances and Mixtures

The chemical and physical properties of matter are used to divide matter into separate categories. The general and specific classes are arranged in Figure 2-3.

2-3 Classification of Matter

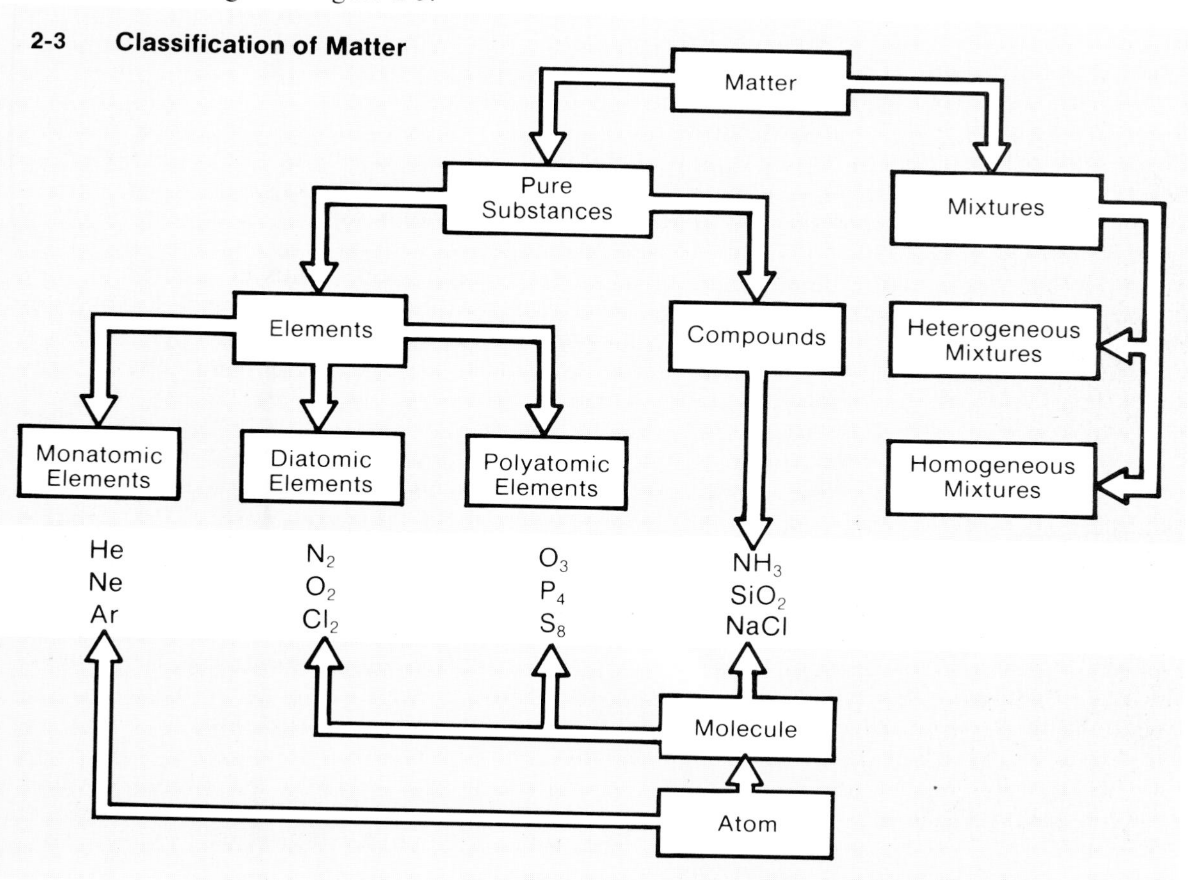

Pure substances are made up of only one kind of particle. Gold contains only gold particles, water contains only water particles. Mixtures contain two or more kinds of basic substances. Bronze has tin and copper particles in it, and sweetened ice tea has, among other things, water particles, sugar particles, and the particles that give that tea flavor. As Figure 2-3 shows, both pure substances and mixtures can be subdivided into smaller, more specific categories.

2–3 Elements and Their Symbols

A pure substance that cannot be broken down into a simpler substance by ordinary chemical means is an **element.** Men have known about several elements, such as gold, silver, sulfur, tin, and lead, since biblical times. Scientists discovered many others shortly after the rise of modern science in the 1800s. In addition, other elements have recently been synthesized in the laboratories of nuclear scientists. You can see these elements represented on any periodic table.

Atoms are the particles in elements. They are the smallest particles that are completely unique to the elements they compose. For example, a lump of sulfur is made up of sulfur atoms.

Elements such as neon, helium, and argon, whose atoms do not naturally bond, are called **monatomic elements.** Monatomic elements are rare, for most atoms bond with other atoms to form molecules. Elements whose atoms bond into two-atom units are called **diatomic elements.** O_2 and H_2 are examples of diatomic elements. By the same line of reasoning, elements composed of multi-atom units are called **polyatomic elements.** For instance, sulfur often exists in the form of eight atoms bonded into an S_8 unit.

Each element has a special **symbol** that represents its name. The first letter of many elements serves as the symbol for their names (H for hydrogen, N for nitrogen, and O for oxygen). Frequently the names of more than one element have the same first letter. To avoid confusion, a second lower-case letter is used in the symbol. The second lower-case letter is usually related to the sound of the element's name. The single letter C is the symbol for carbon, Ca stands for calcium, and Cd represents cadmium.

For some elements that were known in ancient times, the Latin names serve as the basis of the symbols.

Cu (*cuprum*) copper	Hg (*hydrargyrum*) mercury
Fe (*ferrum*) iron	K (*kalium*) potassium
Ag (*argentum*) silver	Na (*natrium*) sodium

FACETS OF CHEMISTRY

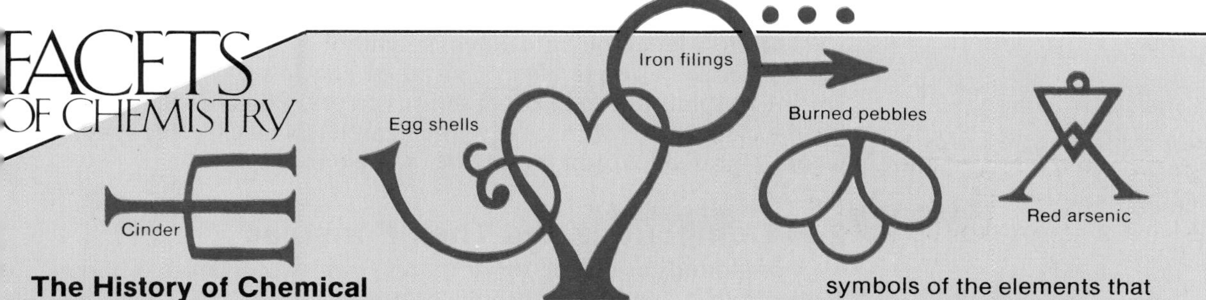

The History of Chemical Symbols

A student in the early 1800s sat down to study his chemistry text. Chemistry was his favorite subject, but reading the text was one task he always dreaded. He began but quickly became mired in a bog of strange symbols that made no sense at all. The student recognized one symbol but then found that another symbol meant the same thing. One book in the university's library used twenty different symbols for mercury. Another book used fourteen different symbols for lead. "This mess of symbols must be cleaned up and replaced with something better," he muttered.

Metallurgists developed the first symbols for elements. The metals they worked with eventually became associated with gods and planets that were known in ancient times. Ancient symbols for the metals tell of the Egyptian, Persian, Greek, and Roman associations.

☉ Gold—The "perfect" metal received the symbol of perfection and divinity.

☽ Silver—The metal with the luster of moonlight received the shape of the moon for its symbol.

♀ Copper—The goddess Venus was supposedly formed near copper mines on Cyprus. The symbol for copper pictures the looking glass of the goddess of beauty.

♄ Lead—This metal was associated with Saturn, the god of harvest, and his scythe.

♂ Iron—The metal used in weapons received a symbol that showed the lance and shield of Mars, the god of war.

♃ Tin—The thunderbolt of Jupiter served as tin's symbol.

☿ Mercury—This flowing liquid metal became associated with Mercury, the messenger of the gods. Mercury's wand was used as the symbol.

The alchemists produced many new symbols. Drawing their symbols often required artistic skill and time. The alchemists probably used their symbols to create a scholarly atmosphere and to hide their ignorance of chemistry.

In the early 1800s John Dalton designed a system of symbols to illustrate the different kinds of atoms. He drew various symbols inside circles to designate the different elements. Dalton represented compounds by combining the symbols of the elements that were in the compounds.

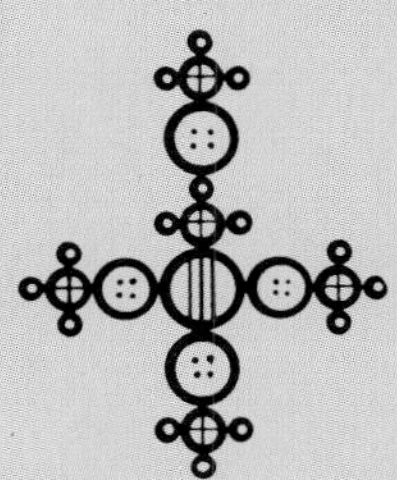

Soon after Dalton introduced his system, a Swedish chemist named Jons Berzelius developed a system of abbreviations. He included several revolutionary ideas in his system: "It is easier to write an abbreviated word than to draw a figure which has little analogy with words. The chemical signs ought to be letters for the greater facility of writing and not disfigure a printed book. I shall therefore take for the chemical sign the initial letter of the Latin name of each chemical element. If the first two letters be common to two metals, I shall use both the initial letter and the first letter they have not in common."

Soon Berzelius's abbreviations became accepted and understood all over the world. Today the conglomeration of confusing symbols has yielded to a unified, reasonable, and understandable system of chemical symbols.

The first letter of an element's symbol is always capitalized, but a second letter is always given in the lower case. Careless writing of symbols can result in serious errors. Consider the symbol for the element cobalt: Co. If written carelessly as CO, this symbol would represent carbon monoxide, a poisonous gas.

2–4 Compounds and Their Formulas

Compounds are made up of atoms from two or more different elements that have been chemically bonded together. As you may have guessed, there are many more compounds than elements. Just as symbols represent elements, formulas represent compounds. **Formulas** tell the type and number of atoms that are present in compounds. Carbon monoxide, a molecule that can bind with the oxygen-carrying portions of red blood cells and destroy their effectiveness, is represented by the formula CO. This formula tells chemists that the individual units of this compound contain one carbon atom that has been bonded to one oxygen atom. Another compound of carbon and oxygen is carbon dioxide (CO_2). This compound consists of one carbon atom bonded to two oxygen atoms. Other common compounds, their formulas, and the atoms they contain are listed in Table 2-4.

Table 2-4

Common Compounds and Their Formulas

Compound	Formula	Atoms
Ammonia	NH_3	1 nitrogen, 3 hydrogen
Rust	Fe_2O_3	2 iron, 3 oxygen
Sucrose	$C_{12}H_{22}O_{11}$	12 carbon, 22 hydrogen, 11 oxygen
Slaked lime	$Ca(OH)_2$	1 calcium, 2 oxygen, 2 hydrogen
Salt	NaCl	1 sodium, 1 chlorine
Water	H_2O	2 hydrogen, 1 oxygen

Numbers written at the lower right of a chemical symbol are called **subscripts.** They indicate the number of atoms or groups of atoms in a formula. A unit of water contains two hydrogen atoms and a single oxygen atom (the 1 is assumed). When a subscript follows a group of symbols that are surrounded by parentheses, it refers to the entire group. $Ca(OH)_2$ contains two OH groups for a total of two oxygen atoms and two hydrogen atoms. A number in front of a formula is called a **coefficient** and refers to the entire unit. Thus $5Fe_2O_3$ refers to five Fe_2O_3 groups, for a total of ten iron atoms and fifteen oxygen atoms.

Sample Problem. How many atoms of each element are present in each of the following groups?

a. $Na_2S_2O_3$ b. $Mg(NO_3)_2$ c. $3CaBr_2$

Solution.

a. The subscripts show that two Na atoms, two S atoms, and three O atoms are present.

b. No subscript after the Mg implies that only one atom is present. The subscript of 2 after the (NO_3) means that two NO_3 groups are present for a total of two N atoms and six O atoms.

c. A single $CaBr_2$ group would have one Ca atom and two Br atoms. The coefficient 3 refers to three of these groups. Tripling the number of atoms in one group gives a total of three Ca atoms and six Br atoms.

Molecules are the smallest independent units in many compounds. A **molecule** consists of two or more atoms that are bonded together. H_2O is a molecule, as is NH_3 and $C_{12}H_{22}O_{11}$. Diatomic and polyatomic elements are also made up of molecules; O_2 and S_8 qualify because they contain two or more atoms.

2-5 Elements, Compounds, and Mixtures

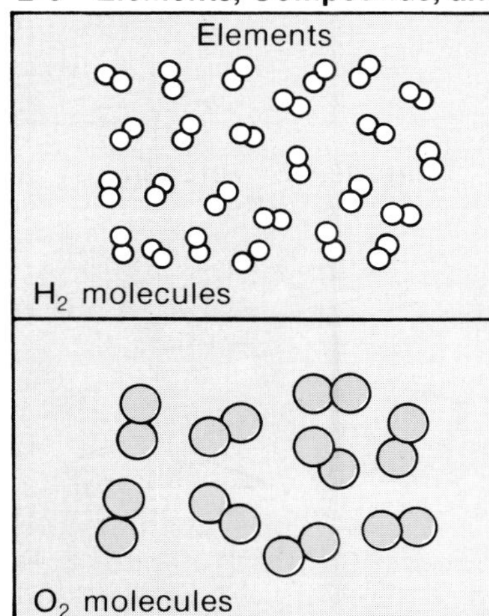

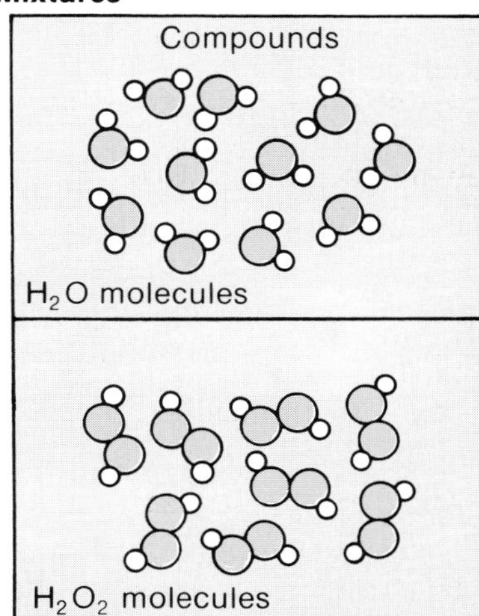

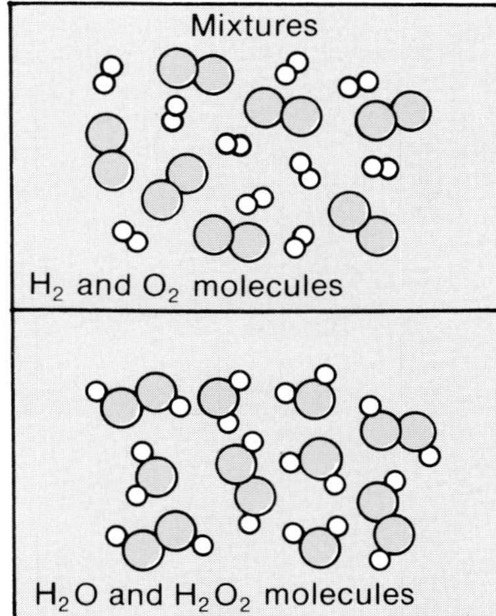

2–5 Heterogeneous and Homogeneous Mixtures

Mixtures are physical combinations of pure substances. Because the ingredients are not chemically combined, each one retains its own characteristics. Because the pure substances can be mixed together in many different proportions, there is no set ratio between the substances. All these properties make mixtures totally unlike compounds.

2-6 This moon rock is a heterogeneous mixture. Distinct regions of minerals can be seen in its cross section.

An examination of several mixtures under a microscope would reveal two distinct groups. One group of mixtures would appear to have distinct regions. A microscopic examination of milk, for example, shows globules of fat and other suspended particles. Mixtures that have distinct regions are called **heterogeneous mixtures.**

The second group of mixtures would not show any distinct regions. These mixtures are classified as **homogeneous mixtures.** In homogeneous materials the chemical and physical properties are the same throughout. Sugar water is a common example of a homogeneous mixture. The sugar is thoroughly mixed in the water so that no distinct regions are present.

Energy in Matter

While chemistry is the study of matter, the subject demands a basic understanding of energy. Every chemical reaction either releases or absorbs energy. Matter that is not undergoing chemical changes can contain energy stored in the form of heat, magnetic fields, electrical energy, chemical energy, nuclear energy, or mechanical energy.

2–6 Forms of Energy

Energy, like matter, seems to defy accurate definitions. Traditionally scientists have called energy "the ability to do work." This definition tells what energy does, not what it is. Nevertheless, it is the best one available. All of the commonly recognized forms of energy can be harnessed in some way to do work. The subject of chemistry is concerned most with the relationships between chemical, thermal, electrical, and nuclear energy, but it relates in some way to all the different kinds of energy.

2–7 Energy Conservation Despite Change

Thermodynamics is the study of the flow of energy, especially heat energy. Several laws that have a great impact on chemistry have been formulated as a result of thermodynamic studies. No exceptions to these laws have been observed; they apply to every field, at all times, in every instance.

The law of energy conservation, or the **first law of thermodynamics,** states that energy cannot be created or destroyed. Apart from divine intervention, the energy content of the universe has remained constant since the sixth day of Creation. All energy changes since then have merely changed one form into another.

The **second law of thermodynamics** deals with the tendency of the universe to "wax old as doth a garment" (Heb. 1:11). It states that during any energy transformation, some energy goes to an unusable form. Sometimes this law is quoted as saying that energy is "lost." Not so. That would contradict the first law of thermodynamics. When a battery discharges its electrical energy through a coil of wires, the energy is not "lost." It is changed into heat energy or possibly light energy if the wires glow. These new forms of energy ultimately become dispersed and unusable. Given enough time and a sufficient number of energy transformations, all the energy of the universe would eventually become dissipated and totally unusable.

Another vital conservation law is an offshoot of the first law of thermodynamics. Called the **law of mass conservation,** it says that during ordinary processes, mass is neither created nor destroyed. The word *ordinary* is included in the law because nuclear changes can convert some mass into energy. Chemical processes, however, merely rearrange atoms. The same number of atoms that enter a chemical reaction will invariably emerge as products.

2–8 Heat, Energy, and Temperature: There Is a Difference!

The energy of motion is called **kinetic energy.** All matter contains particles that are moving. The kinetic energy of the molecules and atoms in a substance is called **thermal energy.** The more motion, or kinetic energy, the particles have, the more thermal energy a material has.

Heat (thermal energy) and temperature are related but are definitely not the same thing. Thermal energy refers to total heat content, or the sum of every particle's kinetic energy. **Temperature** measures the *average* kinetic energy of all the particles in a sample. Which contains more heat: a bathtub full of lukewarm water or a tablespoon of boiling water? Obviously the boiling water has the greater temperature, but the bathtub of water has more thermal energy. The large number of molecules in the bathtub makes up for the relatively low kinetic energy of each molecule.

2-7 The heat energy in an object depends on its temperature and the amount of mass in the object.

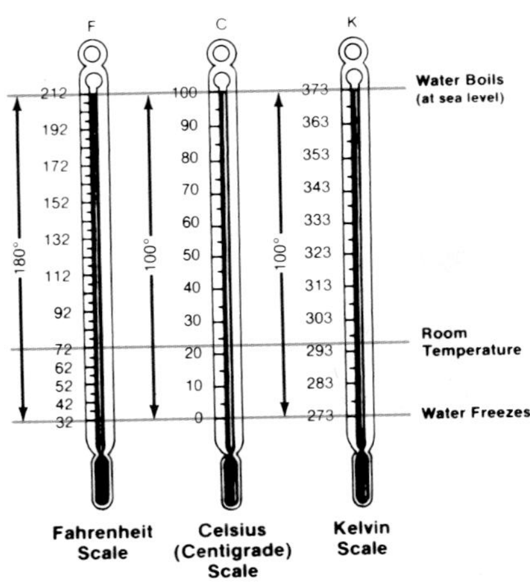

2-8 Three common temperature scales.

2–9 The Measurement of Energy: Important Units

The standard unit of measurement for energy is the calorie. One **calorie** is the amount of energy required to raise the temperature of 1 gram of water 1 degree Celsius. Larger units called kilocalories, which are 1000 times as large, are used for most chemical applications. The kilocalorie is equivalent to the Calorie (note the capital *C*), which is used in reference to foods.

Temperature scales indicate heat energy. The two temperature scales used most often in chemistry are the Celsius and the Kelvin scales. The **Celsius scale** uses the freezing point of water as its zero point and the boiling point of water as 100° C. The **Kelvin scale** uses **absolute zero** (the lowest possible temperature) as its zero point and has degrees that are the same "size" as those on the Celsius scale.

Since absolute zero is equivalent to -273° C, you can use the formulas $C = K - 273$ and $K = C + 273$ to convert between the Kelvin and the Celsius scales. As a rule, the Fahrenheit scale is not used for scientific purposes. But for comparison, you can convert Celsius temperatures to this commonly used scale with the formulas $C = \frac{5}{9}(F - 32)$ and $\frac{9}{5}C + 32 = F$.

Sample Problem. The weatherman announces that the high for the day is expected to be 33° C. What is this temperature in (a) the Kelvin scale and (b) the Fahrenheit scale?

Solution.

a. $K = C + 273$
$= 33 + 273$
$= 306\ K$

b. $F = \frac{9}{5}C + 32$
$= \frac{9}{5}(33) + 32$
$= 91°F$

2–10 The States of Matter

Scientists theorize that all matter is composed of submicroscopic particles (atoms, molecules, and ions) in constant motion. If energy is added to these particles, their motions increase; and the greater the amount of energy added, the faster the resulting motion. Yet if this motion were not in some way limited, matter would simply fly apart. Electrical forces attract atoms toward each other and inhibit the movement of the particles.

Scientists call the above set of ideas the **kinetic theory** (kinetic = motion), since it describes the motion of particles in matter. According to the kinetic theory, particles in solids possess relatively little energy compared to the attractive forces that are present. The attractive forces overpower the movements of the particles. The forces keep the particles of a **solid** in fixed positions with set distances between them.

When a solid is sufficiently heated, its particles gain enough energy to partially overcome their attractive forces, and the solid becomes a **liquid.** While the attractive forces retain their ability to hold the particles closely together, the energy that the particles possess allows limited motion or "flow."

When boiling, the particles of the liquid state gain enough energy to completely overcome their attractive forces, and they exist as a **gas.** The particles of a gas possess a high degree of energy. They move rapidly and randomly across great distances. The average velocity of an oxygen molecule is 480 meters per second, which is equivalent to a rate of speed just over 1700 kilometers per hour.

2-9 A great amount of heat energy is required to change solid rocks into liquid lava.

Table 2-10

The Physical States of Matter

State	Particle Positions	Characteristics
Solid		Definite shape and volume
Liquid		Definite volume; assumes shape of its container
Gas		Restricted only by its container

As the particles of a gas cool down, they slow down. Lacking the necessary energy to resist the attractive forces, the particles pull together into the liquid state.This phase change from gas to liquid is called liquefaction or, more commonly, **condensation.** Condensation occurs frequently in our homes during the winter months when the warm, moist air inside the house comes into contact with a cold window pane. If the particles in a liquid are sufficiently cooled, they solidify. **Freezing,** or solidification, occurs when the liquid molecules lose enough energy to allow the attractive forces to hold the particles in tightly packed, fixed positions. **Melting** is the phase change from solid to liquid. **Sublimation** is a phase change that may be less familiar. Under certain conditions a gas may change directly into a solid without becoming a liquid. The sublimation of ice onto aircraft wings has long been a problem of high-altitude flight. When moisture-laden air contacts the cold surface of the metal wing, gaseous water can sublimate into ice.

2-11 Phase Changes

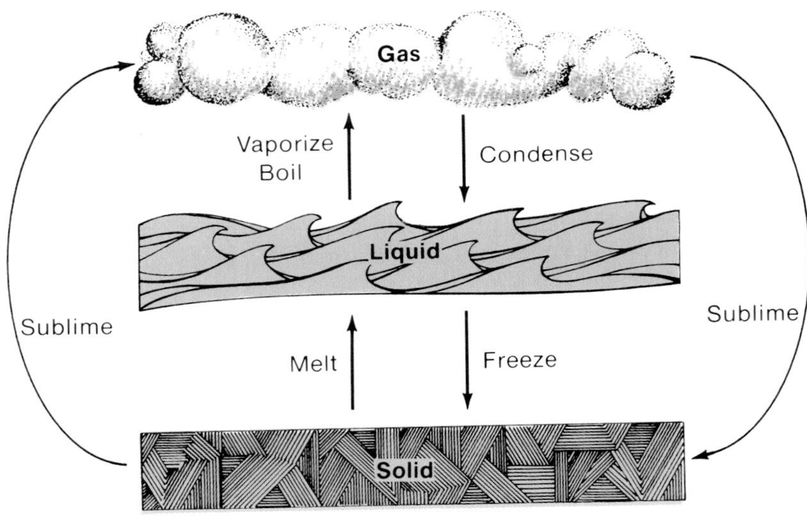

Under normal conditions matter exists in three physical states: solid, liquid, and gas. All matter has the potential of existing in these three states, yet certain substances are often thought of as being only a solid, a liquid, or a gas because they commonly exist in a narrow range of atmospheric conditions. Methane, the main component of natural gas, is one of these "pigeon-holed" substances. Recent evidence suggests that on Titan, Saturn's largest moon, methane coexists in all three of its physical states. Just as water vapor (gas), streams and lakes (liquid), and snow and ice (solid) are found together during the winter months on our own planet, the extremely cold temperatures of Titan allow the coexistence of the solid, liquid, and gaseous states of methane.

The Measurement of Matter

Chemistry is an exacting science. The typical stereotype of a chemist is a wizened old man, armed with a huge slide rule and cryptic ledger sheets full of data, climbing over some fantastically complicated apparatus containing multitudes of test tubes, beakers, and gauges. In a way some of these ideas are correct, for chemists must do a large amount of measuring, calculating, and working with numbers.

This chapter has discussed the characteristics and general classifications of matter. Chemistry, however, involves not only describing matter but also measuring it. **Measurements** consist of numbers and **units.** Units give meaning to the numbers by labeling them. Part of being a skillful chemist is knowing how to work with numbers, equations, and equipment in order to make and communicate accurate measurements.

2–11 Organized Problem Solving

Chemistry provides many opportunities to gain experience in problem solving. Most of these problems are word problems. Word problems scare some students, but they can be conquered and even enjoyed if they are attacked systematically. A systematic approach will not always lead to an immediate solution, but it will give direction in finding the answer. One systematic approach has three steps: (1) identifying what is given, (2) deciding what to do, and (3) deciding how to do it.

Identifying what is given. The essential pieces of information are usually easy to spot; organizing them is the main task. To do this, collect all the numerical information and any important non-numerical (qualitative) information, and record it neatly in an organized way. Occasionally you must weed out pieces of irrelevant data from a problem.

Deciding what to do. After jotting down the information that has been given, look for key words that tell you what to do. *Find, how many, name,* and *identify* point you on the path toward the desired solution.

Deciding how to do it. As you become more experienced in solving problems in chemistry, you will begin to recognize patterns and familiar routes to solutions. Most of the problems will require one of two general approaches: unit analysis (discussed in section 2–13) or the use of an equation. A few systematic steps can make using equations easier. First, neatly write out the equation you will use. Next, rearrange it to isolate the variable you are seeking. Be sure that your steps in rearranging the equation are mathematically valid: that is, do the same thing to both sides of the equation. Once the equation has been transformed, substitute the givens into it, write the units of measurement that apply, and solve for the answer. Finally, express the solution in the correct units.

Sample Problem. Use a systematic approach to solve the following problem: A lead fishing sinker that has a density of 11.3 grams per milliliter has a mass of 51 grams. What volume will the sinker occupy?

Solution.

Identify what is given. D (for density) = 11.3 g/ml; M (for mass) = 51 g

Decide what to do. The equation that relates density, mass, and volume is $D = M/V$. The problem requires that the volume, V, be found.

Decide how to do it. The equation $D = M/V$ must be rearranged in order to isolate V. If both sides of the

equation are multiplied by V, an equation that reads $DV = M$ results. Now if both sides of this equation are divided by D, an equation with V by itself emerges: $V = M/D$. Now the given values with their appropriate units are inserted into this equation. Notice how the mathematical solution results in both the correct number and the correct unit on the number.

$$V = \frac{M}{D} = \frac{51 \text{ g}}{11.3 \text{ g/ml}} = 4.5 \text{ ml}$$

2–12 Metric Units

Measurements consist of numbers that tell "how many" and units that tell "what." A number without a unit is meaningless. Can you imagine being told that the distance to a shopping mall was 7 without being told it was 7 blocks, 7 kilometers, or 7 miles? Measurements in chemistry also demand clearly understandable units. Chemists around the world use metric and SI units because they are common and easy to use.

The letters SI stand for **Système International,** which is a French version of *International System*. This system includes units for time (seconds), temperature (Kelvins), and electrical current (amperes) as well as the usual metric units for length, volume, and mass. The SI system modifies its basic units by putting prefixes on them. Some prefixes make the base units larger; others make them smaller. The SI prefixes and their equivalents are listed in Table 2-13.

Table 2-12

English-Metric Conversions

Length	2.54 cm = 1 in. 1.609 km = 1 mi.
Mass	28.35 g = 1 oz. 1 kg = 2.20 lb.
Volume	16.39 cm^3 = 1 in.^{3} 1 ℓ = 1.06 qt.

Table 2-13

SI Prefixes

Prefix	Symbol	Meaning	Numerical Meaning	Exponential Form
tera	T	trillion	1,000,000,000,000	10^{12}
giga	G	billion	1,000,000,000	10^{9}
mega	M	million	1,000,000	10^{6}
kilo	k	thousand	1,000	10^{3}
hecto	h	hundred	100	10^{2}
deka	da	ten	10	10^{1}
deci	d	tenth	0.1	10^{-1}
centi	c	hundredth	0.01	10^{-2}
milli	m	thousandth	0.001	10^{-3}
micro	μ	millionth	0.000001	10^{-6}
nano	n	billionth	0.000000001	10^{-9}
pico	p	trillionth	0.000000000001	10^{-12}

2–13 Unit Analysis: The Chemist's Secret Weapon

Chemistry problems often involve converting a measurement from one unit to another. **Unit analysis** is an excellent tool for solving this type of problem. Basically it is a powerful, versatile, and organized method of changing units on numbers.

The addition and subtraction of measurements require that the numbers have identical units. Three meters can be added to 5 meters to get 8 meters, but 3 meters cannot be added to 5 centimeters until one of the units matches the other. In multiplication and division the units are multiplied or divided along with the numbers. For example, 3 meters times 5 meters equals 15 square meters (m^2). A car that travels 60 kilometers in one hour moves at a rate of 60 kilometers per hour (km/hr.). The way in which units multiply and divide is the key to unit analysis.

Changing a number with a unit to an equivalent number with another unit involves multiplying the given number and unit by a **conversion factor** equal to 1. Some conversion factors that are equal to 1 appear in the list below. Since the numerator equals the denominator in each case, the result of each division is 1.

$$\frac{1\text{ yd.}}{3\text{ ft.}} \qquad \frac{3\text{ ft.}}{1\text{ yd.}} \qquad \frac{1000\text{ m}}{1\text{ km}} \qquad \frac{1000\text{ ml}}{1\ \ell} \qquad \frac{60\text{ min.}}{1\text{ hr.}}$$

The key to changing a number's units is constructing a conversion factor that allows the undesired units to cancel out in division. For instance, the conversion factor of 1 yard/3 feet is used to change 15 feet into yards.

$$15\text{ ft.} \times \frac{1\text{ yd.}}{3\text{ ft.}} = 5\text{ yd.}$$

Since the *feet* units appear on the top and bottom of the fraction bar, they cancel out. After the numerical operations are done, the resulting number has the unit of yards with it. If the conversion factor of 3 feet/1 yard had been used, it would not have canceled out the units of feet.

$$15\text{ ft.} \times \frac{3\text{ ft.}}{1\text{ yd.}} = \frac{45\text{ ft.}^2}{\text{yd.}}$$

Sample Problem. Convert a length of 123,456 centimeters to kilometers.

Solution.

Starting with the given information—123,456 centimeters—use a succession of conversion factors to obtain the unit of kilometers.

$$123{,}456\text{ cm} \times \frac{1\text{ m}}{100\text{ cm}} = 1234.56\text{ m}$$

$$1234.56\text{ m} \times \frac{1\text{ km}}{1000\text{ m}} = 1.23456\text{ km}$$

Doing the conversions one after the other shortens the operation.

$$123{,}456\text{ cm} \times \frac{1\text{ m}}{100\text{ cm}} \times \frac{1\text{ km}}{1000\text{ m}} = 1.23456\text{ km}$$

2–14 Significant Figures: Telling the Truth with Numbers

Measurements can never be perfect, no matter how meticulous the scientists are or how good their equipment is. In most cases the tools of the scientists, not careless mistakes, limit accuracy. Consequently the numbers that scientists use must indicate the accuracy of the measurements.

Scientists indicate how exact their numbers are by using **significant figures.** Significant figures help people to report their measurements honestly. For instance, if someone measured his weight with a bathroom scale, he could not honestly and accurately report that his weight was 135.67942 pounds. A bathroom scale cannot measure weight that accurately. A reasonable measurement on a bathroom scale might be as accurate as 136 pounds.

2-14 Precise equipment allows for many significant digits.

Four basic rules determine which digits in numbers are significant:

1. All nonzero digits are significant.
2. Zeros that serve as place holders are *not* significant. The zeros in 0.006 and in 300 have no purpose other than to show the location of the decimal point. Both of these numbers contain only one significant digit.
3. All zeros between two significant digits are significant. The zeros in 7008 are significant, but those in 7800 are not.
4. Zeros to the right of the decimal point and other significant figures are significant. For instance, the two zeros in 7.800 centimeters are significant. They show that the measurement could be accurately determined to thousandths of a centimeter and that it is thus highly accurate.

Sample Problem. Determine the number of significant digits in the following measurements:

a. 9.370 kg b. 63,000 g c. 705.06 ml

Solution.

a. Zeros to the right of the decimal point and other significant digits are significant, so the number has four significant digits.

b. Place holders are not significant; therefore, the number has two significant figures.
c. Zeros between other significant digits are significant. The number therefore contains five significant digits.

The number of significant digits in a number must be maintained during mathematical operations. Two simple rules guide the process of keeping significant digits during addition, subtraction, multiplication, and division.

1. After addition and subtraction, the answer cannot be more precise than the least accurate measurement.

   The addition of 50.23, 14.678, and 23.7 yields a preliminary answer of 88.608. Since the least precise addend (23.7) has its most precise digit in the tenths place, the answer must be rounded to 88.6.

2. In multiplication or division the answer must contain the same number of significant digits as the least precise measurement.

   Although $0.238 \times 0.31 = 0.07378$, this number must be rounded off to 0.074 because 0.31 has only two significant figures.

Sample Problem. A metal object's mass was measured to be 30.926 grams, and its volume was measured to be 2.75 milliliters. Calculate the object's density, and report your answer with the appropriate number of significant figures.

Solution.

$$\text{Density} = \frac{\text{Mass}}{\text{Volume}} = \frac{30.926 \text{ g}}{2.75 \text{ ml}} = 11.245818, \text{ or } 11.2 \text{ g}$$

The least precise measurement (2.75 ml) has three significant figures, so the answer must also have three.

Since the purpose for using significant figures is to show the accuracy of measurements, the rules of significant figures apply only to measured numbers. Consider the following problem: A nickel has been measured to have a mass of 5.2 grams; find the mass of six nickels. What would the answer be? Straight multiplication yields a value of 31.2 grams. Should the answer be reported as 31 grams (two significant figures) or as 30 grams (one significant figure)? The answer should be 31 grams, with two significant figures, because the number 6 is not measured—it is a given, an absolute. Significant figures apply to measured numbers only.

2-15 Most modern calculators use this format for scientific notation.

2–15 Scientific Notation: Long Numbers in Short Forms

Chemists constantly work with very large and very small numbers. For example, a certain wavelength of light is 0.0000006 meters. This small number can be written more conveniently in scientific notation as 6×10^{-7} meters (read as "six times ten to the negative seven"). One milliliter of hydrogen gas contains 26,900,000,000,000,000,000 hydrogen molecules. Using scientific notation, scientists express this number as 2.69×10^{19}. Expressing numbers in terms of powers of ten—that is, in **scientific notation**—has several benefits: (1) Numbers in scientific notation clearly show the number of significant figures because all the numbers used are significant; (2) Numbers expressed in scientific notation are easier to work with in multiplication and division problems; and (3) Scientific notation makes it easier to read and to write very large and very small numbers.

A number in scientific notation has two main parts: the mantissa and the characteristic. The **mantissa** is the string of numbers that is multiplied by ten raised to some power. The **characteristic** is the power to which ten is raised. The mantissa tells how many significant figures are in the number, and the characteristic tells where the decimal point is located.

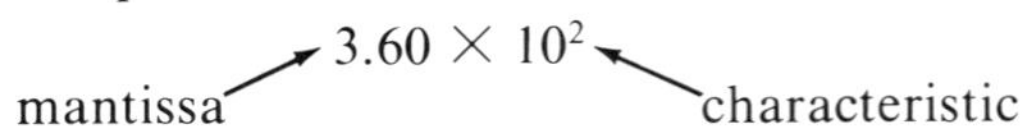

In scientific notation the mantissa appears first. It contains all the significant digits, with the decimal point always placed after the first digit. The mantissa of 36,300 is 3.63. The characteristic shows the number of places the decimal point moved. Because the decimal point moved four places to the left in the previous example, the characteristic is +4. The number should be written as 3.63×10^{4}.

The direction the decimal point moves determines the sign of the characteristic. Movement to the left requires a positive sign, and movement to right, a negative sign. If a number is negative, the mantissa should carry the negative sign. If the number is between one and zero, the characteristic will have a negative sign. For instance, 0.0036 in scientific notation is 3.6×10^{-3}.

Sample Problem. Write the following numbers in scientific notation.

a. -780 b. 0.078 c. -0.0078

Solution.

a. -7.8×10^{2} b. 7.8×10^{-2} c. -7.8×10^{-3}

Adding or subtracting numbers in scientific notation has little advantage except to reduce bulky numbers to a workable size. In these operations all characteristics must be the same before the mantissas can be added or subtracted. For example, the sum of 1×10^{2} and 1×10^{3} is not 2×10^{5} ($100 + 1000 \neq 200{,}000$). The numbers must be rewritten so that they have identical characteristics.

$$\begin{array}{r} 1 \times 10^{2} \\ +\ 1 \times 10^{3} \\ \hline \end{array} \qquad \begin{array}{r} 1 \times 10^{2} \\ +\ 10 \times 10^{2} \\ \hline 11 \times 10^{2} = 1100 \end{array}$$

In multiplication the mantissas are multiplied and the characteristics are added. The characteristics do not have to be alike as in addition and subtraction. Division is similar to multiplication except that the characteristics must be subtracted instead of added.

Sample Problem. Perform the indicated arithmetic operations.

a. $(6.5 \times 10^{4}) + (2.0 \times 10^{3})$

b. $(6.5 \times 10^{4}) \times (2.0 \times 10^{3})$

c. $\dfrac{6.5 \times 10^{4}}{2.0 \times 10^{-3}}$

Solution.

a. Addition and subtraction demand numbers with identical powers.

$$\begin{array}{r} 6.5 \times 10^{4} \\ +\ 2.0 \times 10^{3} \\ \hline \end{array} \qquad \begin{array}{r} 65 \quad \times 10^{3} \\ +\ \ 2.0 \times 10^{3} \\ \hline 67.0 \times 10^{3}, \text{ or } 6.7 \times 10^{4} \end{array}$$

b. Multiply the mantissas, and add the characteristics.

$$(6.5 \times 10^{4}) \times (2.0 \times 10^{3}) =$$
$$(6.5 \times 2.0) \times (10^{4} \times 10^{3}) =$$
$$13 \times 10^{7} = 1.3 \times 10^{8}$$

c. Divide the mantissas, and subtract the characteristics.

$$\frac{6.5 \times 10^{4}}{2.0 \times 10^{-3}} = \frac{6.5}{2.0} \times \frac{10^{4}}{10^{-3}} = 3.3 \times 10^{7}$$

Since you will probably use an electronic calculator to solve most of your problems, you should become familiar with the way in which your calculator works with numbers in scientific notation.

Coming to Terms

matter
physical property
density
malleability
ductility
conductivity
chemical property
physical change
chemical change
chemical reaction
pure substance
element
atom
monatomic element
diatomic element
polyatomic element
symbol
compound
formula
subscript
coefficient
molecule
mixture
heterogeneous mixture
homogeneous mixture
energy
thermodynamics
first law of thermodynamics
second law of thermodynamics
law of mass conservation
kinetic energy
thermal energy
temperature
calorie
Celsius scale
Kelvin scale
absolute zero
kinetic theory
solid
liquid
gas
condensation
freezing
melting
sublimation
measurement
unit
Système International
unit analysis
conversion factor
significant figures
scientific notation
mantissa
characteristic

Review Questions

1. State the definitions of *matter* and *energy*.
2. The concepts of matter and energy are fundamental to the study of chemistry. What is unique about the definitions of both?
3. Why is Creation (*ex nihilo*) a religious belief and not a scientific fact?
4. Tell whether each of the following properties is a physical property or a chemical property.
   a. color
   b. density
   c. radioactivity
   d. ability to conduct electricity
   e. corrosiveness
   f. magnetism
   g. ability to burn rapidly

5. Tell whether each of the following processes involves a physical change, a chemical change, or both.
   a. A block of silicon chips being sliced into wafers to be used in microcomputer chips
   b. An eskimo's igloo melting
   c. Steam condensing on the bathroom mirror as someone takes a shower
   d. Dynamite exploding and destroying an old building
   e. A burning candlewick melting wax
   f. The corroding of spokes on a bicycle's wheels
6. Why do some chemical symbols for elements consist of two letters and others of only one?
7. Some chemical symbols are apparently unrelated to the names of the elements to which they refer. Why? Give an example.
8. How many of each kind of atom is present in each of the following? Example: A single H_2O unit has one O atom and two H atoms.
   a. $CsBr$
   b. $NaNO_3$
   c. $2LiH_2PO_4$
   d. $KC_2H_3O_2$
   e. $K_2Cr_2O_7$
   f. $Al(C_2H_3O_2)_3$
   g. $2H_3PO_4$
   h. $2Ba_3(PO_4)_2$
9. Use the classification scheme to classify the following substances as either elements, compounds, homogeneous mixtures, or heterogeneous mixtures. Example: $MgSO_4$ is a compound.
   a. vegetable soup
   b. air
   c. oxygen
   d. gasoline
   e. sulfuric acid (H_2SO_4)
10. The ideas of men are not always in harmony with the way the universe operates. Identify the law that says that each of the following is impossible.
   a. A perpetual motion machine produces more energy than it consumes.
   b. A frictionless wheel revolves without ever slowing down.
   c. A scientist uses a particle accelerator to convert 50 g of gold into 75 g of gold.
   d. The universe spontaneously created itself.

11. Convert the following temperatures from the scale given to the scale indicated in parentheses.
    a. The weatherman says that today's high temperature will be 75° F. (° C)
    b. A batch of cookies bakes at 325° F. (° C)
    c. Pure water freezes at 32° F. (° C)
    d. The temperature on the sun's surface could be 5820° C. (° F, K)
    e. At atmospheric pressure, water boils at 100° C. (° F)
    f. Nitrogen gas can be liquefied at a temperature of 77 K. (° C, ° F)
    g. Helium exists as a liquid at 4 K. (° C, ° F)

12. Write an equation that states the relationship between the two given units, and then write the conversion factor (or conversion factors) that could be used to convert the first unit to the second. Example: Millimeters and meters are related by the equation 1000 mm = 1 m. The conversion factor 1 m/1000 mm should be used.
    a. grams and milligrams
    b. nanometers and meters
    c. kilograms and grams
    d. liters and milliliters
    e. megahertz and hertz

13. Convert the following measurements from the units given to the units requested with the use of the conversion factors in the previous problem. Example: How many meters wide is 35 mm camera film?

$$35 \text{ mm} \times \frac{1 \text{ m}}{1000 \text{ mm}} = 0.035 \text{ m}$$

    a. How many grams are 5280 mg?
    b. The wavelength of blue light is about 475 nanometers (nm). How many meters is this?
    c. What is the mass in grams of a 72.6 kg man?
    d. How many milliliters of ginger ale are contained in a 2-ℓ bottle?
    e. What is the frequency in hertz of a radio station's 94.5-megahertz (MHz) signal?

14. Use unit analysis to convert the given measurement to the units requested.
    a. How many pounds does a 45.4 kg woman weigh?
    b. How many grams are contained in a ¼-lb. (4-oz.) meat patty?
    c. What is the mass in kilograms of a 4000-lb. automobile?

d. A ship displaces 650 tons of water. How many kilograms of water is this? Express your answer in scientific notation.
e. How many inches are present in 35 km? Express your answer in scientific notation.

15. Add, subtract, multiply, and divide the following measurements, and give your answer with correct units and the correct number of significant figures. Round answers off when necessary.
    a. 5.85 g + 3.2 g
    b. 2.718 cm − 3.50 cm
    c. (6.98 cm − 2.83 cm) × 1.7 cm
    d. 3.14 × 3.5 cm
    e. (2 × 3.14) × 6.83 m^2
    f. 1.70 × 10^3 sec. + 1500 sec.

16. Use unit analysis and a systematic approach to solve the following density problems. Give all answers with correct units and the correct number of significant figures.
    a. Mercury, which is often used in thermometers, has a density of 13.6 g/ml at room temperature. What volume of mercury contains 10.0 g?
    b. How many ounces will 1.00 cup of mercury weigh?
    c. Express the density of mercury in lb./gal.
    d. What mass (in grams) of mercury will fit into a 2.00-ℓ bottle?
    e. At room temperature pure water has a density of 1.00 g/ml. What mass of water (in grams) will fit into a container if 1.00 lb. of mercury completely fills the container?

THREE

ATOMIC STRUCTURE

SMALL-SCALE ARCHITECTURE

DESPITE their not being able to see atoms, scientists have accumulated a surprising amount of information about them. They have used indirect techniques to collect this knowledge. Chemists creatively used bits of fragmented evidence to ingeniously form the theories that are now called atomic models. The theories about atomic structure serve as the foundational ideas for studies of bonding, reactions, and the rest of chemistry.

The Development of Atomic Models: A Historical Perspective

The quantum model, the Bohr model, the plum-pudding model—each of these theories about the structure of atoms is called a model. **Models** are working representations of experimental facts. They are not exactly correct in all points, but then, they do not claim to be. They are mental pictures or simplifications of what is being studied. To further understand models, consider the concept of eternity, which is sometimes likened to traveling in a circle: "There is no start, and there is no stop. It just goes on forever." This analogy is like a scientific model. It is used to visualize an idea and to explain a complex concept. Although this model is crude and does not hold true in many aspects, it is still useful because it helps the human mind to grasp some of the concept.

3–1 The Origin of the Atomic Concept: Greek Ideas

A Greek philosopher named Democritus is credited with being the first to say that matter is discontinuous: it is made of separate, discrete particles. He said that matter contained definite particles and that it could not be divided infinitely without losing its properties. Eventually the dividing process would result in a single particle that could not be divided without losing its properties. Democritus used the term *atoms* (meaning "indivisible") to name these smallest possible particles.

The precise measurement of elements in many compounds paved the way for full acceptance of Democritus's ideas. Chemists observed that a compound always contains a set mass ratio of elements. For instance, when a 9.00-gram sample of water is analyzed, 8.00 grams of oxygen and 1.00 gram of hydrogen are found. The mass ratio here is 8:1. An analysis of an 18.0-gram sample reveals 16.0 grams of oxygen and 2.00 grams of hydrogen. Again the ratio holds true ($8/1 = 16/2$). Any sample of water from any source always contains 8 grams of oxygen for every 1 gram of hydrogen.

Further study showed that every compound has its own unique and definite mass composition. As the evidence began to mount, the trend became clear, and the findings were compiled into the **law of definite composition.** This law states that every compound has a definite composition by weight. The law of definite composition could be explained only one way: definite particles combine in definite numbers to form compounds.

3-1 Democritus **(left);** John Dalton **(right).**

3–2 The First Experimental Model: Dalton's Atomic Theory

An English schoolteacher named John Dalton (1766-1844) was the first to frame an atomic model based on sound experimental evidence instead of mental gymnastics. With incisive logic and new knowledge such as the law of definite composition, Dalton formed his remarkable model. His model may be summarized by the following statements.

1. Elements are made of minute particles called atoms, which are tiny, indestructible spheres.
2. Atoms of different elements have unique sizes and properties.
3. Atoms of one element cannot be changed into atoms of another element.
4. Atoms form compounds by combining with each other.
5. A certain compound always contains the same relative number and kinds of atoms.

The major points of Dalton's theory were his ideas that different combinations of atoms form compounds and that atoms of different elements have different masses. Dalton proceeded to assign relative masses to atoms of various elements. He assigned *relative* masses because he could only determine the sizes of atoms in *relation* to each other. Through painstaking analyses, Dalton and other chemists of his day determined that "oxygen is much heavier than hydrogen, and slightly more massive than carbon" and other important facts about atoms.

The exact values in Dalton's table were not accurate, and in some cases even the order of elements from smallest to largest was not correct. Nevertheless, the fact that Dalton was able to start such an ambitious project is remarkable because he was handicapped by a lack of information. His theory started a trickle of experimentation that soon brought a flood of new information. Today Dalton's model still serves as the foundation for present theories.

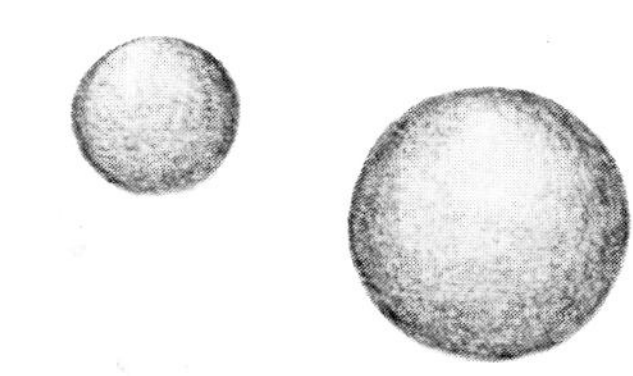

3-2 Dalton's model of the atom featured atoms of different masses.

3–3 Discovery of the Electron: Thomson's Model

Like Democritus, Dalton and others had assumed that atoms were tiny spheres. They "just knew" (or thought they did) that atoms were indivisible, as the Greek word *atoms* implied. Until the 1880s these ideas about atoms were common. Then new clues led men to believe that atoms were made up of even smaller particles and that they could be divided.

The invention of batteries sparked the study of electricity. Scientists found that gases at atmospheric pressure stopped an electrical current. If a gas was sealed in a glass tube under a very low pressure, it could easily carry a current between two electrical contacts. The glass tube was called a gas discharge tube.

3-3 A cathode-ray tube shows that electrons travel in straight lines.

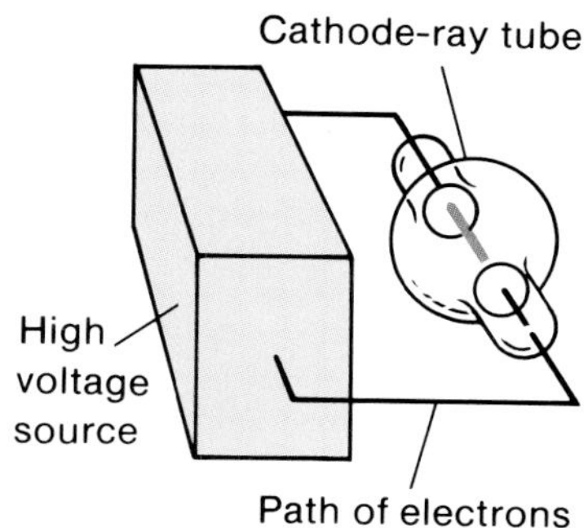

During their efforts to reduce the amount of gas in the discharge tubes, scientists noticed a strange new phenomenon. When almost all the gas molecules were removed by a vacuum pump, the current decreased. This was understandable; fewer molecules could carry less current. When even more gas was removed, scientists saw surprising things happen. The current increased and an eerie green light appeared. Something other than the gas allowed the current to flow. Because this "something" came from the electrical contact called the cathode, it was named **cathode rays.**

Although many men worked with cathode rays, an Englishman named J. J. Thomson did the most extensive experiments. Thomson carried out a series of experiments to examine cathode rays in detail. First, he found out that cathode rays could be deflected by a magnet. This fact told him that the rays were actually little particles. When he passed a stream between two electrically charged plates, the stream bent toward the positively charged plate. Since opposite charges attract, Thomson knew that the particles carried a negative charge. Finally, he deflected the particles by a combination of magnetic and electrical fields. By manipulating the strength of the fields, he was able to determine the charge-to-mass ratio (e/m) of the particle. He found that this ratio was surprisingly large. Compared to the charge, the mass was almost nothing.

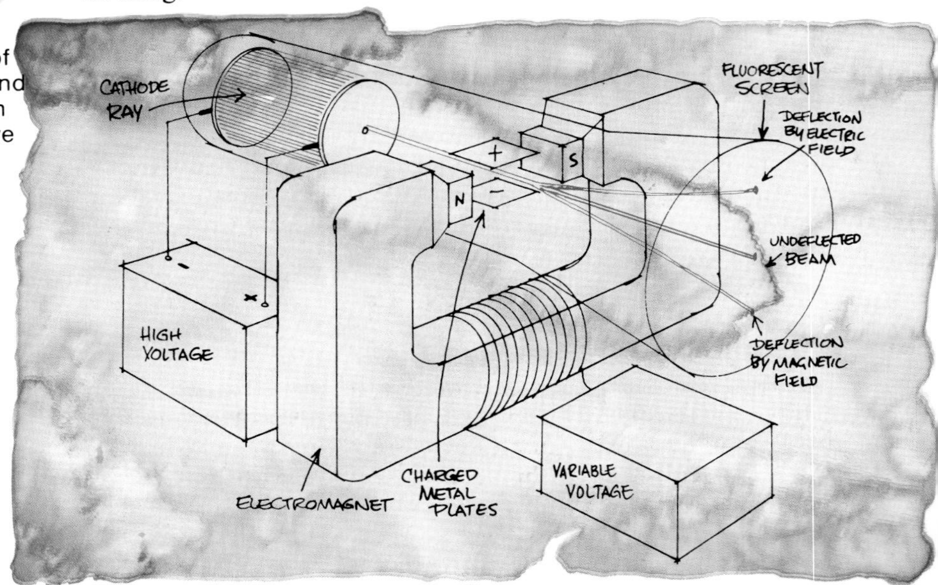

3-4 By bending a beam of electrons with magnets and electrical fields, Thomson proved that electrons have very little mass.

Thomson further proved that the same type of particle was emitted from atoms of every element. Gold, silver, iron, and copper all gave off the same particle. After his experiments were complete, Thomson had proved that every atom contained minute negatively charged particles. These particles were named **electrons.**

Dalton's atomic model could not explain these new facts. It was time for a new model. This new model had to explain (1) how electrically charged particles could exist in an atom, (2) why the atom as a whole was neutral, and (3) how negative charges, but not positive charges, could leave an atom.

Thomson explained these observations by postulating a new atomic model. He said that

1. Electrons exist in a positively charged substance that completely surrounds them.
2. The positive material balances out the negative charges on the electrons so that the atom is neutral.
3. Under certain conditions electrons could be removed from an atom.

A sketch of these ideas looked like the then-famous English plum pudding. The electrons were negatively charged "plums" in a positively charged "pudding." Since Thomson's first experiments, the charge on an electron has been defined as -1, and the mass of an electron has been determined to be a scant 9.11×10^{-31} kilograms.

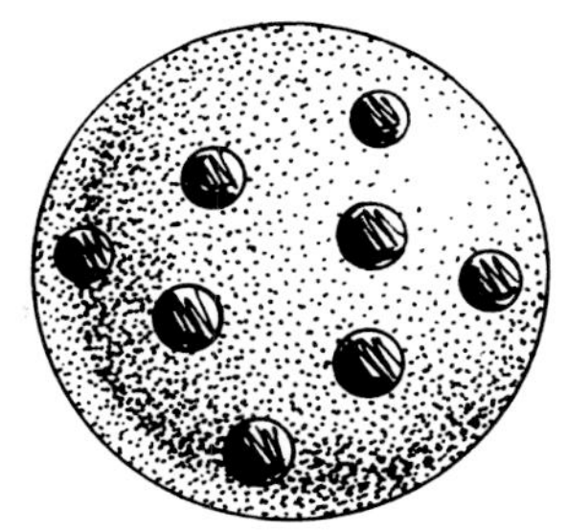

3-5 Thomson's plum-pudding model of the atom.

3–4 Discovery of the Proton: Rutherford's Model

While working with cathode-ray tubes in 1896, Wilhelm Roentgen accidentally discovered x-rays. This discovery triggered further experiments that led to the discovery of radiation and detailed studies of the inner parts of the atom. In the twenty years before World War I, the best minds in the scientific world pioneered the fascinating field of radioactive particles. One of these brilliant scientists was Ernest Rutherford, a professor at Cambridge University in England. His experiments with radioactive particles known as alpha particles led the world to new insights about the atom.

Alpha particles are massive (compared to other nuclear particles), positively charged ions. Radioactive elements emit them at high speeds. Their large mass and high speed combine to give the alpha particle a great amount of energy. Rutherford found that he could mark the passage of one of these particles as it struck a zinc-sulfide screen and produced a brief flash of light.

During his work, Rutherford examined a beam of alpha particles as they struck a thin gold foil. For the most part his results agreed with Thomson's model; most of the particles went straight through. However, a few particles were slightly deflected by the gold atoms. Some even ricocheted back toward the source. According to the Thomson model, this was impossible. No part of the atom should have had enough density or electrical charge to withstand, let alone repel, a speeding alpha particle. It was time for a new atomic model.

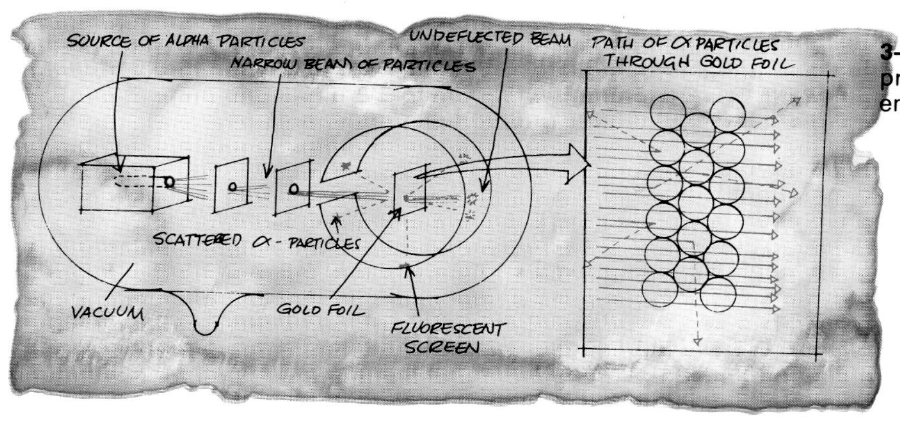

3-6 Rutherford's experiment proved that atoms are mostly empty space.

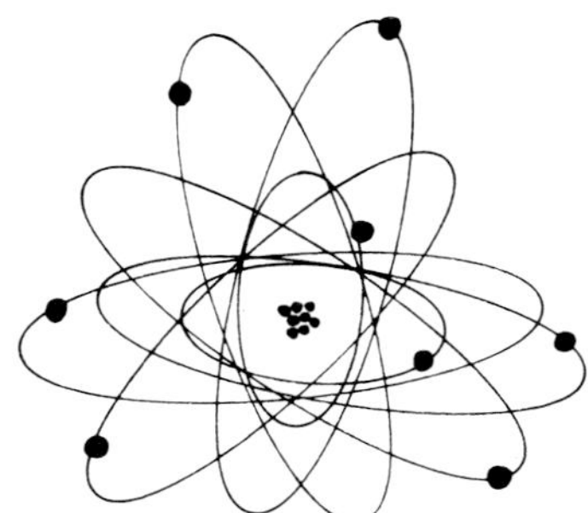

3-7 Rutherford's model of the atom.

Rutherford reasoned that atoms must have an extremely dense, positively charged central portion. What else could reflect an alpha particle? Because only a few alpha particles were greatly affected, the **nucleus,** as Rutherford called it, must be very small. Subsequent calculations indicated that the diameter of a nucleus was only 1/100,000 the size of the entire atom. Atoms and matter are mostly empty space.

Rutherford named the small positively charged particles in the nuclei **protons.** A proton has an electrical charge of +1, exactly opposite the electron's charge. The mass of a proton is approximately eighteen hundred times greater than the mass of an electron. In kilograms the mass is 1.67×10^{-27} kilograms.

3–5 Discovery of the Neutron: Chadwick's Work

Scientists soon realized that atoms were much more massive than expected. The protons and electrons alone could not supply all the mass that was being observed. There had to be something else. Rutherford suggested that a neutral particle could supply the extra mass without bringing an extra positive charge. Unfortunately, since the particle was so small and had no electrical charge, it eluded detection for many years. It was not until 1932 that a physicist named James Chadwick identified neutral particles that existed in the nuclei of atoms. Appropriately enough, these particles were named **neutrons.** A neutron has a mass of 1.68×10^{-27} kilograms, just slightly greater than the mass of a proton. Together neutrons and protons make up the nucleus and contribute almost all of an atom's mass.

3–6 Energy Levels for Electrons: Bohr's Model

3-8 Niels Bohr.

Rutherford's experiments supplied much information about the nucleus. But what about the electrons? Rutherford had simply guessed that electrons must exist at great distances from the nucleus. Many questions were left unanswered. How were the various electrons arranged? Were they moving? If so, in what manner?

Niels Bohr, a young Danish physicist working in Rutherford's laboratory, took up the task of answering some of the nagging questions. He knew that the nucleus had a positive charge. He also knew that electrons had negative charges. What he did not know was why electrons did not fall into the nucleus. The attraction between positive and negative charges should pull the electrons in and collapse the atom. It was assumed that the electrons moved around the nucleus and that their momentum kept them from falling into the nucleus just as the earth's momentum balances the sun's gravitational attraction.

The science of spectroscopy (the study of how atoms absorb and emit light) helped Bohr determine how electrons move around the nucleus. Light from the sun and incandescent bulbs gives off a **continuous spectrum;** that is, the light separates into all the colors of the rainbow after it passes through a prism. In contrast, light that is given off from excited atoms forms spectra that contain definite bands of colored light. Furthermore, each element has its own unique set of colored lines, or a **line spectrum.**

The explanation of these bright lines eluded scientists for several decades. In 1913 Niels Bohr devised an atomic model that helped explain these lines. He said that the electrons could exist only in definite energy levels outside the nucleus. Energy levels close to the nucleus corresponded to lower levels of energy. Levels at greater distances corresponded to higher energy levels.

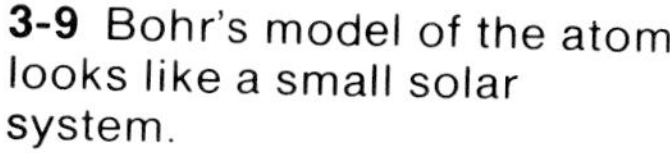

3-9 Bohr's model of the atom looks like a small solar system.

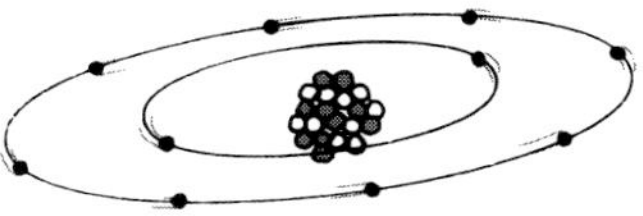

3-10 A continuous spectrum and the bright-line spectrum of hydrogen.

The bright-line spectra of gaseous elements could be explained by electrons' moving between various energy levels. Normally electrons exist in the lowest possible energy level (the ground state). When the right amount of strong light, intense heat, or electricity energizes an atom, the electrons jump up to a higher energy level. This change in energy levels is definite and **quantized.** There is no stopping between levels. Once the electrons are at their higher energy level, they immediately seek to return to their lower energy state. As soon as possible, the electrons fall back into a lower level. The energy the electrons possessed at the higher level is converted into light energy when the electrons return to lower levels. The observed colors in bright-line spectra give valuable clues about the energy levels in atoms. Bohr was actually able to predict the exact wavelengths (which correspond to colors) of the lines in the hydrogen spectrum.

Bohr's energy levels are called **principal energy levels.** They were temporarily envisioned as a set of concentric tracks on which electrons orbited. But this concept was soon replaced by a more accurate picture. Theoretically, many principal energy levels exist. In practice, however, six or seven can be measured. Figure 3-11 shows that upper energy levels crowd so closely together that measuring any difference between them soon becomes impossible. At these high levels an electron may as well be completely separated from the atom (n = infinity).

3-11 Energy Relationships Between Principal Levels

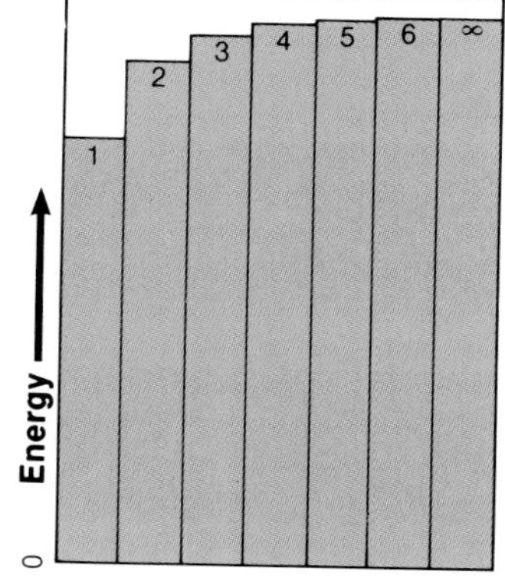

FACETS OF CHEMISTRY

Spectroscopy: Fingerprinting Atoms

Where was the element helium first discovered? If you were to guess that it was isolated from air, found in some mineral, or detected anywhere else on this earth, you would have missed the mark by some 93 million miles. Surprisingly enough, scientists discovered helium in the sun, not the earth. Even more surprisingly, the discovery occurred in 1868—a full century before interplanetary space probes ever ventured from NASA's launching pads. Scientists made this remarkable discovery by using one of the most powerful tools known to science: spectroscopy.

Spectroscopy is the study of how matter interacts with electromagnetic radiation. When atoms are highly energized, they can release light and other forms of radiation. In other instances atoms can absorb electromagnetic radiation. Every element has its own characteristic set of interactions. In a way, the types of light that elements emit and absorb serve as the "fingerprints" of atoms.

Atoms can absorb and emit all kinds of electromagnetic radiation: infrared, visible, ultraviolet, and x-ray. Visible light is the easiest to observe, so this branch of spectroscopy is the most common. When an atom receives a small amount o heat, electricity, or light of the proper wavelength, one or more of its outer electrons becomes "excited." It jumps from its original position to a higher orbital. Electrons in higher orbitals are extremely unstable, so within a fraction of a second, they fall back to some lower orbital. When they fall, they give off a burst of light whose wavelength (or color) depends on the energy difference between the higher and the lower orbitals.

If electrons in an atom always jumped to the same higher orbital and always fell directly back to their "home" orbital, atoms would emit only one type of light. Electrons, however, are not limited to only one transition. On their initial jump upwards, they can go to any one of several orbitals. On

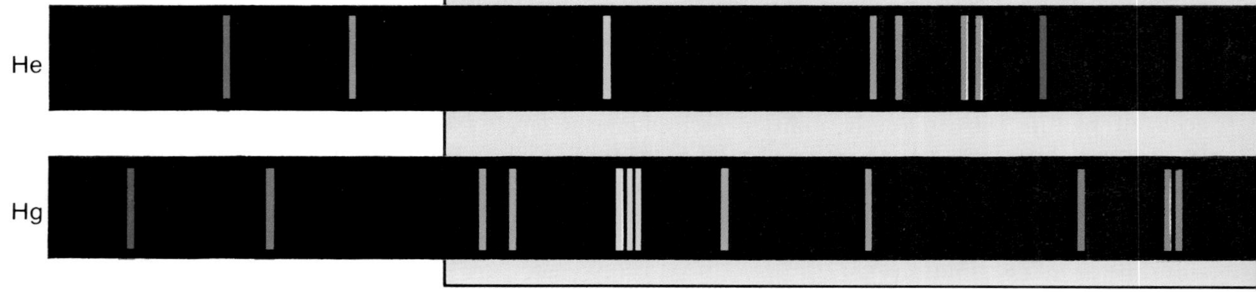

their return to a low-energy, stable state they can fall all the way back to the original orbital in a single step. They can also cascade downward, landing temporarily in some or all of the in-between orbitals. As a result, atoms release an entire set of wavelengths.

Normally these individual colors of light cannot be observed, because they are all mixed together. A prism, however, can separate the colors of light so that they can be easily seen. When light from energized atoms is analyzed, distinct bands of colors appear at specific locations. The set of bright lines is called a bright-line spectrum.

No two elements have exactly the same set of orbitals or the same arrangement of outer-level electrons. As a result, every element has its own unique set of colored lines in its spectrum. Just as police detectives use the fact that no two people have the same fingerprint, scientific detectives rely on the fact that no two elements have the same spectrum.

The simplest device for studying spectra, called the prism spectroscope, was invented in the 1850s by Gustav Kirchhoff and Robert Bunsen at the University of Heidelberg. It consisted of four parts—a flame; an arrangement of lenses; a prism; and a small, movable telescope. The flame energized the atoms in the sample to be tested. The lenses directed the light rays from the flame into a parallel beam. The prism took the unified beam of light and broke it up into its component wavelengths. The telescope swiveled around and detected the colors of light that came from the prism at various angles. Using this early device, Kirchhoff observed a strong yellow line when table salt was placed in the flame. He correctly identified the line as an emission line of the sodium atom. Later Bunsen and Kirchhoff jointly discovered cesium and rubidium by observing emission lines from vaporized mineral waters.

Time has brought numerous improvements in the basic spectroscope. Instead of prisms, scientists now use diffraction gratings to separate the beams of light into their separate components. More sensitive optical detection systems have been provided, and it is now possible to study the spectral lines in great detail. In many cases what was thought to be one line has turned out to be a compilation of many lines. Cameras have replaced the telescope of the old spectroscope, and it is now possible to photograph an entire spectrum instantaneously. No longer must scientists spend hours searching for tiny lines of color by inching a telescope through all the various angles. New instruments have allowed scientists to study infrared and ultraviolet emissions. Armed with these new tools and the basic theory of spectroscopy, scientists can quickly determine what kinds of elements are in a sample of water, in clay from an archaeological relic, or in the plasma of a distant star.

3-12 Production of a Bright-Line Spectrum

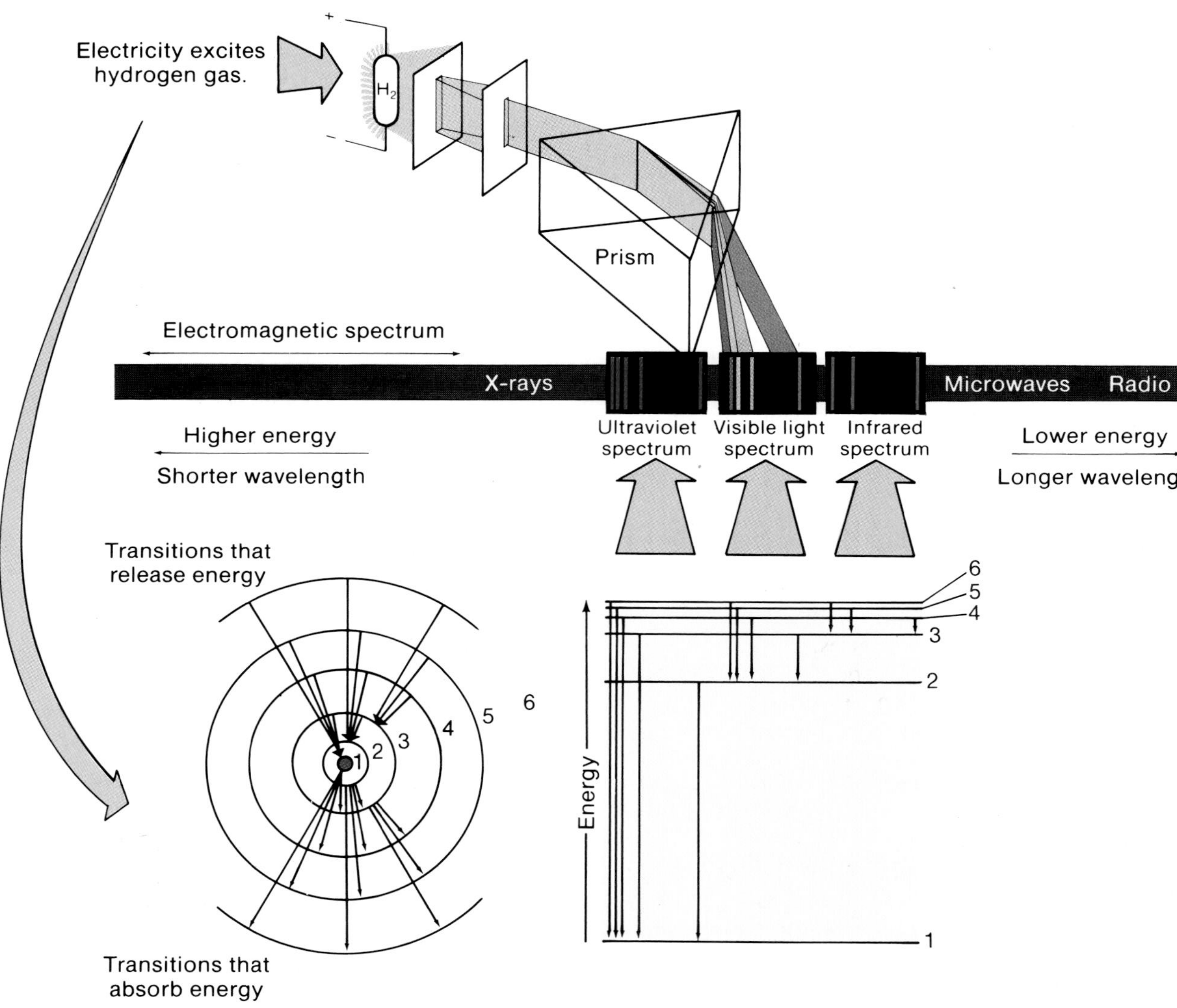

Arrows represent relative amounts of energy released as an electron drops to lower energy levels of a hydrogen atom: the longer the arrow, the more energy released.

Each principal energy level has a maximum number of electrons that it can hold at one time. Table 3-13 gives the capacities of the first seven energy levels.

Table 3-13

Capacities of Principal Energy Levels

Principal Energy Level (n)	Maximum Number of Electrons ($2n^2$)
1	2
2	8
3	18
4	32
5	50* (32)
6	72* (18)
7	98* (8)

*Values are theoretical. The elements in the universe do not have enough electrons to completely fill these levels. The smaller numbers are the observed capacities for known elements in their ground state.

3–7 Evidence for the Quantum Model: New Physics

Bohr's model works well for atoms with one electron: for hydrogen. However, it does not work well for larger atoms that have more electrons. While Bohr's model was a great accomplishment, he soon saw that modifications were necessary. The scientists of the early twentieth century (Bohr included) set about to do this task.

The familiar laws that govern the motion of large objects such as baseballs, planets, and railroad boxcars do not properly describe the movement of electrons. Electrons are so small and move so quickly that a separate, more fundamental set of rules is required to describe their motion. Werner Heisenberg stated one of these rules in 1927. The **Heisenberg uncertainty principle** states that it is impossible to know both the energy (velocity) and the exact position of an electron at the same time. Since an electron moves at incredible speeds, it could easily zigzag or change directions without being detected.

Scientists understood that it was presumptuous to assume that electrons stayed in a set track. They replaced Bohr's precise orbits with a new concept, orbitals. **Orbitals** are the general areas where electrons probably exist. In diagrams orbitals look like fuzzy clouds without definite boundaries. The areas where electrons spend the most time are shaded the darkest. Away from the main part of the cloud, the shading becomes lighter as the chances of finding an electron decrease. As in the Bohr model, principal energy levels are arranged around the nucleus. Orbitals in which the electron's *average* distance from the nucleus is small have low energies. Orbitals in which the electron's average distance from the nucleus is great have high energies.

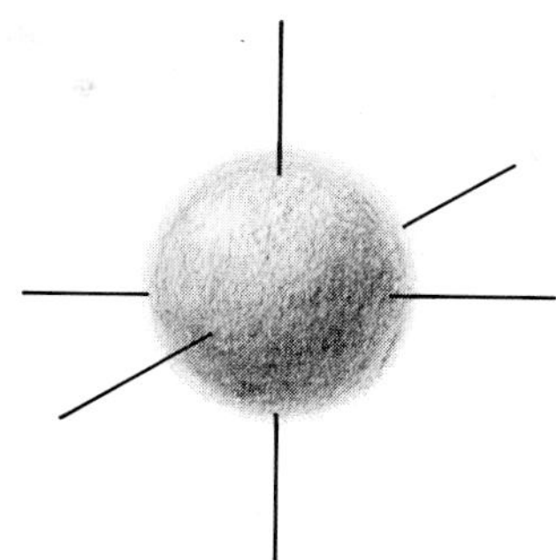

3-14 An orbital is a general area in which an electron can exist.

Recent developments in physics brought about the idea of orbitals, but they also changed what scientists thought about electrons. Are electrons particles or waves? Although Thomson long ago proved that electrons act like particles, a quarter of a century after his work, scientists began to think that electrons could often act like waves. In 1924 Louis de Broglie stated that the matter of an electron was not concentrated at one point but was spread out over the entire orbital. Even though the concept of matter-waves sounds like science fiction, it is firmly rooted in theory and observations.

Is an electron a particle, then, or is it a wave? It is both! The electron is said to have a dual nature. This concept of a dual nature is often difficult to grasp because the human mind is limited. Many things are just too difficult to understand. The limitations of the mind are even more apparent when spiritual matters are considered. Concepts such as the Trinity, predestination, free will, eternity, and the new nature of Christians after salvation are simply beyond understanding. In Romans 7:19 the Apostle Paul pointed out that Christians have a dual nature: "For the good that I would I do not: but the evil which I would not, that I do." Christians have a new nature that strives to obey Christ and an old nature that longs to serve sin. This fact is true but not easy to understand fully. Likewise, the fact that an electron can act like a particle and a wave at the same time is not easy to understand but must be accepted. The idea has become a cornerstone of the very successful quantum model of the atom.

The Quantum Model: Where Are the Electrons?

The latest, but not necessarily the last, idea on atomic structure is the quantum model. This model focuses on the locations of electrons, but it incorporates parts of all the previous atomic models. The wave concept of electrons along with a branch of higher mathematics called wave mechanics allowed scientists to develop a new model of the atom.

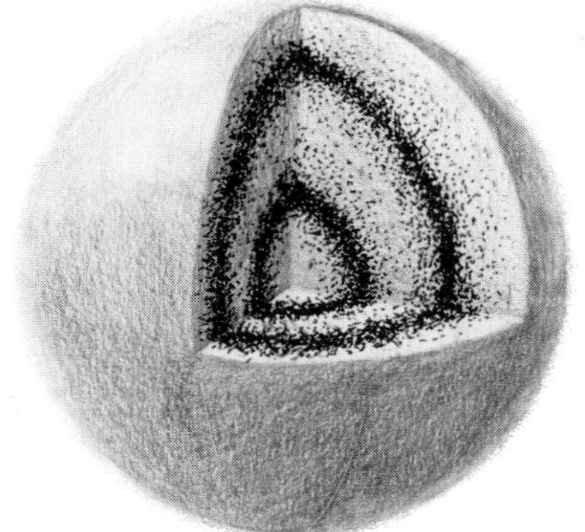

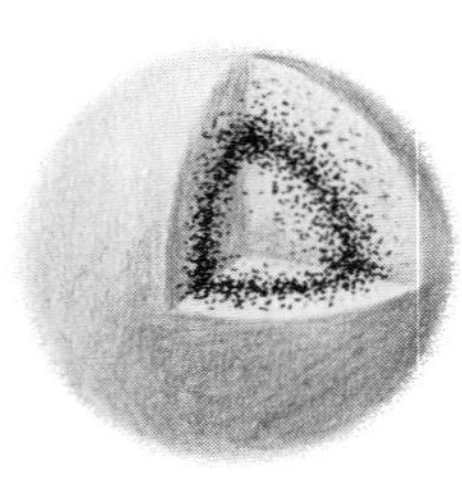

3-15 Orbitals come in different sizes. Large orbitals surround small orbitals.

3–8 Sublevels and Orbitals: Home of the Electrons

Like the Bohr model, the quantum model states that electrons exist in principal energy levels. Unlike the Bohr model, the quantum model subdivides some of the principal energy levels into **sublevels.** These sublevels contain other divisions called orbitals, and the orbitals contain electrons. There are four types of sublevels: *s, p, d,* and *f.*

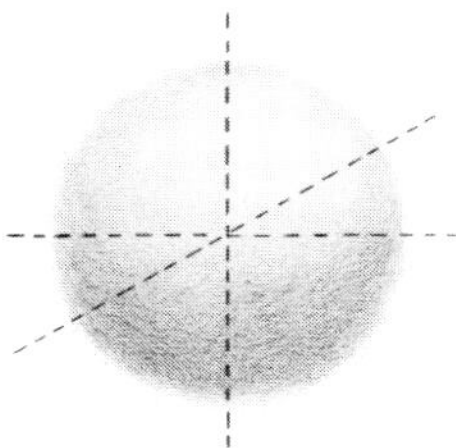

The s *sublevel.* This sublevel is the simplest of all. It has a spherical shape. Unlike other sublevels, it has only one orbital, which can hold two electrons. An orbital never contains more than two electrons.

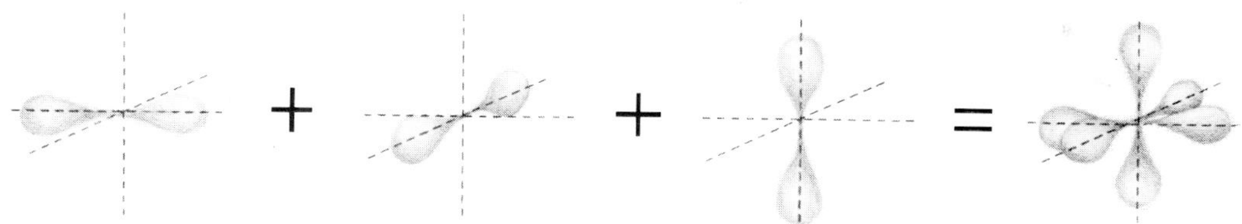

The p *sublevel.* A *p* sublevel looks like three barbells that intersect in the middle. It contains three orbitals: one in the *x* direction on a graph, one in the *y* direction, and one in the *z* direction. Since each orbital can hold two electrons, a complete *p* sublevel can hold six (3 × 2) electrons.

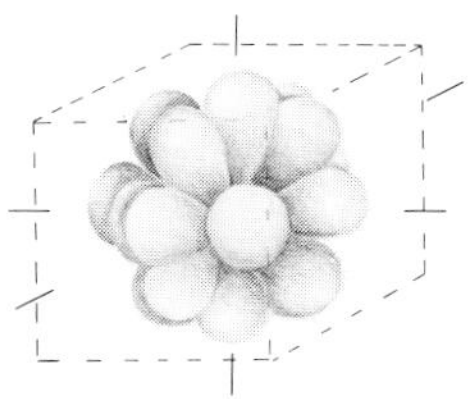

The d *sublevel.* A *d* sublevel has a complicated shape. It is a combination of five orbitals, and its capacity is ten (5 × 2) electrons.

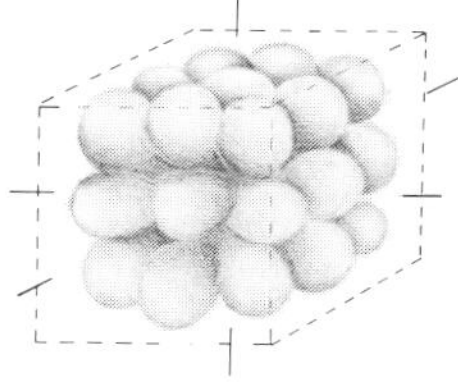

The f *sublevel.* An *f* sublevel is even more complicated than a *d* sublevel. It has seven orbitals and a capacity of fourteen (7 × 2) electrons.

Table 3-16

Sublevels in Energy Levels	
Principal Energy Level	**Possible Types of Sublevels***
1	*s*
2	*s p*
3	*s p d*
4	*s p d f*
5	*s p d f*
6	*s p d*
7	*s p*

*For the first 105 elements.

Not every principal energy level has an *s*, a *p*, a *d*, and an *f* sublevel. Each principal energy level has specific types of sublevels.

The first principal energy level has only an *s* sublevel. The second level contains an *s* and a *p* sublevel. The third level contains *s*, *p*, and *d* sublevels. The fourth and the fifth principal energy levels contain all four types of sublevels. The higher principal energy levels do not normally contain all the sublevels that they could, because the known elements have only a certain number of electrons.

The first principal energy level contains one *s* sublevel. The *s* sublevel has one orbital, which can hold two electrons. The total capacity of the first principal energy level is two electrons. The second principal energy level has an *s* and a *p* sublevel. Since the *p* sublevel can hold six electrons, the total capacity of the second principal energy level is eight electrons. The total capacities of the other principal energy levels can be found by the same procedure.

Table 3-17

Capacities of Energy Levels

Principal Energy Level	Sublevels	Orbitals in Each Sublevel	Electron Capacity of Each Sublevel	Total Electron Capacity
1	*s*	1	2	2
2	*s*	1	2	
	p	3	6	8
3	*s*	1	2	
	p	3	6	
	d	5	10	18
4	*s*	1	2	
	p	3	6	
	d	5	10	
	f	7	14	32
5	*s*	1	2	
	p	3	6	
	d	5	10	
	f	7	14	32
6	*s*	1	2	
	p	3	6	
	d	5	10	18
7	*s*	1	2	
	p	3	6	8

3–9 Energies of Sublevels

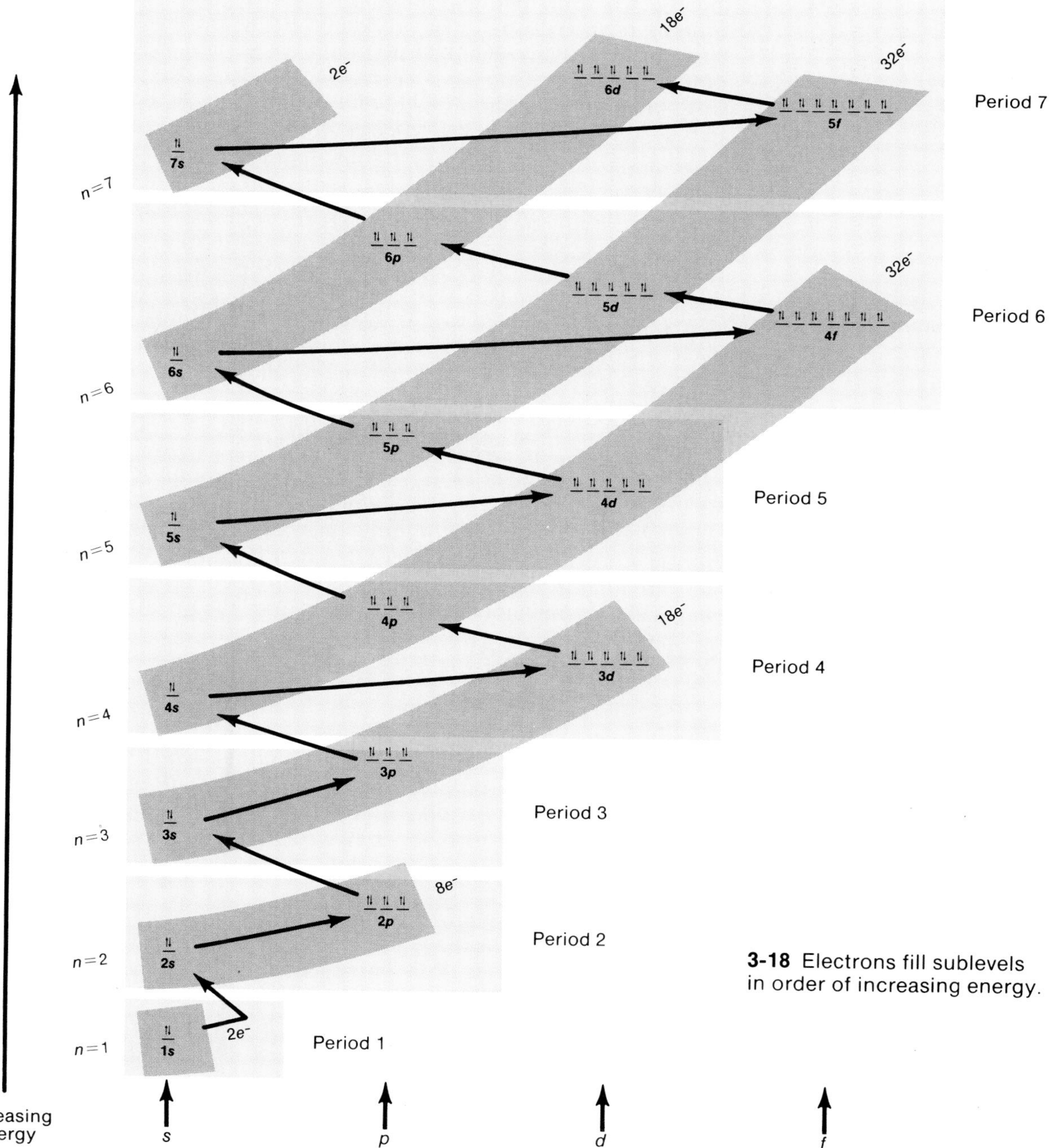

3-18 Electrons fill sublevels in order of increasing energy.

3-19 Mnemonic device for the filling order.

7*s*	7*p*		
6*s*	6*p*	6*d*	
5*s*	5*p*	5*d*	5*f*
4*s*	4*p*	4*d*	4*f*
3*s*	3*p*	3*d*	
2*s*	2*p*		
1*s*			

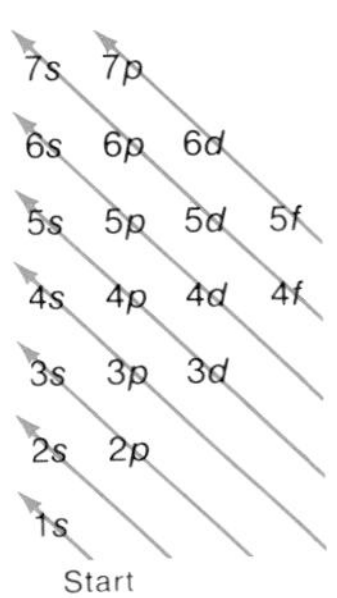

All sublevels can be ranked according to their energies. As expected, the 1*s* sublevel has the least amount of energy. The 2*s* and the 2*p* sublevels have more energy. Note that all three 2*p* orbitals have the same energy. Above them are the 3*s* and the 3*p* sublevels. A careful look at the graph reveals that the 3*d* orbitals do not come next as might be expected. The 4*s* has less energy than the 3*d* does! The graph ranks the sublevels (from bottom to top) in order of increasing energy.

1*s*, 2*s*, 2*p*, 3*s*, 3*p*, 4*s*, 3*d*, 4*p*, 5*s*, 4*d*, 5*p*, 6*s*, 4*f*, 5*d*, 6*p*, 7*s*, 5*f*, 6*d*, 7*p*

Notice that several of the higher principle energy levels "overlap." Memorizing the exact order of the sublevels is tedious, so a mnemonic device (memory aid) called the **diagonal rule** has been devised. To use this device, make a diagram like the one to the left (top), which shows which types of sublevels exist in each principal energy level.

Starting at the lower right corner, draw a diagonal arrow upwards through the 1*s* sublevel. The arrow immediately hits the left border of the structure, so return to the lower right. Draw the next diagonal arrow through the 2*s* sublevel and the third through the 2*p* and then the 3*s* sublevels. Continue this process of drawing parallel diagonal arrows from the lower right to the upper left of the chart. The order in which the diagonal arrows hit the sublevels reveals the energy order. (Read the arrows from bottom to top and from head to tail.) When completed, your diagonal-rule mnemonic device will look like the one to the left.

3–10 The Aufbau Principle: How to Build an Atom

The **Aufbau principle** states that the arrangement of electrons in an atom may be determined by the addition of electrons to a smaller atom. The word *aufbau* is a German word meaning "a building up." In the progression from hydrogen up to the larger elements, each successive element has one additional proton and one additional electron. As a rule, electrons add to the least energetic orbital possible. They must fill low-energy orbitals before they can occupy high-energy orbitals.

Hydrogen's one electron normally resides in the 1*s* sublevel. The **electron configuration,** or the arrangement of electrons, in hydrogen is shown as $1s^1$. The superscript above the 1*s* means that one electron is in the 1*s* sublevel. Chemists often use a picture called **orbital notation** to convey the same meaning. A horizontal line represents the one orbital in the 1*s* sublevel. An arrow pointing upward represents the first electron in the orbital.

	1*s*
H	$\underline{\uparrow}$

Helium has two electrons. The second electron joins the first to fill the 1*s* sublevel. Helium's electron configuration is thus $1s^2$.

	1*s*
He	↑↓

According to the same rules, beryllium's electron configuration is $1s^2\,2s^2$.

Now that electrons fill the 1*s* and 2*s* sublevels, the next electrons must go into the 2*p* orbitals. The orbital notation of boron (with five electrons) is

	1*s*	2*s*	2*p*		
B	↑↓	↑↓	↑	__	__

When determining the electron configuration of carbon, an option arises. The electron configuration is $1s^2\,2s^2\,2p^2$. But what about the orbital notation? Are the two electrons in the 2*p* sublevel in the same orbital, or are they in different orbitals? In orbital notation, is carbon

	1*s*	2*s*	2*p*				1*s*	2*s*	2*p*			
C	↑↓	↑↓	↑↓	__	__	or	↑↓	↑↓	↑	↑	__	?

Hund's rule states that when electrons fill a sublevel, all orbitals receive one electron before any receive two. Apparently electrons prefer to be as far away from each other as possible. By Hund's rule, carbon's orbital notation is the second option. According to Hund's rule, the orbital notation of nitrogen is

	1*s*	2*s*	2*p*		
N	↑↓	↑↓	↑	↑	↑

Oxygen's last electron is forced to pair up.

	1*s*	2*s*	2*p*		
O	↑↓	↑↓	↑↓	↑	↑

The Aufbau principle and Hund's rule can help reveal the electron configuration of any element. The Aufbau principle suggests the order in which electrons fill sublevels. Hund's rule tells whether electrons in the same sublevel will be paired or unpaired.

Sample Problem. Draw the orbital notation of manganese, and give its electron configuration.

Solution.

The twenty-five electrons fill the 1*s*, 2*s*, 2*p*, 3*s*, and 3*p* sublevels. The 3*d* sublevel is partly filled. The 4*s* sublevel is filled with two electrons before electrons are added to the 3*d* sublevel.

3-20 A sodium atom has electrons in the 1*s*, 2*s*, 2*p*, and 3*s* sublevels.

	1s	2s	2p			3s	3p		
Mn	↑↓	↑↓	↑↓	↑↓	↑↓	↑↓	↑↓	↑↓	↑↓

3d					4s
↑	↑	↑	↑	↑	↑↓

To write the electron configuration of an element, simply count the number of electrons in each sublevel.

$$1s^2 2s^2 2p^6 3s^2 3p^6 4s^2 3d^5$$

Hund's rule and the Aufbau principle are not always followed precisely. Chromium and copper are notable exceptions. In these cases the electrons tend to remain unpaired, thus overcoming the Aufbau principle. One electron that normally appears in the $4s$ sublevel shifts up to a $3d$ orbital so that it can remain unpaired. Electron configurations for all the elements may be found in Appendix D.

3–11 Quantum Numbers: Addresses for Electrons

Chemists use numbers called **quantum numbers** to describe the locations and energies of electrons. Each electron in an atom has its own set of four numbers that serves as an "address."

The first quantum number identifies the principal energy level. The number can have a value of 1, 2, 3, 4, or higher.

The second quantum number identifies the type of sublevel in which an electron exists (*s, p, d,* or *f*). The sublevels receive the following numbers: *s*—0; *p*—1; *d*—2; *f*—3.

The third quantum number specifies the electron's orbital. If an electron exists in an *s* sublevel, there is only one possible value: 0. If an electron resides in a *p* sublevel (second quantum number = 1), there are three possibilities: -1, 0, or 1. All *d* sublevels have five orbitals, so there are five possible values for the third quantum number. They are -2, -1, 0, 1, 2.

Table 3-21

Values for the Third Quantum Number

Second Quantum Number	Number of Orbitals	Possibility for the Third Quantum Number
0 (*s* sublevel)	1	0
1 (*p* sublevel)	3	-1, 0, 1
2 (*d* sublevel)	5	-2, -1, 0, 1, 2
3 (*f* sublevel)	7	-3, -2, -1, 0, 1, 2, 3

The fourth quantum number differentiates between the two electrons in a given orbital. One electron is assigned a value of $+\frac{1}{2}$, and the other is assigned a value of $-\frac{1}{2}$. Scientists have described this difference in electrons as the "spin" of the electrons.

Numbers of Atomic Particles: Things We Can Count On

Even though the quantum model could be changed in the future, the "basic" particles in atoms are fairly well agreed upon. The nucleus carries a positive charge and contains most of an atom's mass. It consists of positively charged protons and neutral neutrons. The number of protons in an atom determines the atom's identity; the number of neutrons affects its mass; and the number of electrons affects its electrical charge. Counting the particles in atoms gives valuable information.

3–12 Atomic Mass

Once chemists of Dalton's day started to analyze chemical compounds, they tried to determine the masses of individual atoms. Men knew that carbon atoms were twelve times as heavy as hydrogen atoms and that oxygen atoms were sixteen times as heavy as hydrogen atoms. A few elements with their relative masses are listed in Table 3-23.

Chemists express these masses in **atomic mass units** (abbreviated amu). An amu is defined as 1/12 the mass of a carbon-12 atom, or as 1.66×10^{-27} kilograms. It is approximately the same size as a proton or a neutron (one proton = 1.0073 amu; one neutron = 1.0087 amu). The electron is a scant 0.00055 amu. Adding the number of protons and neutrons gives the approximate mass of an atom. (The electrons can be ignored because their masses are negligible.) The sum of the protons and neutrons in an atom is that atom's **atomic mass number.**

ED FREEMAN, A SIMPLE JANITOR... LATER TO BE REMEMBERED AS THE FIRST MAN TO SEE A PROTON FIRST-HAND.

atomic mass number = protons + neutrons

The number of protons in an atom is vitally important. This number, called the **atomic number,** determines the identity of the atom. If an atom has twenty-nine protons, it must be a copper atom. Conversely, all copper atoms have twenty-nine protons.

atomic number = number of protons

Table 3-23

Element	Average Atomic Mass (in amu)	Atomic Mass Number	Atomic Number
H	1.008	1	1
C	12.01	12	6
O	16.00	16	8
Na	22.99	23	11
S	32.06	32	16
Ca	40.08	40	20
U	238.0	238	92

3–13 Isotopes: Count Those Neutrons!

Even though all atoms of an element must have the same number of protons (atomic number), they do not all have the same mass. Some atoms of the same element have a different number of neutrons. Atoms with the same atomic number but different numbers of neutrons are called **isotopes.**

Isotopic notation is often used to specify the exact composition of an atom. This notation includes the atom's symbol, atomic number, and atomic mass number. A boron atom that has five protons and six neutrons has an atomic mass number of 11 and would be written as

$$^{11}_{5}B$$

Given an atom's isotopic notation, it is easy to calculate the number of protons, neutrons, and electrons. The atomic number at the lower left of the symbol signifies that this atom has five protons. To be electrically neutral, the atom must also have five electrons. The number of neutrons in the atom is the difference between the mass number and the atomic number.

mass number − atomic number = number of neutrons

(protons + neutrons) − protons = neutrons

11 − 5 = 6 neutrons

If this boron atom had five neutrons, its isotopic notation would be

$$^{10}_{5}B$$

Sample Problem. Determine the number of protons, neutrons, and electrons in $^{51}_{24}Cr$.

Solution.

The atomic number tells the number of protons: 24. The number of electrons equals the number of protons in a neutral atom: 24. The number of neutrons is the difference between the mass number and the atomic number.

$$51 - 24 = 27 \text{ neutrons}$$

Sample Problem. An atom has nineteen protons and twenty-two neutrons. Write its isotopic notation.

Solution.

Any atom that has nineteen protons must be a potassium (K) atom. Add the number of protons and neutrons to find the mass number.

$$19 \text{ protons} + 22 \text{ neutrons} = 41$$

The isotopic notation is

$$^{41}_{19}K$$

Most elements are mixtures of isotopes. This explains why their masses are not always whole numbers. **Atomic masses** are the weighted averages of isotopes. They show the average mass of an atom in a sample. For example, a naturally occurring sample of lithium is 7.42 per cent lithium-6 and 92.58 per cent lithium-7. The weighted average is closer to 7 than to 6.

Suppose that you calculated the average atomic mass of 10,000 lithium atoms. The 7.42 per cent of lithium atoms has a mass of 6.015 amu per atom. The 92.58 per cent of lithium atoms has a mass of 7.016 amu per atom. To find the average, first find the total mass of the sample; then divide by the number of atoms. The mass of the entire sample is the sum of the masses of the two isotopes.

mass from lithium-6 atoms:

$$742 \text{ atoms} \times 6.015 \text{ amu/atom} = 4463.13 \text{ amu}$$

mass from lithium-7 atoms:

$$9258 \text{ atoms} \times 7.016 \text{ amu/atom} = 64{,}954.128 \text{ amu}$$

MASS OF ENTIRE SAMPLE	69,417.258 amu

The average mass, or the atomic mass, of an atom in this sample is 69,417 amu/10,000 atoms = 6.9417 amu/atom. As expected, this value is closer to 7 than to 6.

Table 3-24

Naturally Occurring Isotopic Abundances of Common Elements

Isotope	Per cent	Mass (in amu)
H-1	99.985	1.007825
H-2	0.015	2.014
Li-6	7.42	6.01512
Li-7	92.58	7.01600
B-10	19.78	10.0129
B-11	80.22	11.00931
C-12	98.89	12.0000
C-13	1.11	13.00335
Si-28	92.21	27.97693
Si-29	4.7	28.97649
Si-30	3.09	29.97376
P-31	100	30.99376
Br-79	50.54	78.9183
Br-81	49.46	80.9163
Au-197	100	196.9666
U-234	0.0057	234.0409
U-235	0.72	235.0439
U-238	99.27	238.0508

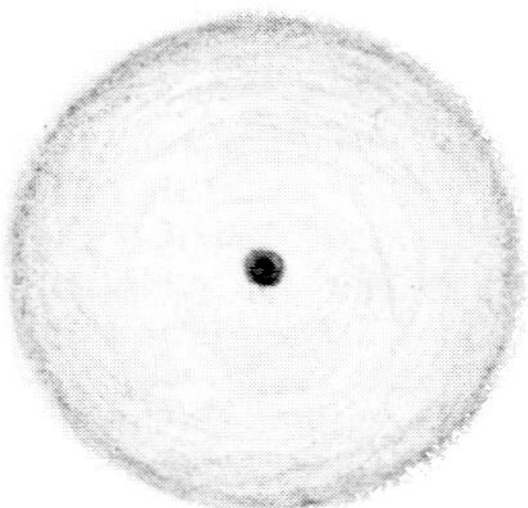

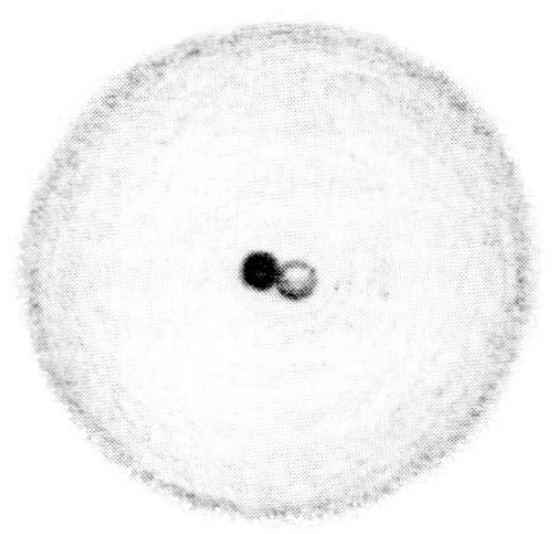

3-25 Isotopes of hydrogen. A few hydrogen atoms have a neutron.

3–14 Valence Electrons: Last, but Not Least

The electrons in the outermost energy level are the most important electrons of an atom. They are the ones that hop between energy levels when atoms get excited. They are the ones that participate in chemical bonds. They are also the ones that give elements their physical properties. The electrons in the outermost energy level of an atom are given a special name: **valence electrons.**

Sample Problem. How many valence electrons do these atoms have?

a. argon

	1*s*	**2*s***	**2*p***	**3*s***	**3*p***
Ar	↑↓	↑↓	↑↓ ↑↓ ↑↓	↑↓	↑↓ ↑↓ ↑↓

b. nickel

	1*s*	**2*s***	**2*p***	**3*s***	**3*p***
Ni	↑↓	↑↓	↑↓ ↑↓ ↑↓	↑↓	↑↓ ↑↓ ↑↓

3*d*	**4*s***
↑↓ ↑↓ ↑↓ ↑ ↑	↑↓

Solution.

a. argon: The orbital notation shows eight electrons in the third energy level.

b. nickel: Even though the 3*d* orbitals were the last to fill, the fourth principal energy level is considered the outermost level. The two electrons in the 4*s* sublevel are the ones that participate most often in chemical reactions. Nickel has two valence electrons.

3–15 Electron-Dot Structures

Since valence electrons determine how atoms bond, the inner electrons can often be ignored. An **electron-dot structure** is a shorthand way of representing only the valence electrons in an atom. Dots that represent the valence electrons are placed around an element's symbol. The first two dots are paired, since they stand for the two electrons in the *s* sublevel. The other electrons remain unpaired if possible (Hund's rule). See Table 3-26 for the conventional arrangement of dots for each number of valence electrons.

Sample Problem. Write electron-dot structures for helium and oxygen.

Solution.

Helium has two valence electrons: He:

Oxygen has six valence electrons: ·Ö:
·

Table 3-26

Electron-Dot Structures

Valence Electrons	Example
1	Na·
2	Mg:
3	Äl·
4	S̈i· (dot below)
5	·P̈· (dot below)
6	·S̈: (dot below)
7	·C̈l: (two dots below)
8	:Är: (two dots below)

3–16 Ions: Charged Atoms

Electrons move between energy levels when they gain or lose energy. Given enough energy, an electron can jump away from an atom. This defection results in an atom that has an unbalanced electrical charge. Such atoms are called **ions.** Changing the number of electrons does not change the identity of the atom. The number of *protons* determines the atom's identity.

Ions may have positive or negative charges. If an atom loses an electron, it will have a positive charge. Positive ions are called **cations.** If an atom gains an electron, it will have an extra negative charge. Negative ions are called **anions.** Electron-dot structures can be used to represent ions. If a fluorine atom gains an electron, it acquires a negative charge. The 1- superscript reminds us of the charge.

$$\cdot\ddot{\underset{..}{F}}: + \text{electron} \longrightarrow :\ddot{\underset{..}{F}}:^{1-}$$

A magnesium atom that lost two electrons would have a +2 charge.

$$Mg: \longrightarrow Mg^{2+} + 2 \text{ electrons}$$

Coming to Terms

model
law of definite composition
cathode rays
electron
nucleus
proton
neutron
continuous spectrum
line spectrum
quantized
principal energy level
Heisenberg uncertainty principle
orbital
sublevel
diagonal rule
Aufbau principle
electron configuration
orbital notation
Hund's rule
quantum number
atomic mass unit
atomic mass number
atomic number
isotope
isotopic notation
atomic mass
valence electron
electron-dot structure
ion
cation
anion

Review Questions

1. Although nobody has seen an atom, scientists assert that atoms exist. What gives them the confidence to do this?
2. Point out one flaw in each of the following statements:
   a. Scientific models do not deal with facts.
   b. Scientific models make predictions, but whether these predictions are reasonable or not makes no difference.
   c. Scientific models merely organize facts.
3. Briefly describe each of the following atomic models:
   a. Dalton's
   b. Thomson's
   c. Rutherford's
   d. Bohr's
   e. Quantum
4. Describe the discoveries or advancements that made each of these atomic models obsolete:
   a. Dalton's
   b. Thomson's
   c. Rutherford's
   d. Bohr's
5. How did observations of spectra lead to conclusions that the energy given off by excited atoms is quantized?
6. Describe what happens to the outermost electron in a sodium atom when that atom is heated and made to give off a line spectrum.

7. Explain how atoms can be electrically neutral even though they contain charged particles.
8. What is the electron capacity of
   a. an orbital?
   b. an *s* sublevel?
   c. a *p* sublevel?
   d. the second principal energy level?
   e. the fourth principal energy level?
9. How many orbitals are in
   a. an *s* sublevel?
   b. a *d* sublevel?
   c. the second principal energy level?
   d. the fourth principal energy level?
10. For each of the following atoms,
   i. write out the orbital notation;
   ii. write out the electron configuration;
   iii. show the number of electrons in each energy level.

   Example: Carbon

   i.

	1*s*	**2*s***	**2*p***		
C	↑↓	↑↓	↑	↑	__

   ii. $1s^2 2s^2 2p^2$
   iii. 2, 4

   a. oxygen
   b. sulfur
   c. potassium
   d. titanium
   e. bromine
   f. barium
11. How many unpaired electrons are found in each of the elements in the previous problem?
12. Draw a blank orbital notation chart that contains all seven energy levels (through the 7*p* subshell). Instead of drawing in arrows, number the blanks according to the filling order. Follow Hund's rule. Example: The first two levels should be labeled as follows:

1, 2	3, 4	5, 8	6, 9	7, 10
1*s*	2*s*		2*p*	

13. What information can quantum numbers give?

14. What are the possible values for the third quantum number for an electron in the following sublevels?

    a. 1*s*
    b. 3*p*
    c. 4*f*
    d. 3*d*

15. If the first quantum number for an electron is 2, what possible values may the other three quantum numbers have?

16. Several of the following lists of quantum numbers are faulty. Pick out the faulty lists, identify which numbers are impossible, and explain why they are impossible.

	First	Second	Third	Fourth
a.	2	1	1	+½
b.	0	0	0	-½
c.	4	4	0	+½
d.	4	3	-2	+½
e.	3	1	2	+½
f.	1	0	0	+½

17. How is the number of electrons in an atom related to the atomic number of the element?

18. What information does the atomic mass number provide?

19. For each of the following atoms, tell how many protons, neutrons, and electrons are present.

    a. $^{9}_{4}Be$
    b. $^{45}_{21}Sc$
    c. $^{127}_{53}I$
    d. $(^{132}_{55}Cs)^{+}$

20. Fill in the blanks in the following chart:

Element	Symbol	Atomic Number	Mass Number	Electrons	Protons	Neutrons
hydrogen	______	______	______	______	______	0
______	______	______	______	______	10	______
______	______	29	65	______	______	______
______	______	______	104	44	______	______

21. Write isotopic notation for the atoms that have these compositions:

    a. 14 protons, 14 neutrons
    b. 1 proton, 1 neutron
    c. 80 protons, 120 neutrons

22. Natural boron contains both B-10 and B-11 isotopes. Considering that boron's average atomic mass is 10.81 amu, which isotope is more common?

23. A naturally occurring sample of the element gallium is a mixture of two isotopes. Calculate the atomic mass of gallium given that 60.4 per cent of the atoms have a mass of 68.9257 amu and that 39.6 per cent of the atoms have a mass of 70.9244 amu.

24. State the number of valence electrons in the following elements:
    a. oxygen
    b. sulfur
    c. potassium
    d. bromine
    e. barium

25. Draw electron-dot structures for each of the elements in question 24.

26. Must all the electrons be removed from an atom for it to become positively charged? Why or why not?

27. State the charge that would be on the ion if a neutral atom were to
    a. gain one electron.
    b. lose one electron.
    c. gain two electrons.
    d. lose two electrons.

FOUR

ELEMENTS

ORGANIZATION AND PROPERTIES

AN exasperated student was told by a friend that the key to passing chemistry was to understand the subject before beginning the course. The student paused and sighed, "If I understood chemistry, I would not have to take this course."

The real key to learning chemistry is understanding the framework of the course. You have learned about the scientific method, the general forms of matter, and the specific structure of the atom. But before you accumulate any more facts about chemistry, you need to understand the framework: how atoms of one element differ from atoms of another. This information is found in an unexpectedly simple form—the **periodic table.**

The Periodic Table

4–1 Early Organizational Attempts: The Table Shapes Up

Imagine a list of all the elements, their atomic structures, and their properties. The great number of facts would be overwhelming even to someone blessed with a photographic memory. Clearly this essential information needs to be organized and presented so that all the needed facts can be at anyone's fingertips.

Chemists began this process long ago by searching for properties that were common to the known elements. One of the first scientists to discover such common properties was Johann Dobereiner. In 1829 this German chemist announced that he had observed several triads, or groups of three similar elements, among the known elements. One of Dobereiner's triads contained Cl, Br, and I. Each of these elements forms a gas with a distinct color and has similar properties.

As more elements were discovered, Dobereiner's concept of triads of chemical elements did not hold up. Elements with similar properties joined the triads to form quartets and quintets. Apparently the number *three* was not significant. Grouping chemical elements into families according to similar chemical properties, however, was an important step.

In 1864 John Newlands presented a classification scheme that added another idea to the groupings of Dobereiner. Newlands arranged the known elements by their increasing atomic masses.

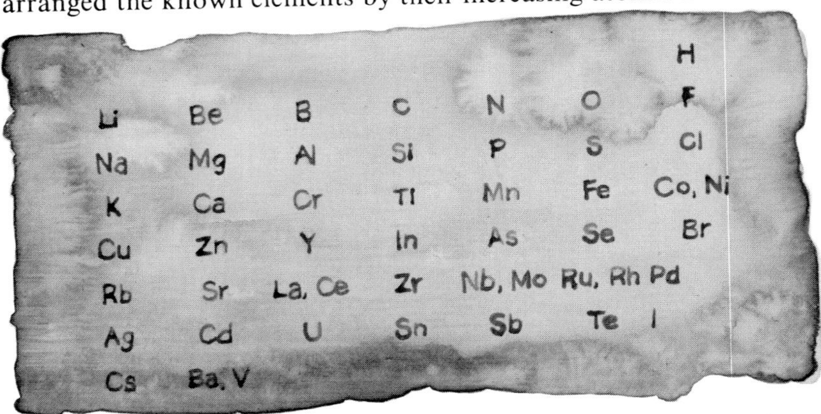

4-1 John Newlands's table aligned similar elements in vertical columns.

It appeared that every eighth element had similar properties. The known elements fell into similar groups when arranged in seven columns. Having extensive musical and scientific training, Newlands saw a correlation between the two worlds of music and science. The arrangement he had uncovered paralleled the octaves in music. He labeled this observed relationship the Law of Octaves. His ideas, however, were not well received, and his parallel to music was subjected to much ridicule. Newlands's idea that atomic mass and chemical properties might be related was correct, but he did not undertake a detailed study of each element's mass and characteristics.

4–2 The Modern Periodic Table: Getting It All Together

Credit for the development of the modern periodic table goes mostly to the Russian chemist Dmitri Mendeleev. Like Newlands, Mendeleev arranged elements by their atomic masses. When an element did not seem to fit into a column, he noted that the atomic mass jumped significantly from that of the last element. He reasoned that undiscovered elements belonged in the gaps, so he left blanks in the chart and placed the known elements in columns in which they fit. Using information about the physical and chemical characteristics of elements, he predicted the properties of the elements that would fit into the blanks. Some of these elements were discovered shortly after he published his table.

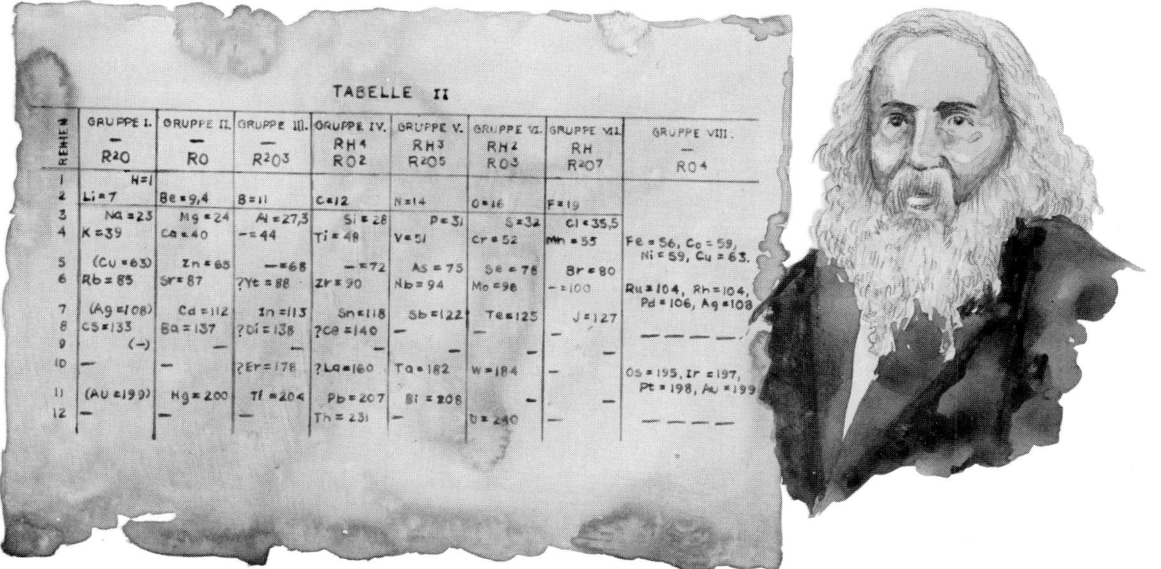

TABELLE II

REIHEN	GRUPPE I. — R^2O	GRUPPE II. — RO	GRUPPE III. — R^2O^3	GRUPPE IV. RH^4 RO^2	GRUPPE V. RH^3 R^2O^5	GRUPPE VI. RH^2 RO^3	GRUPPE VII. RH R^2O^7	GRUPPE VIII. — RO^4
1	H=1							
2	Li=7	Be=9,4	B=11	C=12	N=14	O=16	F=19	
3	Na=23	Mg=24	Al=27,3	Si=28	P=31	S=32	Cl=35,5	
4	K=39	Ca=40	—=44	Ti=48	V=51	Cr=52	Mn=55	Fe=56, Co=59, Ni=59, Cu=63.
5	(Cu=63)	Zn=65	—=68	—=72	As=75	Se=78	Br=80	
6	Rb=85	Sr=87	?Yt=88	Zr=90	Nb=94	Mo=96	—=100	Ru=104, Rh=104, Pd=106, Ag=108
7	(Ag=108)	Cd=112	In=113	Sn=118	Sb=122	Te=125	J=127	
8	Cs=133	Ba=137	?Di=138	?Ce=140	—	—	—	— — — —
9	(—)	—	—	—	—	—	—	
10	—	—	?Er=178	?La=180	Ta=182	W=184	—	Os=195, Ir=197, Pt=198, Au=199
11	(Au=199)	Hg=200	Tl=204	Pb=207	Bi=208	—	—	
12	—	—	—	Th=231	—	U=240	—	— — — —

4-2 Mendeleev's periodic table contained gaps for undiscovered elements.

Another innovation of Mendeleev's chart involved elements called transition metals. These elements did not fit into the major families of the chart, but they all had similar characteristics. Mendeleev put them in the chart but did not let them interfere with the groupings of the other elements. He then summarized his discoveries in a periodic law: the properties of the elements vary with their *atomic masses* in a systematic way.

Even after most of Mendeleev's "missing" elements were found, the table still had some problems. Arranging the elements in order of increasing atomic masses did not always produce a table with

	IA	IIA	IIIB	IVB	VB	VIB	VIIB	VIIIB	VIIIB	VIIIB	IB	IIB	IIIA	IVA	VA	VIA	VIIA	VIIIA
1																		
2																		
3															15 P	16 S	17 Cl	
4								26 Fe	27 Co 58.9	28 Ni 58.7	29 Cu				33 As	34 Se	35 Br	
5								44 Ru	45 Rh	46 Pd	47 Ag				51 Sb	52 Te 127.6	53 I 126.9	
6								76 Os	77 Ir	78 Pt	79 Au							
7																		

4-3 Arranging elements by their atomic masses caused Ni, Co, Te, and I to fall into the wrong columns.

PERIODIC TABL

11 — Atomic number
Sodium — Name
Na — Symbol
22.99 — Atomic mass
- rounded to four significant digits
- mass number of longest known half-life indicated b

2, 8, 1 — Electron structure by energy level

	IA	IIA	IIIB	IVB	VB	VIB	VIIB		
1	1 Hydrogen **H** 1.008 1								
2	3 Lithium **Li** 6.939 2, 1	4 Beryllium **Be** 9.012 2, 2							
3	11 Sodium **Na** 22.99 2, 8, 1	12 Magnesium **Mg** 24.31 2, 8, 2							
4	19 Potassium **K** 39.10 2, 8, 8, 1	20 Calcium **Ca** 40.08 2, 8, 8, 2	21 Scandium **Sc** 44.96 2, 8, 9, 2	22 Titanium **Ti** 47.90 2, 8, 10, 2	23 Vanadium **V** 50.94 2, 8, 11, 2	24 Chromium **Cr** 52.00 2, 8, 13, 1	25 Manganese **Mn** 54.94 2, 8, 13, 2	26 Iron **Fe** 55.85 2, 8, 14, 2	27 C 2
5	37 Rubidium **Rb** 85.47 2, 8, 18, 8, 1	38 Strontium **Sr** 87.62 2, 8, 18, 8, 2	39 Yttrium **Y** 88.91 2, 8, 18, 9, 2	40 Zirconium **Zr** 91.22 2, 8, 18, 10, 2	41 Niobium **Nb** 92.91 2, 8, 18, 12, 1	42 Molybdenum **Mo** 95.94 2, 8, 18, 13, 1	43 ☢ Technetium **Tc** (99) 2, 8, 18, 14, 1	44 Ruthenium **Ru** 101.1 2, 8, 18, 15, 1	45 R 2, 8
6	55 Cesium **Cs** 132.9 —18, 18, 8, 1	56 Barium **Ba** 137.3 —18, 18, 8, 2	57 Lanthanum **La** 138 9 —18, 18, 9, 2	72 Hafnium **Hf** 178.5 —18, 32, 10, 2	73 Tantalum **Ta** 180.9 —18, 32, 11, 2	74 Tungsten **W** 183.9 —18, 32, 12, 2	75 Rhenium **Re** 186.2 —18, 32, 13, 2	76 Osmium **Os** 190.2 —18, 32, 14, 2	77 I —1
7	87 ☢ Francium **Fr** (223) —18, 32, 18, 8, 1	88 ☢ Radium **Ra** 226.0 —18, 32, 18, 8, 2	89 ☢ Actinium **Ac** 227.0 —18, 32, 18, 9, 2	104 ☢ Rutherfordium **Rf** (261)	105 ☢ Hahnium **Ha** (262)	106 ☢ Seaborgium **Sg** (263)	107 ☢ Nielsbohrium **Ns** (262)	108 ☢ Hassium **Hs** (265)	109 Me

Lanthanide series

58 Cerium **Ce** 140.1 —18, 20, 8, 2	59 Praseodymium **Pr** 140.9 —18, 21, 8, 2	60 Neodymium **Nd** 144.2 —18, 22, 8, 2	61 ☢ Promethium **Pm** (145) —18, 23, 8, 2	62 Sa S —
90 ☢ Thorium **Th** 232.0 —18, 32, 18, 10, 2	91 ☢ Protactinium **Pa** 231.0 —18, 32, 20, 9, 2	92 ☢ Uranium **U** 238.0 —18, 32, 21, 9, 2	93 ☢ Neptunium **Np** 237.0 —18, 32, 22, 9, 2	94 P —18

Actinide series

F THE ELEMENTS

	IB	IIB	IIIA	IVA	VA	VIA	VIIA	VIIIA
								2 Helium **He** 4.003 2
			5 Boron **B** 10.81 2, 3	6 Carbon **C** 12.01 2, 4	7 Nitrogen **N** 14.01 2, 5	8 Oxygen **O** 16.00 2, 6	9 Fluorine **F** 19.00 2, 7	10 Neon **Ne** 20.18 2, 8
			13 Aluminum **Al** 26.98 2, 8, 3	14 Silicon **Si** 28.09 2, 8, 4	15 Phosphorus **P** 30.97 2, 8, 5	16 Sulfur **S** 32.06 2, 8, 6	17 Chlorine **Cl** 35.45 2, 8, 7	18 Argon **Ar** 39.95 2, 8, 8
el i , 2	29 Copper **Cu** 63.55 2, 8, 18, 1	30 Zinc **Zn** 65.38 2, 8, 18, 2	31 Gallium **Ga** 69.72 2, 8, 18, 3	32 Germanium **Ge** 72.59 2, 8, 18, 4	33 Arsenic **As** 74.92 2, 8, 18, 5	34 Selenium **Se** 78.96 2, 8, 18, 6	35 Bromine **Br** 79.90 2, 8, 18, 7	36 Krypton **Kr** 83.80 2, 8, 18, 8
um d 4 18	47 Silver **Ag** 107.9 2, 8, 18, 18, 1	48 Cadmium **Cd** 112.4 2, 8, 18, 18, 2	49 Indium **In** 114.8 2, 8, 18, 18, 3	50 Tin **Sn** 118.7 2, 8, 18, 18, 4	51 Antimony **Sb** 121.8 2, 8, 18, 18, 5	52 Tellurium **Te** 127.6 2, 8, 18, 18, 6	53 Iodine **I** 126.9 2, 8, 18, 18, 7	54 Xenon **Xe** 131.3 2, 8, 18, 18, 8
m t 7, 1	79 Gold **Au** 197.0 —18, 32, 18, 1	80 Mercury **Hg** 200.6 —18, 32, 18, 2	81 Thallium **Tl** 204.4 —18, 32, 18, 3	82 Lead **Pb** 207.2 —18, 32, 18, 4	83 Bismuth **Bi** 209.0 —18, 32, 18, 5	84 ☢ Polonium **Po** (209) —18, 32, 18, 6	85 ☢ Astatine **At** (210) —18, 32, 18, 7	86 ☢ Radon **Rn** (222) —18, 32, 18, 8

line of metalloids

Key:

- Alkali metals
- Alkaline-earth metals
- Transition metals
- Post-transition metals
- Metalloids
- Nonmetals
- Halogens (also nonmetals)
- Noble gases
- ☢ Radioactive isotopes

um u 8, 2	64 Gadolinium **Gd** 157.3 —18, 25, 9, 2	65 Terbium **Tb** 158.9 —18, 27, 8, 2	66 Dysprosium **Dy** 162.5 —18, 28, 8, 2	67 Holmium **Ho** 164.9 —18, 29, 8, 2	68 Erbium **Er** 167.3 —18, 30, 8, 2	69 Thulium **Tm** 168.9 —18, 31, 8, 2	70 Ytterbium **Yb** 173.0 —18, 32, 8, 2	71 Lutetium **Lu** 175.0 —18, 32, 9, 2
☢ ium n 5, 8, 2	96 ☢ Curium **Cm** (247) —18, 32, 25, 9, 2	97 ☢ Berkelium **Bk** (247) —18, 32, 26, 9, 2	98 ☢ Californium **Cf** (251) —18, 32, 28, 8, 2	99 ☢ Einsteinium **Es** (254) —18, 32, 29, 8, 2	100 ☢ Fermium **Fm** (257) —18, 32, 30, 8, 2	101 ☢ Mendelevium **Md** (258) —18, 32, 31, 8, 2	102 ☢ Nobelium **No** (259) —18, 32, 32, 8, 2	103 ☢ Lawrencium **Lr** (260) —18, 32, 32, 9, 2

similar elements below each other. For example, nickel resembles paladium and platinum much more than it resembles rhodium and iridium.

A young Englishman discovered a new technique that eventually cleared up discrepancies in the periodic table. In 1912 Henry Moseley developed a way to count the protons in a nucleus. He found that if the elements were arranged in order of increasing atomic numbers, the problems in the table vanished. Moseley's work led to a revision of the **periodic law.** After this revision it read as follows: the properties of an element vary with their *atomic numbers* in a systematic way.

4–3 Parts of the Periodic Table

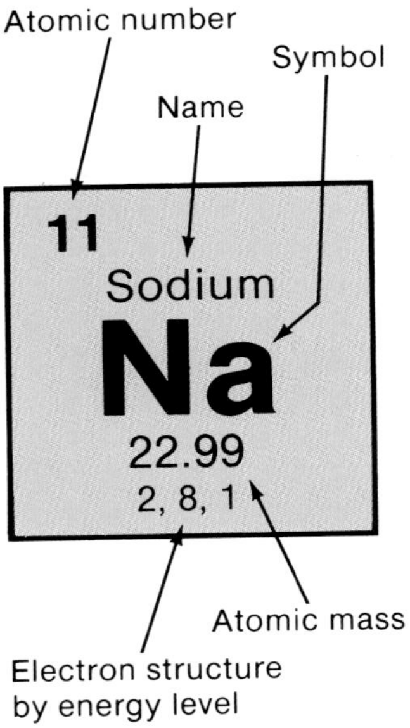

Atomic number | Symbol | Name

11
Sodium
Na
22.99
2, 8, 1

Atomic mass | Electron structure by energy level

4-5 Information found in the periodic table.

The periodic table contains a small block for each element, and each block contains basic information about the element. An element's *atomic number* appears at the top of the block. This number specifies the number of protons in the nucleus. Some tables give the names of the elements along with the symbol. Located under the symbol is the atomic mass. This number gives the average mass of the atom in amu's. Some tables also show the number of electrons in the outer energy levels.

Together the various blocks form vertical columns and horizontal rows. A vertical column of elements is called a **group** or a **family** because the elements are physically and chemically similar. Families have similar properties because their members have similar electron configurations.

A Roman numeral I above the first vertical column indicates that all elements in this family have one valence electron. Likewise, the second family of elements is headed by a Roman numeral II, which shows that each member possesses two valence electrons. The Roman numerals above the families give a reasonably accurate indication of valence electrons. Transition metals, however, are noted for being the exceptions to almost every rule. Each Roman numeral has an accompanying *A* or *B* that tells whether the families are **main groups** (A) or *transition metals* (B).

Horizontal rows of elements are called **periods** or series. The left side of the table contains **metals;** the center holds transition metals; the heavy, stair-step line marks the home of the **metalloids—** elements having characteristics of both metals and nonmetals; and the far right side of the table contains the **nonmetals.**

Sample Problem. What element belongs to family VA and the second period?

Solution. nitrogen

Sample Problem. To what family and period does the element with the atomic number 10 belong?

Solution.

Neon, the tenth element, appears in the far right column and on the second row. It belongs to family VIIIA and the second period.

Two rows of elements, called the lanthanide and the actinide series, have been placed at the bottom of the chart. The lanthanide series extends from element number 58 through number 71, fitting into the table immediately after lanthanum. The actinide series, beginning with thorium (element number 90), fits into the table after actinium. If those elements were in their proper places, the table would be expanded into an unwieldy, bulky shape.

4-6 An awkward shape results when the inner transition metals are inserted into the main body of the periodic table.

	IA	IIA	IIIB	Inner Transition Elements														IVB	VB	VIB	VIIB	VIIIB			IB	IIB	IIIA	IVA	VA	VIA	VIIA	VIIIA
1	H																															He
2	Li	Be																									B	C	N	O	F	Ne
3	Na	Mg																									Al	Si	P	S	Cl	Ar
4	K	Ca	Sc															Ti	V	Cr	Mn	Fe	Co	Ni	Cu	Zn	Ga	Ge	As	Se	Br	Kr
5	Rb	Sr	Y															Zr	Nb	Mo	Tc	Ru	Rh	Pd	Ag	Cd	In	Sn	Sb	Te	I	Xe
6	Cs	Ba	La	Ce	Pr	Nd	Pm	Sm	Eu	Gd	Tb	Dy	Ho	Er	Tm	Yb	Lu	Hf	Ta	W	Re	Os	Ir	Pt	Au	Hg	Tl	Pb	Bi	Po	At	Rn
7	Fr	Ra	Ac	Th	Pa	U	Np	Pu	Am	Cm	Bk	Cf	Es	Fm	Md	No	Lr															

4–4 Predicting Electron Configurations

In its own way, the periodic table gives the electron configurations of the elements. Keeping the filling order of the sublevels in mind, follow the order of the elements in the periodic table. The electrons of hydrogen and helium occupy the 1*s* sublevel. After that the electrons of both lithium and beryllium begin filling the 2*s* sublevel, and the electrons of boron, carbon, nitrogen, oxygen, fluorine, and neon fill the 2*p* sublevel. The outermost electrons of the next ten elements occupy the 3*s*, the 3*p*, and the 4*s* sublevels. Then a group of ten transition metals have outer electrons filling the 3*d* sublevel. Figure 4-7 labels all the regions of the periodic table according to the sublevels that are being filled. Note that the widths (number of elements per row) of the regions match the capacities of the sublevels.

Each *s* sublevel can hold two electrons, and the *s* regions on the periodic table are two elements wide. The *p* sublevels can hold six electrons, and the series of six elements in the *p* regions fill these positions. The center of the periodic table contains series of ten elements whose last electrons fill the ten positions in *d* sublevels. The lanthanide and actinide series have fourteen members whose electrons fill the *f* sublevels.

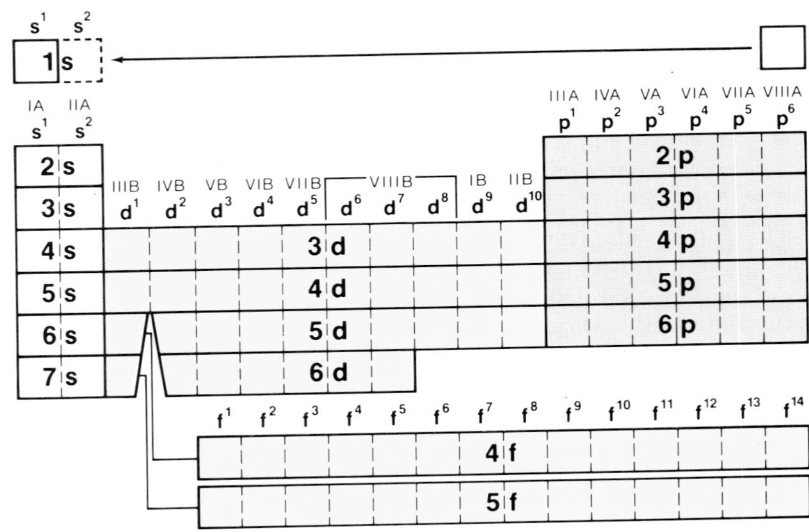

4-7 The periodic table reveals the order in which sublevels are filled.

Sample Problem. Using the periodic table, predict the electron configuration of calcium.

Solution.

To get from the beginning of the periodic table to calcium, you must pass through the 1*s*, 2*s*, 2*p*, 3*s*, 3*p*, and 4*s* regions. Since all these sublevels are filled, the electron configuration of Ca is

$$1s^2 2s^2 2p^6 3s^2 3p^6 4s^2$$

Periodic Trends

Periods are horizontal rows of elements. Each period shows the same general progression in electron configurations. As more electrons join the outermost sublevel, elements become less metallic in character. The sizes of the atoms and their ions result directly from electron configurations. The forces between nuclei and electrons also change regularly as atomic numbers increase. Periodic trends help to reveal the characteristics of the elements.

4–5 Atomic and Ionic Radii

In general, atoms decrease in size as they progress from left to right across the periodic table. This may seem strange, since each atom has more electrons. The atoms become smaller because each successive atom has an additional proton and electron, and the **electrostatic attractions** between positive and negative charges become stronger. Because greater numbers of opposite charges attract each other more, the particles exist closer together. The distance between chlorine's seven valence electrons and its nucleus is smaller than the distance between sodium's one valence electron and its nucleus.

In a progression down the periodic table, the atomic radii in each family become larger. This increase in size occurs because each new period has an additional energy level. Figures 4-8 and 4-9 illustrate the general trends of the atomic radii.

4-8 Atomic and ionic radii.

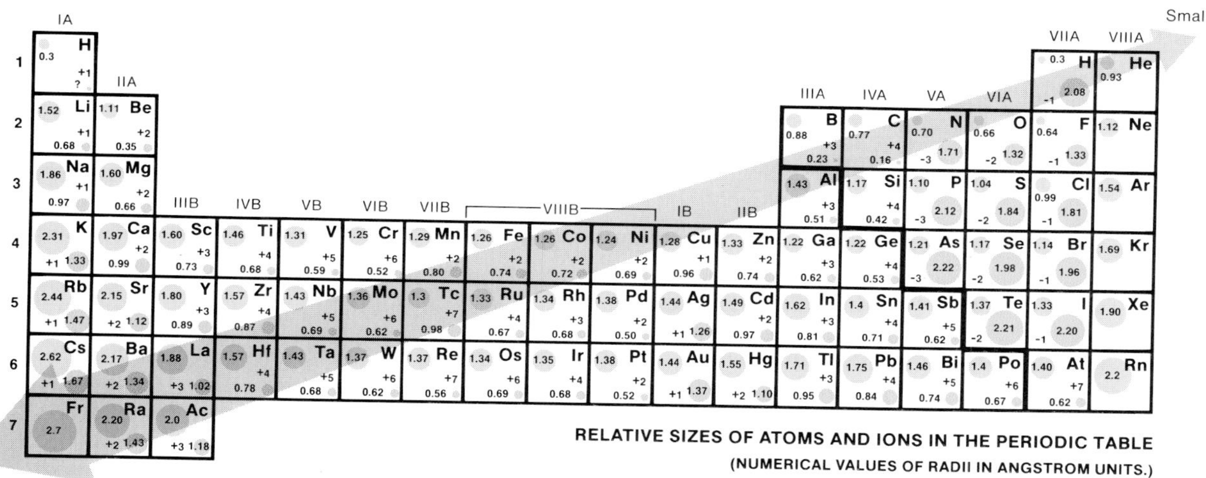

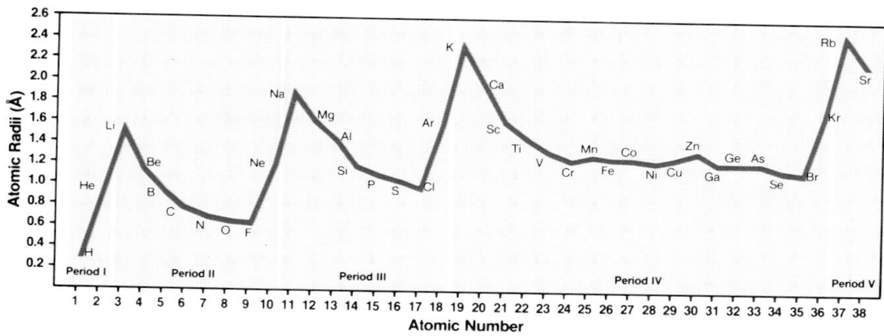

4-9 A graph of atomic radii versus atomic number shows that the changes in size follow a pattern.

Recall that atoms that have gained or lost electrons are called ions. A positive ion—an atom that has lost electrons—is smaller than its parent atom. Negative ions, which have extra electrons, are larger than their parent atoms. Figure 4-8 shows how the sizes of the ions vary.

4–6 Ionization Energy: The Electron "Rip-off"

Some elements lose their electrons easily, whereas others stubbornly hold on to theirs. The minimum energy required to remove an atom's outermost electron and to make the atom an ion is that atom's first **ionization energy.** Figure 4-10 portrays the first ionization energies of the first thirty-eight elements. Note what happens to the values in each period.

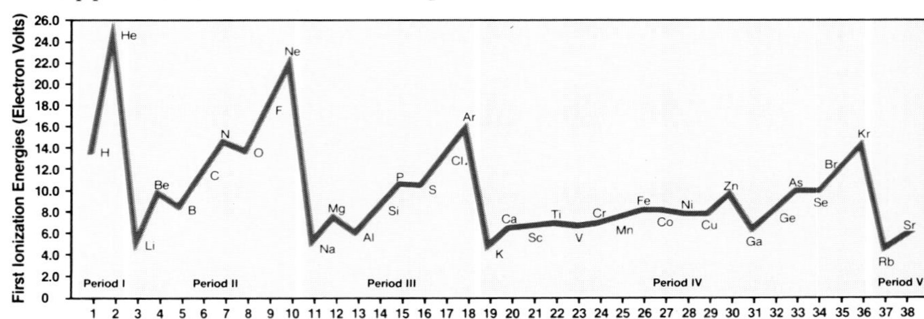

4-10 A graph of ionization energies versus atomic number shows that the changes in ionization energies follow a pattern.

Ionization energies increase from left to right across the periods because electrostatic attractions increase. Strong positive charges tugging on electrons that are close to the nucleus tightly hold the electrons of nonmetals. Ionization energies decrease from the top of the table to the bottom. The reason for this decrease is two-fold. First, the outer electrons are farther away from the nucleus. Second, the outer electrons are somewhat shielded from the positive charges in the nucleus by the electrons in the lower levels.

4–7 Electron Affinity: Electrons Anyone?

Whereas ionization energy is the amount of energy required to remove an electron and form a positive ion, **electron affinity** is the amount of energy *released* when an electron joins an atom to form a negative ion. Electron affinity measures the degree of attraction that an atom has for *additional electrons.* The factors that affect ionization energy also affect electron affinity. Electron affinities increase from left to right on the periodic table and decrease from top to bottom.

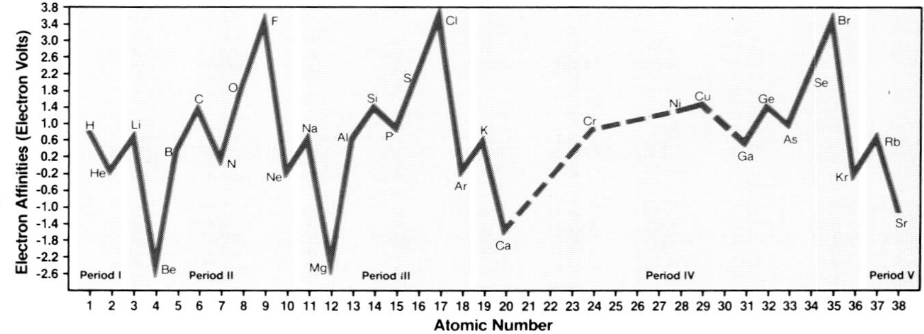

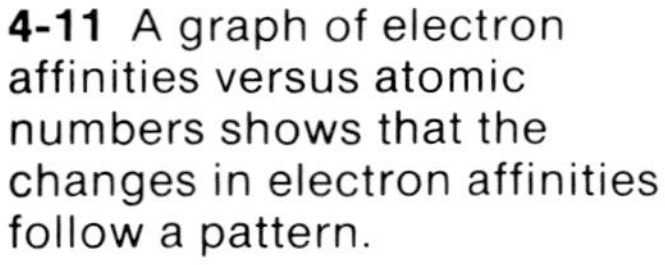

4-11 A graph of electron affinities versus atomic numbers shows that the changes in electron affinities follow a pattern.

4–8 Electronegativity: A Tug of War with Electrons

Electronegativity values reveal the tendency of atoms to attract electrons when they are bonded to other atoms. Electronegativities are related to both ionization energies and electron affinities; thus high electronegativities invariably accompany high ionization energies and high electron affinities.

4-12 Electronegativities of the elements.

	IA	IIA	IIIB	IVB	VB	VIB	VIIB	VIIIB	VIIIB	VIIIB	IB	IIB	IIIA	IVA	VA	VIA	VIIA	VIIIA
1	2.1 H																	He
2	1.0 Li	1.5 Be											2.0 B	2.5 C	3.0 N	3.5 O	4.0 F	Ne
3	0.9 Na	1.2 Mg											1.5 Al	1.8 Si	2.1 P	2.5 S	3.0 Cl	Ar
4	0.8 K	1.0 Ca	1.3 Sc	1.5 Ti	1.6 V	1.6 Cr	1.5 Mn	1.8 Fe	1.8 Co	1.8 Ni	1.9 Cu	1.6 Zn	1.6 Ga	1.8 Ge	2.0 As	2.4 Se	2.8 Br	2.9 Kr
5	0.8 Rb	1.0 Sr	1.2 Y	1.4 Zr	1.6 Nb	1.8 Mo	1.9 Tc	2.2 Ru	2.2 Rh	2.2 Pd	1.9 Ag	1.7 Cd	1.7 In	1.8 Sn	1.9 Sb	2.1 Te	2.5 I	2.6 Xe
6	0.7 Cs	0.9 Ba	1.1 La	1.3 Hf	1.5 Ta	1.7 W	1.9 Re	2.2 Os	2.2 Ir	2.2 Pt	2.4 Au	1.9 Hg	1.8 Tl	1.8 Pb	1.9 Bi	2.0 Po	2.2 At	Rn
7	0.7 Fr	0.9 Ra	1.1 Ac															

Large

Small

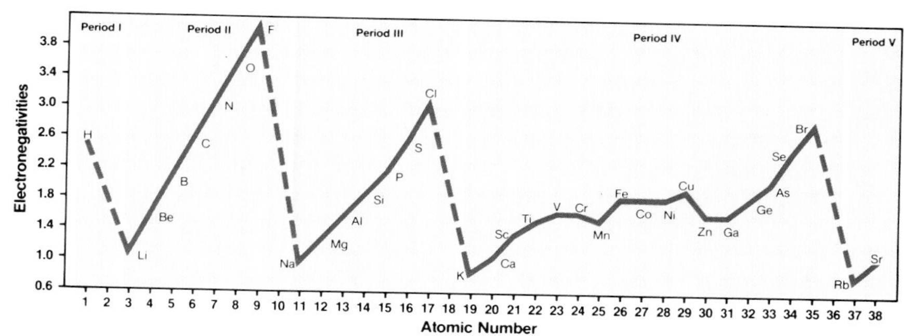

4-13 A graph of electronegativities versus atomic numbers shows that the changes in electronegativities follow a pattern.

The values on the electronegativity chart were not determined experimentally. They were selected arbitrarily on the basis of comparisons with other elements. A Nobel Prize-winning chemist named Linus Pauling devised a scale with a maximum value of 4. The element fluorine received this number, since it is the most electronegative element. Pauling then assigned the values of the other elements. Of the three measures of electrostatic attraction between electrons and the nucleus, electronegativity has the widest use. It plays a central role in predicting *how* atoms chemically combine with each other.

Sample Problem. For each of the following pairs of elements, use a periodic table and your knowledge of the sizes of atoms to predict which element has the higher electronegativity.

a. N or P b. Rb or I

Solution.

a. Nitrogen's outermost electrons are closer to the nucleus than those of phosphorus. Consequently, nitrogen has stronger attractions for electrons than phosphorus does.

b. While rubidium and iodine have the same number

FACETS OF CHEMISTRY

The Case of the Unknown Chemical

A farmer asks, "Does my soil contain enough minerals and nutrients for my crops?"

A laboratory supervisor inquires, "Do my workers absorb excessive amounts of formaldehyde into their blood as they work?"

A school principal wonders, "Does the insulation around the heating pipes in my school contain harmless fiber glass or cancer-causing asbestos fibers?"

A paint manufacturer questions, "Does our new brand of paint contain too much lead to be safely used in homes?"

An archaeologist thinks, "I wish I knew whether the metal alloy used in this ancient plowshare contains tin."

A government worker wonders, "How many phosphate ions are polluting Reedy River?"

In a way, these people each need a detective. They need someone who knows how to search for the right clues, examine the evidence, and identify the "suspect" chemicals. Although police detectives are good at tracking down missing people, they do not trace down elusive chemicals. A different kind of detective, called an analytical chemist, solves these cases.

Identifying the contents of a substance is the main goal of analytical chemistry. One part of analytical chemistry, called *qualitative analysis,* identifies but does not measure the elements in an unknown substance. Chemists use so many liquid solutions in qualitative analysis that they often call it "wet chemistry." The traditional techniques of qualitative analysis involve mixing liquid solutions of various chemicals. After they mix the solutions, the chemists watch for telltale reactions.

Suppose a paint manufacturer wanted to know if a certain pigment contained lead. Analytical chemists in the company's laboratory would first dissolve the substance in water. Then they would treat the solution with dilute hydrochloric acid and watch to see if any reaction occurred. If a solid formed and settled out of the solution, the chemists would know that the solution contained either lead, silver, or mercury ions. To determine which ion was present, the chemists would place some of

of electron levels, iodine has many more protons in its nucleus. The resulting stronger positive charge attracts electrons more strongly.

Descriptive Chemistry

"Science is built up with facts, as a house is built up with stones, but a collection of facts is no more science than a heap of stones is a house." This statement by Henri Poincaré accurately describes the interplay between facts and theories in chemistry. While facts can serve as the foundation or even the polishing touches of chemistry, theories provide the framework by which the facts fit together. Most of this course deals with general theories involving the fundamental questions of chemistry. But the facts needed to answer these fundamental questions are provided by **descriptive chemistry**—the study of elements and the compounds they form.

the precipitate in hot water and some in ammonium hydroxide. If the precipitate dissolved rapidly in the hot water but not in the ammonium hydroxide, the chemists would know that lead was present.

Sometimes knowing which chemicals are present in a substance is not enough—the amounts must also be known. In these cases, *quantitative analysis* of substances is needed. One of the most common ways to measure chemicals is measurement by mass. Measurement of elements by mass is the gravimetric (or weight) method of analysis. Suppose an official in a mining company had to know how much iron was in a batch of iron ore. To determine the exact percentage, chemists would first weigh the sample of iron ore and then dissolve it in hydrochloric acid. They would then add ammonium hydroxide (NH_4OH) because it reacts with iron to form ferric hydroxide ($Fe[OH]_2$). Finally, the chemists would heat the ferric hydroxide to form ferric oxide (Fe_3O_3) and would carefully weigh the ferric oxide on a sensitive balance. By using the formula Fe_2O_3, the chemists would calculate that ferric oxide is 69.94 per cent iron (Fe) by weight. Knowing this fact and the weight of ferric oxide, they would calculate how much iron was present.

Another common method of quantitative analysis is colorimetry. This method measures chemicals by examining the colors of solutions. When the color of a particular solution is intense, chemists know that the concentration of the chemicals in the solution must be high. When the color of the solution is faint, they know that the concentration must be low.

Some chemicals form colored solutions when they are dissolved in water. Many chemicals, however, form solutions that have no color at all. These solutions look just like water. For colorless solutions chemists cannot use colorimetry as a measuring tool. Chemists can overcome this obstacle by producing a color in the solution through a series of chemical reactions. Since the human eye cannot detect small differences in color intensity, chemists use

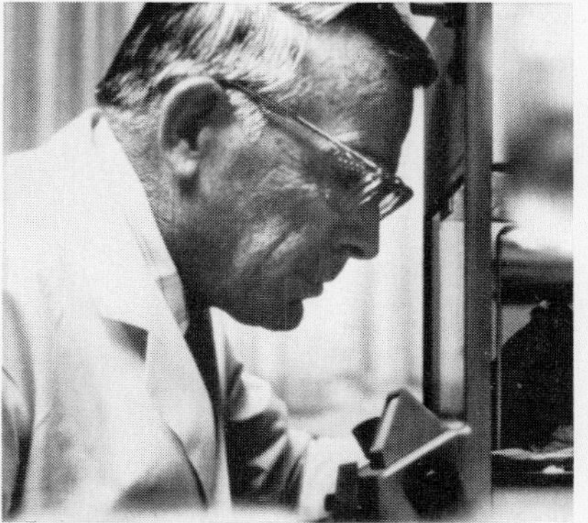

a device called a colorimeter to measure the color. A colorimeter beams light through a sample and measures the amount of light the sample absorbs.

The techniques described here make up only a small percentage of the tools used by chemical detectives. Newly invented instruments and recently discovered reactions constantly provide analytical chemists with more tools. Along with the many traditional techniques, the new methods equip analytical chemists to help the many people who require their services.

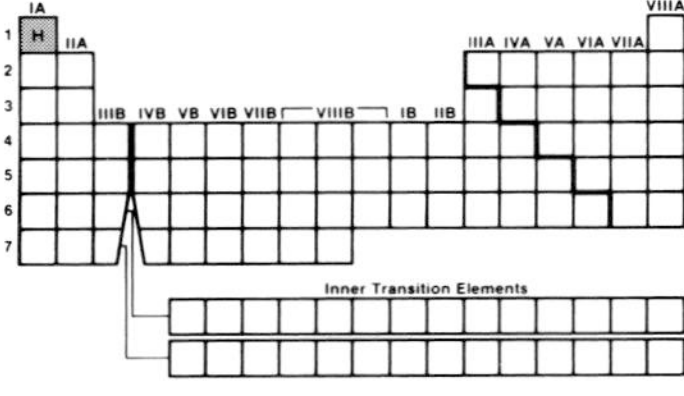

4–9 Hydrogen: A Family by Itself

Hydrogen, the simplest of all the elements, has an electron configuration similar to that of the IA metals. Yet because it displays unique properties, it is often considered to be a family by itself. Although other scientists probably prepared hydrogen gas earlier, an Englishman named Henry Cavendish was the first to collect and study it. In 1766 he prepared the gas by reacting a metal and an acid. The gas burned rapidly, even explosively, so Cavendish called it "inflammable air." Lavoisier later renamed it *hydrogen,* which means "water-former," because its burning with oxygen produces water.

4-14 Hydrogen balloons were used for transatlantic trips until this reaction between hydrogen and oxygen took place in 1937.

Physical Properties. As a gas, hydrogen is colorless, odorless, and tasteless. Because hydrogen is the lightest of all gases, its molecules move at high speeds and diffuse more quickly than other gases. Hydrogen molecules have little attraction for each other, so they stay in the gaseous state even when temperatures go down to -253° C.

Chemical Properties. Hydrogen has unique chemical and physical properties. On the one hand it has a single electron in its lone occupied energy level, so it can act like a group IA metal. On the other hand it is only one electron shy of filling the first energy level, so it can act like group VIIA elements. It is sometimes shown as a member of both families on periodic tables.

Hydrogen atoms do not float freely in the atmosphere. If they have the chance, they immediately bond to other hydrogen atoms to form two-atom molecules (H_2). At room temperature hydrogen molecules usually refuse to react with other elements. But at high temperatures and pressures molecular hydrogen can split apart and become highly reactive. Sparked by a flame or electrical discharge, hydrogen molecules can combine with oxygen to form water. Bonded to nitrogen atoms, hydrogen forms ammonia (NH_3). Acids, including the well-known hydrochloric acid (HCl), form when hydrogen reacts with the VIIA elements.

Occasionally hydrogen reacts with active metals to form compounds called **metallic hydrides.** Lithium hydride (LiH), sodium hydride (NaH), magnesium hydride (MgH_2), and calcium hydride (CaH_2) model this capability.

Uses. Ammonia manufacturers use most of the hydrogen gas produced in the world. Space programs consume large amounts of hydrogen gas as fuels for their rockets. Hydrogen atoms bond with liquid vegetable oils to form solid fats in a process called hydrogenation. Manufacturers of cooking shortenings such as Crisco and Spry carefully monitor the number of hydrogen atoms in their products.

4–10 Alkali Metals: Group IA

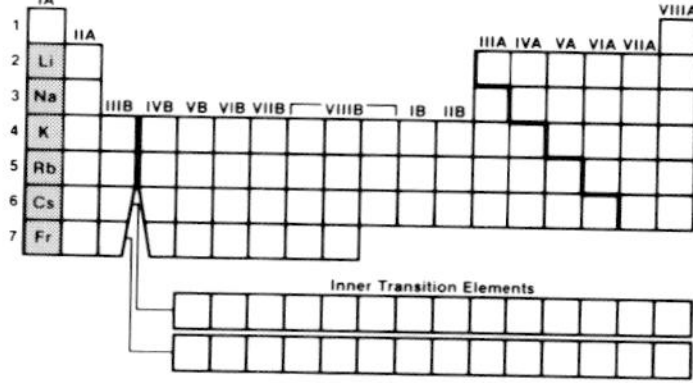

Group IA metals are so reactive that they never exist by themselves in nature. Not until 1807 did Sir Humphrey Davy isolate one of the **alkali metals** from a compound.

Physical Properties. Like typical metals, alkali metals conduct electricity well and have a bright luster when they are freshly cut. Unlike the traditional stereotypes of metals, they have low densities and can be easily cut because they are soft.

Chemical Properties. A solitary, easily lost outermost electron makes this group of elements very reactive. Alkali metals lose their electrons readily to "electron-hungry" elements. Because the largest atoms have the lowest electronegativities, the alkali metals are the most reactive members of metallic families. These metals react violently with water to produce strong, caustic bases. The metals are so reactive that they are usually immersed in kerosene so that they will not react with oxygen or moisture in the air.

Lithium differs from the other alkali metals because of its small size. Its small atomic radius allows the nucleus to hold on tightly to its one valence electron. Some of lithium's chemical and physical properties resemble those of magnesium, a member of the adjoining family, more than those of sodium. This similarity between small elements and elements in neighboring families is called a bridging relationship.

4-15 Alkali metals are soft enough to be cut with a knife.

Uses. Human bodies depend on a balance of sodium and potassium ions to carry electrical signals through the nerves and to trigger muscle contractions. Today's controversy about the amount of salt in diets is really concerned with the level of sodium ions. Commercial "salt substitutes" are actually a potassium salt instead of the more common sodium salt. Potassium compounds serve as main ingredients for many industrial processes such as the production of fertilizers, soaps, and glass. Lithium compounds make modern lubricants water resistant and able to withstand extreme temperatures.

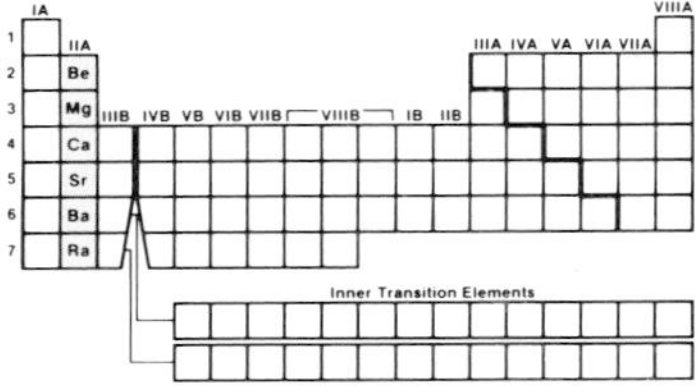

4–11 Alkaline Earth Metals: Group IIA

The chemical term *earth* originally applied to metal-and-oxygen compounds that dissolved slightly in water. Some of these compounds were similar to compounds of alkali metals, so they were given the more specialized name **alkaline earth metals.** Today the term applies to the metals in group IIA. Most people come in contact with alkaline earth metals each time they turn on a faucet. Hard water contains dissolved ions that stop soap from producing lather and suds. Water that percolates through underground deposits of limestone picks up calcium and magnesium ions (Ca^{2+} and Mg^{2+}) that combine with soap to produce an insoluble scum. Water softeners thwart the suds-killing action of these ions.

Physical Properties. Fresh cuts into these metals reveal a common shiny luster under the dull gray coatings. Densities range slightly higher than those of the alkali metals, but these metals are much harder. All the alkaline earth metals are malleable.

Chemical Properties. Each alkaline earth metal has two electrons in its outermost *s* sublevel. Since the alkaline earth metals release two electrons when they react, the ones that hold electrons loosely react the best. Reactivities increase as the alkaline earth metals get larger. Beryllium does not react with water, magnesium can react with hot water, and calcium will react vigorously with even cold water. Like lithium, beryllium resembles a member of an adjacent family. Being a small element, it has properties similar to many of the chemical properties of aluminum, the second member of the IIIA family.

Uses. Special-purpose beryllium alloys make up springs that must endure frequent vibrations. Magnesium is often used to make lightweight alloys for airplanes, automobiles, and boats. Flashbulbs and military flares burn magnesium because it produces a brilliant bright light when it burns. Magnesium compounds in the mineral water of Epsom, England, make up Epsom salts, and magnesium hydroxide gives milk of magnesia its chalky taste and stomach-soothing ability. Although calcium is a necessary part of a balanced

4-16 Stalactites form when water deposits $CaCO_3$ (calcite) onto cave ceilings.

4-17 Strong, lightweight magnesium alloys are used in most modern aircraft.

diet, its major use is for building materials. Limestone, or calcium carbonate, serves as the foundational material for everything from concrete to finishing plaster. This material also has an important aesthetic value in nature. The beautiful daggers of stone known as stalactites and stalagmites consist of limestone. When water containing dissolved carbon dioxide trickles through limestone, it dissolves some of the stone. If that water happens to fall into a cave, the release of carbon dioxide gas triggers the deposition of limestone.

4–12 Transition Metals: The B Groups

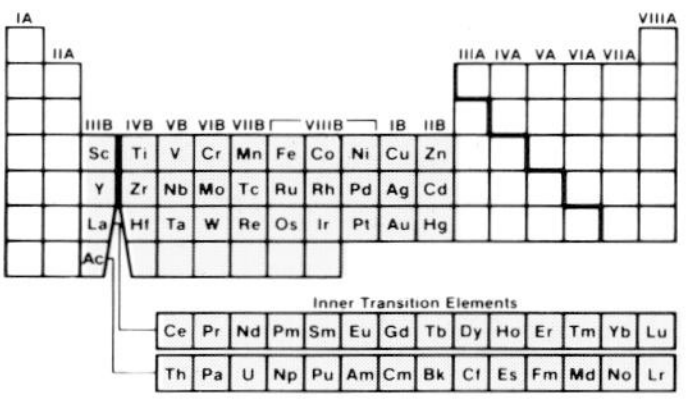

All the B groups on the periodic table belong to the group of elements called **transition metals.** The name for this group of elements stems from a former belief that the properties of these elements progressed in regular graduations to the nonmetals. Today it is known that these elements have characteristics all their own. The term *transition* still has meaning, though, as a label for the physical location in the center of the periodic table. The lanthanide and actinide series are called the **inner transition metals.** The lanthanide series was once called the "rare earths" because these elements resisted extraction from metallic ores. The actinide series has no nickname from the early days of chemistry because most of these elements are manmade.

Physical Properties. The most conspicuous property of the transition elements is that they are the "typical" metals. Unlike the first two families, many of these metals have high densities and considerable strength. They also have a shiny luster, they conduct well, and they conform to desired shapes when pounded or stretched within reasonable limits. Mercury exists as a liquid at room temperature, but all the others are solids.

Chemical Properties. Because their outermost electrons occupy *d* sublevels, transition metals have many different chemical properties. Unreactive metals, like gold, silver, and platinum, can resist corrosion for centuries. Others, like iron and copper, corrode quickly when exposed to moist air. Because the last few energy sublevels of these elements are close to each other, electrons have little difficulty jumping from one sublevel to another, and the same atoms can bond in a variety of ways. The chemistry of the transition metals involves just as many exceptions as common trends.

Uses. Modern society uses transition metals in numberless ways. Trusses that span gymnasiums, I-beams that support skyscrapers, artificial hip joints, shiny chrome finishes on hubcaps, coins, jewelry, and electrical wires all attest to this. In addition, human bodies require certain trace amounts of iron, chromium, cobalt, copper, manganese, and vanadium to operate normally.

4-18 Molten iron that is being poured into an oxygen furnace will soon be refined into steel.

4–13 The Post-Transition Metals and the Metalloids

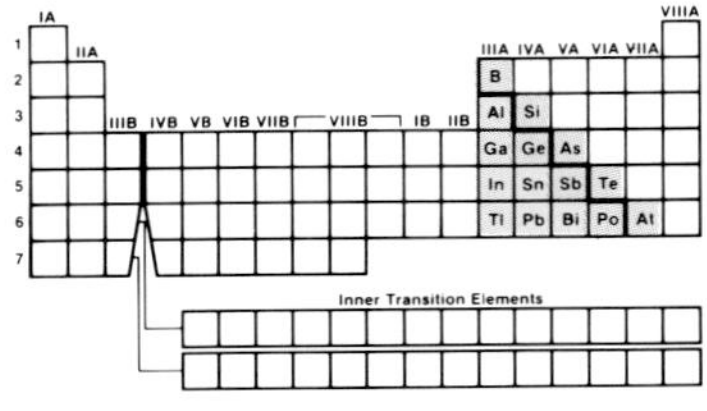

Post-transition metals, as their name implies, follow the series of transition metals on the periodic table. They are found in groups IIIA, IVA, and VA. This group of metals includes well-known elements such as tin, lead, and aluminum as well as obscure elements like thallium, indium, and gallium.

Metalloids have properties of both metals and nonmetals. Aluminum is distinctly metallic, but it also has several metalloid characteristics. Boron, silicon, arsenic, and antimony are the most typical of the metalloids, but germanium, tellurium, and probably polonium and astatine fit in as well. Little is known about polonium and astatine, so their classification is somewhat arbitrary.

Physical Properties. Like metals, the metalloids have a metallic luster. They can conduct electricity, but not very well. Consequently, they are called **semiconductors.**

Chemical Properties. Aluminum is too reactive to be found free in nature; it is usually bonded to oxygen atoms in aluminum ore, which is called bauxite. Like iron, aluminum reacts with oxygen if it is exposed to the atmosphere. How then did aluminum get its reputation for being a durable, corrosion-resistant metal? The difference lies in the nature of the corrosion. Whereas iron oxide is porous and allows new oxygen molecules to penetrate deeper into the metal, aluminum oxide forms an impenetrable shield against further oxidation.

4-19 Extensive mining processes supply society with aluminum ore. Large amounts of electricity must be used to extract pure aluminum from its ore.

Boron is a "bridge" element. It has the electron configuration of the elements in group IIIA but has several properties of silicon, which is in group IVA. The small size of the atom allows the nucleus to hold electrons as if the nucleus had a greater positive charge. Silicon does not react with air, water, or acids at low temperatures. Arsenic may act as a metal and form oxides or chlorides. Like nonmetals, it can form acids.

Uses. Metallurgists use electrical currents to pull pure aluminum from aluminum oxide molecules. Before this process was invented, aluminum was so expensive that a large chunk was included with the crown jewels of England. Napoleon III even ordered a rattle of this priceless metal for Prince Louis. Today this metal vies with steel for the title of "most-used metal." Aluminum can be valuable when its oxides form rubies and sapphires. Fuller's earth, a compound of silicon and aluminum, can remove spots and stains from textiles by absorbing them. A boron compound called borax softens water and helps clean clothes in the laundry. Pyrex glass contains fused sand, aluminum oxide, and borax. The borax gives the glass a low thermal expansion so that sudden changes in temperature do not tear the glass apart. Enamel, a compound of soft glass with colored metallic oxides added, has borax added for the same reason. Antiseptics and bleaching agents can be formed if borax is treated with sodium hydroxide (NaOH) and hydrogen peroxide (H_2O_2). Boric acid, an ingredient in eye-soothing medicines, also contains boron.

Just as carbon is the building block for the animal and vegetable worlds, silicon serves as the fundamental element in the mineral world. Twenty-eight per cent of all the atoms in the earth's crust are silicon atoms, and 97 per cent of the crust's compounds contain silicon. The silicate minerals are the bases of rocks, soils, clays, and sands.

The semiconducting property of silicon and germanium has made them vital materials in electronic transistors and integrated circuits. Microscopic chips of semiconductors control the flow of electrons in digital watches, calculators, and mainframe computers. Although arsenic is usually thought of as a potent poison, it serves our industries in several important ways. Its compounds find applications in the preserving of animal skins, the manufacturing of glass, and sometimes as medicines.

4–14 Carbon: Charcoal, Diamonds, and Graphite

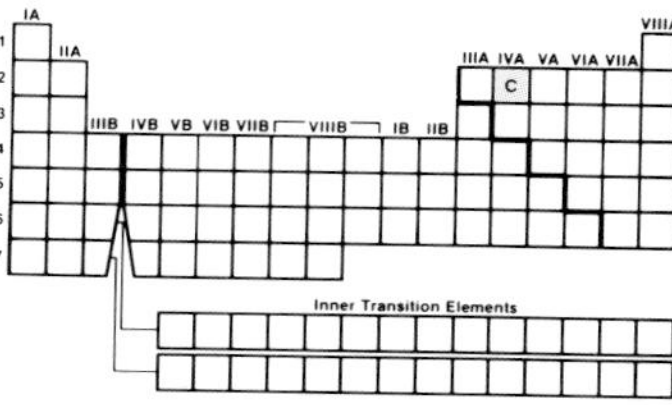

Carbon was well known in the ancient world. Charcoal from fire was probably the earliest recognized form of carbon. The word *carbon* probably comes from the Latin *carbo,* meaning "coal," "charcoal," or "ember." The two naturally occurring forms of elemental carbon were also aptly named. Diamond is named from the Greek *adamas,* meaning "invincible," and graphite comes from the Greek *graphein,* meaning "to write." (Pencil lead contains graphite.)

Carbon constitutes only 0.027 per cent of the earth's crust, yet it is one of the most important elements. Carbon compounds are so numerous and so important that they merit separate consideration as the field of organic chemistry. Important carbon compounds such as carbonates (CO, CO_2), bicarbonates ($NaHCO_3$), and cyanides (NaCN) form the major inorganic carbon compounds.

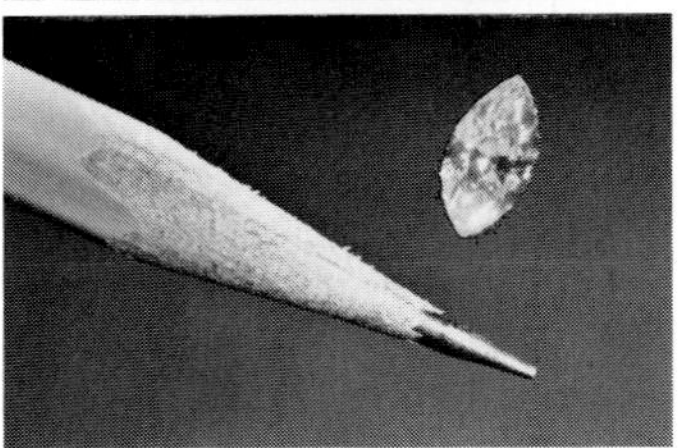

4-20 Charcoal forms when carbon atoms combine randomly **(top)**. Diamond and graphite form when carbon atoms join in different patterns **(bottom)**.

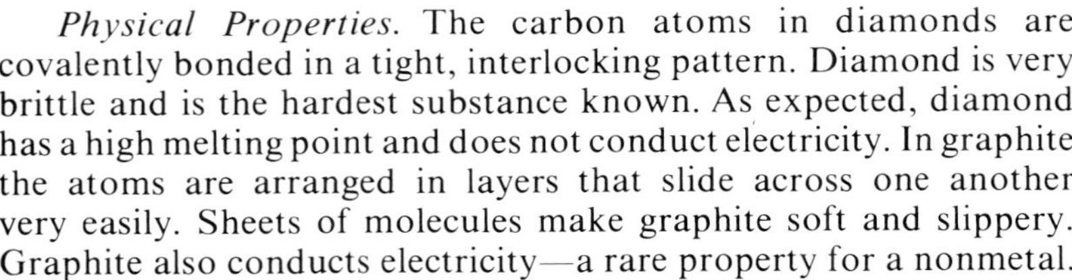

Physical Properties. The carbon atoms in diamonds are covalently bonded in a tight, interlocking pattern. Diamond is very brittle and is the hardest substance known. As expected, diamond has a high melting point and does not conduct electricity. In graphite the atoms are arranged in layers that slide across one another very easily. Sheets of molecules make graphite soft and slippery. Graphite also conducts electricity—a rare property for a nonmetal.

Chemical Properties. Carbon, when found in diamonds and graphite, is relatively unreactive. Graphite, however, does oxidize slowly in the presence of nitric acid and sodium chlorate; charcoal is also rapidly oxidized by this mixture.

Uses. Diamonds can be used in a wide variety of ways. Valuable cut diamonds are used to create beautiful jewelry, and many "worthless" diamonds with imperfections are used as needles in record players, as abrasives for grinding and polishing, and as steel-cutting tools. Graphite is useful in making electrodes for industrial reactions because of its low cost and its resistance to heat and reaction. It is also used in the manufacturing of paints. Charcoal, another form of carbon, is placed in water and air filters to strain out organic impurities that give nasty smells and tastes.

4–15 Nitrogen and Phosphorus: Group VA

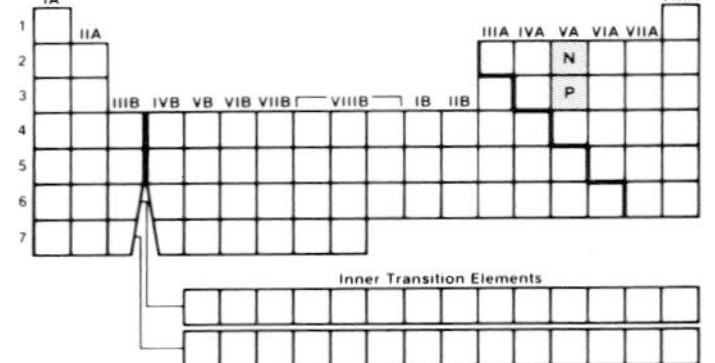

In 1772 a Scottish physician named Daniel Rutherford first recognized nitrogen as an element. Rutherford also showed that nitrogen gas could not support life the way oxygen does for animals or the way carbon dioxide does for plants. The gas was appropriately named *azote,* meaning "lifeless."

About one hundred years before the discovery of nitrogen, a German alchemist had discovered phosphorus. During his experiments, this alchemist heated a concoction of urine (which contains phosphorus compounds), sand, and charcoal. The substance he distilled from this brew glowed in the dark. In later years Lavoisier recognized this substance as an element and named it *phosphorus* from a Greek word meaning "light bearer."

Physical Properties. Nitrogen normally exists as diatomic N_2 molecules in the gaseous state. The gas has no taste, no color, no odor, and accounts for approximately 78 per cent of the earth's atmosphere. Phosphorus exists in one of four or more forms due to different arrangements of the atoms. All the forms are solids, but they have different colors. Some common forms of this element are white (or yellow), red, and black (or violet) phosphorus.

Chemical Properties. Nitrogen molecules rarely enter into chemical reactions. These molecules are tightly bonded together and usually refuse to be split up. In contrast, one of the most important properties of phosphorus is its high chemical reactivity, especially with oxygen. Phosphorus is so reactive that it cannot be found pure in nature.

Uses. Plants and animals require a constant supply of nitrogen atoms. It might seem that the atmosphere would provide an unlimited supply of these atoms. But this is not so. The nitrogen molecules in the air do not usually react to provide the necessary nitrogen atoms. Some nitrogen compounds exist in the soil, and others are provided through artificial fertilizers or decaying organic matter. Some plants coexist with bacteria that can transform atmospheric nitrogen molecules into compounds with ready-to-use nitrogen atoms. Both nitrogen and phosphorus form a variety of gaseous compounds. Ammonia (NH_3) can be used in its gaseous form as a refrigerant or dissolved in water as a cleaner. Phosphine (PH_3) is a colorless, foul-smelling poison that was used in World War I. Nitrogen and oxygen can bond together to produce a variety of compounds such as laughing gas (N_2O) and smog-producing air pollutants (NO and NO_2).

4–16 Oxygen and Sulfur: Group VIA

In 1774 an English clergyman named Joseph Priestley discovered oxygen during a series of experiments in which he decomposed substances with the aid of the sun and a strong lens. When he focused the rays of the sun on mercury oxide (HgO), it decomposed into mercury and a gas that made flames burn brighter and gave an invigorating feeling when inhaled. Lavoisier eventually gave the new element the name *oxygine,* which means "acid producer." When either sulfur or phosphorus was burned in this gas, it produced a compound that formed acids when in water.

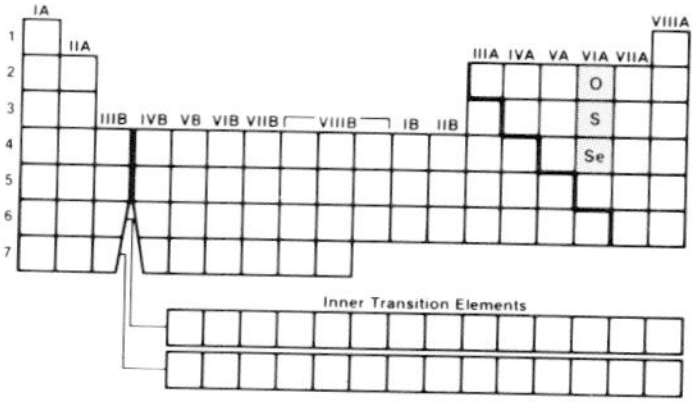

Men of ancient times knew of sulfur because it occurs uncombined in nature. The Bible refers to sulfur fifteen times when it describes brimstone (meaning "burning stone"). These references associate sulfur with hell, the lake of fire, and God's judgment. The acrid fumes and searing blue flame of burning sulfur give a sobering picture of what separation from God for eternity would be like.

Physical Properties. Oxygen is a colorless, odorless, tasteless gas that is slightly soluble in water. Through divine design, enough oxygen dissolves in lakes, rivers, and oceans to sustain fish and aquatic plants. Oxygen liquefies to a pale blue liquid between -183° C and -218° C and solidifies to a pale blue solid below -218° C. Atmospheric oxygen exists in two forms: O_2 gas and ozone (O_3). Lightning can convert odorless O_2 to the pungent O_3, which can often be detected after an electrical storm. God has graciously created a protective layer of ozone in the upper atmosphere to shield the earth from harmful amounts of solar radiation.

Sulfur exists in a variety of forms. Native sulfur is a yellow solid, but when it is heated to 113° C, it melts into a straw-colored liquid that can crystallize into another form. If the molten sulfur is quickly cooled by being poured into water, it forms amorphous globs with a plasticlike consistency.

Chemical Properties. While sulfur and oxygen do not resemble each other physically, their relationship becomes apparent through their chemical properties. Oxygen is one of the most reactive elements, forming compounds called **oxides** with all other elements except those in group VIIIA. Oxygen's electronegativity ranks second only to fluorine, and its strong pull on electrons can be expected to result in chemically active properties. Sulfur is reactive at room temperatures, but it does not match the reactivity of oxygen. Metals such as zinc, calcium, and iron react with sulfur to form compounds called **sulfides.** Sulfur reacts with nonmetals such as oxygen and group VIIA elements to form compounds like sulfur dioxide (SO_2), sulfur dichloride (SCl_2), and sulfur bromide (S_2Br_2).

4-22 Acid rain, caused by the burning of sulfur-containing fuels, brings sulfuric acid to the forest.

Uses. As Lavoisier pointed out, oxygen fuels combustion and supports animal life. Ozone, which has some undesirable effects, can also be beneficial: it can kill bacteria by oxidizing them.

Sulfur atoms bonded into rubber help make today's rubber supple, strong, and pliable in a wide range of temperatures. Sulfur dioxide has a variety of uses ranging from a bleaching agent to a disinfectant. The majority of the sulfur used in industrial countries goes into the production of sulfuric acid. This thick, syrupy, colorless liquid serves as a workhorse of chemical-related businesses. Recently, compounds of sulfur and oxygen released from coal-burning factories have been discovered to be the culprits in the formation of acid rain. The sulfur compounds from the smokestacks mix with water in the clouds and form dilute sulfuric acid that rains down on the earth.

4–17 Halogens: Group VIIA

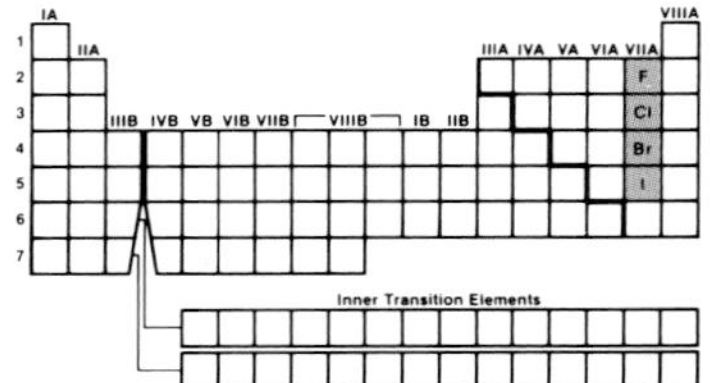

Group VIIA elements carry the name **halogens,** for they form salts when they react with active metals. (*Halogen* comes from a word meaning "salt.") Because these elements are so reactive, they were difficult to obtain in their elemental forms.

Fluorine's electronegativity is greater than that of the other halogens; thus this element gains electrons in chemical reactions more readily than the other group VIIA elements do. Because of its higher reactivity, fluorine was one of the last halogens to be discovered. Chlorine, the second halogen on the periodic table, was first recognized in 1771 when someone reacted hydrochloric acid (HCl) and manganese oxide (MnO_2). The greenish yellow gas that escaped was named *chlorine,* the Greek word for "green." The next element in the family, bromine, stands alone as the only nonmetallic liquid at room temperature. Its irritating, and even poisonous, vapor has a very pungent odor. For this reason its discoverer named it after the Greek word for "stench." Iodine was discovered when seaweed treated with concentrated sulfuric acid gave off a violet-colored vapor that crystallized when it was cooled. Joseph Gay-Lussac, a French chemist and physicist, soon identified the substance as an element and named it after the Greek word for "violet." Astatine, whose name means "unstable," is a highly radioactive element: it has no stable isotopes. It was first isolated in 1940 when it was synthesized from bismuth through a nuclear reaction.

Physical Properties. The halogens show a definite trend in their physical properties. As their atomic numbers increase, their densities, melting points, and boiling points increase and their colors exhibit increasingly darker hues. For example, fluorine is a pale yellow gas with a low density, chlorine is a greenish yellow gas, bromine is a deep, reddish brown liquid, and iodine is a grayish black crystalline solid.

4-23 Halogen headlights are used in many of today's automobiles.

Chemical Properties. Halogens have relatively high reactivities because of their strong electronegativities. Each element exists as a diatomic molecule when it is pure and forms an acid when it reacts with hydrogen. They all form salts when they react with metals.

Since nonmetals share or gain electrons when they react, the ones with strong attractions for electrons exhibit high reactivities. Fluorine is extremely reactive and ignites many substances on contact. The resulting reactions often take the form of spectacular releases of heat and light energy. When fluorine reacts with metals, it often forms a protective layer of metallic fluoride that prevents all the metal from reacting. Violent reactions result when fluorine reacts with hydrogen-containing compounds such as water or organic compounds. As might be expected, the chemical properties of the other halogens are similar to those of fluorine. Larger halogens, though, are less reactive. Note this significant difference between nonmetals and metals: the most reactive nonmetals are those whose atoms are small; the most reactive metals are those whose atoms are large. This difference is due to the fact that metals usually react by *losing* electrons and nonmetals usually react by *gaining* them. Large metal atoms can lose electrons easily, but larger nonmetal atoms do not gain electrons as easily as the smaller family members do.

Uses. The human body benefits from small amounts of halogens, but larger doses are harmful, to say the least. Fluorine compounds help develop decay-resistant teeth, and chlorine kills algae and bacteria in drinking water and swimming pools. Even iodine has a use in the body: small amounts keep the thyroid gland working properly.

Most industrial uses of halogens are obscure, but some items have become familiar household products. Teflon-coated cookware utilizes the nonstick properties of a fluorine compound. Aerosol cans once contained fluorocarbons that served as propellants. Because these compounds were suspected of decomposing the ozone layer in the upper atmosphere, most products now use other propellants. Laundry bleach consists of a chlorine compound—which is why a load of wash with bleach may smell somewhat like a swimming pool.

4–18 Noble Gases: Group VIIIA

The group VIIIA elements were formerly called inert gases but now carry the name **noble gases.** They normally do not react with other elements. Lord Raleigh discovered one of these elements by carefully measuring the constituents of air. He noticed that the nitrogen he isolated from the atmosphere had more mass than the nitrogen he separated from pure ammonia. Suspecting that the atmospheric nitrogen contained some unknown substance, he separated the residual gas and found that it would not react with other elements. Because of its chemical sluggishness, this gas was called argon, meaning "the lazy one." This was the first noble gas to be discovered. More noble gases like argon were discovered, some in significant amounts in the atmosphere. Helium was first discovered in a spectrogram of the sun. Neon was discovered during a purification of oxygen. Scientists also isolated and identified krypton, meaning "hidden element," and xenon, meaning "stranger."

4-24 Deep-sea divers reduce the amount of nitrogen they breathe by mixing helium with their air supply.

Physical Properties. All noble gases are colorless, odorless, and tasteless. Extremely low boiling points and freezing points indicate that the individual atoms of these gases have little attraction for each other.

Chemical Properties. As their name implies, these elements tend to be aloof and separate from the other elements. After many attempts to get noble gases to react with other elements, scientists have been able to force only xenon, radon, and krypton to bond. These elements formed several short-lived compounds such as xenon difluoride (XeF_2), xenon trioxide (XeO_3), krypton tetrafluoride (KrF_4), and radon fluoride (RnF).

Uses. Balloonists prefer helium as their source of lifting power because it has an extremely low density and does not react with oxygen. This may seem unimportant, but helium's inertness rules out the possibility of a disastrous fire. Deep-sea divers also use helium to dilute the amount of nitrogen in the air they breathe. The high pressures at great depths can force nitrogen to dissolve in the bloodstream. When divers resurface with this nitrogen in their blood, it forms bubbles and causes excruciating pains known as the bends. Many colored lights that advertise along busy streets consist of glass tubes filled with neon. When an electric current passes through the gas, it gives off a bright orange light. Fluorescent lights contain a mixture of argon and mercury vapor, and high-speed photographic flashbulbs rely on krypton and xenon. Incandescent light bulbs contain inert gases, but not because these gases give off light. The ability of noble gases to resist a reaction makes them perfect candidates for surrounding the fragile filament to keep it from reacting with oxygen.

4-25 Inert argon gas protects the filaments in light bulbs.

Coming to Terms

periodic table
periodic law
group
family
main group
period
metal
metalloid
nonmetal
electrostatic attraction
ionization energy
electron affinity
electronegativity
descriptive chemistry
metallic hydride
alkali metal
alkaline earth metal
transition metal
inner transition metal
post-transition metal
semiconductor
oxide
sulfide
halogen
noble gas

Review Questions

1. Identify the chemist who
   a. is given credit for having developed the modern periodic table.
   b. formulated the concept of triads.
   c. proposed that elemental properties varied in octaves.

d. predicted the existence of several "missing" elements.
e. determined atomic numbers of many elements.
f. devised the commonly used electronegativity scale.

2. What was wrong with Dobereiner's classification of the elements? What good was it?
3. What is the purpose of the periodic table?
4. Why were several elements in the wrong places in Mendeleev's table? How was the problem corrected?
5. Give the modern statement of the periodic law.
6. Identify each of the following elements as an actinide, an alkali metal, an alkaline earth metal, a halogen, a lanthanide, a metalloid, a noble gas, or a transition metal.

a. lithium
b. antimony
c. bromine
d. tungsten
e. iron
f. cesium
g. cerium
h. calcium
i. argon
j. uranium

7. Give two names for horizontal rows in the periodic table.
8. Give two names for vertical columns in the periodic table.
9. What is the general location of metallic elements on the periodic table? of nonmetals? of metalloids?
10. Use the periodic table to complete the following chart.

Name	Symbol	Atomic Number	Period	Family
cadmium	______	______	______	______
______	______	56	______	______
______	Sn	______	______	______
______	______	______	4	IA

11. Use the periodic table to give the electron configurations of silicon, germanium, and calcium.
12. Use the periodic table to determine which elements have the following electron configurations:

a. $1s^2 2s^2 2p^6 3s^1$
b. $1s^2 2s^2 2p^6 3s^2 3p^6$

13. Explain why sodium ions are smaller than sodium atoms and why chlorine ions are larger than chlorine atoms.
14. Of the eighteen elements in the fourth series, which one

a. has the largest atomic radius?
b. has the smallest ionization energy?
c. has the largest electron affinity?

d. has the lowest electronegativity?
e. has the highest electronegativity?
f. is the most reactive metal?
g. is a semiconductor?
h. is one of the least reactive elements?

15. Tell which of the stable alkaline earth metals (Be, Mg, Ca, Sr, and Ba) fit the following descriptions. (Use the graphs on pp. 79-81; one answer will be an exception to a rule, and you may need to extrapolate.)
    a. has the largest atomic radius
    b. has the smallest ionization energy
    c. has the largest electron affinity
    d. has the smallest electronegativity
16. Given the elements Al, Au, Br, Ca, F, H, He, Hg, I, K, Mg, Na, O, P, S, and Si, which
    a. are gaseous elements at room temperature?
    b. are liquids at room temperature?
    c. are soft metals?
    d. is a constituent of table salt?
    e. is found in salt replacements?
    f. are responsible for making water hard?
    g. is a relatively unreactive solid metal?
    h. is found in glass and many minerals?
    i. is found in a compound called bauxite?
    j. glows in the dark?
    k. is called brimstone in the Bible?
    l. is the most electronegative element?
    m. helps keep thyroid glands working properly?
    n. is used for filling balloons?
    o. is a gas that can behave as an alkali metal?
    p. is a major constituent of stalagmites and stalactites?
17. Why were metals like gold, silver, and copper known in Old Testament times, but metals like sodium, aluminum, and potassium not discovered until recently?
18. Why was Cl_2 isolated before F_2? Can the reason for this be applied to other elements? If so, to which ones?
19. Given the elements Ag, Al, Ar, Au, C, Ca, Cl, Cu, Fe, Hg, O, Pb, U, and W, which
    a. is used as a fuel in nuclear power plants?
    b. fills the tubes of fluorescent lights?
    c. is used in an alloy for light, noncorroding bicycle parts?
    d. may be found in high-quality thermometers and contaminated tuna fish?
    e. helps your body construct strong bones?
    f. can form diamonds, graphite, or charcoal?
    g. is used to disinfect the water in swimming pools?

FIVE

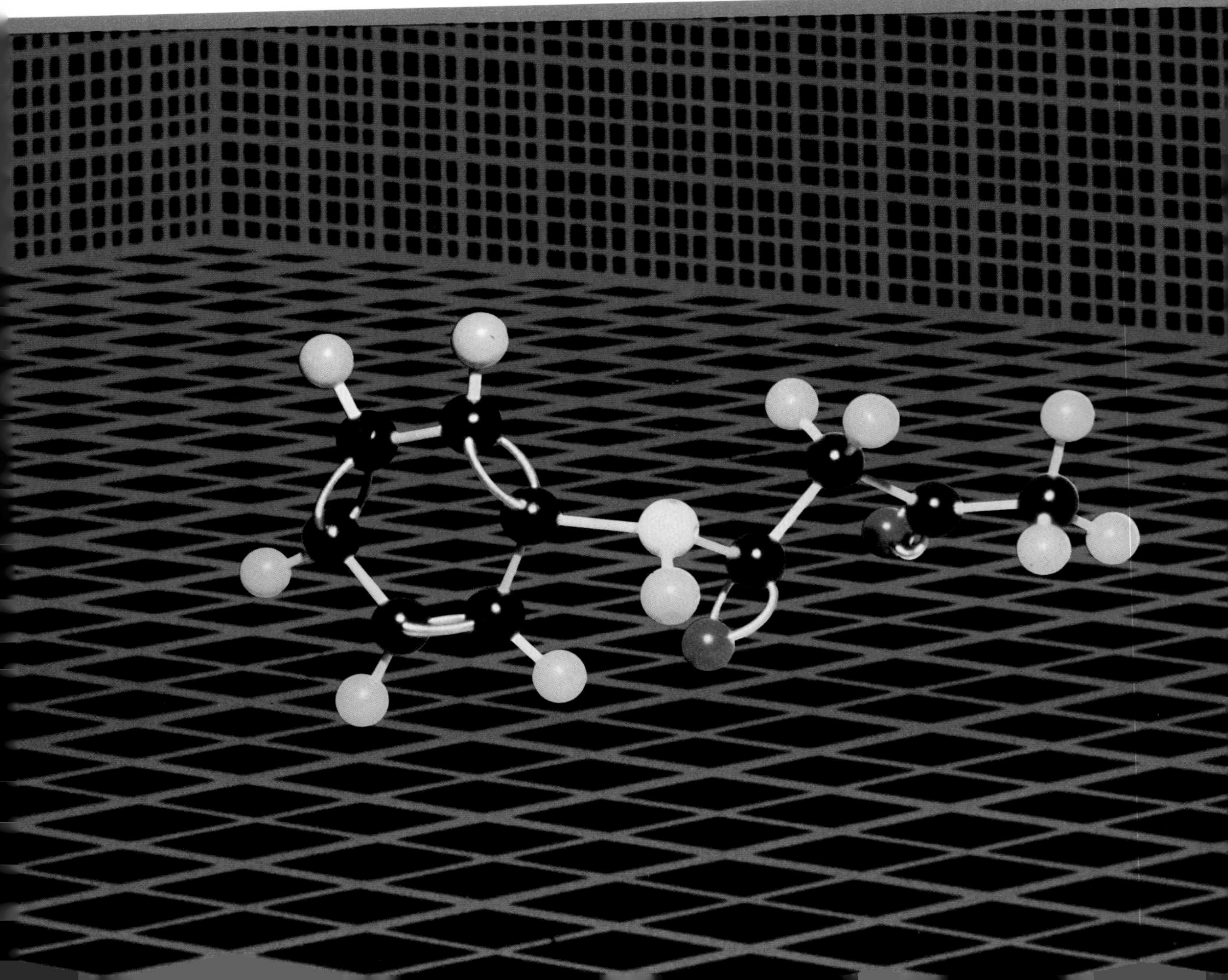

CHEMICAL BONDS

WHEN ATOMS STICK TOGETHER

FEW atoms exist by themselves. Powerful electrostatic attractions called **chemical bonds** link them with other atoms. This chapter addresses some important questions about chemical bonds. Why do they form? How do they hold atoms together? What are the properties of the resulting atomic alliances?

How and Why Atoms Bond

5–1 Why Bond?

The world is decaying. Dead limbs fall to the ground from the treetops; air escapes from tires if nails puncture them; and molten lava cools as it oozes down a volcano's slope. Objects do not gain energy by rising against gravity, compressing themselves, or getting hot spontaneously. It is intuitive that matter goes to low-energy, stable states. Atoms and molecules follow the same trend. The tendency for atoms to seek stable, low-energy states is the key to explaining why they bond. Most unbonded atoms have high-energy, low-stability electron configurations. Bonded atoms have achieved greater stability by losing some of their energy. Favorable bonding processes release energy—often in the form of heat or light.

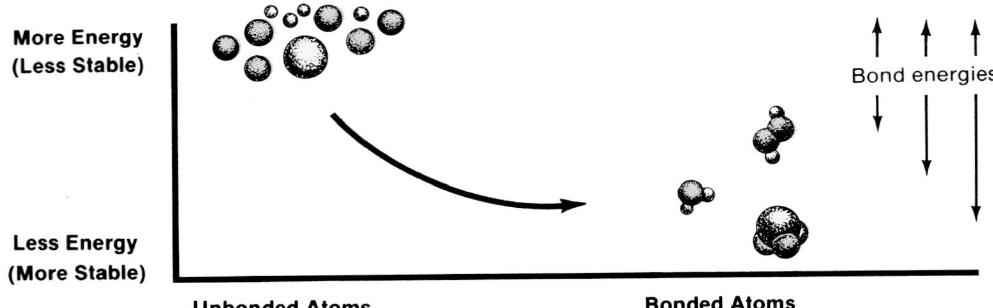

5-1 Favorable bonding processes produce low-energy, stable molecules from high-energy, unstable atoms.

Atoms seek a certain arrangement of electrons. The condition of having eight valence electrons is energetically favorable. Any arrangement that provides less than eight valence electrons is unsatisfactory. The tendency for atoms to react with other atoms until they have eight outer-level electrons is called the **octet rule.** This rule serves as a general guide to chemical bonding processes. How do atoms gain a full octet? They can gain, lose, or even share electrons.

Sample Problem. State several ways in which sodium atoms and oxygen atoms could get eight outer-level electrons.

Solution.

Sodium could get eight outer-level electrons by gaining seven electrons. Another way would be to lose its one valence electron in the third energy level. That way the second energy level with its eight electrons would be the outermost energy level. Oxygen atoms could either gain two electrons or lose six electrons.

Bonding processes rearrange the smallest number of electrons possible. Atoms with less than four valence electrons tend to lose electrons. Atoms with more than four tend to gain electrons.

5–2 Bond Character: What Kind of Bond Am I?

The way atoms get an octet depends on the types of atoms that are involved—particularly on their electronegativities. Three combinations of atoms can be bonded together: metals and nonmetals, nonmetals and nonmetals, and metals and metals. In the first case highly electronegative nonmetals greatly attract electrons toward their nuclei. The valence electrons of the metal transfer to the nonmetal, and an ionic bond forms. In the second case the high electronegativities of both atoms work against each other. The electrons are shared between the atoms in a covalent bond. In the third case neither metal atom strongly attracts the electrons that are involved in the bond. A communal sharing of electrons called metallic bonding occurs.

Table 5-2

Types of Bonds

Combination	Electro-negativities	Electron Action	Type of Bond
Metal/nonmetal	low/high	transfer	ionic
Nonmetal/ nonmetal	high/high	tight sharing	covalent
Metal/metal	low/low	loose sharing	metallic

Sample Problem. Predict the general type of bond that will form when the following atoms bond.

a. N and O   b. Ag and Cu   c. Cs and F

Solution.

a. Both of these elements are nonmetals with high electronegativities. The electrons will be tightly shared in a covalent bond.

b. Both of these atoms are metals with low electronegativities, so they bond metallically.

c. Cesium's electronegativity is extremely low, whereas fluorine's is extremely high. Together they form an ionic bond.

5–3 Ionic Bonds: Transferring Electrons

Picture the way in which metals and nonmetals react with each other. Before reacting, nonmetals are just short of having full octets of electrons in their outermost energy levels. Metals have one or two electrons beyond their last full energy levels. Both kinds of atoms can obtain an octet through a simple transfer of electrons. Nonmetal atoms can gain the electrons they need from metals, and metal atoms can lose their valence electrons and use the full energy levels beneath as their octets. When electrons transfer, ions form. Electrostatic attractions between oppositely charged ions in a solid are called **ionic bonds.**

5-3 Greatly different strengths result in a transfer.

Consider how sodium and chlorine atoms form sodium chloride. Neither atom has an octet before it bonds: sodium has one valence electron, and chlorine has seven. In the reaction that occurs, chlorine acquires a full octet by gaining sodium's one valence electron. In doing so, it becomes a negative ion. Sodium's loss of its valence electron exposes the full second energy level and produces a positive ion. Both atoms benefit because their electron configurations become more stable. Since opposite charges attract, the two ions stick together. Since compounds are electrically neutral, the net electric charge of all the ions must be zero. One Na^+ ion combines with one Cl^- ion.

Atoms before bonding:	$Na^{\times}$	$\cdot\ddot{Cl}:$
Ions after transfer:	Na^{+} →	$[\overset{\times}{\cdot}\ddot{Cl}:]^{-}$
Resulting compound:	$Na^{+}\,[\overset{\times}{\cdot}\ddot{Cl}:]^{-}$	or NaCl

In the formation of calcium chloride, calcium atoms transfer two electrons to chlorine atoms. But it takes two chlorine atoms to receive the electrons from every one calcium atom.

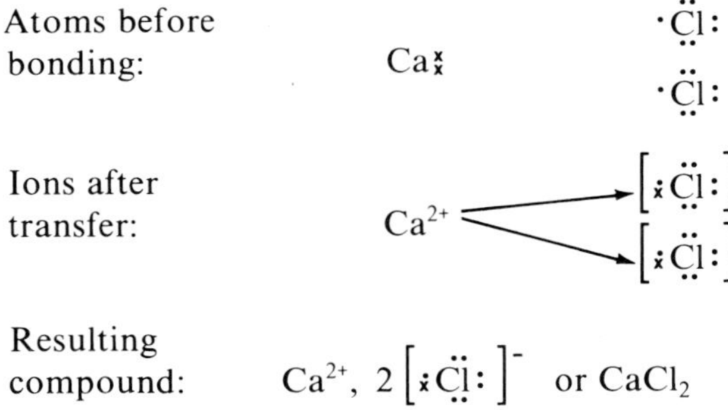

5–4 Ionic Compounds: Opposites Attract

Do not think that only one or two ions are involved in ionic bonding. Millions of ions are formed, and each of these ions interacts with its neighbors. Each positive ion attracts the negative ions in its immediate vicinity. Each negative ion in turn attracts all the neighboring positive ions. As rows and columns of these alternating ions are added, a pattern develops. Solids whose particles are arranged in orderly patterns are called **crystals.**

Sodium and chloride ions pack together in a simple repeating pattern. Each sodium ion has chloride ions on every side. The formula for calcium fluoride is CaF_2. There must be two fluoride ions for every calcium ion that is present in the crystal. Scientists have found that the ions alternate, but not in the same simple pattern that sodium chloride uses.

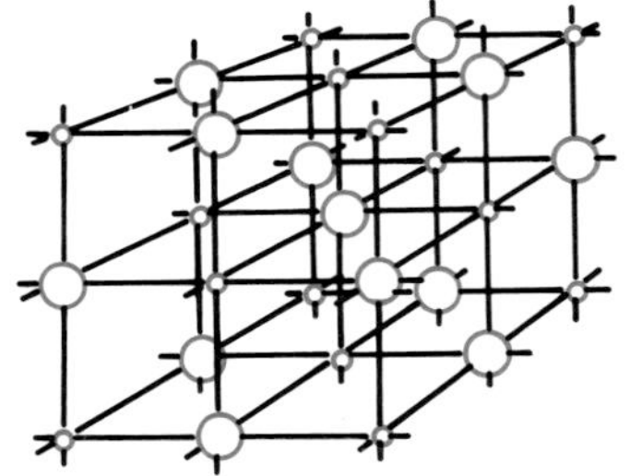

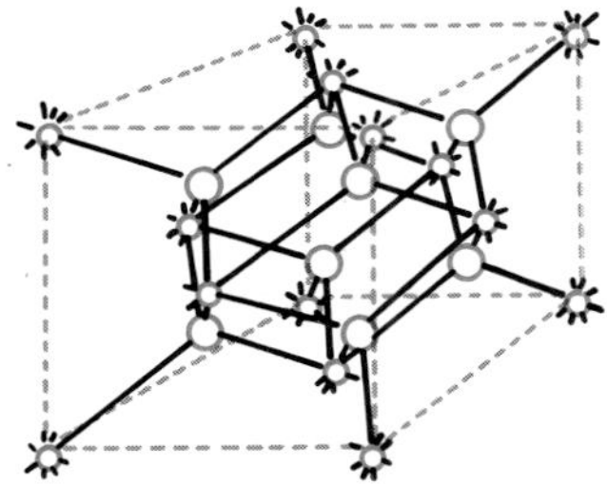

5-4 NaCl and CaF_2 both have ionic bonds, but their crystalline structures are different.

The exact way that the ions pack together depends on their charges and their sizes. The ions position themselves so that they are as near as possible to oppositely charged particles and as far away as possible from similarly charged particles. Ions take the most stable, least energetic positions possible.

Each ion in a crystal structure interacts with all its neighbors. No line can be drawn that separates one part of the crystal from another. The term *molecule* is not appropriate for ionic compounds, because there are no separate, distinct units. There can be no justification for picking one Na^+ and one Cl^- ion out of a large salt crystal and calling it a sodium chloride, or NaCl, molecule. It would be just as valid to form a Na_2Cl_2 or a Na_7Cl_7 molecule. Instead of using the term *molecule,* scientists use **formula units.** These formulas show the relative numbers of atoms in a compound by giving the simplest whole-number ratio between the atoms. The formula unit for sodium chloride is NaCl because there is a one-to-one relationship between the ions. Calcium fluoride's formula unit is CaF_2 because there are two fluorine atoms for every calcium.

Ionic bonds give the compounds they form some very distinct properties. Since ions are held in place by strong electrostatic forces on every side, the compounds are hard solids. The melting points of many of these compounds are near 800° C, illustrating just how strong these bonds are. Because of their orderly structures, crystals of ionic compounds can usually be split, or cleaved, along a straight line.

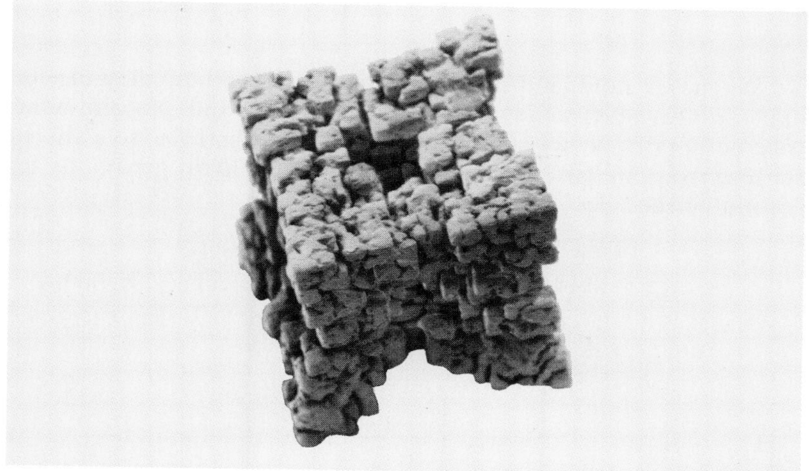

5-5 Large salt crystals are composed of smaller salt crystals.

Ionic compounds are soluble in substances such as water. They are also good conductors of electricity as long as they are not in the solid state. Melting or dissolving the crystals helps free the ions so that they can move. Ions bound in solid crystals cannot carry electrical current.

5-6 Two strong pulls result in a tight sharing.

5–5 Covalent Bonding: Sharing Electrons

In general, nonmetals have high electronegativities. They do not release the electrons needed in ionic bonding. Instead of transferring electrons to gain a full outer energy level, they share them. Bonds consisting of shared electrons are called **covalent bonds.**

The molecules of chlorine gas use covalent bonds to hold two chlorine atoms together. Before bonding, each atom has seven valence electrons. Each needs one more for a full octet. Since both atoms have the same electronegativity, neither one can pull electrons to itself. Instead, both atoms share one of their outer-level electrons. By sharing a pair of electrons, each chlorine atom can effectively have eight outer-level electrons. Because both nuclei strongly attract the shared pair of electrons, the molecule stays together. The covalent bond is often represented by a single line.

$$:\ddot{\underset{..}{Cl}}\cdot + {}^{\times}\underset{\times\times}{\overset{\times\times}{Cl}}{}^{\times}_{\times} \longrightarrow :\ddot{\underset{..}{Cl}}{}^{\times}_{\cdot}\underset{\times\times}{\overset{\times\times}{Cl}}{}^{\times}_{\times} \quad \text{or} \quad Cl{-}Cl$$

Hydrogen atoms also bond covalently. They do not seek an octet, since the first energy level holds only two electrons. They fill the first energy level when they bond.

$$H\cdot + {}^{\times}H \longrightarrow H{}^{\times}_{\cdot}H \quad \text{or} \quad H{-}H$$

Whenever nonmetal atoms are bonded together, they can be expected to have covalent bonds. Hydrogen and oxygen bond together to form water. The oxygen lacks two electrons, so it shares the electrons of two hydrogen atoms. Each hydrogen gains its second valence electron in the process.

$$H^{\times} + H^{\times} + \cdot\ddot{\underset{\cdot}{O}}: \longrightarrow H{}^{\times}_{\cdot}\underset{H}{\ddot{O}}: \quad \text{or} \quad \underset{H}{H{-}O}$$

$$H^{\times} + H^{\times} + H^{\times} + \cdot\dot{\underset{..}{N}}\cdot \longrightarrow H{}^{\times}_{\cdot}\overset{H}{\underset{..}{N}}{}^{\times}_{\cdot}H \quad \text{or} \quad H{-}\overset{H}{N}{-}H$$

Double covalent bonds form when atoms need two additional electrons. Sulfur monoxide (SO) molecules contain a double bond between an oxygen and a sulfur atom. The atoms share two pairs of electrons in a double covalent bond. **Triple covalent bonds** form when atoms share three pairs of electrons. The nitrogen molecules in the air consist of two triply bonded nitrogen atoms.

$$:\ddot{\underset{\cdot}{S}}\cdot + {}^{\times}\overset{\times\times}{\underset{\times}{O}}{}^{\times}_{\times} \longrightarrow \dot{:}\underset{\cdot\cdot}{S}:{}^{\times}_{\times}\overset{\times}{\underset{\times\times}{O}}{}^{\times} \quad \text{or} \quad \dot{:}\underset{\cdot}{S}=\overset{\cdot}{\underset{\cdot}{O}}\dot{:} \quad \text{or} \quad S=O$$

$$:\dot{\underset{\cdot}{N}}\cdot + {}^{\times}\overset{\times}{\underset{\times}{N}}{}^{\times}_{\times} \longrightarrow :N\vdots{}^{\times}_{\times}N{}^{\times}_{\times} \quad \text{or} \quad N\equiv N$$

The following set of steps can be a helpful guide for writing electron-dot structures, especially when the structures are complex.

1. Arrange the atoms in a logical structure. Sometimes there will be only one possible structure; other times you might have to try several arrangements. Often the atom that forms the most bonds serves as the central atom.
2. Count up the number of valence electrons from all the atoms.
3. Distribute some electrons around the atoms by drawing single bonds (one pair of electrons) between each atom.
4. Distribute the rest of the electrons around the atoms so that each atom has a full outer energy level. If there are not enough electrons to go around, form double bonds and triple bonds.

COVALENT BONDING: A NATURAL FOR MR. SMITH

Sample Problem. Draw the electron-dot structure of CCl_4.

Solution.

1. The logical structure would be

$$\begin{array}{ccc} & Cl & \\ Cl & C & Cl \\ & Cl & \end{array}$$

2. Thirty-two valence electrons (seven from each Cl and four from the C) are available.
3. Four single bonds involving eight electrons connect the atoms.

$$\begin{array}{ccc} & Cl & \\ Cl & \overset{\times\cdot}{\underset{\times\cdot}{\,{}^{\times}_{\cdot}C^{\times}_{\cdot}}} & Cl \\ & Cl & \end{array} \quad \text{or} \quad \begin{array}{ccccc} & & Cl & & \\ & & | & & \\ Cl & - & C & - & Cl \\ & & | & & \\ & & Cl & & \end{array}$$

4. The remaining electrons surround the chlorine atoms and give each one a complete octet.

$$\begin{array}{ccc} & :\ddot{\underset{\cdot\cdot}{Cl}}: & \\ :\ddot{\underset{\cdot\cdot}{Cl}} & {}^{\times}_{\cdot}\overset{\times\cdot}{\underset{\times\cdot}{C}}{}^{\times}_{\cdot} & \ddot{\underset{\cdot\cdot}{Cl}}: \\ & :\ddot{\underset{\cdot\cdot}{Cl}}: & \end{array} \quad \text{or} \quad \begin{array}{ccccc} & & :\ddot{\underset{\cdot\cdot}{Cl}}: & & \\ & & | & & \\ :\ddot{\underset{\cdot\cdot}{Cl}} & - & C & - & \ddot{\underset{\cdot\cdot}{Cl}}: \\ & & | & & \\ & & :\ddot{\underset{\cdot\cdot}{Cl}}: & & \end{array}$$

Sample Problem. Draw the electron-dot structure of CF_2O.

Solution.

1. A logical structure is one in which the atom forming the most bonds is in the center of the molecule.

```
F   C   O

    F
```

2. Twenty-four electrons (seven from each F, four from the C, and six from the O) must be placed in bonds around the atoms.
3. Single bonds are drawn between each atom.

```
F:C:O        or      F—C—O
  ..                   |
  F                    F
```

4. The remaining electrons are placed around the atoms so that each atom has eight outer-level electrons.

```
 ..  .  ..               ..  .  ..
:F:C:O·        or      :F—C—O·
 ..  ..  ..              ..     ..
  :F:                       |
   ..                      :F:
                            ..
```

As it now stands, all the atoms do not have octets. A double bond should be placed between the carbon and the oxygen.

```
 ..     .                 ..     .
:F:C::O:       or       :F—C=O:
 ..  ..  .                ..     .
  :F:                        |
   ..                       :F:
                             ..
```

In most covalent bonds each atom contributes one electron. In **coordinate covalent bonds,** however, both of the shared electrons come from the same atom. The only difference between coordinate covalent bonds and normal covalent bonds is the origin of the electrons. Once a coordinate covalent bond forms, it has all the properties of other covalent bonds.

Chloric acid ($HClO_3$) is a compound that contains coordinate covalent bonds. One oxygen atom forms normal covalent bonds with the chlorine and the hydrogen atoms. The other two oxygen atoms use coordinate covalent bonds. Both electrons in these bonds come from the chlorine atom.

```
         ..
        :O:
   ..    xx
 H:O:Cl x     } Coordinate
   ..    xx   } covalent
        :O:   } bonds
         ..
```

5–6 Diatomic Molecules: What a Pair!

The atoms of halogens (F, Cl, Br, and I), hydrogen, oxygen, and nitrogen are not stable by themselves. Samples of these elements are not made of individual atoms but of two-atomed, covalent molecules. Molecules that contain two atoms are called diatomic molecules. The diatomic molecules that are formed from the elements listed above are F_2, Cl_2, Br_2, I_2, H_2, O_2, and N_2. Be familiar with this list; in future chapters it will be necessary to know that atoms of these elements automatically form molecules.

5-8 Bromine consists of diatomic Br_2 molecules.

5–7 Polyatomic Ions: Covalent, Yet Ionic

Some atoms combine to form multi-atom ions. These groups of atoms have electrical charges because electrons must be gained or lost in order for every atom to have a complete octet. Just as a Cl^- ion has one more electron than a chlorine atom, an OH^- ion has one more electron than the oxygen and hydrogen atoms that participate in the covalent bonding.

$$:\ddot{\underset{..}{Cl}}\cdot + \underset{(\mathbf{x})}{\overset{\text{one}}{\text{electron}}} \longrightarrow \left[:\ddot{\underset{..}{Cl}}\overset{\cdot}{\underset{\cdot}{x}}\right]^- \text{ or } Cl^-$$

$$:\dot{\underset{..}{O}}\overset{\cdot}{\underset{\cdot}{x}}H + \underset{(\mathbf{x})}{\overset{\text{one}}{\text{electron}}} \longrightarrow \left[:\overset{x\cdot}{\underset{..}{O}}\overset{\cdot}{\underset{\cdot}{x}}H\right]^- \text{ or } OH^-$$

The electron-dot structures of polyatomic ions can be written according to the same rules that were used for covalent compounds. Just remember that ions have different numbers of electrons than the uncharged atoms have. If an ion has a +1 charge, there is one less electron to work with. If an ion has a -2 charge, two extra electrons are present. Square brackets may be placed around electron-dot structures of the ions for clarity.

Sample Problem. Write the electron-dot structure of the ammonium ion (NH_4^+).

Solution.

Logical structure:

$$\begin{array}{ccc} & H & \\ H & N & H \\ & H & \end{array}$$

When counting electrons, remember that the +1 charge indicates that one electron has been lost. The nitrogen atom has five valence electrons, and each hydrogen has one. The total number of electrons (nine) is decreased by one to account for the +1 charge. Drawing one pair of electrons for each bond results in the following structure.

$$\left[\begin{array}{ccc} & H & \\ H\,{\overset{\times}{\cdot}} & \overset{\times\cdot}{\underset{\times\cdot}{N}} & {\overset{\times}{\cdot}}\,H \\ & H & \end{array}\right]^{+} \quad \text{or} \quad \left[\begin{array}{ccc} & H & \\ H : & \ddot{\underset{\cdot\cdot}{N}} & : H \\ & H & \end{array}\right]^{+} \quad \text{or} \quad \left[\begin{array}{ccccc} & & H & & \\ & & | & & \\ H & — & N & — & H \\ & & | & & \\ & & H & & \end{array}\right]^{+}$$

Polyatomic ions act as units in many chemical reactions. Their stable octets of electrons allow them to go through reactions and form compounds without splitting up. They can even bond with other oppositely charged polyatomic ions to form ionic compounds. When polyatomic ions bond to form ionic compounds, the ratio of positive ions to negative ions must still be such that the overall charge on the compound is zero. When sodium ions (Na^+) and nitrate ions (NO_3^-) combine, they do so in a one-to-one ratio. If sodium and sulfate ions (SO_4^{2-}) combine, there must be two Na^+ ions for every SO_4^- ion.

5-9 Two weak pulls result in a weak sharing.

5–8 Metallic Bonding: Share and Share Alike

What holds the atoms in a piece of metal together? Ionic bonds certainly do not form; all metal atoms have low electronegativities. None of them can pull electrons from other atoms to form ions. What about covalent bonds? No again. Metal atoms do not have enough valence electrons to share them with other needy atoms. A different type of bond must form. The theory that explains how metal atoms stick together also explains why metals have the properties they have.

The theory used to explain the characteristics of metals is called the **electron-sea theory.** In this theory metals are pictured as an

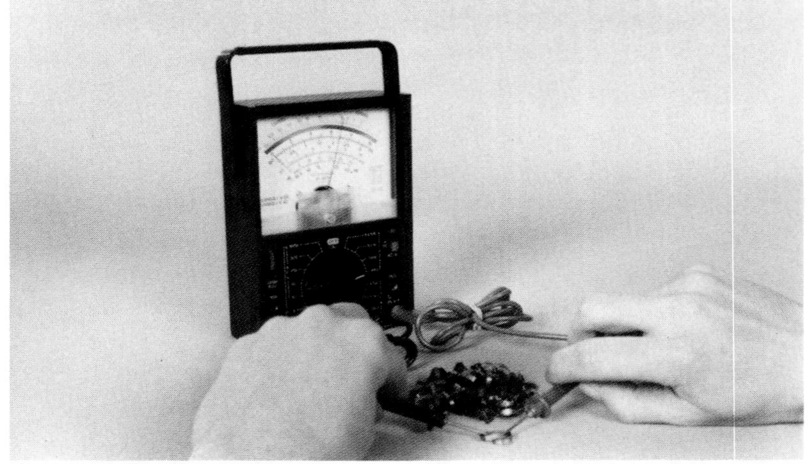

5-10 An ohmmeter is a device used to measure electrical resistance. The electrons in metallic bonds are free to move from one location to another.

extended array of positive ions surrounded by unattached electrons. The positive ions, or cations, are formed when atoms lose their valence electrons. The old valence electrons are mobile electrons that are now shared by all the cations. The metallic bond is a modified form of the covalent bond. Electrons are shared, but not between a mere one, two, or three atoms. They are shared by all the atoms. The situation can be likened to a sea of electrons surrounding islands of positive charges.

The electron-sea theory explains many characteristics of metals. The electrons in the sea are free to carry electrical current and to transfer thermal energy. The luster of metals can be explained by the combination of the ideas of spectroscopy and free electrons. Since electrons are free, they are able to absorb and emit many wavelengths of light. All the wavelengths of light, when reflected together, make up the shiny luster. Metallic bonds allow pieces of metal to be formed into new shapes without shattering. The widespread sharing of electrons allows the cations to shift when under stress. Their positions can be "rearranged" by a swift blow from a hammer.

5-11 The steady pounding of a blacksmith's hammer causes iron atoms to shift, despite their metallic bonds.

The Quantum Model and Bonding

So far, electron-dot structures have been used to study covalent bonds. These simple sketches show the bonding process clearly, but they are so simple that they leave out valuable information about the compounds that form. For instance, they can tell nothing about the three-dimensional shape of a molecule. Is water

$$\mathrm{H:\ddot{\underset{\cdot\cdot}{O}}:H} \qquad \text{or is it} \qquad \begin{array}{c}\mathrm{H:\ddot{\underset{\cdot\cdot}{O}}:}\\ \mathrm{H}\end{array}$$

From electron-dot structures alone, there is no way to tell. For a more complete description of chemical bonds—especially covalent bonds—the quantum model must be used.

5–9 Orbitals and Bonding: The Quantum Model Strikes Again

In the quantum model, electrons are said to exist in various types of sublevels. These sublevels, named *s, p, d,* and *f,* contain varying numbers of orbitals. An orbital is a region in which the probability of finding an electron is great. Each orbital can hold a maximum of two electrons.

In the quantum model a covalent bond is pictured as an overlap of partially filled orbitals. When two orbitals mesh together, the overlapping region is available to both nuclei. Effectively, both atoms have another electron. The term **valence bond theory** is given to the idea that covalent bonds are formed when orbitals of different atoms overlap.

5–10 Bonds: When Orbitals Overlap

The hydrogen molecule (H:H) is a familiar diatomic molecule. According to valence bond theory, the *s* orbitals of each hydrogen atom overlap. A single region of high electron probability forms between the two atoms. This area is shaded darkly because the probability of finding an electron is great.

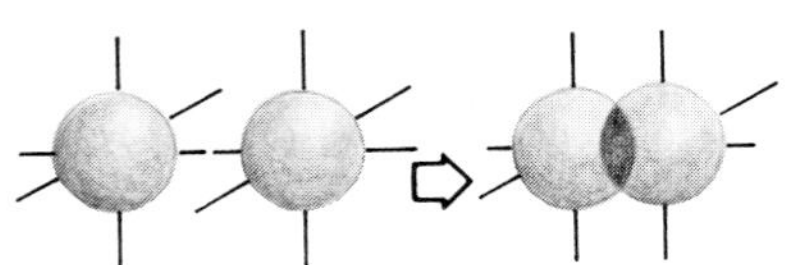

5-12 A single bond forms when orbitals overlap end to end.

Double and triple bonds are formed by the overlapping of more than one set of orbitals. The first overlap is the end-to-end overlap that is common in single bonds. The second bond is different. The *sides* of orbitals pointing in the same direction overlap. Note that a side-by-side overlap results in two regions of high electron probability. Do not let the two regions confuse you. They still represent one bond.

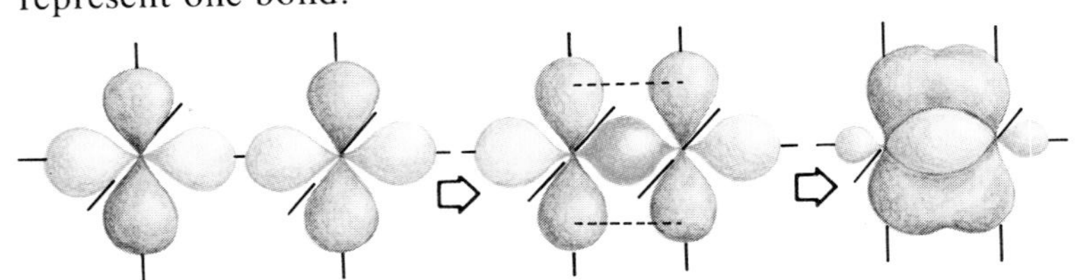

5-13 The second bond in a double bond forms when two orbitals overlap side by side.

A triple bond is made up of one end-to-end overlap and two side-by-side overlaps. A second set of *p* orbitals has a side-by-side overlap.

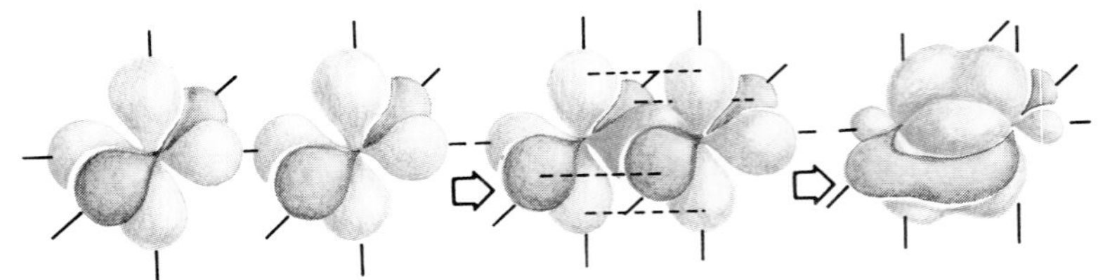

5-14 The third bond in a triple bond forms when another set of orbitals overlaps side by side.

5–11 Hybridization: What Atoms Go Through to Bond

Many observations forced chemists to make bonding theories more complicated than they originally were. One of these observations concerns the bonding of carbon. The electron configuration shows that carbon has two partially filled *p* orbitals.

It would seem probable that carbon would fill these orbitals by forming two bonds; but it does not. In the CH_4 molecule, it forms four equivalent bonds.

In order to bond this way, the electron configuration of the atom must change. It probably shifts from something like

1*s*	**2*s***	**2*p***				**1*s***	**2*s***	**2*p***		
↑↓	↑↓	↑	↑	_	to	↑↓	↑	↑	↑	↑

The process of forming new kinds of orbitals with equal energies from a combination of other orbitals is called **hybridization.** In carbon the *s* and three *p* orbitals combine to form four new orbitals. Scientists believe that most other atoms hybridize before they bond.

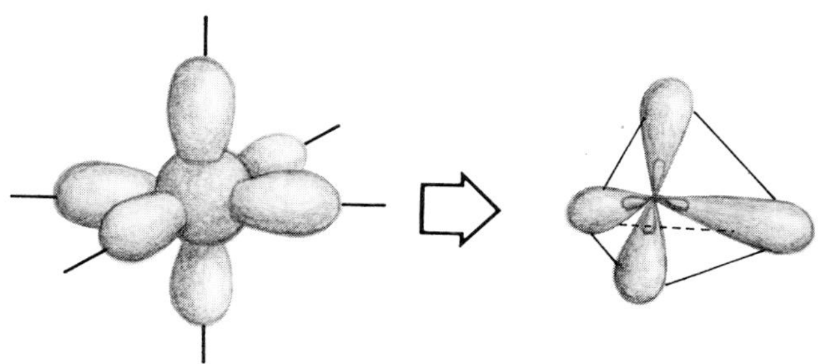

5-15 The hybrid orbitals that form before atoms bond point in new directions and have different shapes from the original orbitals.

5–12 Bonding and Molecular Shape: Keep Your Distance

The **Valence Shell Electron Pair Repulsion theory** (abbreviated VSEPR, which is pronounced "vesper") assumes that regions of electron concentrations in molecules are arranged so that they are separated by the maximum distance possible. This makes sense, since electrons repel each other. The application of this rule is the key to determining the shapes of molecules.

The electron-dot structure can be used to determine the number of electron concentrations around an atom. An electron concentration can be either an unbonded pair, a single bond, a double bond, or a triple bond. CH_4 has four electron concentrations around the carbon atom. CF_2O has three electron concentrations: one double bond and two single bonds.

```
  H
H:C:H        :F:C::O
  H            :F:
```

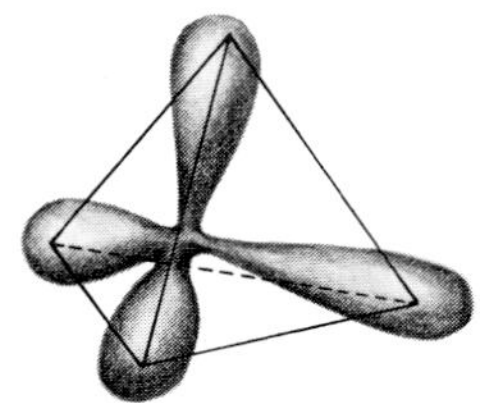

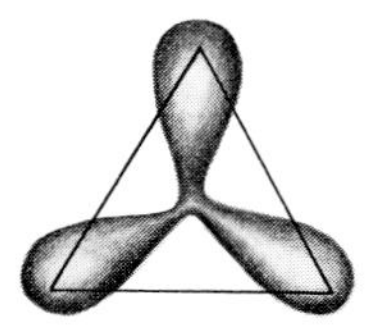

5-16 The distance between hybridized orbitals is as great as possible.

If an atom has four electron concentrations around it, the orbitals point away from each other as much as possible. The orbitals point toward the four corners of a tetrahedron (a four-sided pyramid), with each angle measuring 109.5°. This three-dimensional setup allows more space between the orbitals than any other arrangement does.

The hybridized orbitals around an atom with three electron concentrations point toward the corners of a triangle. The angles between the orbitals all measure 120°, and all the orbitals lie in the same plane.

The hybridized orbitals around an atom with two electron concentrations point in opposite directions, 180° from each other.

Determining the shapes of molecules requires knowing the directions in which hybridized orbitals point and knowing which orbitals bond to other atoms. Consider the following molecules. All of them have four regions of electrons around the central atom. CH_4. The electron-dot structure shows that the molecule has four regions of electrons and must therefore have four hybridized orbitals that point to the corners of a tetrahedron. Hydrogen nuclei are located at the end of each orbital. The resulting shape is called **tetrahedral.**

```
  H
H:C:H
  H
```

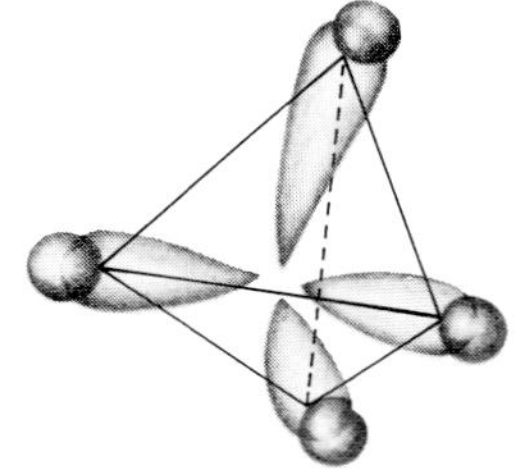

NH_3. Like CH_4, this molecule has four regions of electrons around the central atom. Unlike CH_4, it does not have an atom at the end of one of its orbitals. The orbital is occupied by an unbonded pair of electrons. This molecule's shape is not a full tetrahedron; it is **pyramidal.** The hybridized orbitals still point to the four corners of a tetrahedron, but only three of the corners are occupied.

```
  ..
H:N:H
  H
```

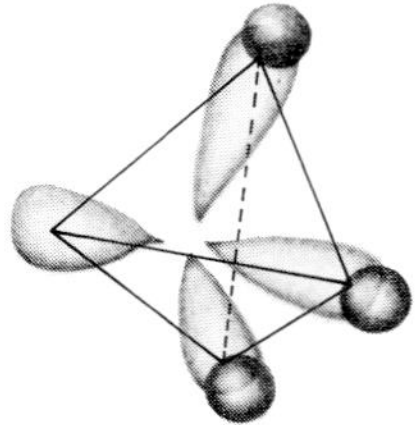

H_2O. Water molecules also have four regions of electrons. The shape of the molecule is determined by the locations of the two hydrogen atoms and the oxygen atom. The positions of the nuclei form a **bent** line. The angles between the bonds are close to 109.5°.

HF. The fluorine atom can be called the central atom. It has four electron concentrations around it. The single bond to the hydrogen atom results in a **linear** shape.

Different shapes can result from the structure that three hybridized orbitals form. If all three orbitals bond to atoms, a **trigonal planar** shape results. The three hybridized orbitals point toward the corners of an equilateral triangle. If only two atoms are bonded to the central atom, the molecule will have a bent shape. The bend in this case is 120°, not the 109.5° of the other bent molecule. If only one orbital is bonded, the linear shape is formed.

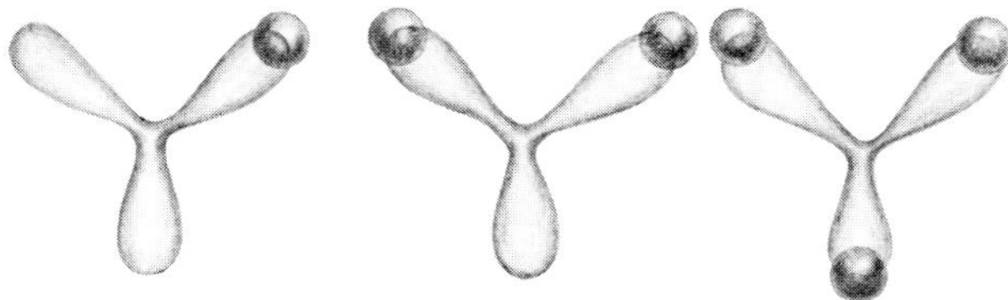

The only possible arrangement for a simple molecule that has two regions of electrons around its central atom is a linear arrangement.

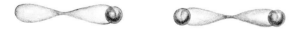

Table 5-17

Molecular Shapes

Number of Electron Regions	Number of Bonds	Diagram	Geometry
4	4		tetrahedral
	3		pyramidal
	2		bent—109.5°
	1		linear
3	3		trigonal planar
	2		bent—120°
	1		linear
2	2		linear
	1		linear

Sample Problem. Predict the shapes of the following molecules.

a. :Ö:S̈::Ö:

b. $[H:\ddot{O}:H]^+$ (with H below O)

c. H:C:::N:

Solution.

a. From the number of electron-concentration regions, you know that the three concentrations of electrons around sulfur point 120° from each other. Since only two of the orbitals are bonded, the bent 120° shape results.

b. Four regions of charge mean that hybridized orbitals point to the four corners of a tetrahedron. Since only three bonds have been formed, the molecule has a pyramidal shape.

c. Two regions of electrons mean that the hybridized orbitals point in a straight line. This shape is called linear.

5–13 Polar Covalent Bonds: Unequal Partnerships

Atoms with similar electronegativities form covalent bonds. But what about atoms with slightly different electronegativities? Do they transfer, or do they share electrons? The answer is that they share, but not equally.

The shared pair of electrons in a hydrogen chloride (HCl) molecule has a unique position. Compared to hydrogen, the chlorine atom is very electronegative. It pulls the shared pair closer to itself. The shifting of electrons results in a semi-ionic condition. The proximity of the electrons to the chlorine atom gives it a partial negative charge. Since the electrons are a good distance from the hydrogen nucleus, the nucleus is left exposed. It therefore has a partially positive charge.

Partial charges on molecules are shown by the lower-case Greek letter delta (δ). The hydrogen chloride molecule should be thought of as

$\overset{\delta^+}{\mathrm{H}}\ \ \overset{\delta^-}{:\ddot{\underset{..}{\mathrm{Cl}}}:}$ instead of as completely covalent $\mathrm{H}:\ddot{\underset{..}{\mathrm{Cl}}}:$

or completely ionic $\mathrm{H}^+\left[:\ddot{\underset{..}{\mathrm{Cl}}}:\right]^-$.

Another way of showing the partial charges is with a crossed arrow. The head of the arrow points toward the negative area of the molecule, and the cross is located near the positive area.

$$\overset{+\!\!\longrightarrow}{\mathrm{H}:\ddot{\underset{..}{\mathrm{Cl}}}:}$$

Objects with two different electrical ends, or poles, are said to be **polar.** Bonds with shared but shifted electrons are called **polar covalent bonds.** These bonds form whenever atoms with different electronegativities share electrons.

Polar bonds often make entire molecules polar. Hydrochloric acid molecules have a positively charged end and a negatively charged end. Polar bonds do not always result in polar molecules, however. The bonds must be arranged unsymmetrically for the entire molecule to have polarity. Carbon tetrachloride (CCl_4) has bonds that are quite polar, but the bonds are arranged symmetrically. As a result the molecule has no discernible regions of charge. The polar bonds cancel each other out. Each chlorine atom draws electrons away from the carbon atom. But since the chlorine atoms are arranged symmetrically around the carbon, no end of the molecule is more negative than another. Table 5-18 shows how this general rule can apply to molecules of different geometries.

Table 5-18

When Molecules Are Polar

Shapes for Four Regions of Electrons	Shapes for Three Regions of Electrons	Shapes for Two Regions of Electrons
Tetrahedral—if outer atoms have different electronegativities 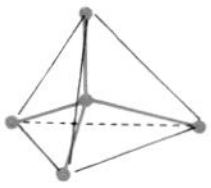		
Pyramidal—always polar 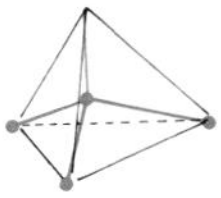	Trigonal planar—if outer atoms have different electronegativities 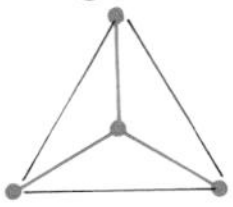	
Bent (109.5°)—always polar 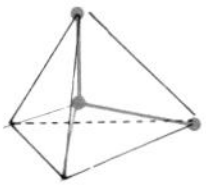	Bent (120°)—always polar 	
Linear—if outer atoms have different electronegativities 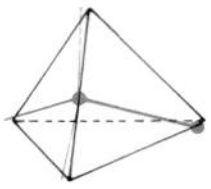	Linear—if outer atoms have different electronegativities 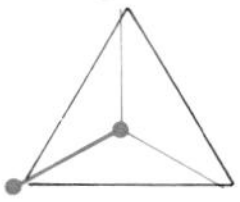	Linear—if outer atoms have different electronegativities 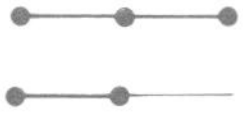

5–14 Dipole Moment: A Measure of Polarity

A **dipole moment** is a measure of polarity used to rate the polarity of molecules and bonds. The abbreviation μ is used for this quantity.

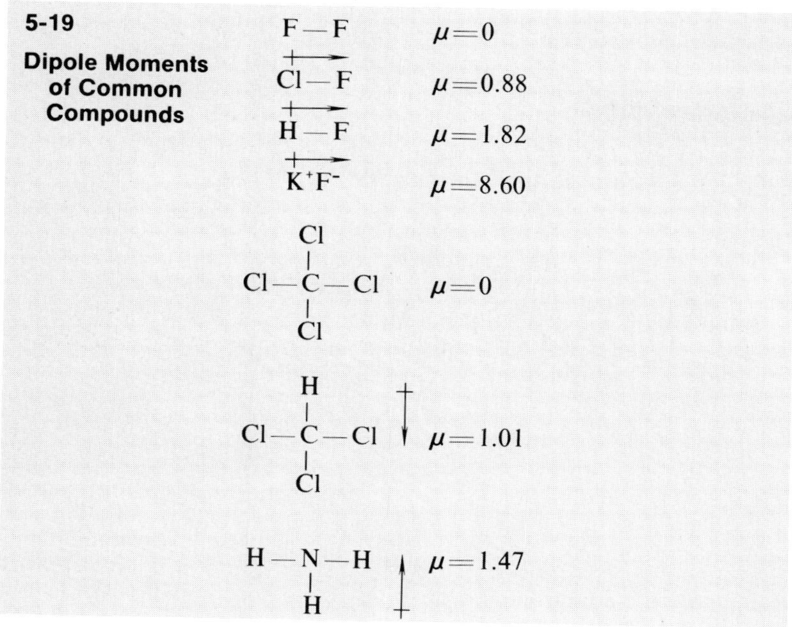

5-19 Dipole Moments of Common Compounds

Sample Problem. Determine whether CO_2, H_2S, and ClBr molecules are polar. If they are, indicate the direction of their dipole moments with a crossed arrow.

:Ö::C::Ö: H:S̈: :C̈l:B̈r:
H

Solution.

H:S̈: :C̈l:B̈r:
H

CO_2 is a linear molecule in which both outer atoms are identical; thus it is nonpolar. H_2S has a bent shape, and this kind of molecule is always polar. The highly electronegative sulfur atom shifts electrons toward itself. The net dipole moment of ClBr points toward chlorine because it has a greater electronegativity.

FACETS OF CHEMISTRY

Molecular Orbital Theory

The head researcher gathered his team of assistants together and informed them of an upcoming experiment. "According to the accepted theories of bonding, oxygen should form a colorless liquid that is not affected by a magnetic field. As you know, a molecule must have at least one unpaired electron before it can have a color or can respond to a magnetic field. The Lewis structure of O_2 predicts that all the electrons in the molecule are paired with other electrons. In our experiments we shall liquefy oxygen and test the validity of these predictions. Our aim is to prove that the accepted Lewis structure for the O_2 molecule is indeed the correct one."

Soon the researcher and his team had pressurized and cooled a sample of O_2 enough to form a liquid. To their great surprise, the liquid O_2 had a pale blue color. Furthermore, liquid O_2 could be held in place by a magnetic field. The researchers could not have been more surprised if the magnet had attracted drops of water. What started as a simple verification of the accepted valence bond theory turned out to provide contradictory, disturbing data.

The lack of a completely satisfactory model of molecules has always frustrated chemists. Many different models have been proposed, but no single model fully explains all that is known about molecules. The Bohr model of the atom explains some of the present knowledge about chemical bonds and molecules. It explains how atoms can lose and gain electrons to form ions. It also helps to explain how covalent bonds form and why molecules contain the atoms they do. Unfortunately, this solar-system model of the atoms cannot explain why molecules have the shapes they do.

The more advanced valence bond (VB) theory explains why molecules have the shapes they do. The orientation of the hybridized orbitals determines the general shape of the resulting molecules. Many chemists, however, are not satisfied with this theory. Experiments with liquid oxygen and some other molecules have supplied data that does not fit the VB theory. According to this theory, oxygen molecules should be colorless and unresponsive to magnetic fields. Since they are colored and they do respond, the VB theory must not be the final word in bonding theories.

A more recent and more complicated theory of bonding has been devised to fill the gaps left by the VB theory. The molecular orbital (MO) theory holds that the orbitals of the individual atoms disappear when a molecule forms. Totally new orbitals form in their place. Each molecule has a unique set of orbitals. Some orbitals encircle two, three, four, or even more atoms. Often they encompass the entire molecule. The MO theory ranks the resulting orbitals in order of increasing energy. Electrons fill low-energy molecular orbitals before they fill high-energy orbitals. The arrangement of electrons in these orbitals tells chemists whether bonds will form; whether they will be single, double, or triple bonds; and whether the bonds will contain unpaired electrons.

The most interesting idea of the MO theory is the concept of antibonding orbitals. When a molecule forms, two things can happen to the electrons in the atomic orbitals. Because the electrons behave like waves, combining orbitals can either reinforce or interfere with each other. When they reinforce each other, bonding orbitals form. Bonding orbitals are located between the nuclei. The electrons in these orbitals serve to stabilize the molecule because they can be shared by both atoms. Antibonding orbitals form when atomic orbitals combine in an unfavorable manner. If the electron waves interfere with each other, an orbital forms on the outside of the molecule, far from the two nuclei. The electrons in an antibonding orbital spend little time between the two nuclei, so these antibonding orbitals destabilize the molecule.

The MO theory successfully predicts whether molecules will be affected by a magnetic field. The ability to predict color and magnetic properties of molecules is a major triumph of the MO theory.

All three models of molecules have a place in chemistry. Obviously, none of them is completely right. Instead, scientists use the one that works best in a particular application. It would, of course, be better to have a single theory that would explain everything. Scientists could then discard the old theories and focus on the one true theory. But because human minds are limited and God's creation is complex, men do not have that luxury.

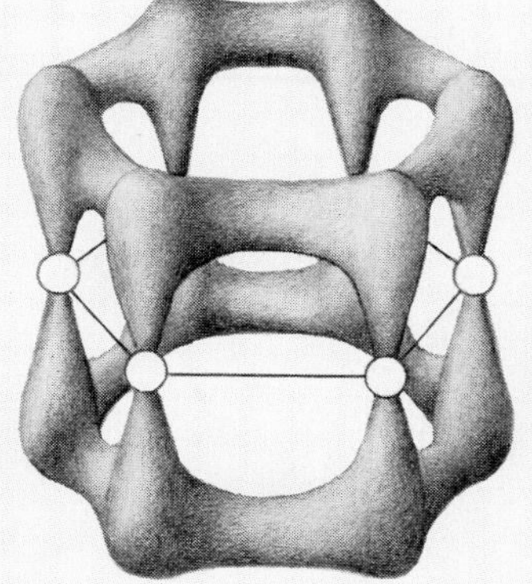

5–15 Intermolecular Forces: Weak but Effective

Molecules interact with each other—some more than others. The electrostatic attractions between molecules are called **intermolecular forces.** Although they are much weaker than the bonds that hold molecules together, they play a major role in determining the physical properties of compounds. Why is hydrogen a gas, water a liquid, and sugar a solid at room temperature? The types and strengths of intermolecular forces determine such physical properties. Intermolecular forces can be classified into three groups, and the existence of each type can be explained by the fact that regions of opposite charge attract each other.

Dipole-dipole interactions. Polar molecules have regions of unevenly distributed electrical charge. The positive areas of one molecule attract the negative areas of other molecules—the stronger the polarity, the stronger the force. The dipole-dipole interactions of polar molecules are similar to the forces in crystals of ionic compounds, but they are not as strong. (In ionic compounds full charges [+1, +2, -1, -2] interact.) Comparing the melting points of sodium chloride (NaCl) and iodine chloride (ICl) crystals exemplifies this point. The sodium chloride units have strong forces between them and can be pulled apart only at a temperature of 801° C. The molecules of iodine chloride have only partial charges on them, and their crystals melt at only 27° C.

Hydrogen bonds. As the name implies, one of the participating atoms is hydrogen. The other member of the bond is a strongly electronegative element. Whenever hydrogen is bonded to a highly electronegative element, the shared electrons shift away from the hydrogen. The hydrogen nucleus, which is actually a proton, is left exposed. Any negatively charged regions of other molecules will quickly interact with the exposed proton. A strong intermolecular force results. Hydrogen bonds are possible whenever hydrogen atoms are bonded to nitrogen, oxygen, fluorine, or chlorine atoms.

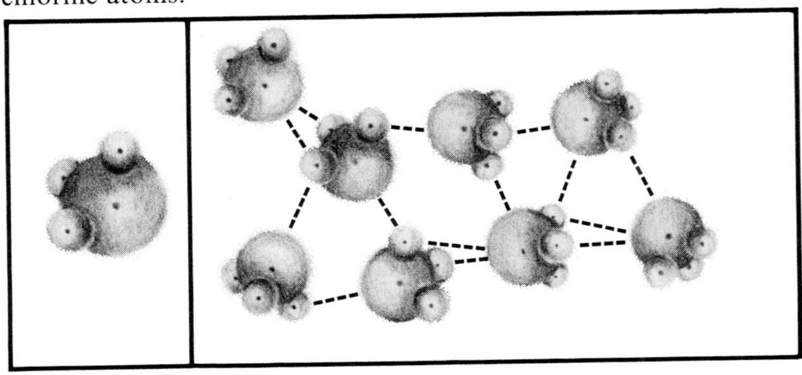

5-20 Hydrogen bonds form in compounds with hydrogen and highly electronegative atoms.

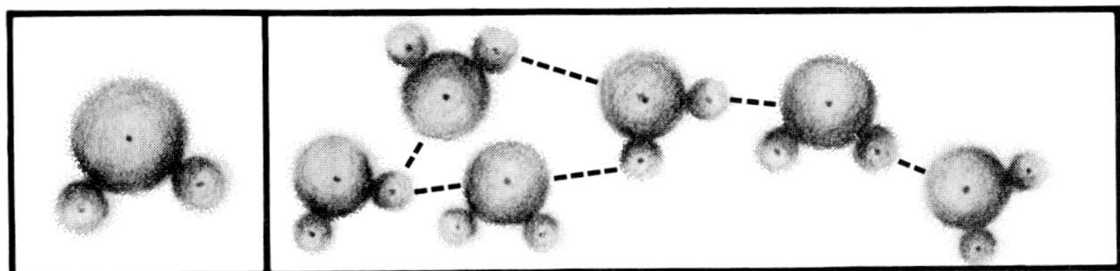

Dispersion forces. Nonpolar substances like wax and gasoline can exist as solids and liquids. This fact shows that dipole-dipole interactions and hydrogen bonds are not the only intermolecular forces. Nonpolar molecules do not have regions of electrical charge, yet they somehow attract each other. A third type of intermolecular force is called a dispersion force. This kind of force allows nonpolar molecules to stick together.

On the average, the electrons in a nonpolar bond spend an equal amount of time around each atom. However, during the course of their movements, electrons can concentrate at one end of the molecule. When this occurs, a temporary region of charge forms. This region of charge can momentarily pull on a neighboring molecule. Dispersion forces result from random, unequal dispersions of electrons.

Dispersion forces work between all kinds of molecules: polar and nonpolar. Dipole-dipole interactions exist only between polar molecules. Hydrogen bonds exist only between polar molecules that have the necessary atoms (H and N, O, F, or Cl).

Sample Problem. List the types of intermolecular forces that act between the molecules of the following compounds:

$\ddot{\underset{\cdot\cdot}{O}}::C::\ddot{\underset{\cdot\cdot}{O}}$ $\qquad$ $H:\ddot{\underset{\cdot\cdot}{Cl}}:$ $\qquad$ $:\ddot{\underset{\cdot\cdot}{Br}}:\ddot{\underset{\cdot\cdot}{Cl}}:$

Solution.

a. CO_2 molecules are nonpolar, so only dispersion forces act.

b. HCl is polar, and it has the elements that are necessary for hydrogen bonds to form. Hydrogen bonds, dipole-dipole, and dispersion forces act.

c. Br Cl molecules are polar, so dipole-dipole forces act in addition to dispersion forces.

Ionic, metallic, and covalent bonds greatly affect the physical properties of the compounds they form. Intermolecular forces also affect these physical properties. Table 5-21 organizes the cause-effect relationships for the three types of compounds.

Table 5-21

Types of Bonding		
Structural Units	**Forces Between Units**	**Properties**
Ions	ionic bonds	very high melting and boiling points; usually soluble in polar solvents; conduct electricity when molten or dissolved but not when in the solid state
Nonpolar molecules	dispersion forces	low melting and boiling points; molecules soluble only in nonpolar solvents; nonconductors of electricity
Polar molecules	dispersion, dipole-dipole, possibly hydrogen bonds	boiling and melting points slightly higher than those of nonpolar molecules; usually soluble in polar solvents; nonconductors of electricity
Cations, mobile electrons	metallic bonds	high melting and boiling points; insoluble; electrical conductors in all states

Sample Problem. Considering the types of chemical bonds and the intermolecular forces that are present, predict the member of each pair that should have the higher boiling point on the basis of the intermolecular forces that are present.

a. KF, BrF b. Cl_2, ICl

Solution.

a. KF is an ionic compound that has extremely strong ionic forces between its units. Its boiling point should be higher than the covalently bonded BrF.

b. Both Cl_2 and ICl are covalently bonded. ICl molecules are slightly polar, while Cl_2 molecules are not. Since ICl molecules have dipole-dipole interactions, it is not surprising that their boiling point (97.4 °C) is higher than the boiling point of Cl_2 (-34.6 °C).

Coming to Terms

chemical bond
octet rule
ionic bond
crystal
formula unit
covalent bond
double covalent bond
triple covalent bond
coordinate covalent bond
electron-sea theory
valence bond theory
hybridization
Valence Shell Electron Pair Repulsion theory
tetrahedral
pyramidal
bent
linear
trigonal planar
polar
polar covalent bond
dipole moment
intermolecular force
dipole-dipole interaction
hydrogen bond
dispersion force

Review Questions

1. What is the general reason that atoms form bonds?
2. State the most probable way in which the following atoms could obtain eight outer-shell electrons.
   a. K
   b. Ca
   c. Ga
   d. Ge
   e. As
   f. Se
   g. Br
   h. Kr
   i. C
3. Identify the types of atoms (metal or nonmetal) in the following substances, and then tell whether the bonds are ionic, covalent, or metallic. Example: P_2O_5 combines nonmetal P and nonmetal O atoms; the bonds are covalent.
   a. NaCl
   b. bronze (a tin, copper, and zinc alloy)
   c. CO_2
   d. $MgBr_2$
   e. brass (a zinc and copper alloy)
4. Draw electron-dot structures of the atoms in the following compounds, the ions that result from the electron transfers, and the resulting ionic compounds. Example: NaCl

Atoms before bonding: Na$\times$ $\cdot\ddot{\underset{..}{Cl}}:$

Ions from the transfer: Na^+ ⟶ $[\overset{\times}{\cdot}\ddot{\underset{..}{Cl}}:]^-$

Resulting compound: $Na^+ [\overset{\times}{\cdot}\ddot{\underset{..}{Cl}}:]^-$

a. LiI
b. MgO
c. $CaBr_2$
d. $FeCl_3$
e. SrF_2

5. Why is it said that ionic compounds do not consist of molecules?
6. Give the correct formula unit for each of the following ionic crystals.

a. $K_{20}Br_{20}$
b. $Al_{15}Cl_{45}$
c. $Na_{12}(PO_4)_4$
d. $Al_{24}O_{36}$

7. The following covalent compounds contain only single covalent bonds. Draw their electron-dot structures.

a. H_2
b. HCl
c. CH_4
d. CF_2Cl_2
e. H_2S

8. The following covalent compounds each contain at least one double or triple bond. Draw their electron-dot structures.

a. H_2CO
b. CS_2
c. CO
d. CO_2
e. C_2H_4
f. C_2H_2

9. Draw electron-dot structures of the polyatomic ions below. Example: SO_4^{2-}

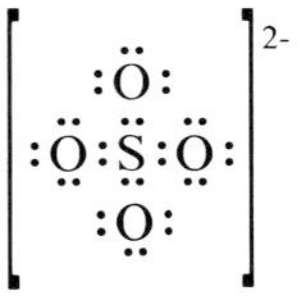

```
[   :Ö:   ] 2-
[ :Ö:S:Ö: ]
[   :Ö:   ]
```

a. OH^-
b. PO_4^{3-}
c. CN^-
d. CrO_4^{2-}
e. SO_3^{2-}

10. Draw electron-dot structures for each of the following compounds containing polyatomic ions. Example: K_2SO_4

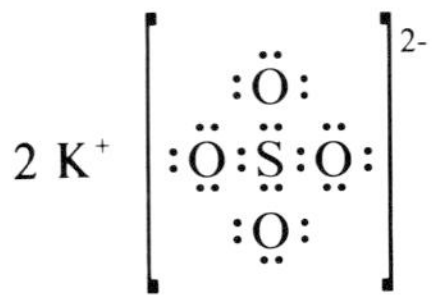

```
      [   :Ö:   ] 2-
2 K+  [ :Ö:S:Ö: ]
      [   :Ö:   ]
```

a. NaOH
b. Na_3PO_4
c. KCN
d. $MgCrO_4$
e. Li_2SO_3

11. Explain how the electron-sea theory accounts for the following properties of metals.
    a. electrical conductivity
    b. thermal conductivity
    c. luster
    d. ductility and malleability
12. Describe how the orbitals in the *s* and the *p* sublevels hybridize when carbon atoms form bonds.
13. How many regions of electron concentrations exist around the central atoms of the molecules in problem 7?
14. Make simple drawings that show how the hybridized orbitals around an atom point when two, three, and four orbitals are present.
15. Predict the molecular shapes for the compounds in problem 7.
16. Predict the molecular shapes for the compounds in problem 8, sections a-d.
17. How many polar bonds are found in each of the molecules below? (Consider a double or triple bond as one bond.)
    a. H_2
    b. HCl
    c. CO_2
    d. CH_4
    e. CF_2Cl_2
    f. H_2S
    g. H_2CO
    h. C_2H_4
    i. C_2H_2
    j. CS_2
    k. CO
18. Which of the molecules in problem 17 are polar (have a dipole moment)?
19. Predict the types of intermolecular forces that may act between molecules in the following substances.
    a. CO_2
    b. NH_3
    c. ICl
    d. HCl
    e. C_3H_8

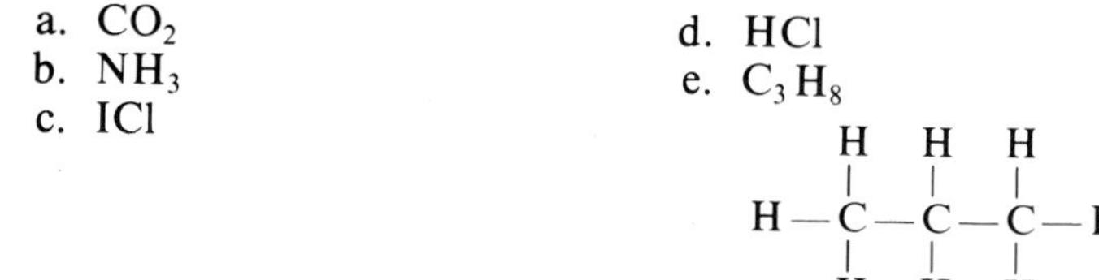

20. Based on your understanding of intermolecular forces, which substance of the following pairs should have the higher boiling point?
    a. NF_3, NH_3
    b. NaCl, HCl
    c. CF_4, CHF_3
    d. Cl_2, C_2H_5Cl

SIX

DESCRIBING CHEMICAL COMPOSITION

NUMBERS, NAMES, AND SOMETHING CALLED A MOLE

COMPOUNDS can be effectively described by formulas, by names, and by measurements of their masses. Formulas serve as a convenient, yet powerful, shorthand system of describing compounds. Systematic names provide additional information about the composition of chemical compounds. Chemists use a concept called the "mole" to describe amounts of compounds.

Oxidation Numbers: Helps in Predicting Formulas

Chemists use **oxidation numbers** to tell how electrons behave during bonding. These numbers tell whether electrons are gained, lost, or shifted. Proficiency with oxidation numbers enables chemists to predict the formulas of chemical compounds.

6–1 Rules for Assigning Oxidation Numbers

Oxidation numbers describe the behavior of electrons in bonding atoms. A clear-cut set of rules governs the assigning of oxidation numbers to the elements in most compounds.

Rule 1. The oxidation number of free atoms and of atoms in pure elements is zero. Individual atoms such as Fe, Na, Ar, and He have oxidation numbers of zero. This rule also applies to Cl_2, H_2, S_8, and other polyatomic elements. The electrons in the covalent bonds of these elements are neither transferred nor shifted, because both atoms have equal electronegativities.

Rule 2. The oxidation number of an ion is equal to the charge of the ion. When a Br atom gains an electron to become a Br^- ion, it has an oxidation number of -1. The -1 shows that one electron has been gained. When a Mg atom loses two electrons to become a Mg^{2+} ion, its oxidation number becomes +2.

Rule 3. The sum of the oxidation numbers of all the atoms in a compound must be zero. Compounds are *not* electrically charged.

When ionic bonds form, negative and positive charges are evenly balanced. Ions with a +1 charge and ions with a -1 charge combine in a 1:1 ratio. A +2 ion combines with two -1 ions to have its charge equalized.

$$\overset{+1}{Na^+} + \overset{-1}{Cl^-} \longrightarrow \overset{+1}{Na}\overset{-1}{Cl}$$

$$\overset{+2}{Mg^{2+}} + 2\,\overset{-1}{Cl^-} \longrightarrow \overset{+2}{Mg}\overset{-1}{Cl_2}$$

This rule applies to covalent bonds as well. Remember that shared electrons can be shifted toward or away from atoms, depending on the electronegativities. If an atom attracts electrons toward itself, that atom is assigned a negative oxidation number. Atoms that lose influence over electrons during bonding become partially positive. They receive positive oxidation numbers.

Rule 4. Alkali metals (Group IA) always have a +1 oxidation number when they are are not free elements. These metals have low electronegativities, so they release their one valence electron when they react.

Rule 5. Alkaline earth metals (Group IIA) always have a +2 oxidation number. These atoms form +2 ions when they bond.

Rule 6. Certain elements have the same oxidation number in almost all their compounds.

a. Halogens (Group VIIA) have an oxidation number of -1 when they are bonded to metals. Since they have seven valence electrons and high electronegativities, they gain an extra electron and form -1 ions. When halogens are bonded to other nonmetals, the element with the highest electronegativity gets the negative number.

b. Hydrogen has a +1 oxidation number in most of its compounds. Only when hydrogen is bonded to metals in compounds called metallic hydrides is hydrogen's number -1.

c. Oxygen has a -2 oxidation number in most of its compounds. Only when oxygen is bonded to highly electronegative elements such as fluorine or another oxygen does it not have its usual -2 number. Oxygen is so electronegative that it pulls electrons from most other elements.

6–2 Applications of Oxidation-Number Rules

The few simple rules just given can be used to determine oxidation numbers in multitudes of compounds. In a situation where one rule contradicts another, the rule that was listed first should be followed. If the oxidation number of an atom is unknown, an algebraic equation can be used to solve for it.

Sample Problem. Determine the oxidation number of each atom in the following compounds.

a. K_2O b. $HMnO_4$

Solution.

a. The sum of the oxidation numbers of all the atoms in the molecule must add up to zero (Rule 3). The potassium atom has a +1 oxidation number as always (Rule 4), and the oxygen atom is -2 as expected (Rule 6c). The sum of two +1s and a single -2 is zero.

The oxidation numbers of all the atoms in the compound are $\overset{+1}{K_2}\overset{-2}{O}$

b. In $HMnO_4$ the only unknown oxidation number is that of manganese. The oxidation numbers of the oxygen and hydrogen atoms are already known to be -2 and +1 respectively. An algebraic equation can be used to solve for the oxidation number of manganese.

$$\text{H's number} + \text{Mn's number} + 4(\text{O's number}) = 0$$
$$+1 + \text{Mn's number} + 4(-2) = 0$$
$$\text{Mn's number} = +7$$

The oxidation numbers of all the atoms in the compound are $\overset{+1}{H}\overset{+7}{Mn}\overset{-2}{O_4}$

Scientists use oxidation numbers as an aid in writing chemical formulas. Given the elements that are in an ionic compound, they can determine how many atoms of each element are present.

Sample Problem. Write the formula of the compound that results when barium and iodine bond.

Solution.

Barium, being an alkaline earth metal, has an oxidation number of +2. Iodine has a -1 oxidation number because it is a halogen bonding with a metal. In order for the sum of the oxidation numbers to equal zero, two iodine atoms must be included in the formula.

$\overset{+2}{Ba}\overset{-1}{I_2}$

6–3 Atoms With Multiple Oxidation States

Some atoms can have more than one oxidation number. Electrons behave differently, depending on the particular atoms in the bond. Transition metals are especially notorious for having more than one oxidation number. Because their outer energy levels are very close to each other, the bonding circumstances determine how many electrons participate in chemical bonds. Iron can form $FeCl_2$ as well as $FeCl_3$. Nonmetals often have more than one oxidation state. If nitrogen, sulfur, phosphorus, or carbon bond to highly electronegative elements, they lose a measure of control over their electrons. If they bond to a less electronegative element, they can attract electrons.

Simple, clear-cut rules rarely work for metals that do not belong to the IA or IIA families. The oxidation numbers of the most common elements must either be memorized or looked up in tables. Figure 6-1 shows the oxidation states of commonly encountered elements. The shaded elements on the chart are the ones used most frequently in this course.

6-1 Oxidation numbers of common elements.

1 **H** +1 -1																	2 **He**
3 **Li** +1	4 **Be** +2											5 **B** +3	6 **C** +4 +2 -4	7 **N** +5 +4 +3 +2 +1 -3	8 **O** -1 -2	9 **F** -1	10 **Ne**
11 **Na** +1	12 **Mg** +2											13 **Al** +3	14 **Si** +4 -4	15 **P** +5 +3 -3	16 **S** +6 +4 +2 -2	17 **Cl** +7 +5 +3 +1 -1	18 **Ar**
19 **K** +1	20 **Ca** +2	21 **Sc** +3	22 **Ti** +4 +3 +2	23 **V** +5 +4 +3 +2	24 **Cr** +6 +3 +2	25 **Mn** +7 +6 +4 +3 +2	26 **Fe** +3 +2	27 **Co** +3 +2	28 **Ni** +2	29 **Cu** +2 +1	30 **Zn** +2	31 **Ga** +3	32 **Ge** +4 -4	33 **As** +5 +3 -3	34 **Se** +6 +4 -2	35 **Br** +5 +1 -1	36 **Kr** +4 +2
37 **Rb** +1	38 **Sr** +2	39 **Y** +3	40 **Zr** +4	41 **Nb** +5 +4	42 **Mo** +6 +4 +3	43 **Tc** +7 +4 +3	44 **Ru** +8 +6 +4 +3	45 **Rh** +4 +3 +2	46 **Pd** +4 +2	47 **Ag** +1	48 **Cd** +2	49 **In** +3	50 **Sn** +4 +2	51 **Sb** +5 +3 -3	52 **Te** +6 +4 -2	53 **I** +7 +5 +1 -1	54 **Xe** +6 +4 +2
55 **Cs** +1	56 **Ba** +2	57 **La** +3	72 **Hf** +4	73 **Ta** +5	74 **W** +6 +4	75 **Re** +7 +6 +4	76 **Os** +8 +4	77 **Ir** +4 +3	78 **Pt** +4 +2	79 **Au** +3 +1	80 **Hg** +2 +1	81 **Tl** +3 +1	82 **Pb** +4 +2	83 **Bi** +5 +3	84 **Po** +2	85 **At** -1	86 **Rn**
87 **Fr** +1	88 **Ra** +2	89 **Ac** +3															

6–4 Oxidation Numbers and Polyatomic Ions: The Charge Makes the Difference

Polyatomic ions are covalently bonded groups of atoms that carry charges. Since polyatomic ions are found in many compounds and reactions, they are included in the oxidation-number rules.

Rule 7. The oxidation numbers of all the atoms in a polyatomic ion add up to the charge on the ion.

An examination of the hydroxide ion (OH^-) shows how this rule works. The oxygen atom has an oxidation number of -2, and the hydrogen atom has a +1 number. The sum of these numbers is -1: the charge on the ion. Polyatomic ions remain intact throughout most chemical reactions. Using the charge of the ion as you would use an oxidation number simplifies many problems.

Sample Problem. What is the oxidation number of the lead atom in $Pb(OH)_2$?

Solution.

$$\text{Pb's number} + 2(\text{OH}^-\text{'s number}) = 0$$
$$\text{Pb's number} + 2(-1) = 0$$
$$\text{Pb's number} = +2$$

The same techniques used to find formulas of two-element ionic compounds can be used for polyatomic ionic compounds. The polyatomic ion is treated as a single unit.

Sample Problem. What is the formula of the compound that contains ammonium (NH_4^+) ions and phosphate (PO_4^{3-}) ions?

Solution.

The oxidation numbers of all the atoms in a compound must add up to zero. Three ammonium ions are required to balance the -3 of the phosphate ion.

$$(\overset{+1}{NH_4})_3\overset{-3}{PO_4}$$

Algebraic equations can be used to find the oxidation numbers of individual atoms in polyatomic ions. The following equation yields the oxidation state of the S atom in a sulfate ion (SO_4^{2-}).

$$\text{S's number} + 4(\text{O's number}) = \text{charge of ion}$$
$$\text{S's number} + 4(-2) = -2$$
$$\text{S's number} + (-8) = -2$$
$$\text{S's number} = +6$$

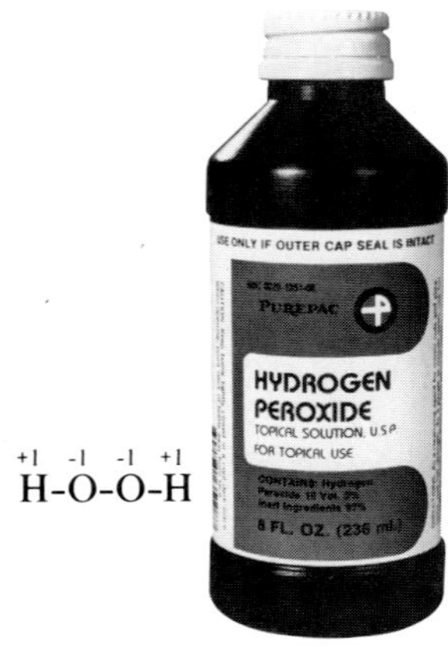

6-2 Hydrogen peroxide is often used to disinfect small cuts. Oxygen atoms in this compound have oxidation numbers of -1 instead of the usual -2.

6–5 Two Important Exceptions

Like the rules of grammar, oxidation-number rules have exceptions. It is helpful to become familiar with a few significant exceptions. Compounds such as LiH and NaH, in which hydrogen is bonded to a metallic atom, are called metallic hydrides. In these compounds the hydrogen atom is the most electronegative element present. Consequently, it attracts the electrons and receives an oxidation number of -1.

Peroxides are a class of compounds in which two oxygens are bonded together. The simplest and most common peroxide is hydrogen peroxide, H-O-O-H. In this compound each oxygen has an oxidation number of -1 instead of the usual -2.

Nomenclature: Naming Compounds

Do the names *soda ash* and *epsomite* mean anything to you? If you can recall the properties of these compounds or the elements they contain, you are relying on a good memory. The names themselves certainly do not give you any clues. Chemical compounds have been given many names throughout history. Some names, like soda ash, came about because they described how a compound looked or how it acted. Other names told where a compound came from. One particular compound was called epsomite because it was often found near the English town of Epsom. In America this compound is now called Epsom salts. Although the backgrounds of these names are interesting, the names do not give much information to someone who sees them for the first time.

As more and more compounds were discovered and synthesized, chemists realized that they could not continue to rely on memorized names. In the twentieth century the International Union of Pure and Applied Chemistry (IUPAC) developed a systematic way to name compounds. This system of names, called a **nomenclature,** allows all compounds to be named according to a common set of rules. The IUPAC names of compounds are packed with information. They tell which elements are present in the compound. Indirectly, they tell about the types of bonds, the intermolecular attractions, and the general properties of the compound.

Today the term *soda ash* is used very little. Instead, people refer to this compound as sodium carbonate. The name epsomite has given way to a more informative name, magnesium sulfate. Some common names are still used, but only when the compound is familiar to many people.

6–6 Using the Greek Prefix System

In this discussion of nomenclature, a graphic device called a **flow chart** will help you determine which rules apply to which compounds. The entire flow chart, presented as Figure 6-3, provides an organized method for identifying an unnamed formula. This discussion will first consider covalent compounds that are not acids. For now, any covalent compound whose formula begins with hydrogen can be considered to be an acid. Covalent compounds that are not acids are named according to a system of Greek prefixes.

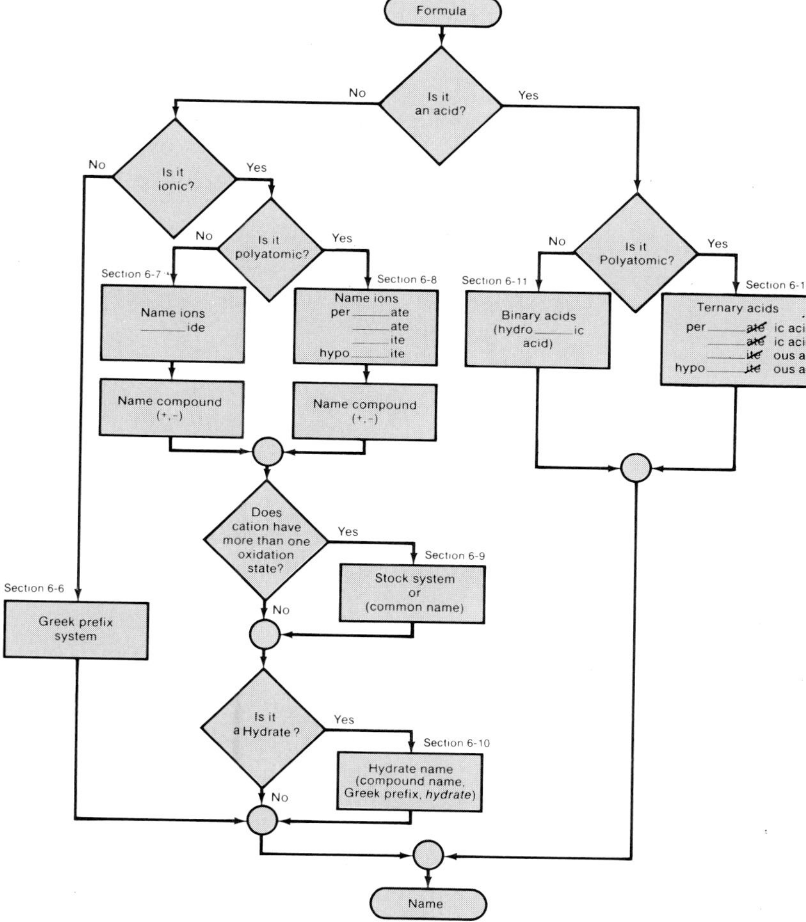

6-3 A flow chart outlines the decisions that must be made in order to name a compound from its formula.

The **Greek prefix system** indicates how many atoms of each element are included in a covalent compound. The commonly used prefixes are listed in Table 6-4. This system omits the prefix *mono* unless it is needed for emphasis or clarity. When it is used, any extra vowels are omitted. (For instance, CO is named carbon monoxide, not carbon mono-oxide.) The least electronegative element is stated first and then the more electronegative element. The ending of the last element changes to *-ide*.

Table 6-4

Greek Prefixes	
mono	1
di	2
tri	3
tetra	4
penta	5
hexa	6
hepta	7
octa	8
nona	9
deca	10

Sample Problem. Name PCl_3.

Solution.

PCl_3 is not an acid, since its formula does not begin with hydrogen. It is not ionic, because all its elements are nonmetals. It should thus be named according to the Greek prefixes. Phosphorus trichloride is the accepted name.

6–7 Binary Ionic Compounds

Ionic compounds are not normally named with Greek prefixes. **Binary compounds** (two-element compounds) that are ionic are named according to each of the two ions that are involved. Positive ions use the same name as their parent atoms (sodium atoms form sodium ions), but negative ions have an *-ide* ending (chlorine atoms form chloride ions). The accepted *-ide* endings for the nonmetals are listed in Figure 6-6.

Table 6-5

Compound	Name (+, -)
NaCl	sodium chloride
MgO	magnesium oxide
Al_2O_3	aluminum oxide
K_2S	potassium sulfide
MgH_2	magnesium hydride

B boride	**C** carbide	**N** nitride	**O** oxide	**F** fluoride
	Si silicide	**P** phosphide	**S** sulfide	**Cl** chloride
		As arsenide	**Se** selenide	**Br** bromide
		Sb antimonide	**Te** telluride	**I** iodide
				At astatide

6-6 Names of Nonmetallic Ions

For a binary ionic compound, the name of the positive ion appears first, followed by that of the negative ion. The names of metallic hydrides start with the active metal and end with *hydride* because hydrogen is the most negative element in these compounds.

6–8 Polyatomic Ions and Their Compounds

Tables 6-7 and 6-8 list the formulas and names of common polyatomic ions. Some generalizations can help make many of these ions easier to learn. The only positive polyatomic ions are NH_4^+, the ammonium ion, and Hg_2^{2+}, the mercurous ion. Most of the negative ions that contain coordinate covalently bonded oxygens (oxyanions) have names that end with *-ate*. Ions that are similar but that have a different number of coordinate covalently bonded oxygens have their names modified by a system of prefixes and suffixes. The prefixes and suffixes depend on the number of oxygen atoms present in the molecule. Although ions may not exist for every name, the system will help name the ones that do exist.

Table 6-7

Common Oxyanions

Charge	Greatest Number of Oxygens per___ate	Base Number of Oxygens ___ate	Fewer Number of Oxygens ___ite	Fewest Number of Oxygens hypo___ite
-1		acetate $C_2H_3O_2^-$		
	perbromate BrO_4^-	bromate BrO_3^-	bromite BrO_2^-	hypobromite BrO^-
	perchlorate ClO_4^-	chlorate ClO_3^-	chlorite ClO_2^-	hypochlorite ClO^-
		cyanate OCN^-		
		hydrogen carbonate (bicarbonate) HCO_3^-		
		hydrogen sulfate (bisulfate) HSO_4^-	hydrogen sulfite (bisulfite) HSO_3^-	
	periodate IO_4^-	iodate IO_3^-		hypoiodite IO^-
		nitrate NO_3^-	nitrite NO_2^-	
	permanganate MnO_4^-			
-2		carbonate CO_3^{2-}		
		chromate CrO_4^{2-}		
		dichromate $Cr_2O_7^{2-}$		
		silicate SiO_3^{2-}		
		sulfate SO_4^{2-}	sulfite SO_3^{2-}	
		thiosulfate $S_2O_3^{2-}$		
-3		arsenate AsO_4^{3-}	arsenite AsO_3^{3-}	
		borate BO_3^{3-}		
		phosphate PO_4^{3-}	phosphite PO_3^{3-}	

Table 6-8

Other Polyatomic Ions

Name	Formula
Ammonium	NH_4^+
Mercurous	Hg_2^{2+}
Amide	NH_2^-
Azide	N_3^-
Cyanide	CN^-
Hydrogen sulfide	HS^-
Hydroxide	OH^-
Thiocyanate	SCN^-

Table 6-9

Compound	Name (+, -)
Na_2SO_4	sodium sulfate
KOH	potassium hydroxide
$Ba(ClO_3)_2$	barium chlorate
$Ca(ClO)_2$	calcium hypochlorite
$Ba(NO_2)_2$	barium nitrite
NH_4Cl	ammonium chloride

Once you have determined the names of the polyatomic ions, you can name **polyatomic compounds** that contain them. Simply name the cation and then the anion.

Some compounds have combinations of metallic ions and hydrogen ions as their cations. The names of these compounds give the name of the most metallic cation first, then the hydrogen, and then the anion. For example, $NaHCO_3$ is called sodium hydrogen carbonate.

Sample Problem. Name NH_4BrO_3.

Solution.

The compound NH_4BrO_3 is not an acid, and it is ionic. The name *ammonium bromate* is formed from the names of the two polyatomic ions included in the formula.

Sample Problem. What is the formula for potassium dichromate?

Solution.

The dichromate ion ($Cr_2O_7^{2-}$) carries a -2 charge. Two potassium atoms (oxidation number of +1) for every dichromate ion can form a neutral compound. The formula must be $K_2Cr_2O_7$.

6–9 Handling Atoms with Multiple Oxidation States

If the metallic element in an ionic compound is one that can have more than one oxidation number (a transition metal), a Roman numeral is placed after the element's name to show the oxidation number. This convention is called the **Stock system** or sometimes the **Roman numeral system.** An older way of identifying the oxidation state of a transition metal is with the suffixes *-ous* and *-ic*. The *-ous* ending refers to the smaller oxidation number, and the *-ic* ending refers to the larger oxidation number. For example, Cu^+ is called the cuprous ion and Cu^{2+} is called the cupric ion.

Table 6-10

Compound	Stock System Name	Common Name
$FeCl_2$	iron (II) chloride	ferrous chloride
$FeCl_3$	iron (III) chloride	ferric chloride
SnO	tin (II) oxide	stannous oxide
SnO_2	tin (IV) oxide	stannic oxide
Hg_2I_2	mercury (I) iodide	mercurous iodide
HgI_2	mercury (II) iodide	mercuric iodide
CuBr	copper (I) bromide	cuprous bromide
$CuBr_2$	copper (II) bromide	cupric bromide

Sample Problem. Name $Hg(BrO_3)_2$ according to the Stock system and the common system.

Solution.

Following the flow chart, you see that $Hg(BrO_3)_2$ is not an acid, is ionic, contains a polyatomic ion, and involves a metal that can have more than one oxidation number. The BrO_3 portion of the formula corresponds to a BrO_3^- ion, so the last part of the name will be *bromate*. Since two -1 ions are present, the mercury atom must have a +2 oxidation number. The Stock system name, therefore, is mercury(II) bromate. Since the +2 is the larger of mercury's two oxidation numbers, the common name of the compound is *mercuric bromate.*

Sample Problem. What is the formula of lead (II) phosphate?

Solution.

The Roman numeral II identifies the +2 oxidation state of lead. Phosphate ions have a -3 charge. A combination of three lead atoms for every two phosphate ions results in an electrically neutral compound. The formula is $Pb_3(PO_4)_2$.

6–10 Hydrates

Hydrates are compounds that have water molecules in their crystalline structures. These compounds hold a characteristic amount of water called the "water of hydration." Formulas of these compounds indicate the presence and number of water molecules by a centered dot and the number of water molecules ($Na_2CO_3 \cdot 7H_2O$). The word *hydrate* with a Greek prefix is added to the usual name of an ionic compound that normally incorporates water molecules into its structure.

Table 6-11

Formula	Name (compound's name, Greek prefix, *hydrate*)
Na_2CO_3	sodium carbonate
$Na_2CO_3 \cdot H_2O$	sodium carbonate monohydrate
$Na_2CO_3 \cdot 7\ H_2O$	sodium carbonate heptahydrate
$Na_2CO_3 \cdot 10\ H_2O$	sodium carbonate decahydrate

6–11 Binary Acids

Binary compounds that show hydrogen as the first element in their formulas can be called binary acids. These acids can have names based on the general rules used for other binary compounds. For example, as a gas, HCl is called hydrogen chloride. When these binary compounds are dissolved in water, however, they form acids and are given different names. These names include the prefix *hydro-* (referring to the hydrogen), the anion name with an *-ic* ending, and the word *acid*. In an aqueous solution HCl is called hydrochloric acid.

Table 6-12

Formula	Common Name (+, -)	Acid Name (hydro___ic acid)
HCl	hydrogen chloride	hydrochloric acid
HBr	hydrogen bromide	hydrobromic acid
H_2S	hydrogen sulfide	hydrosulfuric acid

6–12 Ternary Acids

Ternary acids contain three elements: hydrogen, oxygen, and another nonmetal. The oxygen and the nonmetal are often bound together in a polyatomic ion. The names of ternary acids are derived from the anions in the acids. If the anion's name ends in *-ate*, the ending changes to *-ic* and the word *acid* is added. If the anion's name ends in *-ite*, the ending changes to *-ous* and the word *acid* is added.

Table 6-13

Anion in Ternary Acid		Ternary Acid	
Formula	Name	Formula	Name
ClO_4^-	perchlorate	$HClO_4$	perchloric acid
ClO_3^-	chlorate	$HClO_3$	chloric acid
ClO_2^-	chlorite	$HClO_2$	chlorous acid
ClO^-	hypochlorite	HClO	hypochlorous acid
NO_3^-	nitrate	HNO_3	nitric acid
NO_2^-	nitrite	HNO_2	nitrous acid
SO_4^{2-}	sulfate	H_2SO_4	sulfuric acid
SO_3^{2-}	sulfite	H_2SO_3	sulfurous acid
$C_2H_3O_2^-$	acetate	$HC_2H_3O_2$	acetic acid
CO_3^{2-}	carbonate	H_2CO_3	carbonic acid
PO_4^{3-}	phosphate	H_3PO_4	phosphoric acid

Sample Problem. Name $HBrO_4$.

Solution.

The formula $HBrO_4$ starts with hydrogen and is therefore an acid. Since the compound contains a polyatomic ion, its name is derived from the name of the ion. The BrO_4^- ion is the perbromate ion. The *-ate* ending changes to *-ic,* and the correct name, perbromic acid, results.

The Mole: A Unit Tailor-Made for Tiny Things

Describing the mass of atoms is similar to what a manufacturer might face when buying small ball bearings. When a shipment arrives, how can he know whether it includes all the ball bearings he needs? It would take forever to count them one by one. Instead, he could work in terms of mass. For instance, if 1 kilogram included 500 ball bearings, a 60-kilogram shipment would contain 30,000 bearings. Large units can be used to measure many small items quickly. The large unit that chemists use is called a mole. Molecules, ions, and atoms are some of the things commonly measured in moles.

6–13 What Is in a Mole? Avogadro's Number

A **mole** is the amount of substance contained in 6.023×10^{23} units. The number 6.023×10^{23} is called **Avogadro's number** in honor of the Italian physicist Amedeo Avogadro (1776-1856). This number is used so often that it is often abbreviated N.

$$\begin{aligned}
\text{1 mole of He atoms} &= 6.023 \times 10^{23} \text{ He atoms} \\
\text{1 mole of } H_2O \text{ molecules} &= 6.023 \times 10^{23}\ H_2O \text{ molecules} \\
\text{1 mole of NaCl formula units} &= 6.023 \times 10^{23} \text{ NaCl formula units}
\end{aligned}$$

Because a mole contains such a huge number of items, it is used to measure only very small objects. The reason that no one has ever heard of a mole of bricks or a mole of golf balls is that no one has ever manufactured 602 sextillion of them. Smaller units, such as the dozen, are used to measure large objects. Moles are used for measuring objects on the atomic and molecular scale.

Table 6-14

Objects	Common Group	Number of Items in Group
Socks	pair	2
Eggs	dozen	12
Pencils	gross	144
Sheets of paper	ream	500
Atoms, molecules, and ions	mole	6.023×10^{23}

FACETS OF CHEMISTRY

Quantitative Analysis Solves a Mystery

Just a few strands of hair—most people would consider them insignificant. But to three European scientists, they were the key to unlocking a century-old secret. The mystery involves the untimely death of Napoleon Bonaparte. Although many historians say Napoleon died of cancer or an ulcer, some scientists believe he was murdered. What do they have as proof? A few strands of hair.

For many years Sten Forshufvud had been convinced that the circumstances behind Napoleon's death were not all known. Forshufvud spent many years studying the memoirs of those people associated with Napoleon during his years of exile. Of particular interest to Forshufvud were the memoirs of Louis Marchand. Marchand, a devoted servant and Napoleon's chief valet, took over the complete care of Napoleon during his last months. In his account Marchand gave many details of Napoleon's deteriorating physical condition. From these observations Forshufvud recognized twenty-two out of over thirty generally accepted symptoms of chronic arsenic poisoning. He also concluded that Napoleon's continually changing health from good to bad indicated that the former emperor was poisoned with small doses of arsenic over a long period of time.

In spite of Forshufvud's careful research, he still needed more scientific proof. He soon learned of a new method devised by Hamilton Smith for detecting arsenic and other elements in hair. By determining the level of arsenic in hair, it was possible to calculate the amount of arsenic in the entire body. Fortunately for Forshufvud, Napoleon's valet had shaved off several locks of Napoleon's hair before the emperor was buried in 1821. These locks had been saved and passed down through families, and the researchers were able to obtain permission to use several strands of hair.

The process involved a powerful tool called neutron activation analysis (NAA). With this tool scientists can detect aces of an element in doses as nall as one-billionth of a gram. ɔ determine the arsenic con-nt of Napoleon's hair, Smith aced a single strand of hair ɔout 5 inches long and a stan-ard arsenic solution (included r comparison) in the NAA actor. As neutrons bom-arded the samples, many of e nuclei became radioactive nd began emitting gamma ys. After a twenty-four-hour eriod, Smith removed the ample from the reactor and nalyzed the gamma rays. Since amma rays from different ele-ents display characteristic avelengths and strengths, mith could identify which ele-ents were present as well as eir respective amounts.

The results of these tests ıowed an extremely high level f arsenic. In the first hair ample, for instance, the tests vealed an average of 10.38 arts per million (ppm). The nor-al amount of arsenic in hair is bout 0.5 ppm. Napoleon's hair ɔntained over twenty times the ormal amount of arsenic. If apoleon had been poisoned, ıe arsenic would have per-eated all his body tissues, cluding his hair.

Later Smith refined his tests analyze arsenic levels in spe-fic portions of hair. Since he new when the locks had been ıorn, he could match the rsenic level with specific dates Napoleon's life. Interestingly, orshufvud found that the rsenic was not distributed venly along the hair. It was con-entrated in points every few iillimeters. Doses must have een administered periodically uring the four months before Napoleon died. The results showed that the arsenic content of the emperor's hair ranged from a low of 1.06 ppm to a high of 76.6 ppm. These peaks and valleys coincided perfectly with Napoleon's ever-changing health.

Neutron activation analysis is only one of several modern methods of chemical analysis. Unlike traditional methods of analytical chemistry, modern techniques offer greater speed, a wider range of possible tests, and the ability to use small samples. These improvements allow scientists to gain a better understanding of the present as well as the past.

Sample Problem. How many atoms are in a 4.5-mole sample of helium?

Solution.

The fact that one mole of anything contains 6.023×10^{23} items justifies the formation of a conversion factor that can be used to change 4.5 moles into the number of atoms.

$$4.5 \text{ moles} \times \frac{6.023 \times 10^{23} \text{ atoms}}{1 \text{ mole}} = 2.7 \times 10^{24} \text{ atoms}$$

6–14 Atoms and the Mole

Scientists use Avogadro's number to relate atomic-mass units to the larger units of grams. They can find the mass of a mole of objects by expressing an object's mass in atomic-mass units and changing the unit to grams. A hydrogen atom has a mass of about 1 amu. Scientists have experimentally proved that 6.023×10^{23} hydrogen atoms have a mass of 1 gram. A carbon atom has a mass of 12 amu's; 6.023×10^{23} carbon atoms have mass of 12 grams. If a molecule has a mass of 130 atomic-mass units, a mole of these molecules will have a mass of 130 grams.

Table 6-15

Chemical Unit	Mass of One Unit (amu's)	Number of Units in One Mole	Mass of One Mole (grams)
He atom	4.003	6.023×10^{23}	4.003
H_2O molecule	18.016	6.023×10^{23}	18.016
NaCl formula unit	58.44	6.023×10^{23}	58.44

6-16 One mole of carbon, magnesium, aluminum, sulfur, calcium, iron, and copper. Each sample contains 6.023×10^{23} atoms but has a different mass.

How can one mole of hydrogen atoms have a different mass than one mole of carbon atoms? Compare atoms to varieties of fruits and vegetables for the answer. Suppose that all fruits come in cartons of twelve (one dozen). A dozen apples have a larger mass than a dozen cherries. A dozen cantaloupes have an even larger mass, and the mass of a dozen watermelons is greater still. In the same manner, a mole of carbon atoms has a large mass compared to a mole of hydrogen atoms. A mole of iron atoms has an even larger mass, and a mole of uranium atoms has the greatest mass of them all. Remember that a mole, like a dozen, always contains the same number of objects. The mass of the objects involved determines the mass of one mole.

Sample Problem. Calculate the mass of 0.5 mole of helium atoms.

Solution.

On the average, helium atoms have a mass of 4.003 amu's. This number, expressed in grams, is the mass of 1 mole of helium atoms.

$$0.5 \text{ mole He} \times \frac{4.003 \text{ g He}}{1 \text{ mole He}} = 2.002 \text{ g He}$$

How many copper atoms are in one penny? What is the mass of a single atom? These questions can be answered with the help of the mole concept. The mole also makes it possible to convert between the mass of a chemical sample, the number of moles present, and even the number of chemical units in the sample.

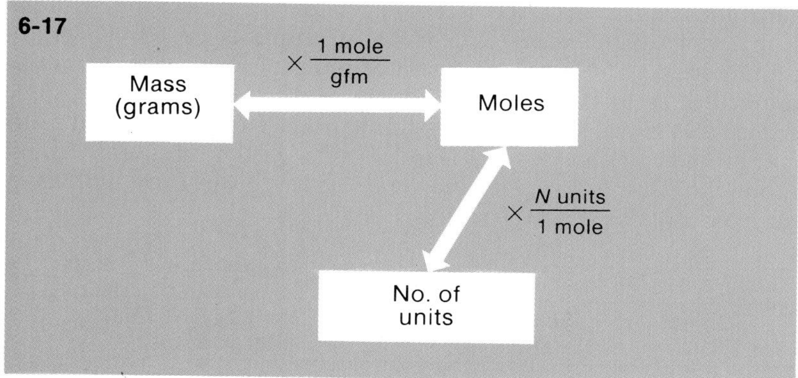

6-17

The arrows between mass, moles, and number of units show possible routes to take when solving a problem. The conversion factors near the arrows are the ones that should be used for the particular operation.

What is the mass of 5 moles of potassium atoms? The given value is expressed in moles (5 moles K), and the value to be calculated is the mass (how many grams). The flow chart shows that the conversion using the conversion factor gram-formula mass/1 mole is the only step that needs to be taken. Each mole of potassium is 39.10 grams.

$$5 \text{ moles K} \times \frac{39.10 \text{ g K}}{1 \text{ mole K}} = 195.5 \text{ g K}$$

How many copper atoms are in a 4.00-gram copper coin? A look at the flow chart shows that there is no step that will convert a mass to the number of units in that mass. The number of moles must be calculated as an intermediate step. Knowing that 1 mole of copper is 63.55 grams allows the use of the following conversion factor.

$$4.00 \text{ g Cu} \times \frac{1 \text{ mole Cu}}{63.55 \text{ g Cu}} = 0.0629 \text{ moles Cu}$$

Once the number of moles has been found, the last step on the flow chart can be taken.

$$0.0629 \text{ moles Cu} \times \frac{6.023 \times 10^{23} \text{ atoms}}{1 \text{ mole Cu}} = 3.79 \times 10^{22} \text{ atoms}$$

6–15 Compounds and the Mole

Several terms are used to refer to the mass in a mole of a substance. Each term that is used specifies the object in the mole. For example, the mass of a mole of atoms is called the **gram-atomic mass.** The mass of a mole of molecules is called the **gram-molecular mass.** The mass of a mole of formula units in an ionic compound is called the **gram-formula mass.** (Remember that ionic compounds are made of formula units, not molecules.) Gram-atomic masses, gram-molecular masses, and gram-formula masses all have units of *grams per mole.*

Table 6-18

Object	Relative Mass (amu's)	Mass of One Mole (grams/mole)
He atom	4.003	gram-atomic mass = 4.003
H_2O molecule	18.016	gram-molecular mass = 18.016
NaCl formula unit	58.44	gram-formula mass = 58.44

Sample Problem. Find the gram-molecular mass of ammonia (NH_3).

Solution.

A mole of NH_3 molecules contains 1 mole of nitrogen atoms and 3 moles of hydrogen atoms. The gram-molecular mass is the sum of all the gram-atomic masses.

$$1 \text{ mole N} \times \frac{14.01 \text{ g N}}{1 \text{ mole N}} = 14.01 \text{ g N}$$

$$3 \text{ moles H} \times \frac{1.008 \text{ g H}}{1 \text{ mole H}} = 3.024 \text{ g H}$$

One mole of NH_3 contains 14.01 grams of nitrogen atoms and 3.024 grams of hydrogen atoms. The gram-molecular mass is the sum of the two masses.

$$14.01 \text{ g} + 3.024 \text{ g} = 17.034 \text{ g}$$

Sample Problem. Find the gram-formula mass of $Al_2(SO_4)_3$.

Solution.

Each formula unit contains two aluminum, three sulfur, and twelve oxygen atoms. A mole of $Al_2(SO_4)_3$ consists of 2 moles of aluminum atoms, 3 moles of sulfur atoms, and 12 moles of oxygen atoms.

$$2 \text{ moles Al} \times \frac{26.98 \text{ g Al}}{1 \text{ mole Al}} = 53.96 \text{ g from Al}$$

$$3 \text{ moles S} \times \frac{32.06 \text{ g S}}{1 \text{ mole S}} = 96.18 \text{ g from S}$$

$$12 \text{ moles O} \times \frac{16.00 \text{ g O}}{1 \text{ mole O}} = 192.00 \text{ g from O}$$

$$342.14 \text{ g total}$$

6–16 Types of Formulas and Per Cent Composition

There are several ways to describe the composition of a chemical substance. **Structural formulas** show the types of atoms involved, the exact composition of each molecule, and where chemical bonds have been formed. These formulas are informative, but they are also difficult to draw, and they take up large amounts of space.

```
H — O          H   H
    |          |   |            Cl — Cl
    H      H — C = C — H
```

Water — Ethene — Chlorine

FINE, BOYS--TOMORROW WE'LL WORK ON GLYCOGEN.

Molecular formulas show the types of atoms involved and the exact composition of each molecule. These formulas are more convenient than structural formulas, but they do not show the shapes of the molecules, the locations of the bonds, or the types of bonds present.

Molecular Formulas

H_2O	C_2H_4	Cl_2
Water	Ethene	Chlorine

Empirical formulas tell what elements are present and give the simplest whole-number ratio of atoms in the compound. Empirical formulas have already been used to describe the composition of ionic compounds. When used for molecular compounds, the empirical formula might represent the actual molecular composition if the molecular formula contains a simple ratio—as in H_2O. On the other hand, the empirical formula of a molecular compound may not represent the make-up of one molecule. Ethene's empirical formula is CH_2 because there are twice as many hydrogen atoms as there are carbon atoms. In this case the molecular formula is not the simplest ratio, so the empirical and molecular formulas are different.

Empirical Formulas

H_2O	CH_2	Cl_2
Water	Ethene	Chlorine

Per cent composition describes the *mass* composition of a compound. All the other formulas describe the numbers of *atoms* in substances. The per cent composition deals with the masses of the atoms. This is an important difference. Look at the per cent composition of water.

H: 11.2%	H: 14.37%	Cl: 100%
O: 88.8%	C: 85.63%	
Water	Ethene	Chlorine

Per cent compositions often look totally different from empirical formulas. Although water has only one oxygen atom, this one atom contains the majority of the compound's mass. The two hydrogen atoms do not contribute much mass, because they are so small. Likewise, ethene has more hydrogen atoms than carbon atoms, but more mass comes from carbon because the carbon atoms are much more massive.

A laboratory analysis of a substance is usually expressed as a per cent composition. Suppose that a 60.00-gram sample of water were decomposed into its elements and that 53.28 grams of oxygen and 6.72 grams of hydrogen resulted. The per cent composition of water could be calculated as follows:

Hydrogen: There are 6.72 grams of hydrogen in 60.00 grams of water.

$$\frac{6.72 \text{ g H}}{60.00 \text{ g } H_2O} = 0.112 \times 100\% = 11.2\%$$

Oxygen: There are 53.28 grams of oxygen in 60.00 grams of water.

$$\frac{53.28 \text{ g O}}{60.00 \text{ g } H_2O} = 0.888 \times 100\% = 88.8\%$$

Sample Problem. A laboratory analysis of a 30.00-gram sample of $Al_2(SO_4)_3$ showed that it contained 4.731 grams of aluminum, 8.433 grams of sulfur, and 16.836 grams of oxygen. What is the per cent composition of this compound?

Solution.

$$\text{Al:}\quad \frac{4.731\text{ g Al}}{30.00\text{ g }Al_2(SO_4)_3} = 0.1577 \text{ or } 15.77\%$$

$$\text{S:}\quad \frac{8.433\text{ g S}}{30.00\text{ g }Al_2(SO_4)_3} = 0.2811 \text{ or } 28.11\%$$

$$\text{O:}\quad \frac{16.836\text{ g O}}{30.00\text{ g }Al_2(SO_4)_3} = 0.5612 \text{ or } 56.12\%$$

Sample Problem. How many grams of oxygen would a 65.00-gram sample of $Al_2(SO_4)_3$ contain?

Solution.

Because of the law of definite composition, any other sample of $Al_2(SO_4)_3$ will have the same per cent composition that the 30.00-gram sample did in the previous problem. The problem could be worked by unit analysis.

$$65.00\text{ g }Al_2(SO_4)_3 \times \frac{56.12\text{ g O}}{100\text{ g }Al_2(SO_4)_3} = 36.47\text{ g O}$$

6–17 Calculations with Empirical Formulas

Empirical formulas contain the information necessary to calculate the per cent composition of compounds. To find per cent composition, the mole ratio in the empirical formula must be converted to a mass ratio through a series of calculations.

The formula H_2O means that there are 2 moles of hydrogen atoms for every 1 mole of oxygen atoms. One mole of water contains 2 moles of hydrogen and 1 mole of oxygen. Expressed in masses, 1 mole of water contains 2.016 grams of hydrogen and 16.00 grams of oxygen.

$$2\text{ moles H} \times \frac{1.008\text{ g H}}{1\text{ mole H}} = 2.016\text{ g H}$$

$$1\text{ mole O} \times \frac{16.00\text{ g O}}{1\text{ mole O}} = 16.00\text{ g O}$$

The total amount of mass being considered is 2.016 grams of hydrogen plus 16.00 grams of oxygen, or 18.016 grams of water. The per cent composition of water can now be found.

$$\frac{2.016 \text{ g H}}{18.016 \text{ g } H_2O} = 0.1119 \text{ or } 11.19\%$$

$$\frac{16.00 \text{ g O}}{18.016 \text{ g } H_2O} = 0.8881 \text{ or } 88.81\%$$

Laboratories often do the reverse process. They first determine the mass composition of an unknown compound and then calculate an empirical formula. Suppose that a chemist is given 100.0 grams of an unknown compound and is told to determine its empirical formula. After a careful analysis in an analytical laboratory, the chemist concludes that 75.00 grams (75%) of the sample's mass is carbon. The other 25.00 grams (25%) is hydrogen. To determine the relative number of atoms that are present, he must use the mole concept.

6-20 Finding the masses of substances before and after reactions can reveal the substances' empirical formulas.

Because carbon atoms have much more mass than hydrogen atoms, the empirical formula is nothing like $C_{75}H_{25}$ or C_3H_1. The key questions are "How many moles of carbon atoms are in the sample?" and "How many moles of hydrogen atoms are present?" These questions must be answered because formulas tell the relative number of atoms, not masses. To determine the mole composition, the mass composition of the sample must be used.

$$75.00 \text{ g C} \times \frac{1 \text{ mole C}}{12.01 \text{ g C}} = 6.245 \text{ moles C}$$

$$25.00 \text{ g H} \times \frac{1 \text{ mole H}}{1.008 \text{ g H}} = 24.80 \text{ moles H}$$

There are 6.245 moles of carbon atoms for every 24.80 moles of hydrogen atoms. The empirical formula could be written as $C_{6.245}H_{24.80}$. Although this formula is numerically accurate, it is not in its final form. Empirical formulas are written as ratios of simple whole numbers. Dividing both numbers by the smallest number gives the simplest form of the ratio.

$$\frac{6.245}{6.245} : \frac{24.80}{6.245} = 1:3.97 \text{ or } 1:4$$

The empirical formula of the compound is C_1H_4 or CH_4.

The steps of the process can be written in a flow chart.

6-21

Per cent composition		Mass composition		Mole composition		Mole ratio		Empirical formula
75.00% C 25.00% H	➧	75.00 g C 25.00 g H	➧	6.245 moles C 24.80 moles H	➧	$\frac{1 \text{ mole C}}{4 \text{ moles H}}$	➧	CH_4

In some problems the mole ratios might not be small whole numbers. If a ratio of 1 : 1.99 resulted from a calculation, it would be logical to round it off to be 1 : 2. Errors in measuring the mass composition are the most common cause of these minute discrepancies. Sometimes ratios such as 1 : 1.5 or 1 : 1.33 result. These should *not* be rounded off. The ratio 1 : 1.5 is equivalent to the whole-number ratio of 2 : 3. The ratio 1 : 1.33 is equivalent to the whole-number ratio 3 : 4. Insight and practice are necessary for knowing when to round off and when to seek another form of the ratio.

Sample Problem. A laboratory analysis of an unknown gas has determined that the gas is 72.55 per cent oxygen and 27.45 per cent carbon by mass. What is the empirical formula of the compound?

Solution.

Per cent composition: 72.55% O
27.45% C

Mass composition: In a 100-gram sample of the gas, there will be 72.55 grams of oxygen and 27.45 grams of carbon. The quantity of 100 grams is chosen because it simplifies the calculation of the mass composition.

Mole composition of sample:

$$72.55 \text{ g O} \times \frac{1 \text{ mole O}}{16.00 \text{ g O}} = 4.534 \text{ moles O}$$

$$27.45 \text{ g C} \times \frac{1 \text{ mole C}}{12.01 \text{ g C}} = 2.286 \text{ moles C}$$

Mole ratio: 4.534 : 2.286 reduced to lowest terms is

$$\frac{4.534}{2.286} : \frac{2.286}{2.286} = 1.983 : 1.000$$

The slight difference between 1.983 and 2.000 can be attributed to experimental error.

Empirical formula: For every 2 moles of oxygen, there is 1 mole of carbon. The empirical formula must be CO_2.

Sample Problem. A 5.000-gram sample of an unknown compound contains 1.844 grams of nitrogen and 3.156 grams of oxygen. Find the empirical formula.

Solution.

The mass composition of the sample is already known.

Mass composition: 1.844 g N
3.156 g O

Mole composition of sample:

$$1.844 \text{ g N} \times \frac{1 \text{ mole N}}{14.01 \text{ g N}} = 0.1316 \text{ moles N}$$

$$3.156 \text{ g O} \times \frac{1 \text{ mole O}}{16.00 \text{ g O}} = 0.1973 \text{ moles O}$$

Mole ratio: 0.1316 : 0.1973

$$\frac{0.1316}{0.1316} : \frac{0.1973}{0.1316} = 1 : 1.499$$

The ratio should be 1 : 1.5.

Empirical formula: The ratio 1 : 1.5 is in its simplest form, but the numbers are not whole numbers. To put the ratio in whole numbers, express the numbers as fractions.

$$1 : 1.5 = 2/2 : 3/2$$

Eliminate the fractions by multiplying through by the common denominator.

$$(2)\,2/2 : (2)\,3/2 = 2 : 3$$

The empirical formula of the compound is N_2O_3.

Coming to Terms

oxidation number
polyatomic ion
peroxide
nomenclature
flow chart
Greek prefix system
binary compound
polyatomic compound
Stock system
Roman numeral system
hydrate
mole
Avogadro's number
gram-atomic mass
gram-molecular mass
gram-formula mass
structural formula
molecular formula
empirical formula
per cent composition

Review Questions

1. Explain why
   a. the oxidation number of F is always negative.
   b. the oxidation numbers of alkali metals are always positive.
   c. elements such as P, N, and S have positive oxidation numbers in some compounds but negative oxidation numbers in others.
2. When the following pairs of atoms bond, which atom gets the positive oxidation number?
   a. H, O
   b. Na, S
   c. N, S
   d. Na, H
3. Give the oxidation numbers of each atom in the following compounds.
   a. $AlCl_3$
   b. $NaIO_3$
   c. N_2O_4
   d. $Na_2SO_4 \cdot 10\ H_2O$
   e. SnF_2
   f. HF
   g. HBrO
   h. IF
   i. HI
   j. HIO_4
   k. $FeBr_3 \cdot 6\ H_2O$
   l. I_2O_5
   m. $FeSiF_6 \cdot 6\ H_2O$
   n. $Ba(ClO_4)_2$
   o. $(NH_4)_2SO_4$
4. Name each of the compounds in problem 3. If a compound contains a metal that can have more than one oxidation number, give both Stock system and common names. Example: $HgBr_2$ is mercury(II) bromide or mercuric bromide. If the compound is a binary acid, name it both as a binary covalent compound and as a binary acid. Example: HCl is hydrogen chloride or hydrochloric acid.

5. Give formulas for the following compounds.
   a. boron trichloride
   b. cobalt(II) chloride hexahydrate
   c. phosphorus pentabromide
   d. magnesium cyanide
   e. ammonium bromate
   f. sodium peroxide
   g. hydrogen bromide
   h. hydrosulfuric acid
   i. potassium hydrogen carbonate
   j. calcium phosphate
   k. cuprous perchlorate
   l. bromic acid
   m. lead(II) acetate decahydrate
   n. dinitrogen pentasulfide
   o. phosphorus trihydride (phosphine)
6. What is Avogadro's number, and what physical significance does it have?
7. Give the gram-atomic mass for H, Sc, As, I, and U. Give your answers with four significant figures and the correct units.
8. How many atoms are in the following:
   a. 12.01 g of C
   b. 16.00 g of O
   c. 1.008 g of H
9. How many moles
   a. of Fe are 37.0 g of Fe?
   b. of Kr are 4.58×10^{20} Kr atoms?
   c. of $AlCl_3$ are 5.00 g of $AlCl_3$?
   d. of $NaIO_3$ are 3.25×10^{26} formula units of $NaIO_3$?
   e. of N_2O_4 are 26.75 g of N_2O_4?
   f. of $Na_2SO_4 \cdot 10\ H_2O$ are in 8.99×10^{24} formula units of Na_2SO_4?
10. Calculate the mass of 1 mole of each compound in problem 3. For each compound, tell whether the mass you calculate is a gram-formula mass or gram-molecular mass.
11. How many
    a. Fe atoms are in 0.256 mole of Fe?
    b. Kr atoms are in 3.87 g of Kr?
    c. $AlCl_3$ formula units are in 6.17 moles of $AlCl_3$?
    d. $NaIO_3$ formula units are in 8.58 g of $NaIO_3$?
    e. N_2O_4 molecules are in 8.16 g of N_2O_4?
    f. $Na_2SO_4 \cdot 10\ H_2O$ formula units are in 3.87 moles of $Na_2SO_4 \cdot 10\ H_2O$?
12. What is the mass (in grams) of
    a. 6.58 moles Fe?
    b. 8.58×10^{28} Kr atoms?
    c. 1.05 moles $AlCl_3$?
    d. 3.17×10^{18} formula units $NaIO_3$?

e. 0.0387 mole N_2O_4?
f. 5.41×10^{26} formula units $Na_2SO_4 \cdot 10\ H_2O$?

13. What is the difference between an empirical formula and a molecular formula?
14. Give the structural, molecular, and empirical formulas of hydrogen peroxide.
15. Ferrous sulfate, $FeSO_4$, is a therapeutic agent for iron-deficiency anemia. It is administered orally as ferrous sulfate heptahydrate. If 0.300 g of $FeSO_4 \cdot 7\ H_2O$ contains 0.0603 g of Fe, 0.0346 g of S, 0.190 g of O, and 0.0151 g of H, what is the per cent composition of $FeSO_4 \cdot 7\ H_2O$?
16. **Dinitrogen oxide, commonly called nitrous oxide or laughing gas, was once commonly used as an anesthetic. N_2O is 63.65% N. What mass of N_2O contains 4.850 g N?**
17. Epsom salts that are used as a laxative consist of $MgSO_4 \cdot 7\ H_2O$. How many grams of Mg are present in 0.0250 mole of $MgSO_4 \cdot 7\ H_2O$, which is 9.86% Mg?
18. Manganese(II) acetate is used to make dyes permanent. $Mn(C_2H_3O_2)_2$ is 27.8% C, 3.50% H, and 37.0% O. What mass of Mn is found in 125 g of $Mn(C_2H_3O_2)_2$?
19. Limestone, which is foundational to cement, consists of calcium carbonate. If 35.80 kg of $CaCO_3$ contain 4.296 kg C, 14.33 kg Ca, and 17.17 kg O, what is the per cent composition of $CaCO_3$?
20. Aspirin is the common name for acetyl salicylic acid. If 100 g of aspirin contain 60.00 g C, 4.480 g H, and 35.53 g O, what is its empirical formula?
21. Most aspirin substitutes in the United States contain acetaminophen as the active ingredient. Acetaminophen is 63.56% C, 6.00% H, 9.27% N, and 21.17% O. What is the empirical formula for acetaminophen?
22. Lidocaine is a widely used local anesthetic. A laboratory analysis of lidocaine reveals that a 5.000-g sample of lidocaine contains 3.588 g C, 0.473 g H, 0.598 g N, and 0.342 g O.
    a. What is the per cent composition of lidocaine?
    b. What is the empirical formula of lidocaine?

SEVEN

DESCRIBING CHEMICAL REACTIONS

EQUATIONS, CLASSIFICATION, AND STOICHIOMETRY

- THE plop, plop of antacid tablets leads to the fizz, fizz of escaping carbon dioxide bubbles.
- Some water softeners cause solid, white calcium carbonate to settle out from hard water.
- Invisible nitric oxide gas from the exhaust of a car turns into reddish brown nitrogen dioxide when it reacts with atmospheric oxygen.
- The combination of natural gas and oxygen releases energy to heat a home.
- The magnesium filament in a flash bulb of an instamatic camera produces a brilliant white light when a picture is taken.

In each of these cases, a chemical reaction occurs. One set of chemical substances forms from some other set of substances. Several visible signals tell of the unseen molecular changes.

1. A gas is released.
2. A solid settles out of solution.
3. A color changes.
4. The temperature changes.
5. Light is produced.

In a way, a chemical reaction is like the change in a man's heart at salvation. The changes themselves are not easily observed, but obvious signs signal that something has happened. Salvation brings a love for God, a desire to do His commands, and many other fruits.

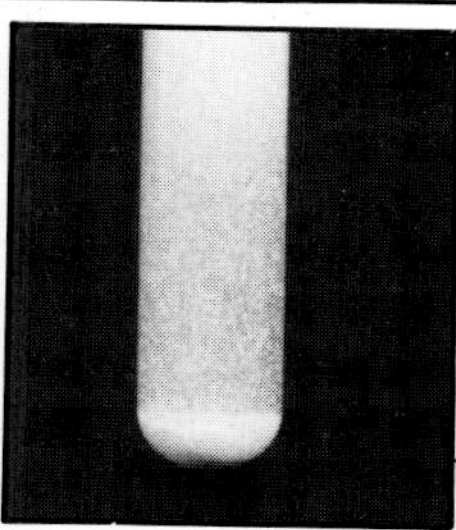

Writing Equations: What Goes in Must Come Out

Knowing when a reaction occurs is just a starting point. What substances go into the reaction? What substances come out of it? When does the reaction occur? How much of each substance is involved? Chemists pack the answers to these questions into shorthand expressions called **chemical equations.**

7–1 What Equations Do

Unlike mathematical equations, chemical equations do not show equalities. Instead, they represent processes called chemical reactions. To tell about reactions, they must do several things.

1. Equations must identify all the substances involved in the reaction. Some water softeners remove calcium salts such as calcium hydrogen carbonate from hard water by adding calcium hydroxide. The two compounds react to form water and calcium carbonate, which settles out of the solution. A word equation shows all the substances that are involved.

   calcium hydrogen carbonate + calcium hydroxide ⟶ water + calcium carbonate

2. Equations must show the composition of the substances. Since molecular and unit formulas are more informative than names, they are used in equations.

   $$Ca(HCO_3)_2 + Ca(OH)_2 \longrightarrow H_2O + CaCO_3$$

3. Equations must account for all the atoms involved in the reaction. The law of mass conservation states that matter cannot be created or destroyed in chemical reactions. Applied to equations, this law says, "What goes in must come out."

As it now stands, the equation above does not show the conservation of atoms. Two calcium atoms, four hydrogen atoms, two carbon atoms, and eight oxygen atoms enter the reaction. After the reaction, the equation shows one calcium atom, two hydrogen atoms, one carbon atom, and four oxygen atoms.

2 Ca atoms ⟶ 1 Ca atom
4 H atoms ⟶ 2 H atoms
2 C atoms ⟶ 1 C atom
8 O atoms ⟶ 4 O atoms

Can sixteen atoms really turn into eight atoms? To be correct, the equation must show equal numbers of atoms before and after the reaction.

Equations that account for all atoms and indicate that the mass of matter involved does not change are called **balanced chemical**

equations. Balancing an unbalanced equation involves adjusting the number of molecules, atoms, or formula units.

$$Ca(HCO_3)_2 + Ca(OH)_2 \longrightarrow 2\ H_2O + 2\ CaCO_3$$

Now each side of the equation has two calcium atoms, four hydrogen atoms, two carbon atoms, and eight oxygen atoms. The equation does what it is supposed to do; it accurately describes the reaction.

7–2 Parts of an Equation

Substances that are present before the reaction are called **reactants.** Substances that emerge from the reaction are called **products.** *Coefficients* tell how many atoms, molecules, or formula units are present. An *arrow* separates the reactants from the products and shows the direction of the reaction.

Reactants Products

$$Ca(HCO_3)_2 + Ca(OH)_2 \longrightarrow 2\ H_2O + 2\ CaCO_3$$

Coefficients

7–3 Special Symbols in Equations

Additional information can be packed into equations with the use of special symbols. Double half-arrows between reactants and products show that the reaction goes forward as well as backward.

$$3\ Fe + 4\ H_2O \rightleftharpoons Fe_3O_4 + 4\ H_2$$

The physical states of the substances can also be indicated. The gaseous state is indicated by a (g) immediately after the formula. If the gas is a product, an upward arrow (↑) is sometimes used. A liquid is represented by an (*l*) after the formula, and a solid is shown by an (s). If the solid falls out of a solution, it is called a **precipitate.** The process of **precipitation** is sometimes noted with a downward arrow (↓).

$$3\ Fe\ (s) + 4\ H_2O\ (l) \rightleftharpoons Fe_3O_4\ (s) + 4\ H_2\ (g)$$

$$3\ Fe\ (s) + 4\ H_2O\ (l) \rightleftharpoons Fe_3O_4 \downarrow + 4\ H_2 \uparrow$$

If a substance is dissolved in water, an (aq), meaning “aqueous,” is placed after the formula.

$$Ag^+\ (aq) + Cl^-\ (aq) \longrightarrow AgCl\ (s)$$

Symbols above and below the reaction arrow are often used to tell about special reaction conditions. A Δ above the arrow means that the reactants are heated. Other descriptions of pressure, light, or specific temperatures can also be placed above the arrow.

Catalysts are substances that change the rate of a reaction but that do not undergo permanent changes themselves. Their symbols or formulas can also be placed above the arrow.

$$2\ KClO_3\ (s) \xrightarrow{\Delta,\ MnO_2} 2\ KCl\ (s) + 3\ O_2\ (g)$$

7–4 Balancing Equations by Inspection

Balancing an equation by inspection involves adjusting coefficients to show how atoms and mass are conserved. The object is to write an equation that has equal numbers of each kind of atom in the reactants and products. Skill in balancing equations will improve with practice, but some general guidelines will be helpful in the meantime.

Consider the reaction that nitrogen oxide goes through when it mixes with oxygen in the atmosphere.

$$\text{nitrogen oxide} + \text{oxygen} \longrightarrow \text{nitrogen dioxide}$$

1. Write the formulas for all reactants and products. The formulas of covalent compounds can often be obtained from their names. (Nitrogen oxide is NO, and nitrogen dioxide is NO_2.) Remember that some elements exist as diatomic molecules. The formulas of ionic compounds can be found with the use of oxidation numbers. Make sure that all the formulas are correct. Once they are, do not even think of changing them.

   $$NO + O_2 \longrightarrow NO_2$$

2. Count atoms of each kind to see whether the equation is already balanced.

   $$\begin{array}{lcl} 1\ \text{N atom} & \longrightarrow & 1\ \text{N atom} \\ 3\ \text{O atoms} & \longrightarrow & 2\ \text{O atoms} \end{array}$$

3. Adjust coefficients until there are equal numbers of atoms on both sides of the arrow. Remember—change *coefficients,* not *subscripts.* The formulas of the reactants and products have already been determined. Never change a compound's formula in order to balance an equation! It is best to start with the most complicated molecules and save simple molecules like O_2 and individual elements until last. In the example more oxygen atoms are needed in the product. The only way to get more oxygen atoms in the product is to add another NO_2 molecule.

   $$NO + O_2 \longrightarrow 2\ NO_2$$

   Now there are two nitrogen atoms in the product but only one in the reactants. An additional NO molecule will supply the needed nitrogen and will balance the oxygen atoms.

   $$2\ NO + O_2 \longrightarrow 2\ NO_2$$

4. Make sure that the coefficients are all whole numbers and that they are in the simplest ratio possible. If the equation looked like $NO + \frac{1}{2} O_2 \longrightarrow NO_2$, it would be numerically correct, but not all coefficients would be whole numbers. You should multiply all the coefficients by a common denominator so that they become whole numbers.

$$2\ NO + 2(\tfrac{1}{2} O_2) \longrightarrow 2\ NO_2$$
$$2\ NO + O_2 \longrightarrow 2\ NO_2$$

If the equation looked like $4\ NO + 2\ O_2 \longrightarrow 4\ NO_2$, it would again be numerically correct, but the coefficients would not be in the simplest possible ratio. Dividing each coefficient by the lowest common factor yields the lowest possible ratio.

$$\tfrac{4}{2}\ NO + \tfrac{2}{2} O_2 \longrightarrow \tfrac{4}{2}\ NO_2$$
$$2\ NO + O_2 \longrightarrow 2\ NO_2$$

Sample Problem. Iron and gaseous chlorine can react to form iron(III) chloride. Write and balance the equation for this reaction.

Solution.

Write the formulas. Iron atoms can react as individual atoms, but chlorine atoms are diatomic molecules. The formula of iron(III) chloride can be found with the aid of oxidation numbers.

$$Fe + Cl_2 \longrightarrow FeCl_3$$

Count the atoms.

1 Fe atom ⟶ 1 Fe atom

2 Cl atoms ⟶ 3 Cl atoms

Adjust the coefficients. More chlorine atoms are needed in the reactants. The addition of another Cl_2 molecule is a start, but it does not yield a balanced equation.

$$Fe + \mathbf{2}\ Cl_2 \longrightarrow FeCl_3$$

At this point you may be tempted to change some formulas, but you would be attempting to alter reality. Additional coefficient changes are necessary.

$$Fe + \mathbf{3}\ Cl_2 \longrightarrow \mathbf{2}\ FeCl_3$$

The chlorine atoms are balanced, but now the iron atoms are not. Another iron atom is needed.

$$\mathbf{2}\ Fe + 3\ Cl_2 \longrightarrow 2\ FeCl_3$$

Check. Atoms are balanced, and all coefficients are whole numbers in the simplest ratio possible.

Sample Problem. Ethane (C_2H_6) burns in oxygen gas to form carbon dioxide and water. Write and balance the equation for this reaction.

Solution.

While writing the formulas, remember that oxygen exists as diatomic molecules.

$$C_2H_6 + O_2 \longrightarrow CO_2 + H_2O$$

Start by balancing carbon and hydrogen atoms, since they are a part of the most complex molecule.

$$C_2H_6 + O_2 \longrightarrow \mathbf{2}\ CO_2 + \mathbf{3}\ H_2O$$

Now seven oxygen atoms are in the products. Since oxygen molecules exist as two-atom units, $3\frac{1}{2}$ (or $\frac{7}{2}$) molecules are needed in the reactants.

$$C_2H_6 + \tfrac{7}{2} O_2 \longrightarrow 2\ CO_2 + 3\ H_2O$$

The coefficient 7/2 is not a whole number. All coefficients should be doubled to complete the balancing act.

$$\mathbf{2}\ C_2H_6 + \mathbf{7}\ O_2 \longrightarrow \mathbf{4}\ CO_2 + \mathbf{6}\ H_2O$$

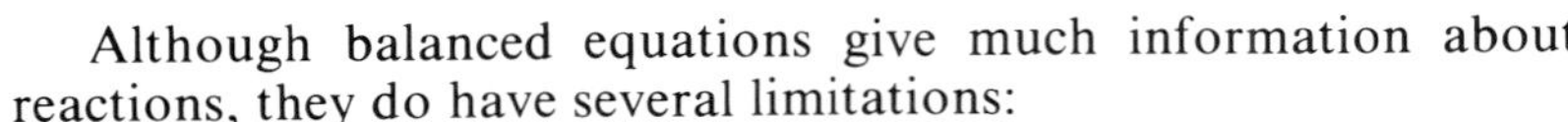

Although balanced equations give much information about reactions, they do have several limitations:

1. The fact that an equation can be written does not mean that the reaction can occur. The equation below is balanced, but the reaction it represents will not occur.

$$Ag + NaCl \longrightarrow Na + AgCl$$

2. Equations do not tell whether a reaction goes to completion. Some reactions leave a mixture of reactants and products.

3. Equations do not show how a reaction occurs. Some reactions involve more than one step. Equations do not show the steps of a reaction or the order in which those steps take place.

A Classification Scheme: Types of Reactions

Most reactions can be classified on the basis of the chemical change that takes place. Classifying reactions leads to generalizations that in turn lead to a better understanding of the reactions. The major classes used in the scheme are composition, decomposition, single replacement, and double replacement reactions.

7–5 Composition Reactions

Composition reactions combine two or more substances into a single product. Because the major effect of the reactions is the production of a new substance, these reactions are often called synthesis reactions. The general equation $A + B \longrightarrow AB$ represents composition reactions.

1. Metals and nonmetals other than oxygen can form compounds called salts.

$$Mg + F_2 \longrightarrow MgF_2$$

2. Metals can combine with oxygen to form metallic oxides.

$$2\ Mg + O_2 \longrightarrow 2\ MgO$$

3. Nonmetals can react with oxygen to form oxides.

$$P_4 + 5\ O_2 \longrightarrow P_4O_{10}$$

4. Water and metal oxides can form metal hydroxides.

$$H_2O + CaO \longrightarrow Ca(OH)_2$$

5. Water and nonmetal oxides can combine to form oxyacids.

$$H_2O + SO_3 \longrightarrow H_2SO_4$$

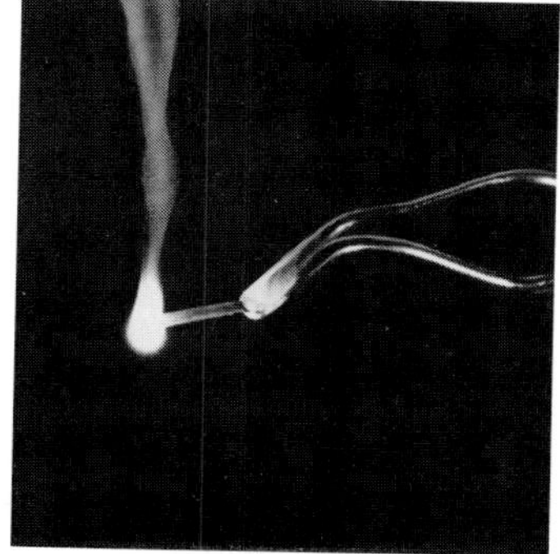

7-2 A composition reaction occurs when magnesium reacts with atmospheric oxygen.

7–6 Decomposition Reactions

The opposite of a composition reaction is a decomposition reaction. Whereas a composition reaction combines substances, a **decomposition reaction** breaks a substance down into two or more substances. Breaking compounds apart usually requires an input of energy. Decomposition reactions have the general form $AB \longrightarrow A + B$.

1. Oxygen can be driven out of some compounds.
   a. Metal oxides are usually very stable, but some can be decomposed by strong heating.

$$2\ HgO \xrightarrow{\Delta} 2\ Hg + O_2$$

   b. Metal chlorates can be heated to produce oxygen.

$$2\ KClO_3 \xrightarrow{\Delta} 2\ KCl + 3\ O_2$$

c. Water can be decomposed by an electric current.

$$2\ H_2O \xrightarrow{\text{elec.}} 2\ H_2 + O_2$$

2. Metal hydroxides can release water when heated.

$$Mg(OH)_2 \xrightarrow{\Delta} MgO + H_2O$$

3. Metal carbonates can release carbon dioxide when heated.

$$CaCO_3 \xrightarrow{\Delta} CaO + CO_2$$

4. Some acids can be decomposed into nonmetal oxides and water.

$$H_2CO_3 \longrightarrow CO_2 + H_2O$$

A carbonated drink goes flat as this reaction occurs. The carbonic acid that gives the tangy taste decomposes at room temperature.

5. Hydrates can release their water molecules when heated sufficiently.

$$BaCl_2{\cdot}2\ H_2O \xrightarrow{\Delta} BaCl_2 + 2\ H_2O$$

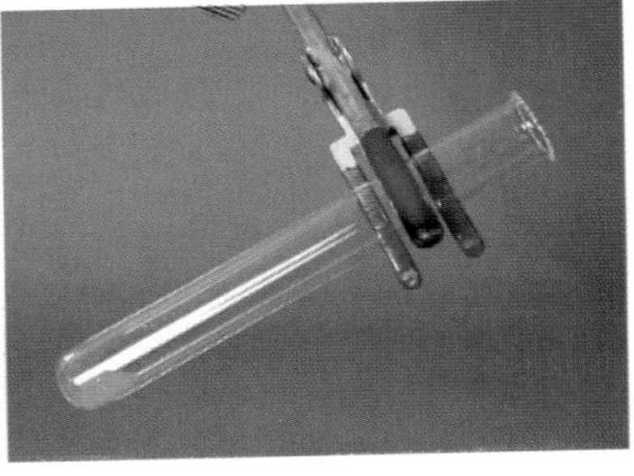

7-3 Orange ammonium dichromate can be decomposed by gentle heating **(left).**

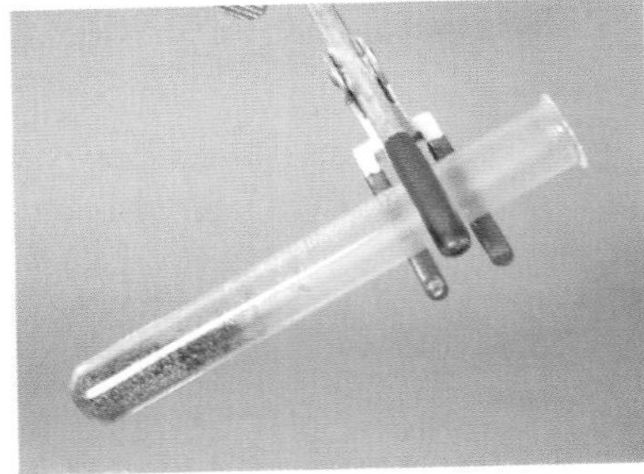

7-4 Green chromium(III) oxide, water vapor, and nitrogen gas result when ammonium dichromate decomposes **(right)**.

7–7 Single Replacement Reactions

In **single replacement reactions,** an active element takes the place of a less active element in a compound. These kinds of reactions are also called displacement or substitution reactions. The general equation $A + BZ \longrightarrow B + AZ$ represents several types of single replacement reactions.

1. Atoms of active metals can replace less active ions from solutions and compounds. When a piece of solid zinc is placed in a copper sulfate solution, the zinc replaces the copper ions in solution and forces them to precipitate out as solid copper.

$$Zn\ (s) + CuSO_4\ (aq) \longrightarrow Cu\ (s) + ZnSO_4\ (aq)$$

Active metals can replace the hydrogen ions of acids. This is why metals placed in acids often react to form bubbles of hydrogen gas. In these reactions metal atoms replace hydrogen ions of acid molecules. The hydrogen bubbles off as H_2 gas, and a salt forms from the acid molecule.

$$Mg\ (s) + 2\ HCl\ (aq) \longrightarrow MgCl_2\ (aq) + H_2\ (g)$$

Very active metals react with water to produce hydrogen gas. In the equation below, HOH is an alternate formula for water. It shows replacement reactions more clearly.

$$2\ Na\ (s) + 2\ HOH\ (l) \longrightarrow 2\ NaOH\ (aq) + H_2\ (g)$$

2. Active halogens can replace less active halogens that are in solution. When chlorine (an active element) gas is bubbled through a sodium bromide solution, chlorine replaces bromine in the solution. Some of the bromine atoms that are replaced escape as Br_2 gas.

$$Cl_2\ (g) + 2\ NaBr\ (aq) \longrightarrow 2\ NaCl\ (aq) + Br_2\ (g)$$

When will a single replacement reaction occur? This depends on the activity of the elements that are involved. An active element can be defined as one that has a strong tendency to lose or gain electrons to form bonds. If unbonded atoms are more active than the bonded atoms, a reaction will probably take place. The more active elements can force the less active elements from the bond. The most active metal listed in Figure 7-5 is potassium; the least active is gold. Other metals can be arranged according to their activities in an **activity series.**

Elements at the top of the list are the most active. Note that hydrogen is included even though it is not really a metal. Predictions about whether a reaction is probable can be based on this series. For instance, will a reaction occur if barium is placed into a tin(II) chloride solution? Ba (s) + $SnCl_2$ $\longrightarrow$? Barium is higher in the activity series, so it can replace tin and force it to precipitate.

$$Ba\ (s) + SnCl_2\ (aq) \longrightarrow BaCl_2\ (aq) + Sn\ (s)$$

Will gold metal react when it is placed in a sodium chloride solution? Gold is at the bottom of the activity series. Its tendency to lose electrons and form ionic bonds is nowhere near that of sodium. Since no reaction will occur, a person can safely dip a gold ring into salt water without losing a fortune.

$$Au\ (s) + NaCl\ (aq) \longrightarrow \text{No reaction}$$

With the aid of an activity series, it is possible to predict which metals will react with acids. If a metal is more active than hydrogen, it can take the place of hydrogen. Because zinc is above hydrogen in the activity series, it will react with dilute sulfuric acid.

$$Zn\ (s) + H_2SO_4\ (aq) \longrightarrow ZnSO_4\ (aq) + H_2\ (g)$$

7-5 Activity Series of Some Common Metals

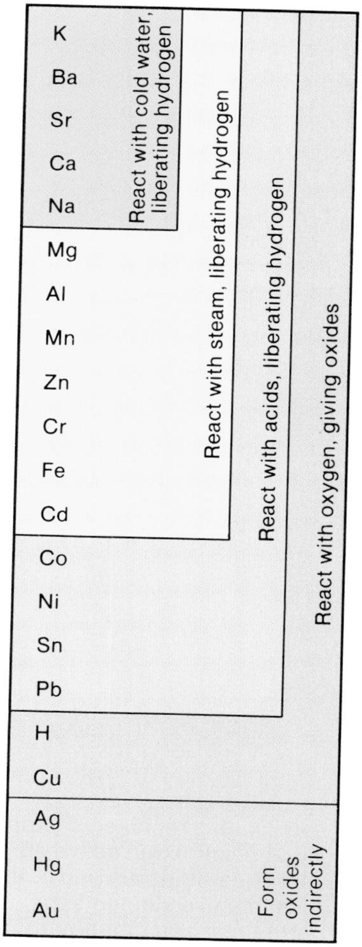

Metals	React with cold water, liberating hydrogen	React with steam, liberating hydrogen	React with acids, liberating hydrogen	React with oxygen, giving oxides
K, Ba, Sr, Ca, Na	✓	✓	✓	✓
Mg, Al, Mn, Zn, Cr, Fe, Cd		✓	✓	✓
Co, Ni, Sn, Pb			✓	✓
H, Cu				✓
Ag, Hg, Au	Form oxides indirectly			

7-6 Halogen Activity Series

F_2

Cl_2

Br_2

I_2

Metals above magnesium readily replace hydrogen in water molecules.

$$2\ Ba\ (s) + 2\ HOH\ (l) \longrightarrow Ba(OH)_2\ (aq) + H_2\ (g)$$

The halogens have their own activity series. A halogen can replace an element below it in the series. Iodine, at the bottom of the series, cannot replace any of the other halogens because of its low activity.

$$Cl_2\ (g) + MgBr_2\ (aq) \longrightarrow MgCl_2\ (aq) + Br_2\ (g)$$

7-7 Single replacement reactions occur when active elements replace less active elements in compounds.

7–8 Double Replacement Reactions

In **double replacement reactions** two compounds switch partners with each other. Equations of double replacement reactions have the general form $AX + BZ \longrightarrow AZ + BX$. Most double replacement reactions occur in an aqueous mixture of two ionic compounds. A precipitate may indicate that a double replacement reaction has occurred.

7-8 Double replacement reactions occur when active elements combine and leave the less reactive elements to form their own compound.

When lead(II) nitrate and potassium chromate solutions are mixed, a double replacement reaction occurs. Solid lead chromate, a brilliant yellow compound that could be used as a pigment in paint, falls out of solution.

$$Pb(NO_3)_2\ (aq) + K_2CrO_4\ (aq) \longrightarrow PbCrO_4\ (s) + 2\ KNO_3\ (aq)$$

An **ionic equation** represents all the particles present before and after the reaction.

Ionic equation:

$$Pb^{2+}\ (aq) + 2\ NO_3^-\ (aq) + 2\ K^+\ (aq) + CrO_4^{2-}\ (aq) \longrightarrow PbCrO_4\ (s) + 2\ K^+\ (aq) + 2\ NO_3^-\ (aq)$$

Ionic equations can include some non-ionic particles and some ions that remain unchanged. **Spectator ions** appear in the reactants and in the products. They do not precipitate or join other ions. They could easily be left out of the equation. **Net ionic equations** show only the ions that actually react; the spectator ions are left out.

Net ionic equation: $Pb^{2+}\ (aq) + CrO_4^{2-}\ (aq) \longrightarrow PbCrO_4\ (s)$

Many neutralization reactions between acids and bases can be classified as double replacement reactions.

$$HCl + KOH \longrightarrow HOH + KCl$$

Ionic equation:

$$H^+\ (aq) + Cl^-\ (aq) + K^+\ (aq) + OH^-\ (aq) \longrightarrow HOH\ (l) + K^+\ (aq) + Cl^-(aq)$$

Net ionic equation: $H^+\ (aq) + OH^-\ (aq) \longrightarrow HOH\ (l)$

Double replacement reactions usually reduce the number of ions in solution. Solid precipitates, such as lead(II) chromate, and the formation of the largely non-ionizable water molecules in acid-base reactions reduce the number of ions.

7-9 When solutions of lead nitrate and potassium dichromate mix, lead dichromate precipitates and potassium nitrate is left in solution.

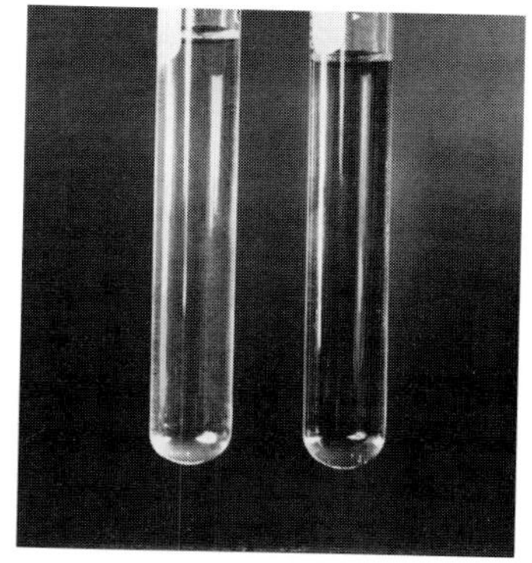

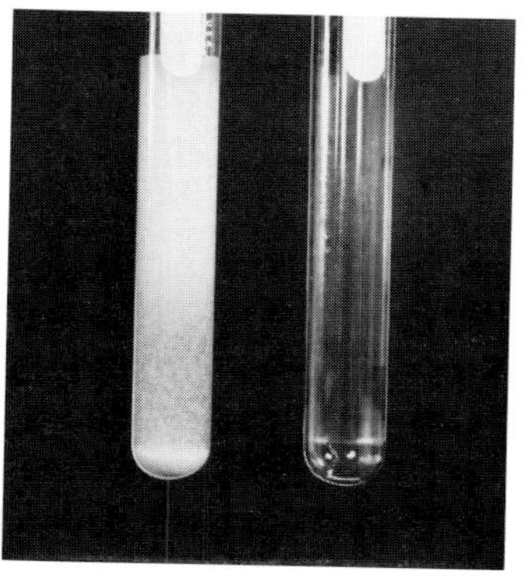

Stoichiometry: Predicting How Much

Ninety per cent of the phosphorus produced in America is used to manufacture phosphoric acid. To form phosphoric acid, chemical engineers burn elemental phosphorus (P_4) in dry air to make diphosphorus pentoxide (P_2O_5). They then mix the diphosphorus pentoxide with water to form the acid (H_3PO_4). The engineers who run this process must keep careful track of all the compounds involved. For instance, if they burn 60 kilograms of phosphorus, they must know what mass of diphosphorus pentoxide will result. They must also know how much phosphoric acid can be produced from the diphosphorus pentoxide. The engineers calculate quantities of reactants and products with the aid of stoichiometry.

Phosphoric acid manufacturers are not the only people who use stoichiometry. Chemists of all types need to measure reactants and products of reactions.

What is stoichiometry? If you guess that it is the measurement of "stoichios," your knowledge of root words has supplied at least half of the definition. The suffix *-metry* means "measurement." *Stoichio* comes from the Greek word *stoicheion,* meaning "elements." In a general sense, **stoichiometry** is the measurement and calculation of amounts of matter in chemical reactions.

7–9 Mole-to-Mole Conversions

Chemical equations show what substances are involved in a reaction. Balanced chemical equations contain the numerical information necessary for detailed calculations. The coefficients in front of each substance show how many atoms, molecules, and moles are involved. The equation $P_4 + 5\ O_2 \longrightarrow 2\ P_2O_5$ means that 1 P_4 molecule + 5 O_2 molecules form 2 P_2O_5 molecules. The coefficients can also represent moles.

$$1 \text{ mole } P_4 + 5 \text{ moles } O_2 \longrightarrow 2 \text{ moles } P_2O_5$$

The coefficients in balanced equations are the key to stoichiometric calculations. They give the numerical relationships between the substances in a reaction. The balanced equation shows that

1 mole P_4 reacts to form 2 moles P_2O_5 (a 1:2 ratio)
1 mole P_4 reacts with 5 moles O_2 (a 1:5 ratio)
5 moles O_2 react to form 2 moles P_2O_5 (a 5:2 ratio)

Even if the original quantities were cut in half, the ratios would still hold true. In each case the coefficients from the balanced equation give the ratios between moles of one substance and moles of another substance.

0.5 mole P_4 reacts to form 1 mole P_2O_5 (a 1:2 ratio)
0.5 mole P_4 reacts with 2.5 moles O_2 (a 1:5 ratio)
2.5 moles O_2 react to form 1 mole P_2O_5 (a 5:2 ratio)

The ratios can be used as conversion factors for calculating moles of one substance from a known number of moles of another substance. Figure 7-10 is a flow chart that illustrates how a mole-to-mole stoichiometric conversion can be done. The chart shows that the coefficients from the balanced equation can be used to calculate an unknown molar amount from a known molar amount.

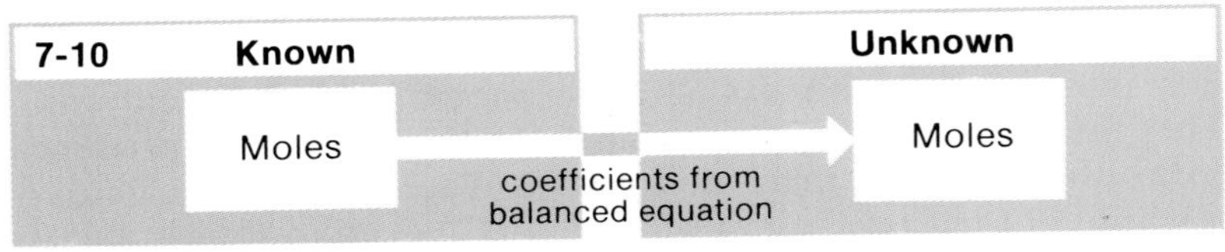

Suppose that a chemical engineer wanted to produce 25.0 moles of diphosphorus pentoxide. How many moles of phosphorus must be burned? The knowledge that 1 mole of phosphorus produces 2 moles of diphosphorus pentoxide enables him to set up and solve the problem.

$$25.0 \text{ moles } P_2O_5 \times \frac{1 \text{ mole } P_4}{2 \text{ moles } P_2O_5} = 12.5 \text{ moles } P_4$$

The amount of oxygen required could be calculated from either the 12.5 moles of phosphorus or from the 25.0 moles of diphosphorus pentoxide. Both methods use ratios formed from the coefficients in the balanced equation.

$$12.5 \text{ moles } P_4 \times \frac{5 \text{ moles } O_2}{1 \text{ mole } P_4} = 62.5 \text{ moles } O_2$$

$$25.0 \text{ moles } P_2O_5 \times \frac{5 \text{ moles } O_2}{2 \text{ moles } P_2O_5} = 62.5 \text{ moles } O_2$$

Sample Problem. If 25.0 moles of diphosphorus pentoxide react with water to form phosphoric acid, how many moles of water are required? The balanced equation of the reaction is $P_2O_5 + 3\ H_2O \longrightarrow 2\ H_3PO_4$.

Solution.

The coefficients on the balanced equation show that 3 moles of water are needed for every 1 mole of diphosphorus pentoxide.

$$25.0 \text{ moles } P_2O_5 \times \frac{3 \text{ moles } H_2O}{1 \text{ mole } P_2O_5} = 75.0 \text{ moles } H_2O$$

7–10 Mass-to-Mole Conversions

Any stoichiometric conversions between substances in a reaction must be done in terms of moles. The mass of a substance must be expressed as moles before any other stoichiometric conversions can be done. The coefficients on balanced equations show *molar* ratios, not *mass* ratios. The flow chart for mass-to-mole conversions shows that the moles of the known substance must be calculated as an intermediate step.

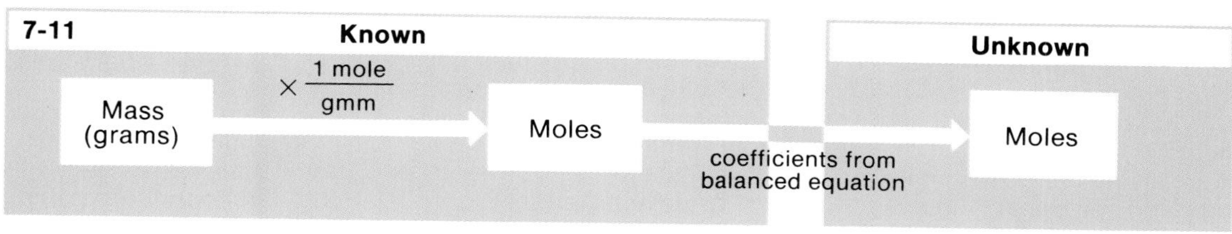

Calculate the quantity of diphosphorus pentoxide that would result from the burning of 1.55 kilograms (1550 g) of phosphorus. Before the conversion factor of 2 moles P_2O_5/1 mole P_4 can be used, the known mass of 1550 grams of phosphorus must be converted to moles. The gram-atomic mass of phosphorus is 123.9 grams/mole.

$$1550 \text{ g } P_4 \times \frac{1 \text{ mole } P_4}{123.9 \text{ g } P_4} = 12.5 \text{ moles } P_4$$

The 12.5 moles of phosphorus can now be converted to moles of diphosphorus pentoxide.

$$12.5 \text{ moles } P_4 \times \frac{2 \text{ moles } P_2O_5}{1 \text{ mole } P_4} = 25.0 \text{ moles } P_2O_5$$

Sample Problem. How many moles of phosphoric acid can be formed from 3550 grams of diphosphorus pentoxide? ($P_2O_5 + 3\,H_2O \longrightarrow 2\,H_3PO_4$)

FACETS OF CHEMISTRY

Chemical Families

Fourteen-year-old Marie Anne Pierretti sat on the edge of her chair and quietly followed the conversation of the prominent men gathered at her father's house. On this evening in 1769, she was particularly interested in one man, Antoine Laurent Lavoisier. Approximately twenty-five, good-looking, keen-minded, and a good conversationalist, the young scientist also noticed her. Less than a year later, the couple were making plans for marriage. They decided that Marie would study English, Latin, and even science so that she could aid her future husband in his work. They also agreed that she could use her artistic ability to illustrate his memoirs. After their marriage, she became his closest collaborator and spent many hours with him in the laboratory, recording notes and making sketches. Eighteen happy years passed, but then the French Revolution came. Antoine Lavoisier's connection with his political father-in-law made him an object of suspicion. In May of 1794 he and his father-in-law were executed at the guillotine. In the following years Marie would marry another scientist named Count Rumford. But the pages of history record that Marie Anne and Antoine Lavoisier were possibly the first husband-and-wife research team.

Perhaps the best-known family research team of all was that of Pierre and Marie Curie. The Curies spent most of their careers discovering radioactive elements. To do this, they laboriously analyzed tons of uranium ore. Eventually they isolated a new element, number 84. They named it polonium after Marie's native land, Poland. A continued probing of the ore finally led to the discovery of radium, an extremely rare element. This research on

Solution.

The 3550 grams of diphosphorus pentoxide must first be expressed as moles. The gram-molecular mass of P_2O_5 is 141.9 grams/mole.

$$3550 \text{ g } P_2O_5 \times \frac{1 \text{ mole } P_2O_5}{141.9 \text{ g } P_2O_5} = 25.0 \text{ moles } P_2O_5$$

Moles of diphosphorus pentoxide can be converted to moles of phosphoric acid according to the ratio of the coefficients.

$$25.0 \text{ moles } P_2O_5 \times \frac{2 \text{ moles } H_3PO_4}{1 \text{ mole } P_2O_5} = 50.0 \text{ moles } H_3PO_4$$

radioactivity earned Marie and Pierre the Nobel prize in physics in 1903. After Pierre was accidentally killed, Marie continued the search and isolated pure radium. She was awarded the Nobel prize in chemistry in 1911 for the discovery of polonium and radium.

Despite the death of her husband, Marie Curie's work with family members was far from over. Throughout World War I Marie and her daughter Irene worked on the application of x-rays for medical diagnoses. As Irene worked in her mother's laboratory, she met a research assistant who later became her husband. Irene and Jean Frederic Joliot also became a famous husband-and-wife research team. Their extensive research on alpha particles led them to discover how to induce radioactivity in nonradioactive substances. For this they were awarded the Nobel prize in chemistry in 1935.

Scattered gaps in Mendeleev's periodic table prompted the German chemist Ida Tacke and her husband-to-be, Walter Noddack, to begin a search. They knew that Mendeleev had predicted the properties of several elements such as gallium, germanium, and scandium. But there were two gaps for which he made no predictions—those representing elements 43 and 75. Both were located below manganese in the seventh column of the table. Since these elements were transition metals, their properties could not be easily predicted. Early investigators had searched for the missing elements in manganese ores but had failed. In 1922 Ida and Walter began their search. Ores containing molybdenum, tungsten, ruthenium, and osmium were concentrated and studied with x-rays. In June of 1925 the Noddack team announced the discovery of element 75. They named the new element rhenium, after the Rhineland. Element 43, on the other hand, never showed itself. To this day it has not been found in nature. Instead, it has been found among the fission products of nuclear reactors. Since this is an artificial means of production, the element has been named technetium, meaning "artificial."

The technicians who control the production of diphosphorus pentoxide and phosphoric acid find mass quantities more convenient to use than molar quantities. Stoichiometric calculations can be used to solve mass-to-mass conversions.

7–11 Mass-to-Mass Conversions

When the mass of one substance in a reaction is known, the mass of a second substance can be calculated. In section 7–10 the number of moles of diphosphorus pentoxide that formed from 1550 grams of phosphorus was calculated. Only one additional step is needed to calculate the mass of diphosphorus pentoxide that would form. The gram-molecular mass of 141.9 grams/mole can be used to convert moles of diphosphorus pentoxide to grams.

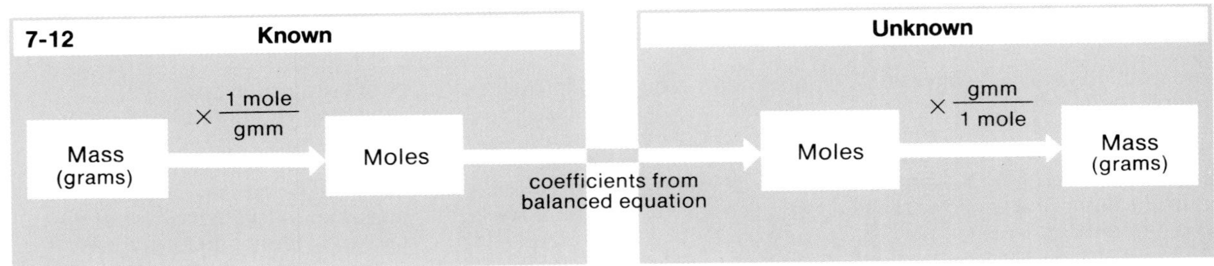

The moles of the known and unknown substances must be determined before the unknown mass can be calculated. Note that the flow chart shows all the previously given stoichiometric conversions (mole-mole, mass-mole, and mass-mass conversions).

$$1550 \text{ g } P_4 \times \frac{1 \text{ moles } P_4}{123.9 \text{ g } P_4} \times \frac{2 \text{ moles } P_2O_5}{1 \text{ mole } P_4} \times \frac{141.9 \text{ g } P_2O_5}{1 \text{ mole } P_2O_5} = 3550 \text{ g } P_2O_5$$

Sample Problem. What mass of water will react with 3550 grams of diphosphorus pentoxide?
($P_2O_5 + 3\ H_2O \longrightarrow 2\ H_3PO_4$)

Solution.

The mass of diphosphorus pentoxide must be expressed as moles before the molar conversion can be done. Once the number of moles of water is known, the mass of water can be calculated.

$$3550 \text{ g } P_2O_5 \times \frac{1 \text{ mole } P_2O_5}{141.9 \text{ g } P_2O_5} \times \frac{3 \text{ moles } H_2O}{1 \text{ mole } P_2O_5} \times \frac{18.016 \text{ g } H_2O}{1 \text{ mole } H_2O} = 1350 \text{ g } H_2O$$

The number of atoms or molecules involved in a reaction can be calculated from known molar quantities. Suppose that the sample problem above asked, "How many water molecules will react with 3550 grams of diphosphorus pentoxide?" The solution to the problem is the same until the step in which the number of moles of water is converted to the mass of water. The conversion factor 6.023×10^{23} molecules/1 mole can be used to convert the number of moles of water to the number of molecules of water.

$$3550 \text{ g } P_2O_5 \times \frac{1 \text{ mole } P_2O_5}{141.9 \text{ g } P_2O_5} \times \frac{3 \text{ moles } H_2O}{1 \text{ mole } P_2O_5}$$

$$\times \frac{6.023 \times 10^{23} \text{ molecules } H_2O}{1 \text{ mole } H_2O} = 4.52 \times 10^{25} \text{ molecules } H_2O$$

With this addition, the flow chart for stoichiometric problems is as follows:

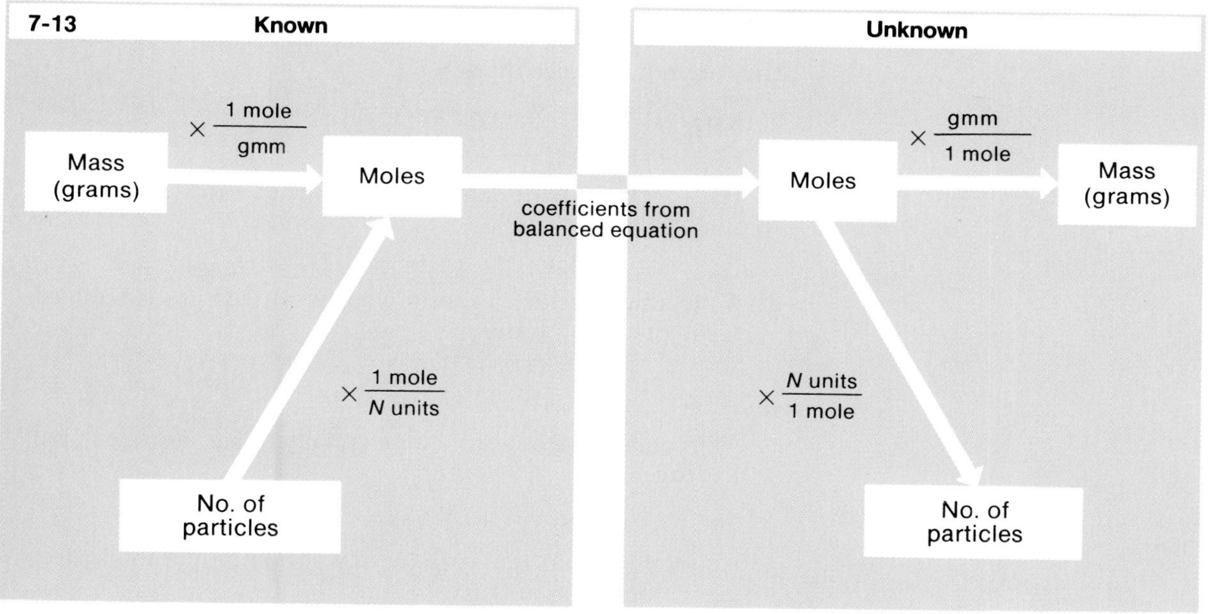

Coming to Terms

chemical equation
balanced chemical equation
reactant
product
precipitate
precipitation
composition reaction
decomposition reaction
single replacement reaction
activity series
double replacement reaction
ionic equation
spectator ion
net ionic equation
stoichiometry

Review Questions

1. List several evidences that tell whether a chemical reaction has occurred.

2. What three criteria must be met before a chemical equation is acceptable?

3. Explain what each underlined term means.

$$2\ AgClO_3\ \underline{(s)} \xrightarrow{\Delta} 2\ AgCl\ (s) + 3\ O_2\ \underline{(g)}$$

4. $HCl\ (aq) + H_2O\ (l) \rightleftharpoons Cl^-\ (aq) + H_3O^+\ (aq)$
   a. Why are two opposing arrows shown?
   b. What does the symbol (*l*) mean?
   c. Why is (aq) written after several of the substances?

5. Determine whether the following equations are balanced. If they are not, balance them.
   a. $BaO_2\ (s) \xrightarrow{\Delta} BaO\ (s) + O_2\ (g)$
   b. $Li\ (s) + H_2O\ (l) \xrightarrow{\Delta} LiOH\ (s) + H_2\ (g)$
   c. Hydrogen peroxide can decompose when exposed to bright sunlight.
   $$H_2O_2\ (l) \longrightarrow H_2O\ (l) + O_2\ (g)$$
   d. A metallic hydride can form when hydrogen gas is bubbled through molten sodium.
   $$Na\ (l) + H_2\ (g) \longrightarrow NaH\ (s)$$
   e. $H_2SO_4 \xrightarrow{\Delta} H_2O + SO_2 + O_2$
   f. Ammonia is produced commercially from nitrogen and hydrogen.
   $$N_2\ (g) + H_2\ (g) \xrightarrow[\text{high pressure}]{\Delta,\ Fe} NH_3\ (g)$$
   g. Ammonium chloride is produced when ammonia and hydrogen chloride vapors mix.
   $$NH_3\ (g) + HCl\ (g) \longrightarrow NH_4Cl\ (s)$$
   h. Carbon black is used in rubber tires and black ink. It is produced by the "cracking" of methane.
   $$CH_4\ (g) \xrightarrow{\Delta} C\ (s) + H_2\ (g)$$
   i. High-purity silicon is used to produce microcomputer chips. One process for producing chip-grade silicon entails three steps. The first step is to obtain impure silicon from molten sand (SiO_2).
   $$SiO_2\ (l) + C\ (s) \longrightarrow Si\ (l) + CO\ (g)$$

j. The second step in the production of pure silicon is to produce silicon tetrachloride from the impure silicon.

$$Si\ (s) + Cl_2\ (g) \xrightarrow{\Delta} SiCl_4\ (l)$$

k. The last step is to pass hot silicon tetrachloride vapor and hydrogen gas through a tube. Pure silicon condenses.

$$SiCl_4\ (g) + H_2\ (g) \xrightarrow{\Delta} Si\ (s) + HCl\ (g)$$

l. Ingested barium sulfate causes the intestinal tract to be emphasized in x-ray pictures. It may be produced when barium reacts with sulfuric acid.

$$Ba\ (s) + H_2SO_4\ (aq) \longrightarrow BaSO_4\ (s) + H_2\ (g)$$

m. Milk of magnesia is an aqueous solution of $Mg(OH)_2$. When ingested, it reduces the amount of hydrochloric acid in the stomach by neutralizing this acid.

$$Mg(OH)_2\ (aq) + HCl\ (aq) \longrightarrow MgCl_2\ (aq) + H_2O\ (l)$$

6. Tell whether each of the reactions in the previous question is a composition, decomposition, single replacement, or double replacement reaction.

7. Predict whether the following single replacement reactions will occur. Base your answers on the activity series given in the text.

a. $BaSO_4 + Ca \longrightarrow CaSO_4 + Ba$
b. $BaCl_2 + Br_2 \longrightarrow BaBr_2 + Cl_2$
c. $Ni(OH)_2 + Mg \longrightarrow Mg(OH)_2 + Ni$
d. $2\ FeCl_3 + 3\ Mg \longrightarrow 3\ MgCl_2 + 2\ Fe$
e. $Al_2(SO_4)_3 + 2\ Fe \longrightarrow Fe_2(SO_4)_3 + 2\ Al$
f. $Ni + 2\ H_2O \longrightarrow Ni(OH)_2 + H_2$ (at room temperature)

8. Complete ionic equations for double replacement reactions are given below. For each equation, identify the spectator ions and write the net ionic equation.

a. Balanced equation:

$$AgNO_3\ (aq) + HCl\ (aq) \longrightarrow AgCl\ (s) + HNO_3\ (aq)$$

Complete ionic equation:

$$Ag^+ + NO_3^- + H^+ + Cl^- \longrightarrow AgCl\ (s) + H^+ + NO_3^-$$

b. Balanced equation:

$$CaCl_2\ (aq) + Na_2CO_3\ (aq) \longrightarrow CaCO_3\ (s) + 2\ NaCl\ (aq)$$

Complete ionic equation:

$$Ca^{2+} + 2\ Cl^- + 2\ Na^+ + CO_3^{2-} \longrightarrow CaCO_3\ (s) + 2\ Na^+ + 2\ Cl^-$$

c. Balanced equation:

$$H_2SO_4\ (aq) + 2\ KOH\ (aq) \longrightarrow K_2SO_4\ (aq) + 2\ H_2O\ (l)$$

Complete ionic equation:

$$2\ H^+ + SO_4^{2-} + 2\ K^+ + 2\ OH^- \longrightarrow 2\ K^+ + SO_4^{2-} + 2\ H_2O\ (l)$$

d. Balanced equation:
$Mg(OH)_2\ (s) + 2\ HCl\ (aq) \longrightarrow MgCl_2\ (aq) + 2\ H_2O\ (l)$
Complete ionic equation:
$Mg(OH)_2\ (s) + 2\ H^+ + 2\ Cl^- \longrightarrow$
$Mg^{2+} + 2\ Cl^- + 2\ H_2O\ (l)$

e. Balanced equation:
$Ba(NO_2)_2\ (aq) + Na_2SO_4\ (aq) \longrightarrow$
$BaSO_4\ (s) + 2\ NaNO_2\ (aq)$

Complete ionic equation:
$Ba^{2+} + 2\ NO_2^- + 2\ Na^+ + SO_4^{2-} \longrightarrow$
$BaSO_4\ (s) + 2\ Na^+ + 2\ NO_2^-$

9. Priestley discovered oxygen when he decomposed mercury(II) oxide into oxygen and mercury.

$$2\ HgO\ (s) \xrightarrow{\Delta} 2\ Hg\ (l) + O_2\ (g)$$

a. If 0.440 mole of HgO reacts, how many moles of O_2 will be produced?
b. If 0.580 mole of Hg is produced, how many moles of O_2 are produced?
c. How many grams of HgO must react to produce 3.75 moles of O_2?
d. How many grams of Hg are produced when 14.7 g of HgO react?
e. How many grams of O_2 are produced when 6.20 g of HgO react?
f. How many grams of HgO must react to produce 2.30 g of Hg?

10. Natural gas consists primarily of methane (CH_4). When natural gas burns in a gas-burning appliance, methane reacts with oxygen to produce carbon dioxide and water.

$$CH_4 + 2\ O_2 \longrightarrow 2\ H_2O + CO_2$$

a. How many moles of CH_4 must react to produce 13.7 moles of H_2O?
b. How many moles of CO_2 will be produced by the reaction of 8.31 moles of O_2?
c. What mass of CH_4 must react to produce 4.00 moles of H_2O?
d. How many grams of CO_2 are produced when 6.00 moles of CH_4 react?
e. How many grams of O_2 will be consumed by the combustion of 2.18 g of CH_4?
f. How many grams of water are produced by the reaction of 139 g of CH_4?

11. Without fertilizers farmers could not give their crops enough nitrogen. Urea (NH_2CONH_2) is used as a common nitrogen

fertilizer. Urea may be produced from ammonia and carbon dioxide.

$$2\ NH_3 + CO_2 \xrightarrow[\text{pressure}]{\Delta} NH_2CONH_2 + H_2O$$

a. How many moles of NH_2CONH_2 are produced when 35.0 moles of CO_2 react?
b. How many moles of NH_3 must react to produce 75.0 moles of H_2O?
c. How many grams of CO_2 will react with 5.75 moles of NH_3?
d. How many moles of NH_2CONH_2 are produced by the reaction of 287 g of CO_2?
e. How many moles of NH_2CONH_2 are produced by the reaction of 603 g of NH_3?
f. How many grams of CO_2 must react to produce 454 g of NH_2CONH_2?

12. Bleach is an aqueous solution of sodium hypochlorite. A bleach solution may be prepared when chlorine gas is bubbled through aqueous sodium hydroxide.

$$2\ NaOH\ (aq) + Cl_2\ (g) \longrightarrow NaCl\ (aq) + NaOCl\ (aq) + H_2O\ (l)$$

a. How many moles of NaOCl will be produced from 5.73 moles of Cl_2?
b. How many moles of NaOH must react to produce 13.7 moles of NaCl?
c. How many grams of H_2O will be produced if 0.750 mole of NaOH react?
d. How many grams of Cl_2 must react to produce 6.70 moles of NaCl?
e. What mass of NaOCl will be produced when 65.5 g of NaOH react?
f. How many grams of NaOH will react with 37.5 g of Cl_2?

13. Hematite, Fe_2O_3, is converted to molten iron in blast furnaces and is then poured into molds.

$$Fe_2O_3\ (s) + 3\ CO\ (g) \longrightarrow 2\ Fe\ (l) + 3\ CO_2\ (g)$$

a. How many moles of Fe_2O_3 must react to produce 262 moles of Fe?
b. How many moles of CO_2 are produced by the reaction of 64.0 moles CO?
c. How many moles of Fe_2O_3 must react to produce 760 kg of Fe?
d. How many grams of CO_2 will be produced when 40.0 moles of CO react?
e. What mass (in kg) of Fe is produced when 299 kg of Fe_2O_3 react?

EIGHT

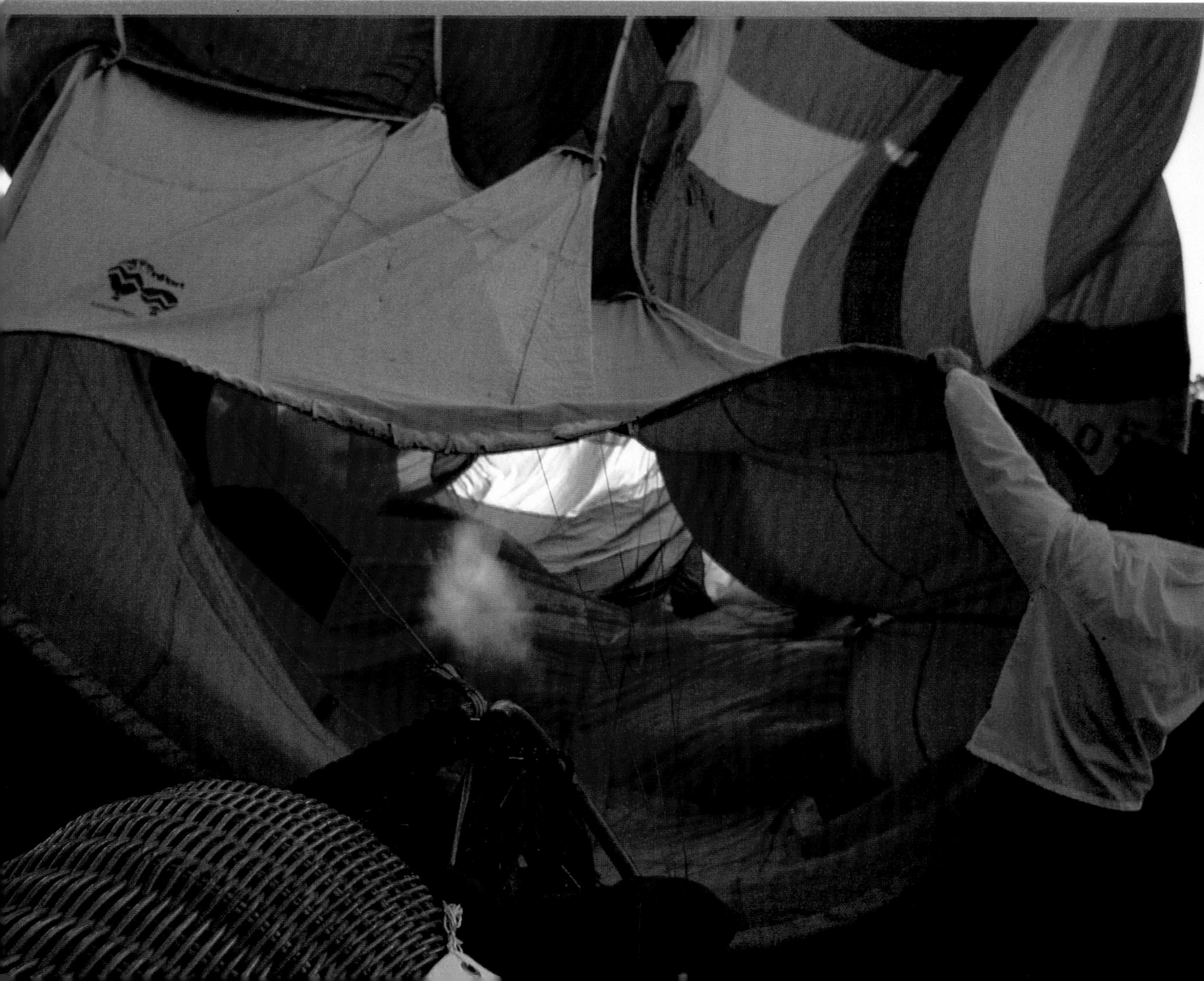

10 T/F
11 mult. choice
7 matching (formulas)
7 problems (2 extra credit)

GASES

MOLECULES ON THE MOVE

THE word *gas* comes from the Greek word *khaos,* meaning "formless matter." Of the three common states of matter, gas particles are the most chaotic. Unlike solids, whose particles are held firmly in place, or liquids, whose particles are in constant contact with each other, gas particles move freely.

The Nature of Gases: My, What Energetic Particles You Have!

8–1 Kinetic Description of Gases

The kinetic theory explains the behavior of matter on the basis of particle motion. According to the kinetic theory,

1. "Gases consist of a vast number of independent particles." These particles have unique sizes and masses.
2. "The particles move at random, with high velocities." The particles move in all directions at many different speeds. At 0°C many hydrogen gas molecules move at speeds of 1500 meters per second. Some move slower, and a few move at speeds near 4000 meters per second. Collisions constantly change the speeds and directions of the molecules.
3. "The particles are separated by great distances." The average distance that oxygen gas molecules travel between collisions

in air at 0°C is 7×10^{-6} centimeters. This distance is great compared to the minute size of the molecules.

4. "Particles do not interact except during momentary collisions." Any gravitational, electrical, or chemical forces between the molecules can be neglected because the particles come near each other only during momentary collisions. It is also important to note that many collisions occur every second. Air molecules at 0°C undergo 5×10^9 collisions every second.
5. "Collisions are elastic." That is, they conserve energy. Two particles leave an impact with the sum of their energies unchanged.

The kinetic theory serves as a remarkably successful basis for explaining the properties of gases.

8–2 The Physical Properties of Gases

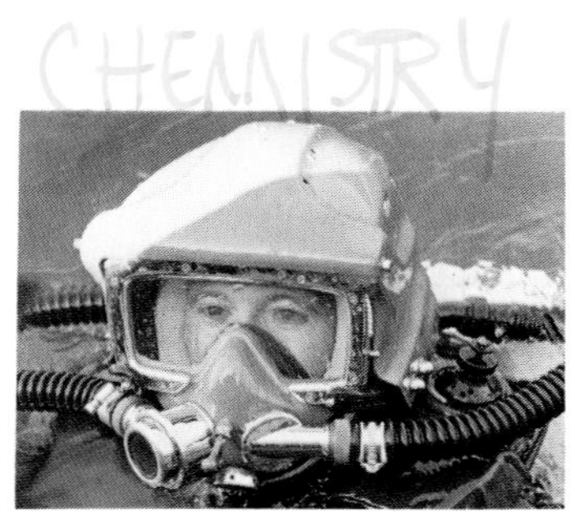

8-1 A demand regulator feeds compressed air to a diver in a self-contained underwater breathing apparatus (scuba).

Low Density. Compared to solids and liquids, gases have hardly any mass per unit of volume. While ice at -25°C has a density of 0.917 gram per milliliter, and liquid water at 25°C has a density of 0.9971 gram per milliliter, steam at 125°C has a density of only 0.000561 gram per milliliter. At 25°C air has a density of 0.001185 gram per milliliter. Some gases, such as hydrogen and helium, have even lower densities. This property is not surprising, since gases have much empty space between their molecules.

Diffusibility and Permeability. When a gas enters a vacuum or another gas, it spreads out to fill the entire volume with an even concentration. This action is called **diffusion.** Diffusion occurs because the gas molecules are in constant motion. **Permeability,** the ability of a gas to mingle with another porous substance, occurs because the constantly moving particles move into the spaces between other molecules.

Compressibility and Expansibility. Whereas liquids do not easily compress, the volumes of gases have the ability to change to fit their containers. High pressures can squeeze gases into smaller volumes. This property is called **compressibility.** When gases encounter a region of low pressure, they quickly expand to fill the available space. This property is called **expansibility.** Gases can expand without limit, and they always fill their containers. The empty spaces between molecules and the constant motion of the molecules make these properties possible.

8–3 How Gases Cause Pressure

Gas molecules can collide with each other billions of times each second. They can also bang into trees, buildings, people, and the walls of their containers. Although individual collisions are not very forceful, they add up to produce a significant force. **Pressure** is the average force exerted per unit area when molecules collide with a boundary. It is the observable result of molecular collisions.

Pressure is measured in units of force per unit area. Normal atmospheric pressure at sea level is 14.7 pounds per square inch. When atmospheric pressure is measured with a **barometer,** another unit of pressure can also be used. Mercury barometers allow air pressure to support a column of mercury. As pressure increases, the column of mercury rises. The pressure and the length of the column can be expressed in **millimeters of mercury.** For example, normal atmospheric pressure at sea level can support a column of mercury 760 millimeters high. This pressure is expressed as 760 millimeters of mercury (760 mm Hg). Another name for a millimeter of mercury is a *torr,* named after Evangelista Torricelli, the inventor of the barometer.

Another measure of pressure that is sometimes used in chemistry is the **atmosphere.** One atmosphere (atm) is simply the normal atmospheric pressure at sea level at 45° latitude. Two atmospheres are double the normal pressure at sea level, and 1/2 atmosphere is half the normal pressure.

$$1 \text{ atm} = 760 \text{ mm Hg} = 760 \text{ torr} = 14.7 \text{ lb./in.}^2$$

The facts above justify the following unit-analysis conversion factors and their reciprocals.

$$\frac{1 \text{ atm}}{760 \text{ mm Hg}} \qquad \frac{1 \text{ atm}}{14.7 \text{ lb./in.}^2} \qquad \frac{760 \text{ mm Hg}}{14.7 \text{ lb./in.}^2}$$

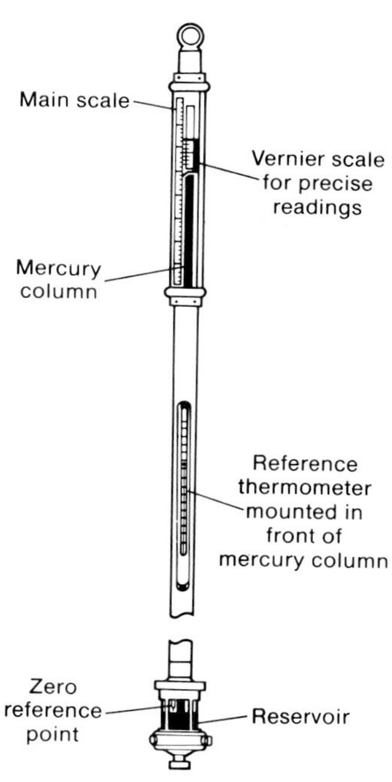

8-2 Mercury barometer.

Sample Problem. Express a pressure of 1.20 atmospheres in millimeters of mercury.

Solution.

Since 1 atmosphere of pressure equals 760 millimeters of mercury, the appropriate conversion factor is 760 mm Hg/1 atm.

$$1.20 \text{ atm} \times \frac{760 \text{ mm Hg}}{1 \text{ atm}} = 912 \text{ mm Hg}$$

8–4 Pressure, Volume, and Temperature: One Good Change Deserves Another

The volume of a gas depends not only on the number of gas molecules but also on the temperature and pressure of the gas. A gas at a given temperature contains molecules moving at many different speeds. The average kinetic energy of the molecules determines the temperature of the gas.

At 0° C many hydrogen molecules move at velocities near 1500 meters per second. Some move slower; some move faster. The average velocity of 1500 meters per second causes the temperature to be 0° C. At 500° C many hydrogen molecules move faster. The average velocity is thus greater.

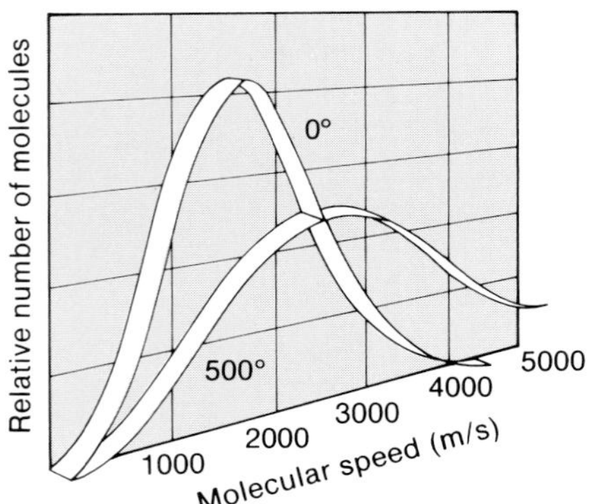

8-3 A frequency distribution of hydrogen molecules at two different temperatures.

This graph describes how gas molecules behave at different temperatures. At higher temperatures gas molecules have a higher average kinetic energy. The molecules move faster, collide more often, and strike with more force. The pressure is bound to increase because of the additional, more forceful collisions. If the gas is confined to a fixed volume, the pressure will increase as the temperature increases.

When external forces act upon a gas, they oppose the effect of all the submicroscopic collisions. When external forces exceed the internal pressure of a gas, they squeeze the gas into a smaller space. Volume therefore decreases when pressure increases. If the external pressure decreases, the volume has the chance to increase. A brief chart summarizes the effects of pressure, temperature, and volume on gases.

Table 8-4

Pressure	Temperature	Volume
1. increase	increase	constant
2. increase	constant	decrease
3. constant	increase	increase

Case 1—A direct relationship. When volume is constant and temperature increases, the pressure also increases.

Case 2—An inverse relationship. When temperature is constant and pressure increases, the volume decreases.

Case 3—A direct relationship. When pressure is constant and temperature increases, the volume also increases.

The Scriptures identify several direct and inverse relationships that affect the lives of Christians. Matthew 24:12 tells of an *inverse* relationship between iniquity and love for God: "And because iniquity shall abound, the love of many shall wax cold." As iniquity increases, the love for God decreases. On the other hand, an increased love for God causes a decrease in iniquity. Luke 12:48 informs us about a *direct* relationship between spiritual knowledge and responsibility: "For unto whomsoever much is given, of him shall be much required: and to whom men have committed much, of him they will ask the more." Advantages such as a good family, a sharp mind, and an early salvation increase a person's responsibility toward God.

Gas Laws: Mathematical Descriptions of Physical Properties

So far the behavior of gases has been described qualitatively—that is, without numbers. However, a series of gas laws, each based on the qualitative kinetic theory, can make these descriptions quantitative. These gas laws make it possible to calculate volumes, pressures, and temperatures of gases at various conditions.

8–5 Standard Conditions: A Reference Point

Because the volume of a gas can change with temperature and pressure, reporting a volume without specifying these conditions would be meaningless. Scientists have defined a standard set of conditions called **standard temperature and pressure** to be used when measuring and comparing gases. Standard temperature is 0° C or 273 K. Standard pressure is 760 millimeters of mercury or 1 atmosphere. The conditions of standard temperature and pressure are often abbreviated *STP.*

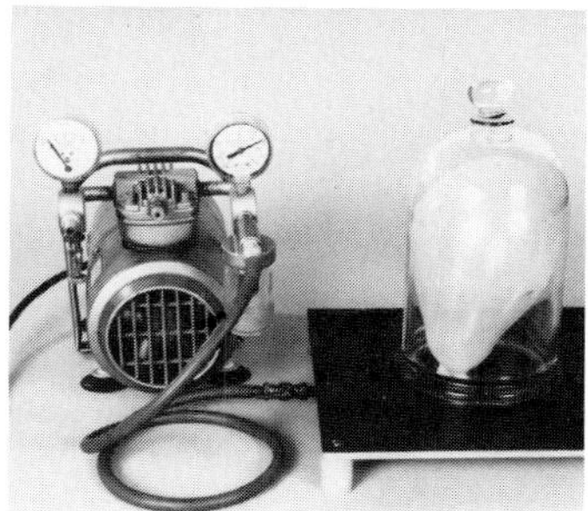

8-5 A balloon under atmospheric pressure **(top)** and in a vacuum **(bottom).**

8–6 Boyle's Law: Pressures and Volumes

Robert Boyle (1627-1691) was the first to measure the effects of pressure on the volume of a gas. He found that increased pressure decreased the volume and that decreased pressure allowed the volume to increase. He also found the mathematical relationship that governed the changes.

Twice the pressure yields half the volume.
Three times the pressure yields one-third the volume.
Half the pressure yields twice the volume.
One-third the pressure yields three times the volume.

Gases: Good and Bad

This world is filled with many kinds of gases. Some of these gases are harmful if breathed, while others are not. For the most part, molecules in harmless gases have strong, stable bonds. In some cases the gases consist of atoms that do not participate in any reactions. When these gases are breathed, no harmful reactions occur.

Gases We Can Breathe

Nitrogen, N_2. This colorless, odorless, tasteless, and relatively inactive gas makes up 78 per cent (by volume) of the lower atmosphere. The gas is slightly lighter than air, and the molecules are extremely stable.

Oxygen, O_2. The active gas in our atmosphere is colorless, odorless, and tasteless. Oxygen makes up 21 per cent of the volume of the lower atmosphere. It is slightly heavier than air. While animals take in a constant supply of oxygen during respiration, plants give off the gas during photosynthesis.

Argon, Ar. The third most abundant component of the earth's atmosphere (1%) is a colorless, odorless, tasteless noble gas. Industries make use of its chemical inactivity. It is used along with nitrogen in light bulbs and radio tubes to protect the filaments. When welding aluminum and stainless steel, arc welders use argon to momentarily shield the molten metals from the atmosphere.

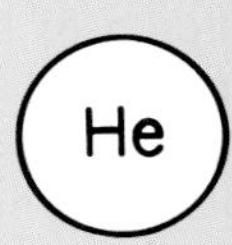

Helium, He. This noble gas is present in the earth but not in the atmosphere. It floats out into space shortly after it escapes from underground deposits or is produced by radioactive processes. Natural gas deposits serve as the primary source of the odorless, tasteless gas. Helium is chemically inert, has an extremely low density, and has the lowest condensation point of all the gases.

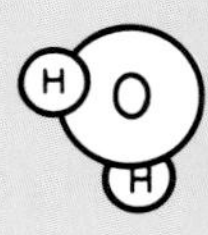

Water vapor, H_2O. Normally a liquid, water molecules are a vital part of the air that is breathed. Without some humidity, throat and lung tissues would dry out. As a drawback, water vapor contributes to the rusting of iron and the corrosion of many other metals.

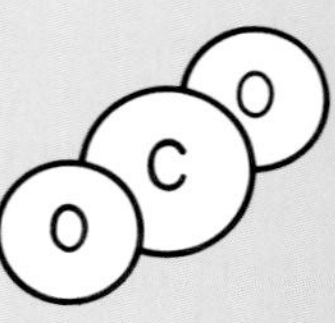

Carbon dioxide, CO_2. This colorless gas has a faint, pungent odor and a slightly sour taste. Plants get the carbon atoms they need from atmospheric CO_2. The burning of fuels, whether in biological respiration or in a car's engine, produces CO_2. The gas is thought to be responsible for keeping solar heat energy from escaping back into space. Some scientists have speculated that recent increases in CO_2 concentrations due to more and more fuels being burned may cause the earth's temperatures to rise in a so-called "greenhouse effect." One-and-one-half times as heavy as air, the gas sinks to a tabletop or floor whenever it is released. It is used to extinguish fires and to make carbonated beverages.

Nitrous oxide (laughing gas), N_2O. The discovery of nitrous oxide and its effects on the

human body marked a great step forward in surgical practice. This colorless gas with a somewhat sweet odor and taste induces mild hysteria and an insensitivity to pain. Widely used as an anesthetic when it was first introduced, it now is used only for short operations and in combination with other gases. Long exposures to N_2O can result in death.

As a rule of thumb, gases that are chemically reactive should not be breathed. Some should not even be touched. Although some of these gases do not cause harmful reactions, they have such irritating odors that it is wise to avoid them.

Gases We Should Not Breathe

Chlorine, Cl_2. Like most harmful gases, chlorine gas is very reactive. This heavy yellowish green gas has a disagreeable, suffocating odor. Chlorine has the dubious distinction of being one of the first poison gases to be used in warfare. Fortunately, the gas can be smelled and detected at levels far below its lethal concentration.

Hydrogen sulfide, H_2S. The decay of organic matter that contains sulfur invariably produces one of the most foul stenches known to man: hydrogen sulfide. This colorless, heavy gas has the odor of rotten eggs. Large amounts of it are produced as refineries remove sulfur-containing impurities from petroleum.

Hydrogen cyanide, HCN. Gas chambers for administering capital punishment use hydrogen cyanide. A dose of 0.05 gram or 200 to 500 parts per million quickly paralyzes the central nervous system. A fatal dose of hydrogen cyanide inhibits respiration by tying up the iron in important enzymes. An odor like that of bitter almonds is characteristic of this gas.

Sulfur dioxide, SO_2. Burning sulfur gives off a heavy, colorless gas having the odor of a freshly struck match. This gas readily dissolves in water to form sulfurous acid, H_2SO_3. Sulfur dioxide is extremely irritating to the nose and throat. Manufacturers use it to bleach straw, paper, silk, and wood.

Carbon monoxide, CO. The incomplete combustion of fuels produces a colorless, odorless, tasteless gas that is extremely dangerous to humans. If carbon monoxide is breathed, it will quickly bind to hemoglobin in the blood and prevent the hemoglobin from carrying oxygen. Many tragic deaths have occurred because concentrations of carbon monoxide built up in garages, cars, and trains.

Chloroacetophenone (tear gas), C_8H_7OCl. Police use tear gas to disperse riots and to flush criminals out of buildings. Although the gas has an odor resembling that of apple blossoms, most people who have smelled it remember the strong irritation to their eyes. Exposure brings tears, eye irritation, and uncontrollable coughing.

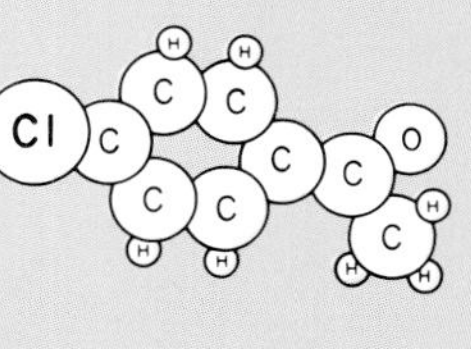

Sarin (nerve gas), $C_4H_{10}O_2FP$. A 1-milligram dose of this poisonous gas paralyzes an entire nervous system in minutes. The gas can be neutralized with applications of water and basic solutions.

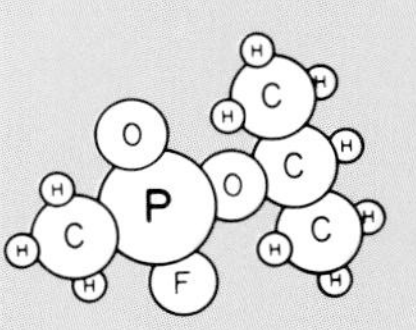

From data such as this, he formulated **Boyle's law:** *The volume of a dry gas is inversely related to the pressure if the temperature is held constant.* Put into an equation, this law appears as

$$\text{Pressure} \times \text{Volume} = k \text{ (a constant value)}$$

The product of pressure and volume remains the same, even at different conditions. The equations listed below are forms of Boyle's law and can be used to solve problems concerning changing pressures and volumes.

$$P_1V_1 = k = P_2V_2$$

$$P_1V_1 = P_2V_2$$ Common form of Boyle's law

8-6

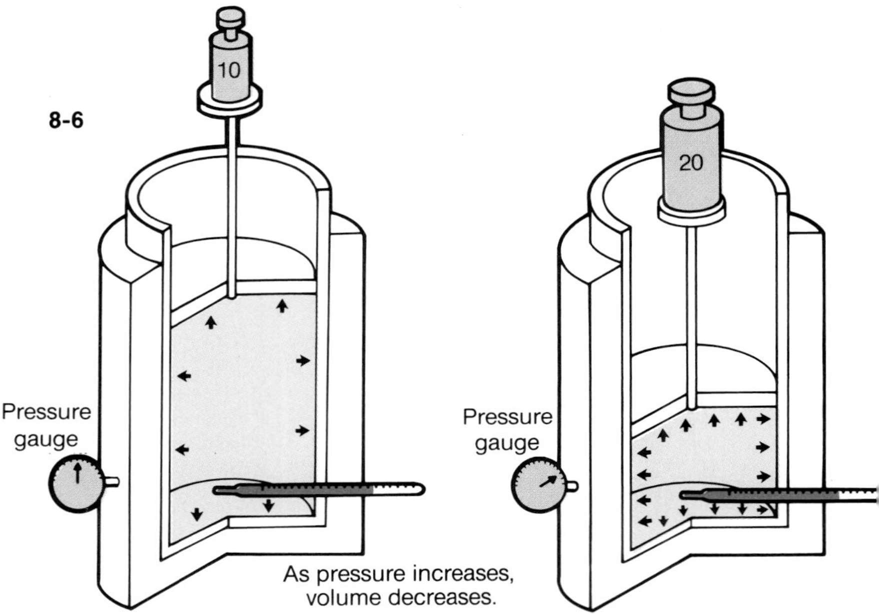

As pressure increases, volume decreases.

Sample Problem. A sample of gas occupies 450 milliliters when it is under a pressure of 780 millimeters of mercury. What volume will it occupy if the pressure is increased to 850 millimeters of mercury?

Solution.

The question asks for the volume at the second set of conditions (V_2). Only one step is necessary to rearrange the common form of Boyle's law into an equation that yields the volume at the new pressure.

$$P_2V_2 = P_1V_1$$

$$V_2 = \frac{P_1V_1}{P_2}$$

The variables P_1 and V_1 correspond to the first set of conditions (780 mm Hg and 450 ml). P_2 is the pressure at the second set of conditions.

$$V_2 = \frac{(780 \text{ mm Hg})(450 \text{ ml})}{850 \text{ mm Hg}}$$

$$V_2 = 413 \text{ ml}$$

As expected, the increased pressure caused the volume to decrease.

8–7 Charles's Law: Temperatures and Volumes

Charles's law deals with the relationship between a gas's temperature and its volume. Careful measurements of the volume of a gas at different temperatures and constant pressures could yield the following data:

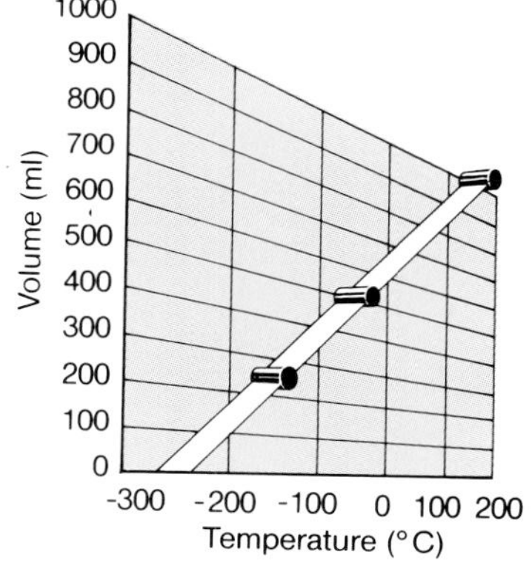

Table 8-7

Temperature	Volume
127°C	1000 ml
-73°C	500 ml
-173°C	250 ml

Volumes keep shrinking as temperatures decrease. The graph shows that the volume would theoretically become zero at a temperature of -273°C. This extrapolation of gas volumes led to the invention of the Kelvin temperature scale. On this scale the lowest temperature that is theoretically possible (-273°C) is labeled 0 K. The two scales are related by the formula K = °C + 273°.

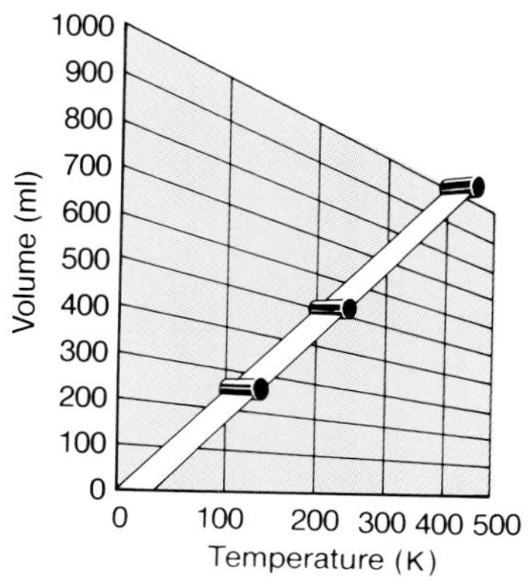

Table 8-8

Temperature	Temperature	Volume
127°C	400 K	1000 ml
-73°C	200 K	500 ml
-173°C	100 K	250 ml

When the Kelvin temperature scale is used, the relationship between temperature and volume can be easily seen. Doubling the temperature from 100 K to 200 K doubles the volume from 250 milliliters to 500 milliliters. When the temperature is doubled again to 400 K, the volume doubles again to 1000 milliliters. Charles's law states that when the pressure on a sample of a dry gas is held constant, the Kelvin temperature and the volume are directly related. Mathematically, this law is stated as

$$\frac{V}{T} = k$$

If the temperature increases, the volume must also increase to keep the constant the same. No matter what changes occur, the ratio between volume and temperature (in the Kelvin scale) will be the same for a given sample of gas at a constant pressure.

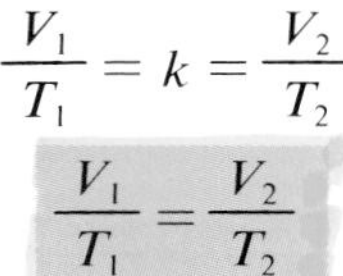

$$\frac{V_1}{T_1} = k = \frac{V_2}{T_2}$$

$$\frac{V_1}{T_1} = \frac{V_2}{T_2}$$

Common form of Charles's law

8-9

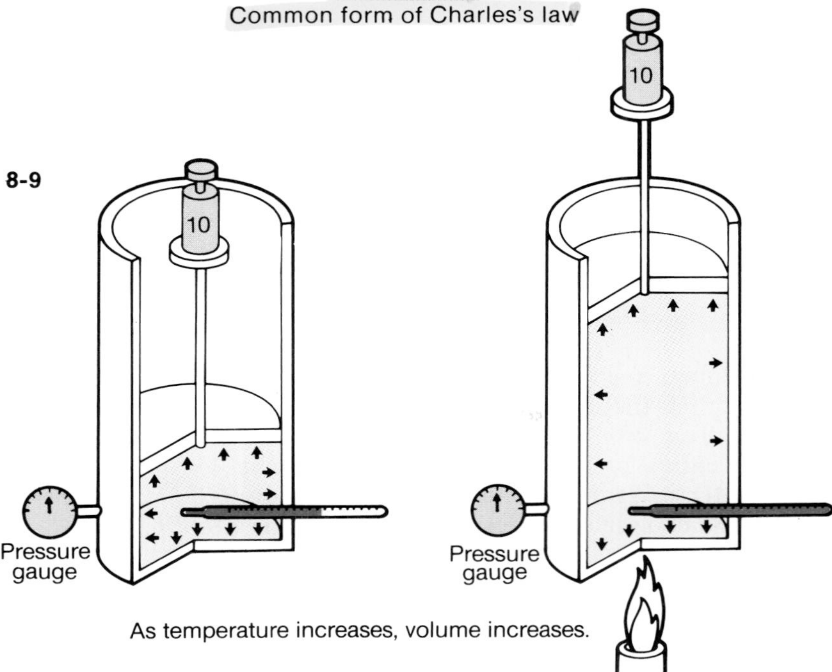

As temperature increases, volume increases.

Sample Problem. A sample of gas occupies 430 milliliters when it is at a temperature of 25° C. What volume will it occupy when it is at standard temperature?

Solution.

Remember that the direct relationship between temperature and volume holds true only when temperature is expressed in the Kelvin scale. All temperatures must be converted to the Kelvin scale.

Set up the equation.

$$\frac{V_2}{T_2} = \frac{V_1}{T_1}$$

$$V_2 = \frac{V_1 T_2}{T_1}$$

Identify the variables.

$V_1 = 430$ ml
$T_1 = 25°C$; $25°C + 273° = 298$ K
$V_2 = ?$
$T_2 =$ standard temperature $= 273$ K

Plug the values in, and solve for the new volume.

$$V_2 = \frac{(430 \text{ ml})(273 \text{ K})}{298 \text{ K}}$$

$$V_2 = 394 \text{ ml}$$

8-10 As Charles's law predicts, the volume of a balloon increases when the balloon is immersed in hot water.

8–8 Gay-Lussac's Law: Temperatures and Pressures

The pressure in a car's tires increases as the tires heat up on a lengthy trip. A basketball loses its "bounce" when it is taken outside on a cold winter day. Both of these changes are examples of **Gay-Lussac's law:** *pressure is directly proportional to Kelvin temperature for a fixed mass of gas held in a constant volume.*

In the first case above, friction with the road raised the temperature of the air in the tires. The gas molecules moved faster, collided more often, and transferred more force to the inner walls of the tires. As a result, pressure increased. In the case of the basketball, the molecules moved more slowly at colder temperatures. The air pressure in the ball decreased accordingly.

The mathematical expression of Gay-Lussac's law is

$$\frac{P}{T} = k$$

As long as the volume is held constant, this equality holds true for many different pressures and temperatures.

$$\frac{P_1}{T_1} = k = \frac{P_2}{T_2}$$

$$\frac{P_1}{T_1} = \frac{P_2}{T_2}$$

Common form of Gay-Lussac's law

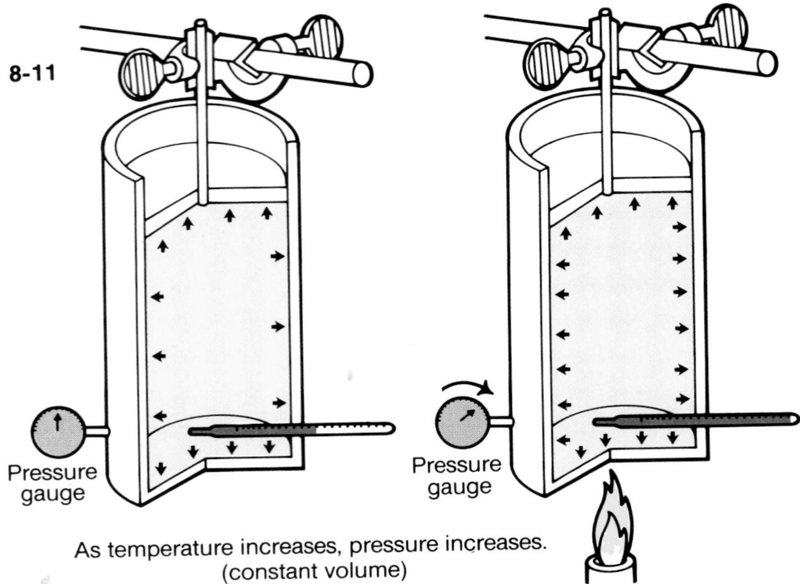

As temperature increases, pressure increases. (constant volume)

Sample Problem. Before Molly Kuhl began a car trip, she measured the air pressure in her car tires and found that it was 32 pounds per square inch at a temperature of 18° C. After two hours of driving, she found that the pressure had increased to 34 pounds per square inch. What was the new temperature of the air in her tires?

Solution.

First set up the equation.

$$\frac{P_1}{T_1} = \frac{P_2}{T_2}$$

$$\frac{1}{T_2} = \frac{P_1}{T_1 P_2}$$

$$T_2 = \frac{T_1 P_2}{P_1}$$

Identify the variables.

$P_1 = 32 \text{ lb./in.}^2$
$T_1 = 18°\text{C}; 18°\text{C} + 273° = 291 \text{ K}$
$P_2 = 34 \text{ lb./in.}^2$
$T_2 = ?$

Plug the values in, and solve for T_2.

$$T_2 = \frac{(291 \text{ K})(34 \text{ lb./in.}^2)}{32 \text{ lb./in.}^2}$$

$$T_2 = 309 \text{ K (or } 36°\text{C)}$$

8–9 Combined Gas Laws: Putting It All Together

The gas laws that have been discussed so far have applied to situations in which one quantity stayed the same.

Boyle's law: $PV = k$, where T is constant.

Charles's law: $V/T = k$, where P is constant.

Gay-Lussac's law: $P/T = k$, where V is constant.

When properly combined, the gas laws form a single equation called the **combined gas law.**

$$\frac{P_1 V_1}{T_1} = \frac{P_2 V_2}{T_2}$$

This equation contains the original three equations. If the temperature is held constant ($T_1 = T_2$), the equation becomes Boyle's law. T_1 and T_2 cancel. If the pressure does not change ($P_1 = P_2$), the two pressures cancel each other algebraically, and Charles's law emerges. When the volume does not change ($V_1 = V_2$), Gay-Lussac's law can be seen. The advantage of the combined gas law is that it allows problems in which pressure, volume, and temperature change to be solved in a single step.

Sample Problem. A gas has a volume of 3.6 liters when it is under a pressure of 1.05 atmospheres and a temperature of -15°C. What will its volume be at STP?

Solution.

First set up the equation.

$$\frac{P_1 V_1}{T_1} = \frac{P_2 V_2}{T_2}$$

$$V_2 = \frac{P_1 V_1 T_2}{T_1 P_2}$$

Identify the variables.

$P_1 = 1.05$ atm
$V_1 = 3.6\ \ell$
$T_1 = -15°\text{C} = 258$ K
$P_2 =$ standard pressure $= 1$ atm
$V_2 = ?$
$T_2 =$ standard temperature $= 273$ K

Solve for V_2.

$$V_2 = \frac{(1.05\ \text{atm})(3.6\ \ell)(273\ \text{K})}{(258\ \text{K})(1\ \text{atm})}$$

$$V_2 = 4.0\ \ell$$

The answer makes sense; both changes should increase the volume.

Pay careful attention to the units on pressure, volume, and temperature when solving gas-law problems. The sample problem above demonstrates how the units on pressure and temperature cancel out. The only unit that is left is liters. Simple checks like this can show whether the equation is set up properly.

8–10 Dalton's Law of Partial Pressures: Mixtures of Gases

The gases in this world are often mixtures. Even the gases that chemists produce in their laboratories contain some impurities. These mixtures complicate gas-law calculations. John Dalton's law of partial pressures describes the behavior of gaseous mixtures.

Suppose that 1 liter of oxygen at STP is added to 1 liter of nitrogen gas at the same pressure. If the two gases are held in a 1-liter jar, the pressure will be 1520 millimeters of mercury—the sum of the two pressures. When molecules of gases do not react with each other, they can behave independently of each other. Thus oxygen molecules exert a pressure of 760 millimeters of mercury just as they did before they were mixed with the nitrogen gas. The nitrogen gas exerts the same pressure, so the total pressure from the two gases is 1520 millimeters of mercury. Dalton's **law of partial pressures** puts these observations into general terms. *The total pressure of a mixture of gases equals the sum of the partial pressures.*

A sample of dry air contains 78 per cent nitrogen, 21 per cent oxygen, and 1 per cent argon. If the mixture exerts a pressure of 760 millimeters of mercury, 78 per cent of the pressure (592.8 mm Hg) comes from nitrogen. Twenty-one per cent of the pressure (159.6 mm Hg) is from oxygen, and 1 per cent of the pressure (7.6 mm Hg) is from argon. The sum of all the partial pressures equals the total pressure of the mixture.

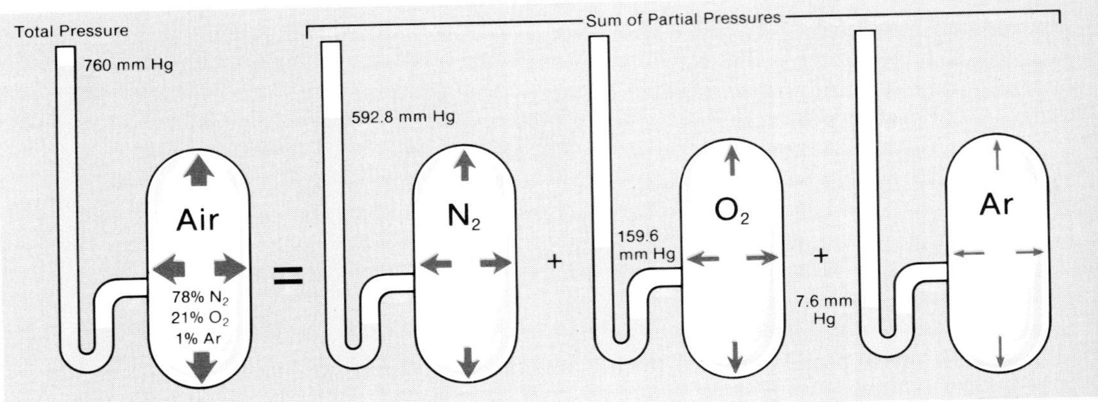

8-12 Air pressure consists of pressure from nitrogen, oxygen, and argon gases.

FACETS OF CHEMISTRY

The Earth Has an Air About It

Suppose that NASA was constructing a domed city on the moon and that you were the engineer responsible for setting up the city's atmosphere. What gases would you include? How much of each would you use? Would you try to improve on the earth's formula? Or would you merely transport liquid air from the earth to the moon and then allow it to vaporize in the enclosed dome?

To begin your work, you might compare the earth's atmosphere with the atmospheres of other planets. You would soon find that no other planet contains the same combination of nitrogen, oxygen, and argon that the earth does. In fact, molecular oxygen that is breathed on the earth is rare in the universe. Venus, the earth's closest neighbor, is surrounded by an envelope of carbon dioxide and nitrogen. Mars, the next closest neighbor, has an atmosphere of carbon dioxide, nitrogen, and argon. The atmospheres of Jupiter and Saturn include the noxious gases methane and ammonia, while those of Uranus and Neptune contain an unsavory mixture of methane and hydrogen. Mercury and Pluto have essentially no atmospheres at all. The earth's oxygen, so far as man can observe, is unique.

The earth's atmosphere contains not only the right gases but also the right concentration of each gas. Oxygen is the active ingredient in the earth's atmosphere. It makes up about 21 per cent of the air's total volume. Nitrogen (78%) and argon (1%) are the inert ingredients in the earth's atmosphere. The presence of nitrogen and argon helps keep the proper concentration of oxygen in the air.

This special balance in the earth's atmosphere is no accident. It is the work of the divine Creator. If the percentage of oxygen in the air ever changed, there would be serious biological consequences. For example, breathing pure oxygen may help some people temporarily, but it is harmful over long periods of time. Symptoms of drunkenness, damage to the eyes, and severe lung damage would follow. The centers of the human brain that regulate breathing would become impaired because they respond to the levels of oxygen and carbon dioxide in the blood. Lower levels of oxygen would cause increased fatigue and shortness of breath, while extremely low levels of oxygen would lead to suffocation. With every breath men take, they should appreciate God's goodness and the provisions He has given.

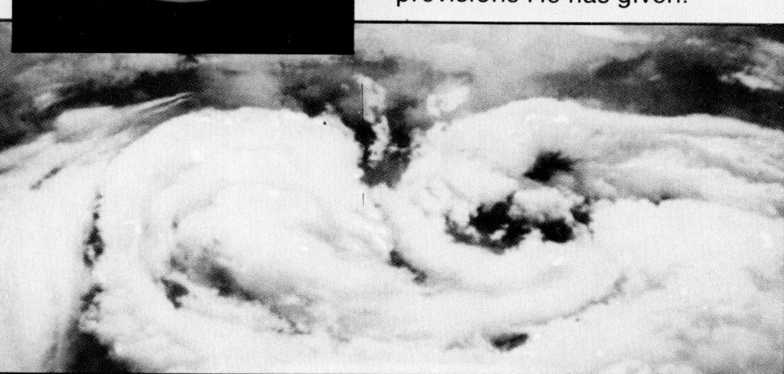

In the laboratory, chemists often collect a sample of a gas by trapping it at the top of a water-filled container. The gas bubbles up through the water, collects at the top, and forces the water out the bottom. This technique is called collecting a gas over water, or collection by water displacement.

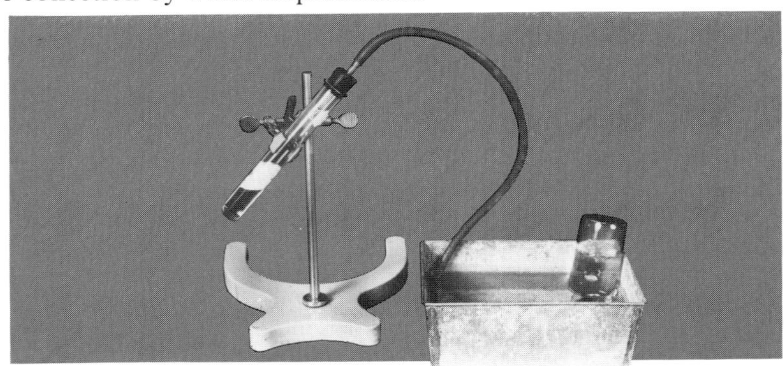

8-13 Collection of a gas over water. Gas from the reaction in the test tube escapes through the tubing and replaces the water in the bottle.

A gas being collected over water may be pure initially, but that quickly changes. As the gas bubbles through the water, some water evaporates and mixes with the gas being collected. Accurate measurements of the gas cannot be made when it is mixed with water vapor. The extra water molecules exert a pressure called **vapor pressure.** The total pressure, which equals the atmospheric pressure, is made up of pressure from the gas and pressure from the water vapor. To find the pressure due to the gas, the pressure from the water vapor must be subtracted from the atmospheric pressure. The pressure from water vapor depends upon its temperature. Table 8-14 lists vapor pressures of water at various temperatures.

$$P_{atm} = P_{H_2O} + P_{gas}$$

$$P_{atm} - P_{H_2O} = P_{gas}$$

Table 8-14

Vapor Pressure of Water at Various Temperatures

Temperature (°C)	Vapor Pressure (mm Hg)
0.0	4.579
5.0	6.543
10.0	9.209
15.0	12.788
20.0	17.535
25.0	23.756
30.0	31.824
35.0	42.175
40.0	55.324
45.0	71.88
50.0	92.51
55.0	118.04
60.0	149.38
65.0	187.54
70.0	233.7
75.0	289.1
80.0	355.1
85.0	433.6
90.0	525.76
95.0	633.90
100.0	760.00

Sample Problem. Forty-six milliliters of oxygen gas is collected above water at 25°C when the atmospheric pressure is 763 millimeters of mercury. What volume of pure oxygen would this be at STP?

Solution.

It is not possible to use the combined gas law with the data given. Since the gas was collected over water, water vapor is mixed with the oxygen. The pressure of oxygen gas must be less than 763 millimeters of mercury. The pressure from water vapor at 25°C can be found in Table 8-14.

$$P_{O_2} = P_{atm} - P_{H_2O} = 763 \text{ mm Hg} - 23.8 \text{ mm Hg}$$
$$= 739 \text{ mm Hg}$$

Thus the oxygen gas occupies a volume of 46 milliliters and exerts a pressure of 739 millimeters of mercury at a temperature of 25°C. This data is ready to use in the combined gas law.

First set up the equation.

$$\frac{P_2 V_2}{T_2} = \frac{P_1 V_1}{T_1}$$

$$V_2 = \frac{P_1 V_1 T_2}{T_1 P_2}$$

Identify the variables.

$P_1 = 739$ mm Hg	$P_2 = 760$ mm Hg
$V_1 = 46$ ml	$V_2 = ?$
$T_1 = 25°C$; $25° + 273° = 298$ K	$T_2 = 273$ K

Plug the values in, and solve for V_2.

$$V_2 = \frac{(739 \text{ mm Hg})(46 \text{ ml})(273 \text{ K})}{(298 \text{ K})(760 \text{ mm Hg})}$$

$$V_2 = 40.98 \text{ ml}$$

8-15 Ambulance equipment humidifies oxygen gas by bubbling it through water. Without this precaution, a patient's mouth, throat, and lung tissues would eventually become dry.

Gases and the Mole

When 1 mole of water is decomposed into its elements, 16 grams of oxygen and 2 grams of hydrogen are produced. Yet, when the gases are collected and their volumes are measured, there is twice as much hydrogen as oxygen. This observation invites further questions about the nature of gases. What is the relationship between the number of molecules, their mass, the volume they occupy, and the gas's density? These questions are the heart of gas stoichiometry.

8-16 Electricity separates water into hydrogen and oxygen gases.

8–11 The Law of Combining Volumes: Gases in Reactions

In addition to his studies of pressure and temperature, Gay-Lussac studied the chemical reactions of gases. In particular, he measured and compared the volumes of gases that reacted with each other. One reaction that he studied was between hydrogen and chlorine ($H_2 + Cl_2 \longrightarrow 2\ HCl$). He found that if the gases had identical pressures and temperatures, 1 liter of hydrogen combined with 1 liter of chlorine to form 2 liters of hydrogen chloride. When he studied the reaction between hydrogen and oxygen ($2\ H_2 + O_2 \longrightarrow 2\ H_2O$), he found different ratios

8-17 Volcanic eruptions involve chemical reactions as well as changes in the temperature, pressure, and volume of gases.

between combining volumes. When another chemist investigated the reaction between nitrogen and hydrogen ($N_2 + 3\ H_2 \longrightarrow 2\ NH_3$), he found yet another set of volume ratios.

$H_2 + Cl_2 \longrightarrow 2\ HCl$ (mole ratio)
$1\ \ell\ H_2 + 1\ \ell\ Cl_2 \longrightarrow 2\ \ell\ HCl$ (volume ratio)

$2\ H_2 + O_2 \longrightarrow 2\ H_2O$ (mole ratio)
$2\ \ell\ H_2 + 1\ \ell\ O_2 \longrightarrow 2\ \ell\ H_2O$ (volume ratio)

$N_2 + 3\ H_2 \longrightarrow 2\ NH_3$ (mole ratio)
$1\ \ell\ N_2 + 3\ \ell\ H_2 \longrightarrow 2\ \ell\ NH_3$ (volume ratio)

In 1808 Gay-Lussac formulated the **law of combining volumes.** He said that under equivalent conditions, the volumes of reacting gases and their gaseous products are expressed in small whole numbers. Although he did not know it at the time, the ratios of these small whole numbers were the ratios between moles of reactants and products. This law along with the law of definite proportion (which says that the *masses* of reactants and products are related by ratios of small whole numbers) eventually led chemists to understand the relationship between atoms, molecules, and compounds.

8–12 The Molar Volume of a Gas

The law of combining volumes led Amedeo Avogadro to propose a principle. He sought to explain why volumes combined in simple ratios. **Avogadro's principle** soon became a fundamental idea of chemistry.

> Under equivalent conditions, equal volumes of gases contain the same number of molecules.

Each volume of gas in a reaction contains the same number of molecules. When hydrogen and chlorine react, one hydrogen molecule reacts with one chlorine molecule to form two hydrogen chloride molecules. The one volume of hydrogen contains the same number of molecules as the one volume of chlorine. Since twice as many hydrogen chloride molecules are produced, twice the volume results.

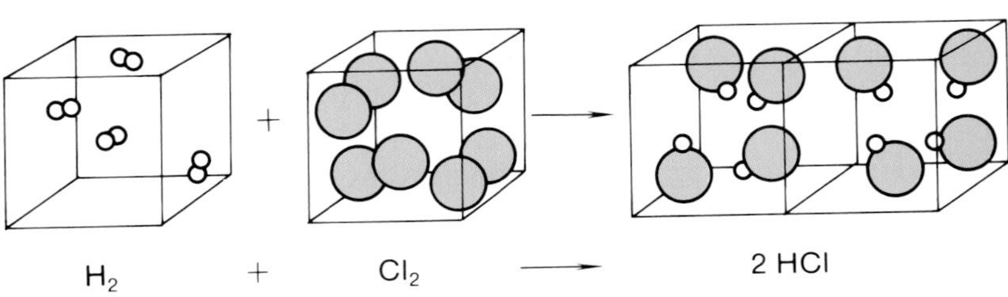

In the formation of water from hydrogen and oxygen, the two volumes of hydrogen contain twice as many molecules as the one volume of oxygen. The two volumes of water vapor contain the same number of molecules as the two volumes of hydrogen and twice the number of molecules as the one volume of oxygen. Likewise, the volumes of gases involved in the formation of ammonia (NH_3) show the relative number of molecules.

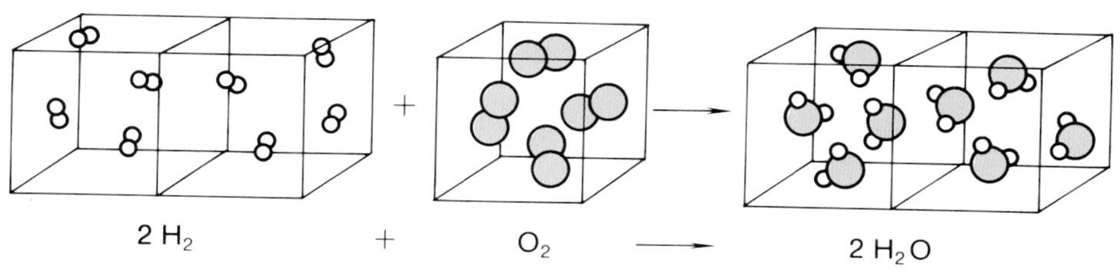

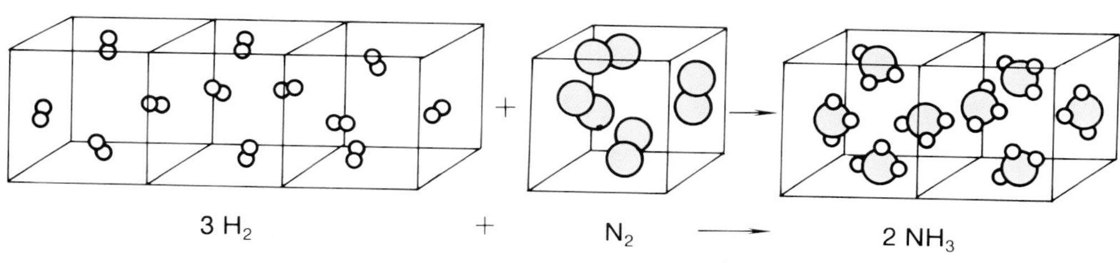

Avogadro's ideas eventually helped establish the idea of a mole. After Avogadro's death, Avogadro's number was determined and named in his honor. Experiments also determined how many molecules were present in a given volume. At STP a volume of *22.4 liters contains 6.023×10^{23} molecules,* or 1 mole, of a gas. For this reason, 22.4 liters is called the **molar volume** of a gas. No matter what type of gas is being considered, 1 mole at STP occupies approximately 22.4 liters.

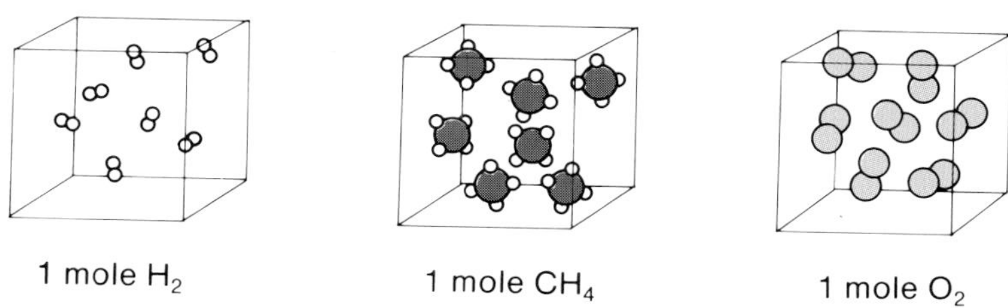

8-18

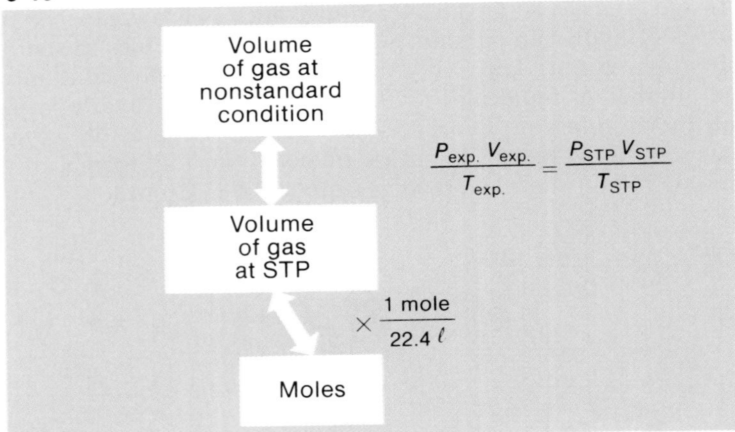

Sample Problem. What volume would 4 moles of ammonia occupy at STP?

Solution.

The fact that 1 mole fills 22.4 liters at STP makes the conversion factor 1 mole NH_3/22.4 ℓ valid.

$$4 \text{ moles } NH_3 \times \frac{22.4\ \ell}{1 \text{ mole } NH_3} = 89.6\ \ell \text{ at STP}$$

Sample Problem. What volume will 2.50 moles of hydrogen gas at 300 K and at a pressure of 400 millimeters of mercury occupy?

Solution.

The conversion factor of 22.4 ℓ/mole changes 2.50 moles of hydrogen to a volume at STP.

$$2.50 \text{ moles } H_2 \times \frac{22.4\ \ell}{1 \text{ mole } H_2} = 56.0\ \ell \text{ at STP}$$

The combined gas law can now be used to adjust this volume to the nonstandard conditions.

$$\frac{P_1 V_1}{T_1} = \frac{P_2 V_2}{T_2}$$

$$V_2 = \frac{P_1 V_1 T_2}{T_1 P_2}$$

$P_1 = 760$ mm Hg $P_2 = 400$ mm Hg
$V_1 = 56.0\ \ell$ $V_2 = ?$
$T_1 = 273$ K $T_2 = 300$ K

$$V_2 = \frac{(760 \text{ mm Hg})(56.0\ \ell)(300 \text{ K})}{(273 \text{ K})(400 \text{ mm Hg})}$$

$$V_2 = 117\ \ell$$

Sample Problem. A sample of oxygen gas occupies 1 liter when its temperature is 190 K and its pressure is 965 millimeters of mercury. How many moles of oxygen are present?

Solution.

The given volume must be first corrected to standard conditions.

$$V_2 = \frac{P_1 V_1 T_2}{T_1 P_2}$$

$P_1 = 965$ mm Hg $P_2 = 760$ mm Hg
$V_1 = 1\ \ell$ $V_2 = ?$
$T_1 = 190$ K $T_2 = 273$ K

$$V_2 = \frac{(965 \text{ mm Hg})(1\ \ell)(273 \text{ K})}{(190 \text{ K})(760 \text{ mm Hg})}$$

$$V_2 = 1.82\ \ell \text{ at STP}$$

Once the gas's volume at STP has been calculated, the number of moles can be found.

$$1.82\ \ell_{\text{STP}} \times \frac{1 \text{ mole } O_2}{22.4\ \ell} = 0.0813 \text{ moles } O_2$$

8–13 The Densities of Gases: Why They Are Different

As with all types of matter, the density of a gas is defined as mass per unit volume. The usual units of gas density are grams per liter. Some people assume that all gases have identical, or at least similar, densities. But this is not so. Hydrogen (0.0899 g/ ℓ) and helium (0.1785 g/ ℓ) have densities so low that these gases can be used to lift weather balloons. Air at 25°C and 1 atmosphere has a density of 1.185 grams per liter. Some gases, such as nitrogen dioxide (1.977 g/ ℓ), have densities so high that they immediately sink in air and roll along the ground.

The molar volume concept explains why gases have different densities. One mole of any gas will occupy 22.4 liters at STP. It is reasonable then that the mass of that mole determines the density of the gas. Gases with small molecules and low gram-molecular masses will have low densities. The density of a gas is a function of the gram-molecular mass. Gases with large molecules have greater densities.

$$\text{Density at STP} = \frac{\text{g}}{\ell} = \frac{\text{g/mole}}{\ell/\text{mole}} = \frac{\text{Gram-molecular mass}}{\text{Molar volume}}$$

This equation is a powerful tool for calculations involving gases. The theoretical density of a gas can be calculated if the gram-molecular mass of the molecules is known.

Sample Problem. What is the density of hydrogen gas (gram-molecular mass = 2.016 g/mole)?

Solution.

$$\text{Density of } H_2 = \frac{\text{Gram-molecular mass}}{\text{Molar volume}}$$

$$= \frac{2.016 \text{ g/mole}}{22.4 \ \ell\text{/mole}}$$

$$= 0.0899 \text{ g/}\ell$$

Have you ever wondered how scientists arrived at the figure of 22.4 liters per mole? If the density and gram-molecular mass of a gas are known, the density equation can be used to determine the molar volume.

$$\text{Density} = \frac{\text{Gram-molecular mass}}{\text{Molar volume}}$$

$$\text{Molar volume} = \frac{\text{Gram-molecular mass}}{\text{Density}}$$

Sample Problem. Given that the density of oxygen gas at STP is 1.429 grams per liter and that the gram-molecular mass is 32.00 grams per mole, find the molar volume of the gas.

Solution.

$$\text{Molar volume} = \frac{\text{Gram-molecular mass}}{\text{Density}}$$

$$= \frac{32.00 \text{ g/mole}}{1.429 \text{ g/}\ell}$$

$$= 22.39 \ \ell\text{/mole}$$

Analytical chemists can use this equation to find the gram-molecular mass of an unknown gas. When given an unknown gas, they measure the density and then solve for the gram-molecular mass.

$$\text{Density} = \frac{\text{Gram-molecular mass}}{\text{Molar volume}}$$

$$\text{Gram-molecular mass} = \text{Molar volume} \times \text{Density}$$

Sample Problem. An unknown gas has a density of 2.144 grams per liter at STP. What is its gram-molecular mass?

Solution.

$$\text{Gram-molecular mass} = \text{Density} \times \text{Molar volume}$$
$$= 2.144 \text{ g}/\ell \times 22.4\ \ell/\text{mole}$$
$$= 48.0 \text{ g/mole}$$

Further tests could have proved that this gas is ozone, which has a gram-molecular mass of 48.00 grams per mole.

8–14 Stoichiometric Conversions with Gases

Chapter 7 showed how the coefficients on balanced chemical equations give the molar ratios between reactants and products. The number of particles and their masses can be calculated once the number of moles is known. The information that 1 mole of a gas at STP occupies 22.4 liters can be added to the flow chart used for stoichiometric problems.

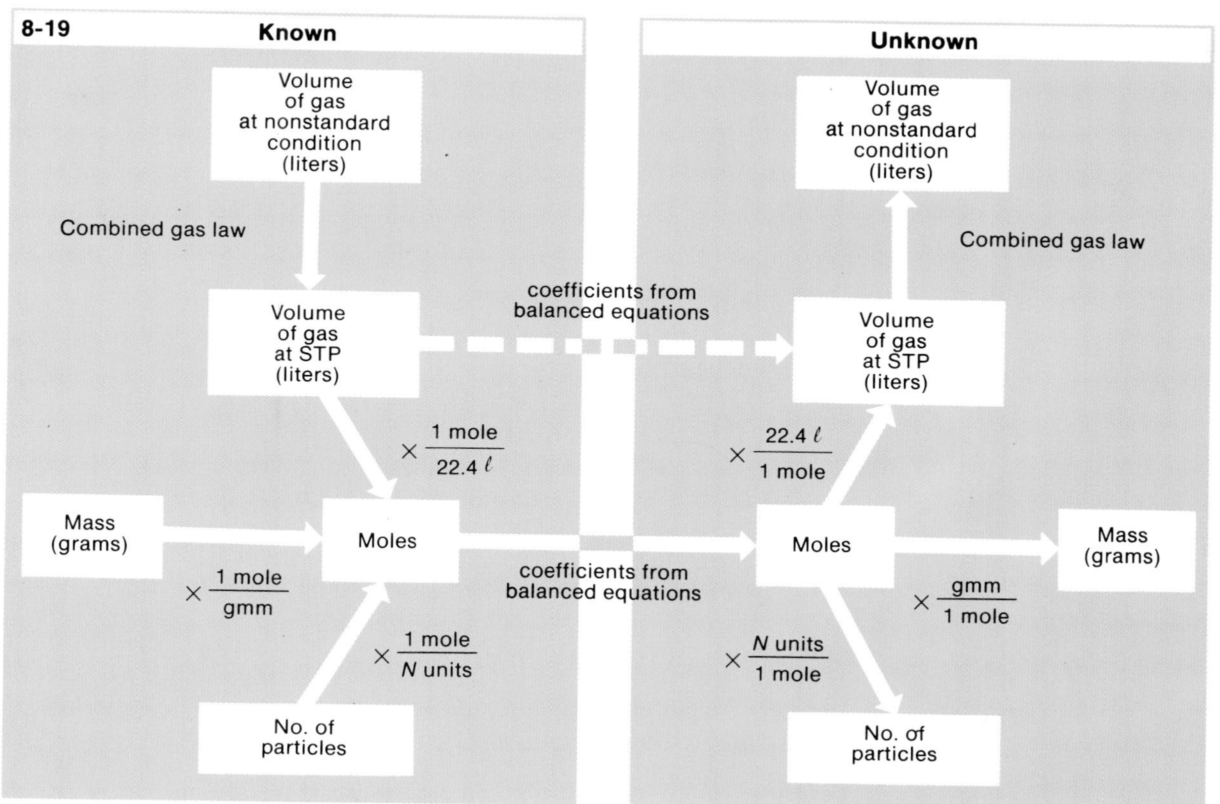

Sample Problem. When 2 moles of calcium react with water ($Ca + 2\ H_2O \longrightarrow Ca(OH)_2 + H_2$), what volume of hydrogen gas at STP will be produced?

Solution.

Moles of calcium can be used to find moles of hydrogen, which can then be converted to the volume of hydrogen.

$$2 \text{ moles Ca} \times \frac{1 \text{ mole } H_2}{1 \text{ mole Ca}} \times \frac{22.4\ \ell}{1 \text{ mole } H_2}$$

$$= 44.8\ \ell\ H_2 \text{ at STP}$$

Sample Problem. How many grams of water will be produced if 0.500 liter of oxygen gas at STP is burned with hydrogen?

Solution.

The balanced equation of the reaction is $2\ H_2 + O_2 \longrightarrow 2\ H_2O$. The volume of oxygen must be converted to moles of oxygen. The moles of oxygen can be used to find moles of water, which can then be converted to the mass of water.

$$0.500\ \ell\ O_2 \times \frac{1 \text{ mole } O_2}{22.4\ \ell} \times \frac{2 \text{ moles } H_2O}{1 \text{ mole } O_2}$$

$$\times \frac{18.016 \text{ g } H_2O}{1 \text{ mole } H_2O} = 0.804 \text{ g } H_2O$$

These conversions apply only to gases at STP. If gases are not at STP, their volumes must be adjusted before they are converted to moles.

8–15 Ideal Gases: They Do Not Exist, but They Are Certainly Useful

Did you know that gas molecules do not have to obey Boyle's law? For that matter, Charles's law holds no authority over gas molecules either. It is important to remember that gas laws do not govern; they describe. Boyle and Charles provided accurate descriptions of volume, pressure, and temperature, but their laws are valid only to the extent that they work. The limitations of these laws point out that science is only man's weak attempt to fathom God's creation. Through science man tries to see patterns and to formulate generalizations about the universe. Although sometimes tedious, the endeavor can be challenging, the work can be exciting, and the discoveries can be exhilarating. Yet science must be kept in its proper perspective. Man does not rule the universe. He rather seeks to understand and use what God allows him to know.

An **ideal gas** is a gas that behaves just as the kinetic theory says it should. Like other ideals on this earth, the perfect ideal gas has yet to be found, but some come very close at certain temperatures and pressures. Because the kinetic theory's description of gases is simple, it cannot describe the behavior of most gases at extreme temperatures and pressures.

The kinetic theory makes several assumptions that are not always accurate.

1. "Gas molecules are extremely small." This statement is true in most cases. Gases with larger molecules behave differently than expected.
2. "Molecules are located great distances away from each other." This assumption is fine for gases under ordinary conditions. Great pressures or extremely low temperatures can force gases to approach the point of liquefaction. Under these conditions the molecules slow down considerably, and the spaces between them become small.
3. "Forces act on the particles only during collisions." Under normal conditions gas molecules move so fast and are so far apart that intermolecular forces have little chance to act. Yet they always act to some degree. When a gas is near liquefaction, dipole-dipole interactions and dispersion forces increase their effects. Consequently, the gas molecules start "sticking" together and actual pressures and volumes are smaller than expected.

8-20 Pressurized gases allow this astronaut to breathe and to maneuver back to the space shuttle.

The molar volume of all gases is 22.4 liters, right? Not exactly. The volume 22.4 liters is only a useful approximation. When gaseous molecules are large, molar volumes decline slightly because intermolecular forces become significant.

Table 8-21

Standard Molar Volumes for Some Common Gases (0 °C)

Gas	Gas Density (g/ℓ)	Molecular Mass (g/mole)	Standard Molar Volume (ℓ)
H_2	0.0899	2.016	22.428
He	0.1785	4.003	22.426
Ne	0.9002	20.18	22.425
N_2	1.251	28.02	22.404
O_2	1.429	32.00	22.394
Ar	1.784	39.95	22.393
CO_2	1.977	44.01	22.256
NH_3	0.7710	17.03	22.094
Cl_2	3.214	70.90	22.063

8–16 The Ideal Gas Law

Boyle's law states that volume is inversely proportional to pressure when temperature remains constant. Charles's law states that volume is directly proportional to the Kelvin temperature when pressure is constant. It is also true that the volume is directly proportional to the number of moles of gas (n) in the sample.

$$V \propto 1/P$$
$$V \propto T$$
$$V \propto n$$

When all these proportions are put together, they form the basis for the ideal gas law.

$$V \propto nT/P$$
$$PV \propto nT$$

With the right numerical constant, this proportion can be made into an equality called the **ideal gas law.**

Ideal Gas Law:

$$PV = nRT$$

R, the **universal gas constant,** relates the units of pressure, volume, temperature, and quantity. Its value and its units depend on the units being used for P, V, n, and T. The ideal gas law can be rearranged to give the value of R.

$$R = \frac{PV}{nT}$$

Since 1 mole of gas at 1 atmosphere of pressure and 273 K occupies approximately 22.4 liters, these values can be substituted into the equation.

$$R = \frac{(1 \text{ atm})(22.4 \ \ell)}{(1 \text{ mole})(273 \text{ K})}$$

$$R = 0.0821 \ \ell \cdot \text{atm}/\text{mole} \cdot \text{K}$$

When pressure is measured in millimeters of mercury instead of atmospheres, R has a value of $62.36 \ \ell \cdot \text{mm Hg}/\text{mole} \cdot \text{K}$.

The equation $PV = nRT$ serves chemists well. Like the combined gas law, it relates pressure, volume, and temperature to each other. It also relates the number of gas molecules. Any problem that can be solved with the combined gas law can also be solved with the ideal gas law. As an added benefit, the equation can be used to solve for the number of molecules (measured in moles) in a sample.

Sample Problem. How many moles of a gas are present in a 2.4-liter sample at 1.25 atmospheres of pressure and 27° C?

Solution.

$$PV = nRT$$

$$n = \frac{PV}{RT}$$

Identify the variables, and express them with the correct units. The units in the constant must match the units on the other variables.

$P = 1.25$ atm
$V = 2.4\ \ell$
$T = 27°\text{C};\ 27°\text{C} + 273° = 300\ \text{K}$
$R = 0.0821\ \ell\cdot\text{atm/mole}\cdot\text{K}$

$$n = \frac{(1.25\ \text{atm})(2.4\ \ell)}{(0.0821\ \ell\cdot\text{atm/mole}\cdot\text{K})(300\ \text{K})}$$

$$n = 0.12\ \text{mole}$$

If chemists measure the mass, pressure, volume, and temperature of an unknown gas, they can find the gas's gram-molecular mass. They first use the ideal gas law to find the number of moles present. They then form a ratio between the mass of the sample and the number of moles in the sample (n). To complete the problem, they reduce the ratio to find the mass of 1 mole. This mass is the gram-molecular mass of the gas.

$$\frac{\text{Mass of the sample}}{\text{Number of moles in sample } (n)} = \frac{\text{Gram-molecular mass}}{1\ \text{mole}}$$

. . . APPARENTLY, NO MOLES WERE PRESENT

8-22 The ideal gas law can be used to determine the number of moles present in a sample of gas.

Sample Problem. A 0.504-gram sample of gas occupies 0.457 liter when under a pressure of 722.5 millimeters of mercury and a temperature of 293 K. What is the gram-molecular mass of this unknown gas?

Solution.

The first step is to use the ideal gas law to determine how many moles are present. Since pressure is given in millimeters of mercury, the constant $R = 62.36\ \ell \cdot \text{mm Hg/mole} \cdot \text{K}$ must be used.

$$PV = nRT$$

$$n = \frac{PV}{RT}$$

$$n = \frac{(722.5 \text{ mm Hg})(0.457\ \ell)}{(62.36\ \ell \cdot \text{mm Hg/mole} \cdot \text{K})(293 \text{ K})}$$

$$n = 0.0181 \text{ mole}$$

Since 0.0181 mole has a mass of 0.504 gram, the mass of 1 mole can be calculated.

$$\frac{0.504 \text{ g}}{0.0181 \text{ mole}} = \frac{27.8 \text{ g}}{1 \text{ mole}}$$

Gram-molecular mass = 27.8 g/mole

Coming to Terms

diffusion
permeability
compressibility
expansibility
pressure
barometer
millimeters of mercury
atmosphere
standard temperature and pressure (STP)
Boyle's law
Charles's law
Gay-Lussac's law
combined gas law
law of partial pressures
vapor pressure
law of combining volumes
Avogadro's principle
molar volume
ideal gas
ideal gas law
universal gas constant

Review Questions

1. Use the kinetic theory of gases to explain why
   a. air has a low density.
   b. on a day with no wind, you can smell a dead skunk that is 500 yards away.
   c. a large volume of air can be pumped into a small bicycle tire.
   d. you can smell coffee and bacon at the same time.
2. Use your knowledge of the gas laws to predict what will happen to the
   a. pressure in a can of hair spray when the gas is heated (no gas escapes).
   b. volume of a balloon as it is warmed (pressure stays the same).
   c. volume of a tire tube when it is immersed in cold water (pressure stays the same).
   d. pressure in a can of spray paint when some of the paint is released (the can remains at a constant temperature).
3. Convert between pressure units to fill in the blanks.

Atm	Lb./in.^{2}	mm Hg
______	______	2300
500.0	______	______
______	32.00	______
______	______	14.7

4. After pumping air into a bicycle tire, you notice that the nozzle on the pump is quite hot. Why? What gas law applies to this situation?
5. Convert the given quantity from the initial conditions to the final conditions given.
   a. A gas at 1.00 atm and 273 K occupies 5.00 ℓ. Under what pressure will the volume be 10.0 ℓ if the temperature remains constant?
   b. A gas occupying 25.0 ℓ has a temperature of 298 K and a pressure of 25.0 lb./in.^{2} What volume will it occupy if the pressure changes to 35.0 lb./in.^{2} while the temperature remains constant?
   c. A 15.0-ℓ volume of gas at 700 mm Hg of pressure has a temperature of 35.0°C. What will its temperature be if the pressure increases to 735 mm Hg and the volume increases to 23.8 ℓ?
   d. A gas occupying 0.500 ℓ at 1200 mm Hg and 16.5°C undergoes a temperature change so that the pressure is now 300

mm Hg. If the volume has remained constant, what is the new temperature?

e. If a gas at 1.2 atm of pressure and 22.0° C occupies 0.350 ℓ, what pressure will hold the same sample of gas in a volume of 0.050 ℓ if the temperature of the gas increases to 25.0° C?

6. A 500-ml flask is filled with Kr at STP.

   a. How many moles of Kr are present?
   b. Calculate the density of Kr at STP.

7. A technician produced H_2 gas by reacting Zn with H_2SO_4 ($2\ Zn\ (s) + H_2SO_4\ (aq) \longrightarrow ZnSO_4\ (aq) + H_2 \uparrow$). He collected the hydrogen in a flask by water displacement. The atmospheric pressure was 737.2 mm Hg, and room temperature was 25.0° C.

   a. What was the vapor pressure of water in the flask?
   b. What was the pressure of H_2 in the flask?
   c. Suppose that a leak in the gas collection tubes accidentally let a small amount of air into the flask. The unwanted air exerts 25.2 mm Hg of pressure in the flask. How much pressure is the H_2 exerting in the flask?

8. A 1.00-ℓ flask is filled with Ar by water displacement at 20.0° C. The atmospheric pressure is 750.6 mm Hg.

   a. After correcting for the water vapor in the flask, determine how many moles of Ar are present.
   b. What is the density of Ar at STP?

9. An unknown gas has a density of 0.714 g/ℓ at STP. What is its gram-molecular mass?

10. What is the gram-molecular mass of a gas whose density is 5.531 g/ℓ at STP?

11. Use the ideal gas law to obtain the answers to the following questions.

    a. How many moles of H_2 occupy 5.00 ℓ at 1.70 atm and 35.6° C?
    b. What is the temperature of 0.257 mole of O_2 occupying 6.78 ℓ at 0.856 atm?
    c. What volume does 35.8 g of CO_2 occupy at 1.56 atm and 125.8° C?
    d. What is the pressure of 25.6 g of Cl_2 occupying 15.6 ℓ at 28.6° C?

12. When nitroglycerine (227.1 g/mole) explodes, N_2, CO_2, H_2O, and O_2 gases are released initially. Assume that the gases from the explosion cool to standard conditions without reacting further.

$$4\ C_3H_5N_3O_9\ (s) \longrightarrow 6\ N_2\ (g) + 12\ CO_2\ (g) + 10\ H_2O\ (g) + O_2\ (g)$$

a. If 16.7 moles of nitroglycerine react, how many liters of N_2 are produced?
b. What volume of CO_2 (at STP) will be produced when 100.0 g of nitroglycerine reacts?
c. What is the total volume of gas (at STP) produced when 1.000 kg of nitroglycerine reacts?

13. A reaction between NH_3 and O_2 is the first step in the preparation of nitric acid (HNO_3) on a commercial scale. The products are produced at 1000° C (1273 K) and at atmospheric pressure.

$$4\ NH_3\ (g) + 5\ O_2\ (g) \xrightarrow{\text{catalyst}} 4\ NO\ (g) + 6\ H_2O\ (l)$$

a. What volume of NO is produced in the reaction vessel by the reaction of 0.500 mole O_2?
b. What mass of H_2O is produced by the reaction of 15.0 ℓ of NH_3?
c. How many liters of O_2 must react to produce 35.5 ℓ of NO?

14. Copper may be found in an ore named chalcocite, which contains copper(I) sulfide (Cu_2S). Crude copper may be obtained by the roasting of chalcocite ($Cu_2S\ (s) + O_2 \longrightarrow 2\ Cu\ (s) + SO_2$). Assume that a smelting plant doing this process is heating some chalcocite to 800° C at an atmospheric pressure of 755 mm Hg. (The O_2 reacts at this temperature and pressure.) Assume also that the SO_2 is being vented from the process at the atmospheric pressure and at 350° C.

a. What volume of SO_2 is released by the reaction of 454 kg of Cu_2S?
b. What mass of copper is produced by the reaction of 8.00×10^6 ℓ of O_2?

NINE

SOLIDS & LIQUIDS

PACKED AND STACKED, HENCE MORE DENSE

THE kinetic theory of matter ranks as one of the foremost theories of science. Like all good models, the kinetic theory organizes many observations. It explains why gases cause pressure and why evaporating liquids feel cool. With this model scientists can understand phenomena such as thermal expansion and melting. Scientists and students alike appreciate the way this model allows them to visualize microscopic events in solids, liquids, and gases.

Solids

9–1 Kinetic Description and Basic Properties of Solids

Particles in solids vibrate, but not over great distances. The particles in solids always have some motion. Temperature affects how much the particles in a solid move. At low temperatures the particles barely vibrate. As temperatures increase toward a solid's melting point, the particles have more kinetic energy and the vibrations increase in magnitude. The strength of the attractive forces between molecules in a solid also affects the movements of particles. Strong forces stifle the motions, whereas weak forces allow the particles to move more freely. Table salt exists as a solid at the scorching temperature of 801°C because attractions between the Na^+ ions and the Cl^- ions are extremely strong. Nonpolar carbon tetrachloride (CCl_4) molecules, with their weak intermolecular forces, can move more freely. Consequently, carbon tetrachloride can melt into a liquid at a much lower temperature than sodium chloride can.

The kinetic theory explains why solids have the properties they do. Because particles in solids are held close together, solids usually have high densities. The particles have little empty space between them, causing the solids to have fixed shapes and definite volumes. For this reason solids resist compression. Atoms, molecules, or ions would have to be deformed for solid matter to be compressed significantly. Because the particles in solids have little motion, solids have low rates of diffusion, and they are not permeable. If a silver coin and a copper coin were clamped together for several years, not many silver atoms would mix with the copper, and vice versa. Most likely, though, none of the atoms would migrate.

9–2 Crystalline and Amorphous Solids: In Line or Jumbled Up

Some solids naturally have orderly shapes. They form regular three-dimensional patterns with distinct edges and sharp angles. When they are shattered, smaller shapes form with similar edges and angles. These solids are called **crystalline solids.** Other solids have no preferred shape. When they are split or shattered, all kinds of fragments result. These solids are called **amorphous solids.**

The differences between crystalline and amorphous solids result from the particular structures of the solids. The particles in crystalline solids such as salt, sugar, and monoclinic sulfur are arranged in orderly patterns. Atoms, ions, or molecules are stacked row on row, column by column. The patterns, when repeated many times, result in the regular shapes of crystals.

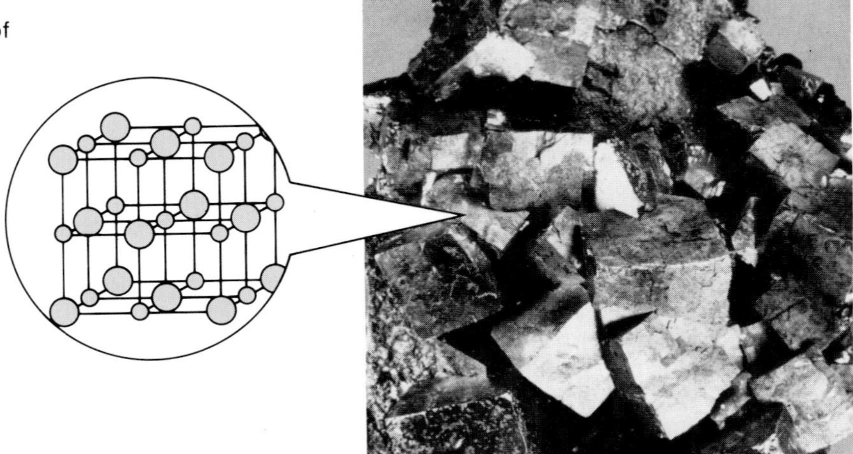

9-1 The internal structure of galena (PbS) is reflected in the external shape of its crystals.

The particles in amorphous solids such as rubber, glass, some plastics, asphalt, paraffin, and amorphous sulfur are not arranged in any particular pattern. Their random positioning results in globular microscopic shapes.

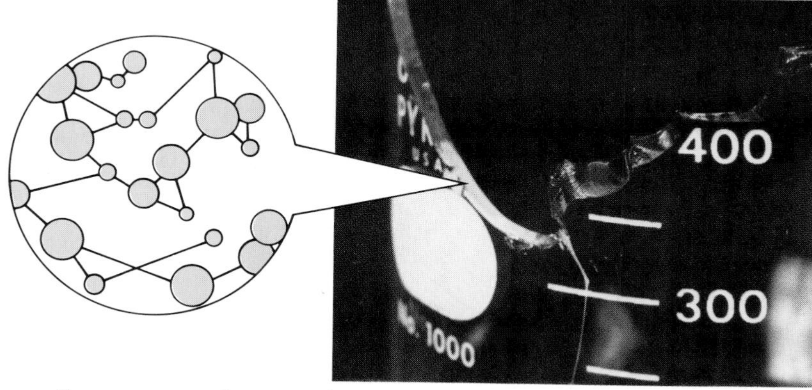

9-2 A random arrangement of particles in glass causes glass fragments to have irregular shapes.

Some amorphous solids are called super-cooled liquids or glasses. If a liquid can be cooled fast enough, its particles may not have time to get into their preferred crystalline pattern before they stop moving. The molecules become fixed in random positions.

9–3 Melting and Freezing: Solid, Meet Liquid

Melting and freezing are changes between the solid and liquid states. Melting is the transition from a solid to a liquid; freezing is the reverse. Although people normally think of these terms in relation to water, every substance can melt and freeze. Furthermore, freezing points do not always occur at cold temperatures.

Lead melts and freezes at the not-so-cold temperature of 327.5° C. When a lump of lead is placed in a ladle and heated, the atoms begin to vibrate more vigorously. Temperature, which is a measure of the vibrations, rises. When the melting point of the lead is reached, the temperature ceases to rise. At this point all the atoms are at the brink of liquefaction. Additional heat overcomes the attractive forces and melts the solid. Not until all the lead is melted will the temperature resume its upward climb.

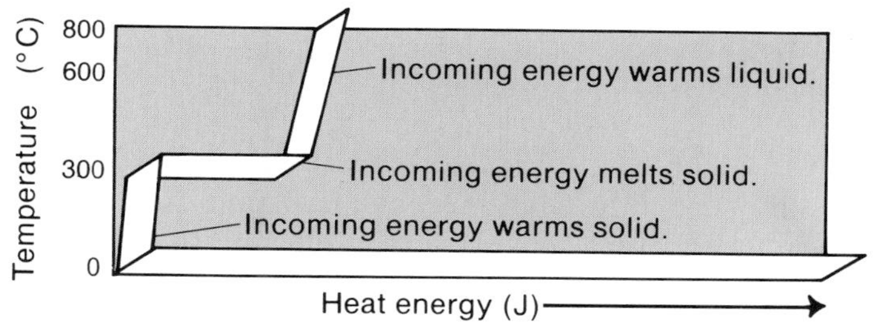

9-3 The warming curve of lead shows how temperature changes as heat energy is added.

The melting of water follows a similar pattern. Ice can be heated until it reaches a temperature of 0° C. Any heat that is added at this point does not raise the temperature. It serves to supply the energy for the breaking of intermolecular bonds. Not until the last piece of ice has melted will the temperature of the water rise above 0° C.

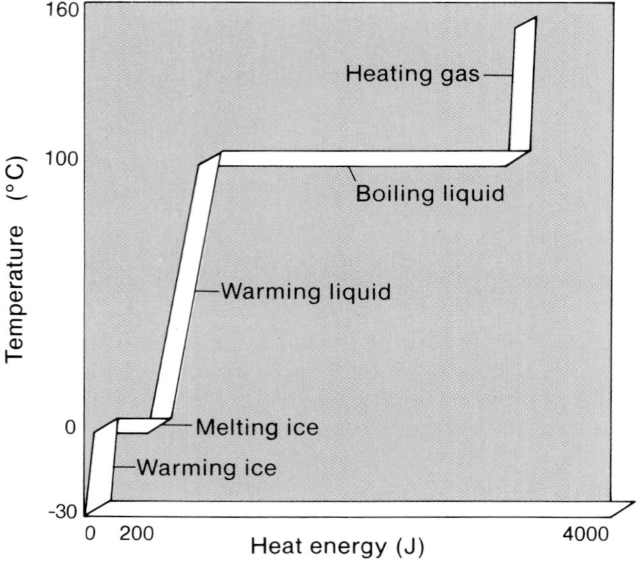

9-4 The warming curve of water shows how temperature changes as heat energy is added.

A significant amount of heat energy must be added to a solid at its melting point to break intermolecular bonds. This heat, called the **heat of fusion,** is different for individual substances. It is defined as the amount of heat required to melt a solid at its melting point without changing its temperature. It is usually expressed in units of calories per grams or kilocalories per mole.

Table 9-5

Heats of Fusion

Substance	(cal/g)	(kcal/mole)
Mercury, Hg	2.8	0.56
Water, H_2O	80	1.4
Salt, NaCl	124	7.3
Aluminum, Al	94	2.5
Gold, Au	15	3.0
Benzene, C_6H_6	30.5	2.4

Crystalline substances such as ice and lead have distinct melting points. Warming-curve graphs show clear plateaus that correspond to sharp melting points. An entire sample melts at a clearly defined temperature because all particles are held by nearly identical forces.

Amorphous solids do not have sharp melting points. Their particles are in random positions at different distances from each other. Since the forces vary with distance, not all particles are held together with identical forces. At a specific temperature during the melting process, only some of the forces will be overcome. Amorphous solids gradually soften as some of the attractive forces are overcome. A warming curve of an amorphous solid could look like this:

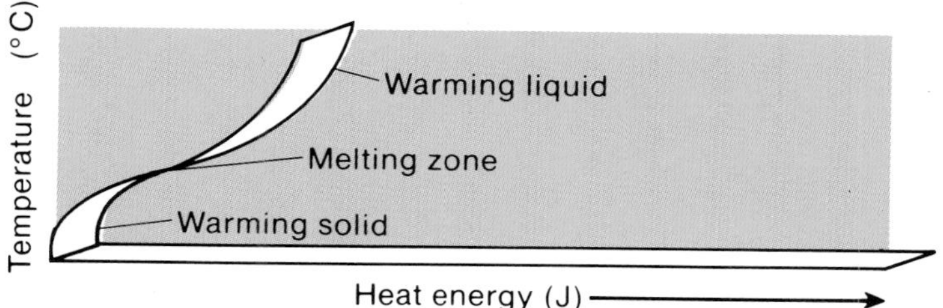

9-6 The warming curve of an amorphous solid lacks a clearly defined melting point.

Analytical chemists use melting points to help determine the identity and purity of compounds. Many pure substances are crystalline, and their melting points are listed in reference tables. Chemists can tell how pure a compound is by observing the melting-point range. A narrow range indicates a pure sample, and a wide range means that impurities are present.

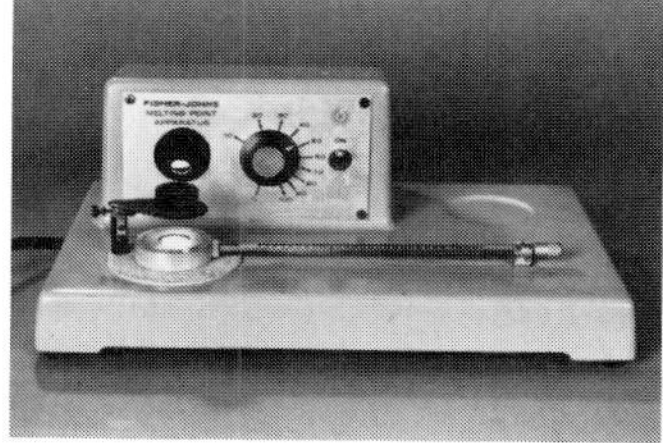

9-7 Melting point apparatus. An optical lens allows chemists to observe the point at which crystals on the heating pad begin to melt.

9–4 Sublimation: Solid, Meet Gas

Many caterers use dry ice (frozen CO_2) to refrigerate their stock. It has a strong advantage over frozen water because when it warms up, it changes into a gas instead of melting into a liquid. This state change by-passes the liquid state and alleviates the problems of messy puddles.

Sublimation is the direct change in state between the solid and gaseous states. Dry ice and many other substances can sublime. It is possible for an occasional molecule to leave the surface of a solid. The smell of naphthalene or paradichlorobenzene moth balls attests to this fact. Substances having many molecules that easily leave the surface sublime readily. Iodine is one of these substances. When heated, the iodine crystals at the bottom of a beaker sublime. The vapor ascends until it hits the cold surface of a watch glass placed on top of the beaker. Here sublimation occurs again when the vapor changes directly to a solid.

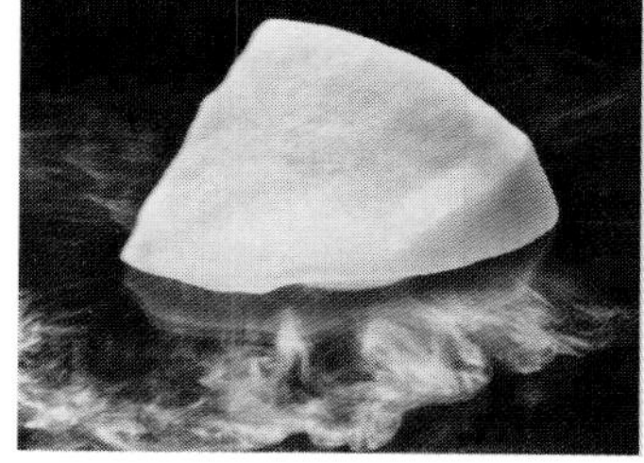

9-8 Frozen carbon dioxide sublimes directly into a gas as it warms up.

9–5 Crystalline Structures: Fourteen Ways to Build a Crystal

The particles in crystals are arranged in orderly, repeating patterns. These patterns vary, as shown by the wide variety of beautiful shapes found in natural crystals. Several factors influence how the particles will be arranged. Solids seek to maximize the distance between similar electrical charges. At the same time they seek to minimize the distance between opposite charges. A crystal's three-dimensional pattern, or **crystal lattice,** depends on the number and kinds of particles, their relative sizes, and their electrical natures. Scientists have found and classified seven basic classes of crystals.

9-9 The seven basic types of crystal structures.

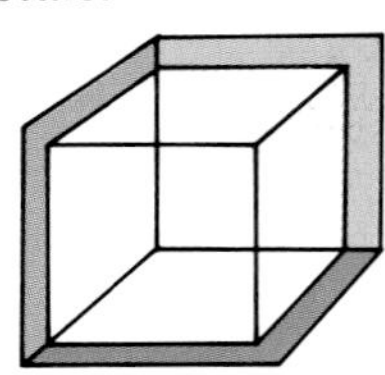

Cubic
All angles are 90°
All lengths are the same.
$(a = b = c)$

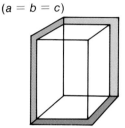

Tetragonal
All angles are 90°.
One length is different.
$(a = b \neq c)$

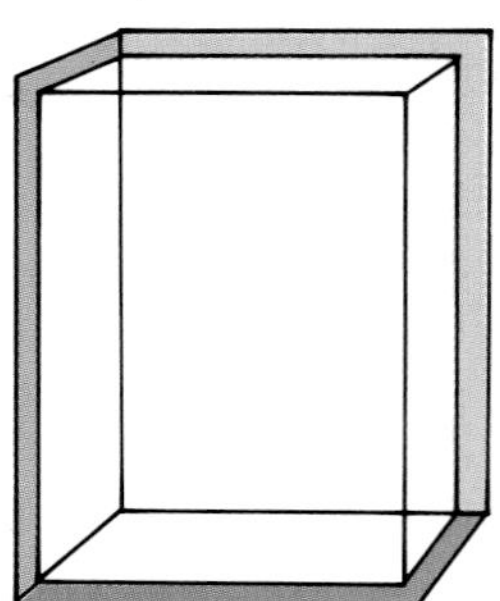

Orthorhombic
All angles are 90°
All lengths are different.
$(a \neq b \neq c)$

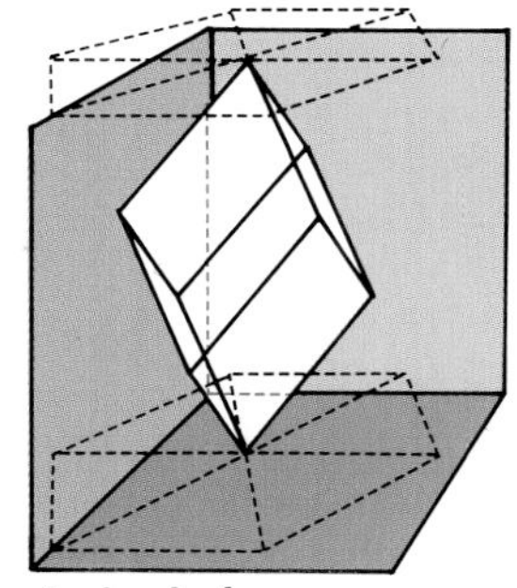

Rhombohedral
All angles are the same, but not 90°.
All lengths are the same.
$(a = b = c)$

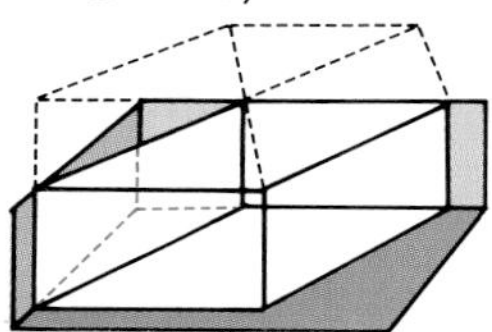

Hexagonal
One angle equals 120°.
One length is different.
$(a = b \neq c)$

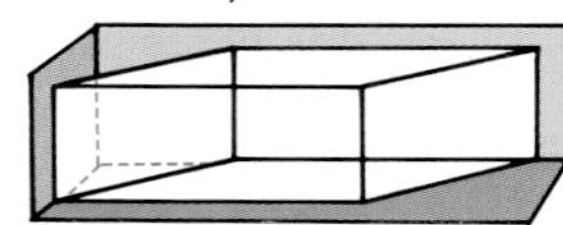

Monoclinic
Only two angles are 90°.
All lengths are different.
$(a \neq b \neq c)$

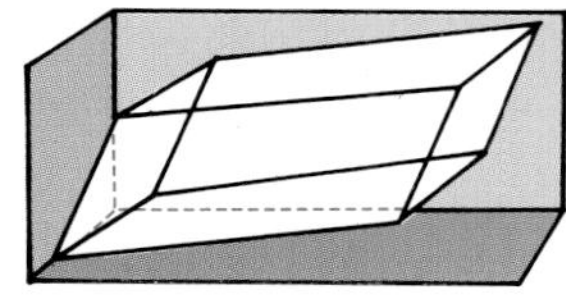

Triclinic
No angles are 90°.
All lengths are different.
$(a \neq b \neq c)$

Some of these classes can be slightly modified by the addition of particles on the faces or interiors. These modifications expand the seven basic classes into fourteen lattices.

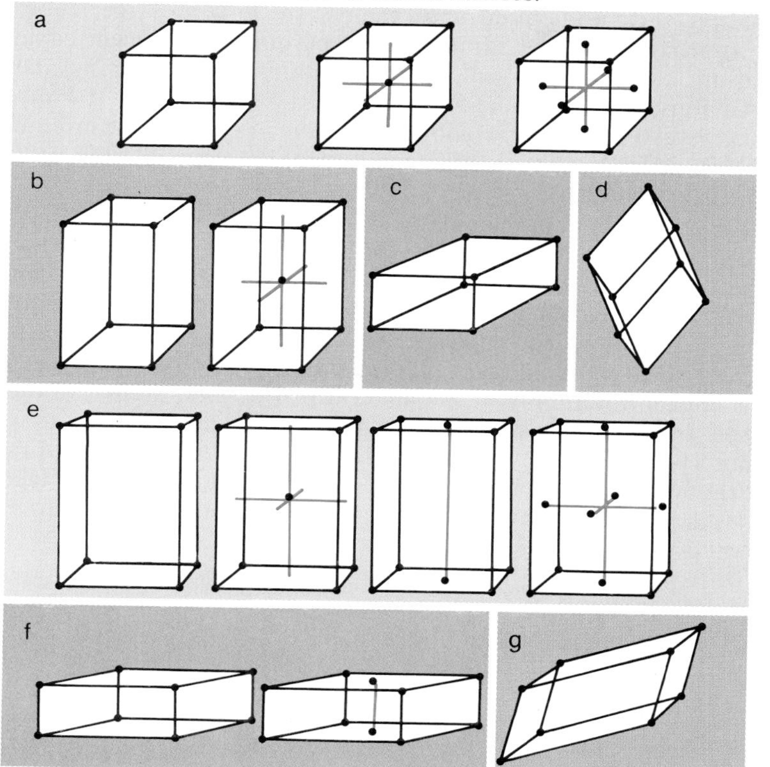

9-10 Modifications of Crystal Structures

(a) Simple, body-centered, and face-centered cubic crystals.

(b) Simple and body-centered tetragonal crystals; (c) hexagonal crystal; (d) rhombohedral crystal.

(e) Simple, body-centered, base-centered, and face-centered orthorhombic crystals.

(f) Simple and base-centered monoclinic crystals.

(g) Triclinic crystal.

Scientists divide the natural structures of crystals into blocks that contain the fundamental patterns of the lattices. These portions of crystals can be compared to the basic pattern in a piece of wallpaper. The wallpaper pattern can be repeated indefinitely to cover large walls. Unit cells, when repeated many times in three dimensions, form crystals. A **unit cell** is the smallest unit of a crystal that can be used as a building block.

9-11 Unit cells can be defined for any type of crystal.

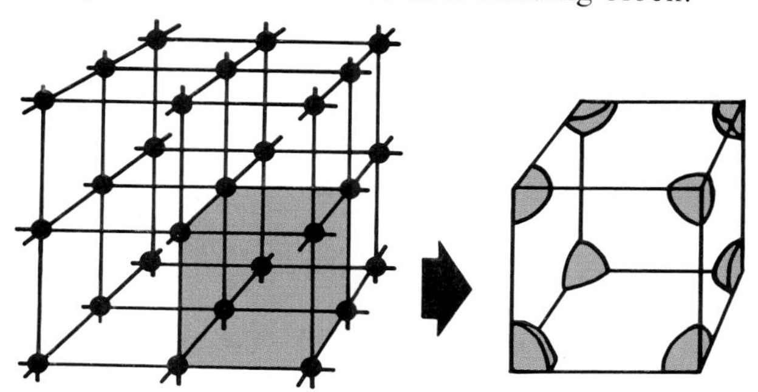

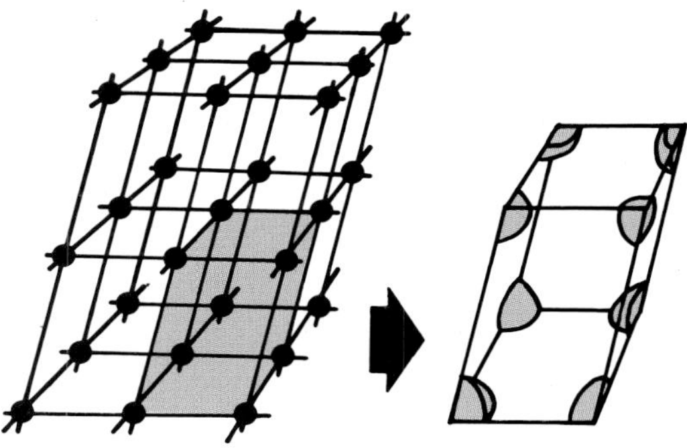

Because crystals are three-dimensional accumulations of unit cells, they often assume the same shape as their unit cells. Salt and sugar crystals appear as tiny cubes because during their formation, their units build upon themselves to form larger cubes with approximately the same number of units along each edge. A sodium chloride unit cell, which contains four Na^+ ions and four Cl^- ions, has a length of 5.6 angstroms (1 **angstrom** $= 10^{-10}$ m). A salt crystal 0.5 millimeters along each edge has nearly one million (10^6) unit cells along each edge and approximately 10^{18} unit cells in its total structure.

Many crystals found in nature do not have the same shape as their constituent unit cells. Due to varying conditions of temperature, pressure, and other environmental interactions, unit cells may stack in such a way that a different external structure forms. Figure 9-12 shows some ways in which cubic unit cells may stack. The eight-sided octahedral or twelve-sided dodecahedral forms appear commonly in the mineral world. The "steps" on the surfaces of the crystals are only a few angstroms wide, so they are not visible to the eye. The crystal faces appear to be smooth even though they are ragged on the atomic scale. Despite the fact that all the known minerals have one of the basic crystal structures, mineral crystals can exhibit a great variety of external forms.

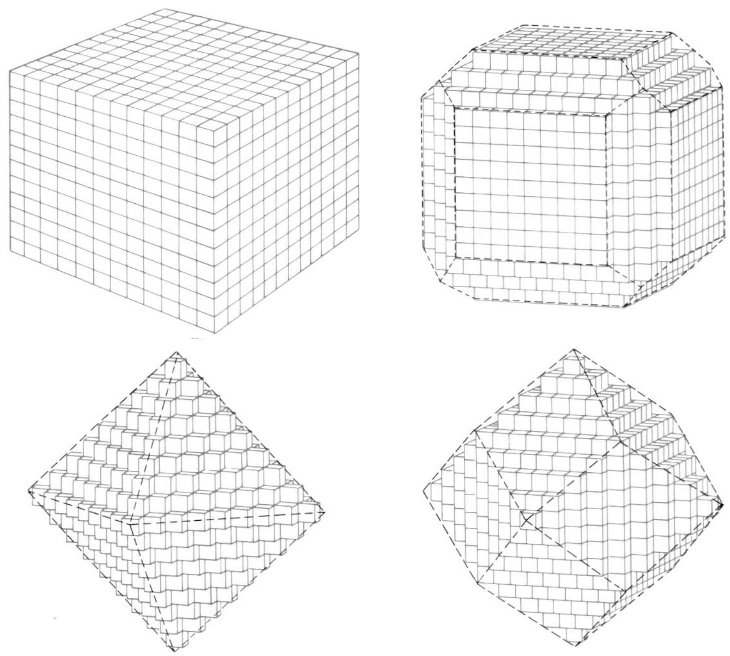

9-12 Unit cells can stack together several ways to produce crystals with different shapes.

9–6 Polymorphs and Allotropes: One Substance, Many Faces

Some substances can form more than one type of crystal lattice. Such elements and compounds are said to be **polymorphous** (*many + forms*). When Ca^{2+} and $CO_3{}^{2-}$ ions crystallize at a low temperature, they fall into a rhombohedral lattice. Mineralogists call this form of calcium carbonate *calcite*. When these same ions crystallize at a high temperature, they orient themselves in an orthorhombic lattice and form a substance called *argonite*.

Polymorphous elements are given the special label **allotropic.** The different forms of allotropic elements are called **allotropes.** Sulfur, phosphorus, and arsenic are a few allotropic elements. When sulfur is in the solid state, it exists as ring-shaped S_8 molecules. These rings can be arranged in either the rhombic or the monoclinic lattices. Rapid cooling of liquid sulfur from 300° C can produce yet another allotrope: amorphous sulfur. This globular form changes into the rhombic crystalline form after a couple of days.

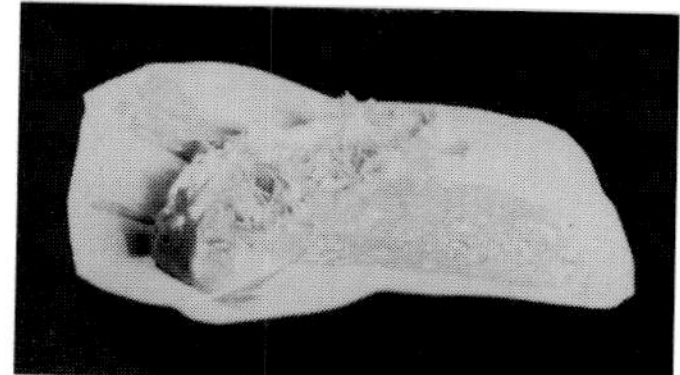

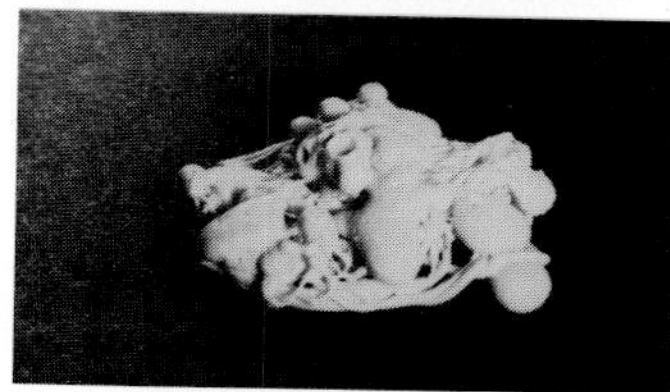

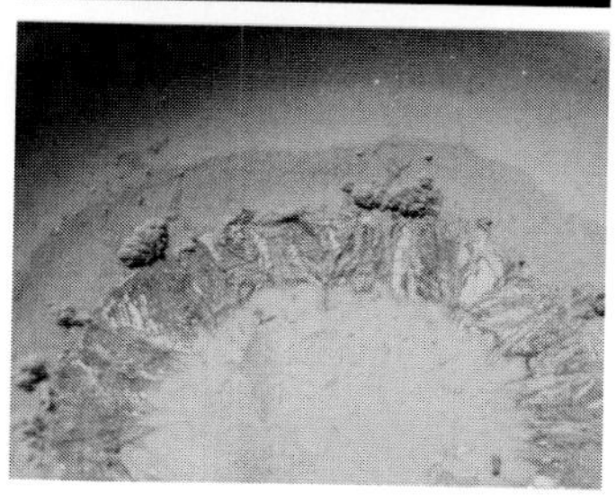

9-13 Three forms of sulfur: needle-shaped monoclinic crystals **(top),** plastic amorphous glob **(middle),** and rhombic crystals **(bottom).**

9–7 Binding Forces in Crystals: What Makes Crystals Strong

Crystals are formed by electrical forces. Oppositely charged regions attract, and similarly charged regions repel each other. The balance between attractions and repulsions determines how tightly the particles in the crystal are bound. If attractions just barely overcome the repulsions, the crystal will have a weak bond. If attractions are much greater than repulsions, the crystal will have strong binding forces.

The **lattice energy** of a crystal is the energy that is released when gaseous particles form crystals. It is equal in magnitude but opposite in sign to the energy that must be supplied to pull a crystal apart. The lattice energy shows the difference in energy between the particles when they are in the crystal and when they are free.

What makes a strong crystal? (In other words, what determines the lattice energy?) It has been found that the number of the electrical charges affects the stability of a crystal. Strong charges, like those in ionic compounds, interact strongly and result in strong crystals. The size of the particles also affects the binding forces. Small particles can be more tightly bound than large particles. Finally, the structure of the crystal affects the binding forces.

Binding forces must be overcome whenever a crystal is melted or dissolved. When a crystal melts, thermal energy is used to overcome binding forces. When a crystal dissolves, attractions between the particles of the crystal and the molecules of the solvent supply the necessary energy.

FACETS OF CHEMISTRY

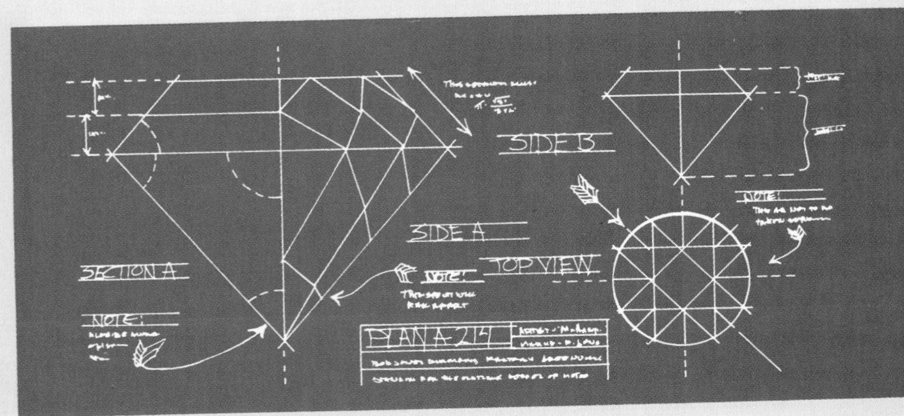

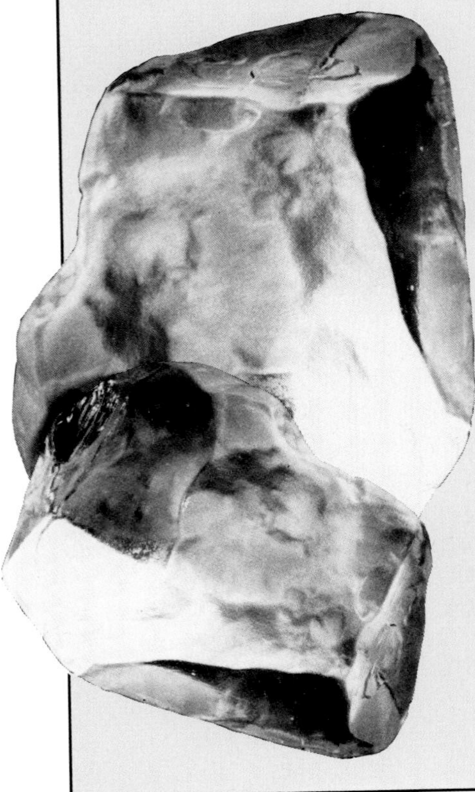

Diamonds: A Girl's Best Friend

In January, 1933, a poor prospector and his native helper were searching the diamond field of Pretoria, South Africa. The helper bent down and picked up an earth-encrusted lump. He handed it to the old prospector, Jacobus Jonker. Jonker, more from long habit than extreme interest, wiped away the mud. Then he stared at his hand in disbelief. He held a rare "blue-white" diamond about the size of a hen's egg. Needless to say, Jonker spent a sleepless night guarding the diamond. He could not relax until he had it safely deposited in the vaults of the Diamond Corporation. Jonker parted with his diamond for $315,000—what seemed like a fantastic amount to him. The new owners, however, knew that $315,000 was a small price to pay. With the proper cutting and polishing, the original stone could yield several gems whose combined value would be several times the price of the rough diamond.

The following year many leading European diamond cutters submitted their plans for cutting the huge diamond. But one lone American expert, Lazare Kaplan, declared that the stone would be ruined if it were cut according to the plans submitted. He was one against many, yet the owners finally decided to trust him with the 726-carat diamond. Kaplan planned, measured, and scrutinized for a year and then announced that he was ready. With the help of his son, Leo, he cut a groove on a line of cleavage. Now came the nerve-racking moment: the famous diamond might be shattered into fragments, or it might split as planned. Leo held a steel rule in the groove and Kaplan gave it one sharp tap. The Jonker diamond fell apart as planned. The first cleavage yielded a 35-carat chunk. After two more cleavages, the rest of the division was done by sawing. All of this

work was done to increase the value of the rough diamond.

To determine the value of a gem, diamond cutters have to consider four *C*'s: carat, clarity, color, and cut. Of these, the weight usually affects the value most. A diamond's weight is measured in carats—a unit of weight equal to 200 milligrams. Surprisingly, the process of cutting usually reduces a diamond's weight by one-half. Diamond owners are compensated for the large weight loss because diamond-cutters increase clarity by removing flaws as they work. A diamond cutter looks for flaws by immersing the diamond in a liquid that bends light rays just as much as diamonds do. This makes the position of any flaws easy to note, and they can be avoided when the diamond is cut. The color is also a factor in the value of the gem. A completely colorless stone, referred to as "blue-white," is the most valuable. Other colors can be valuable only if the color is definite and attractive. Finally, the cut of the diamond influences the value. The shape of the stone should conform to certain proportions, and the facets must be symmetrical, the same size, and well polished.

The cutting of a diamond involves two general steps: dividing and faceting. Although dividing a diamond is only the first step in cutting the diamond, it is the most important step. That is why Kaplan studied the crystal structure of the Jonker diamond for a year before attempting to divide it. Two methods can be used to divide diamonds: cleaving and sawing. A diamond can be cleaved in only four directions. To cleave a diamond, cutters form a small scratch in the crystal with a sharp diamond point. They then insert a steel blade into the groove and give it a sharp blow with a mallet. While a diamond will not cleave in ordinary wear, it will cleave cleanly with correct preparation and a hard blow. A diamond can be sawed in only nine directions. The sawing is accomplished with a thin disk of phosphor bronze that revolves 5000 to 6000 times each minute. Initially a mixture of diamond powder and olive oil serves as the abrasive on the edge of the sawing disk. In time, however, diamond dust from the cut diamond replaces the original dust. The bonds in the crystal are so strong that sawing a one-carat diamond may take as long as eight hours.

The final step in cutting the diamond is faceting. The object of faceting is to grind smooth surfaces that will allow the light to enter through the top and be internally reflected as many times as possible. The facets also break up light into its component colors and give the diamond its characteristic fire. Faceting for the common round brilliant gem begins with grinding the stone on a coarse silicon carbide wheel until it is the general size and shape desired. When the stone is satisfactorily shaped, it is closely examined for surface imperfections and chipping. The diamond is then secured in a holder. The intricate pavilion facets are then cut and polished. Again the gem is closely examined for chipping. The diamond is then turned around in the holder so that crown facets can be cut and polished. After the diamond is cleaned, it is ready for sale.

The process of cutting the Jonker diamond produced a total of twelve gems ready for sale. The largest weighed 143 carats. All were of the finest blue-white color, and their total value was $2,000,000—quite a change from the original price Mr. Jonker received for his lucky find.

Liquids

If liquids were not so familiar, most people would regard them as amazing substances. Drops of water have been seen beading up into spherical globs so often that this action seems perfectly natural. But is it? People intuitively know that rubbing alcohol will evaporate after it is rubbed onto the skin and that it will feel cold. Although many properties of liquids are well known, they are not necessarily well understood by most people. What makes the surface of a liquid in a test tube curve? What holds an insect up as it walks on the surface of a pond?

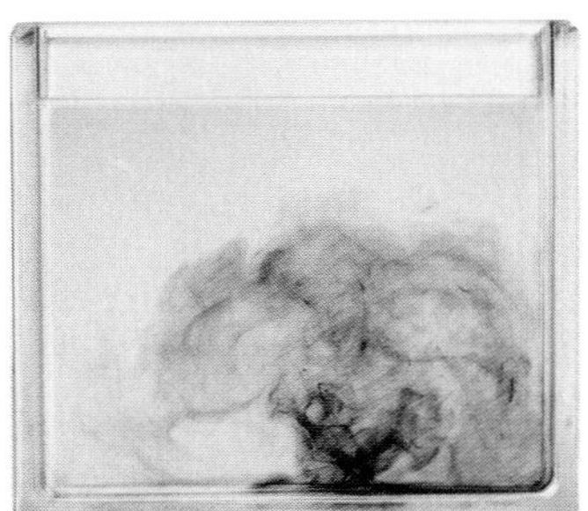

9-14 A drop of food coloring diffusing through water shows that particles in the liquid state are quite mobile and active.

9–8 Kinetic Description of Liquids

Molecules in liquids are held together by intermolecular forces that balance out the kinetic energy of the molecules. The particles move, but not with the reckless motion of gaseous molecules. They have less energy, and they experience stronger restraining forces than gases do. Yet the attractive forces holding the molecules together do not totally dominate. There is enough freedom for liquid particles to roll and slide over each other. The particles are not fixed in any one position.

Liquids are fluids. They flow and match the shape of a container. In this respect liquids are like gases. Other similar properties are diffusibility and permeability. A drop of food coloring spreading throughout a glass of water, or spilled milk seeping into a paper towel provides evidence that liquids consist of moving particles in unfixed positions.

Liquids have densities that are markedly greater than the densities of gases. This is to be expected, since there is little empty space between the molecules of liquids. Unlike gases, liquids do not expand much. They also are not easily compressed. People rely on this latter property every time they touch the brake on an automobile. The pressure that is applied on the liquid near the brake pedal is transferred through the brake line to the brake pads or discs. Since the molecules already touch each other, liquids can transfer the incredible pressures of even the most powerful hydraulic systems without being compressed much. The molecules themselves would have to be crushed before a liquid could be compressed to any great degree.

9-15 Since liquids cannot be compressed much, hydraulic pumps can force fixed volumes of fluid against great resistances.

9–9 Effects of Intermolecular Attractions

The curved surface of a liquid in a test tube, a drop of oil, or a water spider skating across the surface of a pond is evidence of intermolecular forces at work. All these examples show the effects of **surface tension.**

Why should surface molecules form an elastic skin over liquids? The intermolecular forces at the surface are not stronger than those in the interior of the liquid. The "skin" forms because the forces all point in the same direction. A molecule within the bulk of a liquid has neighbors on all sides. Each neighbor holds some attraction, so the molecule experiences forces in all directions. A molecule at the surface, however, has no neighboring molecules on one of its sides. All forces are directed toward the interior of the liquid, and the unbalanced forces bind surface molecules together.

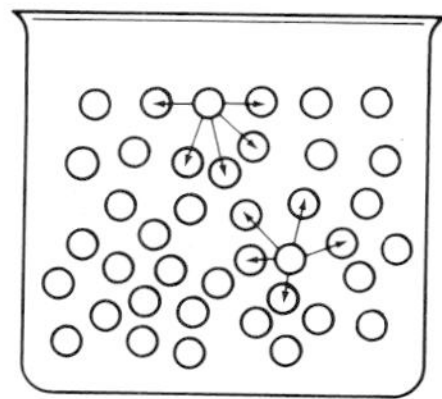

9-16 Unbalanced forces act on molecules on the surface of a liquid.

9-17 Surface tension causes a paper clip to float **(left)** and water droplets to form spheres **(right).**

Surface tension affects the shapes of liquids. The spherical shape of liquid droplets results when these forces pull the liquid into the shape with the least surface area per unit volume. This action minimizes the unbalanced forces.

Liquids are wet, right? Not always. Wetness is a chemical effect that comes into play in certain situations. For instance, water wets a cotton cloth, but not wax candles. Water molecules are polar, so they readily adhere to sugar, cotton, skin, and any other materials that have polar regions on their surfaces. Nonpolar surfaces cause water to bead up and roll away. On the other hand, nonpolar liquids wet nonpolar surfaces but not polar surfaces. In each situation the intermolecular attractions determine whether the liquids are "wet."

Have you ever observed the curved surface of some liquid in a test tube? This surface, called a **meniscus,** results from intermolecular attractions within the liquid and between the liquid and the container. When attractions between the container and the molecules of the liquid exceed the surface tension attractions, the liquid can climb the walls of the container. In narrow glass tubes called capillary tubes, this effect becomes greatly exaggerated. Water rises up narrow capillary tubes easily and exhibits what is called **capillary rise.** Mercury, on the other hand, has little attraction for the glass but has strong internal cohesive forces. These cohesive forces are so strong that the surface molecules are pulled away from the glass. Thus mercury does not exhibit a capillary rise.

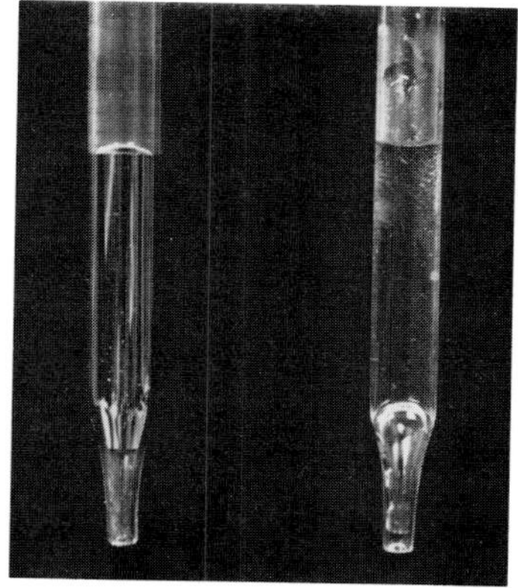

9-18 The surface tension of mercury surpasses mercury's attraction for the glass sides of the dropper. The strong attraction of water molecules for the glass cause the meniscus of the water to curve upward.

9-19 Strong intermolecular forces make some fluids very viscous.

Thickness and *gumminess* are common words for the scientific term **viscosity.** Viscosity is a liquid's ability to resist flowing. It comes about partly because molecules attract each other. The stronger the attractions are, the more viscous the fluid is. Molasses is viscous, so it can be expected to have some strong attractions between its particles. Thinner, less viscous fluids like water and gasoline pour well and spread out quickly because they have weak intermolecular attractions. Temperature often affects the strength of intermolecular forces. For example, at cold temperatures the forces act more strongly on the slow-moving particles. That is why molasses flows so slowly in January.

9–10 Evaporation: The Energetic Ones Come Out on Top

The molecules in a liquid are not all moving at the same speed. Many do move at similar speeds, but random motions rule out complete uniformity. Some molecules are slowed down by a series of head-on collisions. Others are accelerated by a series of favorable shoves. Molecules with above-average speeds can sometimes break away from liquids if they are near the surface. This process, whether it occurs above or below the boiling point, is called **evaporation.** Evaporation can occur at any temperature, but it happens much more readily at higher temperatures.

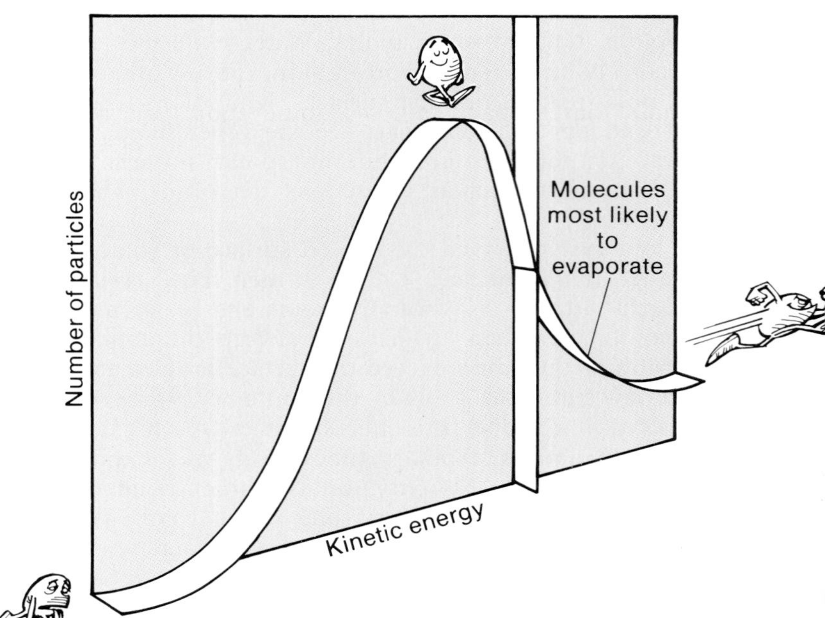

9-20 Frequency distribution of water molecules.

Evaporation is a cooling process. This is evident when someone shivers before drying off after a shower or a swim. The molecules with the most kinetic energy leave. The ones that remain have a lower average kinetic energy. As a result the unevaporated liquid draws heat from the surrounding environment. The incoming heat does not raise the temperature of the unevaporated liquid; it merely replaces the energy that left with the departed molecules.

The amount of heat required to convert a given quantity of a liquid at its boiling point to its vapor at the same temperature is called the **heat of vaporization.** Heats of vaporization differ widely because liquids have different intermolecular attractions. For instance, it takes 540 calories to vaporize 1 gram of water at 100°C and 1 atmosphere. A gram of ethyl alcohol at its boiling point can be vaporized with the addition of 205 calories. Figure 9-21 shows the heats of vaporization for several liquids.

Table 9-21

Heats of Vaporization at Boiling Point

Substance	cal/g	kcal/mole
Water	540	9.73
Ethyl alcohol	205	9.40
Benzene	94.3	7.37
Diethyl ether	84.0	6.23

Molecules that evaporate can easily re-enter liquids. Suppose that a liquid evaporates in a closed jar. At first the molecules evaporate into the space above the liquid. During their random movements, these molecules can bounce back into the surface of the liquid. When enough molecules have evaporated, the number of molecules that go back into the liquid equals the number of molecules that evaporate. At this point the level of the liquid will remain the same. The volume of the liquid stays constant because the opposite process, condensation, nullifies the effect of evaporation. This situation is called a dynamic equilibrium. The two processes of condensation and evaporation oppose each other so that no net effect can be seen.

9–11 Vapor Pressure: The Impact of Evaporated Molecules

When molecules evaporate, they enter the gaseous state. They then move and collide just like any other gaseous molecules. When confined in a closed container, these molecules also exert pressure on the walls of the container. This pressure is called the vapor pressure of the liquid.

The vapor pressure of a liquid is a measure of the number of molecules that evaporate. Vapor pressure increases with the temperature. High temperatures cause molecules to move faster and to evaporate more easily. The intermolecular attractions within a liquid also affect the vapor pressure. Strong attractions restrain particles from evaporating, while weak attractions allow quick evaporation. Suppose that some mercury, some water, and some diethyl ether are spilled in a room at 25° C. The mercury will exert 0.002 millimeters of mercury of vapor pressure; the water, 24 millimeters of mercury; and the ether, 450 millimeters of mercury. These numbers show that the ether will evaporate quickly, the water will take longer, and the mercury will take decades to evaporate.

Table 9-22

Vapor Pressures (mm Hg)

Substance	**0° C**	**25° C**	**50° C**	**100° C**
Mercury	0.000185	0.00185	0.0127	0.273
Water	4.58	23.8	92.5	760
Ethanol	12.2	68	234	1663
Methanol	29.7	122	404	—
Diethyl ether	185	541	1216	4859

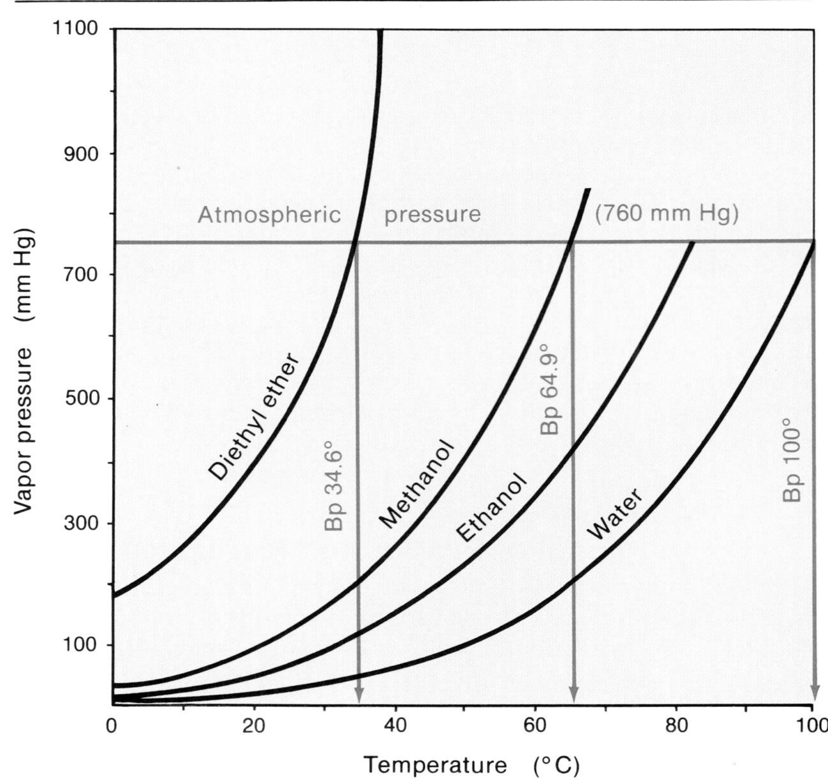

9-23 Vapor pressures of liquids rise steadily with temperature.

9–12 Boiling: Full Steam Ahead Despite the Opposition

Boiling is a rapid state change between the liquid and the gaseous states. Vapor escapes from a liquid's surface, as in evaporation, and it also forms internally and collects in bubbles that rise to the surface.

Boiling occurs when the vapor pressure of a liquid equals the atmospheric pressure. Normally, atmospheric pressure is greater than vapor pressure, and it prevents liquids from boiling. Table 9-22 shows that the vapor pressure of ethanol at 25°C is only 68 millimeters of mercury. The normal atmospheric pressure of 760 millimeters of mercury has no trouble suppressing this weak tendency to vaporize. But when the alcohol is heated to 78.3°C, the story changes. At this temperature the vapor pressure equals normal atmospheric pressure. Now the tendency of ethanol to vaporize wins out, and boiling occurs.

Mountain climbers and users of pressure cookers know from experience that temperature is not the only factor that affects boiling points. Atmospheric pressure affects it too. Climbers at the summit of Mount Everest would find that water boils at 70°C, not at 100°C. At an elevation of 8850 meters (29,000 ft.), the prevailing atmospheric pressure is only 236 millimeters of mercury. This small pressure cannot hold water in its liquid state as long as normal pressure can. If the vapor pressure exceeds 236 millimeters of mercury, the water will boil.

9-24 Large vacuum evaporators make powdered milk. They remove water by boiling it at a greatly reduced pressure, preventing the proteins and sugars from becoming scorched.

LOOK! THE SILLY THING IS JUST 3 FEET OFF THE FLOOR... WHAT'S ELEVATION GOT TO DO WITH ITS BOILING POINT, ANYWAY?!!

9-25 The low atmospheric pressure at high altitudes allows water to boil at lower-than-normal temperatures. Cooks must compensate for this by following special baking instructions.

A pressure cooker raises boiling points by creating a high-pressure "atmosphere" within itself. A clamped lid exerts extra pressure on the liquid's surface. At high pressures, higher-than-normal temperatures are needed to produce matching vapor pressures. Water in a pressure cooker under a pressure of 1520 millimeters of mercury can exist as a liquid at 120°C. It is no wonder that foods cook faster in pressure cookers than in open pans.

9-26 Pressure cookers speed up cooking by forcing water to remain a liquid at temperatures higher than 100° C.

Because boiling points change with pressure, the **boiling point** of a liquid is defined as the temperature at which the vapor pressure equals the applied pressure. The normal boiling point is the temperature at which the vapor pressure equals 760 millimeters of mercury.

Sample Problem. What is the boiling point of water that is subjected to an atmospheric pressure of 500 millimeters of mercury?

Solution.

The graph of vapor pressures shows that the vapor pressure of water equals 500 millimeters of mercury at approximately 89° C. At this temperature the vapor pressure of water can match the given atmospheric pressure, and the water can boil.

9–13 Distillation: Separating Liquids

Condensation is the reverse of vaporization. It occurs when high pressures pack gaseous molecules together and when low temperatures slow down molecules until they collect as liquids. Whereas heat must be supplied to vaporize a liquid, it must be removed to condense a gas. The **heat of condensation** is the amount of heat that must be removed from a vapor to condense it.

$$\text{Liquid} + \text{Heat} \underset{\text{vaporization}}{\overset{\text{condensation}}{\rightleftharpoons}} \text{Vapor}$$

At 100° C and 1 atmosphere of pressure, 9.73 kilocalories of heat must be supplied to vaporize 1 mole of water. The same amount of heat must be removed from a mole of water vapor at 100° C to condense it. The heat of condensation of a substance has the same value but opposite sign as the heat of vaporization.

$$1 \text{ mole } H_2O + 9.73 \text{ kcal} \underset{\text{vaporization}}{\overset{\text{condensation}}{\rightleftharpoons}} 1 \text{ mole } H_2O$$

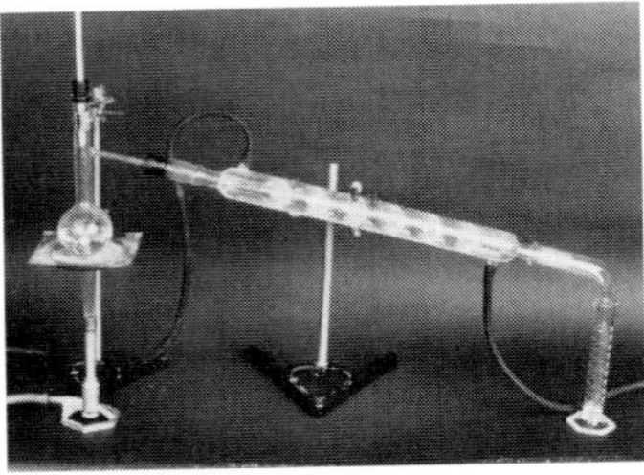

9-27 Distillation apparatus. The vapor that escapes is condensed in a water-cooled tube.

The processes of vaporization and condensation can be linked together and used to separate mixtures. This technique is called **distillation.** Through it salt water can be purified, and combinations of liquids can be separated into pure samples called fractions.

The mixture to be separated is placed into a distilling flask and is heated. The temperature rises steadily until it reaches the boiling point of the liquid that boils first. The vapor of this liquid enters the condenser and flows over its water-cooled glass walls. The vapor soon condenses and drips into a collecting flask. Once the first liquid has been vaporized, the temperature can rise until the boiling point of another substance is reached. The process is repeated and the other liquid is collected in another flask. Dissolved and suspended solids are left behind in the distilling flask. This technique works well as long as the substances in the mixture have distinctly different boiling points and they do not interact with each other too strongly.

9–14 Critical Values: You Can Push a Gas Only So Far

The combustion of 1,444,000 liters of liquid hydrogen and 530,000 liters of liquid oxygen thrusts space shuttles into their orbits. Blood banks can store frozen blood cells for years at the super-cold temperatures of liquid nitrogen. Physicists use liquefied helium to refrigerate metals and to cause them to become superconductors.

Oxygen, hydrogen, nitrogen, and helium are usually thought of as gases because their boiling points are well below normal temperatures. Yet these gases can be liquids under the proper conditions. Low temperatures and high pressures can condense and even solidify any gas. The low temperatures slow the molecules down, and the high pressures pack them together.

Scientists have found that gases cannot be liquefied by high pressures alone. Their temperatures must be lowered past a certain point. This value, called the **critical temperature,** is the highest temperature at which a gas can be liquefied. Each gas has its own characteristic critical temperature.

Hydrogen gas at 35 K cannot be liquefied, even with tremendous pressures. The molecules are moving too quickly. If its temperature is lowered to 33 K, it can be squeezed into a liquid if enough pressure is applied. Gases that have critical temperatures above room temperatures can be liquefied at room temperature by pressure alone. Other gases require a combination of refrigeration and compression.

9-28 Equipment used to liquefy gases. Liquid air can be seen on the left.

FACETS OF CHEMISTRY

Cryogenics

In the bizarre world of cryogenics, rubber balls shatter on impact and bananas are so strong that they can be used to pound nails into wood. Cryogenics is the science of the supercold. This word *cryogenics* comes from the Greek word *kryo,* meaning "frost." Cryogenics does not deal with the "moderately" cold temperatures of a freezer, but with the intensely cold world of -150°C and below. Applications of this fascinating area of study are found in such wide-ranging fields as space, food preservation, and medicine.

Supercooled gases are used extensively in the space industry. Liquid hydrogen and oxygen are used together as a powerful fuel. Life support systems and space refrigeration systems also make ample use of cryogenic techniques.

Another application of cryogenics has been the preservation of food, especially during shipment. Instead of a mechanical refrigerator, liquid nitrogen can be used to cool food. No moving parts are needed, and exceedingly low temperatures are attainable. Nitrogen has the added advantage of being more chemically inert than the oxygen in air. Since it will not react with the food, even perishable foods such as lettuce and strawberries arrive at their destination in perfect condition.

Cryosurgery, the use of a freezing probe in place of a surgeon's scalpel, has been used

The pressure that is required to liquefy a gas at its critical temperature is called the **critical pressure.** Hydrogen gas at its critical temperature can be liquefied under a pressure of 12.8 atmospheres. If the gas is colder than its critical temperature, less pressure will be required to liquefy it.

Table 9-29

Substance	Critical Temperature (K)	Critical Pressure (atm)
Hydrogen, H_2	33.1	12.8
Nitrogen, N_2	126	33.5
Oxygen, O_2	155	50.1
Carbon dioxide, CO_2	304	72.9
Ammonia, NH_3	406	112
Chlorine, Cl_2	417	76.1
Sulfur dioxide, SO_2	431	77.7
Water, H_2O	647	218

with good success for removing warts, tonsils, and cataracts. Cryosurgery offers advantages of less pain and a freedom from hemorrhaging. Many operations that required hospitalization have been replaced by procedures that can be carried out in a doctor's office. Cryogenics also allows cells and tissues to be frozen for later use.

One area involving irresponsible experimentation is cryonics. This is the process of freezing and storing a human body in hopes that the individual can be brought back to life at some future date. Some men hope that people with incurable diseases could be stored in a deep freeze until new medical cures have been developed. This extravagant dream has serious ethical and scientific flaws. Freezing people before they die involves either the sin of murder or suicide. If the freezing is done after the death, there is no real hope of reviving them, since, as far as science has been able to determine, the biological processes of death are irreversible. Leading authorities also seriously doubt that an entire human body could ever be frozen intact. When more than a few cells are frozen, scientists find it impossible to maintain a fast, uniform rate of freezing. Consequently, destructive ice crystals form and destroy the cell membranes. Despite these facts, unscrupulous "freezatorium" operators continue to offer families false hopes and to collect exorbitant sums of money for their futile efforts. It is remarkable how much some people are willing to pay to prolong their lives for a few years when they can have eternal life as a free gift.

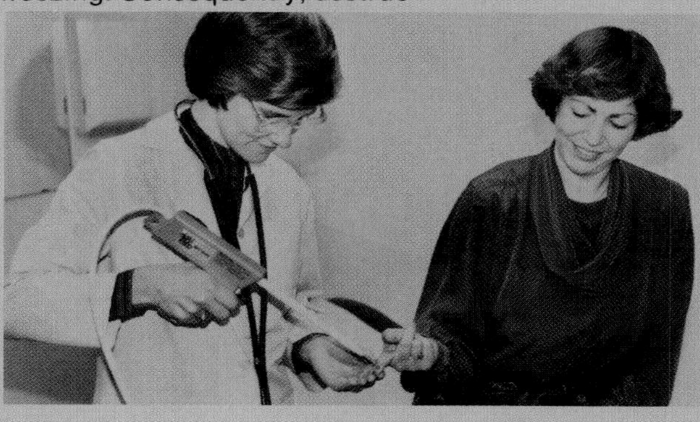

Wart removed by cryosurgery.

9–15 Specific Heats: Hold That Temperature

If an aluminum pan full of water were placed on a stove and the burner were turned on high, after two minutes the pan would get painfully hot before the water would heat up. Why? Although the pan does receive the heat first, there is a more significant reason that it becomes hotter quicker. All substances do not heat at the same rate. The amount of heat energy that raises 1 gram of water 1°C will raise the temperature of 1 gram of aluminum 4.54°C. Given the same amount of heat, aluminum will get hotter.

These differences arise because substances have characteristic specific heats. The **specific heat** of a substance is the amount of heat required to raise the temperature of 1 gram of the substance 1°C. The usual unit for this quantity is calories per gram °C (cal/g °C).

One gram of water can be raised 1°C with the input of 1 calorie. The specific heat of water is 1 calorie per gram °C. A gram of aluminum requires only 0.22 calorie for the same rise in temperature. The specific heat of aluminum is 0.22 calorie per

Table 9-30

Substance	Specific Heat (cal/g °C)
Mercury	0.033
Lead	0.038
Silver	0.056
Copper	0.092
Chlorine	0.11
Carbon	0.12
Aluminum	0.22
Oxygen	0.22
Benzene	0.42
Acetic acid	0.49
Ethyl alcohol	0.58
Water	1.00

gram °C. Specific heats of common substances are listed in Table 9-30. Those substances with high specific heats require large amounts of thermal energy for a given temperature change. Low specific heats indicate that the substances change temperature rapidly.

Like heats of vaporization, specific heats serve as rough indicators of intermolecular attractions. Molecules that are strongly attracted to each other require extra thermal energy to increase their kinetic energies.

The warming curve of a substance reveals the relative specific heats. If the temperature rises quickly with the addition of heat, the specific heat must be low. In this case a small amount of heat results in a large change in temperature. A substance that has a gentle slope on its warming curve has a high specific heat because added heat does not change the temperature very much. The warming curve of water illustrates this well. The specific heat of ice is approximately 0.5 calorie per gram °C at 0°C. Ice heats up twice as quickly as liquid water. The slope of the warming curve that corresponds to the heating of ice is steeper than the portion that corresponds to the heating of the liquid.

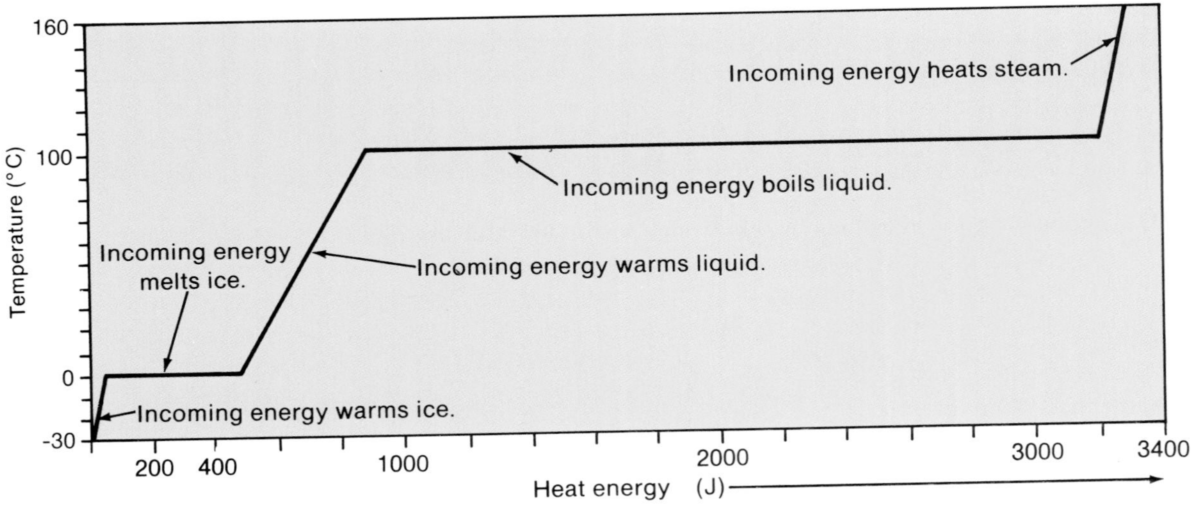

9-31 The slopes of the lines on a warming curve indicate how quickly a substance changes temperature as it is heated.

Coming to Terms

crystalline solid
amorphous solid
heat of fusion
sublimation
crystal lattice
unit cell
angstrom
polymorphous
allotropic
allotrope
lattice energy
surface tension
meniscus
capillary rise
viscocity
evaporation
heat of vaporization
boiling
boiling point
heat of condensation
distillation
critical temperature
critical pressure
specific heat

Review Questions

1. Use the kinetic theory to explain each observation given.
   a. Wax melts near the flame of a burning candle.
   b. Liquid water may be converted into ice cubes in a freezer.
   c. Ginger ale flows to match the shape of the glass.
   d. Water gradually evaporates from a swimming pool.
   e. Water vapor condenses inside house windows on cold days.
   f. Alcohol boils when heated strongly.
   g. Snow gradually disappears, even when the temperature remains below freezing.
   h. Solids and liquids cannot be compressed as much as gases.
2. What is the major difference between a crystal and an amorphous solid?
3. Assume that the particles in table salt (NaCl) vibrate just as forcefully as the particles in Pb. Can you explain why NaCl remains a solid at 500° C while Pb exists as a liquid?
4. When heat is being removed from a liquid, why does the temperature of the liquid at its freezing point remain constant until all of the liquid freezes?
5. What would happen to the temperature and physical state of a mole of benzene (C_6H_6) liquid at its standard boiling point if its molar heat of vaporization (94.3 cal) were added?
6. What is wrong with the statement, "As a solid freezes, it absorbs energy equal in amount to its heat of fusion"?
7. After a jar of liquid has been sealed, the level of the liquid decreases slightly because of evaporation. After a slight decrease, the level of the liquid ceases to change. Why?
8. Name three factors that determine the structure of a crystal.
9. Name three factors that determine the strength of a crystal.

10. Predict which member of the following pairs of crystals has the stronger binding forces. Explain the reasons for your prediction.
    a. NaCl, I_2
    b. KBr, NaBr
    c. CaI_2, KI
11. In terms of attractive forces and kinetic energies of particles, explain what happens during the following phase changes. Example: melting. The particles gain enough kinetic energy to break away from the attractive forces that hold them in fixed positions.
    a. boiling
    b. evaporation
    c. freezing
    d. condensation
    e. sublimation
12. A white powder contains tiny, cube-shaped grains and melts at a temperature between 141.6 and 142.2° C. Is this solid most likely to be a crystalline solid or an amorphous solid?
13. Fill in the following chart, which summarizes the properties of solids, liquids, and gases.

State	Compressible	Fluid	Density
Solid	_____	_____	relatively high
Liquid	_____	yes	_____
Gas	yes	_____	_____

14. What causes surface tension?
15. Water rolls off a duck's back but thoroughly wets a head of human hair. What do these observations reveal about the chemical nature of these two surfaces?
16. Why do raindrops not assume triangular or cubic shapes?
17. Human bodies sweat when they overheat. Why does perspiration on the skin cool a person's body?
18. Why does the surface of water in a glass test tube curve upward at the edges?
19. Automobile engines require low-viscosity oils in extremely cold weather. What causes low-viscosity oil to work better at low temperatures than high-viscosity oils? What can you conclude about the intermolecular attractions in low-viscosity oil?
20. What is the essential difference between boiling and evaporation?
21. Refer to the graph of vapor pressures and boiling points on page 224 to determine

a. the boiling point of ethanol when it is at normal atmospheric pressure.
b. the boiling point of methanol at 720 mm Hg.
c. the atmospheric pressure at which diethyl ether boils at 20° C.

22. Water in a truck's radiator can get hotter than 100° C when the radiator is sealed tight. How is it possible for water to exist as a liquid at temperatures above its normal boiling point?
23. Crude oil is purified through a process called fractional distillation. In this process the different components of oil (lubricating oil, grease, gasoline, natural gas, etc.) are separated by distillation. What do you conclude about the physical properties of the different components?
24. A scientist claims to have a cooling apparatus kept at -100° C by liquid nitrogen. Is this possible?

TEN

WATER

SMALL BONDS HAVE BIG EFFECTS

WHAT could be so spectacular about water that an entire chapter should be devoted to its qualities? It is such an ordinary compound. It has no color, no taste, and no odor. The compound is so harmless that it serves as a home for creatures ranging from amoebas to blue whales. It makes up approximately 65 per cent of the human body. Water is seen everywhere—oceans, lakes, rivers, ice, and clouds. All in all, it has been estimated that there are 1358 million cubic kilometers (1.358×10^{21} ℓ) of water on the earth. That amounts to 7.546×10^{22} moles of water.

Only an amazing compound could be so ordinary. Water must have unique properties that allow it to do so many things in the earth's environment. Indeed, when compared to other compounds that should be similar, water emerges as a unique, fascinating, and intriguing compound.

The Water Molecule

10–1 Structure

Water owes its unique properties to its molecular structure. The atoms, the shape, and the polarity of the molecules cause the compound to act the way it does.

A water molecule is made of two hydrogen atoms that are covalently bonded to an oxygen atom. Before bonding, hydrogen atoms have one valence electron (one short of a full outer energy level), and oxygen atoms have six valence electrons (two short of an octet). Two single bonds allow all the atoms to achieve stable electronic configurations.

H:Ö:
  H

According to the valence bond theory, the orbitals of the oxygen atom change before they bond. The one $2s$ and the three $2p$ orbitals hybridize to form four similar orbitals. Two of the new orbitals contain two electrons, but the other two are only partially filled. The hydrogen atoms bond covalently by sharing electrons in the two unfilled hybridized orbitals.

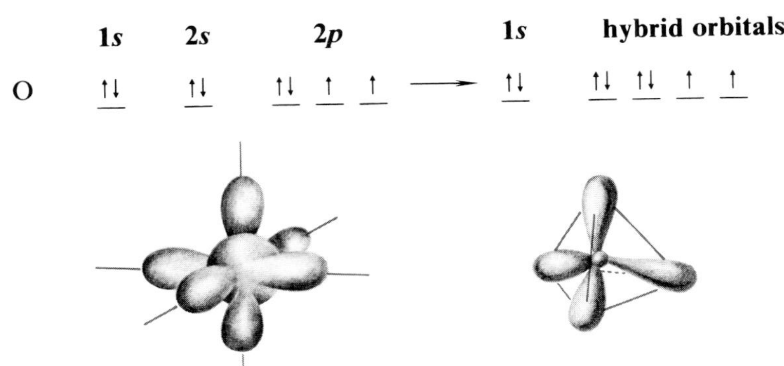

10-1 Oxygen atoms hybridize before they bond.

Because the hybridized orbitals are oriented in the shape of a tetrahedron, the two bonds should form a 109.5° angle. The molecule does have a bent shape, but the angle is 104.5° instead of the expected 109.5°. The difference between the theoretical and the actual bond angle results from the fact that the unbonded orbitals take up more space than the bonded orbitals. Electrostatic repulsions between the electrons in unbonded orbitals are greater than the electrostatic repulsions in bonded orbitals.

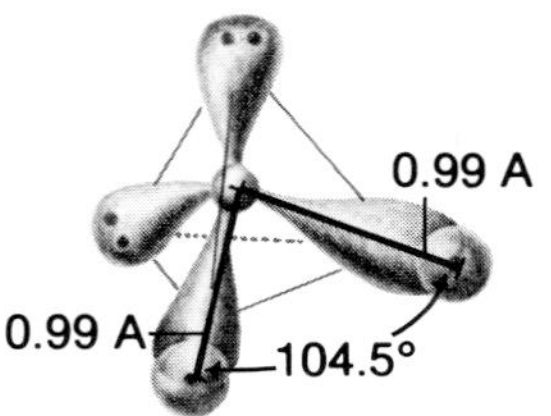

10-2 Bond lengths and angles in water molecules.

10–2 Hydrogen Bonding

An oxygen atom has a high electronegativity (3.5 on the Pauling scale). A hydrogen atom has a low electronegativity—2.1. The combination of oxygen and hydrogen atoms forms a polar bond, and electrons are shifted toward the oxygen atom. The positive charge on each hydrogen nucleus is left partially exposed while the shared electrons are pulled close to the oxygen atom. The polar bonds and the unsymmetrical shape make the water molecule polar. The region of the molecule that contains the exposed hydrogen nuclei is partially positive, and the region that contains the oxygen atom is partially negative.

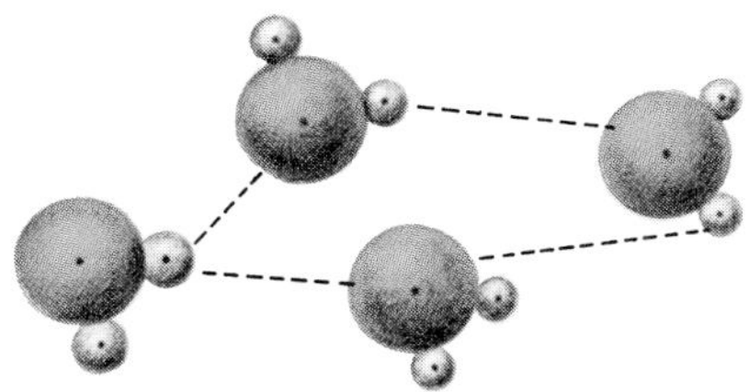

10-3 Hydrogen bonding between water molecules.

Hydrogen bonds form between the hydrogen atoms of one water molecule and the oxygen atom of another water molecule. These bonds, like other intermolecular forces, are not as strong as the covalent bonds that form molecules. While 68.3 kilocalories of energy would be required to break the covalent bonds in a mole of water molecules, only 4 or 5 kilocalories of energy are required to break apart a mole of hydrogen bonds. Between water molecules the average hydrogen-bond length is 1.77 angstroms (compared to 0.99 angstrom for the O-H covalent bond). Despite the apparent weakness of these bonds, they have a great effect on the physical properties of water.

10–3 Physical Properties

Hydrogen bonds raise melting and boiling points. It may seem perfectly natural for water to melt (or freeze) at 0° C and to boil at 100° C, but these facts are actually rather surprising. Look at the series of compounds in which two hydrogen atoms are bonded to elements in the VIA family.

Table 10-4

Compound	Molecular Mass	Melting Point	Boiling Point
H_2Te	129.6	-49.0	-2.0
H_2Se	80.98	-60.4	-41.5
H_2S	34.07	-85.5	-60.7
H_2O	18.02	0.0	100.0

The large mass of each hydrogen telluride (H_2Te) molecule causes the comparatively high melting point of -49° C and boiling point of -2° C. Hydrogen selenide (H_2Se) and hydrogen sulfide (H_2S) have lower melting points because their molecules have less mass. The hydrogen bonds in water raise the boiling point despite

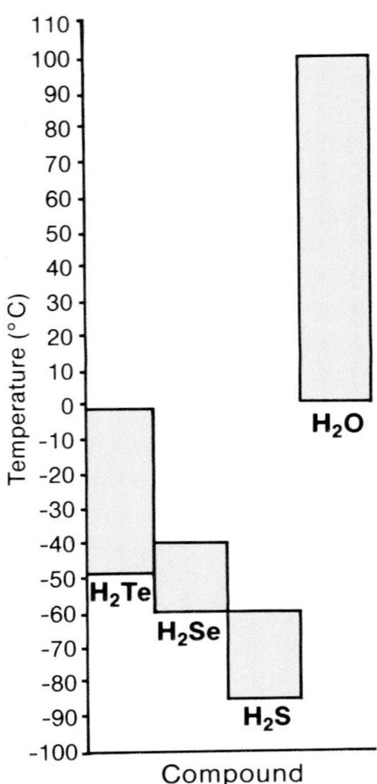

10-6 The temperatures at which water exists as a liquid are much higher than the temperatures at which related compounds exist as liquids.

the low mass of each molecule. The attractions hold water molecules in the solid state at temperatures far above those at which the other compounds vaporize. The hydrogen bonds also hold the water molecules in the liquid state at the surprisingly high temperature of 100° C.

Water changes from a liquid to a gas at 100° C when the atmospheric pressure is 760 millimeters of mercury. At higher pressures, higher temperatures are needed to boil water. Lower-than-normal pressures cause lower boiling temperatures. Figure 10-5 shows the boiling points at different pressures. Note that water can boil even at temperatures near 0° C if the atmospheric pressure is low enough.

10-5 Boiling Point of Water at Different Pressures

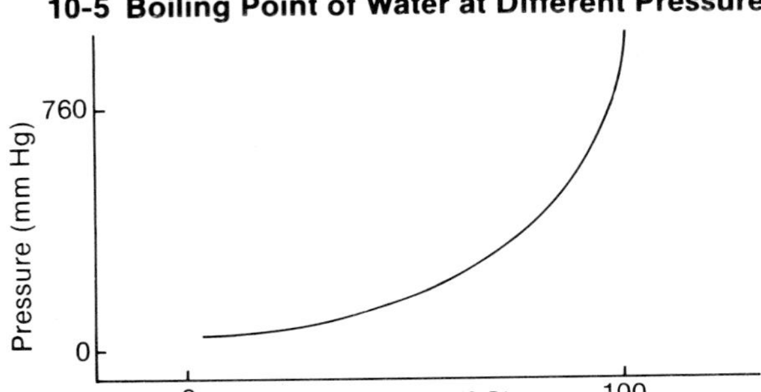

Is it merely coincidental that atmospheric conditions on this planet allow water to exist in the liquid state? Hardly. The Lord providentially engineered the sun's thermal output, the dimensions of the solar system, and the earth's cloud cover to provide conditions that would allow water to exist as a liquid. Other planets do not have appreciable amounts of water. But even if they did, their surface temperatures and pressures would not allow water to exist as a liquid.

Water's melting point (or freezing point) is 0° C. Differences in atmospheric pressure affect the melting point, but not nearly as much as they affect the boiling point. As the pressure rises, the melting point decreases slightly. The almost vertical line in Figure 10-7 shows the melting points at different pressures.

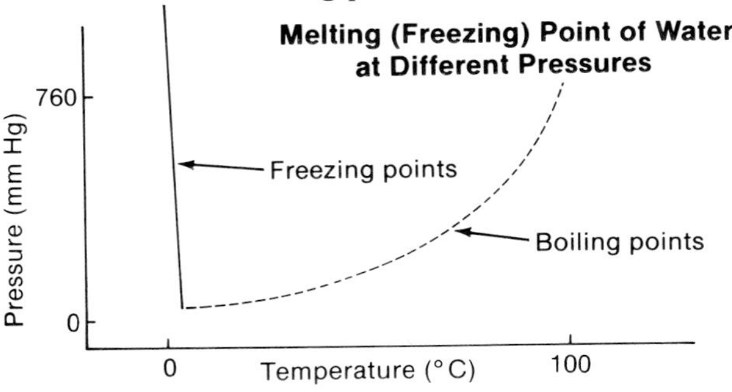

10-7 The freezing point of water changes slightly with pressure.

Figure 10-8 is called a **phase diagram** because it represents the conditions at which water exists as a solid, liquid, or gas.

10-8 Phase Diagram of Water

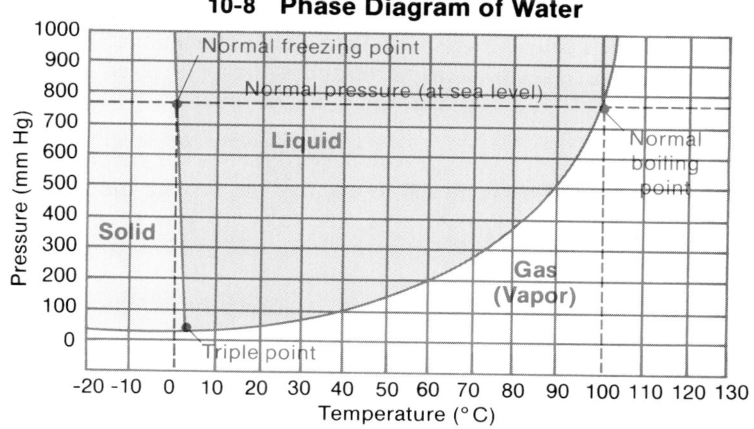

Sample Problem. Determine the state of water at the following conditions.

a. 60° C, 400 mm Hg
b. -10 °C, 1000 mm Hg
c. 80 °C, 200 mm Hg

Solution.

a. The point that corresponds to 60° C and 400 millimeters of mercury is between the line of melting points and the line of boiling points. This region represents the conditions at which water is in the liquid state.

b. The point corresponding to -10° C and 1000 millimeters of mercury is to the left of the line of melting points. Water is a solid under these conditions.

c. The point corresponding to 80° C and 200 millimeters of mercury lies beyond the line of boiling points. Water will exist as a gas under these conditions.

In what phase would water exist at a temperature of 0.01° C and a pressure of 4.6 millimeters of mercury? The line of boiling points and the line of melting points intersect at this point. Under this condition water can exist in all three states: solid, liquid, and gas. The pressure is low enough that some liquid water can change to a gaseous state. At the same time, the temperature is low enough that some liquid water can begin to freeze into a solid. This specific set of conditions is called the **triple point** of water.

Normally the density of water is considered to be 1 gram per milliliter, but that density changes slightly with temperature. The kinetic theory says that particles in matter vibrate less violently at lower temperatures. It logically follows that particles that are vibrating less will occupy less space than other particles. Because of this, most matter "shrinks" as its temperature is lowered. Since the same mass occupies less space, the density increases with lower temperatures.

The volume of water changes in accordance with the kinetic theory when it is cooled from 100°C to 3.98°C. As the molecules lose kinetic energy, they vibrate less and take up less space. But at 3.98°C (approximately 4°C) something surprising happens: water begins to expand. It continues to expand as the temperature falls down to 0°C. When water freezes, it suddenly expands even more. This characteristic is completely unlike the characteristics of most matter because most matter shrinks when it freezes.

10-9 Density of Water vs. Temperature

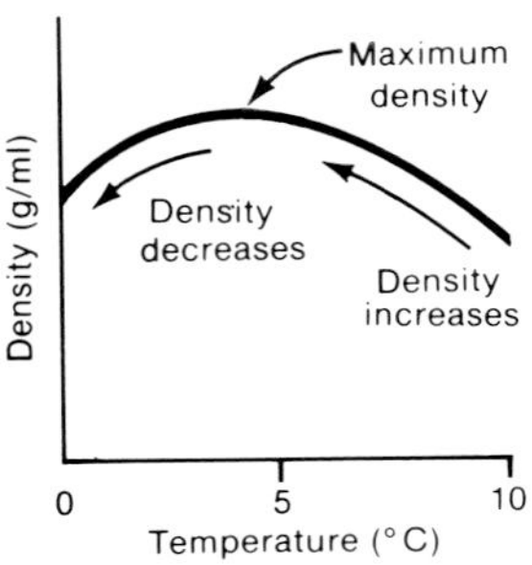

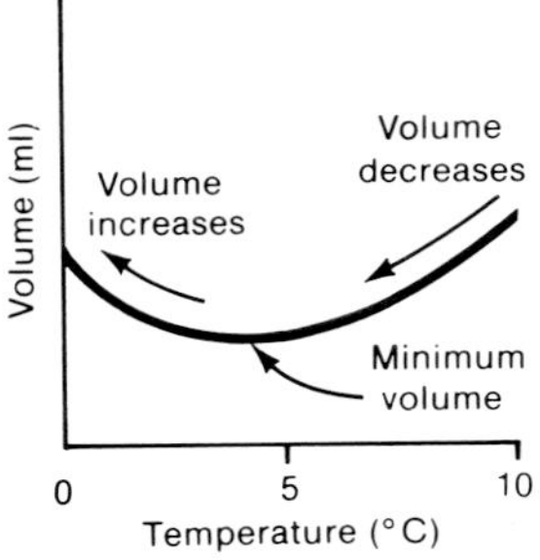

Density is inversely related to volume. As volume increases, density decreases. Conversely, if volume decreases, density increases. This means that water's density is greatest at 4°C and least when water is frozen. Since the density of an object determines whether it will float or sink in water, ice always floats on the top of liquid water. God's wisdom in designing this earth becomes evident. If water did not expand when it froze, ice would sink to the bottom of oceans, lakes, and rivers instead of forming a layer on the surface. Long, cold winters would cause small bodies of water to freeze solid, killing off many fish and plants and disrupting a vital ecological food chain.

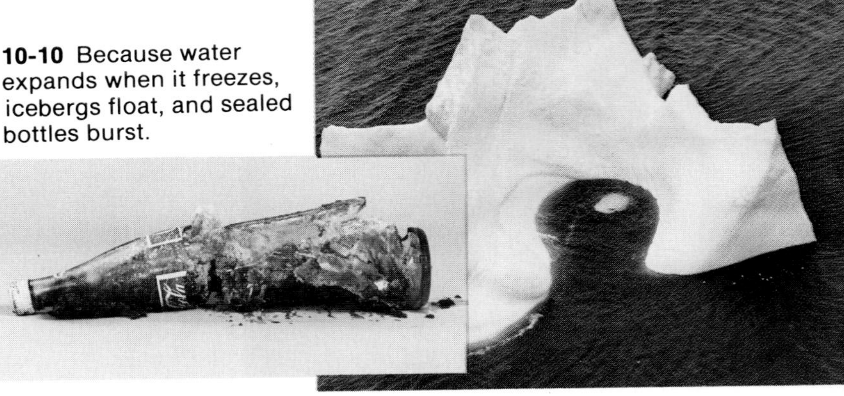

10-10 Because water expands when it freezes, icebergs float, and sealed bottles burst.

Why does water exhibit this novel behavior? Hydrogen bonds and molecular shapes are the causes. When water freezes, molecules fall into an open, hexagonal crystalline lattice. Hydrogen bonds stabilize the structure and hold molecules in place. Note the empty spaces in the structure. If the molecules were free to roll and slide, this space would be filled. But since the hydrogen bonds dictate where the molecules are when they are in the solid state, the space remains empty. It is this empty space that increases the volume and decreases the density of water when it freezes.

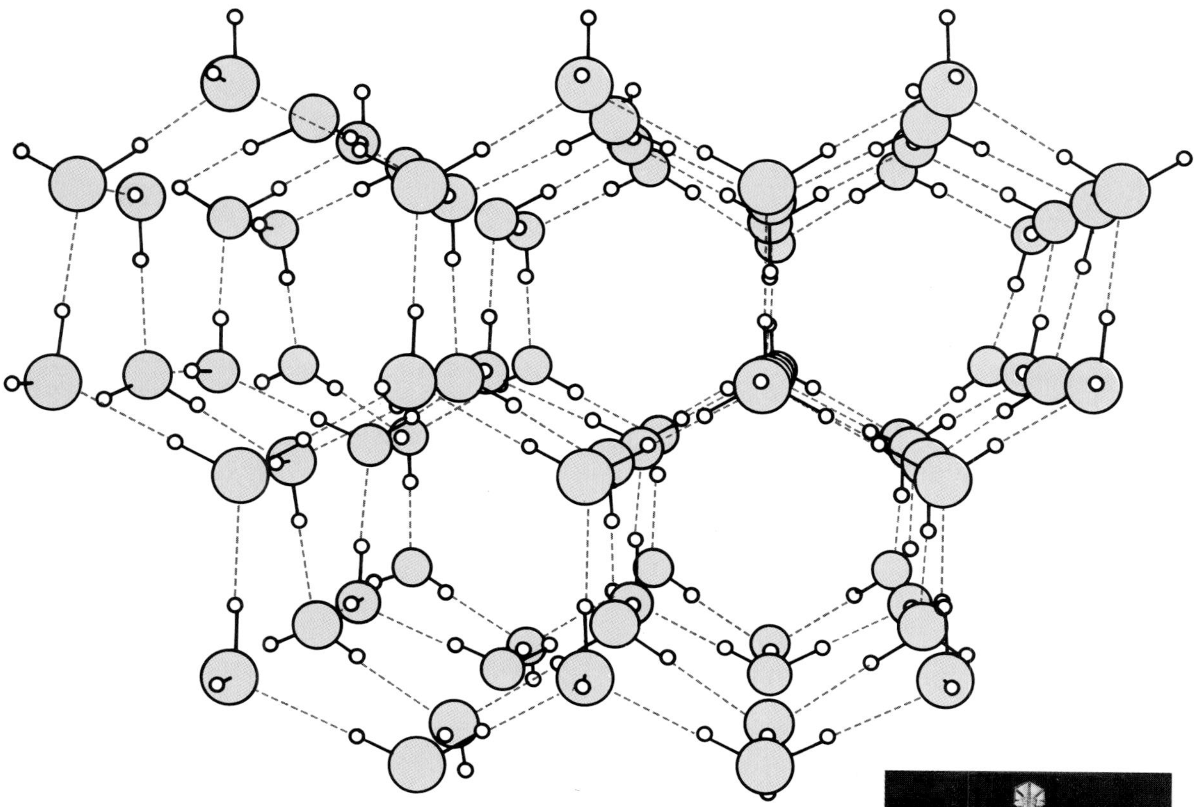

10-11 When ice forms, hydrogen bonds hold water molecules in a hexagonal crystal structure.

The hexagonal structure is seen mostly in solid ice, but some scientists think that it is present to some degree in very cold water. Even while molecules are rolling over one another, they may arrange into the hexagonal form. When the temperature falls below 4° C, the thermal movement decreases and the hydrogen bonds begin to orient the water molecules into the orderly but spacious crystal system.

The extraordinary surface tension of water further illustrates water's strong intermolecular attractions. Of all the common liquids, only hydrazine (N_2H_4), hydrogen peroxide (H_2O_2), and mercury have greater surface tensions.

Another physical property of water has weighty environmental consequences. God has designed water with a high specific heat. That is, a large amount of heat energy must be absorbed before

FACETS OF CHEMISTRY

Water Purification

A small fleet of ships docks to a gigantic iceberg floating in the sea off Antarctica. The crews wrap the iceberg with sheets of insulating plastic, attach mooring cables, and begin towing the iceberg north to the Indian Ocean. By the time the iceberg reaches its destination off the coast of Saudi Arabia, much of it has melted away. Enough ice remains, however, to supply a substantial amount of much-needed pure water.

No one has towed an iceberg to a country that needs pure water, but the idea has been considered. Pure water is a vital commodity in today's society. Consequently, the purification of water is an important industrial process.

The earth's water is purified by a gigantic natural distillation system called the water cycle. Water continually moves from the continents to the oceans. Evaporation takes place from both the continents and oceans, leaving impurities behind. Water vapor rising to colder layers of air condenses to liquid droplets that form clouds. The cycle is completed when the clouds pour the purified water back onto the earth's surface as rain. This divinely engineered system continuously purifies water on a global scale.

Early settlers in the United States were able to meet their water requirements by simply drilling wells. Ground water is available almost anywhere if a person drills to a sufficient depth. Residents of many rural and resort areas still obtain their water from wells. In more densely settled areas, however, it is difficult, if not impossible, to keep sewage and other contaminants out of the ground water. Since it would be impractical for each home owner to have his own water-treatment plant, well water as a source for homes has largely given way to community water supplies with large-scale treatment plants.

Water generally goes through three types of purification operations: (1) coagulation and settling, (2) filtration, and (3) disinfection. Coagulation is accomplished by the addition of alum (aluminum sulfate) to the water. The alum reacts with the water to form aluminum hydroxide, a gelatinous precipitate that slowly settles to the bottom of the container. As it falls, it traps bacteria and impurities that color the water. After the precipitate settles, the water is drawn off and passed through a filter, which often consists of a bed of sand on top of a bed of gravel. Finally the water is disinfected

the temperature of water changes significantly. Water, therefore, can store large amounts of heat energy and resist rapid fluctuations in temperature. The high specific heat of water allows oceans and lakes to act as moderators of the climate. Large bodies of water

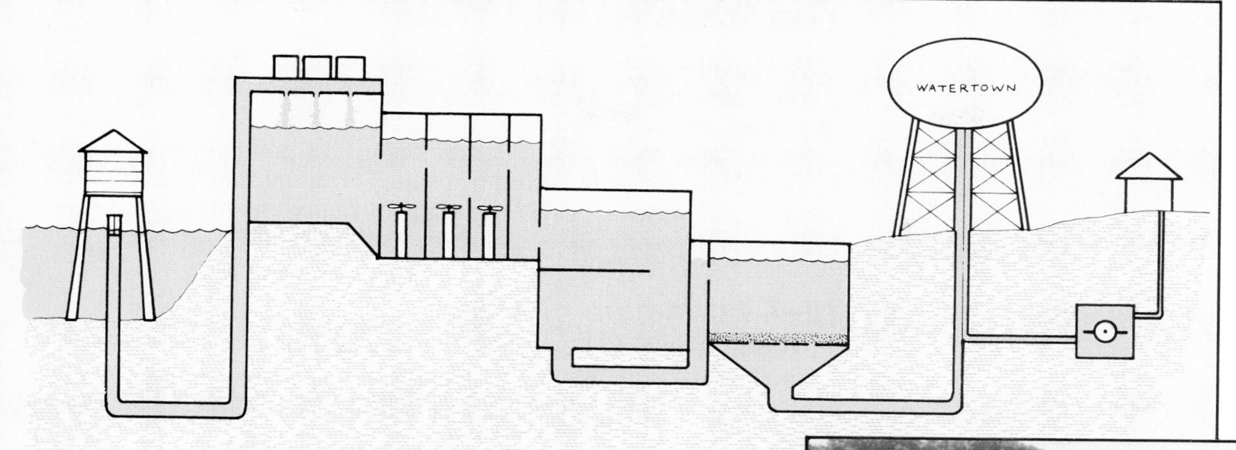

by the addition of a small quantity of chlorine. In some localities where taste or odor is a particular problem, the water is also aerated (mixed with air) or treated with activated charcoal.

Many regions of the world need additional sources of drinking water. Research is continuing on the desalting of seawater (3.5% salt content) and brackish water (less than 3.5% salt content). Distillation is the most straightforward way to purify water containing dissolved solids, but large amounts of thermal energy are required to boil the water. Water may be boiled at a considerably lower temperature than its normal boiling point if the pressure on it is reduced (vacuum distillation). But an additional amount of energy is required to produce the reduced vacuum. Because of the problems associated with distillation, scientists have sought new methods for the desalting of seawater.

In one alternate process called reverse osmosis, salt water is forced under pressure against a semipermeable membrane. Water molecules squeeze through the membrane, but the salt stays behind. In another process salt water is cooled to the freezing point. Crystals of pure ice form while the salt stays in solution. The ice is washed free of salt, then melted for use. Both of these alternate processes work better for brackish water than for seawater, since brackish water contains a lower concentration of impurities. At the present time there is no completely satisfactory method for purifying seawater. Therefore new ideas like towing icebergs are still being entertained.

absorb much of the summer's heat before their temperatures change significantly. When winter comes, the warmed water acts as a heat reservoir long after the air becomes frosty and the ground freezes. Without water's high specific heat, the earth's climate would fluctuate wildly from night to day and from season to season.

The Reactions of Water

Water molecules are stable. Large releases of energy usually accompany their formation. Once water molecules form, it is extremely difficult to break them apart with heat alone (temperatures around 2700° C are required). This great stability makes water an energetically favored product of many reactions. On the other hand, water is also a reactant in many chemical processes. Many reactive substances can react with it despite its stability.

10–4 Formation of Water

It may come as a surprise, but one of the chemicals emitted from an automobile's exhaust pipe is plain water. The combustion of gasoline yields water as a product. In fact, the combustion of any hydrocarbon produces water.

$$2\,C_2H_6 + 7\,O_2 \longrightarrow 4\,CO_2 + 6\,H_2O$$
$$C_3H_8 + 5\,O_2 \longrightarrow 3\,CO_2 + 4\,H_2O$$
$$2\,C_8H_{18} + 25\,O_2 \longrightarrow 16\,CO_2 + 18\,H_2O$$

The combustion of hydrogen also produces water. This combustion reaction releases energy with an explosive force like that from the combustion of hydrocarbons. Because this reaction sidesteps problems associated with the burning of hydrocarbons (problems such as high cost of fuel and the unwanted by-products), scientists have considered it as an alternative source of energy.

10-12 An experimental vehicle burns hydrogen gas instead of gasoline.

$$2\,H_2 + O_2 \longrightarrow 2\,H_2O$$

Reactions between acids and bases also produce water. These two types of compounds can neutralize each other and produce water in the process.

$$\begin{array}{ccccccc} HCl & + & NaOH & \longrightarrow & NaCl & + & H_2O \\ \text{acid} & + & \text{base} & \longrightarrow & \text{salt} & + & \text{water} \end{array}$$

10–5 Electrolysis

The heat and the explosive force that result from the formation of water by combustion attest to the great amount of energy that is given off when hydrogen and oxygen bond. Once water molecules form, a large amount of energy is needed to break them apart. Although heat or chemical energy could be used to split water molecules, the form of energy that is most efficient at this task is electrical energy. It can decompose water in a process called **electrolysis.**

An electrical voltage of at least 1.23 volts is required to pull the water molecules apart. This voltage can be supplied by a dry-cell battery, a lead-storage battery, or any other source of direct current. The voltage is applied to two chemically inert electrodes dipped in the water sample. The electrode connected to the negative terminal (the cathode) adds electrons to water molecules to produce hydrogen gas.

Cathode: $4\ H_2O + 4\ \text{electrons} \longrightarrow 2\ H_2 + 4\ OH^-$

The electrode connected to the positive terminal (the anode) pulls electrons from water molecules to form oxygen.

Anode: $2\ H_2O \longrightarrow O_2 + 4\ H^+ + 4\ \text{electrons}$

The total reaction is the combination of both reactions.

Total:

$$6\ H_2O + 4\ \text{electrons} \longrightarrow 2\ H_2 + O_2 + 4\ OH^- + 4\ H^+ + 4\ \text{electrons}$$

$$2\ H_2O \longrightarrow 2\ H_2 + O_2$$

Figure 10-13 shows an apparatus that is often used to separate and collect the gases that are formed. A small amount of sulfuric acid, hydrochloric acid, sodium chloride, or potassium hydroxide is added to the water being decomposed. These substances do not participate in the electrolysis except to carry the electrical current between the two electrodes. Pure water cannot conduct electricity, so substances that ionize must be present. Moving ions can shuttle electrical current.

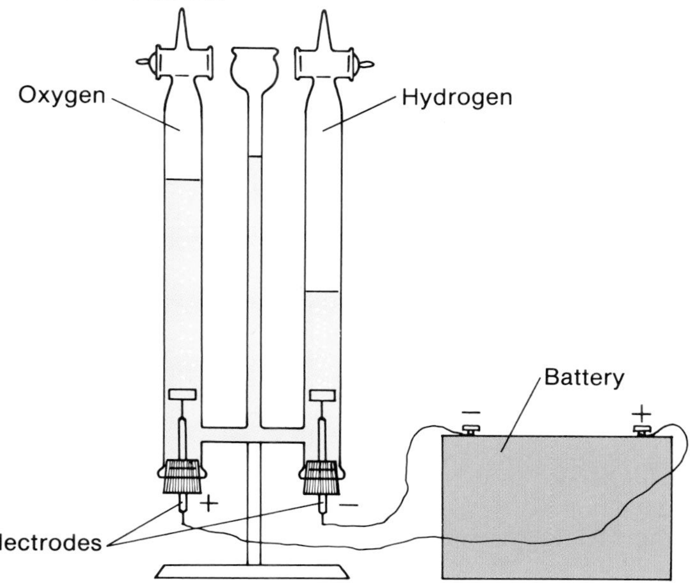

10-13 Electrolysis of water.

10–6 Reactions with Elements

Many of the more active metals can react with water at room temperature. In essence these reactions are single replacement reactions in which the metals replace hydrogen in the water molecule.

The reaction between sodium and water proceeds quickly and explosively.

$$2\,Na + 2\,H_2O \longrightarrow 2\,NaOH + H_2$$

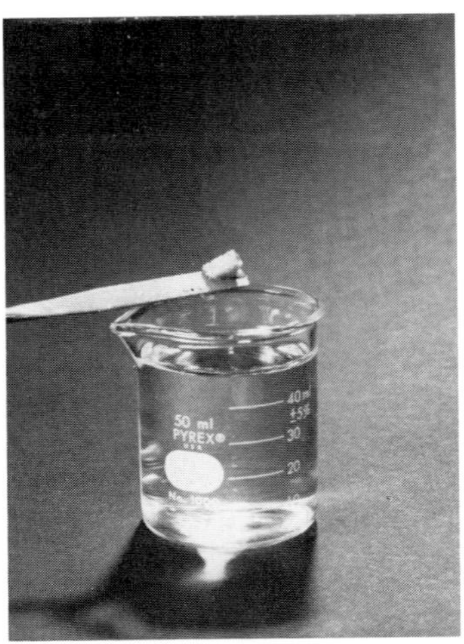

10-14 Sodium reacts violently with water.

Sodium hydroxide (NaOH) splits into Na^+ and OH^- ions in the water solution, and hydrogen gas is released. Potassium undergoes a similar reaction except that it forms potassium hydroxide (KOH) and reacts even faster and more violently than sodium. Calcium metal also reacts with water at room temperatures.

$$Ca + 2\,H_2O \longrightarrow Ca(OH)_2 + H_2$$

Since magnesium is not as reactive as calcium, it requires boiling water to react. As in the other reactions, a metal hydroxide and hydrogen gas are the products.

Moderately reactive metals such as iron, zinc, and aluminum will react with water only when the water is heated into steam.

$$2\,Fe + 6\,H_2O\,(g) \longrightarrow 2\,Fe(OH)_3 + 4\,H_2$$
$$Zn + 2\,H_2O\,(g) \longrightarrow Zn(OH)_2 + H_2$$
$$2\,Al + 6\,H_2O\,(g) \longrightarrow 2\,Al(OH)_3 + 3\,H_2$$

The most significant water-and-nonmetal reactions involve the halogens. Iodine, bromine, and chlorine can react to form acids: the halogen and water molecules are split. The reaction for chlorine illustrates the general form:

$$\begin{array}{l} H-O \\ \quad\;| \\ \quad\;H \end{array} + Cl-Cl \longrightarrow Cl-OH + H-Cl$$

The extremely reactive fluorine molecule is the only halogen that displaces oxygen from a water molecule.

$$2\,F_2 + 6\,H_2O \longrightarrow 4\,H_3O^+ + 4\,F^- + O_2$$

10–7 Reactions with Compounds

Compounds that can react with water in composition reactions are called **anhydrides** (meaning "without water"). Two types of anhydrides will be considered: metal oxides and nonmetal oxides.

10-15 $CaO + H_2O \longrightarrow Ca(OH)_2$. Phenolphthalein in the water is colorless before the reaction. After the reaction it turns pink, signifying the presence of $Ca(OH)_2$ (a base).

The oxides of very active metals such as sodium, potassium, barium, and calcium react to form compounds with basic properties.

$$Na_2O + H_2O \longrightarrow 2\ NaOH$$
$$CaO + H_2O \longrightarrow Ca(OH)_2$$

Potassium oxide and barium oxide undergo similar reactions. Because the products of reactions like these have the properties of bases, metal oxides are called **basic anhydrides.**

Oxides of nonmetals such as sulfur, carbon, and phosphorus react with water to form oxyacids. Because of these reactions, oxides of nonmetals are given the name **acidic anhydrides.**

$$CO_2 + H_2O \longrightarrow H_2CO_3$$
$$SO_3 + H_2O \longrightarrow H_2SO_4$$
$$P_4O_{10} + 6\ H_2O \longrightarrow 4\ H_3PO_4$$

10-16 $SO_3 + H_2O \longrightarrow H_2SO_4$. Burning sulfur produces SO_3 gas, which mixes with the water. The color of an indicator in the water changes to show that an acid forms.

Water in Compounds

Water, water, everywhere,
Nor any drop to drink.

These lines from Samuel Coleridge's *Rime of the Ancient Mariner* were written to show the plight of sailors on a ship stranded in a salty sea. These lines could also describe the presence of water in chemical compounds. Water molecules can be found in many compounds and in surprising numbers. Though not always easily obtained, water *is* nearly everywhere.

10–8 Hydrates

Hydrates are chemical compounds that include water in their crystal structures. Water molecules occupy empty space in some crystals. Electrically charged particles in the crystal structure can interact with the regions of charge in water molecules to hold them in place. In one sense hydrates are like a chemical sponge: they hold water molecules. Yet hydrates are different from sponges in two important aspects: they hold a set amount of water, and they have crystal structures.

The majority of hydrates are salts. Copper sulfate ($CuSO_4$) crystals can bind 5 moles of water molecules for every mole of

FACETS OF CHEMISTRY

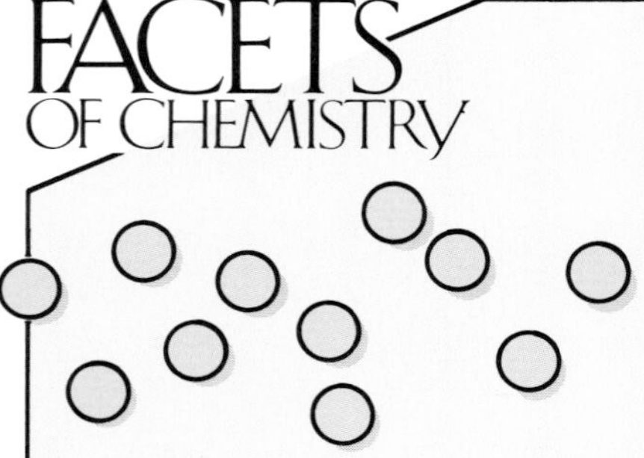

An F^- That Made the Grade

In the early 1900s Dr. Frederick McKay noticed that some of his patients had mottled (spotted) tooth enamel that was harder and more resistant to decay than "normal" enamel. He observed this condition only in individuals who had lived in certain geographical areas during their childhood. Adults who moved into these areas did not show the effect. One locality in particular that came to Dr. McKay's attention was Bauxite, Arkansas. His intuition told him that it was something in the drinking water. In 1931 ALCOA (Aluminum Company of America) detected elevated levels of fluoride ions (F^-) in the water. The cause of the condition had finally been determined.

Later in the 1930s the U.S. Public Health Service made a study of selected localities that had either unusually high or unusually low fluoride levels. On the basis of these investigations, authorities concluded that a level of 1 part per million (ppm) dramatically reduced decay without causing mottling. Several of the investigators suggested that it would be beneficial to raise the fluoride concentration to 1 part per million in regions in which it was low. As a result, community fluoridation was born.

In the mid-1940s three cities were selected for pilot fluoridation projects—Newburgh, New York; Grand Rapids, Michigan; and Brantford, Ontario. Test results were most satisfactory: the occurrence of dental cavities was reduced 41 to 63 per cent. A fourth study undertaken in Evanston, Illinois, in 1947 resulted in reductions ranging from 49 per cent to 75 per cent. The reason for the wide percentage span is that the amount of benefit depends strongly on the age of the individual—the younger the person, the greater the benefit. From Evanston the practice of fluoridation quickly spread to other communities. Even a number of foreign countries soon followed this practice. Today more than half of the population of the United States enjoys the benefits of fluoridated water.

In addition to studying the benefits of fluoridation, higher concentrations of the fluoride ion, none can be documented at the level of 1 part per million. It is now generally agreed that fluoridation as it is presently dispensed is as safe as it is effective.

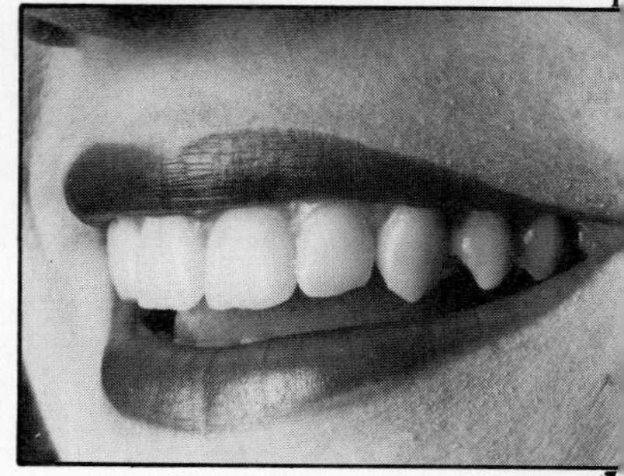

copper sulfate. The water that is incorporated into the crystal structure is called the **water of hydration.**

10-17 $CuSO_4 \cdot 5\ H_2O$ changes color from deep blue to white as it is dehydrated.

Many other compounds naturally hold water in their crystal structures. Recall that hydrated compounds are named according to the same rules that were used for other compounds. The word *hydrate* follows a Greek prefix.

$CuSO_4 \cdot 5\ H_2O$: copper sulfate pentahydrate
$Ba(OH)_2 \cdot 8\ H_2O$: barium hydroxide octahydrate
$Na_2CO_3 \cdot 10\ H_2O$: sodium carbonate decahydrate

Water molecules can be driven out of hydrates with high temperatures or low pressures. Copper sulfate pentahydrate can be dehydrated if it is heated with a Bunsen burner.

$$CuSO_4 \cdot 5\ H_2O \xrightarrow{\Delta} CuSO_4 + 5\ H_2O$$

10–9 Hygroscopic, Deliquescent, and Efflorescent Compounds

Some substances have such a strong tendency to attract water in their structures that they can remove water from the air. These compounds are called **hygroscopic** compounds. Sodium sulfate is hygroscopic. If placed on a balance, its mass can be observed to increase as it pulls water from the air.

The hygroscopic properties of some compounds must be dealt with in the laboratory. If the compounds are left exposed to the air, their masses will change because of the water they collect. Measurements will not be accurate if precautions are not taken. Hygroscopic compounds must be kept in airtight containers called **desiccators.** Yet even this precaution is sometimes not enough. Powerfully hygroscopic compounds, called drying agents, are stored with the compound being protected in a desiccator. Any moisture in the desiccator is captured by the drying agent (usually $CaCl_2$) rather than by the compound being stored.

10-18 A desiccator.

10-19 Dry sodium hydroxide pellets gain moisture and mass when they are exposed to air.

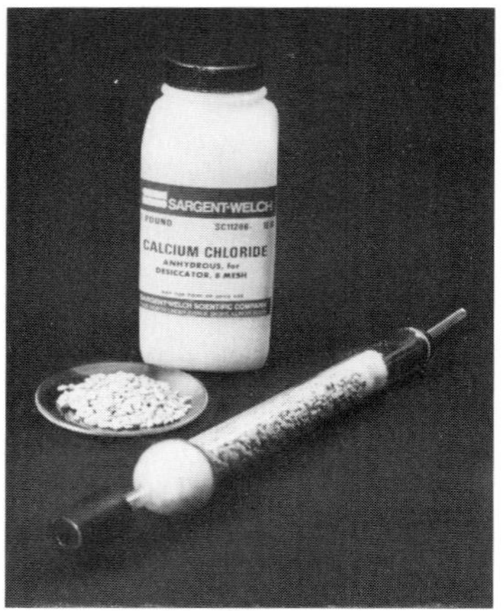

10-20 Air can be dehumidified when it is passed through a tube of $CaCl_2$.

What happens when a compound is highly hygroscopic and also very soluble in water? It dissolves in the water that it captures from the air. The process of attracting enough water to completely dissolve is called **deliquescence.** Compounds that do this become moist. Later the crystals become completely dissolved in a small puddle of water.

Some hydrates lose water when they are exposed to air. This process is called **efflorescence.** Sodium sulfate decahydrate ($Na_2SO_4 \cdot 10\ H_2O$) is one compound that effloresces easily. Copper sulfate pentahydrate effloresces if the humidity is sufficiently low.

Coming to Terms

triple point
phase diagram
electrolysis
anhydride
basic anhydride
acidic anhydride
water of hydration
hygroscopic
desiccator
deliquescence
efflorescence

Review Questions

1. Use your knowledge of the structure and properties of water to explain the following observations.
   a. H_2O molecules are polar.
   b. Of all the group VIA nonmetal hydrides, H_2O has the highest melting and boiling points.
   c. Icebergs float.
   d. Northern coastal cities have warmer winters than do cities located inland at the same latitude.
   e. Snowflakes have crystalline structures.
   f. H_2O molecules are bent.
   g. The angle at which an H_2O molecule is bent is smaller than the angle expected from a tetrahedrally hybridized oxygen.
2. What effect do hydrogen bonds have on the following?
   a. the melting point of water
   b. the boiling point of water
   c. the density of ice
   d. the specific heat of water
3. List three types of reactions that produce water.
4. With the aid of the phase diagram in Figure 10-8, tell what state water exists in under the set of conditions given. If water can exist at more than one state at a set of given conditions, list all possible states.

	Pressure (mm Hg)	Temperature (°C)
a.	780	-25
b.	740	40
c.	500	125
d.	760	0
e.	760	100
f.	300	125
g.	4.60	0.01

5. Complete and balance the following reactions.
   a. $C_5H_{12} + O_2 \longrightarrow$
   b. $H_2 + O_2 \longrightarrow$
   c. $HBr + KOH \longrightarrow$
   d. $Ba(OH)_2 + HNO_3 \longrightarrow$
   e. $Ba(OH)_2 \cdot 8\ H_2O \xrightarrow{\Delta}$
6. If reaction (e) of the previous question occurred spontaneously without heat, the substance would be said to be ____________ and the process would be called ____________.
7. Complete and balance the following reactions.
   a. $Li + H_2O \longrightarrow$
   b. $Mg + H_2O \longrightarrow$
   c. $F_2 + H_2O \longrightarrow$
   d. $Br_2 + H_2O \longrightarrow$
   e. $MgO + H_2O \longrightarrow$
   f. $K_2O + H_2O \longrightarrow$
   g. $SO_2 + H_2O \longrightarrow$
8. What kind of anhydride is
   a. K_2O (see reaction [f] of the previous question)?
   b. SO_2(see reaction [g] of the previous question)?
9. A 2-lb. box of washing soda ($Na_2CO_3 \cdot 10\ H_2O$) manufactured and packaged in Chicago was found to contain only 28 oz. when it was opened in Tempe, Arizona. Assuming that the manufacturer put in a full 2 lb. of washing soda and that the box did not leak, can you explain why the box weighs 4 oz. less?
10. Calculate the gram-formula mass of $CuSO_4 \cdot 5\ H_2O$.
11. Knowing that H_2O is a stable compound, what can you infer about the strength of its chemical bonds?
12. How could you keep a hygroscopic compound anhydrous during several months of storage?
13. If a hygroscopic compound had been left exposed to humid air during storage, what could you do to make it anhydrous?

ELEVEN

SOLUTIONS

CONSISTENTLY MIXED UP

SHAMPOOS, soft drinks, and perfumes are mixtures of many ingredients. Their ingredients do not clump together, separate from each other, or fall to the bottom of the container. These products are not heterogeneous mixtures, since their compositions are uniform. They are not compounds, because no reaction has bound them together.

The substances listed above are **solutions.** In other words, they are homogeneous mixtures of variable composition. The major substance in a solution is called the **solvent.** In shampoo and soft drinks, the solvent is water; in perfume, the solvent is often some type of alcohol. The substances that are dissolved are called **solutes.** Solutes in a solvent make a solution.

The Dissolving Process

People use solutions whenever they add antifreeze to a radiator, salt an icy sidewalk, use sterling silver, disinfect a cut with iodine tincture, or clean windows with ammonia water. They benefit from myriads of products manufactured with and from solutions. Almost every chemical reaction takes place in solution. People breathe a solution called air, and most of the human body is a water solution. The study of chemistry is saturated with solutions.

11–1 Types of Solutions

Most of the common solutions that people come in contact with each day are liquid solutions. The most abundant part of the solution, the solvent, is a liquid. Liquid solvents can dissolve

11-1 Aquarium water must contain dissolved oxygen gas in order for fish to live.

solids, other liquids, and even gases. When sugar is dissolved in tea, a liquid-solid solution is created. Rubbing alcohol, a mixture of 30 per cent water dissolved in 70 per cent isopropyl alcohol, is a common liquid-liquid solution. When two liquids mix to form a homogeneous mixture, they are said to be **miscible.** When they refuse to remain mixed, they are said to be **immiscible.** The oil and vinegar in Italian salad dressing are a common pair of immiscible liquids. No matter how hard oil-and-vinegar salad dressing is shaken, the oil and vinegar separate into two distinct layers. The fact that gases can dissolve in liquids is all-important to fish. Fish "breathe" by removing dissolved oxygen from water with the use of thin, membranous gills.

Solids can also act as solvents. Solids, liquids, and gases can dissolve in solid solvents. The most common solid-solid solutions are alloys. A copper and zinc alloy known as brass blends the two metals into a uniform mixture. Gold and mercury can form a solid-liquid solution that is sometimes undesirable. Liquid mercury will dissolve in gold and will permanently discolor gold rings and bracelets. (For this reason, a person should never work with mercury when wearing gold jewelry.) Hydrogen gas can dissolve in palladium metal and produce a solid-gas solution. Scientists have used this process to purify hydrogen. They allow it to dissolve into the metal, and they then force it out with heat.

A third general type of solution has a gas as the solvent. Although some scientists will argue the point, the only permanent homogeneous mixtures that occur with gas solvents are those in which a gas is also the solute. The solution of gases forming air consists of oxygen, carbon dioxide, and trace amounts of other gases dissolved in approximately 78 per cent nitrogen. Gases cannot serve as solvents for liquid or solid particles, because gases cannot support solid and liquid particles for indefinite periods of time. These combinations form suspensions that will eventually separate.

11–2 Dissolving Mechanisms: Small-Scale Interactions

The water in coffee will eventually dissolve a sugar cube. Although stirring will speed up the process, it is not necessary. The sugar will become evenly distributed throughout the liquid without any outside help. How does this happen? The process of dissolving occurs through molecular interactions called the dissolving mechanism.

For a substance to be dissolved, the attractive forces between particles must be overcome. **Dissociation,** the first step in the dissolving mechanism, does just that. Dissociation is a process of separation. Solute particles, such as sugar molecules, must be pulled away from each other. Attractions between solvent particles must also be overcome. Both of these steps absorb heat; therefore, heat energy must be supplied before the intermolecular forces can be broken.

The next step in the dissolving mechanism is called solvation. **Solvation** is the process in which solvent particles surround and interact with solute particles. In a sugar-and-water solution, positive portions of water molecules attach to negative portions of sugar molecules. The water molecules then pull sugar molecules away from their neighbors. Negative portions of water molecules attract positive parts of sugar molecules in the same manner. Hydrogen bonds form, and dispersion forces take effect. When solute particles are dissolved, energy is released as heat. The process of solvation is called **hydration** when the solvent is water.

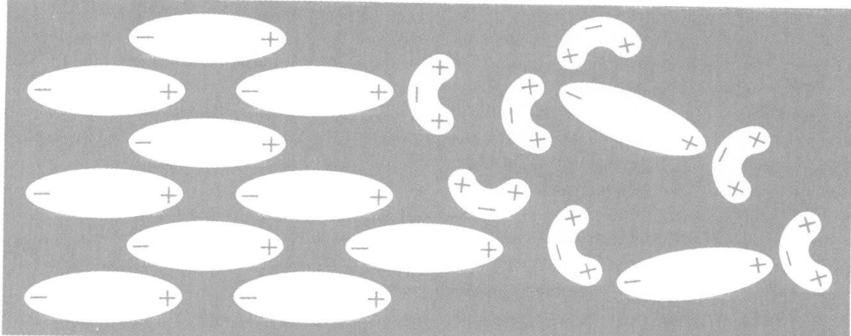

11-2 When sugar dissolves, energy is required to break water-water and sugar-sugar intermolecular forces. Energy is given off when hydrogen bonds form between water and sugar molecules.

The total input or output of heat energy depends on the amount of heat energy required for dissociation and the amount of heat given off in solvation. When dissociation absorbs more heat than solvation releases, the energy change shows up as a decrease in the temperature of the solution. This is called an **endothermic** process. When the process of solvation releases more energy than dissociation absorbs, heat energy is released. The motions of the particles increase, and the temperature of the solution rises. This is called an **exothermic** process.

After solvation, molecular motions carry the dissolved particles throughout the solution. The end result of the solution process is an even concentration of solute particles that will remain in solution.

11–3 Solvent Selectivity: Like Dissolves Like

Acetic acid mixes with water. Oil does not. Why? What determines which substances can mix or dissolve in others? One general rule is that *like dissolves like*. In chemical terms, polar solvents dissolve polar solutes, and nonpolar solvents dissolve nonpolar solutes.

11-3 Miscible combinations.

	Polar	**Nonpolar**
Polar	Miscible	Immiscible
Nonpolar	Immiscible	Miscible

Ionic compounds and covalent molecules with dipole moments are polar because they have regions of electrical charge. The charges can interact with neighboring ions or polar portions of molecules. Water (H_2O), acetic acid ($HC_2H_3O_2$), ammonia (NH_3), and hydrogen chloride (HCl) are all polar substances. They can mix because forces exist between their molecules. Forces can also exist between ions and molecules, as in salt water. Positive Na^+ ions are strongly attracted to the negative portions of water molecules, while negatively charged Cl^- ions are attracted to the positive portions.

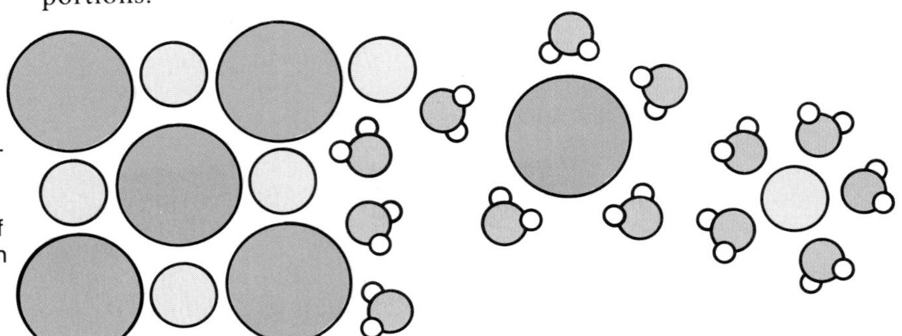

11-4 As sodium chloride dissolves, negative portions of water molecules attach to Na^+ ions. Positive portions of water molecules interact with Cl^- ions.

Nonpolar substances such as carbon tetrachloride, pentane, and petroleum ether cannot mix with polar substances. They lack dipoles, and they cannot form hydrogen bonds. Consequently, they are "squeezed out" of polar solvents.

Sample Problem. Considering the electrical natures of methanol, hexane, and aluminum chloride, which of these substances can dissolve in water?

```
    H              H   H   H   H   H   H
    |              |   |   |   |   |   |
H — C — OH     H — C — C — C — C — C — C — H     [Al]3+ [Cl]3-
    |              |   |   |   |   |   |
    H              H   H   H   H   H   H
```

Methanol | Hexane | Aluminum chloride

Solution.

Polar water molecules can dissolve polar methanol molecules and ionic aluminum chloride, but they cannot dissolve nonpolar hexane molecules.

"Like dissolves like" is only a general rule; there are several exceptions. Salt dissolves in water, but chalk ($CaCO_3$) does not. Both compounds are ionic; so it seems that both should be soluble in a polar solvent like water. Why is there a difference? The strength of the ionic attractions in compounds helps to account for differences in solubility. The process of dissociation must overcome the lattice energy of the crystal. It is possible for ions to be bound together so tightly that they cannot be separated by a solvent.

11–4 Solution Equilibria: More Than Meets the Eye

When a glass is filled half with cold water and half with salt, water molecules immediately begin colliding with the salt, dissociating and hydrating the Na^+ and Cl^- ions in the process. As ions are carried away, additional water molecules move in to pull more of the crystals apart. At this stage more solute can be dissolved, so the solution is said to be **unsaturated.** The heat energy required for the dissociation of salt is greater than the heat given off in hydration. Heat is therefore absorbed in the solution process, and the solution becomes slightly cooler.

$$H_2O\,(l) + NaCl\,(s) + \text{Heat} \longrightarrow Na^+\,(aq) + Cl^-\,(aq)$$

Eventually, however, no more salt appears to dissolve. The temperature and the amount of salt at the bottom of the glass both remain constant. When a solution contains the maximum amount of solute at a given temperature, it is **saturated.** But this condition does not stop the solution process. The water molecules are still moving, dissociating, and hydrating ions. The reason that the amount of salt at the bottom of the glass remains constant is that a reverse process also occurs.

$$Na^+\,(aq) + Cl^-\,(aq) \longrightarrow NaCl\,(s) + \text{Heat} + H_2O\,(l)$$

When both processes occur at the same rate, no noticeable changes occur. This condition is called a dynamic equilibrium.

$$H_2O\,(l) + NaCl\,(s) + \text{Heat} \rightleftharpoons Na^+\,(aq) + Cl^-\,(aq)$$

Equilibria can also exist for liquid-gas solutions. Carbonated drinks are actually solutions of carbon dioxide. When a bottle of carbonated beverage is opened, carbon dioxide gas escapes with a fizz. When the cap is replaced, the escaping gas is again confined in the bottle. As the pressure in the bottle builds up, the rate at which carbon dioxide escapes from the solution decreases. Eventually, the rate at which carbon dioxide re-enters the solution will match the rate at which it leaves the solution. Because the two processes oppose each other, the drink does not lose all of its carbonation.

11-5 Opening a carbonated drink allows carbon dioxide gas to come out of solution.

11–5 Rates of Solution

The rate at which something dissolves depends on two factors. The first is the inherent solubility of the solute. Substances that dissolve well dissolve quickly. The second major factor is the number of collisions that occur between solvent molecules and solute molecules: the more collisions, the faster the process.

The temperature of a solution can affect the number of molecular collisions. Consider a glass of warm, unsweetened tea. Which should be put into the tea first—sugar or ice? If the dissolving process is to occur quickly, the sugar should be put in first. The active molecules in warm tea will dissolve sugar faster than will the more sluggish molecules in iced tea.

Stirring a solvent can increase the number of collisions. A moving spoon more rapidly brings the solvent molecules into contact with the sugar at the bottom of the glass.

The number of collisions also depends on the surface area exposed to solvent action. Which dissolves more quickly in tea—granulated sugar or sugar cubes? The granulated sugar does. In a sugar cube, many sugar molecules are shielded from the solvent. In granulated sugar, many more sugar molecules are exposed. Increased surface area speeds up the rate of solution.

11-6 Solubility curve of $KClO_3$.

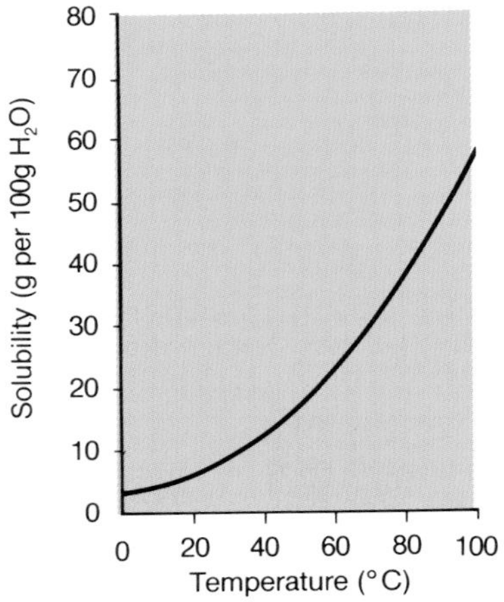

11-7 Solubility curve of CO_2.

0.340
0.300
0.260
0.220
0.180
0.140
0.100
0.060
0.020
Solubility (g per 100g H_2O)
0 20 40 60 80 100
Temperature (°C)

11–6 Factors That Affect Solubility: Temperature and Pressure

Will the solubility of a substance increase or decrease as temperature increases? In general, high temperatures help solids and liquids to dissolve. But this happens only because most solids and liquids require heat to dissolve. Suppose that a saturated solution of potassium chlorate ($KClO_3$) is at equilibrium.

$$KClO_3 + H_2O + \text{Heat} \rightleftharpoons \text{Solution}$$

Adding heat is equivalent to adding more of a reactant. This heat fuels the forward reaction. More potassium chlorate will dissolve until a new equilibrium is established. The graph to the left shows how much can be dissolved in 100 grams of water at various temperatures.

When gases dissolve, they usually release heat.

$$CO_2 + H_2O \rightleftharpoons \text{Solution} + \text{Heat}$$

For this reaction, adding heat is equivalent to increasing the amount of products. This heat fuels the reverse reaction and causes carbon dioxide to escape from the solution until a new equilibrium is established. The graph to the left shows how much carbon dioxide dissolves in 100 grams of water at various temperatures.

Pressure also affects solubility. The effect of pressure on the solubility of solid and liquid solutes is minimal. Its effect on the solubility of gases, however, can be drastic. **Henry's law** states that the solubility of gases increases with the partial pressures of the gases above the solutions. This law is illustrated vividly when a bottle of carbonated soft drink is opened. When the pressure above the beverage is removed, the solubility of carbon dioxide in the beverage decreases, and the excess gas escapes with a fizz.

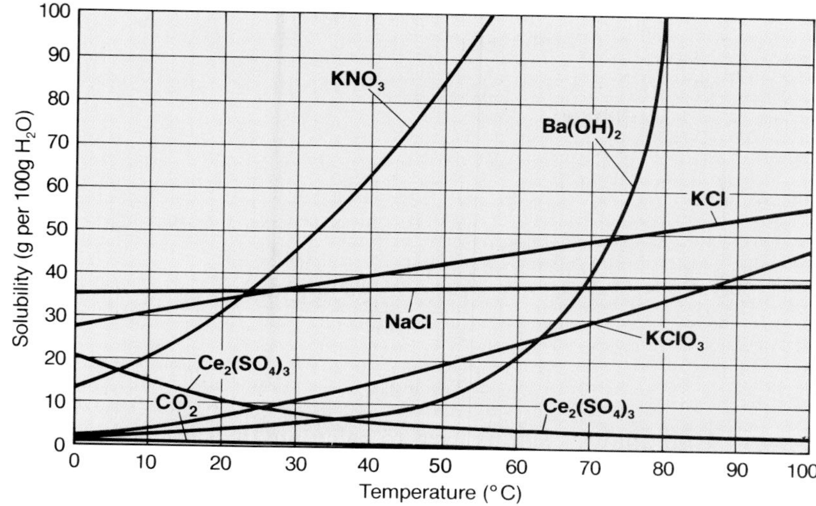

11-8 Solubilities of common compounds.

Measures of Concentration

What is the best way to express the concentration of a solution? Terms such as **dilute** and **concentrated** refer to small and large amounts of solute in a solvent. These terms are easy to understand, but they do not describe concentrations precisely. Quantitative measurements of solutes are much more useful in chemistry. Many methods can be used, but the most common are per cent by mass, molarity, molality, and normality. Each expression has its own advantages and unique uses.

11–7 Per Cent by Mass

One of the most common methods of expressing concentrations compares the mass of the solute to the mass of the solution. **Per cent by mass** is used on the ingredient labels of many household products. Vinegar is approximately 5 per cent acetic acid by mass. That means that acetic acid contributes 5 grams for every 100 grams of solution.

$$\% \text{ by mass} = \frac{\text{Mass of solute}}{\text{Mass of solution}} \times 100\% = \frac{5 \text{ g}}{100 \text{ g}} = 5\%$$

Sample Problem. Concentrated hydrochloric acid is 37.2 per cent hydrogen chloride by mass. How much hydrogen chloride is in 500.0 milliliters of the acid (the solution has a density of 1.19 g/ml)?

Solution.

The given volume can be converted to mass, since the density is known.

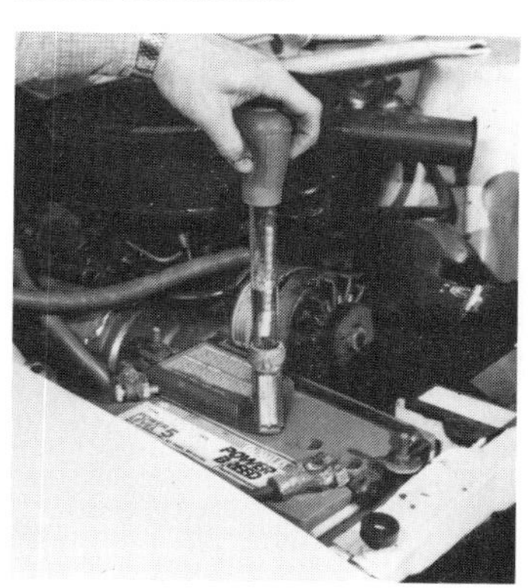

11-9 A hydrometer gauges the concentration of a solution by measuring the density. A float inside the tube rises more in dense, concentrated solutions.

$$500.0 \text{ ml acid} \times \frac{1.19 \text{ g acid}}{1 \text{ ml acid}} = 595 \text{ g acid}$$

The amount of hydrogen chloride in the acid can now be calculated.

$$\frac{\text{Mass of solute}}{\text{Mass of solution}} \times 100\% = \% \text{ by mass}$$

$$\text{Mass of solute} = \frac{(\% \text{ by mass})(\text{Mass of solution})}{100\%}$$

$$= \frac{(37.2\%)(595 \text{ g})}{100\%}$$

$$= 221 \text{ g HCl}$$

Unit analysis can be used to calculate the same answer.

$$500.0 \text{ ml acid} \times \frac{1.19 \text{ g acid}}{1 \text{ ml acid}} \times \frac{37.2 \text{ g HCl}}{100 \text{ g acid}} = 221 \text{ g HCl}$$

Sample Problem. A chemical reaction requires 40.0 grams of hydrogen chloride. What volume of the hydrochloric acid in the previous sample problem should be added?

Solution.

$$40.0 \text{ g HCl} \times \frac{100 \text{ g acid}}{37.2 \text{ g HCl}} \times \frac{1 \text{ ml acid}}{1.19 \text{ g acid}} = 90.4 \text{ ml acid}$$

11-10 Laboratory solutions are usually measured in units of molarity.

11–8 Molarity

The most common measure of concentration deals not with mass but with moles. The **molarity** of a solution is the number of moles of solute per liter of solution. The word *molar* is abbreviated with an *M*, as in a 6 *M* HCl solution.

Sample Problem. What is the molarity of a solution that contains 3.40 moles of solute in 245 milliliters of solution?

Solution.

After expressing the volume in units of liters, you can write the ratio 3.40 moles/0.245 liters. This ratio can be divided by the denominator to yield the number of moles in 1 liter.

$$\frac{3.40 \text{ moles}}{0.245 \ \ell} = \frac{13.9 \text{ moles}}{1 \ \ell} = 13.9 \ M$$

Solutions measured by molarity are convenient to use in chemical reactions. They make it easy for a chemist to measure out a precise number of atoms, molecules, or ions.

FACETS OF CHEMISTRY

An In-Depth Look at the Dead Sea

It is a landlocked lake, yet people call it a sea. Certain microscopic bacteria seem to thrive in its waters, yet people call it "dead." Together, these misnomers form the name of a most unusual body of water: the Dead Sea.

Nestled in the hills of Judea, the Dead Sea lies 1296 feet below sea level. It covers an area 48 miles long and 10 miles wide. A peninsula divides the sea into two unequal basins. The large, northern basin averages about 1000 feet deep. The smaller, southern basin has an average depth of only 20 feet.

The Dead Sea receives its water from the Jordan River and four minor streams. The water from these sources picks up many chemicals as it mixes with hot sulfur springs and flows through the region's salty soil. Unlike many other lakes, the Dead Sea has no outlets. Scorching temperatures keep the water level constant by evaporating as much as six million tons of water per day. Sometimes so much water evaporates that heavy clouds form above the surface of the water. While evaporation removes water, it leaves many dissolved minerals behind. Over the centuries, minerals have accumulated and increased in concentration. Dissolved minerals now account for nearly 30 per cent of the water's weight. This is seven-and-one-half times the concentration of salts in the oceans. The brine is so concentrated that it leaves a feeling of nausea if it is tasted; an oily, slippery feeling if it is touched; and a white crust of chemicals after it dries.

The water of the Dead Sea is not evenly mixed. Different areas of water contain different minerals. The upper layer, for example, is rich in sulfates and bicarbonates, whereas the lower zone contains hydrogen sulfide and strong concentrations of magnesium, potassium, chlorine, and bromine. The concentration of salts increases with depth. Concentrated salt solutions are more dense than pure water, so they sink toward the bottom. Sodium chloride saturates the deep waters of the Dead Sea so much that it remains permanently on the bottom. The floor of the sea is covered with salt crystals.

If the waters of the Dead Sea could speak, they could add many exciting details to biblical history. Much history lies beneath the murky waters of the southern basin. Here the cities of Sodom and Gomorrah once existed. When their wickedness became too great for Jehovah to tolerate, He rained fire and brimstone (burning sulfur) upon the cities. Today the waters of the southern basin cover the sites of these ancient cities.

The many valuable chemicals in the Dead Sea's waters have attracted several mining operations. Today the area near historical Sodom is the site of a large chemical industry. The first chemical plant established at Sodom was begun in 1929. At that time a Jewish engineer secured the rights to extract minerals from the Dead Sea. Two years later he marketed the first purified potassium chloride. By World War II, half of Britain's total annual supply of potassium chloride was coming from this source. Unfortunately the 1948-49 Arab-Israeli war largely destroyed the chemical plant. In 1952 a new company called the Dead Sea Works, Ltd., was founded. In a greatly expanded operation, it now extracts large quantities of chlorides, bromides, chlorates, and bromates, as well as many other chemicals.

Sample Problem. A chemical reaction requires 0.180 moles of silver nitrate ($AgNO_3$). How many milliliters of a 0.800 molar solution should be added to the reaction vessel to provide this amount?

Solution.

$$0.180 \text{ mole } AgNO_3 \times \frac{1\ \ell \text{ solution}}{0.800 \text{ mole } AgNO_3} \times \frac{1000 \text{ ml}}{1\ \ell}$$

$$= 225 \text{ ml solution}$$

11–9 Molality

The **molality** of a solution is defined as the number of moles of solute per kilogram of solvent. It is different from the molarity of the solution, and it is used in different instances. The word *molal* is abbreviated with an *m,* as in a 6 *m* NaCl solution.

Sample Problem. What is the molality of a solution composed of 30.0 grams of sodium nitrate ($NaNO_3$) and 400 grams of water? The gram-formula mass of sodium nitrate is 85.00 grams.

Solution.

First, express the quantity of sodium nitrate in moles.

$$30.0 \text{ g } NaNO_3 \times \frac{1 \text{ mole } NaNO_3}{85.00 \text{ g } NaNO_3} = 0.353 \text{ mole } NaNO_3$$

The ratio 0.353 mole sodium nitrate/0.400 kilogram water can be changed to determine how many moles per kilogram of water are present.

$$\frac{0.353 \text{ mole } NaNO_3}{0.400 \text{ kg } H_2O} = \frac{0.883 \text{ mole } NaNO_3}{1 \text{ kg } H_2O} = 0.883\ m$$

11–10 Equivalents and Normality

Another measure of concentration is called normality. Before this third measure of concentration can be understood, a more fundamental concept called "chemical equivalents" must be learned. When a mole of hydrochloric acid reacts with a mole of sodium hydroxide, they can neutralize each other. Chemists say that 1 mole of hydrochloric acid and 1 mole of sodium hydroxide are chemically equivalent. When sulfuric acid (H_2SO_4) reacts with sodium hydroxide, only 1/2 mole of sulfuric acid is needed for each mole of sodium hydroxide. One mole of sodium hydroxide is equivalent to 1/2 mole of sulfuric acid.

In chemistry the term **equivalent** refers to the combining capacity of a substance in a specific reaction. There are several similar ways to define the term, depending on the type of reaction being considered. When reactions transfer electrons, an equivalent is defined as the amount of substance that gains or releases 1 mole of electrons. By this definition sodium has 1 equivalent per mole when it reacts with bromine to form sodium bromide.

$$2\ Na + Br_2 \longrightarrow 2\ NaBr$$

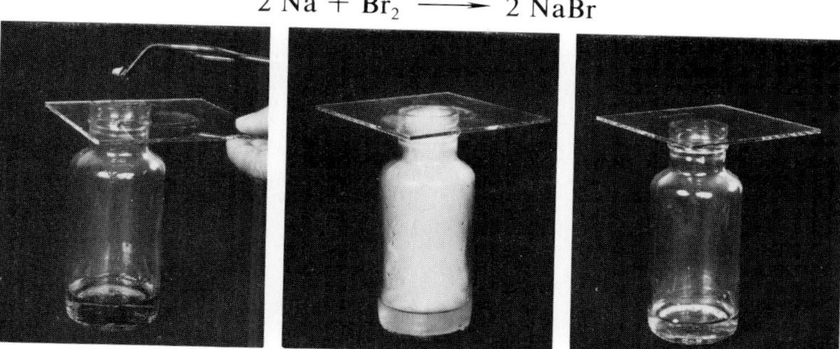

11-11 Sodium reacts with a solution of bromine, removing the solution's color.

Each mole of sodium loses 1 mole of electrons. The **gram-equivalent mass** of a substance is the mass of an equivalent expressed in grams. The gram-equivalent mass of sodium in this reaction is easily calculated with unit analysis.

$$\frac{22.99\ g\ Na}{1\ mole\ Na} \times \frac{1\ mole\ Na}{1\ eq\ Na} = \frac{22.99\ g\ Na}{1\ eq\ Na}$$

When copper sulfate reacts with zinc metal, each mole of copper sulfate releases 2 moles of electrons. Since 1 mole of copper sulfate contains 2 equivalents, the gram-equivalent mass of copper sulfate is one-half its gram-formula mass.

$$\frac{159.61\ g\ CuSO_4}{1\ mole\ CuSO_4} \times \frac{1\ mole\ CuSO_4}{2\ eq\ CuSO_4} = \frac{79.805\ g\ CuSO_4}{1\ eq\ CuSO_4}$$

In acid-base reactions, an equivalent is defined as the quantity that donates or accepts 1 mole of hydrogen ions. When hydrogen chloride is dissolved in water, each hydrogen chloride molecule splits into a H^+ ion and a Cl^- ion.

$$HCl \longrightarrow H^+ + Cl^-$$

One mole of hydrochloric acid gives up a mole of hydrogen ions. The gram-equivalent mass of this substance is identical to its gram-molecular mass. Each molecule of sulfuric acid gives away two hydrogen ions when it dissociates completely in water.

$$H_2SO_4 \longrightarrow SO_4^{2-} + 2\ H^+$$

A half a mole of sulfuric acid would give up 1 mole of hydrogen ions. The gram-equivalent mass of sulfuric acid in this reaction is 49.04 grams per equivalent (one-half of its gram-molecular mass).

While molarity expresses concentration in moles/liter, normality does so in equivalents/liter. The **normality** of a solution is the number of equivalents of solute per liter of solution. The word *normal* is abbreviated with an *N*, as in a 6 *N* HCl solution.

Sample Problem. What is the normality of an 875-milliliter sulfuric acid solution that contains 126 grams of sulfuric acid and reacts with sodium hydroxide (H_2SO_4 + 2 NaOH ⟶ Na_2SO_4 + 2 H_2O)?

Solution.

In this reaction each mole of sulfuric acid donates 2 moles of hydrogen ions. The conversion factor 1 equivalent per 1/2 mole sulfuric acid must be used.

$$\frac{126 \text{ g } H_2SO_4}{0.875\ \ell \text{ solution}} \times \frac{1 \text{ mole } H_2SO_4}{98.08 \text{ g } H_2SO_4} \times \frac{1 \text{ eq } H_2SO_4}{\frac{1}{2} \text{ mole } H_2SO_4}$$

$$= \frac{2.936 \text{ eq}}{\ell \text{ solution}} = 2.94\ N$$

Colligative Properties: The Effects of Solutes

The presence of solutes causes solutions to behave differently from their pure solvents. Freezing points, boiling points, vapor pressures, and osmotic pressures all change. It makes no difference what type of solutes are present; the new properties, called **colligative properties,** depend on the number, not the type, of particles in solution.

11–11 Decreased Vapor Pressures

At the surface of a solution, solute particles fill positions that are normally occupied by solvent molecules. Fewer solvent molecules are exposed to the surface, so fewer have the chance to evaporate. The result of this is that the vapor pressure of the solution is lower than the vapor pressure of the pure solvent.

Pure water has a set of vapor pressures that increase with temperature. If a mole of sugar were added to a liter of water, the vapor pressures would be lower than those of pure water. If a mole of sodium chloride were added to a liter of water, the vapor pressures would be even lower. Sodium chloride units dissociate into Na^+ and Cl^- ions, and these extra particles lower the vapor pressures. If aluminum chloride ($AlCl_3$) were dissolved in a liter of water, 4 moles of particles for every 1 mole of salt would be released, decreasing the vapor pressures even more.

These effects can be summarized in a single statement called **Raoult's Law:** The lowering of the vapor pressure of a solvent is directly proportional to the number of solute particles.

11-12 Vapor pressures of solutions decrease as the number of solutes increases.

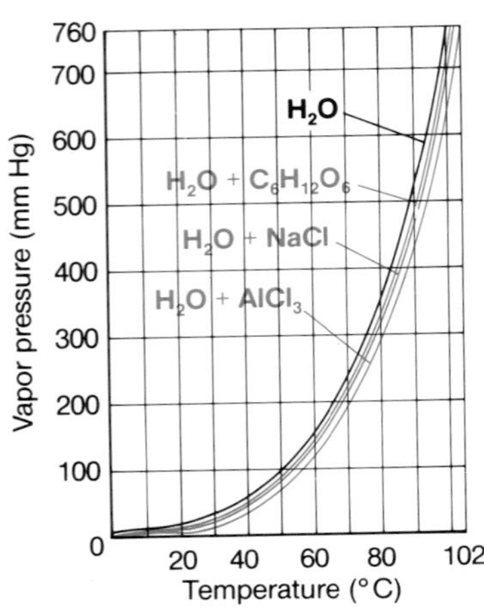

11–12 Boiling Point Elevation

When solute particles lower vapor pressures, they make it difficult for solutions to boil. Higher-than-normal temperatures are then necessary to raise vapor pressures up to atmospheric pressures. The effect that solute particles have on the boiling points of substances is called **boiling point elevation.**

A 1-molal solution of sugar in water boils at 100.512° C—0.512° C higher than usual. The boiling point elevation is represented by the symbol ΔT_{bp}. Δ is the capital Greek letter delta. It stands for the words *change in.* The change in boiling temperature is the difference between the new boiling point and the original boiling point.

$$\Delta T_{bp} = bp_{new} - bp_{original}$$

It has been found that 1 mole of particles—molecules, atoms, or ions—in 1 kilogram of water elevates the boiling point of water 0.512° C. This value is called the **molal boiling point elevation constant** (K_{bp}) for water. Other solvents have their own unique molal boiling point elevation constants. Note that concentration is always measured in molality for these constants.

11-13 Boiling points of 1-molal solutions.

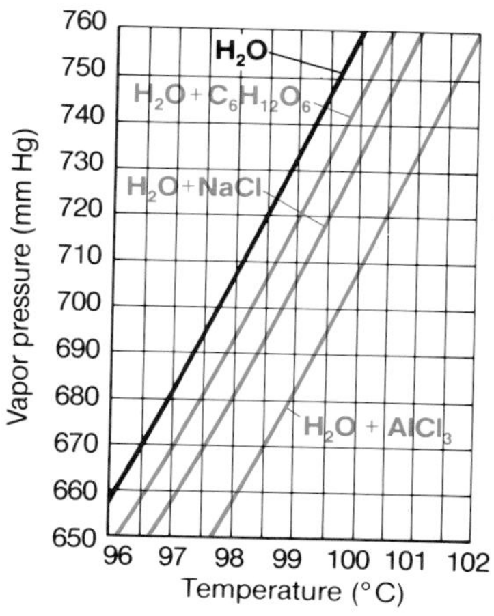

11-14 A concentrated sugar solution boils at a temperature well above 100° C.

Table 11-15

Boiling Point Elevations of Solvents

Solvent	Normal Boiling Point (° C)	Molal Boiling Point Elevation Constant (° C/molal)
Acetic acid	117.9	3.07
Acetone	56.00	1.71
Benzene	80.15	2.53
Carbon tetrachloride	76.50	5.03
Ethanol	78.26	1.22
Ether	34.42	2.02
Phenol	181.8	3.56
Water	100.0	0.512

The more concentrated the solution is, the greater the boiling point elevation will be. Exactly how much higher depends on the precise concentration and the molal boiling point elevation constant of the solvent.

$$\Delta T_{bp} = K_{bp}\, m$$

Sample Problem. What is the boiling point of acetone when 0.500 moles of naphthalene are added to 1 kilogram of acetone?

Solution.

A solution of 0.500 mole naphthalene per kilogram of acetone constitutes a 0.500-molal solution. The molal boiling point elevation constant of acetone is 1.71°C/*m*.

$$\Delta T_{bp} = K_{bp}\, m$$
$$\Delta T_{bp} = (1.71°\text{C}/m)(0.500\ m)$$
$$\Delta T_{bp} = 0.855°\text{C}$$

To find the new boiling point, add the temperature change to the original boiling point of acetone.

$$56.00°\text{C} + 0.855°\text{C} = 56.855 \text{ or } 56.86°\text{C}$$

Ionizable solutes increase the concentration of particles in solution. This fact must be considered when working colligative-property problems.

Sample Problem. If 425 grams of magnesium chloride ($MgCl_2$) are added to 675 grams of hot water, what is the boiling point of the solution?

Solution.

Before the salt ionizes, 4.46 moles of magnesium chloride are present. This is equivalent to a 6.61-molal solution.

$$\frac{425 \text{ g } MgCl_2}{0.675 \text{ kg } H_2O} \times \frac{1 \text{ mole } MgCl_2}{95.21 \text{ g } MgCl_2} = \frac{6.61 \text{ moles } MgCl_2}{1 \text{ kg } H_2O}$$

Because each mole of magnesium chloride ionizes to form 1 mole of Mg^{+} ions and 2 moles of Cl^{-} ions, the effective concentration is tripled. The "working" concentration of the solution is 3 × 6.61, or 19.8 moles per kilogram.

$$\Delta T_{bp} = K_{bp}\, m$$
$$\Delta T_{bp} = (0.512°\text{C}/m)(19.8\ m)$$
$$\Delta T_{bp} = 10.14°\text{C}$$

The new boiling point is 110.14°C.

11–13 Freezing Point Depression

Solutions freeze at lower temperatures than their pure solvents do. A 1-molal solution of sugar in water freezes at -1.86°C, or 1.86°C lower than the normal freezing point of water. The change in freezing point is called the **freezing point depression** and is represented by the symbol ΔT_{fp}. As with molal boiling point elevation constants, each solvent has its own characteristic **molal freezing point depression constant** (K_{fp}).

Table 11-16

Freezing Point Depressions of Solvents

Solvent	Normal Freezing Point (°C)	Molal Freezing Point Depression Constant (°C/molal)
Acetic acid	16.6	3.90
Benzene	5.48	5.12
Ether	-116.3	1.79
Phenol	40.9	7.40
Water	0.00	1.86

11-17 The icy salt water outside the canister is cold enough to freeze ice cream.

Sample Problem. How much will the freezing point of phenol change if 4.00 moles of naphthalene are dissolved in 2.00 kilograms of phenol?

Solution.

Four moles of naphthalene in 2.00 kilograms of phenol is equivalent to 2.00 moles per kilogram, or a 2.00-molal solution. The molal freezing point depression constant of phenol is 7.40°C/*m*.

$$\Delta T_{fp} = K_{fp}\, m$$
$$\Delta T_{fp} = (7.40°\text{C}/m)(2.00\ m)$$
$$\Delta T_{fp} = 14.80 \text{ or } 14.8°\text{C}$$

The freezing point will be 14.80°C lower than the freezing point of pure phenol.

Calcium chloride, rather than sodium chloride, is the salt used on icy roads. The reason calcium chloride is used lies partly in the fact that it lowers the freezing point of water more, and it melts ice at lower temperatures. It does this because it releases more ions upon dissolution than sodium chloride does. When a mole of calcium chloride dissociates, 3 moles of ions can be released into solution. The effective concentration of the solution is tripled, rather than doubled, so there is a greater change in freezing point.

Sample Problem. Compare the freezing points of a 3.00-molal calcium chloride solution and a 3.00-molal sodium chloride solution.

Solution.

The concentration of the calcium chloride solution will be effectively tripled when it dissolves; the concentration of the sodium chloride solution will be doubled.

$$\Delta T_{fp} = K_{fp}\, m$$
$$\Delta T_{fp} = (1.86°C/m)(9.00\ m)$$
$$\Delta T_{fp} = 16.74 \text{ or } 16.7°C$$

The freezing point of the calcium chloride solution is 16.7°C lower than the normal freezing point of water, or -16.7°C.

$$\Delta T_{fp} = K_{fp}\, m$$
$$\Delta T_{fp} = (1.86°C/m)(6.00\ m)$$
$$\Delta T_{fp} = 11.16 \text{ or } 11.2°C$$

The sodium chloride solution freezes at -11.2°C.

FACETS OF CHEMISTRY

How Old Are the Oceans?

An hourglass measures time as grains of sand fall at a constant rate. An observer looking at the pile of sand in the bottom of the glass can tell how much time has elapsed since the grains started to fall because the grains fall at a constant rate. In a similar fashion, rivers carry dissolved ions from eroded minerals into the ocean at a reasonably constant rate. Theoretically, it should be possible to determine how long the salts have been flowing into the ocean by measuring how much salt is present. Although this method of age-dating appears simple, it does have problems.

Dividing the amount of ions by the rate at which they are presently flowing into the oceans results in different ages for the oceans. Calculations show that the amount of sodium in the oceans could have accumulated in 260 million years. Yet this does not prove that the earth is that old. Similar calculations show that the manganese in the oceans could have accumulated in only 1400 years. Calculations for other elements also yield greatly different ages.

Element	Time Necessary for Accumulation at Present Rate
Lithium	2.0×10^7 years
Beryllium	150 years
Sodium	2.6×10^8 years
Magnesium	4.5×10^7 years
Potassium	1.1×10^7 years
Manganese	1.4×10^3 years
Iron	140 years
Copper	5.0×10^5 years
Gold	5.6×10^5 years
Mercury	4.2×10^4 years
Lead	2.0×10^2 years

11–14 Osmotic Pressure

Wrap the end of a tube with a sheet of semipermeable membrane—cellophane will do. Pour a concentrated sugar solution into this tube, and quickly dip the tube into a sample of pure water.

Osmosis, the process in which water moves across a selectively permeable membrane, begins immediately. The semipermeable membrane allows the small water molecules to pass through it, but it retains the larger sugar molecules. Only a few water molecules leave the sugar solution. Many more enter the solution from the pure water outside. As a result, the level of liquid in the tube gradually rises above the level of the water outside the tube. Eventually the level of the solution ceases to rise because the weight of the liquid column pushes water molecules out of the tube as fast as they enter.

The **osmotic pressure** of a solution is the amount of pressure required to prevent osmosis from occurring. The more solute particles there are in a solution, the higher the osmotic pressure will be and the higher the column will rise. The osmotic pressure of a solution is a colligative property because it depends on the number of particles in solution.

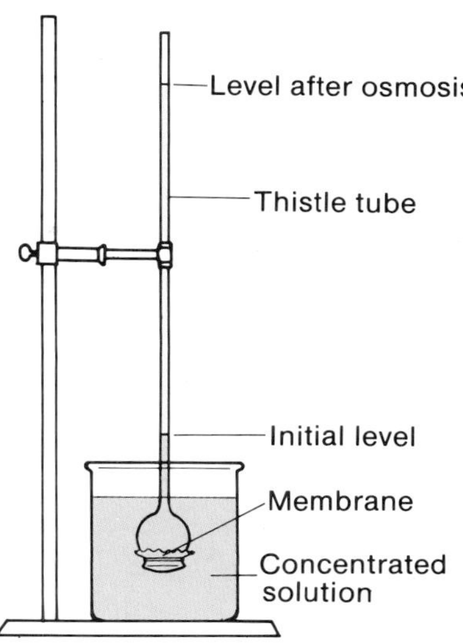

11-18 Osmotic pressure experiment.

Since not all of these widely different answers can be correct, it is obvious that this is not a particularly accurate dating method. Why is there such a wide variety of ages? First, this method of age-dating assumes that no ions were originally in the oceans. That is, the first oceans had to have been freshwater. But the oceans may have been created salty. Second, it assumes that every ion entering the oceans remains dissolved in the water. But this is not true for some of the ions. For example, mollusks use large amounts of calcium ions to build their shells. Third, although scientists can measure present rates of ion inflow, there is no guarantee that these rates remained constant throughout history. Rates may have increased as new sources were tapped, or they may have decreased as old sources became depleted.

In spite of the problems with this method, these measurements can still tell us something. The data clearly fit the creationist model of the earth's origin better than the evolutionary model. Creationists can readily explain the ions that are present in high concentration by assuming that the oceans were created salty. They can also explain the ions that are present in low concentration by saying that the earth is relatively young. Ions that do not erode quickly or that resist being transported have not had enough time to reach the ocean. Evolutionists, on the other hand, have serious trouble with the data. If the oceans are really billions of years old, why have the oceans not become saturated? Precipitates hundreds of feet deep should cover the ocean floor. But no such precipitates are found. Evolutionists have no reasonable explanation for the "short supply" of so many ions.

Good gardeners must recognize that concentrated solutions have high osmotic pressures. Commercial fertilizers consist of salts such as ammonium nitrate (NH_4NO_3). Heavy applications of fertilizer can form concentrated salt solutions around the roots of plants. Because of its high osmotic pressure, the concentrated fertilizer solution can "pull" water from the plants. Too much fertilizer can "burn," or dehydrate, the plants it was intended to nourish. Consequently, good gardeners fertilize, but they do it with caution. They also water the area immediately afterwards so that they can dilute the fertilizer solution around the plants and reduce its osmotic pressure.

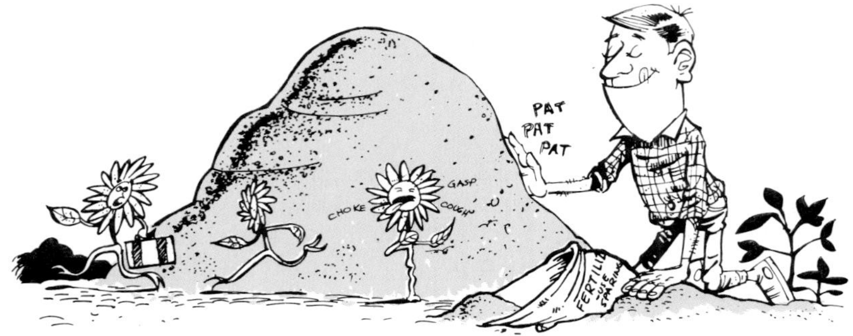

11-19 Osmotic pressure can kill.

Colloids: Almost Solutions, but Not Quite

Some mixtures cannot be classified as solutions or suspensions. The mixture of water in air that is called fog appears to have a uniform consistency. Is it a solution? Not really. The water molecules have not been completely separated from each other. Groups of molecules float through the air without becoming dissociated. Is fog a suspension? Again the answer is no. Fog has a uniform consistency and does not readily separate like suspensions do. A class of mixtures called colloids lies between solutions and suspensions.

11–15 What Are Colloids?

Colloids are mixtures that contain small particles dispersed in a medium. Since colloids are different from solutions, terms such as *solute, dissolved,* and *solvent* do not apply.

The colloidal particles that are dispersed in the medium usually exceed 10 angstroms—the approximate size limit on dissolved particles. The size of particles in a colloid cannot exceed 10,000 angstroms, since particles of this size would quickly settle out from their medium. Intermolecular collisions can buffet particles smaller than 10,000 angstroms enough to counteract the constant tug of gravity.

Colloids are commonly found in everyday surroundings. Colloids can be solids, liquids, or gases. All combinations of solids, liquids, and gases except one can be colloids. Gas-gas mixtures are always solutions. The other eight combinations can form colloids.

Table 11-20

Mixture	Particle Size
Solution	less than 10 Å
Colloid	between 10 and 10,000 Å
Suspension	greater than 10,000 Å

Table 11-21

Types of Colloids

Particles	Medium	Common Name	Examples
Liquid	gas	aerosol	fog, clouds, mist
Solid	gas	aerosol	smoke, dust in the air
Gas	liquid	foam	shaving cream, whipped cream
Liquid	liquid	emulsion	milk, mayonnaise
Solid	liquid	sol, gel	paint, pudding
Gas	solid	solid foam	Styrofoam, marshmallows
Liquid	solid	solid emulsion	cheese, butter
Solid	solid	solid sol	colored gems

11–16 The Properties of Colloids

In 1869 a Scottish physicist named John Tyndall demonstrated that the particles in colloids were large enough to scatter light waves. This effect, called the **Tyndall effect** in his honor, is often used to distinguish colloids from solutions. A beam of light will pass through a solution without being seen. The particles that are small enough to be dissolved are too small to disturb light waves. When a beam of light goes through a colloid, its outline shows up distinctly. This effect can be seen when automobile headlights shine through air into a patch of fog. The outline of the beams does not show up in the air, because air is a solution. However, the beams show up clearly in fog, since it is a colloid.

11-22 The Tyndall effect. Mist droplets (a colloid) scatter light waves, but the molecules in air (a solution) do not.

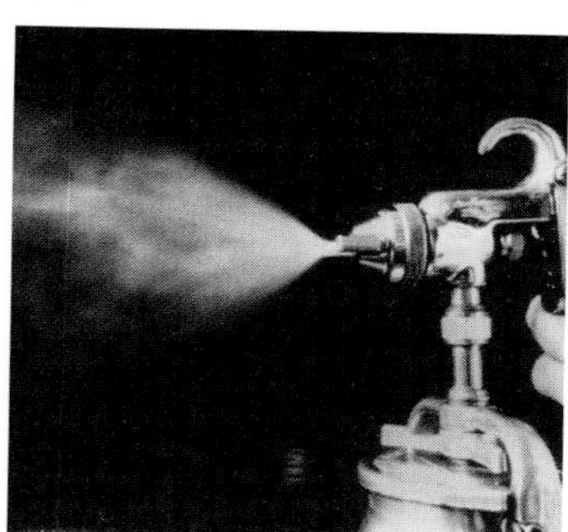

A British botanist named Robert Brown discovered a major proof of the kinetic theory by observing a colloid. In 1827 he watched pollen particles that were dispersed in water. He saw that the pollen particles moved slightly, as if they were being jostled by many small collisions. This movement, called **Brownian**

movement, results from colloidal particles' being buffeted by molecular collisions. This observation led scientists to conclude that matter is made of moving particles.

The intermediate size of colloidal particles allows them to pass through most filtering systems. Most membranes can catch suspended particles, but special membranes are needed to catch particles smaller than 10,000 angstroms.

The chemistry of colloids is largely determined by the electrical charges on the surfaces of the particles. What is on the surface of the particles is important because colloidal particles have a great amount of surface area compared to their volume.

Mayonnaise is an emulsion of oil and water (from milk). The oil in mayonnaise particles does not naturally combine with the water medium. Makers of mayonnaise must use a chemical principle called adsorption to keep the oil and water together. **Adsorption** is the attachment of charged particles to the particles in a colloid. In mayonnaise, oil and water are "tied together" by an emulsifying agent in egg yolks. A protein from the egg covers the oil particles and makes them compatible with the aqueous medium. Without the emulsifier in the eggs, mayonnaise could not be a stable emulsion.

Coming to Terms

solution
solvent
solute
miscible
immiscible
dissociation
solvation
hydration
endothermic
exothermic
unsaturated
saturated
Henry's law
dilute
concentrated
per cent by mass
molarity
molality
equivalent
gram-equivalent mass
normality
colligative property
Raoult's law
boiling point elevation
molal boiling point elevation constant
freezing point depression
molal freezing point depression constant
osmosis
osmotic pressure
colloid
Tyndall effect
Brownian movement

Review Questions

1. Identify the solvent and solute in the following solutions.
   a. salt water used for gargling
   b. carbonated water
   c. air
   d. carbon steel (1% Mn, 0.9% C, 98.1% Fe)
2. Predict whether each of the following pairs of liquids is miscible or immiscible.
   a. popcorn oil and vegetable oil
   b. gasoline and water
   c. iced tea and salt water
   d. popcorn oil and tea
3. Will the following substances dissolve in water or in an oil?
   a. carbon tetrachloride (CCl_4)
   b. LiCl
   c. NaBr
   d. methanol (CH_3OH)

```
      H
      |
  H — C — OH
      |
      H
```

4. Using the kinetic theory, explain each of the following observations.
   a. Sugar dissolves more quickly in hot coffee than in cold coffee.
   b. Finely ground salt dissolves more quickly than large chunks of salt.
   c. Powders dissolve more quickly when stirred.
   d. Popcorn oil and vegetable oil mix more quickly than do vegetable oil and sugar.
5. When ice cream is made with an old-fashioned ice-cream maker, salt is added to the ice that cools the ingredients. Considering the heat of solution for NaCl, explain why this is done.
6. Will a carbonated drink go "flat" faster if it is heated? Why?
7. Thimerosal is an organic compound (gram-molecular mass = 404.8 g/mole) used to inhibit bacterial growth. A 0.100% solution of thimerosal is sometimes used as an antiseptic. Assume that this solution has a density of 1.00 g/ml.
   a. How many grams of thimerosal are found in 0.500 g of 0.100% solution?

b. How many grams of thimerosal are required to make 50.0 g of 0.100% solution?
c. What mass of thimerosal must be mixed with 25.0 g of water to make a 0.100% solution?
d. How many grams of thimerosal are required to make 75.0 ml of 0.100% solution?
e. What volume of 0.100% solution contains 0.750 g of thimerosal?

8. An aqueous solution of sodium borate (201.2 g/mole) is sometimes used to fire-proof wood.
   a. What is the molarity of 2.50 ℓ of solution that contain 1.85 moles of sodium borate?
   b. What is the molarity of 45.0 ℓ of solution that contain 6.78 kg of sodium borate?
   c. How many moles of sodium borate are in 600.0 ml of a 1.57 *M* sodium borate solution?
   d. A chemist needs 50.8 g of sodium borate for a reaction. How many milliliters of 1.87 *M* solution contain this mass?

9. Sodium monofluorophosphate (144.0 g/mole) is the fluoride component in some modern fluoride-containing toothpastes. What is the molality of a solution containing
   a. 1.85 kg of H_2O and 1.00 mole of sodium monofluorophosphate?
   b. 125.0 g of H_2O and 0.356 g of sodium monofluorophosphate?
   c. 500.0 g of solution and 12.0 g of sodium monofluorophosphate?

10. Consider a reaction in which phosphoric acid (H_3PO_4) (97.99 g/mole) donates two H^+ ions to two NaOH units.

$$H_3PO_4 + 2\,NaOH \longrightarrow Na_2HPO_4 + 2\,H_2O$$

   a. How many equivalents per mole of H_3PO_4 are in this reaction?
   b. What is the gram-equivalent mass of H_3PO_4 in this reaction?
   c. What is the normality of a 365-ml solution that contains 76.8 g of H_3PO_4?

11. From each set pick the solution that has the *lowest* vapor pressure.
   a. 1.8 m CH_3OH, 0.7 m CH_3OH, 2.9 m CH_3OH, 0.2 m CH_3OH
   b. 0.5 m Na_3PO_4, 0.5 m $MgCl_2$, 0.5 m NaCl, 0.5 m $Al_2(SO_4)_3$

12. A housewife reads that eggs will boil faster if salt is added to the hot water.
   a. Suggest an explanation for this fact.
   b. What is the boiling point of 1.00 ℓ of water in which 10.0 g of NaCl (58.44 g/mole) have been dissolved?

c. How many grams of NaCl must be added to a liter of water to raise its boiling point to 105.00° C?
d. In light of the answers to questions (b) and (c), do you think that adding salt to water is a convenient method for decreasing the cooking time of eggs?

13. At what temperature will a solution consisting of 100.0 ml of H_2O and 2.50 g of sucrose ($C_{12}H_{22}O_{11}$) (342.3 g/mole) freeze?

14. Explain why
    a. red blood cells that are placed in pure water absorb water until they explode but are fine when they are surrounded by blood plasma.
    b. red blood cells shrink when they are in a very concentrated salt solution.

15. How can you determine whether a substance is a solution or a colloid? Why does this method of determination work?

16. Automobile antifreeze consists primarily of ethylene glycol ($C_2H_6O_2$) (62.07 g/mole). Small amounts of dye and anti-corrosion substances are also added.
    a. The coldest temperature of the year in Augusta, Maine, is expected to be -26.0° C. What must the molality of $C_2H_6O_2$ in an automobile radiator fluid be to prevent it from freezing?
    b. How many grams of $C_2H_6O_2$ must be added to 4.00 ℓ of H_2O to attain this molality?
    c. How many quarts of antifreeze is this? Assume that the density of antifreeze is 1.11 g/ml, and ignore the fact that small amounts of other substances are present.
    d. Why is it important to have a solution of antifreeze in the radiator during the summer?

TWELVE

THERMODYNAMICS & KINETICS

TO REACT OR NOT TO REACT

DETERMINING whether reactions can occur is crucial in the study of chemistry. Thermodynamics, which is the study of energy changes, is the tool that chemists use for this purpose. A reaction that involves a favorable energy change can be spontaneous. It may not "go boom" when the reactants are mixed, but there is a good chance that it will proceed on its own. If the energy changes required for a reaction are unfavorable, the reaction cannot occur on its own. It is therefore nonspontaneous.

The fact that a reaction can occur does not mean that it will occur at an observable rate when the reactants combine. Questions about the speed at which reactions occur and the way in which they get started are answered in a field of chemistry called kinetics. While thermodynamics answers the basic question "Can it react?" kinetics answers the broader questions "Will it react?" and "How fast will it react?"

Thermodynamics: Can Things React?

12–1 Chemical Energy: Stored in Bonds

Chemical bonds possess stored energy. As long as the bonds do not break or change, the energy that they contain cannot be observed. When the bonds are broken, energy can take more observable forms. A pile of gunpowder does not look any more energetic than a pile of sand. Yet experience reveals that the bonds in gunpowder are much more energetic.

In chemistry the most common, and usually most important, energy transformations are between chemical bonds and heat. Although some reactions involve significant amounts of light energy, electrical energy, or physical work, these transformations are minimal when compared to the heat energy transformations. For the sake of simplicity, thermodynamics usually concentrates on transformations of heat energy and ignores the others.

12–2 Conservation: The First Law of Thermodynamics

After six days of Creation, God saw that the universe was good and pronounced it complete. With the possible exception of some miracles, the total energy content of the universe has been preserved. The replenishment of oil and meal for the widow of Zarephath (I Kings 17) and Christ's feeding of the multitudes (Mark 6, 8) may well have entailed the creation of matter. Scientists have found that energy is conserved in every natural process. This observation has been generalized into the first law of thermodynamics: energy can be neither created nor destroyed.

The explosion of TNT releases great amounts of energy. This reaction and all others that release heat energy are called *exothermic reactions.* Do these reactions violate the first law? No, they do not. The energy present before the reaction equals the energy present after the explosion, but the energy after the reaction is in a much more visible form.

$$\underset{\text{High energy content}}{\text{TNT}} \longrightarrow \underset{\text{Low energy content}}{CO_2 + CO + H_2O + N_2} + \text{Heat} + \text{Energy}$$

12-1 Explosions change stored chemical energy into light, heat, and kinetic energy.

Red Runs the River, Unusual Films

Endothermic reactions absorb energy from their surroundings. Photosynthesis requires the input of light energy. Again the amount of energy present before the reaction matches the amount of energy present after the reaction. The first law of thermodynamics has no exceptions.

$$6\ CO_2 + 6\ H_2O + \text{Light} \longrightarrow C_6H_{12}O_6 + 6\ O_2$$

$$\underset{\text{content}}{\text{Low energy}} + \text{Energy} \longrightarrow \underset{\text{content}}{\text{High energy}}$$

12–3 Enthalpy: Heat Content of Compounds

All substances contain energy. **Enthalpy** (H) is a thermodynamic quantity that describes the energy of a substance at constant pressure. Scientists sometimes call the change in enthalpy that occurs during a reaction the *heat of reaction,* and they represent it by the symbol ΔH. The enthalpy change of a reaction is the difference between the enthalpy of the products and the enthalpy of the reactants.

$$\Delta H = H_{\text{products}} - H_{\text{reactants}}$$

An exothermic reaction releases energy; the products have less enthalpy than the reactants. The formation of water from its two elements illustrates this process. When 1 mole of hydrogen gas is ignited in the presence of 1/2 mole of oxygen gas, an explosive reaction that forms 1 mole of water occurs. Careful measurements reveal that 68.3 kilocalories of heat are released in the explosion.

$$H_2 + \tfrac{1}{2}O_2 \longrightarrow H_2O + 68.3\ \text{kcal}$$

Exothermic reactions have negative ΔHs. When the large enthalpy of the reactants is subtracted from the small enthalpy of the products, the difference is negative. Figure 12-2 illustrates the energy changes that are common for exothermic reactions. The products have less enthalpy than the reactants, and the difference is released as heat.

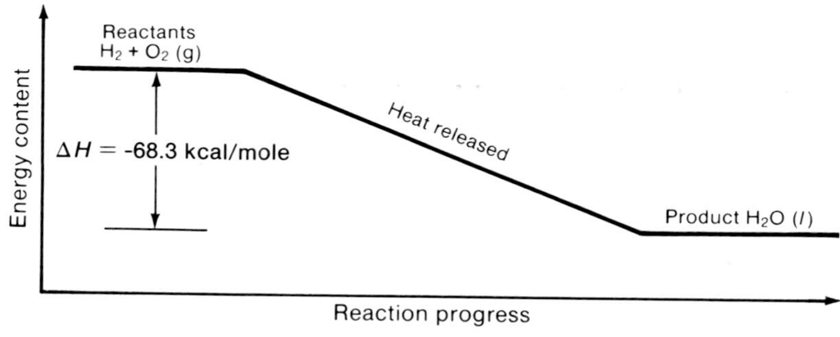

12-2 The products of exothermic reactions have less enthalpy than the reactants do.

Products of endothermic reactions have more enthalpy than the reactants. The formation of a mole of benzene from its elements requires an input of 11.78 kilocalories.

$$6\ C + 3\ H_2 + 11.78\ \text{kcal} \longrightarrow C_6H_6$$

Endothermic reactions have positive ΔHs. A graph illustrates the difference in energies between the reactants and the products of an endothermic reaction.

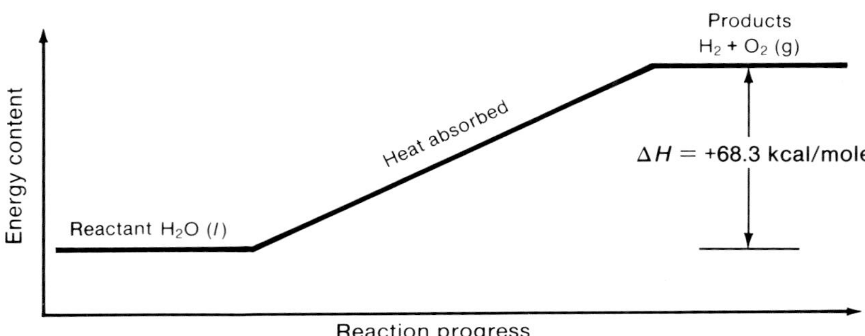

12-3 The products of endothermic reactions have more enthalpy than the reactants do.

If the ΔH of a reaction is known, the ΔH of the reverse reaction can be easily calculated. The ΔH of the reverse reaction has the same magnitude as the ΔH of the forward reaction, but it has the opposite sign. The reaction that formed water had a ΔH of -68.3 kilocalories. The breakdown of water has a ΔH of +68.3 kilocalories.

12-4 Laboratory calorimeters measure heat exchanges during reactions.

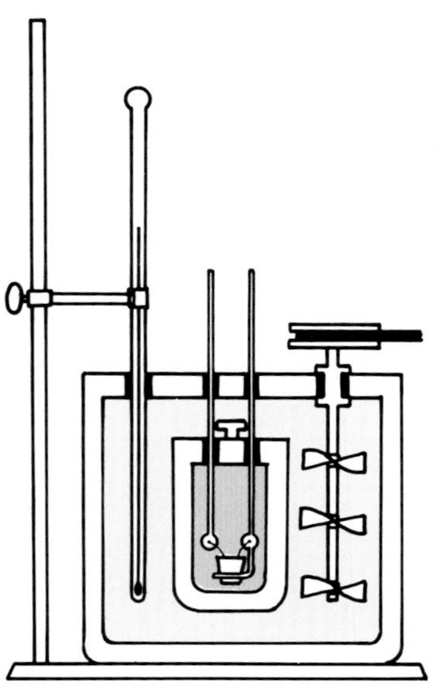

12–4 Calculating Enthalpy Changes

Chemists could measure the change in enthalpy for all the thousands of known reactions. Needless to say, this would be difficult, and the data would fill several volumes of books. Chemists have devised a quick technique for calculating changes in enthalpy for reactions. They use a table that lists enthalpies of formation for common compounds. A compound's **enthalpy of formation,** also called the heat of formation, is the change in enthalpy that occurs when 1 mole of the compound is formed from its elements. The enthalpy of formation of water is -68.3 kilocalories.

$$H_2 + \tfrac{1}{2}O_2 \longrightarrow H_2O; \quad \Delta H = -68.3\ \text{kcal}$$

The amount of enthalpy in a substance varies slightly with temperature and pressure, so these conditions must be specified. In thermodynamics the **standard state** is defined to be 25°C, or 298 K, and 1 atmosphere of pressure. The **standard molar enthalpy of formation,** ΔH_f°, is defined as the enthalpy change for the reaction that produces 1 mole of a compound in its standard state from its elements in their standard states. The degree symbol in

ΔH_f° signifies that this ΔH refers to standard conditions. Table 12-5 lists many standard molar enthalpies of formation.

Table 12-5

Standard Molar Enthalpies of Formation

Compound	ΔH_f° (kcal/mole)	Compound	ΔH_f° (kcal/mole)	Compound	ΔH_f° (kcal/mole)
AgBr	-23.8	CO	-26.4	NaF	-136.0
AgCl	-30.4	CO_2	-94.1	NaOH	-102.0
AgI	-14.9	H_2O (*l*)	-68.3	NH_3	-11.0
Al_2O_3	-399.1	H_2O (g)	-57.8	NH_4Cl	-75.4
$BaCl_2$	-205.6	H_2O_2	-44.8	NH_4NO_3	-87.3
$BaCO_3$	-291.3	H_2SO_4	-193.9	NO	+21.6
BaO	-133.4	HBr	-8.7	NO_2	+8.1
$Ba(OH)_2$	-226.2	HgS	-13.9	$PbCl_2$	-85.9
$BaSO_4$	-350.2	HCl (g)	-22.1	PbO	-52.1
$CaCl_2$	-190.0	KBr	-93.7	PCl_3	-73.2
$CaCO_3$	-288.5	KCl	-104.2	PCl_5	-95.4
CaO	-151.9	$KClO_3$	-93.5	SiO_2	-205.4
$Ca(OH)_2$	-235.8	KOH	-101.8	$SnCl_2$	-83.6
$CaSO_4$	-342.4	$MgCl_2$	-153.4	SnO_2	-138.8
CCl_4	-33.3	MgO	-143.8	SO_2	-71.0
CH_4	-17.9	$Mg(OH)_2$	-221.0	SO_3	-94.5
C_2H_4	+12.5	$MgSO_4$	-305.5	ZnO	-83.2
C_2H_6	-20.24	MnO	-92.0	ZnS	-48.5
C_6H_6	+19.8	NaBr	-86.0		
C_2H_5OH	-66.37	NaCl	-98.2		

Most of the ΔH_f°s are negative. Thus the reactions that produce most of the commonly known compounds are exothermic. Compounds with large negative numbers release large amounts of energy when they form. Note that the chart does not include molecules such as Cl_2, H_2, and O_2. Because these substances are elements, not compounds, they have no enthalpies of formation.

Sample Problem. What is the ΔH° for $N_2 + 2\ O_2 \longrightarrow 2\ NO_2$?

Solution.

Table 12-5 shows that the standard molar enthalpy of formation of nitrogen dioxide is +8.1 kilocalories per mole. The given reaction forms 2 moles of nitrogen dioxide.

$$2 \text{ moles } NO_2 \times \frac{+8.1 \text{ kcal}}{\text{mole } NO_2} = +16 \text{ kcal}$$

A reaction has two hypothetical steps. The first step involves the breaking down of the reactants. The second step is the formation of the products. The following reaction between lead oxide and carbon monoxide illustrates these two steps.

$$PbO + CO \longrightarrow Pb + CO_2$$

The first step in the reaction is the breakdown of lead oxide and carbon monoxide. The ΔH_f° for the formation of lead oxide at standard conditions is -52.1 kilocalories per mole. The breakdown of lead oxide, which is the reverse reaction, requires +52.1 kilocalories. The ΔH_f° for the breakdown of carbon monoxide is +26.4 kilocalories per mole. The ΔH° for the first part of the reaction is +78.5 kilocalories.

The second part of the reaction is the formation of products. The ΔH°s for these changes can be easily found in the table of ΔH_f°s. Since lead is an element, its ΔH_f° is zero. The ΔH_f° for the formation of 1 mole of carbon dioxide from its elements at standard conditions is -94.1 kilocalories. The total ΔH° for the formation of products is -94.1 kilocalories.

The ΔH° for the entire reaction is the sum of the ΔH_f° for the reactant breakdowns and the ΔH_f° for the product formation.

$$+78.5 \text{ kcal} + (-94.1 \text{ kcal}) = -15.6 \text{ kcal}$$

The ΔH° for the reaction is -15.6 kilocalories. This result shows that the reaction is exothermic.

In the previous problem, calculating the ΔH° of a reaction involved combining the ΔH°s of two partial reactions. A law of thermochemistry called Hess's law justifies this method of calculation. **Hess's law** states that the enthalpy change of a reaction equals the sum of the enthalpy changes for each step of the reaction. The example shows how one reaction could be thought of as the sum of two other reactions.

$$\begin{array}{rlll}
PbO + CO & \longrightarrow & Pb + O_2 + C & \Delta H^\circ = +78.5 \text{ kcal} \\
Pb + O_2 + C & \longrightarrow & Pb + CO_2 & \Delta H^\circ = -94.1 \text{ kcal} \\
\hline
PbO + CO & \longrightarrow & Pb + CO_2 & \Delta H^\circ = -15.6 \text{ kcal}
\end{array}$$

The enthalpy change of the total reaction equals the sum of the two enthalpy changes. The mathematical version of this statement is

$$\Delta H^\circ_{\text{reaction}} = \Delta H^\circ_{\text{product formation}} + \Delta H^\circ_{\text{reactant breakdown}}$$

Because the table refers to the formation of compounds, the values for reactant-breakdown enthalpies will be opposite in sign to those listed. The equation can be changed to a form that uses the data in Table 12-5 without changing the signs of the numbers. The symbol Σ in this equation is the Greek letter sigma. It signifies a summation of numbers.

$$\Delta H^\circ_{\text{reaction}} = \Sigma\Delta H^\circ_{f\,\text{products}} - \Sigma\Delta H^\circ_{f\,\text{reactants}}$$

Sample Problem. Estimate the ΔH° for the combustion of methane, using standard enthalpies of formation.

$$CH_4 + 2\,O_2 \longrightarrow CO_2 + 2\,H_2O$$

Solution.

The equation requires the use of the following data from the table of enthalpies of formation.

$$\Delta H^\circ_f \text{ of } CO_2 = \text{-94.1 kcal/mole}$$
$$\Delta H^\circ_f \text{ of } H_2O = \text{-68.3 kcal/mole}$$
$$\Delta H^\circ_f \text{ of } CH_4 = \text{-17.9 kcal/mole}$$
$$\Delta H^\circ_f \text{ of } O_2 = 0$$

Two moles of water and 2 moles of oxygen participate in the reaction. This fact must be dealt with when calculating the enthalpy change of the entire reaction.

$$\Delta H^\circ_{\text{reaction}} = \Sigma\Delta H^\circ_{f\,\text{products}} - \Sigma\Delta H^\circ_{f\,\text{reactants}}$$
$$\Delta H^\circ_{f\,\text{products}} = \Delta H^\circ_{f\,CO_2} + 2(\Delta H^\circ_{f\,H_2O})$$
$$= \text{-94.1 kcal} + 2(\text{-68.3}) \text{ kcal}$$
$$= \text{-231 kcal}$$

The last term in the equation can be calculated in a similar manner.

$$\Delta H^\circ_{f\,\text{reactants}} = \Delta H^\circ_{f\,CH_4} + 2(\Delta H^\circ_{f\,O_2})$$
$$= \text{-17.9 kcal} + 2(0)$$
$$= \text{-17.9 kcal}$$

The two terms can now be combined in the original equation.

$$\Delta H^\circ_{\text{reaction}} = \Sigma\Delta H^\circ_{f\,\text{products}} - \Sigma\Delta H^\circ_{f\,\text{reactants}}$$
$$\Delta H^\circ_{\text{reaction}} = (\text{-231 kcal}) - (\text{-17.9 kcal})$$
$$\Delta H^\circ_{\text{reaction}} = \text{-213 kcal}$$

The reaction is highly exothermic.

12–5 Bond Enthalpies: The Bigger the Better

The **enthalpy of bond formation,** or bond enthalpy, is defined as the ΔH° that occurs when a mole of bonds in a gaseous compound is broken. For example, an input of 46 kilocalories is necessary to break apart a mole of Br—Br bonds.

$$Br_2 + 46 \text{ kcal} \longrightarrow Br + Br; \quad \Delta H^\circ = 46 \text{ kcal/mole}$$

Because bonded atoms are more stable than unbonded atoms, energy is always required to break bonds. Consequently, all bond enthalpies are positive numbers. Conversely, the formation of bonds always releases energy and is thus exothermic.

Bond enthalpies can help explain why some reactions give off energy and others require energy. Strong bonds are stable bonds; large amounts of energy are necessary to break them. The bond enthalpies of strong bonds are thus quite high. Strong bonds also give off large amounts of energy when they form. Weak bonds can be broken with small amounts of energy. Predictably, they give off small amounts of energy when they form. The bond enthalpies of weak bonds are relatively low.

A reaction that breaks strong bonds and forms weak bonds will require energy. More energy is required to break the strong bonds than is released when the weak bonds form. As a result, reactions that produce compounds with weaker, less stable bonds are endothermic.

$$\text{Stronger bonds} \longrightarrow \text{Weaker bonds}; \quad \Delta H > 0, \text{ Endothermic}$$

A reaction that forms stable, low-energy compounds from compounds with high-energy, weak bonds releases energy. The amount of energy that must be used to break the weak bonds is small compared to all the energy that is given off when the strong bonds form.

$$\text{Weaker bonds} \longrightarrow \text{Stronger bonds}; \quad \Delta H < 0, \text{ Exothermic}$$

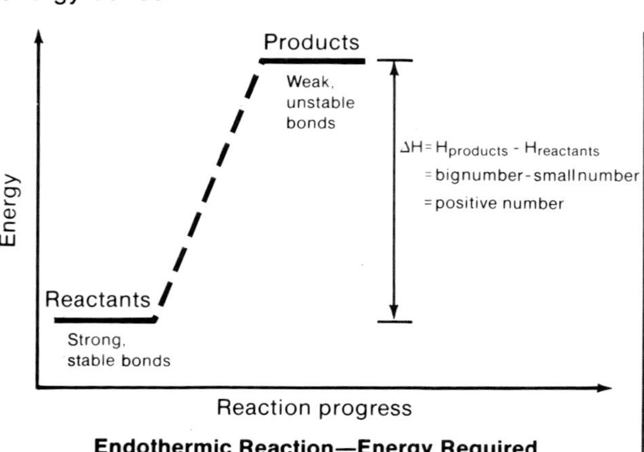

Endothermic Reaction—Energy Required

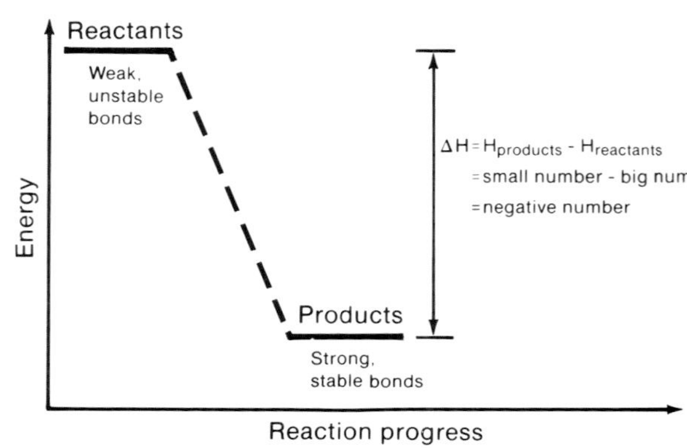

Exothermic Reaction—Energy Released

12-6 Exothermic reactions form stable, low-energy bonds. Endothermic reactions form unstable, high-energy bonds.

12–6 Entropy: The Chaos Factor

12-7 Natural processes in the universe automatically increase entropy.

In most cases exothermic processes proceed spontaneously, and endothermic ones do not. But this rule does not always hold true. More than a negative ΔH is necessary in order for a process to be spontaneous. An example of an endothermic process that proceeds on its own is the releasing of compressed gas into the atmosphere. As gas under high pressure is released, it gets colder. Something besides changes in heat influence spontaneity.

Two natural tendencies govern all spontaneous processes. The first is that matter seeks stable, low-energy states. The second is that natural processes decrease the order of the universe. The latter is a statement of the second law of thermodynamics.

Could the universe have formed spontaneously? Not according to the laws of thermodynamics. The first law shows that it could not have begun itself, because energy cannot be created or destroyed. The second law forbids the spontaneous evolution of the universe because the orderliness of this world could not have arisen on its own. The universe could only have been created.

Entropy (S) is a measure of randomness (disorder). Disordered substances have high entropies; very ordered substances have low entropies. Crystalline solids have particles arranged in definite, repeating, organized systems; these substances have low entropies. Gases, with their free-flying molecules, have high entropies. Dissolved substances usually have higher entropies than their crystalline counterparts. The entropy of substances increases with temperature. As the temperature becomes greater, the increased kinetic energy gives the particles greater motion.

The amount of entropy in a substance varies with the temperature and pressure, so these conditions must be specified. Table 12-8 lists the entropies per mole of common substances at standard conditions. Although elements are not listed in tables of enthalpies (see Table 12-5), they are included in tables of entropies because all substances have some entropy.

Table 12-8

Standard Molar Entropies (at 298 K and 1 atm)					
Compound	Entropy (cal/mole·K)	Compound	Entropy (cal/mole·K)	Compound	Entropy (cal/mole·K)
Ag (s)	10.21	Cu (s)	8.0	Mn (s)	7.6
AgBr (s)	25.6	CuO (s)	10.4	MnO (s)	14.4
AgCl (s)	23.0	Cu_2O (s)	24.1	MnO_2 (s)	12.7
AgI (s)	27.3	CuS (s)	15.9	N_2 (g)	45.8
Ag_2O (s)	29.1	$CuSO_4$ (s)	27.1	Na (s)	12.2
Ag_2S (s)	34.8	F_2 (g)	48.6	NaBr (s)	20.8
Al (s)	6.77	Fe (s)	6.5	NaCl (s)	17.3
Al_2O_3 (s)	12.2	Fe_2O_3 (s)	21.5	NaF (s)	14.0
Ba (s)	40.7	Fe_3O_4 (s)	35.0	NaI (s)	23.5
$BaCl_2$ (s)	30.0	H_2 (g)	31.2	NaOH (s)	15.4
$BaCO_3$ (s)	26.8	HBr (g)	47.44	NH_3 (g)	46.0
BaO (s)	16.8	HCl (g)	44.6	NH_4Cl (s)	22.6
$BaSO_4$ (s)	31.6	HCl (aq)	13.2	NiO (s)	57.0
Br_2 (*l*)	36.4	HF (g)	41.5	O_2 (g)	49.0
C (s)	1.4	HI (g)	49.3	O_3 (g)	56.8
Ca (s)	10.0	HNO_3 (*l*)	37.2	P (red) (s)	5.45
$CaCl_2$ (s)	27.2	H_2O (g)	45.1	Pb (s)	15.5
$CaCO_3$ (s)	22.2	H_2O (*l*)	16.7	$PbBr_2$ (s)	38.6
CaO (s)	9.5	H_2O_2 (*l*)	26.2	$PbCl_2$ (s)	32.6
$Ca(OH)_2$ (s)	18.2	H_2S (g)	49.2	PbO (s)	16.2
$CaSO_4$ (s)	25.5	H_2SO_4 (*l*)	37.5	PbO_2 (s)	18.3
CCl_4 (*l*)	51.3	Hg (*l*)	18.5	Pb_3O_4 (s)	50.5
CH_4 (g)	44.5	HgO (s)	17.2	PCl_3 (g)	74.5
C_2H_2 (g)	48.0	HgS (s)	18.6	PCl_5 (g)	84.3
C_2H_4 (g)	52.5	I_2 (s)	27.9	S_8 (s)	7.6
C_2H_6 (g)	54.85	K (s)	15.2	Si (s)	4.5
C_3H_8 (g)	64.5	KBr (s)	23.1	SiO_2 (s)	10.0
$CHCl_3$ (*l*)	48.5	KCl (s)	19.8	Sn (s)	10.7
CH_3OH (*l*)	30.3	$KClO_3$ (s)	34.2	$SnCl_4$ (*l*)	61.8
C_2H_5OH (*l*)	38.4	KF (s)	15.9	SnO (s)	13.5
Cl_2 (g)	53.3	KOH (s)	18.9	SnO_2 (s)	12.5
CO (g)	47.3	Mg (s)	7.8	SO_2 (g)	59.4
CO_2 (g)	51.1	$MgCl_2$ (s)	21.4	SO_3 (g)	61.2
Co (s)	6.8	$MgCO_3$ (s)	15.7	Zn (s)	10.0
CoO (s)	10.5	MgO (s)	6.4	ZnO (s)	10.5
Cr (s)	5.7	$Mg(OH)_2$ (s)	15.09	ZnS (s)	13.8
Cr_2O_3 (s)	19.4	$MgSO_4$ (s)	21.9		

12–7 Calculating Entropy Changes

From the data in Table 12-8 the entropy changes of many reactions can be calculated. An entropy change is the difference between the entropy of the products and the entropy of the reactants.

$$\Delta S^\circ = \text{Total entropy in products} - \text{Total entropy in reactants}$$

$$\Delta S^\circ = \Sigma S^\circ_{\text{products}} - \Sigma S^\circ_{\text{reactants}}$$

A reaction with a positive $\Delta S°$ increases entropy. The products have more entropy than the reactants. Negative $\Delta S°$s signify a decrease in entropy.

Sample Problem. Does the reaction $NH_3 + HCl \longrightarrow NH_4Cl$ increase or decrease entropy?

Solution.

$$\Delta S° = \Sigma S°_{\text{products}} - \Sigma S°_{\text{reactants}}$$

$$\Sigma S°_{\text{products}} = S°_{NH_4Cl} = 22.6 \text{ cal/K}$$

$$\Sigma S°_{\text{reactants}} = S°_{NH_3} + S°_{HCl} = 46.0 \text{ cal/K} + 44.6 \text{ cal/K} = 90.6 \text{ cal/K}$$

$$\Delta S° = \Sigma S°_{\text{products}} - \Sigma S°_{\text{reactants}} = 22.6 \text{ cal/K} - 90.6 \text{ cal/K} = -68.0 \text{ cal/K}$$

Since the $\Delta S°$ value is negative, the amount of entropy has decreased. The product (a solid) is more ordered than the reactants (gases).

12-9 Solid NH_4Cl forms when HCl and NH_3 vapors mix.

Natural processes tend to increase the entropy of the universe. A positive $\Delta S°$ aids spontaneity. A reaction with a negative $\Delta S°$ goes against this tendency and attempts to decrease entropy. What can force a reaction to violate the trend toward disorder?

12–8 The Driving Force of Reactions: Free-Energy Change

Two tendencies drive reactions. The first is the tendency to decrease enthalpy, and the second is the tendency to increase entropy. Reactions can be either exothermic or endothermic, and they can either increase or decrease entropy. Four possible enthalpy/entropy combinations exist.

1. Exothermic and increasing entropy ($-\Delta H$, $+\Delta S$)
2. Exothermic and decreasing entropy ($-\Delta H$, $-\Delta S$)
3. Endothermic and increasing entropy ($+\Delta H$, $+\Delta S$)
4. Endothermic and decreasing entropy ($+\Delta H$, $-\Delta S$)

Reactions are driven by the combined effects of ΔH and ΔS. A single expression that relates ΔH and ΔS is needed to determine how they combine. J. Willard Gibbs, a brilliant American physicist and mathematician of the 1800s, formulated a single criterion of spontaneity. He combined the change in enthalpy and the change in entropy into a single term called **free energy,** which is sometimes called Gibbs free energy (G) in his honor. The **free-energy change,** ΔG, for a reaction can be calculated by the equation $\Delta G = \Delta H - T\Delta S$, where T is temperature in kelvins.

ΔG is the change in free energy. It is the difference between the free energy of the products and the free energy of the reactants. A negative ΔG indicates an overall release of energy and signifies that a reaction may occur naturally. A positive ΔG indicates a net energy gain and signifies that a reaction is unfavorable.

The free-energy change can be negative under several conditions. Negative ΔHs always contribute to a negative ΔG; so do positive ΔSs. When the two tendencies oppose each other, the temperature often determines which one will win.

Table 12-10

When Is ΔG Negative?

	ΔH	ΔS	ΔG
1.	−	+	$-\Delta H - T(+\Delta S) = -\Delta G$ at all Ts
2.	−	−	$-\Delta H - T(-\Delta S) = -\Delta G$ at low Ts
3.	+	+	$+\Delta H - T(+\Delta S) = -\Delta G$ at high Ts
4.	+	−	$+\Delta H - T(-\Delta S) = +\Delta G$ at all Ts

Case 1 shows that exothermic reactions that increase entropy ($-\Delta H$, $+\Delta S$) are always spontaneous. They are favorable on both counts. They release energy, and they increase disorder. ΔG for such reactions is always negative.

Case 2 shows that exothermic reactions that decrease entropy ($-\Delta H$, $-\Delta S$) may or may not be spontaneous. The two tendencies oppose each other. In cases like this, the temperature determines whether the reaction is favorable. The entropy change hinders the reaction less at low temperatures than it does at high temperatures, so ΔG is negative at low temperatures.

Case 3 represents endothermic reactions that increase entropy ($+\Delta H$, $+\Delta S$). These reactions can be favorable if the entropy change is greater than the change in enthalpy. High temperatures magnify the effect of the entropy change and make ΔG negative. As a result, the reaction can proceed.

Case 4 shows that endothermic reactions that decrease entropy ($+\Delta H$, $-\Delta S$) do not occur naturally. To proceed naturally, these reactions would have to store energy in chemical bonds and increase order. Reactions that exhibit positive enthalpy changes can be forced if other types of energy are used.

12-11 In this analogy of a reaction, gravity is like ΔH, and the magnetic force represents ΔS. The two forces can interact in four different ways to control the motion of the ball.

Spontaneous

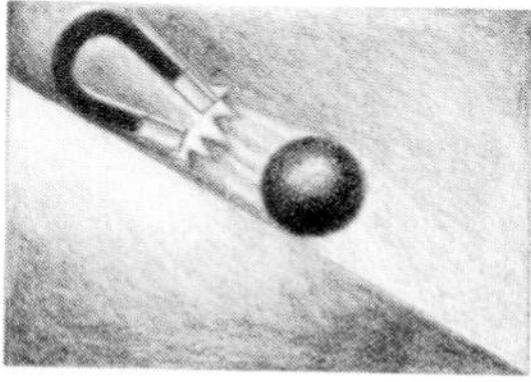

Spontaneous if gravity overcomes magnetism

Spontaneous if magnetism overcomes gravity

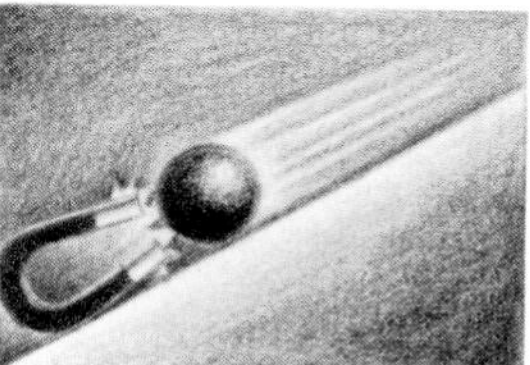

Not spontaneous

The ΔG of a reaction can be calculated from the values for ΔH, ΔS, and T, which can be plugged into the free-energy equation. For practice, calculate the free-energy change for the reaction $Mg(OH)_2 \longrightarrow MgO + H_2O$. Once the change in free energy is known, the probability of the reaction can be determined. At 25° C the $\Delta H°$ of the reaction is +19.4 kilocalories. The $\Delta S°$ is +36.41 calories per mole·K. Note that the two values are not expressed in similar units. Expressing the $\Delta S°$ in kilocalories per mole·K can remedy this problem.

$$\begin{aligned} \Delta G &= \Delta H - T\Delta S \\ &= +19.4 - 298(0.03641) \\ &= +8.55 \text{ kcal/mole} \end{aligned}$$

Since the ΔG is positive, the reaction cannot be spontaneous at 298 K. At a higher temperature the favorable ΔS has a greater effect. This can be seen in the calculation of ΔG at 1000 K.

$$\begin{aligned} \Delta G &= \Delta H - T\Delta S \\ &= 19.4 - 1000(0.03641) \\ &= -17.01 \text{ kcal/mole} \end{aligned}$$

Sample Problem. Determine whether the reaction between ammonia and hydrogen chloride ($NH_3 + HCl \longrightarrow NH_4Cl$) is probable at 298 K and whether it is probable at 1000 K. The ΔH° of the reaction is -42.3 kilocalories per mole, and the ΔS° is -0.068 kilocalories per kelvin.

Solution.

To find the ΔG at 298 K, plug the appropriate values into the free-energy equation.

$$\begin{aligned}\Delta G &= \Delta H - T\Delta S \\ &= -42.3 \text{ kcal} - 298 \text{ K}(-0.0680 \text{ kcal/K}) \\ &= -22.0 \text{ kcal}\end{aligned}$$

Since the ΔG is negative, the reaction is favorable at this temperature. To determine whether the reaction is favorable at 1000 K, insert 1000 K into the free-energy equation and solve for ΔG.

$$\begin{aligned}\Delta G &= \Delta H - T\Delta \text{S} \\ &= -42.3 \text{ kcal} - 1000 \text{ K}(-0.0680 \text{ kcal/K}) \\ &= +25.7\end{aligned}$$

The positive ΔG shows that the reaction is unfavorable at this temperature.

12-12 Grinding substances with a mortar and pestle often helps the substances to react more quickly.

Kinetics: Will Things React?

The fact that a reaction is thermodynamically favorable does not mean that it will proceed automatically. Some reactions proceed at an extremely slow rate, some need a push to get started, and some go on their own. Consider three reactions. All of them have negative ΔGs, so they are all favorable.

1. The oxidation of a diamond: $\Delta G = -94.7$ kilocalories
2. The burning of methane: $\Delta G = -138.9$ kilocalories
3. The mixing of $Ba(OH)_2$ and H_2SO_4: $\Delta G = -31.3$ kilocalories

The first reaction does not proceed at a significant rate. The second reaction does not start unless it is given an energetic push (from a lighted match, for example). The third reaction proceeds as soon as the reactants are mixed together. Something besides thermodynamics must be used to explain why reactions have such a wide variety of rates. **Kinetics** is the study of the rates of reactions and the steps by which they occur.

12–9 Energy Diagrams: Mapping Energy Changes

Thermodynamics determines the difference between the free energy of the reactants and the free energy of the products. Thermodynamics does not, however, determine what happens *during* a reaction. In kinetics scientists strive to determine what happens between the start and finish of a reaction. Are the energy changes during a reaction simple and direct? Or must the reactants gain some energy before the reaction can proceed?

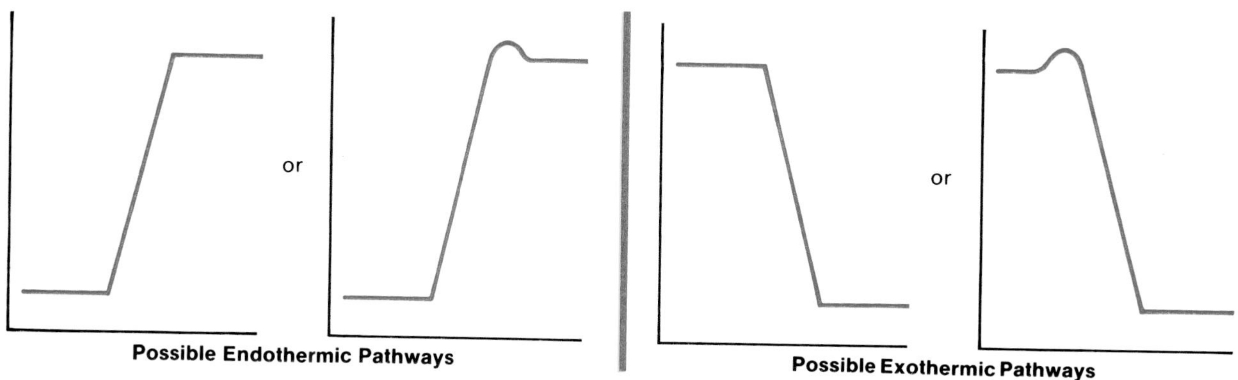

12-13 Possible reaction pathways.

Energy diagrams are commonly used in kinetics to illustrate complex ideas. The vertical scale represents the energy of a particular chemical entity. Usually the energy scale does not have any specific units. The horizontal scale represents the progress of the reaction being considered.

12–10 Collision Theory: Prerequisites for Reactions

An oxygen molecule careens off the inside glass wall of a camera flashbulb. It ricochets over to the magnesium wire mounted in the center of the bulb. The collision is mild, so there is no reaction with the reactive metal. Suddenly, the photographer snaps the shutter button. An electrical current surges through the wire and heats it to a searing temperature. The nearby oxygen molecule, now full of kinetic energy, slams back into the hot metal. Each atom in the oxygen molecule contacts a magnesium atom. The stage is set for a reaction.

The forceful collision disrupts the electron orbitals, and for a brief moment, four atoms hang in one highly energized group. The bonds in the oxygen molecule quiver and shake. Energized electrons scramble toward the oxygen atoms in search of stable positions. Then, with a flash of white light that illuminates the photographer's scene, the entire group of atoms splits. The newly fused magnesium and oxygen atoms shower downward as a portion of the ashes from the burned filament.

This imaginative account attempts to narrate the steps in the reaction that burns the filament of a flashbulb. It points out a fundamental principle of kinetics: things must collide before they react. However, a collision alone does not guarantee a reaction. The collision must be (1) forceful enough, and (2) properly oriented. The **collision theory** explains why reactions go at greater rates, depending on reaction conditions. Any factor that increases the number of effective collisions increases the rate of a reaction.

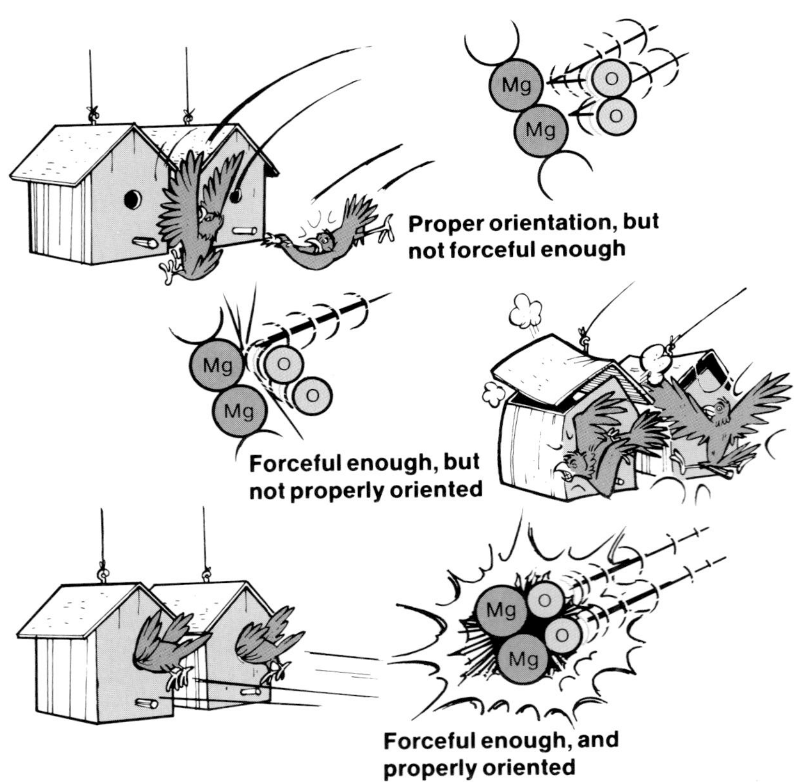

12-14 Two conditions must be met before reactions can occur.

Before the electrical current heated the wire, the collisions were too mild. Yet even forceful collisions might not cause a reaction. Suppose that the end of an oxygen molecule hit the magnesium so that only one oxygen atom contacted the magnesium. This improper orientation would doom any chance of a reaction, since two oxygen atoms are necessary to react with one magnesium atom. Reactions follow forceful, properly oriented collisions.

12–11 Activated Complex: Over the Hump!

Magnesium does not automatically burst into flames when exposed to oxygen. Despite the negative ΔG, (-60.3 kcal/mole), the reaction is not totally spontaneous. The overall reaction is favorable, but something restrains the release of energy.

Recall that a reaction can be pictured as a two-step process: (1) the breaking of bonds, and (2) the formation of bonds. Tearing magnesium atoms away from the wire and breaking the bonds in the oxygen molecules requires energy. Not until this step is completed can the magnesium and oxygen atoms form bonds and release energy.

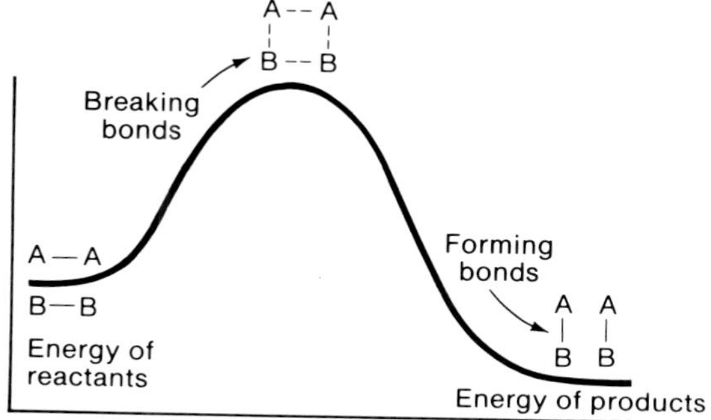

12-15 Reactions must often overcome an initial energy barrier before they can proceed.

Molecules need kinetic energy before their collisions can be forceful enough to cause reactions. This energy, called the **activation energy,** is the minimum amount of kinetic energy that must be possessed by the reactants before they can react.

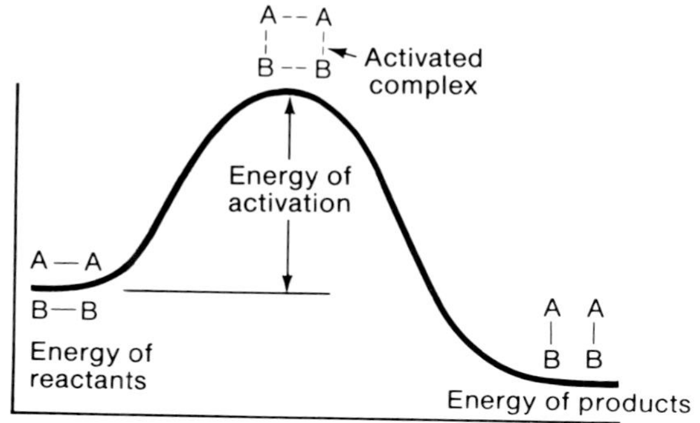

12-16 An activated complex is a transitional structure.

Colliding reactants can form a transitional structure between reactants and products. This structure, called an **activated complex,** is an unstable, intermediate group of reactants. Its high energy content makes it extremely unstable. The activated complex can break up to form the products of the reaction, or it can revert back to the separate reactants. If the activated complex goes on to complete the reaction, a large amount of energy will be released. In exothermic reactions, this energy activates more reactants, and the reaction becomes self-sufficient. No additional energy input is necessary.

In conclusion, the activation energy plays a crucial role in determining whether a reaction proceeds on its own. A large activation energy can prevent a thermodynamically favorable reaction from proceeding. The following figures show energy diagrams for several reactions. Which reaction is most likely to proceed?

12-17 Reaction pathways.

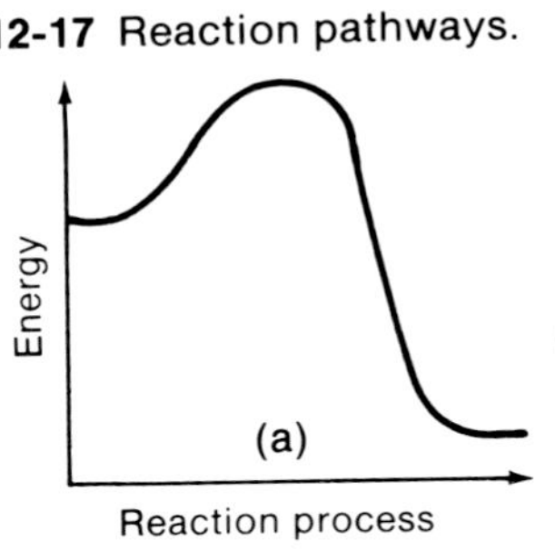

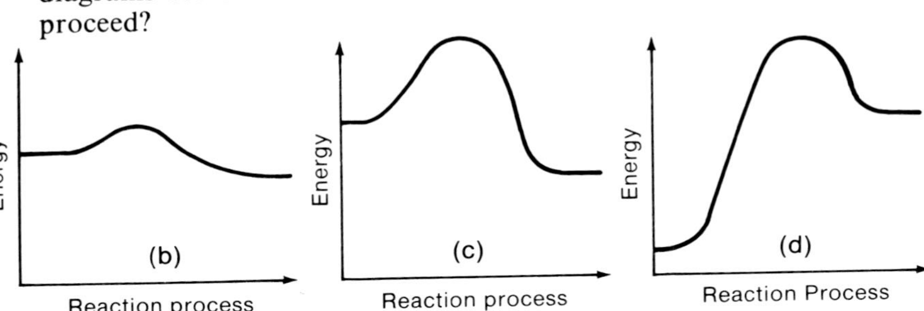

Reaction (d) requires a large initial input and a net gain in energy; it is doubtful that such a reaction will proceed on its own. The other reactions release energy but must overcome the activation-energy barrier to do so. Reaction (b) has the smallest barrier to overcome, so it is the most likely to proceed as soon as reactants combine.

12–12 Rates of Reactions

During a reaction the concentrations of reactants and products change constantly. At the beginning of a reaction, the reactants are packed together in high concentrations. As the reaction progresses, product concentrations increase as reactants are consumed. Consider the reaction between iodine chloride and hydrogen: $2\ ICl\ (g) + H_2\ (g) \longrightarrow I_2\ (g) + 2\ HCl\ (g)$. Figure 12-18 shows how the concentrations of the substances in this reaction vary with time.

12-18

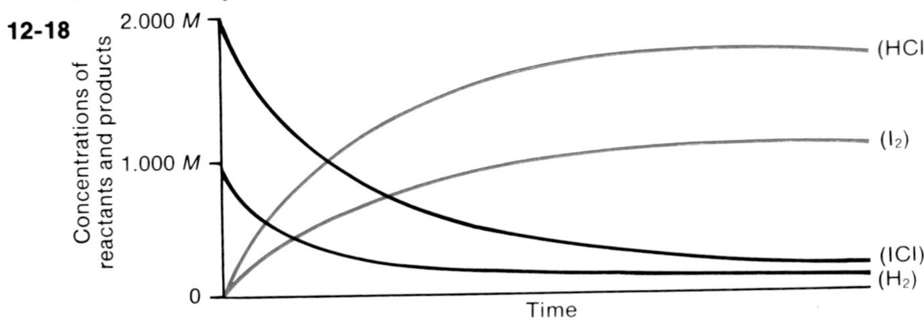

Reaction rates tell how fast reactants change into products. They can describe how fast the reactants disappear or how fast the products appear. Although reaction rates may be measured in many different units, they usually tell how fast concentrations change with time. Units such as molarity per second or moles per liter per hour are common.

12–13 Factors that Affect Reaction Rates

The most obvious factor that controls the rate of a reaction is the chemical nature of the reactants. Logically enough, reactive substances react quickly. The chemical nature of reactants cannot be changed, but other factors can. The rate of a given reaction can be modified by changes in concentration, temperature, the amount of surface area, and the presence of catalysts.

Concentration. The typical test for the presence of oxygen gas relies on the fact that high concentrations of reactants improve the rate of a reaction. A glowing splint is thrust into a gas-collection bottle. If the bottle contains pure or relatively pure oxygen gas, the glowing splint will burst into flames. The atmosphere contains only 21 per cent oxygen. This small amount of oxygen supports the slow smoldering while the splint is glowing. An atmosphere of 100 per cent oxygen increases the reaction rate; the combustion thus proceeds more quickly.

12-19 Glowing splint test for oxygen gas.

The effect of concentration on the reaction rate varies from reaction to reaction. Doubling the concentration of a reactant in one reaction might not affect the rate at all. Doubling the concentration of a reactant in a second reaction could double its rate or even quadruple the rate of a third reaction. No rule can predict the effect of concentration changes on reaction rates. Reactions must be studied individually.

Temperature. One rule of thumb in kinetics states that reaction rates double for every 10° C rise in temperature. Although the rule has many exceptions, it illustrates the vital role that temperature plays in determining the rates of reactions. Higher temperatures increase reaction rates in two ways. First, they increase the number of collisions between reactants. Second, the collisions that do occur are more forceful. In the final analysis, higher temperatures increase the number of effective collisions.

The decomposition of lactose (a sugar in dairy products) into lactic acid turns fresh milk into a foul-smelling fluid. The lactic acid that is produced gives old milk its distinctive sour taste. Can this reaction be stopped? Not totally; but it can be greatly slowed down if the milk is kept cool in a refrigerator. The lower temperature in the refrigerator extends the usable period of milk by lowering the reaction rate.

Surface Area. Small particles have greater surface area per unit volume than do large particles. If a large lump of coal is placed into a furnace, the molecules buried deep within the lump have no chance to burn. Crushing the coal into smaller pieces exposes additional molecules and allows the rate of the reaction to increase. Further crushing, to the point of producing powdered coal, exposes multitudes of molecules and results in even faster reaction rates. Coal miners are all too familiar with this problem. Tragic coal-

FACETS OF CHEMISTRY

Spontaneous Combustion

It had been a hot day in North Arlington, New Jersey. Swimmers seeking relief from the oppressive heat thronged a beach along a riverbank. Between them and the road was a storehouse full of pyroxylin—a highly combustible material. Across the road was the Atlantic Pyroxylin Waste Company. Here workers sorted pyroxylin scraps collected from surrounding factories so that they could be used again. At 9:12 P.M. lingering swimmers noticed fire coming from the roof of the factory. With a puff, both ends of the building blew out, and a vast flame swept over the surrounding area. The flames crossed the road and set fire to the small storehouse beside the beach. Another puff occurred, and flames engulfed the beach. The burning of the Atlantic Pyroxylin Waste Company is a classic example of spontaneous combustion.

Spontaneous combustion fires start without a flame or spark. They start because of the role that heat plays in speeding up reaction rates. The Atlantic Pyroxylin Waste Company stored pyroxylin scraps swept up from factory floors. These scraps often had machine oil on them. The heat necessary for the fire to start came from the reaction between this oil and atmospheric oxygen. The reacdust explosions can rip through mines if powdered coal is ignited by a stray spark. Even grain dust is potentially explosive if the surface area is great enough. Large amounts of easily combustible dust can collect in grain elevators. If enough dust starts to react, the reaction rate can increase to the point that it explodes an entire elevator.

12-20 The ceiling, walls, and floor of this coal mine have been sprayed with powdered limestone to prevent coal dust from collecting and exploding.

tion does not normally generate great amounts of heat, because it occurs slowly. Whatever heat is produced is released gradually. However, if the heat from the oxidation cannot escape, it accumulates and the temperature increases. The increased temperature causes the reaction to proceed faster and to produce more heat. This vicious cycle repeats itself until the reaction proceeds fast enough to generate temperatures above the kindling point of the surrounding material.

Spontaneous combustion can occur in places other than factories. For example, spontaneous combustion occurs in soft coal, especially if powdered coal covers a mass of lump coal. As the coal slowly reacts with oxygen, the heat cannot dissipate. The temperature increases until the coal ignites. Soft coal should be spread over a large area to allow the heat to escape.

Farmers must also be aware of the dangers of spontaneous combustion. If they pack freshly cut hay into a barn before it is properly dried, oxidation will continue in the confined space. When a certain temperature is reached, the hay will burst into flames. Hay should be stored in a cool, dry, well-ventilated barn.

Oily, paint-saturated rags pose a threat to many homes and workshops. As paint dries, the linseed oil it contains reacts with oxygen and forms an elastic solid. This reaction produces heat as the paint dries. A pile of oily rags provides the perfect conditions for a cycle of higher temperatures and faster reaction rates to be set up. Again the temperature increases until the rags catch fire. Paint rags should be hung outdoors where there is good air circulation, and they should then be stored in a metal can.

Preventing spontaneous combustion fires is a matter of controlling the rates of chemical reactions. Caution should be taken with combustible materials in powdered forms. The large amount of surface area allows reactions to proceed more quickly. More importantly, combustible materials should be stored in well-ventilated places where heat can be removed faster than it is produced. This will prevent heat from accumulating in a place where it can increase the rate of the reaction.

(a) Reactants enter the active site of the enzyme.

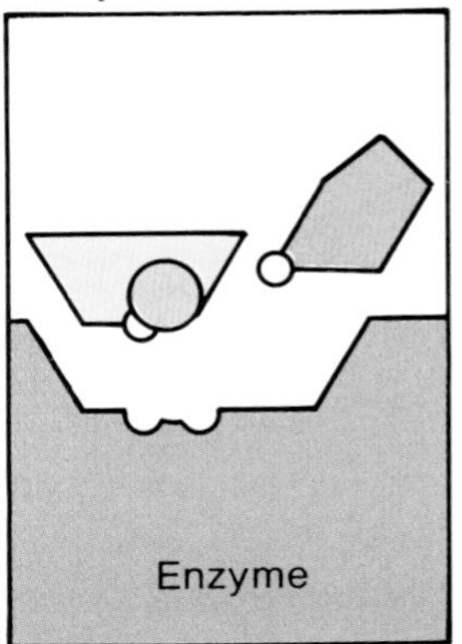

(b) The reaction occurs.

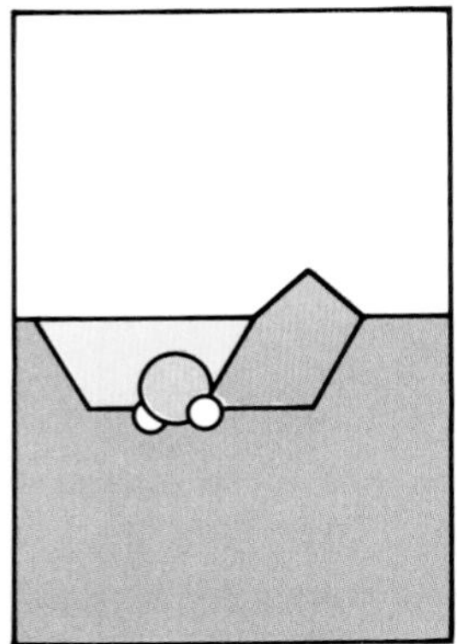

(c) One product leaves the active site.

(d) A water molecule leaves the active site.

12-21 The lock-and-key model of enzyme action for a reaction in which two large molecules join together by releasing a water molecule.

Catalysts. A **catalyst** is a substance that changes a reaction rate without being permanently changed by the reaction. It is present during the reaction, but it is neither a reactant nor a product. In the reaction between hydrogen and oxygen gases, water is the product. Normally a spark of some kind must start the reaction. A catalyst such as powdered platinum metal allows the reaction to start at room temperature.

How do catalysts work? Chemists think that catalysts hold reactants in niches and pockets on their surfaces. Theoretically, catalysts provide sites for reactions by holding reactants in just the right positions for favorable collisions. Catalysts lower the activation energy of a reaction.

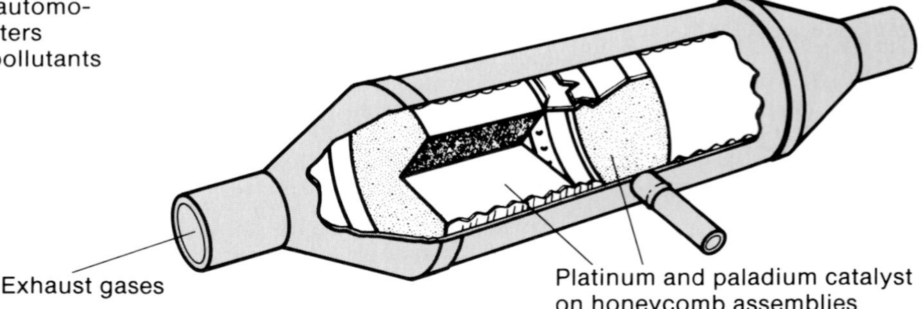

12-22 Reactions in automobile catalytic converters reduce the level of pollutants in exhaust gases.

12–14 Mechanisms: One Step at a Time

Chemists can easily identify the substances that go into reactions. They can also routinely analyze the compounds that emerge. The fragments of molecules that exist during reactions are much more difficult to pinpoint. For chemists, observing reactions is like looking at a factory from the outside. They can see the raw materials going in and the finished products coming out, but they cannot see the "assembly line"—the individual steps in the reactions. The series of steps that make up a reaction is called a **reaction mechanism.**

The reaction between hydrogen and iodine gases was one of the first to be studied in the field of kinetics. Scientists all knew that $H_2 + I_2 \longrightarrow 2\ HI$. What they did not know was what actually happened during the reaction. Did two molecules collide to form an activated complex that split into two hydrogen iodide molecules? Did the atoms in both molecules split and then rearrange themselves? Or did an atom of one molecule split off, join another molecule, and cleave it? Theoretically, any one of these proposed mechanisms could produce hydrogen iodide from hydrogen and iodine. As it turns out, experimental evidence proves the third mechanism to be correct.

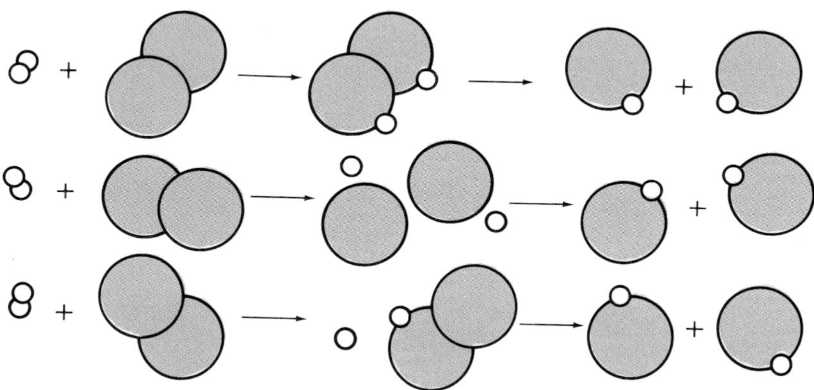

12-23 Possible mechanisms for $H_2 + I_2 \longrightarrow 2\ HI$

12–15 Rate Laws: Equations that Describe Reaction Rates

As stated before, the concentrations of reactants influence reaction rates. The effect of concentration varies from reaction to reaction. For example, the rate of $H_2 + I_2 \longrightarrow 2\ HI$ is directly proportional to the concentration of hydrogen gas in the reaction vessel. The concentration of reactants in terms of moles per liter (molarity) is often signified by square brackets. Doubling the concentration of hydrogen, $[H_2]$, doubles the reaction rate. Tripling the concentration triples the reaction rate. The rate of this reaction is also directly proportional to the concentration of iodine gas.

$$\text{Rate} \propto [H_2][I_2]$$

This expression, called a rate law, becomes an equality when a numerical constant is inserted. A **rate law** is an equation that mathematically describes how fast a reaction occurs. Each reaction has its own rate constant (k).

$$\text{Rate} = k[H_2][I_2]$$

The reaction between nitrogen dioxide and carbon monoxide at low temperatures has a completely different rate law.

$$NO_2 + CO \longrightarrow NO + CO_2; \quad \text{Rate} = k[NO_2]^2$$

Changing the concentration of carbon monoxide has no effect on the rate of the reaction. Therefore, the concentration of carbon monoxide does not appear in the rate law. The exponent on the $[NO_2]$ term indicates that the concentration of nitrogen dioxide plays the crucial role in determining how fast the reaction goes. If the concentration of nitrogen dioxide is doubled, the rate quadruples. If the concentration of nitrogen dioxide is tripled, the rate speeds up by a factor of nine.

Table 12-24

Rate Laws for Several Reactions

Reaction	Rate law
$2\,H_2 + 2\,NO \longrightarrow N_2 + 2\,H_2O$	Rate $= k[H_2][NO]^2$
$2\,NO + Br_2 \longrightarrow 2\,NOBr$	Rate $= k[NO]^2[Br_2]$
$O_3 + NO \longrightarrow NO_2 + O_2$	Rate $= k[O_3][NO]$
$2\,NO + O_2 \longrightarrow 2\,NO_2$	Rate $= k[NO]^2[O_2]$

Coming to Terms

enthalpy
enthalpy of formation
standard state
standard molar enthalpy of formation
Hess's law
enthalpy of bond formation
entropy
free energy (Gibbs free energy)
free-energy change
kinetics
collision theory
activation energy
activated complex
reaction rate
catalyst
reaction mechanism
rate law

Review Questions

1. What two tendencies influence all chemical reactions?
2. Which of the following situations are possible according to the laws of thermodynamics?
   a. Insect larvae automatically emerging from rotting meat
   b. The human body converting the energy in food to other forms of energy
   c. The energy and matter in the universe coming into being from nothing without any interference from God
   d. The invention of an automobile engine that is 100 per cent efficient
3. For each of these reactions, give the enthalpy of reaction and tell whether the reaction is endothermic or exothermic.
   a. $C\ (s) + O_2\ (g) \longrightarrow CO_2\ (g)$
   b. $CO_2\ (g) \longrightarrow C\ (s) + O_2\ (g)$
   c. $2\ C\ (s) + 2\ H_2\ (g) \longrightarrow C_2H_4\ (g)$
   d. $C_2H_4\ (g) \longrightarrow 2\ C\ (s) + 2\ H_2\ (g)$

For the next nine questions, refer to these reactions:

a. $N_2\ (g) + 3\ H_2\ (g) \longrightarrow 2\ NH_3\ (g)$
b. $Ca(OH)_2\ (s) \longrightarrow CaO\ (s) + H_2O\ (g)$
c. $2\ KClO_3\ (s) \longrightarrow 2\ KCl\ (s) + 3\ O_2\ (g)$
d. $SnO_2\ (s) + 2\ H_2\ (g) \longrightarrow Sn\ (s) + 2\ H_2O\ (l)$

4. For each reaction, calculate the total standard enthalpies of formation for all reactants. (Give your answer in kcal.)
5. For each reaction, calculate the total standard enthalpies of formation for the products. (Give your answer in kcal.)
6. Calculate the standard change in enthalpy ($\Delta H°$) for each reaction, and tell whether the reaction is endothermic or exothermic.
7. Calculate the total standard entropy in the reactants for each reaction. (Give your answer in cal/K and kcal/K.)
8. Calculate the total standard entropy in the products for each reaction. (Give your answer in cal/K and kcal/K.)
9. Calculate the standard entropy change for each reaction. (Give your answer in cal/K and kcal/K.)
10. Calculate the change in free energy (ΔG) for each reaction at 25.0°C, and tell whether the reaction is energetically favorable or unfavorable at this temperature.
11. Calculate ΔG for each reaction at 1000 K, and tell whether the reaction is energetically favorable or unfavorable at this temperature.

12. Calculate the temperature (if any) at which the reactions change from being energetically favorable to energetically unfavorable (the temperature at which ΔG equals zero).
13. Based on your calculations of ΔG at 298 K and 1000 K for the four reactions, graph ΔG versus temperature. Graph ΔG on the y-axis and temperature on the x-axis. Based on the trend from the graph, state whether the reaction is more or less spontaneous at higher temperatures.
14. The reactants for a thermodynamically favorable reaction are mixed, but no reaction occurs. Suggest an explanation for the nonreaction.
15. Give two reasons that a collision between two reactive molecules might not result in a reaction.
16. According to the collision theory,
    a. why does increased temperature increase the reaction rate?
    b. why does a greater concentration of reactants increase the reaction rate?
    c. why do powders react more quickly than crystals?
    d. why will a reaction involving the collision of three molecules proceed more slowly than one involving the collision of two molecules (all other things being equal)?
17. Sugar needs temperatures much higher than 98.6° F in order to burn. Yet sugar can be "burned" in your digestive tract at this temperature. What is responsible for the ability of your body to burn sugar at this low temperature? Draw energy diagrams that illustrate the difference between the two situations.

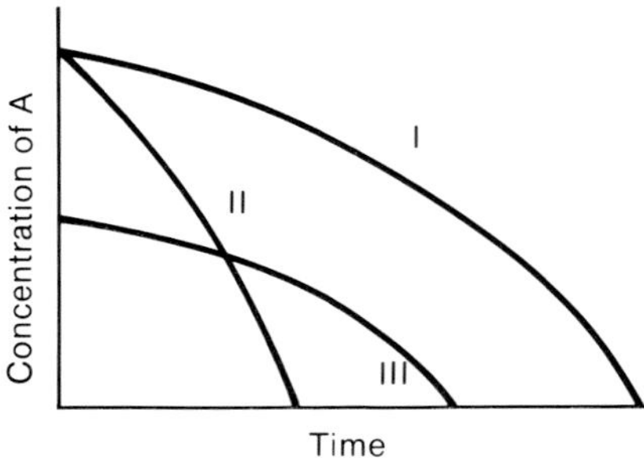

18. This diagram shows how fast an unnamed substance (A) reacts. Curves I, II, and III correspond to the reaction under different conditions.
    a. Under which set of conditions does the reaction proceed at the highest rate?
    b. Of reaction conditions I and III, which starts with the highest reactant concentration?

c. If reaction conditions I and II occur without a catalyst, which one probably occurs at the higher temperature?
d. If the temperatures for I and II are identical, which occurs in the presence of a catalyst?

19. The two curves in the following energy diagram represent the reaction 2 $KClO_3$ (s) $\longrightarrow$ 2 KCl (s) + 3 O_2 (g) occurring under two different sets of reaction conditions.

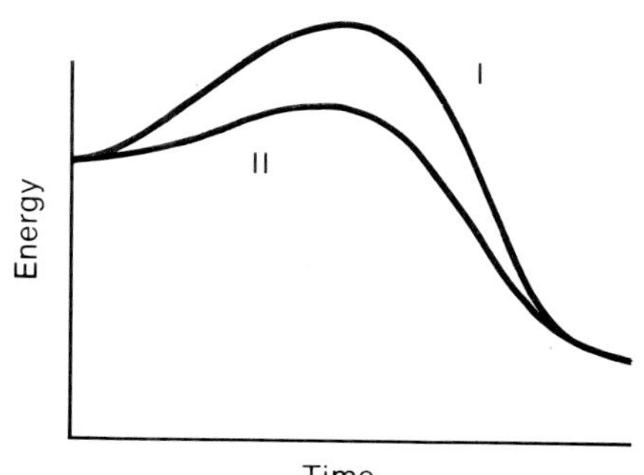

a. Which set of conditions requires the lowest activation energy?
b. Which reaction pathway benefits from a catalyst?
c. Which reaction pathway requires higher temperatures?

20. The reaction 2 NO (g) + 2 H_2 (g) $\longrightarrow$ N_2 (g) + H_2O (*l*) occurs in two steps, which could be either

A. (1) 2 NO (g) + H_2 (g) $\longrightarrow$ N_2 (g) + H_2O_2 (*l*)
   (2) H_2O_2 (*l*) + H_2 (g) $\longrightarrow$ 2 H_2O (*l*)

or

B. (1) 2 NO (g) + H_2 (g) $\longrightarrow$ N_2O (g) + H_2O (*l*)
   (2) N_2O (g) + H_2 (g) $\longrightarrow$ N_2 (g) + H_2O (*l*)

a. Processes A and B are called two possible __________ of the reaction.
b. Scientists can decide whether A or B is correct by ________.

21. Propose a possible two-step mechanism for the decomposition of HgO: 2 HgO (s) $\longrightarrow$ 2 Hg (*l*) + O_2 (g)

22. A scientist postulates that two possible rate laws for the reaction given in question 20 are as follows:

$$\text{Rate} = k[\text{NO}]^2[\text{H}_2]$$

and

$$\text{Rate} = k[\text{NO}]^2[\text{H}_2]^2$$

a. What is *k* called?
b. How could you tell which rate law is correct?

THIRTEEN

CHEMICAL EQUILIBRIUM

CONSTANT EXCHANGE WITHOUT ANY CHANGE

CHEMICAL reactions transform reactants into products. Warning: this simple statement may be misleading. When most students think about chemical reactions, they think about reactions that go to completion. These are reactions in which the reactant or reactants are completely changed to produce one or more products. It is often thought that all reactions are **irreversible reactions.** In reality, many natural processes are **reversible reactions.** While products form, some simultaneously revert into reactants. Having forward and reverse reactions going at the same time means that

1. reactants and products will always be mixed together;
2. the ratio in which reactants and products are mixed depends on the speed of each reaction;
3. changing the rate of one reaction changes the ratio of products and reactants in the reaction mixture.

Theories of Chemical Equilibrium

A chemical equilibrium results when forward and reverse reactions proceed simultaneously. This idea ranks as one of the premier concepts in chemistry. Like the kinetic theory and the atomic theory, it helps to explain many observations. While the study of thermodynamics tries to answer the question "Can the reaction occur?" and kinetics seeks to determine "How fast will the reaction occur?" the study of equilibria seeks to answer "How far will the reaction go?"

13-1 Physical equilibria feature balanced forces, but they do not have opposing processes as do chemical equilibria.

13–1 Dynamic Equilibrium: Opposing Processes

The term *equilibrium* often evokes images of fixed or static situations such as the balance of forces in a stalemated tug-of-war or a balanced scale. Yet these examples describe only one type of equilibrium: the static equilibrium of balanced physical forces. In chemistry the term *equilibrium* refers to balanced *changes*, not balanced *forces*.

A **chemical equilibrium** exists when two opposing reactions occur simultaneously at the same rate. Unlike the previous examples of physical equilibria, chemical equilibria are *dynamic*. Particles constantly move and react. Microscopic activity continues at a hectic pace even though macroscopic changes have ceased.

Consider the reaction $A + B \longrightarrow C + D$. A, B, C, and D represent particles of the reactants and products. As particles of A and B mix, they collide and produce some C and D particles. As particles of C and D accumulate, the chances that they will collide with each other increase. Some of these collisions will result in the re-formation of A and B particles. As more C and D particles accumulate, more A and B particles re-form.

$A + B \longrightarrow C + D$; the formation of C and D particles
$C + D \longrightarrow A + B$; the formation of A and B particles

Eventually the two reactions will proceed at the same rate. To an observer it will seem that the amounts of A, B, C, and D remain constant; yet at the molecular level, the two opposing processes continue. The total system is designated by an equation with a special equilibrium sign.

$$A + B \rightleftharpoons C + D$$

Dynamic equilibria have been presented in earlier chapters. Water molecules in a sealed jar continue to evaporate even after the air is completely saturated. The vapor molecules condense at the surface of the water at the same rate that others evaporate.

$$\text{Liquid} \rightleftharpoons \text{Vapor}$$

Dissolving processes also reach dynamic equilibria at their saturation points. Particles leave and rejoin an undissolved solid at the bottom of the solution at equal but opposing rates.

$$\text{Solid particles} \rightleftharpoons \text{Dissolved particles}$$

Chemical equilibria are vitally important, for many industrial processes are made profitable through the control of reversible reactions. However, before applications of equilibrium chemistry are discussed, the way in which chemical equilibria are measured and are influenced by reaction conditions must be studied.

13–2 Shifted Equilibria: Which Way Did that Reaction Go?

Some, but not many, equilibria contain a 50:50 mixture of reactants and products. Ratios of 60:40, 98:2, 1:99, or even 0.001:99.999 are possible. The ratios between products and reactants reflect the speed at which the forward and reverse reactions can go. A modern fable may help explain how equal but opposing rates can allow the substances on one side of an equilibrium to outnumber substances on the other side.

Bob and Betty, two of Ace Catering Service's finest employees, had received the distasteful assignment of serving punch at Mrs. Tisdale's garden party. The party itself was not drudgery; it was the 95-degree weather that made the job miserable.

The scorching sun soon made both servers wish for a cool spot in the shade. Suddenly Bob speculated that if he emptied his punch bowl into Betty's bowl, he would be free for a long-desired rest. He grabbed a large ladle and began scooping punch into Betty's bowl. Realizing what Bob was doing, Betty began to scoop her punch into Bob's bowl. But poor Betty had no large ladle to scoop with. All she had was a serving spoon. Soon Bob's greater rate of transfer allowed him to scoop most of the punch into Betty's bowl. Betty tried gamely, but her rate of transfer was much slower.

13-2 Punch bowl equilibrium.

Just as Bob was feeling confident of victory, he noticed that his large scoop was not working as well as it had before. He could not get a full scoop when there was only a small amount of punch in his bowl. Soon Bob could scoop up only what Betty gave him with her serving spoon. Their two rates of transfer were equal. Realizing that they had set up a dynamic equilibrium, the two called it a draw and went back to serving punch for Mrs. Tisdale.

Equal but opposing rates resulted in a dynamic equilibrium that favored the transfer of punch to Betty's bowl. This equilibrium is said to favor the forward reaction.

$$\text{Punch in Bob's bowl} \rightleftharpoons \text{Punch in Betty's bowl}$$

A reaction that favors the formation of products is said to be shifted toward the right and is represented in the chemical equation with a long half-arrow pointing to the right. Conversely, a reaction that favors the formation of reactants is shifted to the left and is represented by a long half-arrow pointing to the left.

A spiritual "equilibrium" exists between the old nature and the new nature in a Christian (old nature $\rightleftharpoons$ new nature). Each Christian possesses an old and a new nature. The strengths of the two natures constantly change throughout a Christian's walk with God. The equilibrium can shift to the old nature if the Christian practices sin and neglects to fellowship with God. The equilibrium can shift to the new nature if the Christian stays in fellowship with God and avoids sin.

13–3 Equilibrium Constants: Describing Mixtures with Numbers

Chemists must often describe an equilibrium in terms of the ratio of products to reactants. To do this, they use a number called an equilibrium constant. Return to the reaction $A + B \rightleftharpoons C + D$. Suppose that experimentation shows that the rate law for the forward reaction (formation of products) is $R_{\text{fp}} = k_{\text{fp}}[A][B]$ and that the rate law for the reverse reaction (formation of reactants) is $R_{\text{fr}} = k_{\text{fr}}[C][D]$. Square brackets signify concentration in units of moles per liter. By definition chemical equilibrium is attained when the forward reaction rate matches the reverse reaction rate ($R_{\text{fp}} = R_{\text{fr}}$). As a result, the two rate laws can be equated.

$$R_{\text{fp}} = R_{\text{fr}}$$

$$k_{\text{fp}}[A][B] = k_{\text{fr}}[C][D]$$

A few algebraic operations can rearrange this equation to a new form.

$$\frac{k_{\text{fp}}}{k_{\text{fr}}} = \frac{[C][D]}{[A][B]}$$

Both k_{fp} and k_{fr} are constants. Therefore, their quotient is also a constant. This quotient of rate constants is called an **equilibrium constant** and is denoted by an upper-case K.

$$\frac{k_{\text{fp}}}{k_{\text{fr}}} = K = \frac{[C][D]}{[A][B]}$$

An equilibrium constant tells the ratio of products to reactants. If the value of K is large, the concentrations of products (in the numerator) are greater than the concentrations of the reactants (in the denominator). If the value of K is small, the reverse reaction predominates and the concentration of products is small compared to the concentration of reactants.

The form of an equilibrium constant is determined from the stoichiometry of the reaction. The concentration of each substance is raised to a power that matches the coefficient of that substance in a balanced equation.

$$aA + bB \rightleftharpoons cC + dD$$

$$K = \frac{[C]^c[D]^d}{[A]^a[B]^b}$$

$$I_2\ (g) + H_2\ (g) \rightleftharpoons 2\ HI\ (g)$$

$$K = \frac{[HI]^2}{[I_2][H_2]}$$

Sample Problem. Write the equilibrium constant for the formation of ammonia from its elements ($3\ H_2 + N_2 \rightleftharpoons 2\ NH_3$).

Solution.

$$K = \frac{[NH_3]^2}{[H_2]^3[N_2]}$$

Writing equilibrium constants for reactions that involve solids or solvents requires an additional bit of knowledge. The concentrations of solids and solvents are defined to be 1, so these substances do not affect equilibrium constants. For instance, the equilibrium between solid silver chloride and its dissolved ions in a saturated solution is not affected by the amount of undissolved solid present.

$$AgCl\ (s) \rightleftharpoons Ag^+\ (aq) + Cl^-\ (aq)$$

The equilibrium constant for this reaction could include the AgCl, but since the concentration of the solid, [AgCl], is defined to be 1, it drops out of the expression. This seemingly arbitrary mathematics makes sense. The amount of dissolved silver chloride that remains at the bottom of a saturated solution does not affect the equilibrium. The concentration of dissolved ions would remain the same if an entire handful of silver chloride were added.

$$K = \frac{[Ag^+][Cl^-]}{[AgCl]}$$

$$K = [Ag^+][Cl^-]$$

When acetic acid molecules mix with water, some of them release hydrogen ions. The reaction adds hydrogen ions to some water molecules. Since an insignificant amount of water is used up in the reaction, the concentration of water molecules is defined to be 1. Although the equilibrium constant could include the concentration of water, it should be left out.

$$HC_2H_3O_2\ (l) + H_2O\ (l) \rightleftharpoons C_2H_3O_2^-\ (aq) + H_3O^+\ (aq)$$

$$K = \frac{[C_2H_3O_2^-][H_3O^+]}{[HC_2H_3O]}$$

Sample Problem. Write the equation for the equilibrium constant for the precipitation of zinc hydroxide.

$$Zn^{2+}\ (aq) + 2\ OH^-\ (aq) \rightleftharpoons Zn(OH)_2\ (s)$$

Solution.

Since zinc hydroxide is a solid, its concentration is 1 in the equilibrium constant.

$$K = \frac{1}{[Zn^{2+}][OH^-]^2}$$

The numerical value of an equilibrium constant must be determined experimentally. Suppose that 5 liters of sulfur dioxide and 4 liters of oxygen are placed in a 1-liter container and allowed to react to form sulfur trioxide. After the reactants reach equilibrium with the sulfur trioxide, the various concentrations are measured. It is found that 1 mole of sulfur trioxide, 4 moles of sulfur dioxide, and 3.5 moles of oxygen are present.

$$2\ SO_2 + O_2 \rightleftharpoons 2\ SO_3$$

$$K = \frac{[SO_3]^2}{[SO_2]^2[O_2]}$$

$$K = \frac{(1)^2}{(4)^2(3.5)}$$

$$K = 0.02$$

The equilibrium constant 0.02 describes the ratio between products and reactants under a specified temperature and pressure.

Sample Problem. Calculate the numerical value of K for the equilibrium involved in the formation of ammonia from nitrogen and hydrogen. When a mixture of the gases reaches equilibrium, $[H_2] = 0.05\ M$, $[N_2] = 0.05\ M$, and $[NH_3] = 50\ M$.

$$N_2\ (g) + 3\ H_2\ (g) \rightleftharpoons 2\ NH_3\ (g)$$

Solution.

$$K = \frac{[NH_3]^2}{[H_2]^3[N_2]}$$

$$K = \frac{(50)^2}{(0.05)^3(0.05)}$$

$$K = 4 \times 10^8$$

13–4 Le Chatelier's Principle: How Equilibria Handle Stress

In 1884 a French chemist named Henri Le Chatelier questioned how equilibria behave when they are disturbed by an external change. The answer that he found has served the field of chemistry so well that it has been named **Le Chatelier's principle** in his honor. This principle says that when a reversible process is disturbed, it will proceed in the direction that relieves the stress.

13-3 Chemical engineers often use Le Chatelier's principle to obtain greater yields as they manufacture chemicals.

13–5 The Effect of Concentration

Before applying Le Chatelier's principle to chemical reactions, consider how it would work in the story of the two punch bowls in section 13–2. Go back to the point where Bob had put most of the punch into Betty's bowl and had set up the dynamic equilibrium.

$$\text{Punch in Bob's bowl} \rightleftharpoons \text{Punch in Betty's bowl}$$

This equilibrium could be disturbed in several ways. First, if someone added a large amount of punch to Bob's bowl, Bob's rate of transfer could increase. The large scoop would quickly convey the extra punch over to Betty's bowl until an equilibrium was reestablished. Second, if Betty disturbed the equilibrium by doubling the number of times she scooped up punch, the equilibrium would temporarily shift to the left.

Changes in concentration definitely affect chemical equilibria. Return to the $2\ SO_2 + O_2 \rightleftharpoons 2\ SO_3$ equilibrium. At one set of conditions, the K has been measured to be 0.02.

$$K = \frac{[SO_3]^2}{[SO_2]^2[O_2]} = 0.02$$

Suppose that more sulfur dioxide were added to the container. The system would be temporarily disturbed from equilibrium. Le Chatelier's principle predicts that the forward reaction would proceed to reduce the extra sulfur dioxide. This reaction would increase the concentration of sulfur trioxide but decrease the concentration of oxygen. Despite all the changes, the original constant would remain unchanged.

If sulfur trioxide were added, the reverse reaction would work to dissipate the added substance. If some sulfur trioxide were removed, the forward reaction would work to restore the lost amount. Of course, the concentrations of sulfur dioxide and oxygen would decrease when the forward reaction predominated. This action would keep the value of the equilibrium constant the same.

Original equilibrium

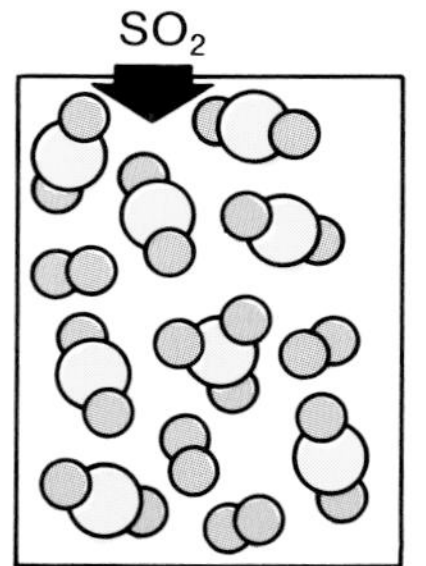

Equilibrium disturbed

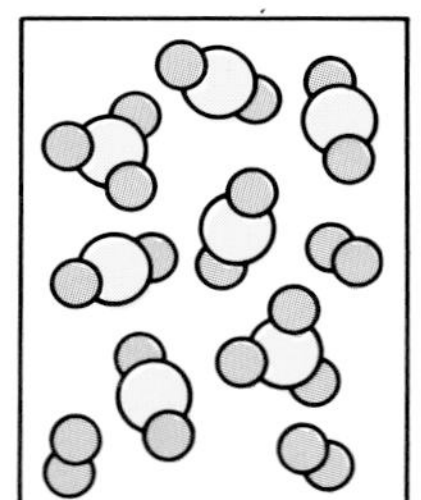

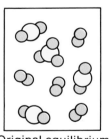

Equilibrium reestablish

13-4 Additional SO_2 causes the equilibrium to shift forward.

13–6 The Effect of Pressure

Some, but not all, gaseous reactions are affected by changes in pressure. Recall that 1 mole of a gaseous substance occupies 22.4 liters at STP. In the equilibrium $2\ SO_2 + O_2 \rightleftharpoons 2\ SO_3$, 2 moles of sulfur trioxide are produced for every 3 moles of gaseous reactants. Since there are fewer gas molecules in the product than in the reactants, the forward reaction has the effect of decreasing the pressure.

Suppose that some additional pressure were placed on the equilibrium. Le Chatelier's principle predicts that the reaction that relieves the stress will predominate. The forward reaction would lower the pressure by producing 2 moles of sulfur trioxide from 2 moles of sulfur dioxide and 1 mole of oxygen. If the equilibrium were depressurized, the reverse reaction would act to fill the void: more sulfur dioxide and oxygen would be produced.

Some gaseous reactions are not affected by pressure changes. $H_2 + I_2 \rightleftharpoons 2\ HI$ has two moles of gas in the products for every two moles of gas in the reactants. The pressure of the entire system does not change with either the forward or the reverse reaction. Extra pressure on this equilibrium will not drive it in either direction.

Sample Problem. Will the formation of ammonia be helped or hindered by high pressures?

$$3\ H_2 + N_2 \rightleftharpoons 2\ NH_3$$

Solution.

The balanced equation shows that four moles of gaseous reactants combine to form two moles of gaseous products. High pressures cause the reaction that produces the smallest volume to predominate. Thus high pressures aid the formation of ammonia gas.

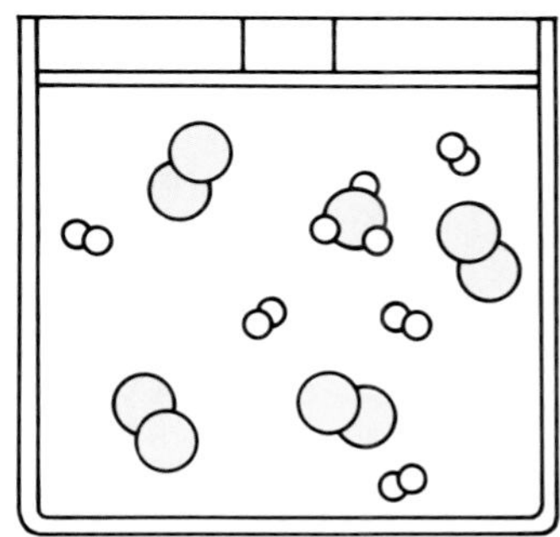

Equilibrium at low pressure

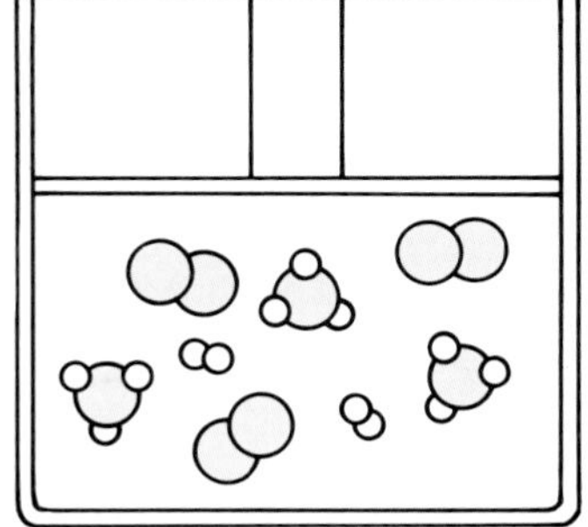

Equilibrium at high pressure

13-5 $3\ H_2 + N_2 \rightleftharpoons 2\ NH_3$. Additional pressure shifts the equilibrium forward.

13–7 The Effect of Temperature

Heat may be thought of as a participant in chemical reactions. The exothermic reaction between sulfur dioxide and oxygen produces sulfur trioxide and heat. Similarly, an endothermic reaction may be written with heat as one of its reactants.

$$2\ SO_2 + O_2 \rightleftharpoons 2\ SO_3 + \text{Heat}$$

$$H_2 + I_2 + \text{Heat} \rightleftharpoons 2\ HI$$

Le Chatelier's principle predicts how temperatures affect each of these equilibria. When heat acts as a reactant, it helps the forward reaction. The equilibrium of hydrogen, iodine, and hydrogen iodide will shift to produce more hydrogen iodide if heat is added to the reaction. Since $2\ SO_2 + O_2 \rightleftharpoons 2\ SO_3$ + heat is exothermic, heat is a product. Extra heat can be relieved only if the reverse reaction uses heat to form more sulfur dioxide and oxygen.

FACETS OF CHEMISTRY

Scientists and Their Faith

The popular image of scientists as totally objective, unbiased information processors is a myth. All scientists, no matter how objective or unbiased they are, are influenced by something that has nothing to do with scientific evidences. What could this influence be? The beliefs that scientists have about the universe, God, and man invariably affect their work. Simply put, personal philosophy guides scientific work.

Pagan men who worship temperamental, whimsical spirits have little reason to study science. Their beliefs serve as handy explanations for natural events that they do not understand. When pagans observe planets that "wander" through the sky, see comets and meteors that arrive unannounced, and endure natural calamities that seem to strike without warning, they simply assume that evil spirits are sending omens. Men with this faith see no need to study science.

The lives of the men who founded modern science illustrate the link between personal beliefs and scientific work. Generally, the "giants of science" were scientists who believed in God. Many, in fact, were Christians. Francis Bacon, the seventeenth-century philosopher who pioneered the scientific method, knew that the Bible was the main source of knowledge for the Christian. "There are two books laid before us to prevent our falling into error," he stated; "first, the volume of the Scriptures, which reveal the will of God; then the

Sample Problem. The formation of ammonia is exothermic. Will high temperatures help or hinder the forward reaction?

$$3\ H_2 + N_2 \rightleftharpoons 2\ NH_3 + \text{Heat}$$

Solution.

Heat is one of the products, so additional heat would encourage the reverse reaction and would hinder the forward reaction.

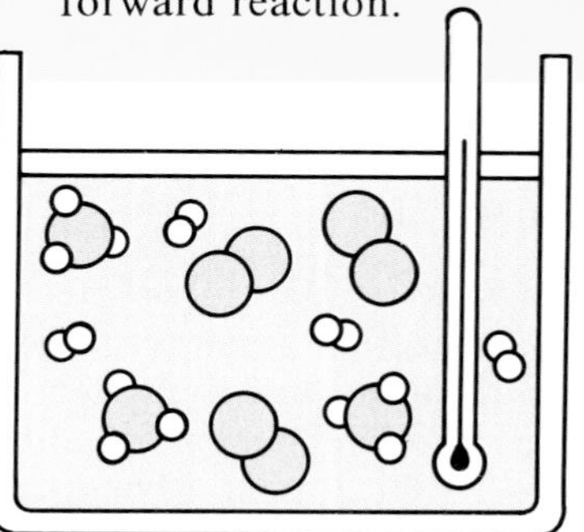

Equilibrium at low temperature

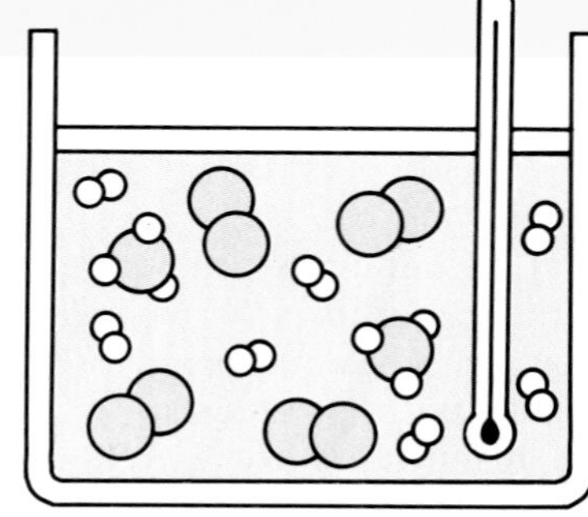

Equilibrium at high temperature

13-6 $3\ H_2 + N_2 \rightleftharpoons 2\ NH_3$. Additional temperature helps the reverse reaction.

volume of the Creatures, which express His power." Robert Boyle, often called the "father of chemistry," was a humble Christian and a diligent student of the Bible. Lord Kelvin, noted among other things for establishing the Kelvin temperature scale, was a dedicated Christian and a staunch creationist who frequently did battle with the evolutionists of his day. "If you think strongly enough," he said, "you will be forced by science to the belief in God."

A faith in God showed these men that the universe must be orderly and knowable—like its Creator. Their faith convinced them that it would be possible to find out how the universe worked. They believed that if they looked hard enough, gathered the right data, and arranged their information correctly, they could understand the universe.

Many of today's scientists no longer believe that the universe was created. Do these men do their scientific investigations without being influenced by their beliefs? Hardly. Most present-day scientists have substituted a faith in evolution, humanism, or science for a faith in God.

An example of how evolutionary beliefs guide scientific activities is seen in the ongoing searches of outer space for signs of intelligent life. A 1982 issue of *Science* magazine (October 29) contained a petition that called for systematic searches of other galaxies for signs of extraterrestrial intelligence. In 1982 Congress authorized 1.5 million dollars for studies that would explore new worlds and seek out new civilizations. At this moment, space probes search for evolving life forms on other planets, and radio telescopes listen for signals from supercivilizations in other parts of the galaxy. The men who conduct such searches are guided by their faith. Their faith in evolution leads them to search for evidences of evolution.

People who do not see the link between personal beliefs and scientific practice may interpret the antagonism of many scientists toward God as a conflict between science and the Bible. People begin to wonder whether science and the Bible conflict. Regrettably, most scientists oppose the truth of God. But the battle between scientists and the Bible stems from personal beliefs, not scientific evidence. True science and the Bible are always in perfect agreement.

Applications of Equilibrium Chemistry

Chemical industries supply society with such diverse products as medicines, pesticides, fertilizers, paints, textiles, detergents, cosmetics, plastics, fuels, and building materials. Because the molecular transformations involved are usually reversible, the laws of equilibrium chemistry govern the processes. Methods of describing and controlling equilibria become indispensable tools in the fast, efficient production of consumer goods.

13–8 Equilibria Between Molecules: Milking Reactions for All They Are Worth

The characteristic flavors and odors of fruits are the results of naturally occurring compounds called esters. Manufacturers of artificial flavorings seek to form esters by reacting alcohols and organic acids.

$$\text{Alcohol} + \text{Organic acid} \rightleftharpoons \text{Ester} + \text{Water}$$

The reaction works well, but it is very easily reversed. Neither the forward nor the reverse reaction dominates. This situation presents several obstacles to the efficient production of esters.

Instead of going to completion, the reaction converts only a part of the reactants into the products. Rather than accept the reduced yields, manufacturers produce more esters per batch of reactants by forcing the forward reaction to prevail.

Manufacturers can shift the equilibrium by continually adding a reactant, removing a product, or both. If either the acid or the alcohol is inexpensive, huge quantities can be added to drive the equilibrium forward. Sometimes manufacturers can easily remove a product by boiling it off as it forms. This too results in a shifted equilibrium. Regardless of the technique that is used, the end result is increased ester production.

Huge quantities of ammonia are used every year in fertilizers, cleaning compounds, and explosives. Until World War I, industrial countries obtained nitrogen atoms by importing mined saltpeter (KNO_3 and $NaNO_3$). All countries had access to nitrogen molecules in the atmosphere, but no one knew how to liberate the atoms from the stable molecules. A way was sought to form ammonia from atmospheric nitrogen.

13-7 Nitrogen fertilizers are responsible for the great productivity of modern farms.

Finding the appropriate reaction was no problem: $N_2 + 3\ H_2 \rightleftharpoons 2\ NH_3$ seemed perfect. The huge equilibrium constant of this reaction (4.0×10^8 at 25°C) indicated that the production of ammonia was the favored direction of the reaction. The problem was that nitrogen, hydrogen, and ammonia took an incredibly long time to reach equilibrium. A few years before World War I, a German chemist named Fritz Haber found a way to manipulate the equilibrium and overcome this difficulty. He invented the **Haber process** that supplied the Kaiser's war machine with ammonia-based explosives. Today the Haber process provides ammonia for use in numerous industries.

$$N_2 + 3\ H_2 \rightleftharpoons 2\ NH_3 + \text{Heat}$$

Because 2 moles of gas are formed from 4 moles of gas, the products take up less space than the reactants. Le Chatelier's principle predicts that high pressures favor the production of ammonia. Because the forward reaction is exothermic, it proceeds best at low temperatures. Le Chatelier's principle says that the forward reaction will predominate when conditions of high pressure and low temperature are supplied.

In the Haber process the reaction is performed under high pressures (200-600 atm), at high temperatures (450-600°C), and with a catalyst. High temperatures shift the equilibrium slightly away from the formation of ammonia, but they more than compensate for the loss by speeding up the reaction. A catalyst (mostly Fe_3O_4 with traces of K_2O and Al_2O_3) also speeds up the reaction. To increase the yield, ammonia is removed by liquefaction as it forms. This continual removal keeps the forward reaction going.

13-8 The Haber Process

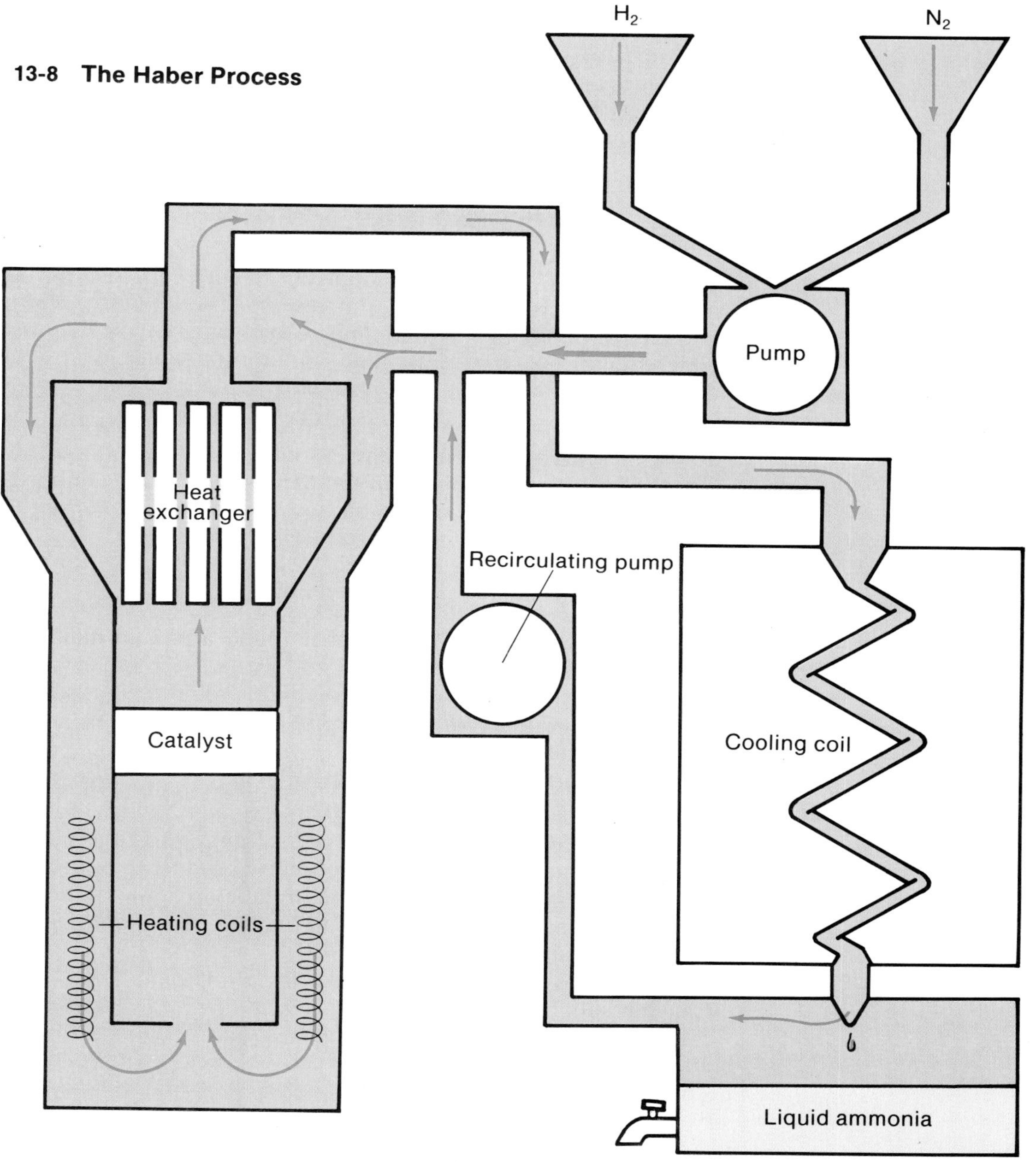

13–9 Equilibria Between Ions: Writing K_{sp}s

Saturated solutions have equilibria between undissolved solids and aqueous ions. Some salts, such as calcium sulfate, are slightly soluble. Others, such as lead phosphate, dissolve so little that for all practical purposes they are insoluble.

$$CaSO_4\ (s) \rightleftharpoons Ca^{2+}\ (aq) + SO_4{}^{2-}\ (aq)$$
$$Pb_3(PO_4)_2\ (s) \rightleftharpoons 3\ Pb^{2+}\ (aq) + 2\ PO_4{}^{3-}\ (aq)$$

The forward reaction is dissolution, and the reverse reaction is precipitation. As with all equilibria, the rate of the forward reaction matches the rate of the reverse reaction. The relative amounts of dissolved ions and undissolved solids can be expressed with equilibrium constants. The equilibrium constant for the dissolution of $Pb_3(PO_4)_2$ is expressed as

$$K = [Pb^{2+}]^3[PO_4{}^{3-}]^2$$

As in other equilibrium expressions, solids are left out. The $[Pb_3(PO_4)_2]$ term is omitted in the expression of the equilibrium constant, and the resulting solubility equilibrium constant is given the special name **solubility product constant (K_{sp}).** The concentrations of the ions are raised to the appropriate powers as in other equilibrium constant expressions.

$$K_{sp} = [Pb^{2+}]^3[PO_4{}^{3-}]^2$$

13–10 Solubilities and Equilibria: K_{sp}s Are the Guides

K_{sp}s provide a description of salt solubilities. Large numbers of ions in solution will cause the solubility product to be relatively large (much greater than 1). Small numbers of ions in solution cause the K_{sp}s to be small (less than 1). The K_{sp}s of some slightly soluble salts are listed in Table 13-9.

K_{sp} values can be determined from measured solubilities. Calcium sulfate has a solubility of 4.95×10^{-3} moles/liter. When calcium sulfate dissolves, each formula unit releases 1 Ca^{2+} ion and 1 $SO_4{}^{2-}$ ion.

$$4.95 \times 10^{-3}\ \text{moles}\ CaSO_4 \rightleftharpoons 4.95 \times 10^{-3}\ \text{moles}\ Ca^{2+} + 4.95 \times 10^{-3}\ \text{moles}\ SO_4{}^{2-}$$

$$K_{sp} = [Ca^{2+}][SO_4{}^{2-}]$$
$$K_{sp} = (4.95 \times 10^{-3})(4.95 \times 10^{-3})$$
$$K_{sp} = 2.45 \times 10^{-5}$$

Table 13-9

Salt	Product	K_{sp} at 25° C
$AgCl$	$[Ag^+][Cl^-]$	1.8×10^{-10}
Ag_2CO_3	$[Ag^+]^2[CO_3^{2-}]$	8.2×10^{-12}
Ag_3PO_4	$[Ag^+]^3[PO_4^{3-}]$	1.8×10^{-18}
Ag_2S	$[Ag^+]^2[S^{2-}]$	1×10^{-50}
$Al(OH)_3$	$[Al^{3+}][OH^-]^3$	5×10^{-33}
$BaCO_3$	$[Ba^{2+}][CO_3^{2-}]$	1.6×10^{-9}
$BaSO_4$	$[Ba^{2+}][SO_4^{2-}]$	1.0×10^{-10}
Bi_2S_3	$[Bi^{3+}]^2[S^{2-}]^3$	1×10^{-70}
$CaCO_3$	$[Ca^{2+}][CO_3^{2-}]$	6.9×10^{-9}
$CaSO_4$	$[Ca^{2+}][SO_4^{2-}]$	2.4×10^{-5}
CoS	$[Co^{2+}][S^{2-}]$	5×10^{-22}
CuS	$[Cu^{2+}][S^{2-}]$	4×10^{-36}
$Fe(OH)_3$	$[Fe^{3+}][OH^-]^3$	6×10^{-38}
$Fe(OH)_2$	$[Fe^{2+}][OH^-]^2$	2×10^{-15}
FeS	$[Fe^{2+}][S^{2-}]$	4×10^{-17}
$MgCO_3$	$[Mg^{2+}][CO_3^{2-}]$	4×10^{-5}
$Mg(OH)_2$	$[Mg^{2+}][OH^-]^2$	8.9×10^{-12}
$PbCO_3$	$[Pb^{2+}][CO_3^{2-}]$	1.5×10^{-13}
$Pb_3(PO_4)_2$	$[Pb^{2+}]^3[PO_4^{3-}]^2$	3.0×10^{-44}
PbS	$[Pb^{2+}][S^{2-}]$	4×10^{-26}
$PbSO_4$	$[Pb^{2+}][SO_4^{2-}]$	1.3×10^{-8}
SnS	$[Sn^{2+}][S^{2-}]$	1×10^{-24}
$Zn(OH)_2$	$[Zn^{2+}][OH^-]^2$	5×10^{-17}
ZnS	$[Zn^{2+}][S^{2-}]$	1×10^{-20}

If the K_{sp} of a substance is known, it can be used to determine the solubility in units of moles per liter. The K_{sp} of lead (II) phosphate is known to be 3.0×10^{-44}.

$$K_{sp} = [Pb^{2+}]^3[PO_4^{3-}]^2$$
$$3.0 \times 10^{-44} = [Pb^{2+}]^3[PO_4^{3-}]^2$$

Notice that when a mole of lead (II) phosphate dissolves, 3 moles of Pb^{2+} ions and 2 moles of PO_4^{3-} ions are released. The number of Pb^{2+} ions in a saturated solution must be three times the amount of $Pb_3(PO_4)_2$ units that were dissolved. Likewise, there must be twice as many PO_4^{3-} ions as the number of dissolved formula units. The concentration of the Pb^{2+} ions can be expressed as $3S$, where S stands for the solubility of the salt. The concentration of PO_4^{3-} ions can be expressed as $2S$. The concentrations of the ions can now be expressed in terms of the solubility of the salt.

$$K_{sp} = [Pb^{2+}]^3 [PO_4^{3-}]^2$$
$$K_{sp} = (3S)^3 (2S)^2$$

To find the solubility of the salt, plug in the value of the K_{sp} and solve for S.

$$3.0 \times 10^{-44} = (3S)^3 (2S)^2$$
$$= 27S^3 \times 4S^2$$
$$= 108S^5$$
$$7.7 \times 10^{-10} = S$$

The solubility of lead (II) phosphate is 7.7×10^{-10} moles/liter. This amount is so small that the salt is, for all practical purposes, insoluble.

Sample Problem. Given that the K_{sp} of silver chloride is 1.8×10^{-10}, determine the solubility (moles/ℓ) of silver chloride.

Solution.

$$AgCl \rightleftharpoons Ag^+ + Cl^-$$
$$K_{sp} = 1.8 \times 10^{-10}$$
$$K_{sp} = [Ag^+][Cl^-]$$

Since each silver chloride unit releases one Ag^+ ion and one Cl^- ion, the $[Ag^+]$ and the $[Cl^-]$ equal the solubility of the salt in a saturated solution.

$$K_{sp} = [S][S]$$
$$1.8 \times 10^{-10} = S^2$$
$$1.3 \times 10^{-5} = S$$

Thus 1.3×10^{-5} moles of silver chloride can be dissolved in 1 liter of water.

The K_{sp} provides a quick way to see whether a solution is unsaturated, saturated, or supersaturated. If the product of ion concentrations equals the K_{sp}, the solution must be saturated. If the product of ion concentrations is less than the K_{sp}, the solution is unsaturated. A product greater than the K_{sp} indicates a supersaturated solution.

Sample Problem. Suppose that 2×10^{-6} moles of zinc hydroxide, $Zn(OH)_2$, are dissolved in a mole of water. Use the K_{sp} of zinc hydroxide to determine whether the solution is unsaturated, saturated, or supersaturated.

Solution.

When dissolved, 2×10^{-6} mole of zinc hydroxide produces 2×10^{-6} mole of Zn^{2+} ions and $2(2 \times 10^{-6})$ mole of OH^- ions. The product of these concentrations is

$$
\begin{aligned}
&[Zn^2][OH^-]^2 \\
&= [2 \times 10^{-6}][2(2 \times 10^{-6})]^2 \\
&= 3.2 \times 10^{-17}
\end{aligned}
$$

This product is less than the K_{sp} of 5×10^{-17}, so the solution must be unsaturated.

13–11 Common-Ion Effect: An Overpopulation Problem

Picture an unsaturated silver chloride solution. Less than the allowed 1.34×10^{-5} mole per liter has dissolved, and the product of the silver- and chloride-ion concentrations is less than the K_{sp}. Now imagine what happens when a handful of sodium chloride is added to the solution.

Sodium chloride is very soluble (it does not appear on the list of slightly soluble salts). It dissolves and dissociates into sodium and chloride ions. The sodium ions have little or no effect on the original solution, but the chloride ions do. The chloride ion is called the common ion because both silver chloride and sodium chloride contain it. Additional chloride ions push the reverse reaction in the $AgCl\ (s) \rightleftharpoons Ag^+\ (aq) + Cl^-\ (aq)$ equilibrium to produce more solid silver chloride. The increased concentration of chloride ions raises the solubility product ($[Ag^+][Cl^-]$) above the K_{sp} value. The result of the **common-ion effect** is that the less soluble salt precipitates.

13-10 Common ion effect. The addition of concentrated hydrochloric acid to a saturated salt solution causes sodium chloride to precipitate.

13–12 K_{sp} and Precipitation Reactions: Some Ions Just Cannot Stay Apart

Mixing two solutions can sometimes cause a precipitate to form. For instance, suppose that hydrochloric acid and silver nitrate ($AgNO_3$) were mixed together. The solution would contain H^+, Cl^-, Ag^+, and NO_3^- ions. Hydrogen chloride and silver nitrate are relatively soluble. However, an alternate combination of ions, Ag^+Cl^-, is not. A silver chloride precipitate will form if enough of these ions are in the solution. How much is enough? That depends on the K_{sp} of silver chloride. If the value of $[Ag^+][Cl^-]$ in the solution exceeds the K_{sp} for silver chloride, a precipitate will form. Thus, the K_{sp} of a salt can be used to predict whether precipitation (a double replacement reaction) will occur.

Sample Problem. Will a precipitate form when 5.0×10^{-5} molar barium nitrate—$Ba(NO_3)_2$—is mixed with 1.0×10^{-3} molar sodium carbonate—Na_2CO_3?

Solution.

Both barium nitrate and sodium carbonate are soluble salts. At this low concentration, they will both be completely dissolved. The first step is to calculate the theoretical concentration of each ion after both salts completely dissolve.

$$Ba(NO_3)_2 \longrightarrow Ba^{2+} + 2\ NO_3^-$$

$$[Ba^{2+}] = 5.0 \times 10^{-5}\ M$$

$$[NO_3^-] = 2(5.0 \times 10^{-5})\ M$$

$$Na_2CO_3 \longrightarrow 2\ Na^+ + CO_3^{2-}$$

$$[Na^+] = 2(1.0 \times 10^{-3})\ M$$

$$[CO_3^{2-}] = 1.0 \times 10^{-3}\ M$$

The next step is to check the table of slightly soluble salts to determine which combination of ions is most likely to precipitate. Both original combinations are very soluble, and so is sodium nitrate. Barium carbonate is the only salt formed by a combination of the ions in this solution that appears in the table of slightly soluble salts ($K_{sp} = 1.6 \times 10^{-9}$). The final step is to determine whether the value of $[Ba^{2+}][CO_3^{\,2-}]$ exceeds the given K_{sp}. In the mixture,

$$[Ba^{2+}][CO_3^{\,2-}] = (5.0 \times 10^{-5})(1.0 \times 10^{-3})$$
$$= 5.0 \times 10^{-8}$$

Since 5.0×10^{-8} is larger than the K_{sp} of 1.6×10^{-9}, a precipitate will form.

Coming to Terms

irreversible reaction
reversible reaction
chemical equilibrium
equilibrium constant
Le Chatelier's principle
Haber process
solubility product constant
common ion effect

Review Questions

1. What is the difference between a dynamic equilibrium and a static one?
2. When a bottle of soft drink is shaken violently, CO_2 gas escapes from solution and exerts increased pressure on the interior of the bottle. If the bottle is opened in this condition, the beverage will spurt out of the bottle. If the bottle is allowed to sit for a short amount of time, the interior pressure subsides. Why does the pressure decrease with time?

3. Write the equilibrium constant for each reaction.
   a. Laughing gas can decompose into nitrogen and oxygen: $2\ N_2O\ (g) \rightleftharpoons 2\ N_2\ (g) + O_2\ (g)$.
   b. Carbon monoxide can be converted into methane in the process of converting coal into a gas: $CO\ (g) + 3\ H_2\ (g) \rightleftharpoons CH_4\ (g) + H_2O\ (g)$
   c. Methanol can be synthesized from carbon monoxide: $CO\ (g) + 2\ H_2\ (g) \rightleftharpoons CH_3OH\ (l)$.
   d. Baking soda can extinguish fires because it can decompose to produce water and carbon dioxide, both of which smother combustion: $2\ NaHCO_3\ (s) \rightleftharpoons Na_2CO_3\ (s) + H_2O\ (l) + CO_2\ (g)$.
4. A scientist does experiments to determine the equilibrium constant for the Haber process at 450°C.
   a. After permitting a reaction mixture of N_2 and H_2 to reach equilibrium, he finds that $[N_2] = 0.100$, $[H_2] = 0.0300$, and $[NH_3] = 0.000200$. Calculate K at this temperature.
   b. The scientist repeats the experiment under the same conditions with different amounts of gas in the reaction vessel. The scientist finds that $[H_2] = 0.0375$ and $[NH_3] = 0.000318$. Use the value of K already determined to calculate $[N_2]$.
5. Acetic acid ($HC_2H_3O_2$) is the compound that gives vinegar its distinctive smell and taste. When dissolved in water, it can ionize.

$$HC_2H_3O_2\ (aq) + H_2O\ (l) \rightleftharpoons C_2H_3O_2^-\ (aq) + H_3O^+\ (aq)$$

   The equilibrium constant for this reaction is

$$K = \frac{[C_2H_3O_2^-][H_3O^+]}{[HC_2H_3O_2]}$$

   a. A chemist working in a clinical research lab dissolves some acetic acid in water (at 25°C) and finds that $[H_3O^+] = 1.01 \times 10^{-5}$, $[C_2H_3O_2] = 1.01 \times 10^{-5}$, and $[HC_2H_3O_2] = 5.67 \times 10^{-6}$. What is the value of K?
   b. If $[H_3O^+] = 3.6 \times 10^{-3}$ and $[C_2H_3O_2^-] = 3.6 \times 10^{-3}$, what is the concentration of un-ionized acetic acid?
   c. What equation gives the equilibrium constant for the reverse reaction?
   d. What is the value of the equilibrium constant for the reverse reaction?
6. Name three factors that can shift equilibria.
7. Predict the effect of increasing the pressure on each of the four equilibria given in problem 3.

8. Lithium carbonate (Li_2CO_3) is less soluble in hot water than in cold.
   a. Do you think the dissolution of Li_2CO_3 is exothermic or endothermic? Explain.
   b. What will happen if a saturated solution of Li_2CO_3 at 25°C is heated to 100°C? Explain.
9. Write K_{sp} expressions for the dissolution of the following:
   a. $BaSO_4$
   b. MgF_2
   c. $Al(OH)_3$
   d. $Pb_3(PO_4)_2$
   e. $Mg(OH)_2$
10. A scientist measures the solubility of $Mg(OH)_2$. The concentration of the Mg^{2+} ions in a saturated solution at 18°C is 1.44×10^{-4} *M*, and the concentration of OH^- in the same solution is 2.88×10^{-4} *M*. What is the value of the K_{sp} at this temperature?
11. A saturated solution of Li_2CO_3 has both Li^+ and CO_3^{2-} ions in it. What will happen if some solid LiCl is added to the solution? (LiCl is much more soluble than Li_2CO_3.)
12. Will a precipitate form if the following solutions are mixed? If so, what substances will precipitate? (Hint: First determine whether each substance is soluble or only minimally soluble. If a salt is minimally soluble, refer to its K_{sp}.)
   a. 0.05 *M* NaCl and 0.05 *M* LiCl
   b. 6.3×10^{-4} *M* $MgCO_3$ and 1.0×10^{-4} *M* $Mg(OH)_2$
   c. 0.5 *M* NaOH and 2.0×10^{-5} *M* $Mg(OH)_2$
13. Barium sulfate ($BaSO_4$) is administered to people when x-rays of their digestive systems are taken, despite the fact that the Ba^{2+} ion is toxic to humans. Suggest the method by which $BaSO_4$ could be administered without the danger from the Ba^{2+} ions. Base your method on the common-ion effect.
14. The K_{sp} of AgCl at 50°C is 1.32×10^{-9}. Predict whether AgCl will precipitate if $AgNO_3$ and NaCl solutions of the following concentrations are mixed.
   a. 1.00×10^{-5} *M* $AgNO_3$ and 1.00×10^{-5} *M* NaCl
   b. 1.00×10^{-5} *M* $AgNO_3$ and 1.32×10^{-4} *M* NaCl
   c. 1.00×10^{-5} *M* $AgNO_3$ and 4.00×10^{-4} *M* NaCl

FOURTEEN

ACIDS, BASES, & SALTS

IONS MAKE THE DIFFERENCE

ACIDS, bases, and salts all release ions when in water. Most acids release H^+ ions. Bases usually release OH^- ions. Salts also release ions: metal cations and nonmetal anions. These ions lack the corrosiveness that the H^+ and OH^- ions have. Different types and numbers of various ions give acids, bases, and salts their unique properties.

Definitions and Descriptions

14–1 Arrhenius Definitions: H^+ and OH^- Ions

What determines whether a compound is an acid, a base, a salt, or none of the above? Acids and bases are often regarded as fuming, caustic, and generally nasty. This impression holds true in many cases, but it is wrong in many others. Scientists focus on chemical behaviors as the basis for definitions.

The earliest of the modern acid-base definitions was proposed in the 1880s by the Swedish chemist Svante Arrhenius. **Arrhenius acids** release hydrogen ions (H^+) into aqueous solutions. Note that a hydrogen ion is just a proton, or a hydrogen nucleus. **Arrhenius bases** are substances that release hydroxide ions (OH^-) into aqueous solutions. According to the Arrhenius definitions, HCl, HCOOH, and H_2SO_4 are acids and NaOH, $Mg(OH)_2$, and $Al(OH)_3$ are bases.

Hydrogen-containing compounds that do not donate protons are not acids. Methane (CH_4) has four hydrogen atoms, but none of them is bonded in such a way that it can be easily released.

No protons are released from methane under ordinary circumstances; so methane is not an acid. Likewise, compounds with OH groups in their formulas are not always bases. Methanol (CH_3OH) does not normally release its OH group.

The Arrhenius definitions deal only with compounds in aqueous solutions. Normally this is not a great limitation, but modern chemistry has started exploring some reactions that take place in nonaqueous solutions and some that take place without the aid of any solvents at all. The Arrhenius definition of bases does not recognize compounds such as ammonia as being bases, because these compounds do not have an OH group. Nevertheless, ammonia exhibits properties that are generally thought of as being basic. Although the Arrhenius definitions find some use, they are restrictive and are not used as often as other definitions.

14-1 Svante Arrhenius.

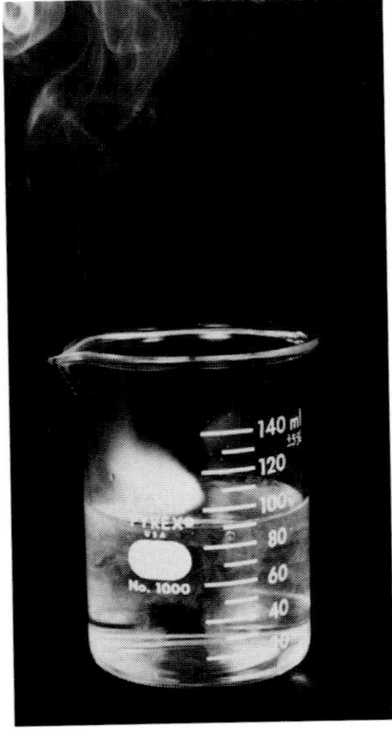

14-2 The reaction of potassium with water forms potassium hydroxide (KOH), a strong base.

14–2 Brönsted-Lowry Definitions: Trading Protons

In 1923 a Danish chemist named J. N. Brönsted and a British chemist named T. M. Lowry proposed new definitions of acids and bases. A **Brönsted-Lowry acid** is a substance that donates protons, and a **Brönsted-Lowry base** is a substance that accepts protons. A released proton does not float freely in water. Instead, it immediately joins a water molecule to make it a hydronium ion (H_3O^+). The process of losing a proton is called **deprotonation,** and the process of gaining a proton is called **protonation.**

$$H^+ + H_2O \longrightarrow H_3O^+$$

Brönsted-Lowry acids and bases exist in pairs called **conjugate pairs.** An acid that loses a proton forms a substance capable of accepting a proton. This base is called the **conjugate base** of the acid. The **conjugate acid** of a base is the substance formed by the protonation of the base. Examples of Brönsted-Lowry acids and bases with their conjugates are shown in Table 14-3.

Table 14-3

Conjugate Pairs of Brönsted-Lowry Acids and Bases

Name of Conjugate Acid	Conjugate Acid	Conjugate Base	Name of Conjugate Base
Acetic acid	$HC_2H_3O_2$	$C_2H_3O_2^-$	acetate ion
Hydrochloric acid	HCl	Cl^-	chloride ion
Perchloric acid	$HClO_4$	ClO_4^-	perchlorate ion
Water	H_2O	OH^-	hydroxide ion
Sulfuric acid	H_2SO_4	HSO_4^-	hydrogen sulfate ion
Hydrogen sulfate ion	HSO_4^-	SO_4^{2-}	sulfate ion

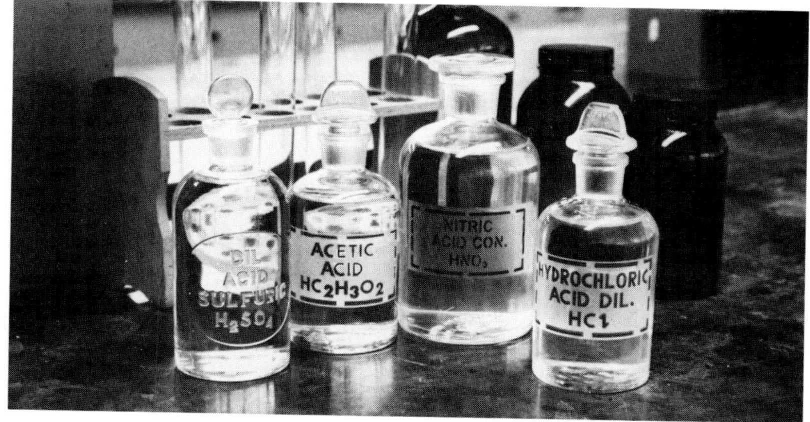

14-4 Common laboratory acids release hydrogen ions into solutions.

The Brönsted-Lowry definitions of acids and bases encompass all Arrhenius acids and bases plus many others. The Brönsted-Lowry definition of acids is essentially the same as the Arrhenius definition, but the definition of bases differs greatly. The Brönsted-Lowry definition greatly expands the number of substances called bases because it includes many substances without OH groups.

14–3 Lewis Definitions: Electron Pairs

The Lewis theory of acids and bases is named after Gilbert N. Lewis, an American chemist who also published his ideas in 1923. A **Lewis acid** is any substance that can accept a pair of electrons, and a **Lewis base** is a substance that can donate a pair of electrons. Another way of saying this is that an acid has at least one empty orbital and a base has at least one lone (unbonded) pair of electrons. The formation of an ammonium (NH_4^+) ion entails a reaction between a Lewis acid and a Lewis base. A hydrogen ion acts as a Lewis acid by accepting an electron pair. The electron pair comes from the ammonia molecule, which acts as a Lewis base. When Lewis acids and bases combine, coordinate covalent bonds form. One coordinate covalent bond forms in the ammonium ion when the nitrogen of the ammonia molecule supplies both electrons in the bond.

14-5 Ammonia is a Lewis base because it can donate a pair of electrons in the formation of a coordinate covalent bond.

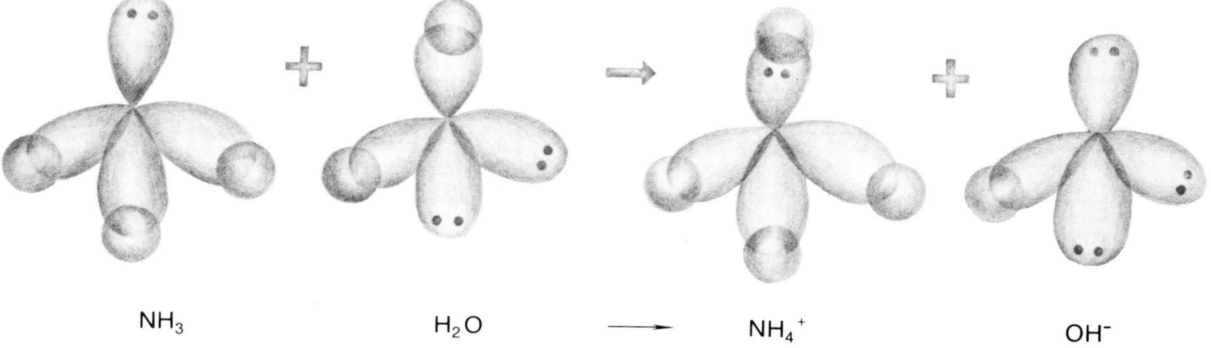

Lewis acids include many more substances than do Arrhenius or Brönsted-Lowry acids. Despite this fact, the Lewis definitions are not used as commonly as the Brönsted-Lowry definitions.

14-6 The Lewis definitions of acids and bases include more substances than the other definitions do.

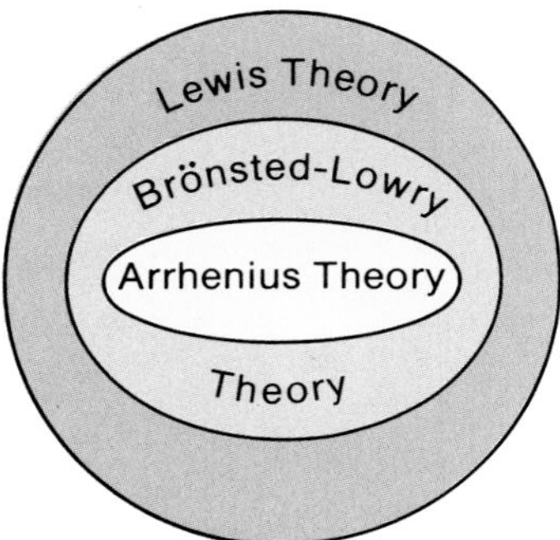

14–4 Observable Properties of Acids and Bases

Aqueous solutions of acids and bases have distinctive properties. Arrhenius and Brönsted-Lowry acids release hydrogen ions that impart several unique characteristics to acids. Citric acid in fruit juices has a tart, sour taste; so do other acids. The putrid, sour taste of lactic acid identifies sour milk. Acetic acid is responsible for vinegar's sharp, sour taste.

Acids react with active metals to produce hydrogen gas and a salt. If the metal is above hydrogen in the activity series, it will replace the hydrogen ion of the acid. The reaction between magnesium and hydrochloric acid illustrates this characteristic.

$$Mg\,(s) + 2\,HCl\,(aq) \longrightarrow Mg^{2+}\,(aq) + 2\,Cl^{-}\,(aq) + H_2$$

Acids can also be identified by their reactions with compounds that change colors. One such compound is litmus, which turns red in the presence of an acid. A final characteristic of acids is that they neutralize bases.

Accidental tastes of soap confirm the fact that basic solutions tend to be bitter. Hydroxide ions interact with taste buds to produce an effect described very well by the word *yucky*. The ions also contribute to that slippery sensation that is felt when bases are touched. Bases react with red litmus to turn it blue, and they react with acids to neutralize them.

14-7 The reaction of magnesium and hydrochloric acid produces hydrogen gas and dissolved magnesium chloride ($MgCl_2$).

14-8 Acids turn litmus red; bases turn litmus blue.

Equilibria, Acids, and Bases

The deprotonation of acids and the protonation of bases are reversible processes. Equilibrium constants describe the extent to which an acid gives up a proton and how readily a base acquires a proton. Equilibrium chemistry explains why it is all right to use boric acid as an eyewash but why it is unsafe to touch the sulfuric acid in the battery of a car. The equilibrium constants of acid-base reactions provide the theoretical basis for the pH system.

14–5 The Autoprotolysis of Water: H_2O Splits Up

In addition to all its unique physical properties, water has one intriguing chemical property: it can react with itself. The reaction is an acid-base reaction in which one water molecule donates a proton to another water molecule. One molecule acts as an acid, and the other acts as a base. This reaction is called the **autoprotolysis** of water. It is also called the autoionization, or self-ionization, of water.

$$H_2O + H_2O \rightleftharpoons OH^- + H_3O^+$$

The reaction is an equilibrium in which the reverse reaction predominates. Only a few molecules produce protons. As with all reversible reactions, this one can be described with an equilibrium constant.

$$K = \frac{[H_3O^+][OH^-]}{[H_2O]^2} = [H_3O^+][OH^-]$$

The concentration of water is eliminated from the equation. The resulting constant is given the special name **autoprotolysis constant of water** and the special symbol K_w. Experimental evidence has shown that the concentrations of hydronium and hydroxide ions are both 1×10^{-7} mole per liter in pure water at 25°C. Only 1 out of 555 million water molecules is dissociated at a given instant in time. The product of these two concentrations makes the value of the constant 1×10^{-14}.

$$\begin{aligned} K_w &= [H_3O^+][OH^-] \\ &= (1 \times 10^{-7})(1 \times 10^{-7}) \\ &= 1 \times 10^{-14} \end{aligned}$$

Despite its small size, 1×10^{-14} is a very important number. Whether a solution is acidic, basic, or neutral, the concentration of hydronium ions times the concentration of hydroxide ions always equals 1×10^{-14}.

Sample Problem. The concentration of hydronium ions in a mild acid is found to be 5×10^{-7} mole per liter. What is the concentration of hydroxide ions?

Solution.

$$K_w = [H_3O^+][OH^-]$$

$$\frac{K_w}{[H_3O^+]} = [OH^-]$$

$$\frac{1 \times 10^{-14}}{5 \times 10^{-7}} = [OH^-]$$

$$2 \times 10^{-8}\ M = [OH^-]$$

14–6 The pH Scale

The concentrations of hydronium and hydroxide ions in aqueous solutions frequently range between 1 and 1×10^{-14} mole per liter. The wide range and the small size of these numbers make working with decimal numbers and scientific notations a chore. Soren P. L. Sorensen, a Danish chemist, proposed the pH scale in 1909 to provide a clear, concise, and convenient way of describing the concentrations of these ions. The **pH** of a solution is the negative logarithm of the hydronium ion concentration.

$$pH = -\log [H_3O^+]$$

A pure sample of water has a hydronium ion concentration of 1×10^{-7} moles per liter. The logarithm of 1×10^{-7} is -7. Since -(-7) is +7, the pH of pure water is 7. Table 14-9 shows hydronium ion concentrations of several solutions, the logarithms of these concentrations, and the pH values.

Table 14-9

$[H_3O^+]$	$\log [H_3O^+]$	pH, or $-\log [H_3O^+]$
1×10^{0}	0.0	0.0
5×10^{-3}	-2.3	2.3
1×10^{-7}	-7.0	7.0
5×10^{-10}	-9.3	9.3
1×10^{-14}	-14.0	14.0

Sample Problem. The hydronium ion concentration in a shampoo is 2×10^{-5} mole per liter. What is the pH of this shampoo?

Solution.

$$\begin{aligned} pH &= -\log [H_3O^+] \\ &= -\log (2 \times 10^{-5}) \\ &= -(-4.7) = 4.7 \end{aligned}$$

Just as the pH system describes the hydronium ion concentration, a pOH system describes the hydroxide ion concentration. The **pOH** of a solution is the negative logarithm of the hydroxide ion concentration. Table 14-10 shows the hydroxide ion concentrations of several solutions, the logarithms of these concentrations, and the pOH values.

Table 14-10

$[OH^-]$	$\log [OH^-]$	pOH, or $-\log [OH^-]$
1×10^{-14}	-14.0	14.0
2×10^{-12}	-11.7	11.7
1×10^{-7}	-7.0	7.0
2×10^{-5}	-4.7	4.7
1×10^{0}	0.0	0.0

Because the hydronium and hydroxide ion concentrations are related, pH and pOH are also related. The pH plus the pOH always equals 14.

Table 14-11

$[H_3O^+]$	pH	pOH	$[OH^-]$
1×10^{0}	0.0	14.0	1×10^{-14}
5×10^{-3}	2.3	11.7	2×10^{-12}
1×10^{-7}	7.0	7.0	1×10^{-7}
5×10^{-10}	9.3	4.7	2×10^{-5}
1×10^{-14}	14.0	0.0	1×10^{0}

Many commonly encountered substances contain acids or bases. Table 14-12 lists some of these solutions and their pHs.

Table 14-12

The pH of Some Common Substances

$[H_3O^+]$	pH	Examples
10^{0}	0	HCl (1 mole/ℓ)
10^{-1}	1	HCl (0.1 mole/ℓ), gastric juice
10^{-2}	2	lemon juice
10^{-3}	3	a nonalkaline shampoo, vinegar, carbonated drink
10^{-4}	4	tomato juice, orange juice, apple juice
10^{-5}	5	boric acid, black coffee
10^{-6}	6	urine, milk
10^{-7}	7	saliva, pure water, blood (pH = 7.35-7.45)
10^{-8}	8	soap solution, baking-soda solution, seawater
10^{-9}	9	0.1 *N* borax
10^{-10}	10	powdered household cleaner, milk of magnesia
10^{-11}	11	household ammonia
10^{-12}	12	lime water, ($Ca[OH]_2$ solution)
10^{-13}	13	NaOH (0.1 mole/ℓ)
10^{-14}	14	NaOH (1 mole/ℓ)

All solutions with a pH less than 7 are called **acidic solutions** because the hydronium ion concentration is greater than the hydroxide ion concentration. All solutions with a pH greater than 7 are called **basic solutions** because the hydroxide ions outnumber the hydronium ions. When a solution has a pH of 7, it is a **neutral solution.**

14-13 pH meters use electrical currents to measure the number of ions in solution.

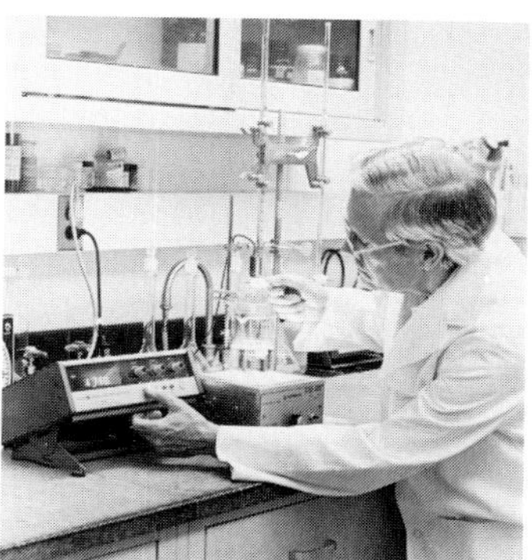

14–7 pH and pOH Calculations

The relationships between $[H_3O^+]$, $[OH^-]$, pH, and pOH are used in many calculations. Figure 14-14 is a flow chart that shows how the various conversions can be made.

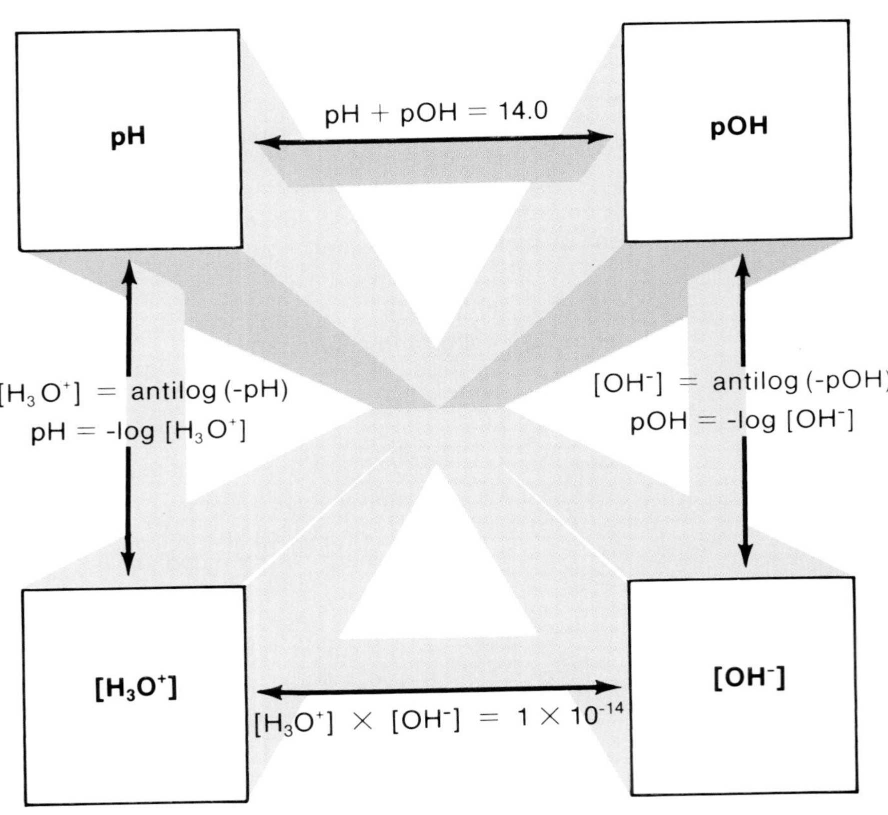

pH
pOH
pH + pOH = 14.0
$[H_3O^+]$ = antilog (-pH)
pH = -log $[H_3O^+]$
$[OH^-]$ = antilog (-pOH)
pOH = -log $[OH^-]$
$[H_3O^+]$
$[OH^-]$
$[H_3O^+] \times [OH^-] = 1 \times 10^{-14}$

14-14 Flow chart for pH and pOH calculations.

Household ammonia solutions used for cleaning are aqueous solutions of ammonia (NH_3). In water, ammonia produces ammonium hydroxide, which makes the solution basic (pH = 11.7). The concentration of hydronium ions can be calculated with the use of antilogs. Finding the antilog of a number (x) means finding the number (y) whose log is x. Finding the negative antilog of 11.7 will not give the correct answer. The antilog of -11.7 must be found.

$$-\log [H_3O^+] = \text{pH}$$
$$[H_3O^+] = \text{antilog}(-\text{pH})$$
$$= \text{antilog}(-11.7)$$
$$= 2 \times 10^{-12}$$

The pOH and the hydroxide ion concentration of the solution can be calculated directly from the pH, since pH + pOH = 14.

$$\begin{aligned} pOH &= 14 - pH \\ &= 14 - 11.7 \\ &= 2.3 \end{aligned}$$

The hydroxide ion concentration equals the antilog of -2.3.

$$\begin{aligned} [OH^-] &= \text{antilog}(\text{-pOH}) \\ &= \text{antilog}(-2.3) \\ &= 5 \times 10^{-3}\ M \end{aligned}$$

Sample Problem. A 0.1-molar hydrochloric acid solution has a hydronium ion concentration of 1×10^{-1} moles per liter. Calculate the pH, the hydroxide ion concentration, and the pOH.

Solution.

The pH can be found first.

$$\begin{aligned} pH &= -\log(1 \times 10^{-1}) \\ &= -(-1) \\ &= 1 \end{aligned}$$

$$\begin{aligned} pOH &= 14 - pH \\ &= 14 - 1 \\ &= 13 \end{aligned}$$

The hydroxide ion concentration can be calculated from the pOH.

$$\begin{aligned} [OH^-] &= \text{antilog}(\text{-pOH}) \\ &= \text{antilog}(-13) \\ &= 1 \times 10^{-13} \end{aligned}$$

14–8 Describing Acid-Base Strengths: Equilibrium Constants Again

The strength of an acid depends on how easily it releases protons. **Strong acids** give up protons easily and ionize completely. Surprisingly, only six common acids may be classified as strong acids: $HClO_4$, HI, HBr, HCl, H_2SO_4, and HNO_3. **Weak acids** do not completely ionize. Only a portion of their molecules lose protons. Acetic acid, in which only 1 out of 24 molecules loses a proton, is a familiar weak acid.

The strength of a base depends on how easily it accepts protons. Whereas **weak bases** (such as the Cl^- ion) are poor proton acceptors, **strong bases** (such as the OH^- ion) accept protons readily. The hydroxides of active metals—LiOH, NaOH, KOH, RbOH, CsOH,

FACETS OF CHEMISTRY

When the Weather Turns Sour—Acid Rain

The earth groaned and then suddenly spewed forth cinders, ashes, molten lava, and a variety of gases. A volcanic mountain formed. In the sulfur-laden atmosphere, oxides of sulfur combined with moisture from the air to form acids. Then it rained—acid rain. Although it is normal for rain to be slightly acidic, this rain with a pH lower than 5.6 was cause for concern.

In a similar manner, gases from industrial smokestacks can cause acid rain. Sulfur released when fossil fuels are burned combine with oxygen. The sulfur dioxide that forms can eventually form sulfuric acid,

$$SO_2 + NO_2 \longrightarrow SO_3 + NO;$$
$$SO_3 + H_2O \longrightarrow H_2SO_4,$$

which falls on the countryside.

This situation is causing serious problems in industrialized countries such as West Germany, Sweden, Norway, Japan, Great Britain, Canada, Russia, and the United States. Studies in Europe, where acid rain has been a problem longer than it has been in the United States, have documented extensive damage to forests downwind from the industrial Ruhr valley. There is evidence that acid rain in these regions has removed vital nutrients such as calcium and magnesium from the soil. There is also evidence that the resulting acidic groundwater is beginning to liberate aluminum from the soil. Aluminum is poisonous to the root hairs of plants, crippling their ability to extract water from the soil. Reforestation efforts in acid-rain regions are failing because of the unhealthy state of the soil. Alarmingly, some of the same symptoms appear in the mountains of Vermont, where industries from midwestern cities pollute the rain. Acid rain that percolates into the groundwater eventually flows into streams and lakes. Drinking water has been contaminated in some areas, and certain species of fish have reportedly had their

$Mg(OH)_2$, $Ca(OH)_2$, $Sr(OH)_2$, and $Ba(OH)_2$—are the best sources of the hydroxide ion, so they are commonly called strong bases.

The conjugate base of a strong acid is always weak; it does not readily accept protons to form a strong acid. Perchloric acid ($HClO_4$) is a strong acid that readily gives up a hydrogen ion. Once the hydrogen and the chloride ions are apart, they do not readily rejoin to form perchloric acid. Therefore, the perchlorate ion is a weak conjugate base. On the other end of the acid scale are the weak acids. Their conjugate bases are strong. The ammonium ion (NH_4^+), for example, has a weak tendency to release a hydrogen ion. The conjugate base (NH_3) is a strong base because it seeks to gain and hold a hydrogen ion.

populations decimated. A number of Swedish lakes are now claimed to be totally devoid of any living fish as a result of pollutants from the British Isles and continental Europe.

One localized solution that has been successfully employed in Sweden is the addition of large quantities of lime to some of the lakes. Through a massive titration, the pH of the water has been raised as much as three full units.

A truly effective solution to the acid rain problem, however, must attack its source—the industrial plants. In this country most of the pollution seems to come from coal-fired power plants. Thus, an elegant solution to the problem would be a changeover to nuclear power. Nuclear power is clean and efficient. However, building new nuclear plants is extremely costly and time-consuming, and scientists are still struggling with the problem of disposing of nuclear waste. But the alternatives are also costly. One option is the addition of "scrubbers" to existing plants. These tall towers mix the escaping gases with water and lime so that the gases emerge "clean." Another approach to the problem places marble-sized pieces of limestone and burning coal in a stream of compressed air at the bottom of the furnace. When sulfur dioxide forms, it immediately reacts with the limestone.

The problem of acid rain does not appear to have a single simple solution, yet it cannot be ignored. After God created the earth, He entrusted it to man's keeping (Gen. 1:28). While man should use the resources God has supplied, he must not recklessly abuse them and deface the environment. More research is needed to explore the workability of new, untried technologies for attacking the problem at its source.

Acid strengths are described by dissociation equilibrium constants. The **acid dissociation constant** (K_a) describes the extent of the forward reaction in the equilibrium.

$$\text{Acid} + H_2O \rightleftharpoons H_3O^+ + \text{Base}$$

$$K_a = \frac{[H_3O^+][\text{Base}]}{[\text{Acid}]}$$

Stronger acids have higher K_as because the forward reaction dominates and many hydrogen ions are released. Table 14-15 lists acids, dissociation constants, and their deprotonation reactions in order from strong to weak. Because the stronger acids have weaker conjugate bases, the bases at the top of the column are the weakest.

Table 14-15

Acid	Ka	Equilibrium	Base
Perchloric acid	very large	$HClO_4 \longrightarrow H^+ + ClO_4^-$	perchlorate ion
Hydriodic acid	very large	$HI \longrightarrow H^+ + I^-$	iodide ion
Hydrobromic acid	very large	$HBr \longrightarrow H^+ + Br^-$	bromide ion
Hydrochloric acid	very large	$HCl \longrightarrow H^+ + Cl^-$	chloride ion
Sulfuric acid	very large	$H_2SO_4 \longrightarrow H^+ + HSO_4^-$	hydrogen sulfate ion
Nitric acid	very large	$HNO_3 \longrightarrow H^+ + NO_3^-$	nitrate ion
Sulfurous acid	1.7×10^{-2}	$H_2SO_3 \rightleftharpoons H^+ + HSO_3^-$	bisulfite ion
Hydrogen sulfate ion	1.2×10^{-2}	$HSO_4^- \rightleftharpoons H^+ + SO_4^{2-}$	sulfate ion
Phosphoric acid	7.5×10^{-3}	$H_3PO_4 \rightleftharpoons H^+ + H_2PO_4^-$	dihydrogen phosphate ion
Hydrofluoric acid	3.5×10^{-4}	$HF \rightleftharpoons H^+ + F^-$	fluoride ion
Formic acid	1.8×10^{-4}	$HCHO_2 \rightleftharpoons H^+ + CHO_2^-$	formate ion
Acetic acid	1.8×10^{-5}	$HC_2H_3O_2 \rightleftharpoons H^+ + C_2H_3O_2^-$	acetate ion
Carbonic acid	4.2×10^{-7}	$H_2CO_3 \rightleftharpoons H^+ + HCO_3^-$	hydrogen carbonate ion
Hypochlorous acid	3.2×10^{-8}	$HClO \rightleftharpoons H^+ + ClO^-$	hypochlorite ion
Boric acid	5.8×10^{-10}	$H_3BO_3 \rightleftharpoons H^+ + H_2BO_3^-$	dihydrogen borate ion
Ammonium ion	5.7×10^{-10}	$NH_4^+ \rightleftharpoons H^+ + NH_3$	ammonia
Hydrocyanic acid	4.0×10^{-10}	$HCN \rightleftharpoons H^+ + CN^-$	cyanide ion
Hydrogen carbonate ion	4.8×10^{-11}	$HCO_3^- \rightleftharpoons H^+ + CO_3^{2-}$	carbonate ion
Hydrogen peroxide	2.6×10^{-12}	$H_2O_2 \rightleftharpoons H^+ + HO_2^-$	hydroperoxide ion
Water	1×10^{-14}	$H_2O \rightleftharpoons H^+ + OH^-$	hydroxide ion

Sample Problem. On the basis of dissociation constants, which acid is stronger, hydrofluoric or hydriodic acid?

Solution.

The dissociation constant of hydriodic acid is too large to be measured, whereas the constant for hydrofluoric acid is 3.5×10^{-4}. Hydriodic acid is the stronger acid.

Boric acid, which has a low dissociation constant, is a weak acid. Since it does not release many hydrogen ions, the dilute eyewash solutions that contain boric acid will not burn people's eyes. On the other hand, sulfuric acid in car batteries releases enough hydrogen ions to blister skin.

14–9 Causes of Acid-Base Strengths: Unhand That Proton!

Dissociation constants *describe* acid strengths; they do not determine them. The factors that cause one acid to be strong and another to be weak are electrical in nature. The location of shared electron clouds and the charge on an acid determine how easily a proton (H^+ ion) can be released.

To be easily ionizable, the nucleus of a hydrogen atom must be exposed and open to attack. The negatively charged electron cloud of the covalent bond must be shifted away from the hydrogen and toward a more electronegative atom in the center of the molecule. The series of compounds shown below illustrates how a highly electronegative element can make acids strong by shifting electrons and exposing hydrogen nuclei. The hydrogen atoms in the methane molecule are virtually surrounded by negative charges. The highly electronegative fluorine atom pulls shared electrons to itself. Consequently, hydrofluoric acid is the strongest acid of this series.

Table 14-16

Compound	Electronegativity of Central Atom	
CH_4	2.4	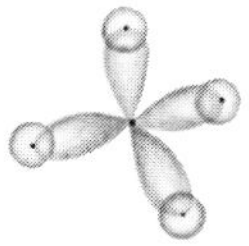
NH_3	3.0	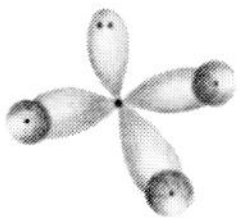
H_2O	3.5	
HF	4.0	

Besides electron-cloud location, electrical charges determine the strengths of acids. The sulfuric acid molecule (H_2SO_4) has a neutral charge and is a strong acid. The hydrogen sulfate (HSO_4^-) ion has an ionizable proton, but this negative ion has little tendency to release another hydrogen ion. Similarly, H_3PO_4, $H_2PO_4^-$, and HPO_4^{2-} have decreasing acidic strengths. Anions hold protons more strongly than neutral molecules.

The same factors that make acids strong make bases weak. Conversely, factors that weaken acids make bases stronger. Strong acids release protons easily; strong bases accept protons easily.

Strong acids . . .	Strong bases . . .
1. have exposed hydrogen nuclei.	1. have exposed electron pairs.
2. have a minimum of negative charges.	2. may have strong negative charges.

THEY THINK IT'S ONE OF OURS, HERB--THEY THINK SOMEONE HERE IN BASEVILLE IS TURNING INTO AN ACID-- DID YOU EVER HEAR OF SUCH A THING?

14–10 It's an Acid! It's a Base! It's Amphiprotic!

Amphiprotic substances can act both as Brönsted-Lowry acids or bases. Whether an amphiprotic substance behaves as an acid or a base depends on the reaction conditions. For example, the hydrogen carbonate ion accepts a proton when an acid is added to the solution. Under those circumstances, therefore, the hydrogen carbonate ion is a base.

$$HCO_3^- + H_3O^+ \rightleftharpoons H_2CO_3 + H_2O$$

When a base is added to the solution, the hydrogen carbonate ion acts as an acid by donating a proton.

$$HCO_3^- + OH^- \rightleftharpoons CO_3^{2-} + H_2O$$

Water is an amphiprotic substance, as is demonstrated by its reactions with perchloric acid and ammonia.

$$H_2O + HClO_4 \rightleftharpoons H_3O^+ + ClO_4^-$$
$$H_2O + NH_3 \rightleftharpoons NH_4OH$$

While in the first reaction water acts as a Brönsted-Lowry base by receiving a proton from perchloric acid, it acts as an acid in the second reaction when it donates a proton to ammonia.

14–11 Polyprotic Acids: Protons Galore!

Monoprotic Brönsted-Lowry acids can donate only one proton. **Polyprotic** acids can donate more than one proton. Each ionization is characterized by a different equilibrium constant. Carbonic acid (H_2CO_3) is an example of a **diprotic** acid, which can donate two protons. The K_a for the first ionization is called K_{a1}, and that for the second ionization is called K_{a2}.

$$H_2CO_3 + H_2O \rightleftharpoons HCO_3^- + H_3O^+$$

$$K_{a1} = \frac{[HCO_3^-][H_3O^+]}{[H_2CO_3]} = 4.3 \times 10^{-7}$$

$$HCO_3^- + H_2O \rightleftharpoons CO_3^{2-} + H_3O^+$$

$$K_{a2} = \frac{[CO_3^{2-}][H_3O^+]}{[HCO_3^-]} = 5.6 \times 10^{-11}$$

All polyprotic acids have at least one amphiprotic substance in their series of ionizations. In carbonic acid the hydrogen carbonate ion is amphiprotic. Furthermore, the K_{a2} is always smaller than the K_{a1}. The first ionization involves separation of a proton from an uncharged carbonic acid (H_2CO_3) molecule, and the second involves separation of a proton from the -1 charged hydrogen carbonate (HCO_3^-) ion. Because the strength of attraction between opposite charges depends on the magnitude of the charges, the second ionization is less favorable than the first. In general, $K_{a1} > K_{a2} > K_{a3}$. Acids with three ionizable protons are called **triprotic** acids.

Several more examples of polyprotic acids are shown below. The values of K_a are for the reactions at 25° C.

Table 14-18

Polyprotic Acids	Acid-Base Reaction	K_a
Chromic acid	$H_2CrO_4 \rightleftharpoons H^+ + HCrO_4^-$	1.8×10^{-1}
	$HCrO_4^- \rightleftharpoons H^+ + CrO_4^{2-}$	3.2×10^{-7}
Hydrosulfuric acid	$H_2S \rightleftharpoons H^+ + HS^-$	1.1×10^{-7}
	$HS^- \rightleftharpoons H^+ + S^{2-}$	1.0×10^{-14}
Phosphoric acid	$H_3PO_4 \rightleftharpoons H^+ + H_2PO_4^-$	7.5×10^{-3}
	$H_2PO_4^- \rightleftharpoons H^+ + HPO_4^{2-}$	6.2×10^{-8}
	$HPO_4^{2-} \rightleftharpoons H^+ + PO_4^{3-}$	4.8×10^{-13}
Sulfurous acid	$H_2SO_3 \rightleftharpoons H^+ + HSO_3^-$	1.3×10^{-2}
	$HSO_3^- \rightleftharpoons H^+ + SO_3^{2-}$	6.3×10^{-8}

14–12 Indicators: Color-Coded Chemicals

Indicators are substances that change colors when the pH of a solution changes. Indicators are usually weak acids or bases whose conjugates have different colors. Some indicators change colors at low pHs, some at high pHs. Some are polyprotic, so they may exhibit more than one color change. Examples of indicators, their colors, and the pH range over which their colors change are given in Table 14-20.

14-19 Colors of Common Indicators

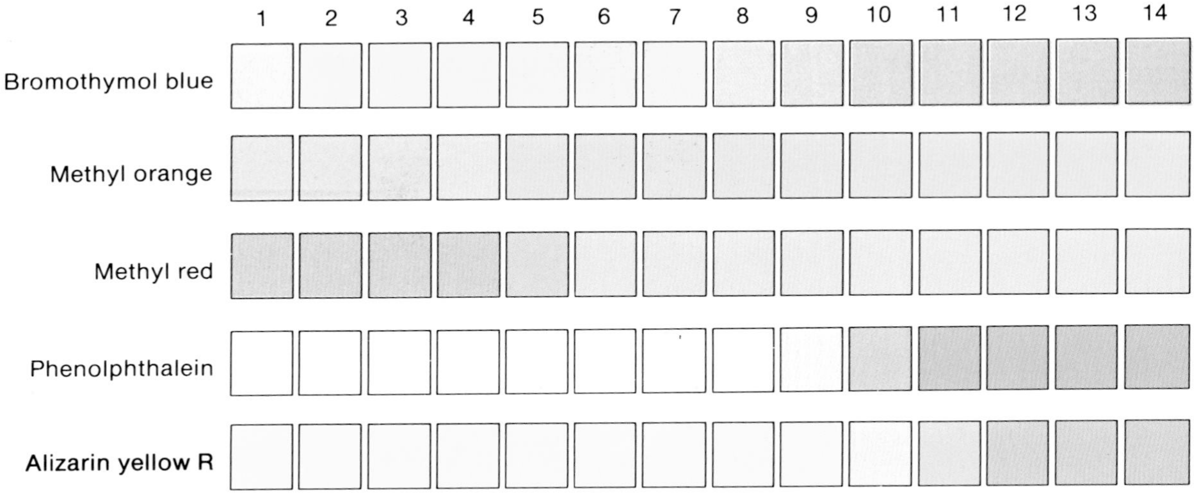

	1	2	3	4	5	6	7	8	9	10	11	12	13	14
Bromothymol blue														
Methyl orange														
Methyl red														
Phenolphthalein														
Alizarin yellow R														

Table 14-20

Common Indicators

Indicator	Color of Conjugate Acid	Color of Conjugate Base	pH Range for Color Change
Methyl green	yellow	blue	0.2-1.8
Thymol blue	red	yellow	1.2-2.8
	yellow	blue	8.0-9.6
Bromophenol blue	yellow	blue	3.0-4.6
2,4-dinitrophenol	colorless	yellow	2.8-4.0
Congo red	blue	red	3.0-5.0
Methyl orange	red	yellow	3.2-4.4
Methyl red	red	yellow	4.2-6.2
Alizarin	yellow	red	5.6-7.2
	red	purple	11.0-12.4
Brilliant yellow	yellow	orange	6.6-7.8
Meta-cresol purple	yellow	purple	7.4-9.0
Phenolphthalein	colorless	red	8.2-10.0
Alizarin yellow R	yellow	red	10.1-12.0
TNT	colorless	orange	11.5-13.0

Indicators give rough estimates of pHs. For instance, if a solution is yellow in 2,4-dinitrophenol but turns blue with congo red, then the pH must be between 3 and 4. Indicators usually show pH changes over a narrow range. Congo red changes color when a solution has a pH between 3 and 5. Once the pH is past 5, the color remains essentially constant. The congo red indicator tells nothing about how basic the solution is. This problem may be overcome by the use of carefully chosen combinations of indicators called universal indicators. More accurate values can be obtained when large numbers of indicators are used, but this is tedious. Instruments called pH meters give accurate pH measurements of solutions by measuring electrical properties that depend on the number of ions present.

14-21 Universal indicator paper can be used to measure a wide range of pHs because it contains several indicators.

The Bible, I John in particular, lists several indicators of spirituality. Observable traits such as (1) obedience to God's commandments, (2) love for others, and (3) separation from the world reveal a person's true colors.

Neutralization: When Acids and Bases Mix

The pain and discomfort of heartburn are usually associated with meals that were either too large or too spicy. The burning sensation under the breastbone comes not from oregano or green peppers, but from excess hydrochloric acid. This acid, which is normally confined to the stomach, irritates the tissues of the esophagus if some splashes past the upper part of the stomach. To relieve this pain, a person can neutralize the acid with an antacid (a base). The mixing of two active chemicals results in a set of harmless products.

14-22 The floor, walls, and ceiling of this salt mine are solid sodium chloride.

14–13 Salts: Products of Neutralizations

Antacids that contain magnesium hydroxide neutralize stomach acid according to the reaction $Mg(OH)_2 + 2\ HCl \longrightarrow MgCl_2 + 2\ H_2O$. Sodium hydroxide is much too corrosive to be used as an antacid, but it too neutralizes acids: $2\ NaOH + H_2SO_4 \longrightarrow Na_2SO_4 + 2\ H_2O$. According to the Arrhenius definitions, the heart of every **neutralization reaction** is the formation of water from hydronium and hydroxide ions. The hydronium ions of acids and the hydroxide ions of bases combine to form two water molecules.

$$H_3O^+ + OH^- \longrightarrow 2\ H_2O$$

Metal cations and nonmetal anions are present, but they are not involved in the neutralization reaction. If the resulting solution is evaporated, these ions will crystallize into a salt.

A **salt** is a substance formed when the anion of an acid and the cation of a base combine. In the antacid reaction Cl^- (the acid's anion) combines with Mg^{2+} (the base's cation) to form $MgCl_2$ (the salt). Many different salts can be produced in neutralization reactions. Sodium chloride, zinc bromide, and potassium fluoride are all examples of salts. Most salts, like these three, are composed of a metal and a nonmetal, but this is not always true. Ammonium chloride (NH_4Cl), potassium sulfate (K_2SO_4), and aluminum phosphate ($AlPO_4$) contain polyatomic ions.

Sample Problem. Write a neutralization reaction that could produce the salt zinc chloride ($ZnCl_2$).

Solution.

Salts are made from the anions of acids and the cations of bases. In this case the most common acid that releases the chloride ion is hydrochloric acid. Zinc hydroxide is a likely source for the zinc ion.

$$2\ HCl + Zn(OH)_2 \longrightarrow ZnCl_2 + 2\ H_2O$$

Sample Problem. What salt results from the neutralization of barium hydroxide by acetic acid ($HC_2H_3O_2$)?

Solution.

$$2\ HC_2H_3O_2 + Ba(OH)_2 \longrightarrow Ba(C_2H_3O_2)_2 + 2\ H_2O$$

Barium acetate forms from the barium and acetate ions.

Salts are divided into three general classes: neutral, acidic, and basic. The formulas of **neutral salts** show no H or OH groups. They cause no change in pH when they are dissolved in water. **Acidic salts** have hydrogen atoms in their formulas. They result from the partial neutralization of polyprotic acids. For instance, sodium hydrogen carbonate ($NaHCO_3$) results when H_2CO_3 is partially neutralized by sodium hydroxide. The substance $CuCO_3 \cdot Cu(OH)_2$ has been classified as a **basic salt** because it contains OH groups. Basic salts are not as common as acidic salts.

14–14 Acid-Base Titrations: Finding Unknown Concentrations

Acid-base **titrations** are controlled reactions in which scientists determine the unknown strength of a solution by measuring its capacity to react with a solution of known strength. Suppose that a chemist has 100 milliliters of a hydrochloric acid solution, but he does not know its exact concentration. He can find the concentration by adding small volumes of a precisely measured 1-molar sodium hydroxide solution until the pH of the solution rises to 7. A graph called a **titration curve** shows how pH changes when an acid or base is added to a solution. Figure 14-23 shows how the pH of a solution of unknown concentration changes with the addition of 1-molar sodium hydroxide.

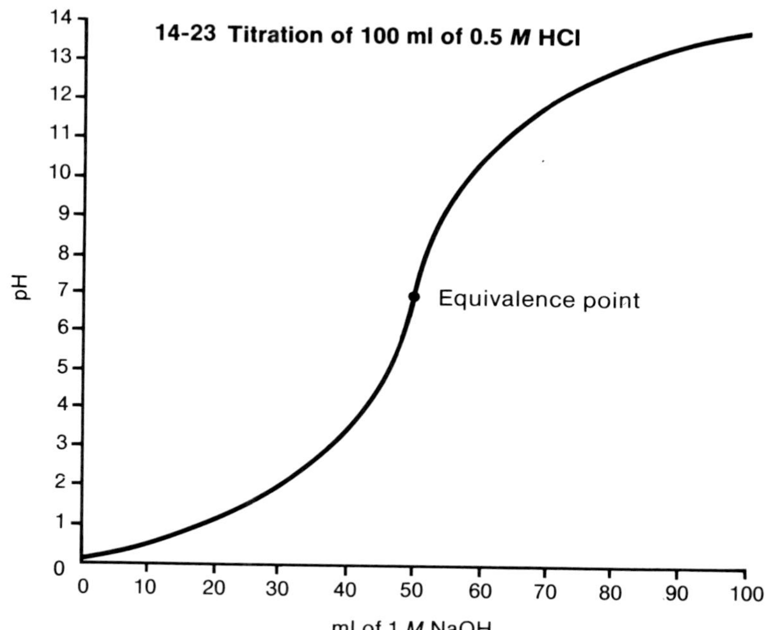

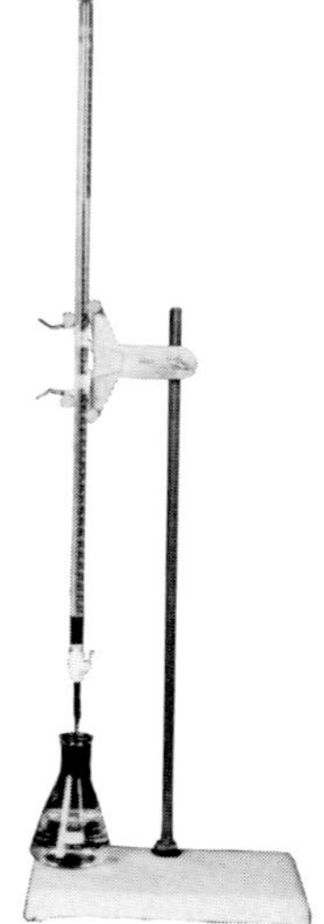

14-24 In titrations, burettes deliver precise amounts of an acid or a base.

Fifty milliliters of the sodium hydroxide raise the pH of the acid to 7; so 50 milliliters of 1-molar sodium hydroxide is chemically equivalent to 100 milliliters of the acid. With this information, the chemist knows that the 1-molar sodium hydroxide is twice as concentrated as the hydrochloric acid. He can then calculate that the hydrochloric acid has a concentration of 0.5 moles per liter.

The concepts of chemical equivalents and normality are used extensively in acid-base titrations. Remember that normality indicates concentration in gram-equivalents per liter of solution. By way of review, the gram-equivalent mass of an acid or base is the amount of substance that accepts or releases 1 mole of protons. The gram-equivalent masses of sodium hydroxide and hydrochloric acid are the same as their gram-molecular masses because 1 mole of sodium hydroxide can accept 1 mole of protons, and 1 mole of hydrochloric acid releases 1 mole of protons. The gram-equivalent mass of sulfuric acid (H_2SO_4) is one-half its gram-molecular mass because each 1/2 mole of acid can release a full mole of protons.

Sample Problem. Calculate the normality of a 1.00-liter solution made with 30.0 grams of phosphoric acid (H_3PO_4).

Solution.

Since each mole of phosphoric acid can release three protons, 1 mole equals 3 equivalents.

$$\frac{30.0 \text{ g } H_3PO_4}{1.00\ \ell \text{ solution}} \times \frac{1 \text{ mole } H_3PO_4}{98.00 \text{ g } H_3PO_4} \times \frac{3 \text{ eq}}{1 \text{ mole } H_3PO_4} = 0.918\ N$$

A simple mathematical equation relates the normalities of solutions and the volumes involved in titrations. The subscript k stands for "known," and the subscript u stands for "unknown."

$$\text{Normality}_k \times \text{Volume}_k = \text{Normality}_u \times \text{Volume}_u$$

$$N_k \times V_k = N_u \times V_u$$

The above equation can be transformed to solve for an unknown normality.

$$N_u = \frac{(N_k)(V_k)}{V_u}$$

Putting the values for the volumes and the strength of the base into this equation gives the strength of the acid.

$$N_u = \frac{(1.0\ N)(50 \text{ ml})}{100 \text{ ml}}$$

$$= 0.50\ N$$

Sample Problem. The addition of 108 milliliters of 5.00×10^{-3} N sodium hydroxide solution can neutralize 36.0 milliliters of a nitric acid solution. What is the concentration of the nitric acid?

Solution.

$$N_u = \frac{(N_k)(V_k)}{V_u}$$

$$= \frac{(5.00 \times 10^{-3}\ N \text{ NaOH})(108 \text{ ml})}{36.0 \text{ ml}}$$

$$= 0.0150\ N$$

14–15 Buffers: Solutions That Are Anti-acid and Anti-base

During the course of a single day, most people probably eat substances with remarkably different pHs. A glass of orange juice has a pH of 4, while the milk of magnesia that follows a late-night pizza has an approximate pH of 10.5. It is obvious that the human stomach can handle a wide range of pHs. The bloodstream, however, cannot tolerate this wide pH range. Its pH must stay between 7.35 and 7.45. God designed the bloodstream with an ingenious protective feature: a buffer system.

Buffers are solutions that resist pH changes despite small additions of hydronium or hydroxide ions. Water is not a buffer; a small amount of acid or base changes its pH dramatically. An addition of 0.01 mole of hydrochloric acid or sodium hydroxide to a liter of pure water changes the pH by 5 units. The same substances added to a liter of blood change the pH only 0.1 unit.

Buffer systems usually consist of a weak acid and its conjugate base or a weak base and its conjugate acid. For example, blood is buffered by a mixture of carbonic acid (H_2CO_3), which is a weak acid, and hydrogen carbonate ions (HCO_3^-), its conjugate base. This combination of solutes keeps the pH relatively constant by reacting with hydronium or hydroxide ions.

When an acid intrudes on the buffer system, hydrogen carbonate ions snare the hydronium ions.

$$H_3O^+ + HCO_3^- \longrightarrow H_2CO_3 + H_2O$$

When a base disturbs the equilibrium of the buffer system, carbonic acid molecules spring into action and remove the hydroxide ions.

$$H_2CO_3 + OH^- \longrightarrow H_2O + HCO_3^-$$

Table 14-25

Common Buffer Systems

Components	Usable pH Range
Formic acid + sodium formate	2.6-4.8
Citric acid + sodium citrate	3.0-6.2
Acetic acid + sodium acetate	3.4-5.9
Sodium hydrogen carbonate + sodium carbonate	9.2-10.6
Sodium hydrogen carbonate + sodium hydroxide	9.6-11.0

Buffers are most effective in regulating slight pH changes. If an enormous amount of acid or base is added to a buffered solution, the buffer will be depleted and the pH will change drastically.

Coming to Terms

Arrhenius acid
Arrhenius base
Brönsted-Lowry acid
Brönsted-Lowry base
deprotonation
protonation
conjugate pair
conjugate base
conjugate acid
Lewis acid
Lewis base
autoprotolysis
autoprotolysis constant of water
pH
pOH
acidic solution
basic solution
neutral solution
strong acid
weak acid
weak base
strong base
acid dissociation constant
amphiprotic
monoprotic
polyprotic
diprotic
triprotic
indicator
neutralization reaction
salt
neutral salt
acidic salt
basic salt
titration
titration curve
buffer

Review Questions

1. Fill in the blanks.
   a. $Al(OH)_3$ is an Arrhenius ________ and therefore must be a Brönsted-Lowry ________.
   b. H_2SO_4 is an Arrhenius ________ and therefore must be a Brönsted-Lowry ________.
   c. NH_3 can be classified as a ________ base and a ________ base, but not as a ________ base.
   d. The Cl^- ion can be classified as a ________ base or a ________ base, but not as a ________ base.
2. True or False
   a. All Lewis acids donate protons.
   b. Brönsted-Lowry acids accept protons.
   c. Arrhenius bases donate protons.
   d. All Brönsted-Lowry acids are Lewis acids.
   e. All Arrhenius acids are Lewis acids.
3. Formic acid (HCO_2H) ionizes in water to form a formate ion and a hydronium ion.

$$HCO_2H\ (aq) + H_2O\ (l) \rightleftharpoons H_3O^+\ (aq) + CO_2H^-\ (aq)$$

   a. What is the conjugate acid in the forward reaction?
   b. What is the conjugate base in the forward reaction?
   c. What is the name of the process by which formic acid loses a proton?

4. Two reactions describe the stepwise ionization of H_2SO_4:

$$H_2SO_4\ (l) + H_2O\ (l) \rightleftharpoons HSO_4^-\ (aq) + H_3O^+\ (aq)$$

$$HSO_4^-\ (aq) + H_2O\ (l) \rightleftharpoons SO_4^{2-}\ (aq) + H_3O^+\ (aq)$$

   a. What is the conjugate acid in the first reaction?
   b. What is the conjugate base in the first reaction?
   c. What is the conjugate acid in the second reaction?
   d. What is the conjugate base in the second reaction?

5. Fill in the blanks.
   a. Aqueous solutions of Arrhenius acids taste ________.
   b. Aqueous solutions of Arrhenius ________ are slippery.
   c. Arrhenius acids react with active metals to produce ________ gas.
   d. An aqueous solution of an Arrhenius base tastes ________.

6. What ion gives H_2SO_4 the ability to react strongly with many substances? What ion is responsible for the corrosiveness of strong bases like NaOH?

7. List four common properties of acids and four common properties of bases.

8. What particles other than H_2O molecules are always present in pure water?

9. Write the equation for the equilibrium constant that describes the reaction of water with itself. What is the numerical value of this constant?

10. Can water molecules act like acids, bases, both, or neither?

11. A young scientist measures $[H_3O^+]$ and $[OH^-]$ in an aqueous solution at 25° C. He reports that $[H_3O^+] = 1 \times 10^{-8}$ and $[OH^-] = 1 \times 10^{-8}$. His supervisor tells him to go back to the lab and make the measurements again. Why?

12. What advantage does the pH scale offer that scientific notation does not?

13. All the following substances can undergo deprotonation reactions. Write the equations for their dissociation constants.
    a. $HClO_4$
    b. H_2CO_3
    c. H_3BO_3

14. Calculate the $[H_3O^+]$ and the pH of each solution.
    a. $1 \times 10^{-5}\ M\ HNO_3$
    b. $5 \times 10^{-3}\ M\ HCl$
    c. $1 \times 10^{-1}\ M\ HClO_4$
    d. $1 \times 10^{-5}\ M\ H_2SO_4$

15. Calculate the pOH and the $[OH^-]$ of each solution in problem 14.

16. What is $[H_3O^+]$ in each of the following solutions?
    a. orange juice, pH = 4.0
    b. black coffee, pH = 5.0
    c. pure water, pH = 7.0
    d. phosphate detergent solution, pH = 9.5
    e. seawater, pH = 8.0
17. Classify each of the solutions in the previous question as acidic, neutral, or basic.
18. Choose the correct answer.
    a. (Strong, Weak) acids ionize incompletely.
    b. (Strong, Weak) acids have large K_as.
    c. Strong (acids, bases) accept protons easily.
    d. The conjugate base of a strong acid is a (strong, weak) base.
19. Referring to Table 14-15, tell which of each pair of the following pairs of acids is the stronger.
    a. $HClO_4$ or H_3PO_4
    b. formic acid or acetic acid
    c. hydrocyanic acid or formic acid
    d. NH_4^+ or HSO_4^-
    e. NH_4^+ or H_2O
20. Choose the member of each pair that should be the stronger acid and then write a brief justification for your choice.
    a. $HBrO_4$, HBr
    b. PH_3, H_2S
21. Is the HCO_3^- ion an acid, a base, both, or neither? Explain.
22. Write the equation that shows how the ions in acids act to neutralize the ions in bases during a neutralization reaction.
23. A NaOH solution contains 1.000 mole NaOH/ℓ of solution. If 25.00 ml of this solution neutralizes 27.00 ml of a HCl solution of unknown concentration,
    a. what is the normality of the HCl?
    b. what is the molarity of the HCl?
24. How many milliliters of 2.00 *M* H_2SO_4 will be required to neutralize 45.0 ml of 3.00 *N* KOH?
25. A careless laboratory assistant set out to determine the concentration of a perchloric acid ($HClO_4$) solution. He found that 50.00 ml of 1.000 *N* NaOH neutralized 0.5000 ℓ of the $HClO_4$ solution. His calculations were as follows:

$$N_u = \frac{(50.00 \text{ ml})(1.000\ N)}{0.5000\ \ell} = 100.0\ N\ HClO_4$$

    Another laboratory assistant insists that the calculation is incorrect. Why? What is the correct answer?

26. A salad-dressing manufacturer desires to make tangy salad dressing by using vinegar with an acetic acid concentration of at least 1 *N*. The quality control department examines a sample of vinegar and determines that 300.0 ml of 0.100 *N* sodium hydroxide neutralizes the acetic acid in 25.00 ml of the vinegar. Does this vinegar meet the manufacturer's requirements?
27. You wish to determine the point at which a chemical reaction raises the pH of a solution past 8.8. Exactly how could you do this?
28. What happens to excess H_3O^+ ions when an acid is added to a solution buffered by a combination of acetic acid and sodium acetate?
29. What happens to excess OH^- ions when a base is added to a solution buffered by a combination of acetic acid and sodium acetate?

FIFTEEN

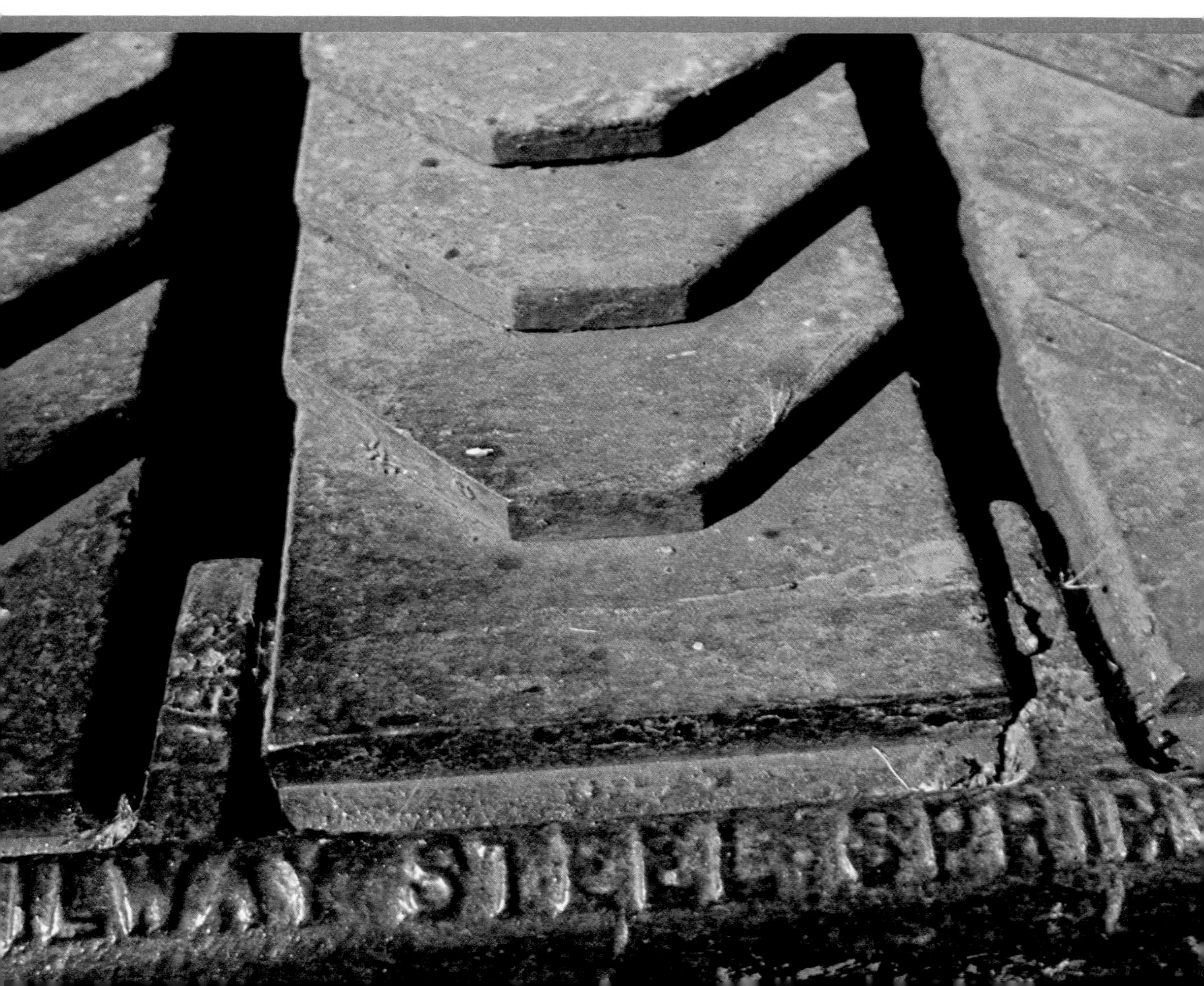

OXIDATION-REDUCTION

ELECTRONS ON THE MOVE

REACTIONS that involve transfers or shifts of electrons occur in every branch of chemistry. In living cells and test tubes, the substances that gain and lose electrons are mixed together. In other cases the substances are separated, and the electrons travel through wires, flow out of batteries, split compounds, or help put metal platings onto objects. This is the realm of oxidation, reduction, and electrochemistry.

Redox Reactions

How do the chemicals on photographic film record the presence of light? At the heart of the film-developing process is the transfer of electrons between different compounds. Some compounds undergo the process of reduction, and some go through oxidation. The result of these processes is a set of compounds with different colors arranged to record images on film. Because electrons move around in so many reactions, the study of these movements has become an important part of chemistry.

15–1 Oxidation: Loss of Electrons

The general name **oxidation-reduction reactions** is given to reactions in which electrons move between atoms. The shortened form of this name is **redox reactions.** Many redox reactions have already been presented. The formation of magnesium oxide as

15-1 A bitten apple oxidizes when exposed to air.

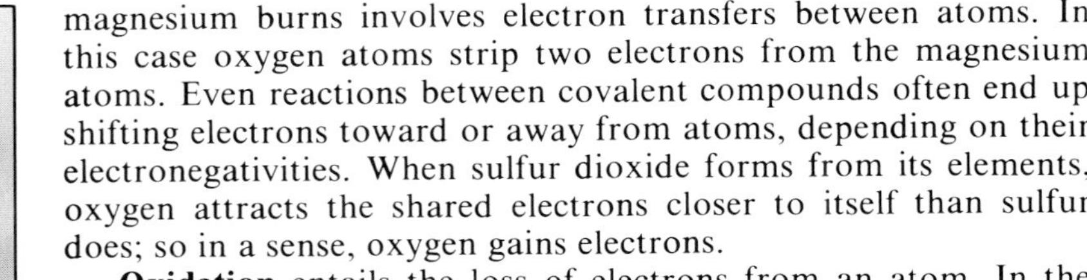

magnesium burns involves electron transfers between atoms. In this case oxygen atoms strip two electrons from the magnesium atoms. Even reactions between covalent compounds often end up shifting electrons toward or away from atoms, depending on their electronegativities. When sulfur dioxide forms from its elements, oxygen attracts the shared electrons closer to itself than sulfur does; so in a sense, oxygen gains electrons.

Oxidation entails the loss of electrons from an atom. In the reaction between magnesium and oxygen, magnesium atoms are oxidized.

$$\text{Mg:} \longrightarrow \text{Mg}^{2+} + 2\,e^-$$

Because electrons with their negative charges are lost, the oxidation numbers of atoms that get oxidized always become more positive. The oxidation number of magnesium is 0 before it reacts and +2 after it reacts. The oxidation number of magnesium increased by two in this reaction because each atom of magnesium lost two electrons.

$$2\,\overset{0}{\text{Mg}} + \text{O}_2 \longrightarrow 2\,\overset{+2}{\text{Mg}}\text{O}$$

At this point, it may seem logical to assume that all oxidation reactions involve oxygen. While oxygen usually causes atoms to lose electrons because of its high electronegativity, other atoms can do the same. The reaction between sodium and chlorine provides a good example of an oxidation reaction that does not involve oxygen. Chlorine causes the sodium atoms to be oxidized.

$$2\,\overset{0}{\text{Na}} + \overset{0}{\text{Cl}_2} \longrightarrow 2\,\overset{+1}{\text{Na}^+} + 2\,\overset{-1}{\text{Cl}^-} \longrightarrow 2\,\overset{+1\ -1}{\text{NaCl}}$$

15–2 Reduction: Gain of Electrons

15-2 Silver ingots to be used in photographic film. Silver ions are mixed into an emulsion that holds them onto film and photographic prints **(inset).**

The electrons lost by atoms in oxidation reactions must go somewhere. They are gained by other atoms. An atom that gains electrons in a reaction is said to be reduced, and the process of gaining electrons is called **reduction.** In the reaction between magnesium and oxygen, each oxygen atom is reduced because it gains two electrons. Reduction causes oxidation numbers to become smaller as more negative charges join atoms. The oxidation number of oxygen reduces from 0 to -2.

Black-and-white photography is based on the reduction of silver from Ag^+ to Ag. Photographic film contains grains of a silver halide such as silver bromide. When exposed to light, silver ions in the silver bromide grains are sensitized. These sensitized ions are more prone to be reduced during the developing process than those in areas not struck by light. The film is developed in a solution containing substances that cause the sensitized silver ions to gain electrons.

$$\overset{+1}{\text{Ag}^+} + \text{electron} \longrightarrow \overset{0}{\text{Ag}}$$

The silver appears as black areas on the developed film. This stage of development produces a negative on which light objects in the scene being photographed appear dark. Conversely, dark objects in the scene appear light on the negative. The film is subjected to a fixing procedure that prevents further blackening. To produce a positive, or print, that looks like the scene that was photographed, a light is shined through the negative to produce an image on paper treated with a silver halide. The paper is then developed with the same procedure used on the film. Although color photography is a shade more difficult to explain, it also is based on reduction processes.

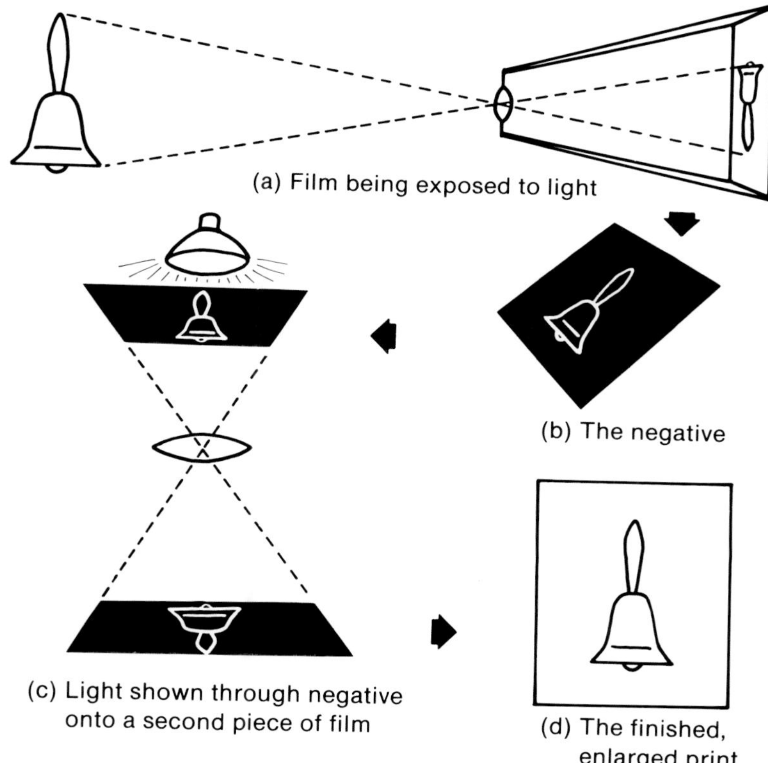
(a) Film being exposed to light
(b) The negative
(c) Light shown through negative
onto a second piece of film
(d) The finished,
enlarged print

15-3 Production of a photographic print.

Is the reaction that forms magnesium oxide a reduction process? Is it an oxidation process? Actually, it is both. Oxygen atoms gain electrons and are reduced. But the magnesium atoms lose electrons and are oxidized. Oxidation and reduction always occur simultaneously. As electrons leave one atom, they must join another. As they shift away from one atom, they must migrate toward another.

15-4 Chemists have devised the phrase "LEO the lion says GER" to help keep definitions of oxidation and reduction straight. LEO stands for "Loss of Electrons is Oxidation," and GER stands for "Gain of Electrons is Reduction."

15–3 Identifying Redox Reactions: Oxidation Numbers Are the Key

The only reactions that qualify as redox reactions are those in which oxidation numbers of atoms change. The absence of changes indicates that neither oxidation nor reduction has occurred.

Sample Problem. Are either of the following reactions redox reactions?

a. $HCl + H_2O \rightleftharpoons H_3O^+ + Cl^-$

b. $2\ KClO_3 \longrightarrow 2\ KCl + 3O_2$

Solution.

a. After assigning oxidation numbers to each atom, you can see that the oxidation numbers of all the atoms remain the same before and after the reaction. The reaction is not a redox reaction.

$$\overset{+1\ -1}{HCl} + \overset{+1\ -2}{H_2O} \rightleftharpoons \overset{+1\ -2}{H_3O^+} + \overset{-1}{Cl^-}$$

b. A determination of the oxidation numbers before and after the reaction shows that both oxygen and chlorine atoms change their numbers. This reaction involves oxidation and reduction.

$$2\ \overset{+1\ +5\ -2}{KClO_3} \longrightarrow 2\ \overset{+1\ -1}{KCl} + 3\ \overset{0}{O_2}$$

15–4 Oxidizing and Reducing Agents

A **reducing agent** is a substance that causes something else to be reduced. Recall that the development steps in photography involve the use of one or more reducing agents. They caused silver ions to be reduced to silver atoms. Because reduction cannot occur without oxidation, reducing agents contain atoms that donate electrons. Because magnesium donates electrons, it is a reducing agent in the reaction between magnesium and oxygen.

$$2\ Mg + O_2 \longrightarrow 2\ MgO$$

Remember that oxidation and reduction always occur simultaneously. If magnesium acts as a reducing agent, it donates electrons. If magnesium loses electrons, it is oxidized (Loss of Electrons is Oxidation). Reducing agents are *always* oxidized in redox reactions. There are no exceptions.

Oxidizing agents are substances that cause other atoms to be oxidized. Many oxidizing agents are commonly used as cleaners and disinfectants. Chlorine, for instance, is an oxidizing agent

FACETS OF CHEMISTRY

The Early Atmosphere

Scripture reveals that during the six-day Creation period the world was fully prepared for man's use. The atmosphere was formed on the second day in preparation for the plants that appeared on the third day. Animals and man were then created on the fifth and sixth days. At the end of the sixth day God viewed everything He had made and pronounced it "very good," implying a state of completeness. From this statement man can deduce that the earth's earliest atmosphere contained oxygen. However, the evolutionists have a different idea about how things originated.

Several decades ago evolutionists became aware of a serious problem in their imagined development of life. They could not explain why oxygen in the early atmosphere did not oxidize the first sugars and amino acids into carbon dioxide as soon as they formed. Serious rethinking of the entire hypothetical process became necessary. A.I. Oparin, a Russian biochemist, suggested that the earth's atmosphere was at one time without oxygen. This idea was a radical change from earlier thinking, but other evolutionists accepted it and began to use it. Oparin proposed that the earth's original atmosphere consisted of methane, ammonia, hydrogen, and water vapor. This is called a reducing atmosphere, in contrast to the present oxidizing atmosphere. The early reducing atmosphere supposedly existed millions of years ago but then was replaced by the present atmosphere.

What observations support the idea of an early reducing atmosphere? Evidence about the early atmosphere of the earth exists, but it shows an oxidizing atmosphere. Rocks that evolutionists claim to be ancient contain large amounts of calcium carbonate ($CaCO_3$)

and iron oxide (Fe_2O_3). These compounds could have formed only if large amounts of oxygen were present.

Two other problems face the idea of a reducing atmosphere. The first is that ultraviolet radiation from the sun would have decomposed ammonia long before the envisioned life-forming reactions could have taken place. The second problem is that the build-up of oxygen could never have taken place short of a miracle, and evolutionary theorists do not tolerate miracles, even as a last resort. Two general approaches have been used in an effort to explain the build-up of oxygen in the atmosphere; both miss the mark. The first holds that plants formed the oxygen by photosynthesis. It is unrealistic to think that plants could have appeared before the oxygen, but assuming that they could, another difficulty would arise. Photosynthesis produces not only oxygen but also organic matter. When the organic matter decayed, the oxygen would have gotten used up again.

The second idea that has been used to explain the oxygen build-up is that steam from volcanoes was decomposed to hydrogen and oxygen by ultraviolet energy from the sun. The hydrogen then presumably escaped into space, leaving the oxygen behind. However, this scheme could not have worked unless the early sun had several hundred times its present ultraviolet output. The idea is obviously based more on wishful thinking than it is on solid science.

Evolutionists have had free reign in contriving theories of earth history. Since these theories have been known to change with the whims of the times, it is possible that the reducing atmosphere may not be a permanent feature of evolutionary theory. Efforts will be made to patch it up for a time, but if it is finally deemed hopeless, it will be replaced by something else.

Stanley Miller produced amino acids by subjecting a reducing atmosphere to electrical shocks. Oxygen gas must be removed for this experiment to work.

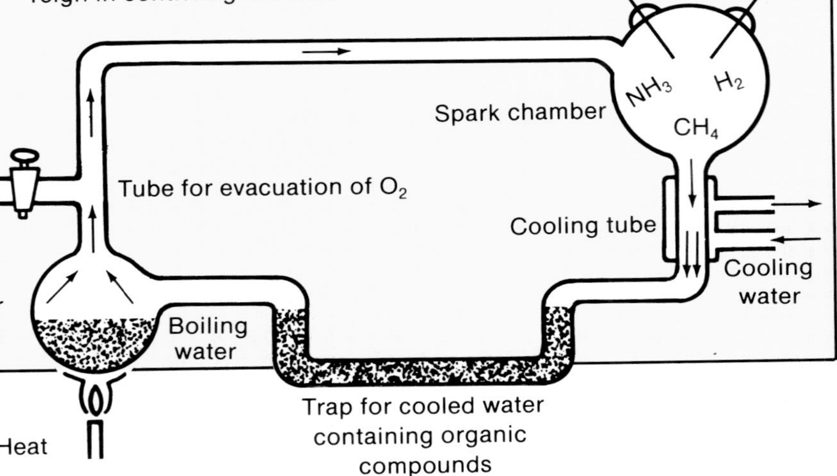

frequently added to swimming pools to kill bacteria, algae, and fungi. Chlorine acts as an oxidizing agent by taking electrons from these little creatures. In the process, chlorine atoms are reduced to chloride ions.

$$Cl_2 + 2\,e^- \longrightarrow 2\,Cl^-$$

Because chlorine gains electrons in this reaction, it is reduced (Gain of Electrons is Reduction). Oxidizing agents are *always* reduced in redox reactions.

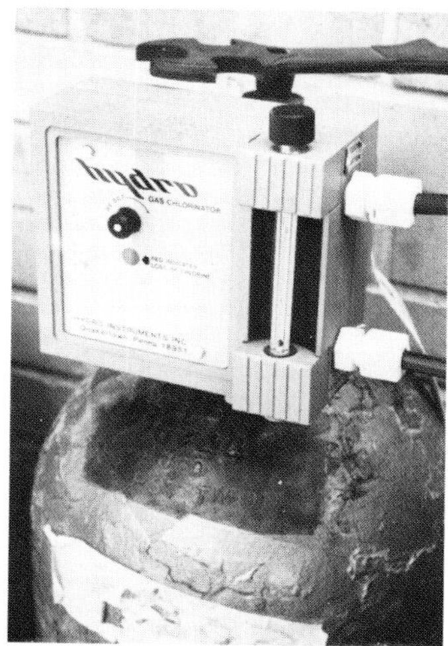

15-5 Equipment that adds chlorine gas to swimming-pool water.

Sample Problem. Tell which substances in the following reaction are reducing agents and which are oxidizing agents.

$$2\,Na + 2\,H_2O \longrightarrow 2\,NaOH + H_2$$

Solution.

The oxidation number of sodium goes from 0 in sodium to +1 in sodium hydroxide. The oxidation number of hydrogen goes from +1 in water to 0 in hydrogen gas. Sodium was oxidized, and hydrogen was reduced. The hydrogen in water, therefore, is acting as an oxidizing agent, and sodium is acting as a reducing agent.

Household bleach is an aqueous solution of sodium hypochlorite (NaOCl). Sodium hypochlorite is an effective oxidizing agent. It is reduced in redox reactions according to the following equation.

$$NaOCl + H_2O + 2\,e^- \longrightarrow NaCl + 2\,OH^-$$

Bleach is normally used to eliminate stains and make dirty white clothes clean and white again. The molecules in stains possess electrons that can move around easily. These molecules are colored because they absorb visible light energy that hits them and energizes their electrons. When a dirty article of clothing is bleached, the sodium hypochlorite in the bleach grabs the easily moved electrons from the molecules in the stains. When these electrons are removed, the molecules no longer absorb visible light. Consequently, the color disappears and the cloth is nice and white. In effect, bleach does not remove stains, it merely decolorizes them. Because sodium hypochlorite can also oxidize hair and stained dentures, it is found in commercial products used for these purposes.

15-6 NaOCl decolorizes cloth.

15–5 Balancing Redox Reactions: The Half-Reaction Method

Balanced chemical equations accurately describe the quantities of reactants and products in chemical reactions. They serve as the basis of stoichiometry by showing how atoms and mass are conserved during reactions. Oxidation and reduction reactions need to be balanced just as all other reactions do, but they are often quite complicated. Balancing redox reactions involves balancing not only atoms but also positive and negative charges. Balancing either the atoms or the charges is not hard, but the process becomes difficult when both must be balanced simultaneously. Chemists have developed a way to balance redox reactions in organized and straightforward procedures.

Redox reactions that are difficult to balance can be managed more easily if the processes of oxidation and reduction are considered separately before they are considered together. In the **half-reaction method,** the redox reaction is split into two hypothetical parts called **half-reactions.** The oxidation half-reaction deals with all the substances that become oxidized and all the electrons they lose. The reduction half-reaction involves substances that become reduced and all the electrons they gain.

The half-reaction method consists of seven steps that help balance reactions in an organized fashion. This method can reduce the task of balancing even complicated reactions such as the one between nitric acid and copper oxide to a series of manageable procedures.

$$HNO_3 + Cu_2O \longrightarrow Cu(NO_3)_2 + NO + H_2O$$

Step 1. Assign oxidation numbers to all atoms, and determine which atoms are oxidized and which ones are reduced. Since the oxidation numbers of hydrogen and oxygen remain unchanged unless a metal hydride or a peroxide forms, ignore them for now and focus on the other atoms. The oxidation number of nitrogen changes from +5 in nitric acid to +2 in nitrogen(II) oxide; so nitrogen is reduced. The oxidation number of copper changes from +1 in copper(I) oxide to +2 in copper nitrate; so copper is oxidized.

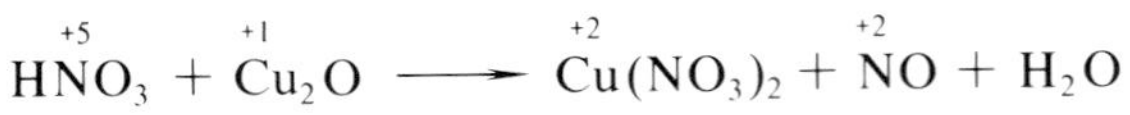

$$H\overset{+5}{N}O_3 + \overset{+1}{Cu}_2O \longrightarrow \overset{+2}{Cu}(NO_3)_2 + \overset{+2}{N}O + H_2O$$

15-7 Electrical energy is involved in many chemical reactions. Lightning can cause oxygen (O_2) to form ozone (O_3).

Step 2. Write one half-reaction for the oxidation process and one for the reduction process. The oxidation half-reaction includes only those substances containing the atom that is oxidized. Since the oxidation number of copper went from +1 to +2, it was oxidized. All the compounds with copper atoms in them should be included in the oxidation half-reaction. Balance the atoms being oxidized in the half-reaction.

$$Cu_2O \longrightarrow \mathbf{2}\ Cu(NO_3)_2$$

The reduction half-reaction includes only those substances containing the atoms that are reduced. Even though copper nitrate contains nitrogen, it is not included in the reduction half-reaction because the nitrogen in copper nitrate is not reduced.

$$HNO_3 \longrightarrow NO$$

Step 3. Balance all other atoms by inspection. Most redox reactions (at least all the ones that will be considered in this text) take place in acidic solutions where there is an unlimited supply of hydrogen ions and water molecules. When needed, these particles can be added to one side of the equation or the other. Since the oxidation half-reaction has some NO_3 groups in the products, some nitric acid can be added to the reactants to balance the nitrogens.

$$\mathbf{4}\ HNO_3 + Cu_2O \longrightarrow 2\ Cu(NO_3)_2$$

The extra oxygen can be balanced by the addition of one water molecule to the right-hand side. The extra hydrogens can be balanced by the addition of two hydrogen ions to the right-hand side.

$$4\ HNO_3 + Cu_2O \longrightarrow 2\ Cu(NO_3)_2 + \mathbf{H_2O} + \mathbf{2\ H^+}$$

The balancing of the reduction half-reaction involves balancing the hydrogen and the oxygen atoms.

$$HNO_3 + \mathbf{3\ H^+} \longrightarrow NO + \mathbf{2\ H_2O}$$

Step 4. Balance the charges in each half-reaction by adding electrons until the total charge is the same on both sides. In this reaction the left side of the reduction half-reaction has three positive charges, and the right side has no charge. Make the left side match the right side by adding electrons.

$$HNO_3 + 3\ H^+ + \mathbf{3\ e^-} \longrightarrow NO + 2\ H_2O$$

Match the right side of the oxidation half-reaction to the neutral charge of the left side by adding electrons. Both sides of the oxidation half-reaction should now have identical charges.

$$4\ HNO_3 + Cu_2O \longrightarrow 2\ Cu(NO_3)_2 + H_2O + 2\ H^+ + \mathbf{2\ e^-}$$

Step 5. Multiply each half-reaction by an appropriate whole number so that the number of electrons produced by the oxidation half-reaction equals the number used by the reduction half-reaction. In this case, multiply all the coefficients in the oxidation half-reaction by three.

$$\mathbf{12}\ HNO_3 + \mathbf{3}\ Cu_2O \longrightarrow \mathbf{6}\ Cu(NO_3)_2 + \mathbf{3}\ H_2O + \mathbf{6}\ H^+ + \mathbf{6}\ e^-$$

To make both half-reactions show the same number of electrons, multiply all the quantities in the reduction half-reaction by two.

$$\mathbf{2}\ HNO_3 + \mathbf{6}\ H^+ + \mathbf{6}\ e^- \longrightarrow \mathbf{2}\ NO + \mathbf{4}\ H_2O$$

Step 6. Add the oxidation and reduction half-reactions together. Add the reactants from both reactions together and put the result on the left-hand side. The products from both half-reactions are then summed up and put on the right-hand side.

$$12\ HNO_3 + 3\ Cu_2O \longrightarrow 6\ Cu(NO_3)_2 + 3\ H_2O + 6\ H^+ + 6\ e^-$$

$$+\quad 2\ HNO_3 + 6\ H^+ + 6\ e^- \longrightarrow 2\ NO + 4\ H_2O$$

$$14\ HNO_3 + 3\ Cu_2O + 6\ H^+ + 6\ e^- \longrightarrow 6\ Cu(NO_3)_2 + 2\ NO + 7\ H_2O + 6\ H^+ + 6\ e^-$$

Step 7. Cancel any quantities that appear on both sides of the overall reaction. Extra electrons, hydrogen ions, and water molecules will usually be present after the two half-reactions are added together. Since there are six hydrogen ions and six electrons on both sides, they cancel out.

$$14\ HNO_3 + 3\ Cu_2O \longrightarrow 6\ Cu(NO_3)_2 + 2\ NO + 7\ H_2O$$

The reaction is balanced. The result is the same as the one that would have been obtained by the old balance-by-inspection method, but the extra steps help to keep you on the right track through all the necessary changes. Balancing redox reactions may seem difficult at first, but do not despair; practice makes perfect.

Sample Problem. Sulfite ions and permanganate ions can react to form sulfate ions and manganese ions. Balance this reaction, using the half-reaction method.

$$SO_3^{2-} + MnO_4^- \longrightarrow SO_4^{2-} + Mn^{2+}$$

Solution.

Step 1. Assign oxidation numbers.

$$\overset{+4}{S}O_3^{2-} + \overset{+7}{Mn}O_4^- \longrightarrow \overset{+6}{S}O_4^{2-} + \overset{+2}{Mn}{}^{2+}$$

Step 2. Identify half-reactions.

Oxidation half-reaction:

$$SO_3^{2-} \longrightarrow SO_4^{2-}$$

Reduction half-reaction:

$$MnO_4^- \longrightarrow Mn^{2+}$$

Step 3. Balance all atoms.

Oxidation half-reaction:

$$SO_3^{2-} + H_2O \longrightarrow SO_4^{2-} + 2\ H^+$$

Reduction half-reaction:

$$MnO_4^- + 8\ H^+ \longrightarrow Mn^{2+} + 4\ H_2O$$

Step 4. Balance charges in each half-reaction. The -2 charge on the left side of the oxidation half-reaction should be matched by a -2 on the right side.

Oxidation half-reaction:

$$SO_3^{2-} + H_2O \longrightarrow SO_4^{2-} + 2\ H^+ + 2\ e^-$$

The right side of the reduction half-reaction has a +2 charge; so the total charge on the left side should also be +2.

Reduction half-reaction:

$$MnO_4^- + 8\ H^+ + 5\ e^- \longrightarrow Mn^{2+} + 4\ H_2O$$

Step 5. Multiply coefficients. In this case the oxidation half-reaction should be multiplied by five, and the reduction half-reaction by two.

Oxidation half-reaction:

$$5\ SO_3^{2-} + 5\ H_2O \longrightarrow 5\ SO_4^{2-} + 10\ H^+ + 10\ e^-$$

Reduction half-reaction:

$$2\ MnO_4^- + 16\ H^+ + 10\ e^- \longrightarrow 2\ Mn^{2+} + 8\ H_2O$$

Step 6. Add the half-reactions.

$$5\ SO_3^{2-} + 5\ H_2O \longrightarrow 5\ SO_4^{2-} + 10\ H^+ + 10\ e^-$$

$$+\ 2\ MnO_4^- + 16\ H^+ + 10\ e^- \longrightarrow 2\ Mn^{2+} + 8\ H_2O$$

$$5\ SO_3^{2-} + 2\ MnO_4^- + 5\ H_2O + 16\ H^+ + 10\ e^- \longrightarrow 5\ SO_4^{2-} + 2\ Mn^{2+} + 8\ H_2O + 10\ H^+ + 10\ e^-$$

Step 7. Cancel. All electrons, ten hydrogen ions, and five water molecules cancel from both sides.

$$5\ SO_3^{2-} + 2\ MnO_4^- + 6\ H^+ \longrightarrow 5\ SO_4^{2-} + 2\ Mn^{2+} + 3\ H_2O$$

15–6 Redox Titrations: Finding Unknown Concentrations

A titration is an experiment in which chemists react a solution of known concentration with a solution of unknown concentration in order to determine the unknown concentration. A redox titration is a titration in which one of the reacting substances is an oxidizing agent and the other is a reducing agent. As with acid-base titrations, the concentrations and volumes of the two reacting substances are related to each other by the equation

$$V_u \times N_u = V_k \times N_k$$

The concentrations are measured in normality (the number of equivalents per liter of solution). In the context of redox chemistry, an equivalent is defined as the number of moles of the substance that either loses or gains 1 mole of electrons in a balanced half-reaction. The gram-equivalent mass is simply the mass in grams of 1 equivalent of the substance.

Sample Problem. Calculate the gram-equivalent masses of copper(I) oxide and nitric acid in the following reaction.

$$14\ HNO_3 + 3\ Cu_2O \longrightarrow 6\ Cu(NO_3)_2 + 2\ NO + 7\ H_2O$$

The gram-formula mass of copper(I) oxide is 143.1 grams per mole, and that of nitric acid is 63.02 grams per mole.

Solution.

The balanced half-reactions for this redox reaction have been determined earlier in the chapter.

$$3\ Cu_2O + 12\ HNO_3 \longrightarrow 6\ Cu(NO_3)_2 + 3\ H_2O + 6\ H^+ + 6\ e^-$$

$$2\ HNO_3 + 6\ H^+ + 6\ e^- \longrightarrow 2\ NO + 4\ H_2O$$

In the oxidation half-reaction, 3 moles of copper(I) oxide produce 6 moles of electrons (a 1:2 ratio). There are thus 2 equivalents in 1 mole of copper(I) oxide in this reaction.

$$\frac{143.1\ \text{g}}{\text{mole}} \times \frac{1\ \text{mole}}{2\ \text{eq}} = \frac{71.55\ \text{g}\ Cu_2O}{\text{eq}}$$

In this reaction each mole of nitric acid reacts with 3 moles of electrons. Thus there are 3 equivalents in 1 mole of nitric acid.

$$\frac{63.02\ \text{g}}{\text{mole}} \times \frac{1\ \text{mole}}{3\ \text{eq}} = \frac{21.01\ \text{g}\ HNO_3}{\text{eq}}$$

The calculations involved in redox titrations follow the same patterns as those for acid-base titrations. The equation $V_u \times N_u = V_k \times N_k$ is used in both cases. Remember that the calculations of normalities use gram-equivalent masses calculated in terms of electrons.

Sample Problem. One liter of a solution contains 4.74 grams of potassium permanganate ($KMnO_4$). If 0.030 liter of this solution titrates 0.032 liter of a sodium sulfite (Na_2SO_3) solution, what is the normality of the sodium sulfite solution? The reaction in the titration is

$$5\ SO_3^{2-} + MnO_4^- + 6\ H^+ \longrightarrow 5\ SO_4^{2-} + 2\ Mn^{2+} + 3\ H_2O$$

Solution.

Before you can use the relationship $V_u \times N_u = V_k \times N_k$ to find the normality of the sodium sulfite solution, you must calculate the normality of the potassium permanganate solution. Before you calculate the normality, you must know the gram-equivalent mass for potassium permanganate in this particular half-reaction. The balanced half-reaction that includes the permanganate (MnO_4^-) ion was previously determined in section 15—5.

$$2\ MnO_4^- + 16\ H^+ + 10\ e^- \longrightarrow 2\ Mn^{2+} + 8\ H_2O$$

In this reaction the permanganate ion has 5 equivalents per mole. Since each potassium permanganate formula unit contains one permanganate ion, potassium permanganate also has 5 equivalents per mole. The gram-equivalent mass of potassium permanganate can now be calculated.

$$\frac{158.04\ g}{mole} \times \frac{1\ mole}{5\ eq} = \frac{31.61\ g}{eq}$$

The normality of the potassium permanganate is

$$\frac{4.74\ g}{\ell} \times \frac{1\ eq}{31.61\ g} = 0.150\ N$$

You can calculate the normality of sodium sulfite by plugging the given volumes and the normality of the potassium permanganate into the standard equation.

$V_u = 0.032\ \ell$ $\qquad N_u = x$

$V_k = 0.030\ \ell$ $\qquad N_k = 0.150\ N$

$$V_u \times N_u = V_k \times N_k$$

$$N_u = \frac{(V_k)(N_k)}{V_u} = \frac{(0.030\ \ell)(0.150\ N)}{0.032\ \ell} = 0.141\ N\ Na_2SO_3$$

15-8 Purple $KMnO_4$ reacts with clear Na_2SO_3. When all the Na_2SO_3 reacts, the solution in the Erlenmeyer flask will remain colored.

Electrochemical Reactions

Electrochemistry deals with redox reactions that are manipulated to either produce or consume electricity. It includes the operation of batteries, the electroplating of metal objects, and the liberation of useful elements from their stable compounds.

15–7 Electrochemical Cells: Wires, Electrodes, and Electrolytes

Metals can conduct electricity because metallic bonds allow electrons to move freely throughout a piece of metal. Some solutions can conduct electricity, but not for the same reason. Water can conduct electricity only when some ionic substance is dissolved in it. An **electrolyte** is any substance that, when dissolved in water, allows the resulting solution to conduct electricity. When an electrolyte is dissolved in water, anions (negative ions) and cations (positive ions) are formed. The ions move freely in the solution and therefore may carry charge. Solutions of strong electrolytes conduct electricity well. Most salts, strong acids, and strong bases fill the list of strong electrolytes (NaCl, HCl, H_2SO_4, HNO_3, and NaOH). Substances that do not ionize completely, such as weak acids, weak bases, and hard-to-dissolve salts, classify as weak electrolytes. Solutions of weak electrolytes conduct electricity but not as well as solutions of strong electrolytes. Nonionic substances such as sugar, alcohol, and oxygen might dissolve in water, but they cannot conduct electricity. For this reason, such substances are called **nonelectrolytes.**

All electrochemical techniques rely on combinations of metals and solutions that conduct electricity. In order to be useful in a variety of ways, however, these substances must be put together in just the right way. The fundamental apparatus used in

15-9 Solutions of a strong electrolyte (HCl), a weak electrolyte (acetic acid), and a nonelectrolyte (sugar) have different electrical conducting properties.

electrochemistry is the electrochemical cell. An **electrochemical cell** consists of two electrical contacts, called **electrodes,** immersed in an electrolyte solution with a wire joining the electrodes. The electrodes are nothing more than metal rods or wires. They are commonly made of metals such as zinc, platinum, or copper.

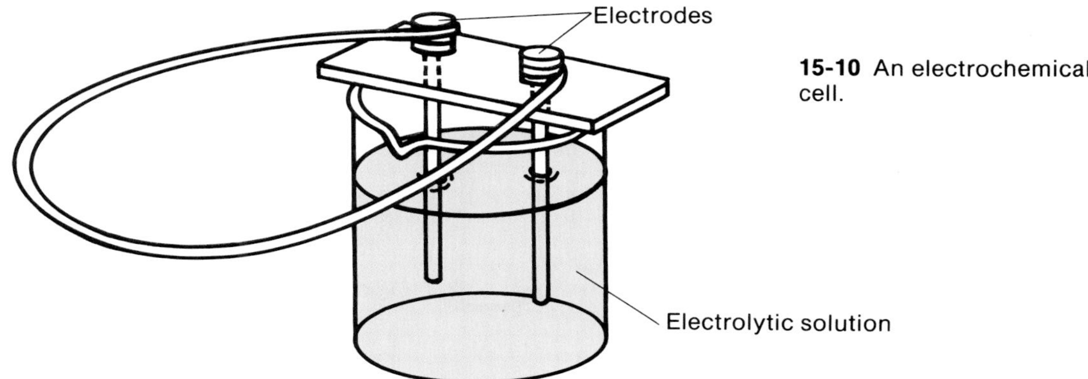

15-10 An electrochemical cell.

15–8 Electrolysis: Using Electricity in Reactions

Electrolysis is the process of forcing an otherwise non-spontaneous redox reaction to occur with the aid of an electrical current in an electrochemical cell. Normally, stable water molecules can be pulled apart by an electrical current to produce hydrogen and oxygen gases. Current can be passed through an electrolytic cell when a source of electricity is hooked to two electrodes immersed in water. When an electrochemical cell is used to split compounds, it is called an **electrolytic cell.**

What happens when electrons flow through the cell? First, the battery attempts to push electrons into the electrode called the **cathode,** giving it a negative charge. The electrons in the cathode become available for reduction reactions. The battery pulls electrons from the other electrode, which is called the **anode.** The lack of electrons in the anode gives it a positive charge and makes the anode the place where substances are oxidized. Since any anions in the solution are negatively charged, they migrate to the positively charged anode. Similarly, positively charged cations migrate to the negatively charged cathode. If the electrical forces between the two electrodes are large enough, electrons at the surface of the cathode will jump onto the particles surrounding the cathode; as a result, reduction occurs. On the other side the anode grabs electrons from the particles around it. Oxidation occurs here.

15-11 An electrolytic cell.

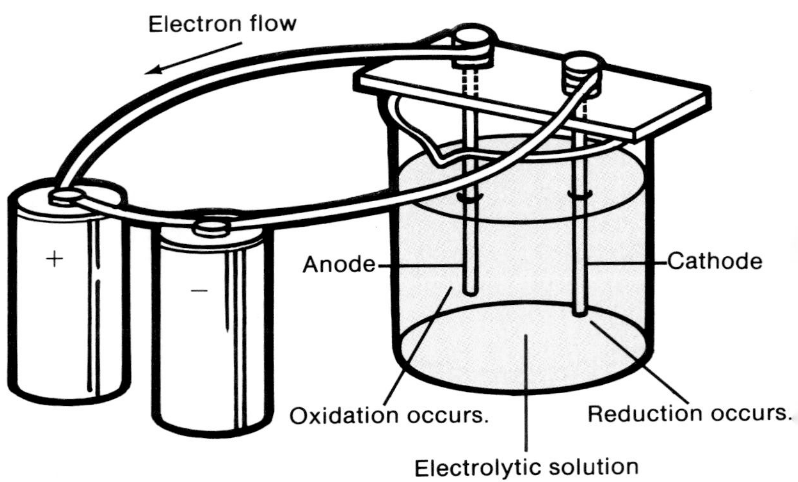

Chemical engineers use electrolysis to purify active metals. Metals such as copper, tin, and iron, which are low on the activity series, can be freed from their natural compounds by chemical means. Active metals such as sodium, lithium, and aluminum bond too strongly for those "mild" techniques to work, so engineers must separate the compounds in electrolytic cells. In nature aluminum atoms are oxidized by oxygen atoms in an ore commonly known as bauxite. To get pure aluminum metal from the very stable aluminum oxide (Al_2O_3), the natural oxidation reaction must be reversed—electrons must be forced back into the aluminum ions.

15-12 Electrolysis of aluminum.

The electrolysis process used to produce aluminum in industry is called the Hall-Héroult process. This process is named after Charles Hall and Paul Héroult, who developed the process independently in 1886. In the Hall-Héroult process, aluminum oxide is dissolved in molten cryolite and electrolyzed with carbon electrodes.

$$3\,C + 4\,Al^{3+} + 6\,O^{2-} \longrightarrow 4\,Al + 3\,CO_2$$

Electrolysis is also used to free sodium metal and chlorine gas from sodium chloride. A carbon anode and an iron cathode are used in this process. Sodium ions are reduced to metallic sodium at the cathode.

$$Na^+ + e^- \longrightarrow Na$$

At the anode chloride ions lose electrons, are oxidized, and produce gaseous chlorine.

$$2\,Cl^- \longrightarrow Cl_2 + 2\,e^-$$

The chlorine gas is vented to a storage container, and the sodium metal is removed and stored. Both products are used in various manufacturing processes. The entire apparatus used in this process is called a Downs cell, which is shown in Figure 15-13.

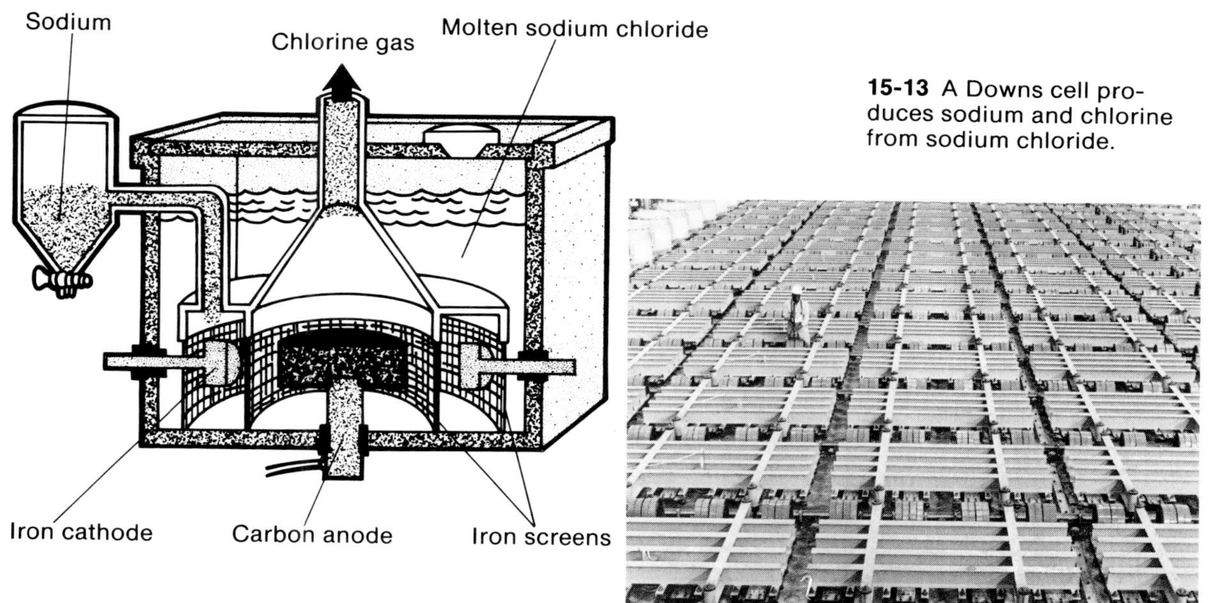

15-13 A Downs cell produces sodium and chlorine from sodium chloride.

15–9 Batteries: Getting Electricity from Reactions

Electrolytic cells force nonspontaneous redox reactions forward by driving them with electricity. **Batteries,** however, do the opposite and use spontaneous redox reactions to produce electricity. Batteries are collections of **voltaic cells,** which are simply two reactants positioned so that a reaction between them will transfer electrons. Voltaic cells were named after Alessandro Volta, the Italian gentleman who invented them around 1800.

All voltaic cells have a negative electrode and a positive electrode. The negative electrode collects electrons because it is connected to a substance that wants to give up electrons. The positive electrode lacks electrons because it is connected to a substance that desires to gain them. All voltaic cells contain an anode that loses electrons, a cathode that gains electrons, and some electrolyte between them.

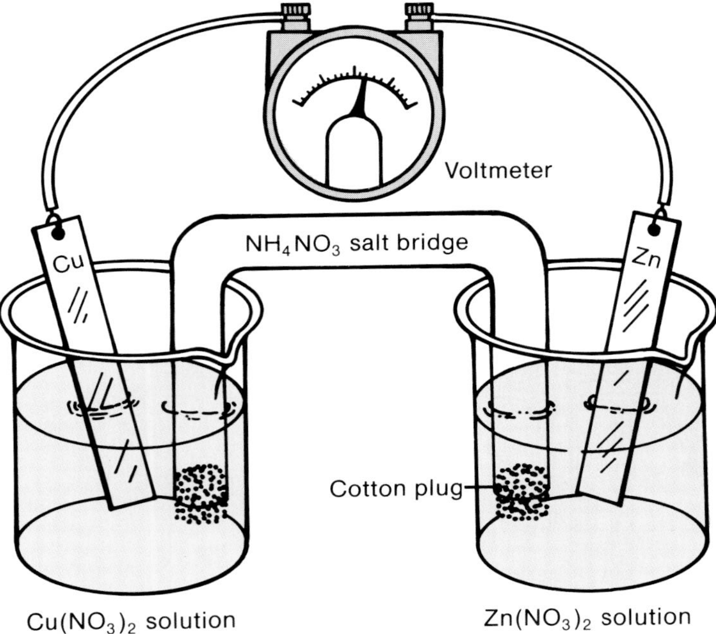

15-14 A voltaic cell.

Just as in electrolysis, an oxidation half-reaction occurs at the anode and a reduction half-reaction occurs at the cathode. In the cell diagramed in Figure 15-14, the reaction occurring at the anode is the oxidation of zinc.

$$Zn \longrightarrow Zn^{2+} + 2\,e^-$$

The electrons from the oxidation half-reaction travel along the wire to the cathode. At the cathode copper(II) is reduced to metallic copper by the electrons coming from the anode. The steady flow of electrons from the anode to the cathode can be harnessed to make a light bulb glow or to power a small radio.

$$Cu^{2+} + 2\,e^- \longrightarrow Cu$$

The salt bridge (shown in the diagram) does not generate electricity. The only thing it does is provide a way for ions to migrate between the two solutions. The solutions must be connected so that excess amounts of charge do not accumulate and stop the current from flowing. Current flows between the solutions in the form of migrating ions. As zinc is oxidized, excess zinc ions accumulate in the solution around the anode. Nitrate ions migrate from the salt bridge toward the concentration of positive charges and keep the solution close to neutral. As copper(II) is reduced to metallic copper at the cathode, positive charges are removed from the solution around the cathode. Ammonium (NH_4^+) ions migrate from the salt bridge into the solution and prevent an excess of negative charges from accumulating. Without the salt bridge, current would not flow. Furthermore, if the connection between the electrodes were to break, current would cease to flow.

A common type of battery is the dry cell. The diagram of a dry cell shown in Figure 15-15 shows that the cell consists of a zinc can filled with an electrolyte paste (made of MnO_2, $ZnCl_2$, NH_4Cl) and some binder that keeps it all together. The zinc can just inside the cardboard tube acts as the anode and loses electrons. Inserted into the electrolyte paste is a graphite (carbon) rod that acts as the cathode.

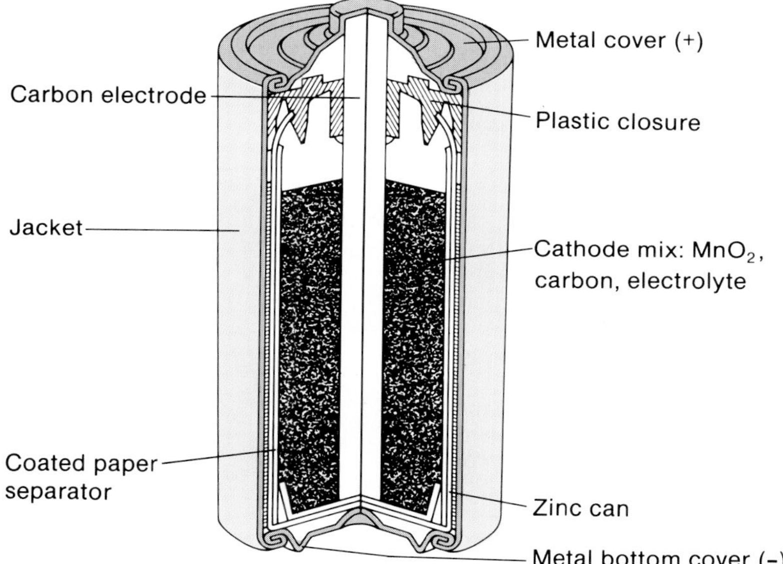

15-15 Dry cell battery.

Although the reactions occurring at these electrodes are complicated, they can be summarized as follows: the anode reaction is $Zn \longrightarrow Zn^{2+} + 2\,e^-$; the cathode reaction is $2\,NH_4^+ + 2\,MnO_2 + 2\,e^- \longrightarrow Mn_2O_3 + H_2O + 2\,NH_3$.

Automobiles get their starting power from a series of six lead storage cells linked together so that the voltages add to each other. The cathode of a lead storage cell consists of a series of lead-antimony alloy plates permeated with lead(IV) oxide (PbO_2). The anode is a series of lead-antimony alloy plates filled with spongy lead. The cathode and anode are immersed in sulfuric acid. The oxidation half-reaction is $Pb + SO_4^{2-} \longrightarrow PbSO_4 + 2\,e^-$. The reduction half-reaction is $PbO_2 + 4\,H^+ + SO_4^{2-} + 2\,e^- \longrightarrow PbSO_4 + 2\,H_2O$.

15-16 A series of batteries could be used to power automobiles.

As strange as it seems, lead atoms are oxidized on one plate and reduced on another. Lead is oxidized to Pb^{2+} at the anode, and Pb^{4+} is reduced to Pb^{2+} at the cathode.

FACETS OF CHEMISTRY

The Battle Against Corrosion

Corrosion is a general term applied to the chemical destruction of a metal by its immediate surroundings. In order for iron to rust, it must be in contact with both air and moisture. Dry air alone will not corrode iron, nor will pure water that is free of dissolved oxygen. Rusting is also aided by impurities (such as carbon) in the iron, impurities (such as acids or other electrolytes) in the water, heat, physical strains in the metal, and the presence of a metal that is less active than iron. As a general rule, when two metals are in contact with each other, the more active metal undergoes corrosion while the less active is protected.

In spite of man's advanced knowledge of chemistry, losses by corrosion in the United States alone run into billions of dollars annually. Iron may be safeguarded from corrosion by being connected electrically to a metal such as zinc or magnesium. The more active metal in such an arrangement is called the sacrificial anode. The Alaskan oil pipeline is a large-diameter iron pipe that is protected by heavy zinc wires. Ships having exposed metal surfaces underwater are similarly protected from the corrosive action of seawater by zinc anodes.

Another strategy used to discourage corrosion is the alloying of iron with other metals. Stainless steel, an alloy noted for its resistance to rust and tarnish, is a mixture of iron and chromium. Finally, there are several materials that can be used to coat iron to protect it against corrosion. The well-known "tin can" is actually an iron can coated with tin. Galvanized iron is iron coated with zinc. It is used for such items as trash cans and chain-link fences. Paints, lacquers, and varnishes are also used to protect the surfaces of iron and steel. Paints containing red lead or zinc chromate are especially effective for preventing corrosion.

Mercury batteries, alkaline batteries, and nickel-cadmium batteries are common on shelves in stores. These batteries are based on redox reactions that are different from the one just studied.

To recharge a battery such as a lead storage battery, current is made to flow from the cathode to the anode. This reverses the redox reaction and regenerates the cell. Some cells cannot be recharged, because their redox reactions are irreversible. Mercury batteries and dry cells cannot be recharged. Alkaline batteries, lead

Chemical alteration of the surface of iron can also form a protective coating. When red-hot iron is treated with steam, a thin coating of black iron oxide (Fe_3O_4) is formed. The black color of stovepipes results from this process. The iron oxide coating affords good protection to the metal even at high temperatures.

The battle against corrosion is a never-ending one. Corrosion is a relentless degenerative process. Many theologians think that it is a consequence of the curse that was placed on the earth after man first sinned. Others hold the view that corrosion is a necessary result of the way the laws of nature were established from Creation. Whichever the case, a study of corrosion should serve to illustrate the futility of putting faith in the material objects of this world. The sight of rust should remind men of the Lord's admonition in Matthew 6:19-20: "Lay not up for yourselves treasures upon earth, where moth and rust doth corrupt, and where thieves break through and steal: But lay up for yourselves treasures in heaven, where neither moth nor rust doth corrupt, and where thieves do not break through nor steal."

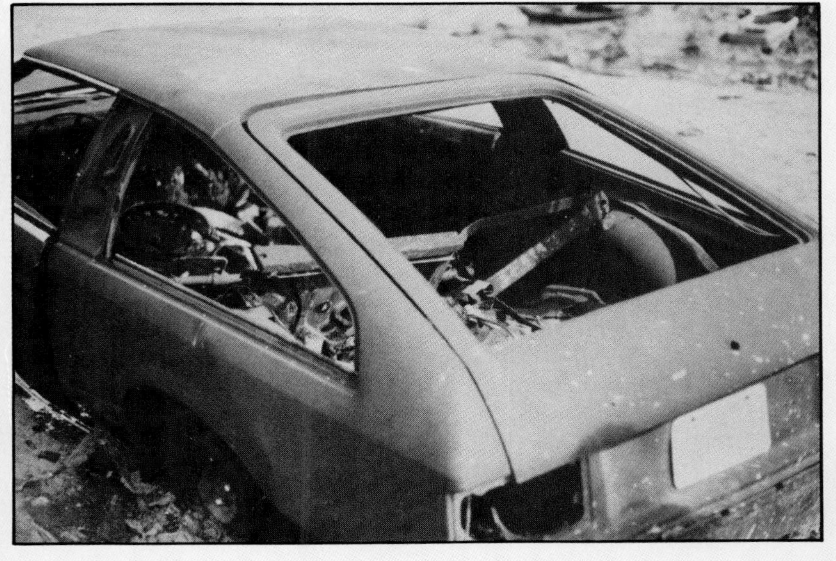

storage cells, and nickel-cadmium batteries are rechargeable. Some manufacturers put a label on their alkaline batteries to warn the customers against recharging the batteries. They do not mean that alkaline batteries *cannot* be recharged; they mean that they *should not* be recharged, because to do so would be dangerous. Even though the redox reaction in an alkaline cell is reversible, recharging produces some gases. Since some alkaline cells have no vents to release gases, they could explode if someone tried to recharge them.

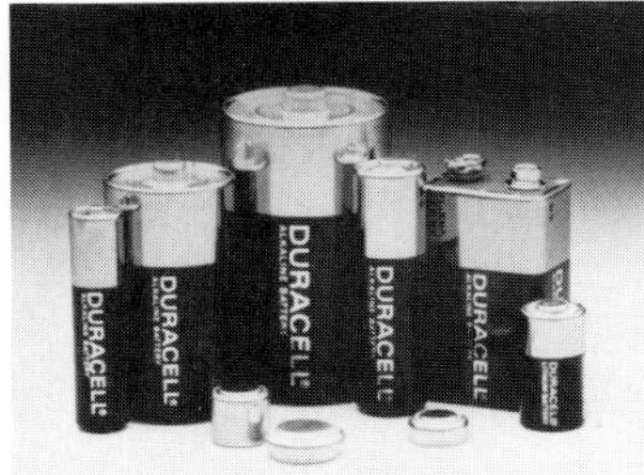

15-17 Different combinations of electrodes and electrolytic pastes result in a wide variety of batteries.

15–10 Electroplating: A Cover-up

Sterling silver is at least 92.5 per cent silver. Less expensive silverware is made of some common metal that is plated with a thin layer of silver. How is the thin silver layer deposited onto the inexpensive metal? One could pound, melt, or glue the silver onto the metal, but there is a much better way. Metallic ions in solution can be forced to cling to metal knives and forks. The electrochemical process of depositing one metal onto another is called **electroplating.**

Electroplating is a type of electrolysis. The cathode consists of the metal item, such as a knife, to be plated. The anode is made out of the metal that is to be plated onto the cathode. Silver plating is performed with a silver anode. The electrolyte solution contains silver ions. When the current in the cell is turned on, silver ions migrate to the cathode and are reduced to metallic silver. The silver plates onto the knife.

$$Ag^{+} \longrightarrow Ag$$

15-18 A technician electropolishing a plutonium-contaminated part from a nuclear reactor. The contaminated piece, immersed in phosphoric acid, acts as the anode. An electric current causes the surface of the piece to dissolve. After the process, the part has a smooth surface that resists recontamination.

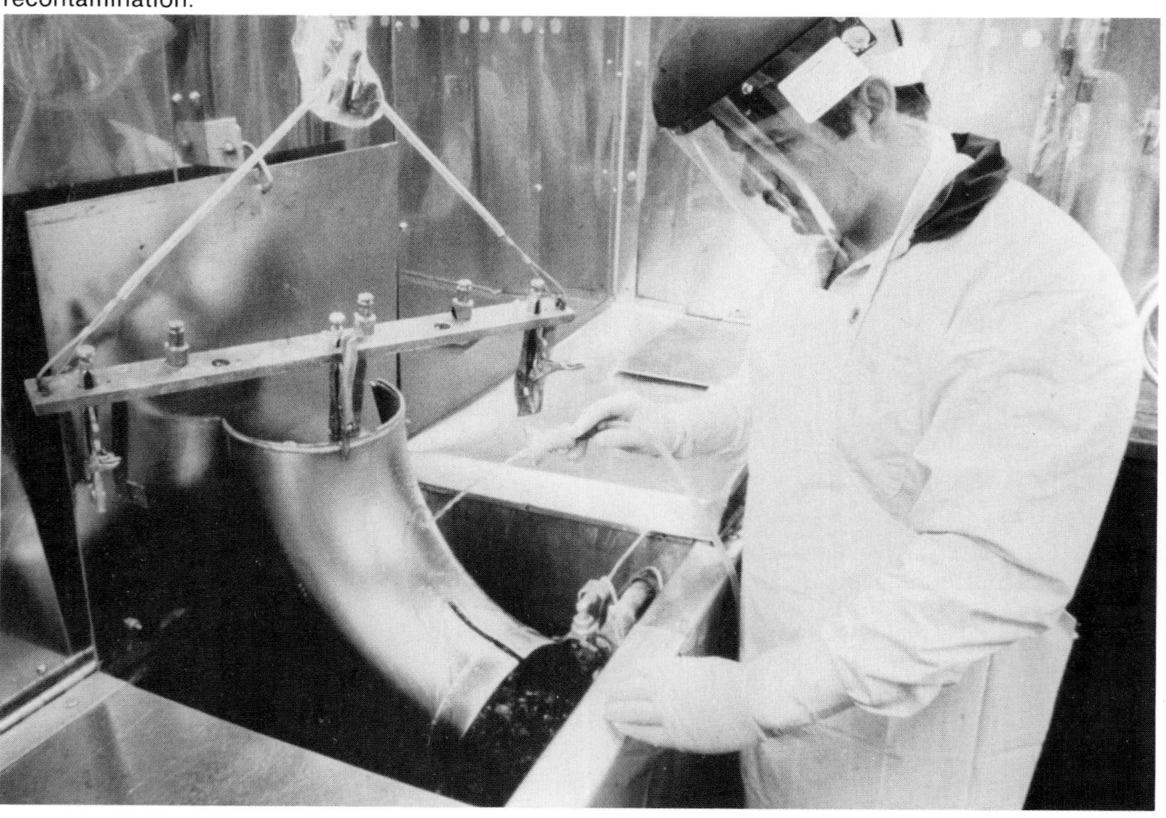

Zinc is sometimes electroplated onto steel to protect the steel against rust. Galvanized steel is steel that has been electroplated with zinc. Zinc corrodes, but the corrosion product does not flake off; it protects the zinc from further oxidation. Therefore, the layer of zinc protects the iron in the steel from being oxidized. Even if a small crack forms in the zinc plating, the iron is still protected because zinc is more easily oxidized than iron. Any oxidation that occurs will be the oxidation of zinc.

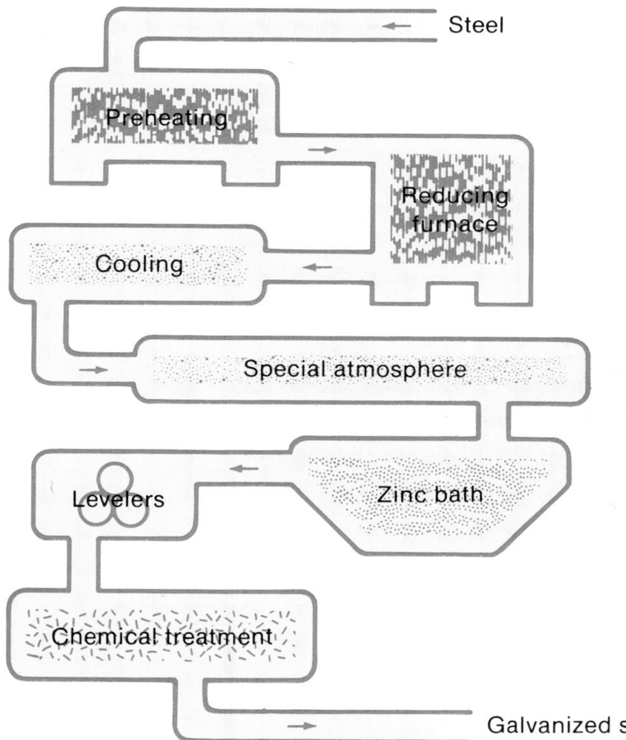

15-19 Steel dipped in a zinc bath in a galvanizing line.

Coming to Terms

oxidation-reduction reaction
redox reaction
oxidation
reduction
reducing agent
oxidizing agent
half-reaction method
half-reaction
electrolyte
nonelectrolyte
electrochemical cell
electrode
electrolysis
electrolytic cell
cathode
anode
battery
voltaic cell
electroplating

Review Questions

1. Does the process of chemical oxidation require that oxygen atoms be present?
2. Tell whether each reaction is a redox reaction.
   a. $2\ Fe\ (s) + 3\ Cl_2\ (g) \longrightarrow 2\ FeCl_3\ (s)$
   b. $CaO\ (s) + 2\ HCl\ (g) \longrightarrow CaCl_2\ (s) + H_2O\ (l)$
   c. $2\ C_2H_6\ (g) + 7\ O_2\ (g) \longrightarrow 4\ CO_2\ (g) + 6\ H_2O\ (l)$
   d. $Zn\ (s) + CuSO_4\ (aq) \longrightarrow Cu\ (s) + ZnSO_4\ (aq)$
   e. $2\ Ba\ (s) + 2\ H_2O\ (l) \longrightarrow Ba(OH)_2\ (s) + H_2\ (g)$
   f. $Pb\ (s) + H_2SO_4\ (aq) \longrightarrow PbSO_4\ (s) + H_2\ (g)$
   g. $AgNO_3\ (aq) + HCl\ (aq) \longrightarrow AgCl\ (s) + HNO_3\ (aq)$

Questions 3-7 refer to the following unbalanced redox reactions.

a. $SO_4^{2-} + Zn \longrightarrow Zn^{2+} + SO_2$
b. $S_2O_3^{2-} + OCl^- \longrightarrow Cl^- + S_4O_6^{2-}$
c. $I^- + SO_4^{2-} \longrightarrow I_2 + H_2S$
d. $H_2S + CrO_4^{2-} \longrightarrow S + Cr^{3+}$
e. $SO_2 + MnO_4^- \longrightarrow SO_4^{2-} + Mn^{2+}$
f. $MnO_4^- + Fe^{2+} \longrightarrow Mn^{2+} + Fe^{3+}$
g. $SO_4^{2-} + C \longrightarrow CO_2 + SO_2$

3. Identify the substance being oxidized in each reaction.
4. Identify the substance being reduced in each reaction.
5. Identify the oxidizing agent in each reaction.
6. Identify the reducing agent in each reaction.
7. Balance each reaction.
8. A chemist titrates a solution of sodium oxalate ($Na_2C_2O_4$) with a solution of $KMnO_4$. The balanced half-reactions occurring during the titration are

$$5\ Na_2C_2O_4 \longrightarrow 10\ CO_2 + 10\ Na^+ + 10\ e^-$$

and

$$2\ KMnO_4 + 16\ HCl + 10\ e^- \longrightarrow 2\ MnCl_2 + 8\ H_2O + 2\ KCl + 10\ Cl^-$$

The gram-formula mass of $Na_2C_2O_4$ is 134.00 g/mole, and that of $KMnO_4$ is 158.04 g/mole.

   a. What is the gram-equivalent mass of $Na_2C_2O_4$ in this reaction?
   b. What is the gram-equivalent mass of $KMnO_4$ in this reaction?
   c. If 3.580 g of $KMnO_4$ are dissolved in 1.000 ℓ of solution, what is the normality of the $KMnO_4$?
   d. If 87.58 ml of 0.1000 N $KMnO_4$ are required to titrate 63.87 ml of $Na_2C_2O_4$ solution, what is the normality of the $Na_2C_2O_4$ solution?

9. A bologna manufacturer uses $NaNO_2$ as a preservative in his product. To determine how much $NaNO_2$ is in a solution being used in the process, an official from the Food and Drug Administration (FDA) titrates the solution with a $K_2Cr_2O_7$ solution. The balanced half-reactions that occur during the titration are

$$3\ NaNO_2 + 3\ H_2O \longrightarrow 3\ NaNO_3 + 6\ H^+ + 6\ e^-$$

and

$$K_2Cr_2O_7 + 14\ HCl + 6\ e^- \longrightarrow 2\ CrCl_3 + 7\ H_2O + 2\ KCl + 6\ Cl^-$$

The gram-formula mass of $NaNO_2$ is 69.00 g/mole, and that of $K_2Cr_2O_7$ is 294.20 g/mole.

   a. What is the gram-equivalent mass of $NaNO_2$ in this reaction?
   b. What is the gram-equivalent mass of $K_2Cr_2O_7$ in this reaction?
   c. If 5.000 g of $K_2Cr_2O_7$ are dissolved in 1.000 ℓ of solution, what is the normality of the $K_2Cr_2O_7$?
   d. If 38.73 ml of 0.3270 N $K_2Cr_2O_7$ are required to titrate 45.00 ml of the $NaNO_2$ solution, what is the normality of the $NaNO_2$?

10. Identify the electrical charge on an anode, the type of ion that migrates toward the anode, and the process (oxidation or reduction) that occurs at the surface of the anode.

11. Identify the electrical charge on a cathode, the type of ion that migrates toward the cathode, and the process (oxidation or reduction) that occurs at the surface of the cathode.

12. What is the difference between a voltaic cell and an electrolytic cell?

13. Describe how the Hall-Heroult process frees aluminum atoms from bauxite.

14. Why did a special process have to be invented for the purification of active metals such as aluminum and sodium when other metals were being purified from their ores by heating and chemical reactions?

15. Why is a salt bridge used in voltaic cells?

16. Why are some batteries considered nonrechargeable even though they are based on the same reversible redox reactions as those in rechargeable batteries?

17. A zinc plating will protect steel from corroding even if the plating is cracked. Give an explanation for this fact.

SIXTEEN

ORGANIC CHEMISTRY

SPOTLIGHT ON CARBON

BRUSSELS sprouts, hormones, DDT, wood, Novocain, polyvinyl chloride, aspirin, TNT, and skin have at least one thing in common. They all contain carbon. Because they contain carbon, they belong to the most extensive branch of chemistry: organic chemistry.

Hydrocarbons

16–1 Structural Formulas: Small Sketches for Big Molecules

Organic chemists study more than the types of atoms in molecules. They also study how the molecules are arranged. If an analytical chemist announced that he had isolated a compound with the molecular formula C_2H_6O, his colleagues would not know what compound he was talking about. C_2H_6O could be the debilitating liquid known as alcohol, or it could be dimethyl ether, a gas used in some refrigerators. The arrangement of the atoms in the molecule makes the difference. For this reason structural formulas are often used in organic chemistry. Many times, to make things simpler, the hydrogen atoms are left out of the drawing.

Table 16-1

Name	Molecular Formula	Structural Formula
Ethanol	C_2H_6O	H H H:C:C:O:H H H or H H | | H—C—C—OH | | H H or | | —C—C—OH | |
Dimethyl ether	C_2H_6O	H H H:C:O:C:H H H or H H | | H—C—O—C—H | | H H or | | —C—O—C— | |

These formulas quickly show that each carbon atom has four bonds, each oxygen atom has two bonds, and each hydrogen atom has one bond.

16–2 The Unique Carbon Atom: Multitudes of Bonds

The 105 elements other than carbon can combine to form several hundred thousand compounds. Contrast that number to the four million compounds that incorporate the carbon atom. It seems amazing that the number of compounds that contain carbon is at least ten times greater than the number of compounds of all the other elements. What makes the carbon atom so versatile?

Carbon atoms form so many compounds because they have unique bonding abilities. A look at carbon's electron-dot structure

$(\cdot\dot{\underset{\cdot}{C}}\cdot)$ shows that it has four valence electrons. It must form four bonds to obtain an octet. Most other atoms form only one, two, or three bonds.

Since carbon is located in the middle of the second period on the periodic table, it has an intermediate electronegativity. It is not strong enough to pull electrons from other atoms, nor is it so weak that it will give up its electrons. Instead, carbon shares its electrons in covalent bonds with many elements.

Carbon can bond to a wide variety of atoms, including other carbon atoms. Carbon atoms bonded together can form chains of various lengths. Chains may be straight, or they may be branched. Carbon atoms can even form rings. In addition to this collection of possibilities, numerous others can result from double and triple bonds, making the possibilities seem endless.

16-2 Variations in carbon-carbon bonding.

```
                     |   |   |
Straight chains    — C — C — C —
                     |   |   |

                           |                                |
                         — C —                            — C —
                       |   |   |   |           |   |   |   |   |   |   |
Branched chains      — C — C — C — C —       — C — C — C — C — C — C — C —
                       |   |   |   |           |   |   |   |   |   |   |
                                                                 — C —
                                                                   |

                        \ /
                      |  C  |
                       /   \
                     C       C
                    /|       |\
Rings                |       |
                    \C       C/
                       \   /
                      |  C  |
                        / \

                     |   |   |   |
Multiple bonds     — C — C = C — C —         — C ≡ C — C —
                     |           |                     |
```

Carbon-carbon bonds in the "backbones" of the molecules account for only two of the four bonds. The remaining bonds are supplied by seemingly endless combinations of hydrogen, halogens, phosphorus, oxygen, nitrogen, sulfur, and other atoms.

16-3 Friedrich Wöhler.

16–3 Classification: A Map Through a Jungle of Compounds

"Organic chemistry nowadays almost drives me mad. To me it appears like a primeval forest full of the most remarkable things, a dreadful endless jungle into which one dare not enter for there seems to be no way out."

Friedrich Wöhler, 1835

If Wöhler were alive today, he would be amazed to see how much larger the "jungle" has grown. Approximately seventy-five thousand new compounds are synthesized for the first time each year. If a person is to find his way through this ever-growing jungle, he must use some guidelines. A classification scheme that organizes compounds into easily identifiable groups serves as the map through the jungle.

Organic compounds can be divided into two large groups: aliphatic compounds and aromatic compounds. **Aliphatic compounds** include straight-chain compounds and those rings that could be formed by the bending and closing of the straight chains. **Aromatic compounds,** like benzene, have ringed shapes, but they are unlike aliphatic rings in one important aspect. Their electrons are not held down to specific bonds; instead, they can migrate in circular clouds above and below the carbon atoms.

This chapter will first survey the simplest aliphatic and aromatic compounds: hydrocarbons. As their name implies, **hydrocarbons** contain only hydrogen and carbon. The chapter will also survey some of the ways in which hydrocarbons can be modified by other elements.

16-4 Coal is the raw material from which many hydrocarbons are extracted.

The classification scheme of Figure 16-5 was determined from the structures of compounds. All compounds in a class have a common structural feature. Usually, compounds in the same class also have similar physical and chemical properties.

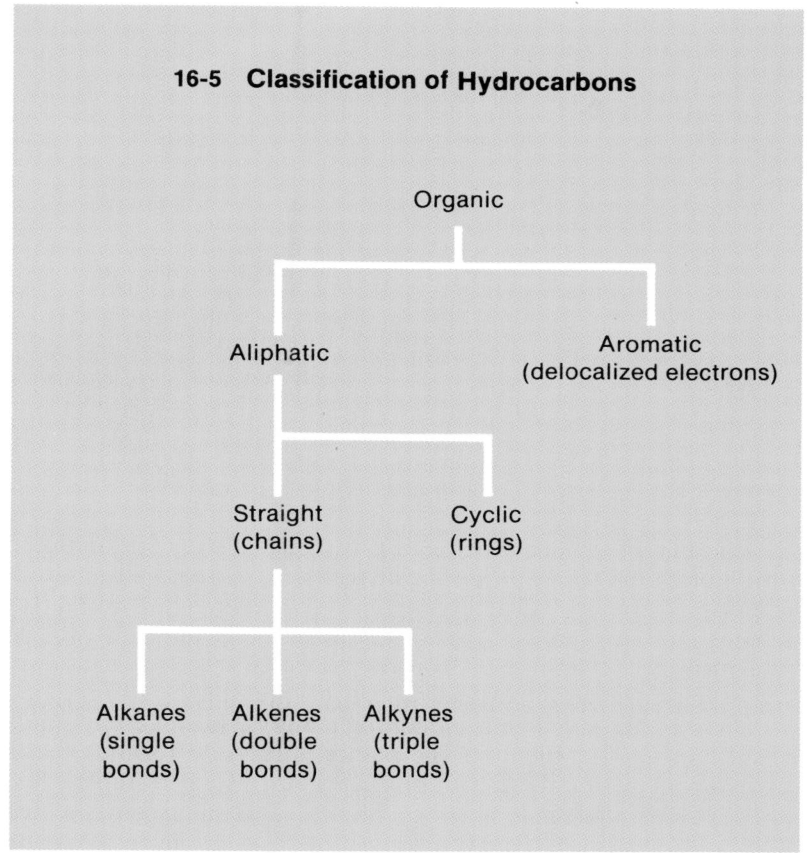

16–4 Alkanes: Chains with Single Bonds

Alkanes are the fuels on which society relies. The natural gas used to heat homes contains methane; portable barbecue grills use bottles of pressurized propane; and automobiles burn a mixture of alkanes called gasoline. All of these compounds contain only carbon and hydrogen. They have structural formulas that resemble open chains, and they have only single bonds. According to the terms on the classification chart, **alkanes** are aliphatic, open-chained hydrocarbons that contain only single bonds.

Methane (CH_4) is the simplest alkane. Its one carbon atom is bonded to four hydrogen atoms. Other alkanes are formed as additional carbons lengthen the chain. Ethane (C_2H_6) has two carbons, propane (C_3H_8) has three, and butane (C_4H_{10}) has four. Each carbon atom in an alkane is surrounded by four other atoms—the maximum number possible. For this reason, the molecules of alkanes are said to be **saturated.**

$$\begin{array}{ccccccccc} & & H & & H & & H & & H & & \\ & & | & & | & & | & & | & & \\ H & - & C & - & C & - & C & - & C & - & H \\ & & | & & | & & | & & | & & \\ & & H & & H & & H & & H & & \end{array}$$

16-6 Straight-chain alkane molecules actually have a zig-zag shape because of the carbon atoms' tetrahedral bonding angles.

A group of chemists belonging to the IUPAC (International Union of Pure and Applied Chemistry) has devised a system that accurately names organic compounds. The system works for alkanes and all the other types of organic molecules that will be studied in this chapter. The system relies on a series of prefixes that indicate the number of carbon atoms present.

Table 16-7

Numerical Prefixes	
C_1	meth
C_2	eth
C_3	prop
C_4	but
C_5	pent
C_6	hex
C_7	hept
C_8	oct
C_9	non
C_{10}	dec

These prefixes will help in naming many classes of compounds in addition to the alkanes. The names, structural formulas, and some properties of the first ten alkanes are listed in Table 16-8.

Are these molecules polar or nonpolar? Bonds between two carbon atoms are not polar, because both atoms have the same electronegativity. The bonds between carbon and hydrogen are arranged symmetrically, so whatever polarity they have is canceled. Alkanes dissolve well in nonpolar solvents such as carbon tetrachloride. In polar substances such as water, however, alkanes form a slimy oil slick.

Crude oil straight from the well contains several types of alkanes. Chains from four carbons up to twenty carbons are thrown together into one seemingly inseparable mixture. Fractions of the mixture must be separated so that they can be used for lubricating oils, gasoline, and kerosene. How do chemical engineers separate the individual compounds? Petroleum engineers use the fact that the boiling points of alkanes rise about 20-30° C for each additional carbon that is added to the chain.

First, a batch of crude oil is heated and dumped into the bottom of a fractional distillation tower. The mixture is heated even further until a large percentage of the compounds has boiled into vapor. The vapors then rise through the cooling tower. Alkanes with high

Table 16-8

Straight-Chained Alkanes

Name	Structural Formula	Melting Point (°C)	Boiling Point (°C)
Methane	$\begin{array}{ccc} & H & \\ & \vert & \\ H - & C & - H \\ & \vert & \\ & H & \end{array}$	-183	-162
Ethane	$\begin{array}{cccc} & H & H & \\ & \vert & \vert & \\ H - & C - & C & - H \\ & \vert & \vert & \\ & H & H & \end{array}$	-172	-88.5
Propane	$\begin{array}{ccccc} & H & H & H & \\ & \vert & \vert & \vert & \\ H - & C - & C - & C & - H \\ & \vert & \vert & \vert & \\ & H & H & H & \end{array}$	-187	-42
Butane	$\begin{array}{cccccc} & H & H & H & H & \\ & \vert & \vert & \vert & \vert & \\ H - & C - & C - & C - & C & - H \\ & \vert & \vert & \vert & \vert & \\ & H & H & H & H & \end{array}$	-138	0
Pentane	$\begin{array}{ccccccc} & H & H & H & H & H & \\ & \vert & \vert & \vert & \vert & \vert & \\ H - & C - & C - & C - & C - & C & - H \\ & \vert & \vert & \vert & \vert & \vert & \\ & H & H & H & H & H & \end{array}$	-130	36
Hexane	$\begin{array}{cccccccc} & H & H & H & H & H & H & \\ & \vert & \vert & \vert & \vert & \vert & \vert & \\ H - & C - & C - & C - & C - & C - & C & - H \\ & \vert & \vert & \vert & \vert & \vert & \vert & \\ & H & H & H & H & H & H & \end{array}$	-95	69
Heptane	$\begin{array}{ccccccccc} & H & H & H & H & H & H & H & \\ & \vert & \vert & \vert & \vert & \vert & \vert & \vert & \\ H - & C - & C - & C - & C - & C - & C - & C & - H \\ & \vert & \vert & \vert & \vert & \vert & \vert & \vert & \\ & H & H & H & H & H & H & H & \end{array}$	-90.5	98
Octane	$\begin{array}{cccccccccc} & H & H & H & H & H & H & H & H & \\ & \vert & \vert & \vert & \vert & \vert & \vert & \vert & \vert & \\ H - & C - & C - & C - & C - & C - & C - & C - & C & - H \\ & \vert & \vert & \vert & \vert & \vert & \vert & \vert & \vert & \\ & H & H & H & H & H & H & H & H & \end{array}$	-57	126
Nonane	$\begin{array}{ccccccccccc} & H & H & H & H & H & H & H & H & H & \\ & \vert & \vert & \vert & \vert & \vert & \vert & \vert & \vert & \vert & \\ H - & C - & C - & C - & C - & C - & C - & C - & C - & C & - H \\ & \vert & \vert & \vert & \vert & \vert & \vert & \vert & \vert & \vert & \\ & H & H & H & H & H & H & H & H & H & \end{array}$	-54	151
Decane	$\begin{array}{cccccccccccc} & H & H & H & H & H & H & H & H & H & H & \\ & \vert & \vert & \vert & \vert & \vert & \vert & \vert & \vert & \vert & \vert & \\ H - & C - & C - & C - & C - & C - & C - & C - & C - & C - & C & - H \\ & \vert & \vert & \vert & \vert & \vert & \vert & \vert & \vert & \vert & \vert & \\ & H & H & H & H & H & H & H & H & H & H & \end{array}$	-30	174

boiling points (the large molecules) condense near the bottom of the tower. Smaller alkanes rise further into the tower before they condense into liquids. By regulating the temperatures of the different portions of the tower, chemical engineers can collect distinct fractions of alkanes.

Natural gas is a naturally occurring mixture of methane, ethane, propane, and butane. Usually the mixture is cooled and liquefied until the butane and propane condense into liquids. The ethane and methane are piped off as natural gas, and the propane and butane are sold as bottled gas.

16-9 Fractional Distillation of Petroleum

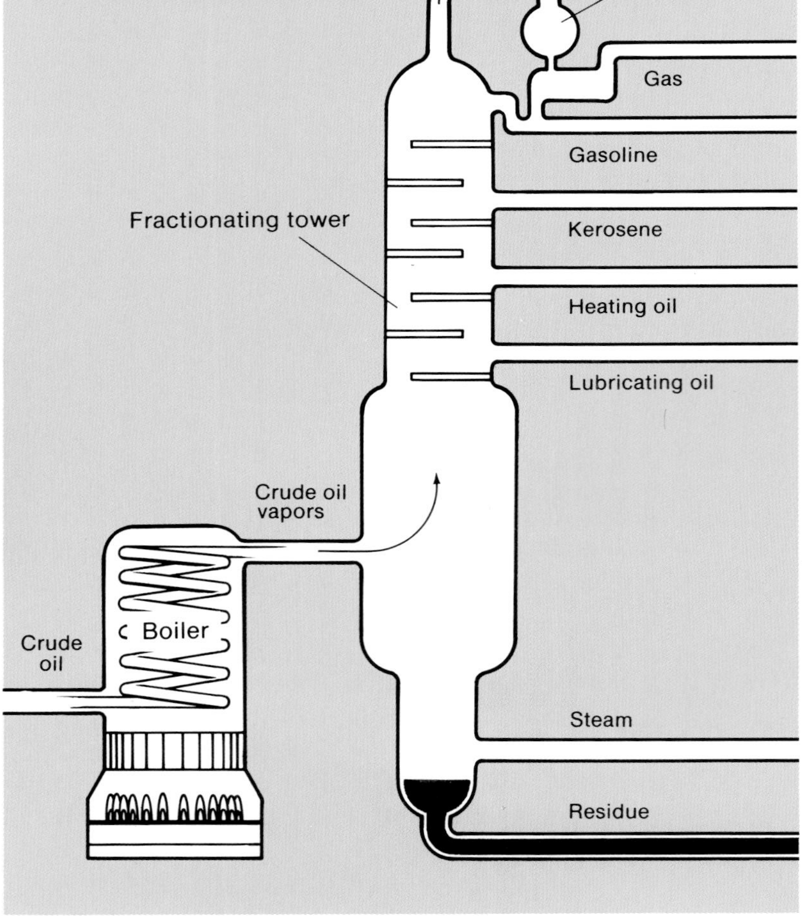

Condenser
Gas
Gasoline
Fractionating tower
Kerosene
Heating oil
Lubricating oil
Crude oil vapors
Boiler
Crude oil
Steam
Residue

16-10 Propane **(top),** hexane **(middle),** and paraffin **(bottom).** Small alkanes are gases, medium-sized alkanes are liquids, and large alkanes are solids.

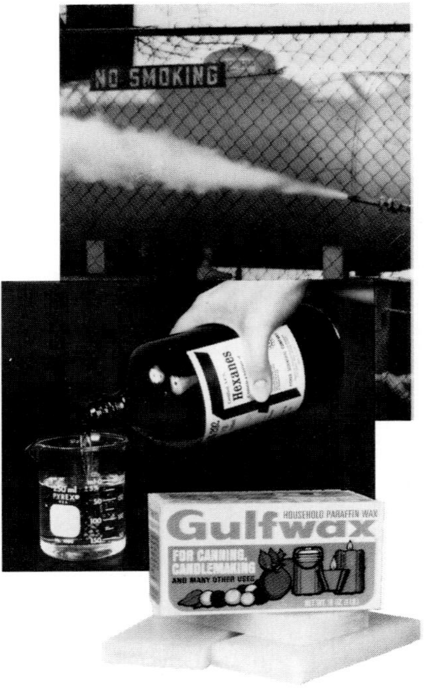

16–5 Structural Isomers: Variations on the Alkane Theme

The carbon chains of alkanes do not have to be straight. Some alkanes have branched-chain structures. The molecular formulas of the two substances listed below are identical, but the molecules are obviously different. Compounds that have the same molecular formulas but different structural formulas are called **structural isomers.** Normal butane (the straight-chained form) and its structural isomer would be expected to have slightly different physical properties, and indeed they do.

Table 16-11

Comparison of Butane's Isomers

Isomer	Structural Formula	Melting Point	Boiling Point	Density	Solubility
Butane (straight-chained)	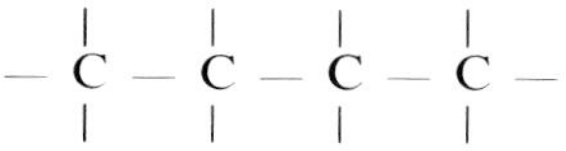 —C—C—C—C— (each C with bonds above and below)	-138.4° C	-0.5° C	0.579 g/ml	1813 ml/100 ml ethanol
Butane (branched)	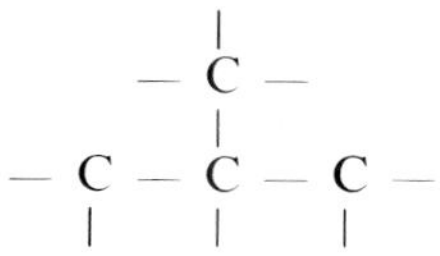 —C—C—C— with —C— attached above the middle C	-159° C	-12° C	0.549 g/ml	1320 ml/100 ml ethanol

Sample Problem. Draw structural formulas for all the structural isomers of pentane (C_5H_{12}).

Solution.

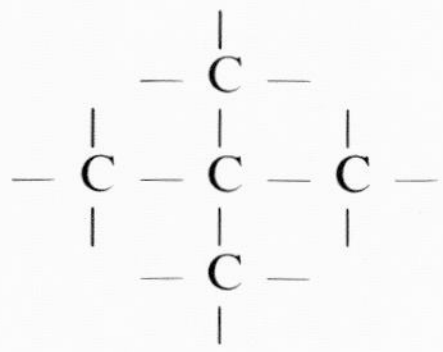

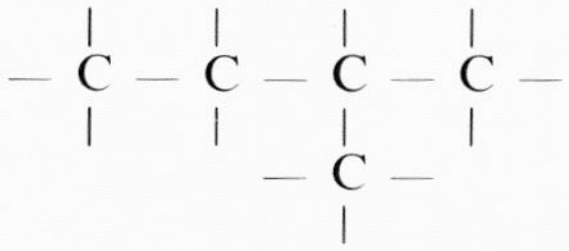

```
          |
        — C —
    |     |     |
  — C  —  C  —  C —
    |     |     |
        — C —
          |
```

```
    |     |     |     |
  — C  —  C  —  C  —  C —
    |     |     |     |
              — C —
                |
```

```
    |     |     |     |     |
  — C  —  C  —  C  —  C  —  C —
    |     |     |     |     |
```

Prefixes before the name of the longest straight chain in a structural isomer identify the locations, numbers, and kinds of side chains. For instance, the structural isomers of pentane are named pentane, 2-methylbutane, and 2,2-dimethylpropane.

16–6 Alkenes: Chains with Double Bonds

Carbon does not always form single bonds. Double bonds appear quite frequently. The simplest hydrocarbon that contains a double bond is ethene.

16-12 Lewis structure and structural formula of ethene.

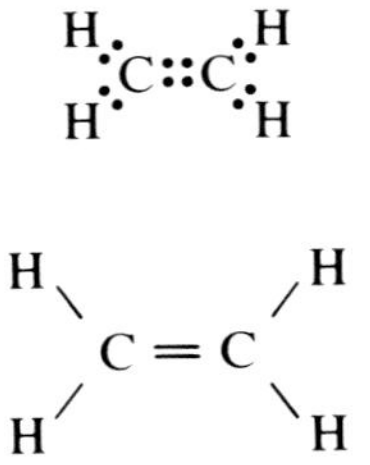

H:C::C:H (each C also bonded to a second H)

$H_2C=CH_2$

Table 16-13

Alkenes

Name	Structural Formula	Boiling Point (°C)	Melting Point (°C)
Ethene	—C=C—	-104	-169
Propene	—C=C—C—	-47	-185
1-butene	—C=C—C—C—	-6.3	-185
2-butene	—C—C=C—C—	4	-139.3
1-pentene	—C=C—C—C—C—	30	-138
2-pentene	—C—C=C—C—C—	37	-151
1-hexene	—C=C—C—C—C—C—	63	-140

Hydrocarbons that contain double bonds are called **alkenes.** Because double bonds reduce the number of hydrogen atoms in the molecules, alkenes are said to be **unsaturated.** As in the alkane series, new compounds result when more singly bonded carbons are added to the chain. These molecules are named with the appropriate prefix and the ending *-ene,* which means that the compound has a double bond. Ethene contains only two carbons. When the carbon chain is longer than three carbons, the double bond could be in several locations. An alkene's name pinpoints the location of the double bond by giving the number of the first carbon that is doubly bonded.

The physical properties of alkenes are very much like those of alkanes. The first few are gases at room temperature. Pentene and larger compounds are liquids at room temperature because of greater intermolecular attractions. Alkenes are relatively nonpolar.

16–7 Alkynes: Chains with Triple Bonds

A triple bond between two carbon atoms identifies a member of the **alkyne** family. The most common alkyne is also the simplest. Ethyne, commonly called acetylene, consists of two carbons joined by a triple bond. This compound is often used as a fuel for welding torches and as an ingredient for polymers.

16-14 Lewis structure and structural formula of ethyne. Ethyne (acetylene) is used in welding.

$$H \overset{\bullet}{\times} C \overset{\bullet}{\times} \overset{\bullet}{\times} \overset{\bullet}{\times} C \overset{\times}{\bullet} H$$

or

$$H{-}C{\equiv}C{-}H$$

Larger alkynes have additional carbons. Names of alkynes are formed from a prefix that tells how many carbons are in the molecule. The suffix *-yne* signifies that a triple bond is present. When necessary, a number is used to tell where the triple bond occurs.

Physically, alkynes are similar to other hydrocarbons. They are practically nonpolar, so they are insoluble in water and very soluble in nonpolar solvents. Their boiling points rise as the carbon chains get longer.

Table 16-15

Alkynes

Name	Structural Formula	Boiling Point (°C)	Melting Point (°C)
Ethyne (acetylene)	$-C\equiv C-$	-84	-81
Propyne	$-C\equiv C-\overset{\mid}{\underset{\mid}{C}}-$	-23	-101.5
1-butyne	$-C\equiv C-\overset{\mid}{\underset{\mid}{C}}-\overset{\mid}{\underset{\mid}{C}}-$	8	-126
2-butyne	$-\overset{\mid}{\underset{\mid}{C}}-C\equiv C-\overset{\mid}{\underset{\mid}{C}}-$	27	-32
1-pentyne	$-C\equiv C-\overset{\mid}{\underset{\mid}{C}}-\overset{\mid}{\underset{\mid}{C}}-\overset{\mid}{\underset{\mid}{C}}-$	40	-90
2-pentyne	$-\overset{\mid}{\underset{\mid}{C}}-C\equiv C-\overset{\mid}{\underset{\mid}{C}}-\overset{\mid}{\underset{\mid}{C}}-$	56	-101
1-hexyne	$-C\equiv C-\overset{\mid}{\underset{\mid}{C}}-\overset{\mid}{\underset{\mid}{C}}-\overset{\mid}{\underset{\mid}{C}}-\overset{\mid}{\underset{\mid}{C}}-$	72	-132
2-hexyne	$-\overset{\mid}{\underset{\mid}{C}}-C\equiv C-\overset{\mid}{\underset{\mid}{C}}-\overset{\mid}{\underset{\mid}{C}}-\overset{\mid}{\underset{\mid}{C}}-$	84	-90
3-hexyne	$-\overset{\mid}{\underset{\mid}{C}}-\overset{\mid}{\underset{\mid}{C}}-C\equiv C-\overset{\mid}{\underset{\mid}{C}}-\overset{\mid}{\underset{\mid}{C}}-$	81	-103
1-heptyne	$-C\equiv C-\overset{\mid}{\underset{\mid}{C}}-\overset{\mid}{\underset{\mid}{C}}-\overset{\mid}{\underset{\mid}{C}}-\overset{\mid}{\underset{\mid}{C}}-\overset{\mid}{\underset{\mid}{C}}-$	100	-81
1-octyne	$-C\equiv C-\overset{\mid}{\underset{\mid}{C}}-\overset{\mid}{\underset{\mid}{C}}-\overset{\mid}{\underset{\mid}{C}}-\overset{\mid}{\underset{\mid}{C}}-\overset{\mid}{\underset{\mid}{C}}-\overset{\mid}{\underset{\mid}{C}}-$	125	-79
1-nonyne	$-C\equiv C-\overset{\mid}{\underset{\mid}{C}}-\overset{\mid}{\underset{\mid}{C}}-\overset{\mid}{\underset{\mid}{C}}-\overset{\mid}{\underset{\mid}{C}}-\overset{\mid}{\underset{\mid}{C}}-\overset{\mid}{\underset{\mid}{C}}-\overset{\mid}{\underset{\mid}{C}}-$	151	-50
1-decyne	$-C\equiv C-\overset{\mid}{\underset{\mid}{C}}-\overset{\mid}{\underset{\mid}{C}}-\overset{\mid}{\underset{\mid}{C}}-\overset{\mid}{\underset{\mid}{C}}-\overset{\mid}{\underset{\mid}{C}}-\overset{\mid}{\underset{\mid}{C}}-\overset{\mid}{\underset{\mid}{C}}-\overset{\mid}{\underset{\mid}{C}}-$	174	-36

16–8 Cyclic Aliphatic Compounds: Chains in Rings

Petroleum from California is unique. For some unknown reason it contains an unusually large amount of carbon compounds whose chains have been bonded into rings. Such compounds are called **cyclic aliphatic compounds.**

A great variety of rings is possible, but five-carbon and six-carbon rings with single bonds are the most abundant. Simple alkenes and alkenes with more than one double bond multiply the number of possible structures. A few structures and their names are shown below.

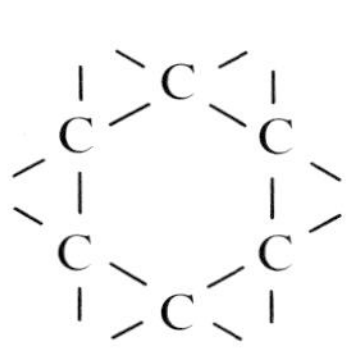

Cyclohexane

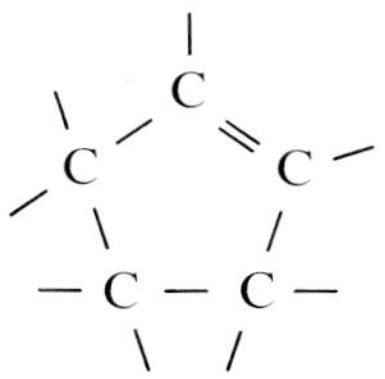

Cyclopentene

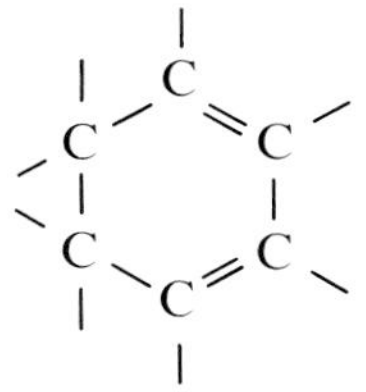

1,3-cyclohexadiene

Some very unusual structures are possible when several rings are combined.

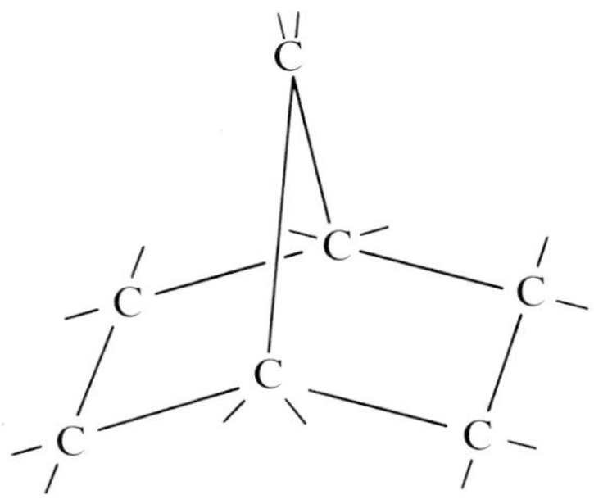

Bicyclo [2.2.1] heptane

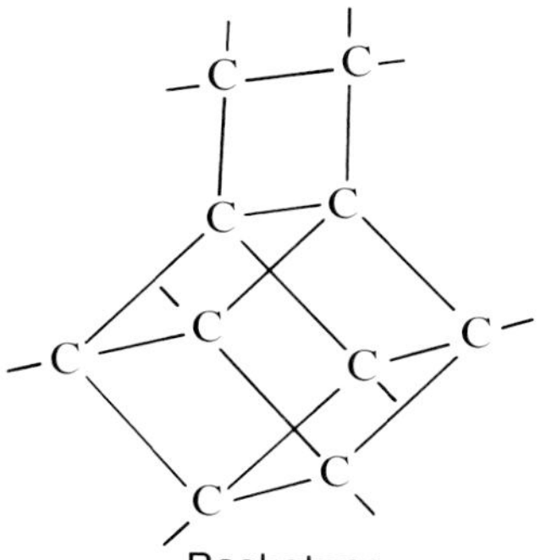

Basketane

The chemical activity of cyclic compounds is about the same as that of other members of their parent families. Cycloalkanes act like alkanes; cycloalkenes act like alkenes. Cyclic compounds have had several unique uses. Cyclopropane is used as an anesthetic. Cyclopentane works well as a cleaner in the fuel system of a car. Added to the gasoline, it dissolves deposits in the intake system, carburetor, cylinders, and top piston valves. Cyclohexane serves as a paint and varnish remover.

FACETS OF CHEMISTRY

Octane Numbers

"Use high-octane gas to stop knocking, pinging, and harmful engine run-on." This line is often heard but little understood. If you have ever pumped gasoline, you have probably noticed on the pump a sticker bearing a number between eighty-seven and ninety-three. This number is important because it rates the quality of the gasoline you are putting into your car. Unless you get the right gas, your car will not run smoothly.

The cylinders of your engine are filled at fixed intervals with a mixture of gas vapor and air. The piston, which slides back and forth in the cylinder, compresses the fuel. When the fuel is then ignited by a spark from the spark plug, it should burn rapidly in a smooth explosion. The expanding gases that are produced drive the piston back down into the cylinder. The back-and-forth motion of the piston ultimately makes the wheels turn.

Some blends of gasoline burn irregularly in certain engines. As the fuel mixture is compressed, some of it may ignite on its own—without the spark from the spark plug. When the undesired flame hits the one produced by the spark plug, tremendous pressures and temperatures are produced. Needless to say, this gives the piston quite a jolt. You hear these detonations in the form of engine knocks, especially when the engine is straining to accelerate or is climbing a steep hill. The overheating and mechanical rattling is hard on any engine.

16–9 Aromatic Substances: Roaming Electrons

Aromatic substances played an important role in early societies: wealthy folks used them instead of soap and water. Since clean water was scarce in many areas, not many people bothered to take frequent baths. The poor learned to accept the odor, but the wealthy fought their accumulated body odors with layers of perfumes. Since many of these perfumes contained benzene compounds, any compound that contained a form of benzene was soon classified as aromatic, or good-smelling. Eventually, however, this rule failed. Chemists found several benzene compounds that had odors far from pleasant—some were actually quite foul. Chemists also found other substances that smelled good even though they did not contain benzene. Nevertheless, by this time the term *aromatic* had been associated with benzene compounds for so long that the name stuck.

The tendency of a fuel to burn prematurely is described by the octane number. 2,2,4-trimethylpentane (an isomer of octane) is a great fuel because it resists knocking very well. This isomer was arbitrarily assigned an octane number of 100. Normal heptane is a poor fuel because it causes a great deal of knocking; it was assigned an octane number of 0. Other fuels are rated by comparison to a mixture of these two standards. If a gasoline blend performs as well as a mixture of 87 per cent 2,2,4-trimethylpentane and 13 per cent normal heptane, it is given an octane number of 87.

Each component of gasoline contributes to the overall octane number. The trick is to find a gasoline that has the right ingredients for your car. Straight-chained alkanes tend to have low octane numbers. Branched alkanes, alkenes, and aromatic compounds have high octane numbers and increase the quality of the fuel. But there is one problem. Gasoline that comes straight from fractional distillation contains several straight-chained alkanes. The octane number of this fuel mixture would be too low for today's car engines. The fuel must be modified in some way.

In 1922 a team of researchers at General Motors discovered that adding a small amount of tetraethyl lead—$(C_2H_5)_4Pb$—greatly increased the octane number. Leaded gasoline soon became so widely used that it picked up the name "regular." This additive worked fine until the government required the addition of catalytic converters (pollution-control devices) to modern automobiles. Unfortunately, lead ruins the catalysts. The petroleum industries had to find another way to increase the octane numbers of their fuels.

The quality of gasoline that comes directly from the fractional distillation of crude oil is upgraded by additional refining. In the refining process the proportion of high-octane components is increased. Straight-chained molecules are converted to branched chains. High-octane hydrocarbons are synthesized from other less desirable hydrocarbons. Chemists can even produce blends of gasoline designed specifically for a geographic area of the country or a particular season of the year. But all this chemistry costs money and boosts the price of a gallon of gasoline. Just compare the cost of unleaded gas to regular gas!

Which gasoline is right for your car? You should get the gas with the lowest octane number that does not cause knocking. Higher octane gasolines are more expensive and probably will not provide any added benefit.

Benzene was isolated in 1825 by Michael Faraday. An analysis of the elements in benzene and a determination of its molecular weight showed that the molecular formula was C_6H_6. This compound is the simplest aromatic compound known. Today it is one of industry's most important compounds.

The structural formula of benzene puzzled scientists for thirty years after Faraday discovered the compound. Many clues were gathered, but they did not seem to fit together. The molecular formula C_6H_6 led chemists to believe that the molecule must have several double or triple bonds. Yet the chemical reactions of benzene did not support this idea. It behaved like an alkane, not an alkene or alkyne. When scientists determined the bond lengths between the carbon atoms, they found that the distances were not those of single or double bonds: they were in between. It was as if benzene used one-and-one-half bonds. Furthermore, it became known that the carbons were arranged in a ring and that all the carbon atoms had identical bonds.

In 1865 August Kekulé proposed a structure that could account for most of the observations. He described benzene in terms of two symmetrical ring structures.

Each benzene molecule was thought to switch rapidly back and forth between the two forms. The bonds were mobile, not tied down to one location. The development of the quantum model of atoms modified this concept. Chemists realized that electrons existed in orbitals and that in benzene these orbitals overlapped and became one big, doughnut-shaped area of electron concentration. The electrons in these clouds are free to roam throughout the entire "doughnut." For this reason, they are called **delocalized electrons.**

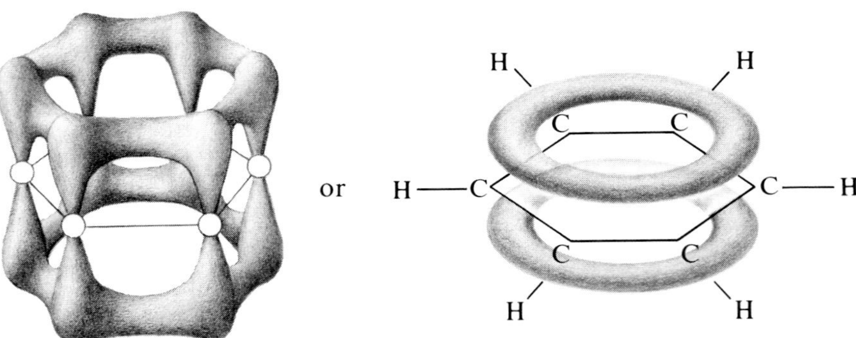

Because the electrons are not bound between any two carbon atoms, chemists now draw the structure of benzene as

or, more simply, like this

The modern definition of aromatic compounds has nothing to do with their smell. Rather, it deals with the nature of the bonds between atoms. All aromatic compounds have cyclic clouds of delocalized electrons. Benzene is the parent compound for a huge number of substances, many of which are used commercially.

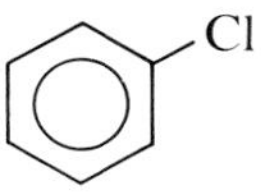

Chlorobenzene

p-dichlorobenzene (moth repellent)

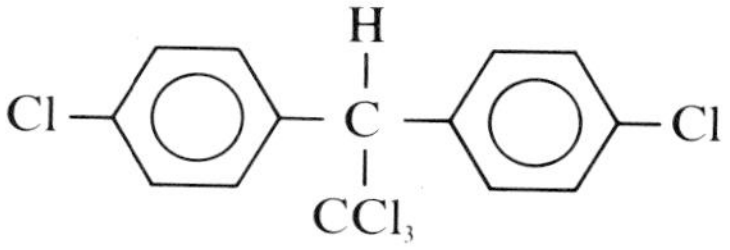

Dichlorodiphenyl Trichloroethane (DDT, insecticide)

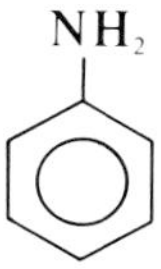

Aniline (used in dyes)

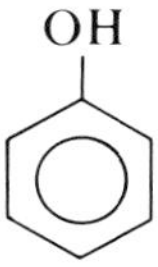

Phenol (disinfectant)

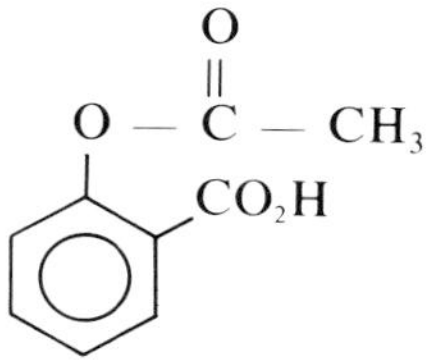

Aspirin (acetyl salicylic acid)

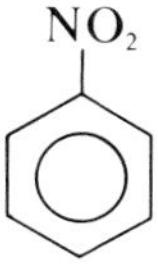

Nitrobenzene

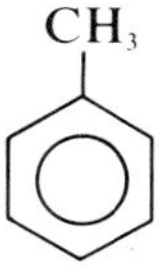

Toluene

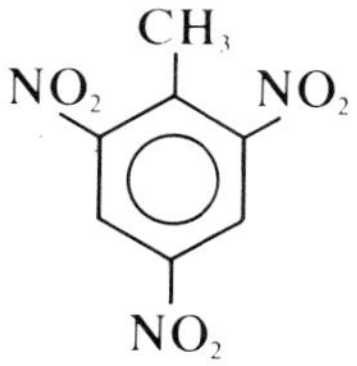

Trinitrotoluene (TNT explosive)

Many other compounds contain multiple benzene rings that are fused together.

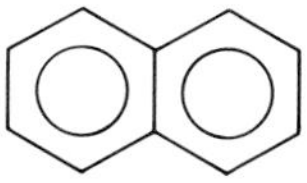

Naphthalene (mothballs)

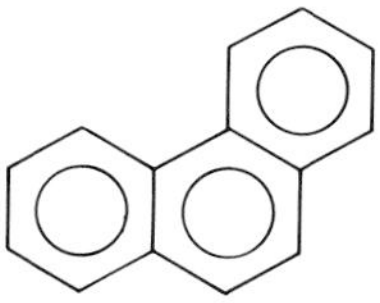

Phenanthrene (dyes, explosives)

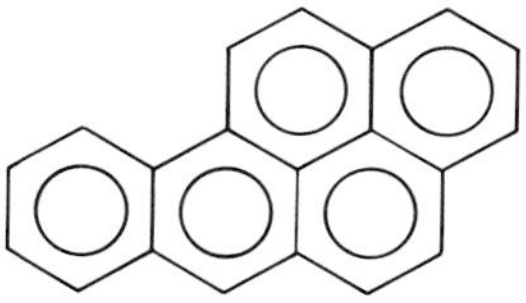

3,4-benzpyrene (a carcinogen found in cigarette smoke and smog)

Finally, many ointments, perfumes, and oils contain aromatic compounds. One of the ointments used instead of the daily bath in the Middle Ages was made from crushed vanilla beans. The good-smelling aromatic compound is named vanillin.

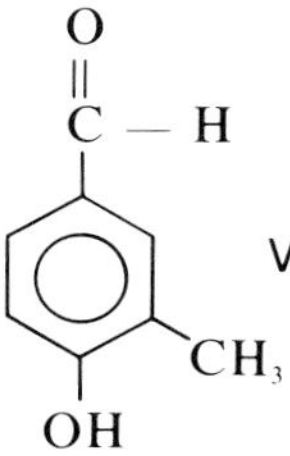

Vanillin

Substituted Hydrocarbons

16-16 Chemists modify hydrocarbons for use in common household products.

Functional groups are the hot spots of chemical activity on an organic molecule. They greatly modify the behavior of hydrocarbons. In alkenes and alkynes the reactive sites are the multiple bonds. The electrons in the bonds are available for a variety of chemical reactions. The multiple bonds give the molecules characteristic structures and chemical properties. There are many kinds of functional groups. Some contain sulfur; some contain halogens. Most functional groups in organic chemistry contain arrangements of oxygen or nitrogen atoms. In each case the functional group greatly influences the molecule's properties.

16–10 Halides: Hydrocarbons Plus Halogens

When a halogen and an alkyl group are combined, an alkyl halide is formed. An **alkyl group** is an alkane chain with one hydrogen atom missing. An **alkyl halide** is a combination of an alkyl group and a fluorine, chlorine, bromine, or iodine atom. When a halogen is attached to an **aryl group** (an aromatic group that lacks a hydrogen atom), the resulting molecule is called an **aryl halide.** Several halides are used by today's industries.

Table 16-17

Name	Structural Formula	Application
Trichloromethane (chloroform)	Cl | H — C — Cl | Cl	early anesthetic
Tetrachloromethane (carbon tetrachloride)	Cl | Cl — C — Cl | Cl	nonpolar solvent
Triiodomethane (iodoform)	I | H — C — I | I	veterinary antiseptic
Dichlorodifluoromethane (freon-12)	Cl | F — C — Cl | F	compressor gas used in refrigerators

Many other halides serve as intermediates in the synthesis of other compounds.

Table 16-18

Name	Structural Formula	Applications
Chloroethene (vinyl chloride)	$H(H)C{=}C(H)Cl$	building block for polyvinyl chloride (phonograph records, credit cards, plastic pipes)
1,1-dichloroethene (vinylidene chloride)	$Cl_2C{=}CH_2$	building block for Saran plastic wrap
Tetrafluoroethene	$F_2C{=}CF_2$	building block for Teflon

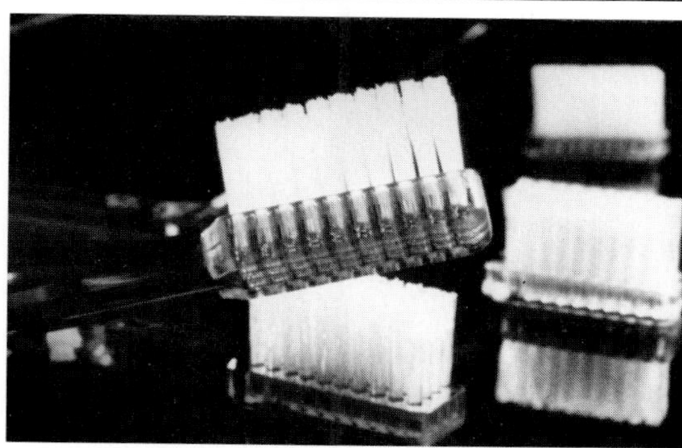

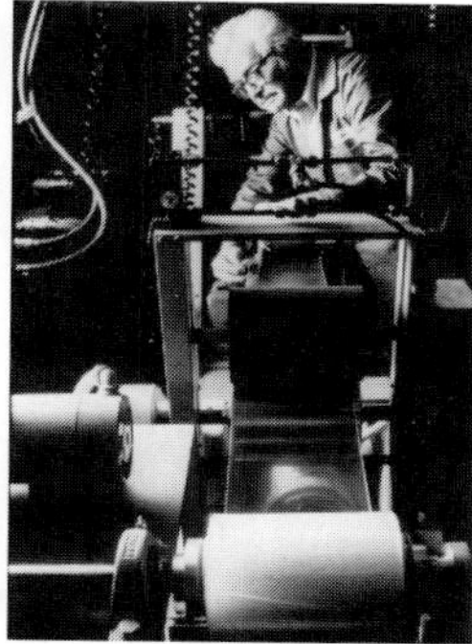

16-19 Alkyl halides are ingredients in polymer plastics.

16–11 Alcohols: Molecules with OH Groups

To most people the word *alcohol* evokes images of society's most abused drug. The teenage casualties of drunk driving, the dismal atmosphere that surrounds bars, and multitudes of fragmented families all reflect the influence of alcohol. Many people do not realize that this misused substance is just one member of a very useful family of organic compounds.

Compounds that have a covalently bonded OH group attached to an alkyl group are classified as **alcohols.** The general formula for the whole family is R-OH, where R represents an alkyl group. The simplest alcohol is methanol. In this case the R group is the smallest one possible, CH_3.

$$\begin{array}{c} \quad H \\ \quad | \\ H - C - OH \\ \quad | \\ \quad H \end{array}$$

Table 16-20

Name	Structural Formula	Applications
Methanol	$-\overset{\vert}{\underset{\vert}{C}}-OH$	solvent, fuels
Ethanol	$-\overset{\vert}{\underset{\vert}{C}}-\overset{\vert}{\underset{\vert}{C}}-OH$	solvent, intoxicant
Propanol	$-\overset{\vert}{\underset{\vert}{C}}-\overset{\vert}{\underset{\vert}{C}}-\overset{\vert}{\underset{\vert}{C}}-OH$	solvent, antifreezes, aftershave lotions
2-propanol (rubbing alcohol) (isopropyl alcohol)	$-\underset{\vert}{C}-\overset{\overset{OH}{\vert}}{\underset{\vert}{C}}-\underset{\vert}{C}-$	solvent, antifreezes, aftershave lotions
Butanol	$-\overset{\vert}{\underset{\vert}{C}}-\overset{\vert}{\underset{\vert}{C}}-\overset{\vert}{\underset{\vert}{C}}-\overset{\vert}{\underset{\vert}{C}}-OH$	solvent, shellacs, varnishes

Alcohol names consist of the standard prefixes that tell how long the carbon chain is plus an *-ol* ending. If the OH group is attached to a carbon other than the end carbon, its position is indicated by a numerical prefix. For instance, what is commonly called rubbing alcohol is a three-carbon chain with the OH group attached to the middle carbon. The IUPAC name is 2-propanol.

The physical properties of alcohols are a result of two factors: the polar OH group and the nonpolar alkyl group. The combination of these two opposites determines the behavior of each specific molecule. If the hydrocarbon chain is relatively short, the OH group dominates the molecule. As a result, it behaves as a polar molecule. If the hydrocarbon chain is very long, the chain dominates and imparts nonpolar characteristics to the molecule. Small alcohols, under the influence of the OH groups, form hydrogen bonds, have high boiling points, and are soluble in water. Large alcohols, under the influence of their hydrocarbon chains, are insoluble in water and soluble in nonpolar solvents.

16-21 Shampoos, facial creams, and deodorants contain many different alcohols.

Alcohols that contain more than one OH group are called polyhydroxy alcohols. One common polyhydroxy alcohol is 1,2-ethanediol (also called ethylene glycol), which is used as an antifreeze in a car radiator. Another common alcohol—1,2,3-propanetriol (glycerol)—is put into moisturizers in cosmetics.

```
 OH  OH
 |   |
-C - C-
 |   |
```

Ethylene glycol

```
 OH  OH  OH
 |   |   |
-C - C - C-
 |   |   |
```

Glycerol

Industries use alcohols as solvents, paint thinners, antifreezes, and ingredients in aftershave lotions. When ethanol is required, manufacturers and chemists face the prospects of paying the same stiff taxes that are imposed on liquor. To avoid these extra costs, they denature the ethanol, or make it totally unfit to drink. Poisons and foul-tasting substances such as gasoline, methanol, or 2-propanol are added to the ethanol. It may surprise some people to know that other alcohols are much more toxic than ethanol. Ingestion of rubbing alcohol causes headaches, nausea, comas, and possibly death. Methanol typically brings the same symptoms with one significant addition. It can cause chronic eye problems and even blindness because it can dissolve the fatty sheath around the optic nerve.

16–12 Ethers: Molecules with -O- Links

Compounds that have the general formula R_1-O-R_2 are called **ethers.** R_2 stands for a second alkyl group. Ethers are distinguished by the oxygen bridge between two carbon chains. The name of an ether includes the names of the alkyl groups on each side of the oxygen (smaller one first) and the word *ether* on the end.

```
 |   |       |   |
-C - C - O - C - C-
 |   |       |   |
```

Diethyl ether

```
 |       |
-C - O - C-
 |       |
```

Dimethyl ether

```
 |       |   |
-C - O - C - C-
 |       |   |
```

Methyl ethyl ether

More complicated ethers have been synthesized, but diethyl ether is by far the most common. When people say "ether," they are usually referring to this compound. A Georgian doctor named Crawford Long made this ether famous when he painlessly removed a tumor from a patient's neck in 1842. The reason that the operation was painless was that ether is an anesthetic: it puts a person "out." Ether served the medical professionals for a long period of time until other anesthetics that had fewer side effects were developed. Ethers are now used as solvents for perfumes, primers for gasoline engines, and reagents in organic syntheses.

Working with ethers in the laboratory requires great caution. Ethers vaporize quickly, and the vapors are very flammable. Since the vapors are more dense than air, they sink to a table top or floor and then spread out over a great area. For this reason, there should be no open flames in the laboratory when ethers are present.

16–13 Aldehydes: Molecules with C=O Groups on the End

Aldehydes are organic compounds that contain a doubly bonded oxygen on the end carbon. Their general structure is

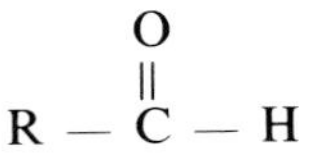

$$R-\overset{\overset{\displaystyle O}{\|}}{C}-H$$

All aldehydes contain the C=O group, which is called the **carbonyl group.** According to the IUPAC rules, the name of an aldehyde is formed with an *-al* ending on the name of the corresponding alkane.

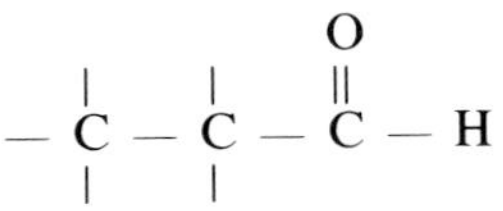

$$-\underset{|}{\overset{|}{C}}-\underset{|}{\overset{|}{C}}-\overset{\overset{\displaystyle O}{\|}}{C}-H$$

Propanal

$$-C-C-C-\underset{\underset{\displaystyle -\underset{|}{C}-}{|}}{C}-\overset{\overset{\displaystyle O}{\|}}{C}-H$$

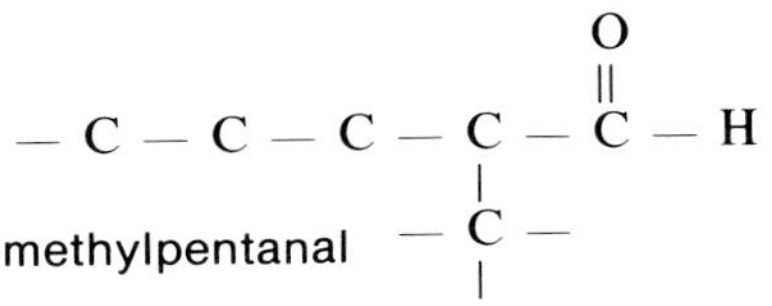

2-methylpentanal

The simplest aldehyde (and one of the most important ones in industry) is known by its common name—formaldehyde. Its IUPAC name is methanal. The substance is a colorless gas with a piercing odor. Since the gas is difficult to handle, it is often dissolved in water to make a 37 per cent solution called formalin. This is the solution that preserves frogs, fetal pigs, and other creatures destined to be dissected in biology labs. The solution is also used as an embalming fluid. It reacts with proteins and starches to form insoluble compounds. Other important aldehydes give unique flavors.

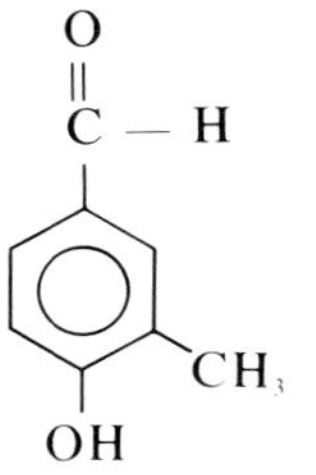

O
||
C — H
(benzene ring with CH_3 and OH substituents)

Vanillin
(vanilla)

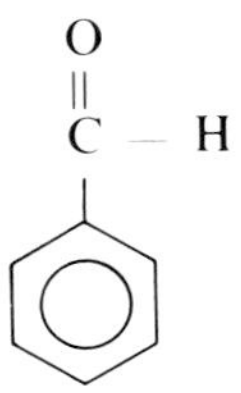

O
||
C — H
(benzene ring)

Benzaldehyde
(almonds)

| | O ||
C = C — C —
(benzene ring)

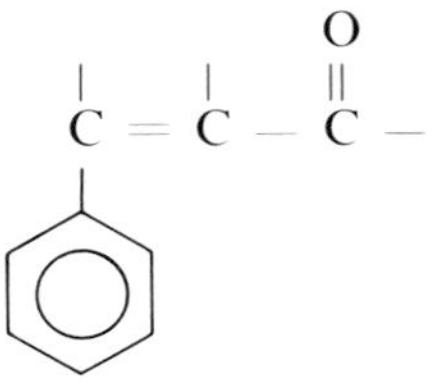

Cinnamaldehyde
(cinnamon)

16–14 Ketones: Molecules with C=O Groups in the Middle

If a doubly bonded oxygen is attached to a carbon that is not on the end of the chain, the compound is called a **ketone.** The general formula of ketones is

$$R_1 - \overset{\overset{\displaystyle O}{\|}}{C} - R_2$$

The simplest ketone is commonly called acetone. According to IUPAC rules, its name is propanone. The name of a ketone is derived from the name of the alkane that has the same number of carbon atoms; the *-e* ending of the alkane is changed to *-one*. For chains over four carbons long, the location of the carbonyl group is shown by a numerical prefix.

$$- \underset{|}{\overset{|}{C}} - \overset{\overset{\displaystyle O}{\|}}{C} - \underset{|}{\overset{|}{C}} -$$

Acetone

$$- \underset{|}{\overset{|}{C}} - \underset{|}{\overset{|}{C}} - \overset{\overset{\displaystyle O}{\|}}{C} - \underset{|}{\overset{|}{C}} -$$

Butanone

Acetone is an excellent solvent. While the molecule's methyl groups are nonpolar, the carbonyl group is polar. As a result, acetone dissolves most organic compounds but still mixes well with water. Acetone is widely used as a solvent for lacquers, paint removers, explosives, plastics, and disinfectants. It is also the active ingredient in nail-polish removers.

Since both ketones and aldehydes have the C=O group, it is not surprising that they have similar physical and chemical properties. As a rule, though, aldehydes are slightly more chemically reactive because their functional group is exposed on the end of the carbon chain.

16–15 Carboxylic Acids: Ant Bites, Bee Stings, and Vinegar

The Ant

The ant has made himself illustrious
Through constant industry industrious.
So what?
Would you be calm and placid
If you were filled with formic acid?

Ogden Nash

A carboxylic acid puts the "fire" in fire ants and the "ouch" in bee stings. Because of their abundance in nature, carboxylic acids were among the first organic compounds to be studied in detail. Since the IUPAC rules were still decades away from being formulated, the acids acquired common names from their most familiar sources. The Latin word for vinegar was *acetum,* so the acid in vinegar was called acetic acid. Butyric acid (from the Latin *butyrum*) gives rancid butter, aged cheese, and human perspiration their nasty odors. The Latin word for ant is *formica.* Consequently, the stinging acid of ants was called formic acid.

All **carboxylic acids** have the general formula

$$R-C\begin{matrix}{\,}^{/\!/O} \\ {}_{\setminus OH}\end{matrix}$$

The COOH group is called the **carboxyl group.** According to IUPAC nomenclature, the *-e* ending of the corresponding alkane is changed to *-oic,* and the word *acid* is added to form the name of a carboxylic acid.

$HCOOH$	CH_3COOH	$CH_3(CH_2)_2COOH$
$-C\begin{matrix}{\,}^{/\!/O} \\ {}_{\setminus OH}\end{matrix}$	$-\overset{\vert}{\underset{\vert}{C}}-C\begin{matrix}{\,}^{/\!/O} \\ {}_{\setminus OH}\end{matrix}$	$-\overset{\vert}{\underset{\vert}{C}}-\overset{\vert}{\underset{\vert}{C}}-\overset{\vert}{\underset{\vert}{C}}-C\begin{matrix}{\,}^{/\!/O} \\ {}_{\setminus OH}\end{matrix}$
Formic acid (methanoic acid)	Acetic acid (ethanoic acid)	Butyric acid (butanoic acid)

The smaller carboxylic acids are liquids at room temperature and have sharp or unpleasant odors. The acids with longer carbon chains are usually waxy solids. When the carbon chains are between twelve and twenty carbon atoms long, the compounds are often called **fatty acids.** Carboxylic acids are quite polar. They can form hydrogen bonds between themselves and other molecules. This explains why even the smallest members of the family are liquids at room temperature. Since they form hydrogen bonds with water, carboxylic acids are soluble in water—unless their hydrocarbon chains are so long that they dominate the molecules.

To be an acid, a compound should have an ionizable hydrogen. The hydrogen that gets ionized in a carboxylic acid is the one in the functional group. Since only a small fraction of carboxylic acid molecules dissociate, these acids are weak: only four out of one hundred acetic acid molecules ionize. The dissociation constant is only 1.754×10^{-5}. Although they are weak acids, carboxylic acids react quickly with strong bases to form salts. Many of these salts are used commercially. Most soaps are sodium or potassium salts of long-chain (fatty) acids.

16–16 Esters: Sweet-Smelling Chemicals

If the hydrogen of a carboxyl group is replaced with an alkyl group, an **ester** forms.

$$R_1 - C \overset{\displaystyle /\!\!/ O}{\underset{\displaystyle \backslash O - R_2}{}}$$

Unlike their cousins the carboxylic acids, esters generally have appealing smells. These compounds are responsible for the flavors of many fruits and the fragrances of many flowers. In the naming of an ester, the R_2 group is indicated with its alkyl name, and the carboxylic acid part is given an *-oate* ending.

Table 16-22

IUPAC Name	Structural Formula	Flavor or Odor
2-methylpropyl methanoate	$-C(=O)-O-C-C(-C-)-C-$	raspberry
Pentyl ethanoate	$-C-C(=O)-O-C-C-C-C-C-$	banana
Octyl ethanoate	$-C-C(=O)-O-C-C-C-C-C-C-C-C-$	orange
Pentyl propanoate	$-C-C-C(=O)-O-C-C-C-C-C-$	apricot
Ethyl butanoate	$-C-C-C-C(=O)-O-C-C-$	pineapple
Ethyl heptanoate	$-C-C-C-C-C-C-C(=O)-O-C-C-$	grape

16–17 Amines and Amides: Nitrogen Compounds

Nitrogen can bond into organic molecules in several different ways. The **amines** are a family of organic compounds that have ammonia as their parent. Derivatives are formed when the hydrogen atoms are replaced with other atoms or groups of atoms. One, two, or even three hydrogens may be replaced. The names of the compounds that result commonly have the word *amine* after the names of the alkyl groups.

$$\diagup \overset{N}{|} \diagdown CH_3$$

Methylamine

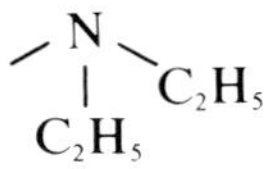

$$\diagup \overset{N}{\underset{C_2H_5}{|}} \diagdown C_2H_5$$

Diethylamine

$$CH_3 \diagup \overset{N}{\underset{CH_3}{|}} \diagdown CH_3$$

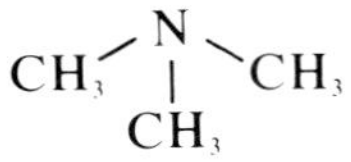

Trimethylamine

Another family of compounds that contain nitrogen is called the **amides.** All the members of this group have the following structure in common.

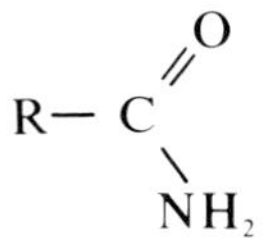

$$R-C\begin{matrix} \diagup\!\!\diagup O \\ \diagdown NH_2 \end{matrix}$$

This structure is especially important because it is what holds the amino acids in proteins together.

16–18 Organic Reactions

There are a huge number of organic compounds and multitudes of reactions that these compounds can participate in. Most of life's processes rely on chemical reactions between organic molecules. They are responsible for the movement of muscles, the digestion of food, the transmission of nerve impulses, and even the sensing of light upon the retina. Industrial chemists manipulate molecules to form plastics, fuels, synthetic fabrics, and a host of other products. Needless to say, some of these reactions are quite complicated. For now, this text will survey a few of the reactions that characterize organic compounds.

16-23 Families of Organic Compounds

Hydrocarbons

alkane	alkene	alkyne	cyclic	aromatic
—C—C—C—	—C=C—C—	—C≡C—C—	cyclo C—C—C ring	benzene ring
propane	propene	propyne	cyclopropane	benzene

Substituted Hydrocarbons

Family	Structural Formula	Suffix or Group Name	Typical Compound	Name of Compound
halide	R—C—X	chloro, bromo, fluoro, iodo	F—C—C—C—	fluoropropane
alcohol	R—C—OH	-ol	—C—C—C—OH	1-propanol
ether	R_1—O—R_2	ether	—C—O—C—	dimethyl etner
aldehyde	R—C=O	-al	—C—C—C(=O)	propanal
ketone	R_1—C(=O)—R_2	-one	—C—C(=O)—C—	propanone
carboxylic acid	R—C(OH)=O	-oic acid	—C—C—C(=O)—OH	propanoic acid
ester	R_1—C(=O)—O—R_2	-oate	—C—C—C(=O)—O—C—	methyl propanoate
amine	R_1—N(R_2)—R_3	amine	—C—N—C—C—	methylethyl amine
amide	R—C(=O)—NH_2	amide	—C—C—C(=O)—N—	propanamide

16-24 Rapid oxidation of fatty acids in a potato chip.

Oxidation-Reduction. These two types of reactions were discussed in Chapter 15. Oxidation is the loss of electrons, and reduction is the gain of electrons. Whenever oxygen and carbon atoms bond, the carbon is oxidized. Since oxygen atoms have high electronegativities, they pull shared electrons away from carbon. This means that the addition of oxygen always makes the oxidation number of carbon more positive. Adding hydrogen atoms reduces carbon atoms.

Combustion oxidizes all the carbon atoms in an organic molecule to carbon dioxide. All hydrocarbons burn in oxygen to form carbon dioxide, water, and plenty of heat. The energy from these combustion reactions is used in engines to move cars, in furnaces to heat homes, and in gas lanterns to light up dark campsites.

Fatty acid chains in food are oxidized by the human body in much the same way that other hydrocarbons are burned. Providentially, the body precisely controls the oxidation so that only small amounts of energy are released at any instant. This regulation keeps the temperatures during oxidation tolerable and allows the body to use most of the released energy.

Substitution. **Substitution reactions** replace one part of a molecule with another part. Typically, most of the reactions of unreactive compounds are substitution reactions. Alkanes are not very reactive, but this is not surprising. Every carbon is already saturated with four single bonds. Furthermore, each of these bonds is very stable. When alkanes are heated to high temperatures or exposed to energetic ultraviolet light, hydrogen atoms can be replaced by other atoms. For example, methane and chlorine can react to form a variety of substitution products.

16-25 Substitution of Cl atoms for H atoms in CH_4.

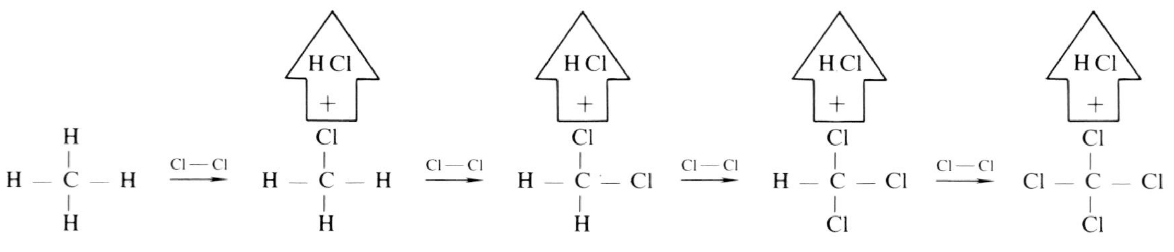

Methane | Chloromethane | Dichloromethane | Trichloromethane (chloroform) | Tetrachloromethane (carbon tetrachloride)

Various groups can replace one or more of the hydrogens of aromatic compounds. Benzene can be nitrated, halogenated, or even alkylated.

16-26 Substitution reactions of benzene.

$$C_6H_6 + HO-NO_2 \longrightarrow C_6H_5NO_2 + HOH$$

Nitrobenzene

$$C_6H_6 + Br-Br \xrightarrow{Fe} C_6H_5Br + HBr$$

Bromobenzene

$$C_6H_6 + Cl-CH_2-CH_3 \xrightarrow{AlCl_3} C_6H_5-CH_2-CH_3 + HCl$$

Ethylbenzene

Addition. Compared to carbon-carbon single bonds, double bonds and triple bonds are very reactive. Consequently, the double and triple bonds in a molecule react first and determine the molecule's behavior. An **addition reaction** is a reaction in which a multiple bond is broken and two atoms or groups of atoms are added. This is a characteristic reaction of unsaturated molecules.

16-27 Addition reactions of propene.

$$H_2C=CH-CH_3 + H_2 \xrightarrow[\text{or Ni}]{\text{Pt, Pd,}} CH_3-CH_2-CH_3$$

$$H_2C=CH-CH_3 + Br-Br \longrightarrow CH_2Br-CHBr-CH_3$$

$$H_2C=CH-CH_3 + HOH \longrightarrow CH_3-CH(OH)-CH_3$$

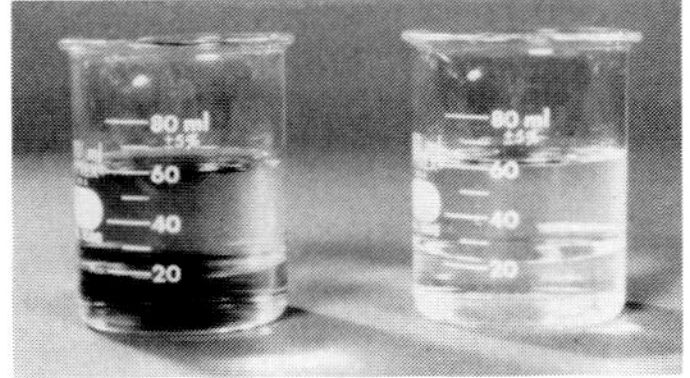

16-28 A bromine solution is added to an alkane and an alkene **(top).** The alkene reacts with the bromine and the color disappears **(bottom).**

Alkanes and alkenes look alike, but they can be distinguished by their chemical reaction with bromine. When bromine in carbon tetrachloride is first added to a hydrocarbon, the resulting mixture is reddish brown. If the reactive double bonds of alkenes are present, the bromine will be added to the molecule, and the color will disappear. If only carbon-carbon single bonds are present, the reddish brown color will remain because alkanes are unreactive under normal conditions.

Condensation and Hydrolysis. Like oxidation and reduction reactions, these reactions are opposites. Reactions in which molecules combine with each other and lose a water molecule are called **condensation reactions.** Two identical alcohol molecules can be made to join together to form an ether under special reaction conditions.

$$R - OH \quad + \quad H - OR \xrightarrow{H_2SO_4} R - O - R \quad + \quad HOH$$

Esters form when carboxylic acids and alcohols go through a condensation reaction. This condensation reaction is called **esterification.** An artificial banana flavoring can be made when ethanoic (acetic) acid and pentanol are mixed.

$$-\overset{|}{\underset{|}{C}} - C\genfrac{}{}{0pt}{}{/\!\!/ O}{\backslash OH} \quad + \quad -\overset{|}{\underset{|}{C}}-\overset{|}{\underset{|}{C}}-\overset{|}{\underset{|}{C}}-\overset{|}{\underset{|}{C}}-\overset{|}{\underset{|}{C}}- OH \longrightarrow$$

Ethanoic acid (acetic acid) Pentanol

$$-\overset{|}{\underset{|}{C}} - C\genfrac{}{}{0pt}{}{/\!\!/ O}{\backslash O-\overset{|}{\underset{|}{C}}-\overset{|}{\underset{|}{C}}-\overset{|}{\underset{|}{C}}-\overset{|}{\underset{|}{C}}-\overset{|}{\underset{|}{C}}-} \quad + \quad HOH$$

Pentyl ethanoate

A condensation reaction is responsible for much of the clothing that people wear. **Polymers** are substances that consist of huge molecules that have repeating structural units. Dacron polyester, one of the more common polymers, forms when ethylene glycol and terephthalic acid condense.

$$\sim OCH_2CH_2O-\overset{O}{\overset{\|}{C}}-\langle\bigcirc\rangle-\overset{O}{\overset{\|}{C}}-OCH_2CH_2O-\overset{O}{\overset{\|}{C}}-\langle\bigcirc\rangle-\overset{O}{\overset{\|}{C}}-O\sim$$

Dacron polyester

Hydrolysis is the reverse process of condensation. A water molecule works its way into the functional group of a large molecule and splits it. The OH group of the water attaches to one of the newly formed molecules, and the hydrogen attaches to the other molecule. The artificial banana flavoring made by a condensation reaction exists in equilibrium with a hydrolysis reaction.

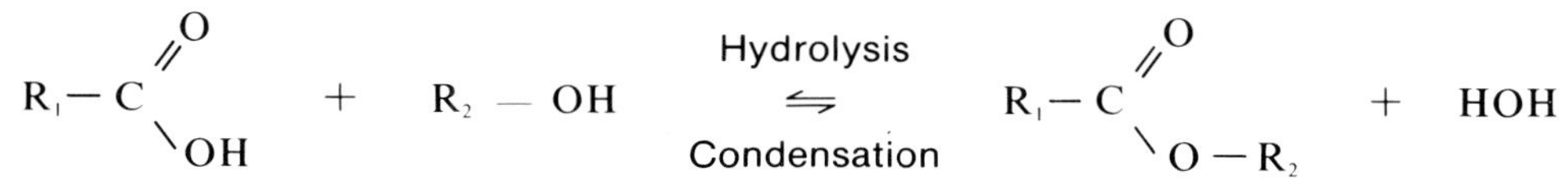

$$\underset{\text{Carboxylic acid}}{R_1-C\begin{matrix}{}^{/\!/O}\\ {}_{\backslash OH}\end{matrix}} + \underset{\text{Alcohol}}{R_2-OH} \underset{\text{Condensation}}{\overset{\text{Hydrolysis}}{\leftrightharpoons}} \underset{\text{Ester}}{R_1-C\begin{matrix}{}^{/\!/O}\\ {}_{\backslash O-R_2}\end{matrix}} + \underset{\text{Water}}{HOH}$$

Soap making, or **saponification,** illustrates hydrolysis. The large molecule to be split is a fat molecule with three ester linkages. Each ester link is susceptible to hydrolysis. When steam hits the fats, water molecules split the large fat molecules.

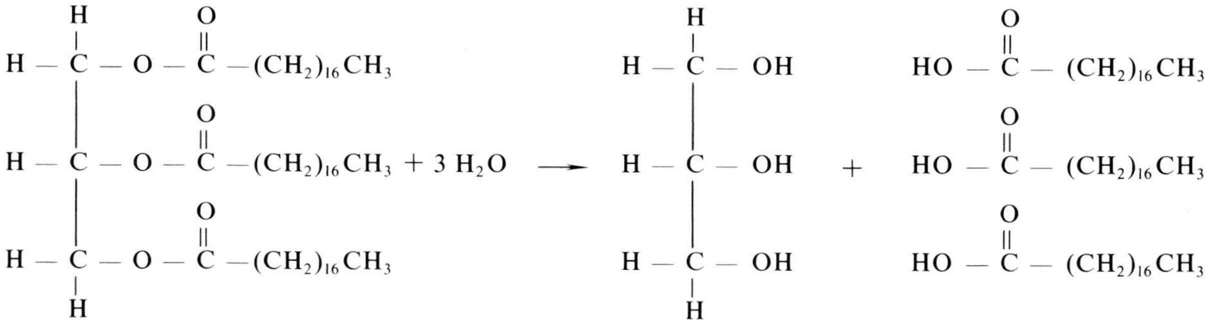

$$\underset{\text{Fat}}{\begin{matrix} H-\underset{|}{\overset{H}{\overset{|}{C}}}-O-\overset{O}{\overset{\|}{C}}-(CH_2)_{16}CH_3 \\ H-\underset{|}{\overset{|}{C}}-O-\overset{O}{\overset{\|}{C}}-(CH_2)_{16}CH_3 \\ H-\underset{H}{\underset{|}{C}}-O-\overset{O}{\overset{\|}{C}}-(CH_2)_{16}CH_3 \end{matrix}} + 3\,H_2O \longrightarrow \underset{\text{Glycerol}}{\begin{matrix} H-\overset{H}{\overset{|}{C}}-OH \\ H-\overset{|}{\underset{|}{C}}-OH \\ H-\underset{H}{\underset{|}{C}}-OH \end{matrix}} + \underset{\text{Fatty acids}}{\begin{matrix} HO-\overset{O}{\overset{\|}{C}}-(CH_2)_{16}CH_3 \\ HO-\overset{O}{\overset{\|}{C}}-(CH_2)_{16}CH_3 \\ HO-\overset{O}{\overset{\|}{C}}-(CH_2)_{16}CH_3 \end{matrix}}$$

Once the fatty acids have been separated, a strong base can be easily added. The result is the salt of a fatty acid, otherwise known as soap. In early American days fats and oils were boiled with lye (NaOH) for many hours in great kettles. The hydrolysis and the reaction with the sodium hydroxide base occurred at the same time.

16-29 Structural formula of a soap molecule.

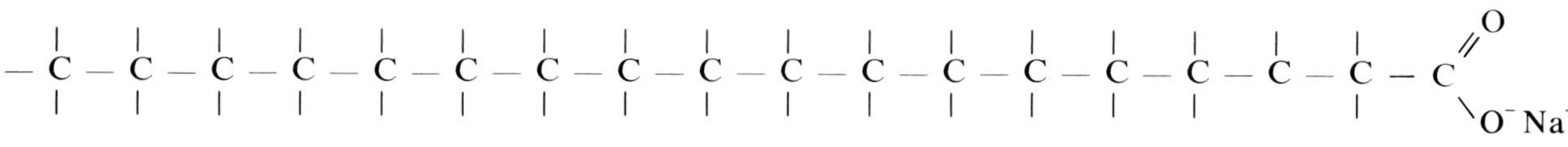

$$-\underset{|}{\overset{|}{C}}-\underset{|}{\overset{|}{C}}-\underset{|}{\overset{|}{C}}-\underset{|}{\overset{|}{C}}-\underset{|}{\overset{|}{C}}-\underset{|}{\overset{|}{C}}-\underset{|}{\overset{|}{C}}-\underset{|}{\overset{|}{C}}-\underset{|}{\overset{|}{C}}-\underset{|}{\overset{|}{C}}-\underset{|}{\overset{|}{C}}-\underset{|}{\overset{|}{C}}-\underset{|}{\overset{|}{C}}-\underset{|}{\overset{|}{C}}-\underset{|}{\overset{|}{C}}-\overset{|}{C}-\underset{|}{\overset{|}{C}}-C\begin{matrix}{}^{/\!/O}\\ {}_{\backslash O^-Na^+}\end{matrix}$$

Coming to Terms

aliphatic compound
aromatic compound
hydrocarbon
alkane
saturated
structural isomer
alkene
unsaturated
alkyne
cyclic aliphatic compound
delocalized electrons
functional group
alkyl group
alkyl halide
aryl group
aryl halide
alcohol
ether
aldehyde
carbonyl group
ketone
carboxylic acid
carboxyl group
fatty acid
ester
amine
amide
substitution reaction
addition reaction
condensation reaction
esterification
polymer
hydrolysis
saponification

Review Questions

1. What characteristic of carbon enables it to be found in millions of compounds?
2. Modify the structural formula of the alkane 2-methylbutane to create the various kinds of compounds requested. Remember that carbon atoms always have four bonds. Add or delete hydrogens when necessary.

```
   |   |   |   |
 — C — C — C — C —
   |   |   |   |
     — C —
       |
```

   a. an alkene
   b. an alkyne
   c. an alkyl halide containing one iodine atom
   d. an alcohol
   e. an aldehyde
   f. a ketone
   g. a carboxylic acid
   h. an ester (Use an ethyl group to modify the carboxylic acid drawn in part [g].)
   i. an amine
   j. an amide (Modify the carboxylic acid drawn in part [g].)

3. Classify each of the following compounds according to its general family.

a.
```
    |   |
  — C — C — Br
    |   |
```

b.
```
            O
    |   |   ||  |
  — C — C — C — C —
    |   |       |
```

c.
```
                  O
    |   |        //
  — C — C — C
    |   |        \
      — C —       OH
        |
```

d.
```
        |
      — C —
    |   |   |   |      O
  — C — C — C — C — C //
    |   |   |   |      \
                        NH2
```

e.
```
                |
              — C —
    |           |   |
  — C — C ≡ C — C — C —
    |           |   |
```

f.
```
    |   |   |
  — C — C — C — NH2
    |   |   |
```

g.
```
        |   |
      — C- -C —
    |   |   |   |   |
  — C — C — C — C — C —
    |   |   |   |   |
          — C —
            |
```

h.
```
                O
    |          //
  — C — C            |
    |          \
                O — C —
                    |
```

i.
```
        |
      — C —
    |   |   |   |   |
  — C — C — C — C — C — OH
    |   |   |   |   |
      — C —
        |
```

j.
```
    |   |   |   |
  — C — C = C — C —
    |           |
```

k. Chlorobenzene ring (Cl attached to a benzene ring)

Cl

l.
```
        |           |
      — C —       — C —
    |   |           |   |
  — C — C — O — C — C —
    |   |           |   |
```

4. Draw the structural formula for each of the following compounds. Assume that the carbon chain is straight in each case.

   a. hexane
   b. 1-heptene
   c. 2-octyne
   d. 1-pentanol
   e. butanol
   f. 1-chloropropane
   g. ethyl butanoate
   h. hexanoic acid
   i. 3-octanone
   j. methyl ethyl ether
   k. butylamine

5. Name each of the following compounds.

```
a.    |   |
    — C — C —
      |   |

b.    |   |   |   |
    — C = C — C — C —
              |   |

c.    |   |
    — C — C — OH
      |   |

d.    |   |   |
    — C — C — C — Cl
      |   |   |

e.    |   |   |   |
    — C — C — C — C —
      |   |   |   |
              OH

f.            O
      |      //
    — C — C
      |      \
              O — C — C —
                  |   |

g.    |   |   |   |      O
    — C — C — C — C — C //
      |   |   |   |      \OH

h.  / N \
      |   CH3
```

```
        |               |
i.  — C — C ≡ C — C —
        |               |
```

```
        |     |     |           |     |     |
j.  — C — C — C — O — C — C — C —
        |     |     |           |     |     |
```

```
                     O
        |     |     ||     |     |     |
k.  — C — C — C — C — C — C —
        |     |            |     |     |
```

6. Name a class of organic compounds that contains a substance that can be used as
   a. a fuel for welding.
   b. a fuel in automobiles.
   c. an antifreeze.
   d. a refrigerator coolant.
   e. an ingredient in soap.
   f. a lacquer paint finish.
7. Why do straight-chained alkanes have higher boiling points than alkanes with branched chains?
8. How can you tell when two compounds are structural isomers?
9. Draw an electron-dot structure of propyne. Would you expect this molecule to be polar or nonpolar? Why?
10. What is unique about the carbon-carbon bonds in benzene and other aromatic compounds?
11. Methane (CH_4) is a gas at room temperature, whereas methanol (CH_3OH) is a liquid. Aside from the difference in molecular masses, can you suggest an explanation for their different melting and boiling points?
12. Methanol is soluble in water, but larger alcohols like octanol are not. Why is this?
13. Alcohols and metallic hydroxides both have OH groups in their structural formulas. Why are metallic hydroxides such as NaOH much more caustic than alcohols?
14. How are HCl and CH_3COOH similar? How are they different?
15. Give one way in which NaCl and soap are similar and one way in which they are different.
16. Draw a structural formula of acetic acid (CH_3COOH), and identify the hydrogen atom that is ionized.

SEVENTEEN

BIOCHEMISTRY

THE MIRACULOUS CHEMISTRY OF LIFE

BIOCHEMISTRY is a springboard; no one who studies it in depth can stay secluded in the field of chemistry for long. The subject naturally leads its students to wider, more comprehensive thought. As its name implies, the subject of biochemistry leads students from the study of traditional chemistry into a field where many sciences blend together. The distinctions between biology, chemistry, and mathematics quickly become blurred. The marvelous complexities of life cannot be studied within the confines of a single subject area.

Biochemistry leads from strictly scientific matters into the realm of philosophical and spiritual issues. As scientists unravel the mysteries of DNA, they begin to see some sobering capabilities of genetic engineering. Can genetic material be altered? Can new forms of life be produced from old forms? Can humans be cloned? These questions naturally lead to the question, "*Should* these things be done?" Science may be able to tell how something can be done, but it cannot tell whether something is right. Scientists, biochemists in particular, need Bible-based ethical and moral guidelines that stem from true spiritual wisdom to direct their work.

Finally, and most critically, biochemistry diverts attention from man to God. The infinite wisdom of the Creator is on display in the precise architecture of a protein chain, the complexity of a metabolic pathway, and the efficiency of an enzyme. Every molecule witnesses to the power, engineering ingenuity, and foresight of God. Man has been granted the privilege of making many discoveries in the field of biochemistry. These discoveries are exciting, but they are also humbling, for they reveal an omniscient, omnipotent Creator. The field of biochemistry can extend man's thoughts to the problems that face society, the fundamental issues of life, and ultimately, the character of God.

Carbohydrates

Carbohydrates are the most abundant biological compounds. Sugars and starches make up a large part of the human diet. Each year photosynthetic processes in plants convert water and carbon dioxide into one hundred billion tons of carbohydrates. The exoskeletons of all the insects, crabs, and lobsters on this planet contribute even more carbohydrates to this already impressive amount.

17–1 What Carbohydrates Are and What They Do

Carbohydrate literally means "water of carbon." The name stems back to the days when these compounds were thought to be hydrates of carbon (water and carbon are produced when carbohydrates are heated). All carbohydrates have several of the OH (hydroxy) groups that are common to alcohols. They also have the C=O (carbonyl) group of aldehydes and ketones. Concisely stated, **carbohydrates** are polyhydroxy aldehydes or ketones.

The three major functions of carbohydrates are energy storage, energy supply, and structural support. Plant cells store energy from the sun by using it to build carbohydrates from carbon dioxide and water. Carbohydrates supply energy (for animals) when they are broken down and oxidized during the processes of cellular respiration. Carbohydrates called cellulose and chitin provide structural support. Fibers and bundles of these materials support giant redwoods and protect lobsters from their enemies.

17-1 Common carbohydrates.

17–2 Monosaccharides

Carbohydrates may be classified into three groups according to the number of units they contain. **Monosaccharides,** or simple sugars, have one polyhydroxy aldehyde or ketone. All known monosaccharides, and there are many of them, are colorless, crystalline solids that dissolve in water. Most have a sweet taste. They rarely occur in nature as free molecules but are usually bonded to a protein, a fat, or another carbohydrate. Two significant exceptions that exist as free molecules are glucose and fructose.

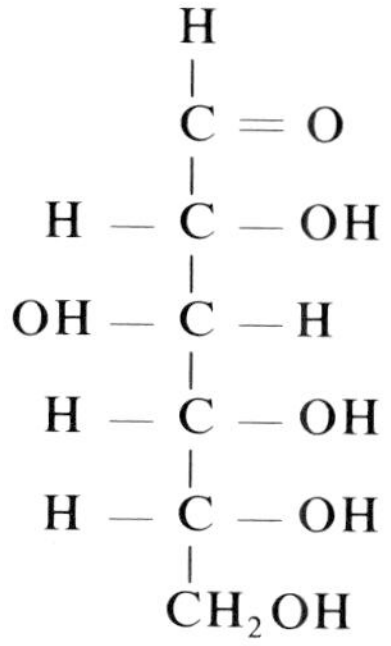

```
        H
        |
        C = O                  CH2OH
        |                        |
   H  — C — OH                   C = O
        |                        |
  OH  — C — H             OH  —  C — H
        |                        |
   H  — C — OH             H  —  C — OH
        |                        |
   H  — C — OH             H  —  C — OH
        |                        |
      CH2OH                    CH2OH
```

Glucose 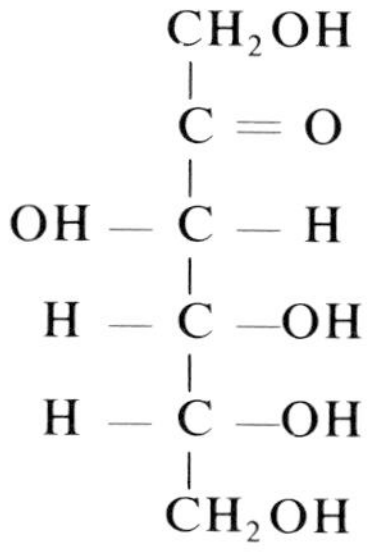   Fructose

Glucose is the most abundant sugar in nature. Ripe berries, grapes, and oranges contain 20 to 30 per cent glucose. The human body maintains a reasonably constant level of 80 to 120 milligrams of glucose per 100 milliliters of blood. Glucose is also the fundamental building block of the most common long-chain carbohydrates. Fructose may be found in ripe fruits and honey.

Monosaccharides are not always straight, chainlike molecules. They usually exist in rings that form when atoms near the end of the chain bond to atoms near the beginning of the chain. Glucose in an aqueous solution exists in an equilibrium between the two ring forms and the straight-chain form. The equilibrium lies strongly in favor of the ring forms.

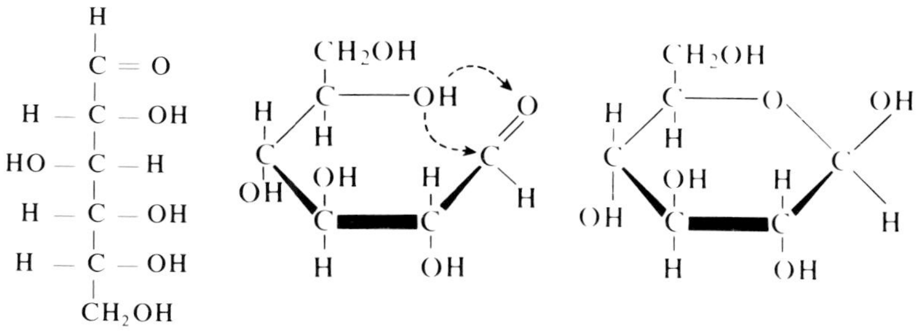

```
        H
        |
        C = O
        |
   H  — C — OH
        |
  HO  — C — H
        |
   H  — C — OH
        |
   H  — C — OH
        |
      CH2OH
```

Straight form   Bent form   Ring form

17-2 Formation of the ring structure in glucose.

17-3 Glucose molecules exist in one of three forms.

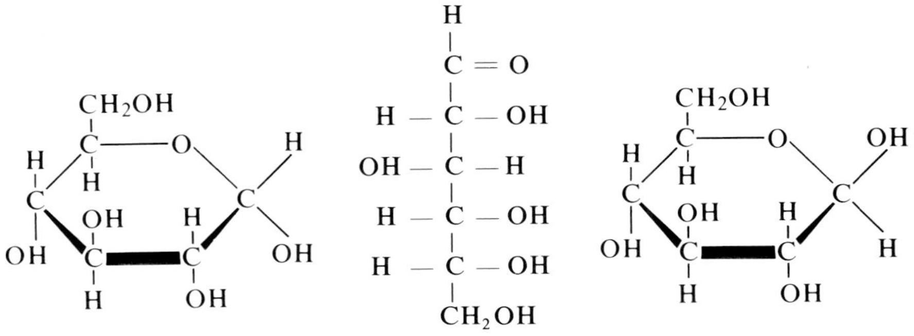

36%   less than 0.1%   63%

Fructose also forms ring structures when it is in solution. Since the carbonyl group is not at the end of the carbon chain, the ring that forms has only five members.

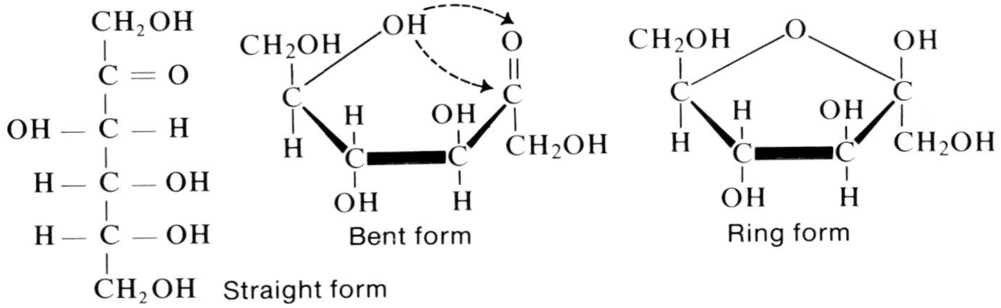

17-4 Formation of the ring structure in fructose.

Straight form   Bent form   Ring form

17–3 Disaccharides: Table Sugar and Other Goodies

As their name implies, **disaccharides** contain two monosaccharide units. An oxygen bridge between the two monosaccharides holds the two units together. While a large number of monosaccharides exist, an even larger number of disaccharides can be formed from combinations of monosaccharides. Of the numerous possibilities, three disaccharides play an important part in the human diet: maltose, lactose, and sucrose.

17-5 Formation of a disaccharide from two monosaccharides. The bond that joins the two units may point in one of two directions.

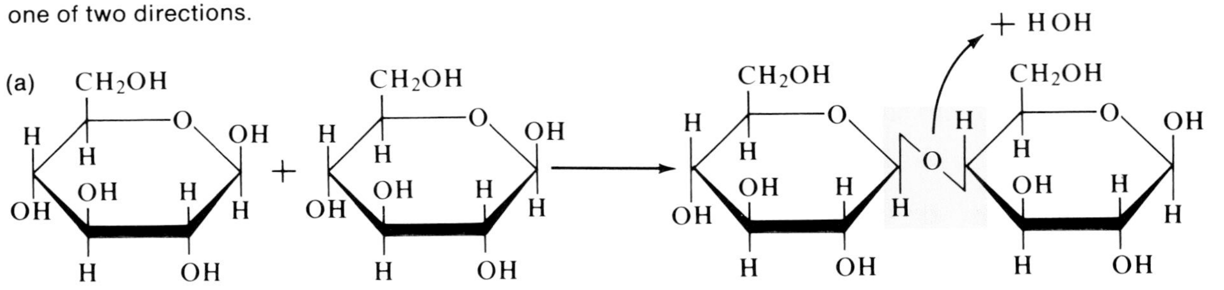

(a) + HOH

(b)

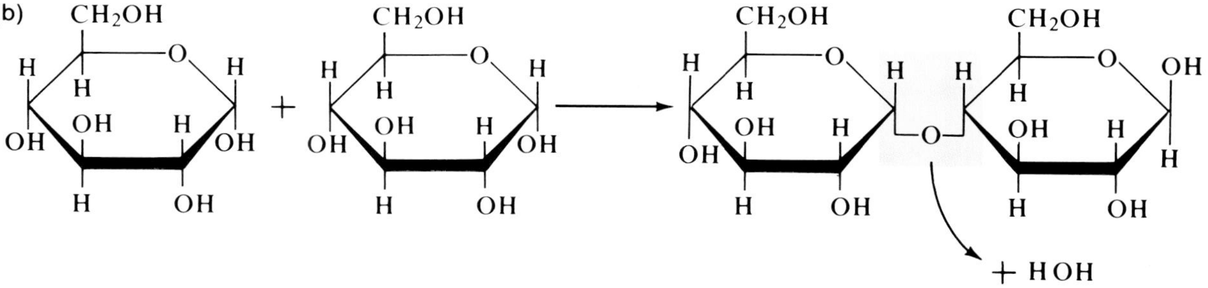

+ HOH

Maltose is the name given to two glucose molecules that are bonded together. The bond forms between the first carbon of one molecule and the fourth carbon of the other. Maltose is found in germinating grain and is produced during the digestion of starches.

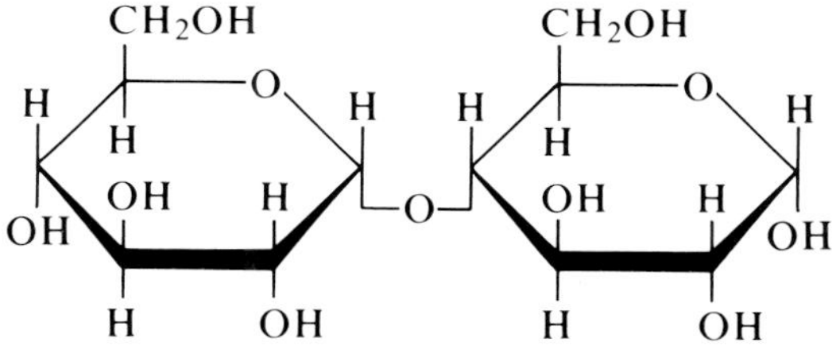

+HOH

Maltose

Lactose is a dissaccharide found only in milk. It consists of an isomer of glucose joined to a glucose molecule. The sugar is not very sweet, but it is an important ingredient in milk. If milk has become sour, it is because the lactose has broken down into lactic acid.

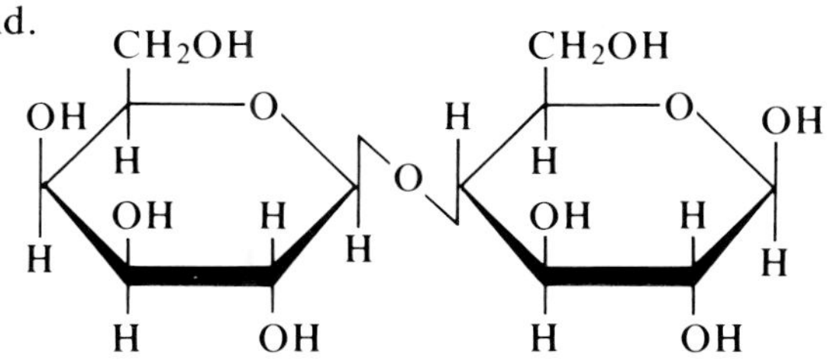

Lactose

Sucrose, the common household sugar that many Americans love so much, consists of glucose and fructose molecules. A bond links the first carbon of glucose to the second carbon of fructose.

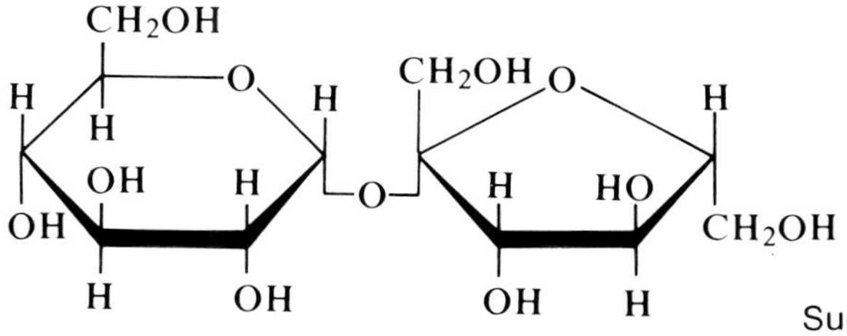

Sucrose

17-6 A hydrolysis reaction sweetens homemade preserves.

Sucrose occurs abundantly in nature; fruits, sugar cane, sugar beets, and nectar are the major sources. This disaccharide can be split by a hydrolysis reaction if it is boiled in the presence of an acid or is acted upon by an enzyme (biological catalyst). People who make jellies and jams at home frequently use this reaction. A small amount of lemon juice is commonly added to preserves before they are cooked. Traditionally, people say that this action serves to make the jam sweeter. How can this be? Everyone knows that lemon juice is sour. Lemon juice contains citric acid. The citric acid hydrolyzes the sucrose in the fruit. The result of this reaction is two sugar molecules (one glucose and one fructose) instead of one sucrose molecule. The extra sugar molecules make the jam sweeter than it would have been if the lemon juice had been left out. Honeybees cause the same type of reaction to occur when they make honey. They catalyze the reaction by secreting a special enzyme that splits sucrose molecules at hive temperatures.

17–4 Polysaccharides: Starch, Glycogen, and Cellulose

17-7 Wheat grain consists of complex polysaccharides.

Polysaccharides are molecules that contain many sugar units. This is evident from their large molecular masses (up to several million amu). Multitudes of sugar units are bonded into long chains. Polysaccharides may be built from several different monosaccharides, but this text will concentrate on the polymers of glucose.

Plants such as rice, potatoes, wheat, and oats store food in polysaccharide deposits called starch. **Starch** is a mixture of two glucose polymers: a straight chain and a branched chain. Together these polysaccharides supply nearly three-fourths of the world's food energy. The straight chain is an extended pattern of maltose disaccharide units. The bonds between the maltose units twist the long chain into a long spiral, or helix. It might seem that these long chains of sugar molecules would taste sweet; but this is not so. Polysaccharide molecules are apparently too large to activate the sweetness receptors on the tongue.

17-8 Several units in a straight-chained starch molecule.

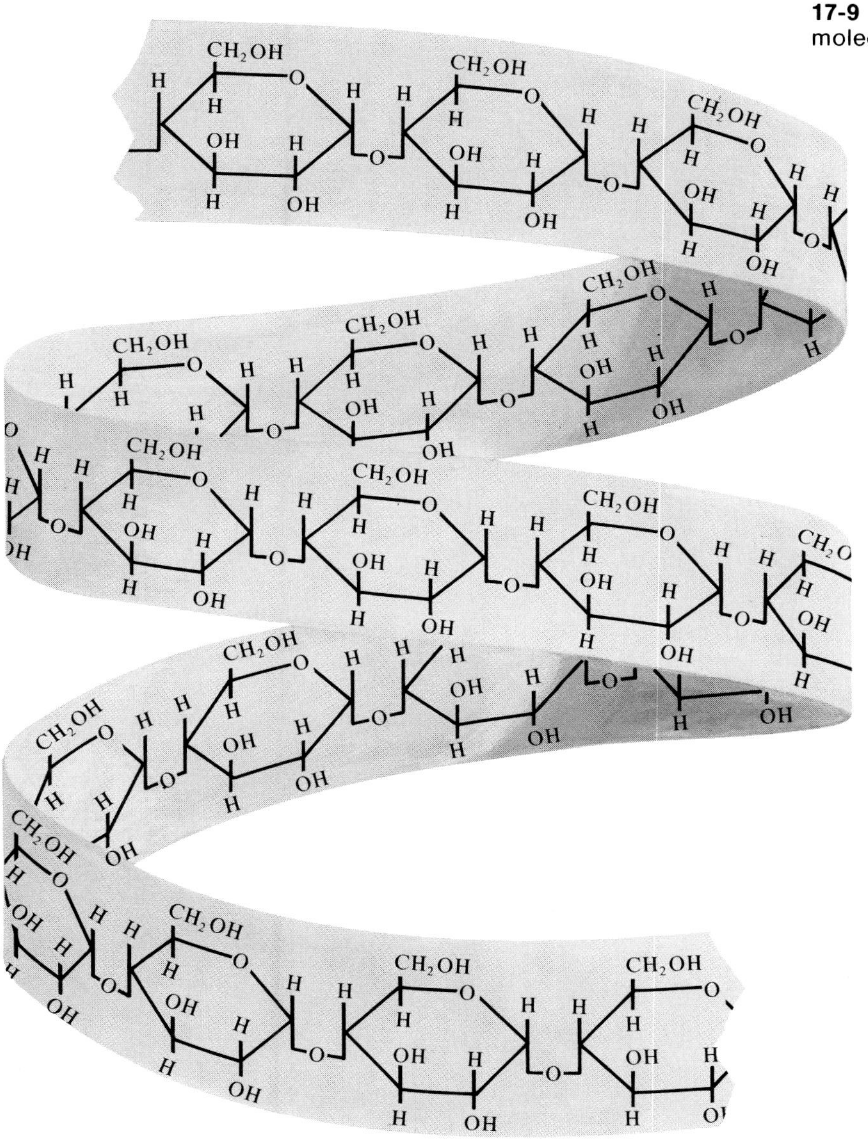

17-9 Straight-chained starch molecules coil into a helix.

The branched polymer has the same backbone of glucose molecules as the straight chain. Branches off this main chain occur when the sixth carbon of a glucose in the chain bonds to the first carbon of another glucose.

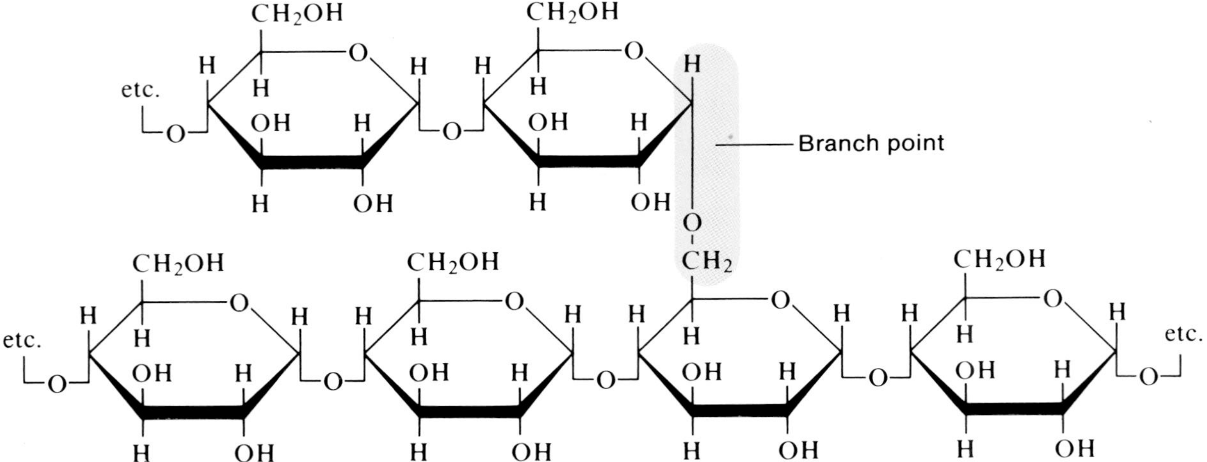

17-10 Several units in a branched starch molecule.

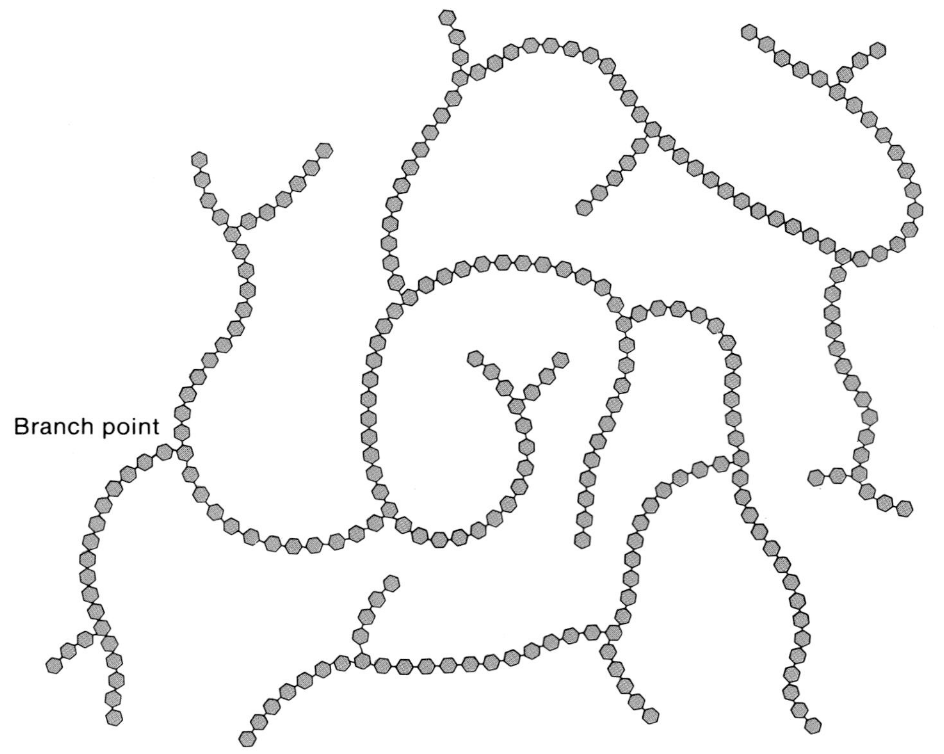

17-11 Branched starch molecules form complex networks.

Animals store food in the form of **glycogen,** not starch. Glycogen is a branched polymer of glucose in which the branches occur more frequently.

Horses, cows, and sheep eat grass. Why do humans not eat it? Aside from the taste consideration, the reason that humans do not eat such plants lies in the structure of the cellulose polymer. Cellulose, the major structural material of plants, is actually a glucose polysaccharide that is similar to starch and glycogen. In the polysaccharides that humans eat, the bonds between glucose units point downward, but the bonds in cellulose point upward. The difference between the starch in a tasty potato and the cellulose fibers in grass or a splintery piece of wood is the orientation of the bonds.

17-12 Cellulose contains glucose molecules like starch, but the bonds between the glucose units point in a different direction.

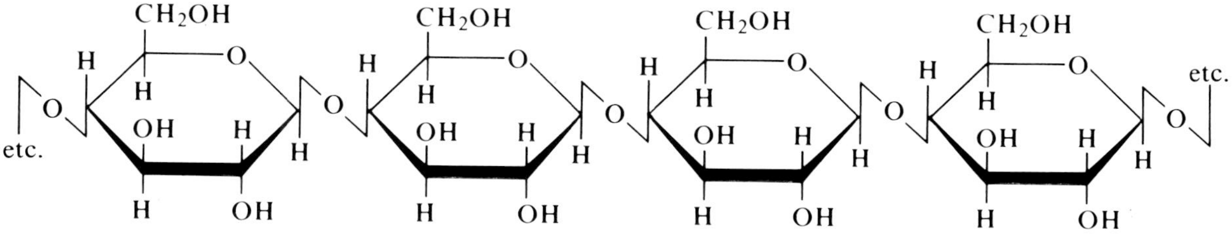

Human digestive tracts contain enzymes that can hydrolyze bonds that point downward. However, they have no such enzymes for the bonds that point upward. Cows, horses, and sheep are blessed with colonies of special bacteria that supply the needed enzymes in their intestines. The task of finding an enzyme that could break down cellulose in humans is a worthy challenge for anyone interested in eliminating the world's hunger problems, winning a Nobel prize, and revolutionizing the world's agricultural economy.

17-13 Cows can hydrolyze the bonds between the glucose units in cellulose.

Proteins

The Greek word *protos* means "first," and the French word *proteine* means "primary substance." It is not surprising, then, that the English word *protein* refers to one of the most important substances in the bodies of animals and man. Proteins serve as the building blocks for muscles, hair, blood cells, skin, spider webs, silk, enzymes, insulin, and snake venom. They are essential nutrients, and they have many life-sustaining functions. Protein chains exhibit an intricate architecture that is marvelous to behold.

17–5 Amino Acids: The Building Blocks

Amino acids are the building blocks of proteins. As their name suggests, they are molecules that contain an amine (NH_2) group

FACETS OF CHEMISTRY

You Like Milk, But Does Milk Like You?

A tall glass of cool, refreshing milk may hit the spot for you, or it may not. For some people, milk seems to be the perfect beverage. It contains important nutrients and brings a full, contented feeling. To others, it automatically brings gas, stomach cramps, and even prolonged diarrhea. The difference between these two outcomes depends on the enzymes in the small intestine.

Milk contains water, proteins, fats, and sugars. The proteins and fats can be digested without much trouble. But the major sugar in milk, lactose, requires a special enzyme to be broken down. Without this enzyme, the lactose in milk cannot be digested in the small intestine. Instead, it passes down into the lower intestine.

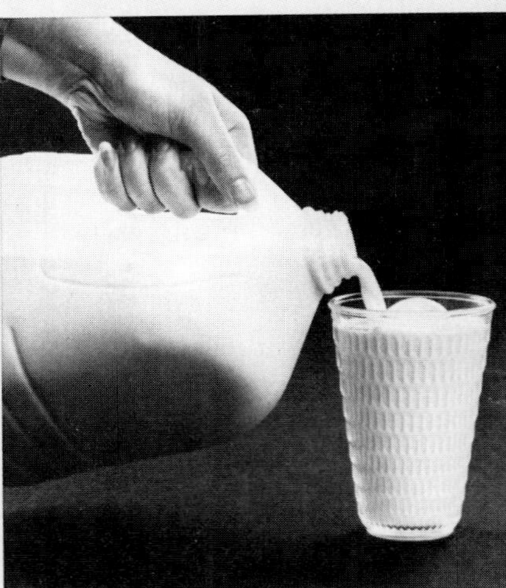

Here bacteria ferment the milk sugar into lactic acid and large quantities of carbon dioxide. The carbon dioxide gas balloons the intestine and causes a painful, bloated sensation. Severe cramps and diarrhea result if too much milk has been drunk.

Babies do not have the enzyme needed to digest lactose until just before they are born. Most babies develop large amounts of the necessary and the carboxyl (COOH) group of carboxylic acids. Various side chains (R groups) attached to the carbon adjacent to the nitrogen atom result in twenty different common amino acids.

$$
\begin{array}{ccccc}
 & & R & & O \\
 & & | & & \| \\
H_2N & - & C & - & C - OH \\
 & & | & & \\
 & & H & &
\end{array}
$$

Amino group — Carboxyl group

17-14 General formula of amino acids.

enzyme just after birth. A minority of babies do not have the enzyme, and therefore cannot tolerate milk. After three years, the production of the enzyme starts to decrease. Some adults become totally intolerant of milk, while others just cannot drink very much of it. Scientists have noted that malnutrition, diseases, and drugs can hasten the departure of the enzyme.

Interestingly enough, the ability to digest lactose is a racial trait. Adult blacks and Asians normally cannot drink milk. Only northern Europeans consistently retain the ability to drink milk when they are adults. If someone really wants to drink milk despite his bad experiences with it, he can build up a certain level of tolerance by consistently drinking milk. Most people, however, do not wish to endure the consequences of such a plan. Besides, the tolerance that is built up can quickly go away.

Knowing about the importance of enzymes in milk digestion may spare you some digestive problems. This knowledge can also clarify the scriptural analogy between milk and the fundamental doctrines of the Bible. I Peter 2:2 exhorts new Christians to "desire the sincere milk of the word, that ye may grow thereby." Yet milk is not designed to be food for adults. Christians must progress to other foods as they mature. Hebrews 5:13-14 states that "every one that useth milk is unskilful in the word of righteousness: for he is a babe. But strong meat belongeth to them that are of full age, even those who by reason of use have their senses exercised to discern both good and evil."

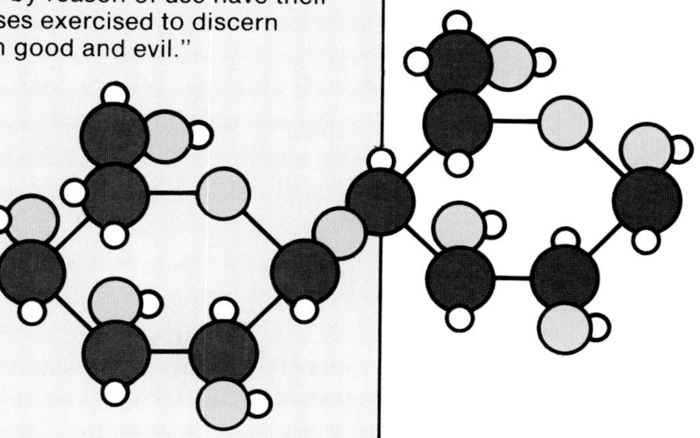

Some side chains are fragments of alkanes, and others contain aromatic rings. Still others have acidic (COOH) or basic (NH_2) groups on them. Two amino acids have side chains that contain a sulfur atom.

17-15 Selected amino acids.

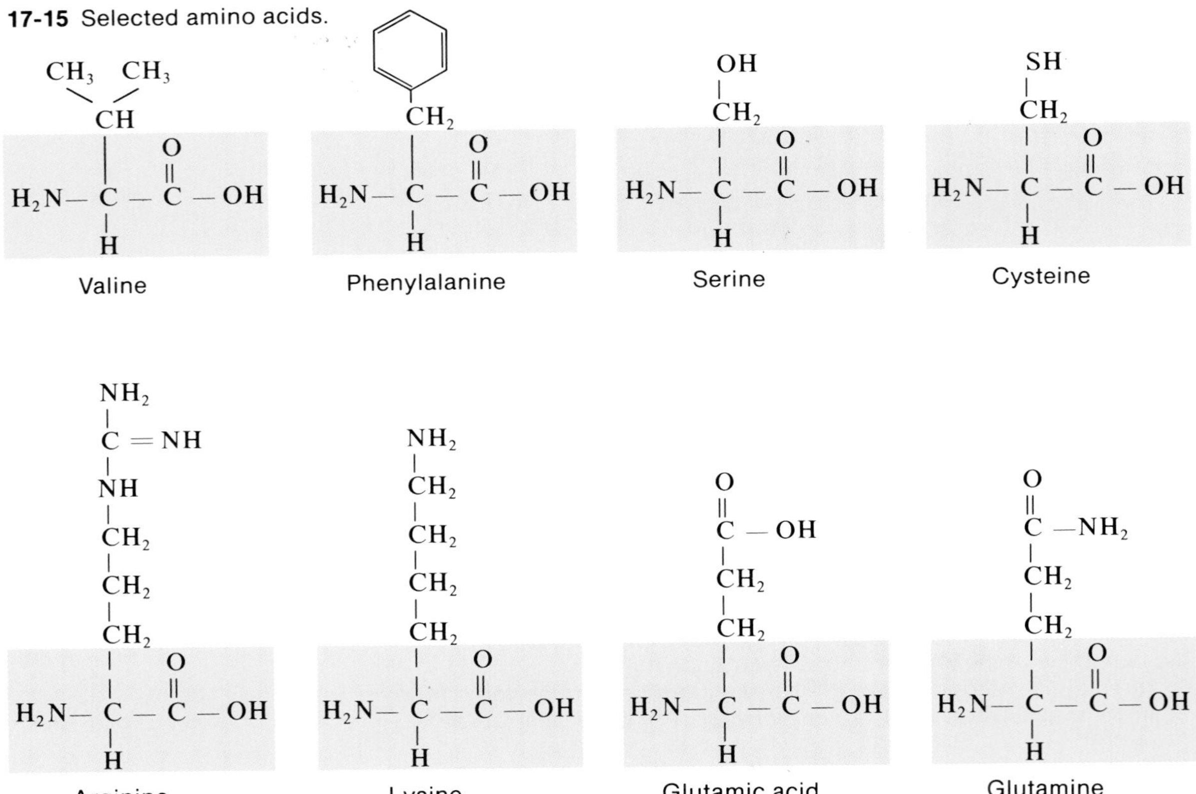

17–6 Polypeptide Chains

Amino acids join together when the amine group of one amino acid reacts with the carboxyl group of another. The bond that links the two amino acids is called a **peptide bond.** Molecules that contain two amino acids are called **dipeptides. Polypeptide** chains contain between three and approximately seventy amino acids.

A **protein** consists of one or more polypeptide chains. Some proteins contain only several hundred amino acids; others have many thousands of these building blocks. Even with a comparatively short chain, the possible number of different proteins is staggering. From the twenty common amino acids, a series of fifty amino acids could be arranged in 3×10^{64} different sequences,

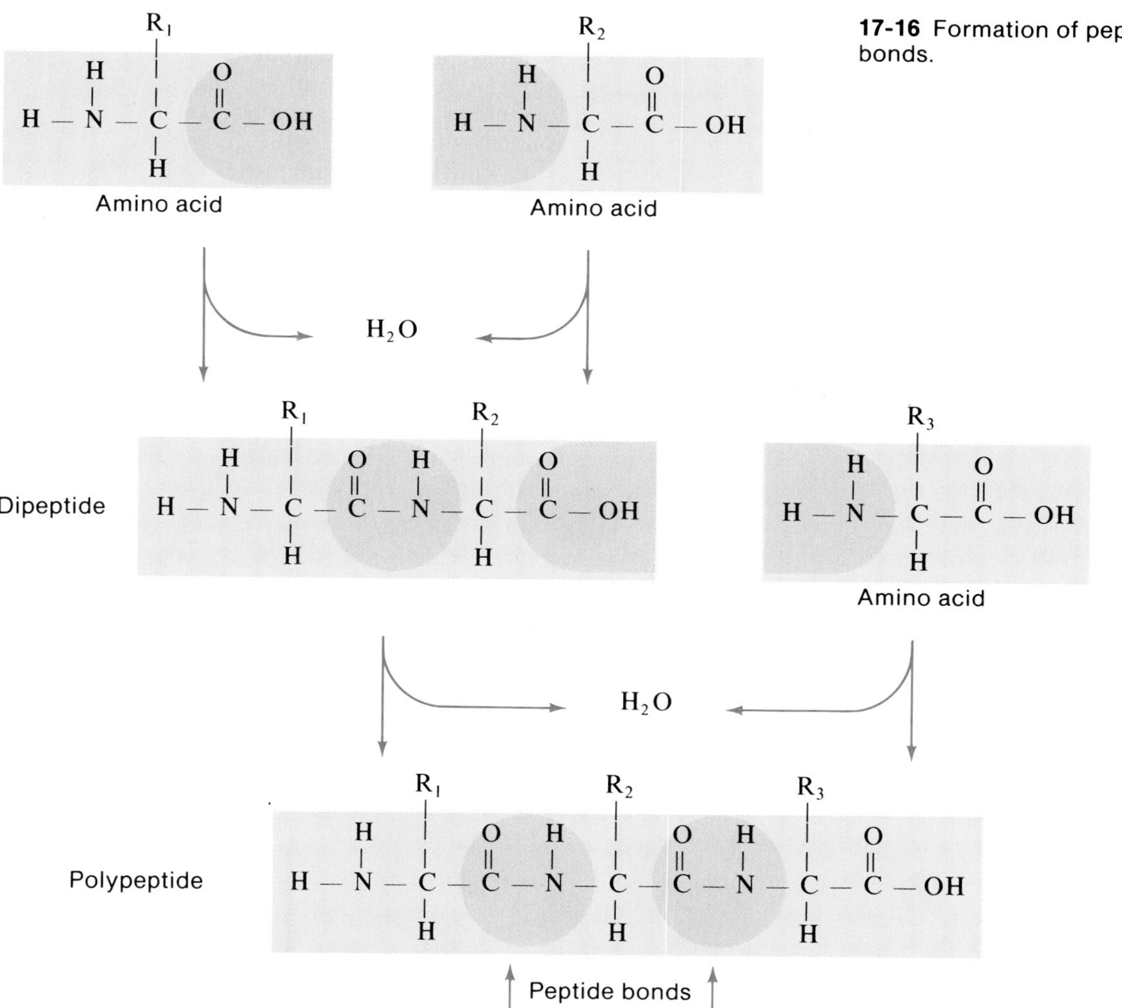

17-16 Formation of peptide bonds.

with each sequence forming a different protein. When one considers that most proteins are much longer, the complexity and variety of proteins in God's creation become apparent.

Like polysaccharides, polypeptides tend to form regular shapes. The exact conformation of the chain depends on the amino acids that are present and the order in which they appear. The shapes and electrical natures of amino acids cause many proteins to coil themselves into helixes. This tight spiral of amino acids is held in place by hydrogen bonds between certain atoms in the amino acid backbone of the protein. A hydrogen in one amino acid forms a hydrogen bond with an oxygen of the amino acid four positions away. The side-chains of each amino acid extend like spokes from the surface of the helix. It is amazing that these intricate coils get their form from ordinary, but carefully arranged, hydrogen bonds. The structure truly is a masterpiece of art and engineering. Helixes known as alpha helixes impart toughness to hair, wool, nails, claws, antlers, hooves, and turtle shells. In most of these instances, alpha-helix coils wind around each other to form larger strands and fibers.

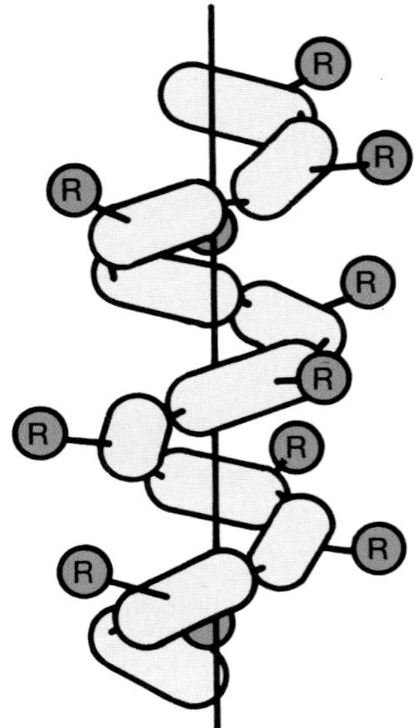

17-17 Helical arrangement of amino acids around an axis with the side chains extending outward.

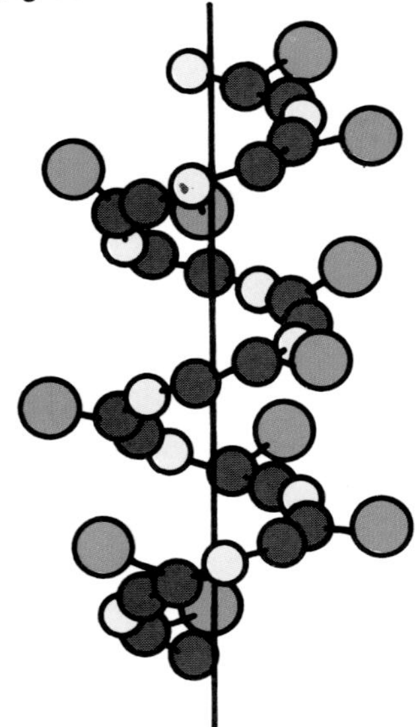

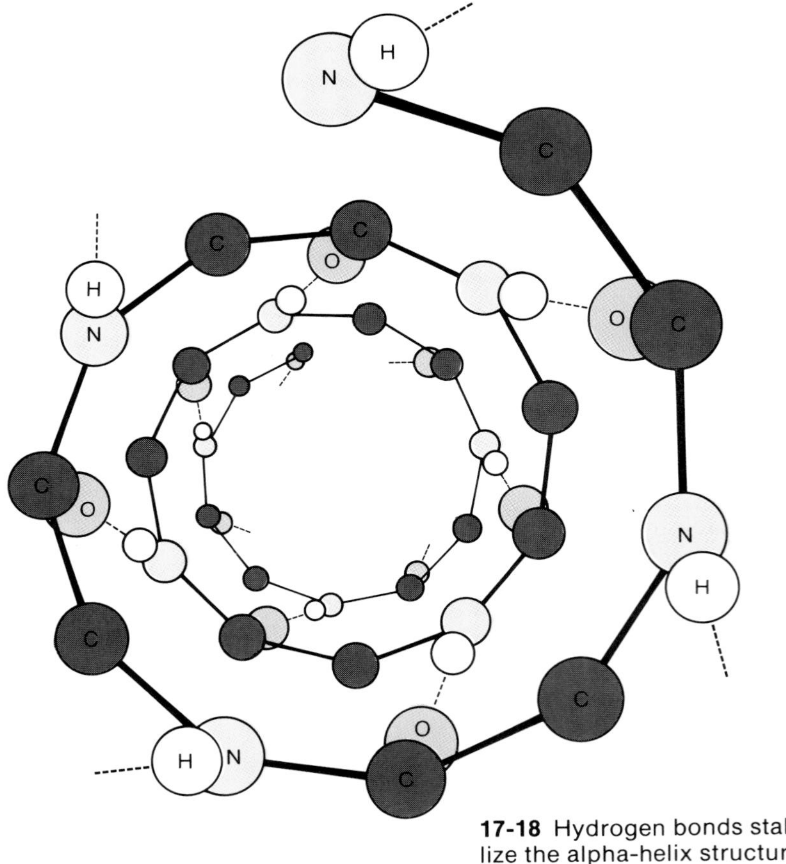

17-18 Hydrogen bonds stabilize the alpha-helix structure of proteins.

Another preferred shape of polypeptide chains is that of a pleated sheet. The chains stretch out in an almost flat, but folded, pattern. Hydrogen bonds, this time between amino acids in different chains, hold the structure together. Pleated sheets of proteins are largely responsible for the resilience of spider webs, silk, and feathers.

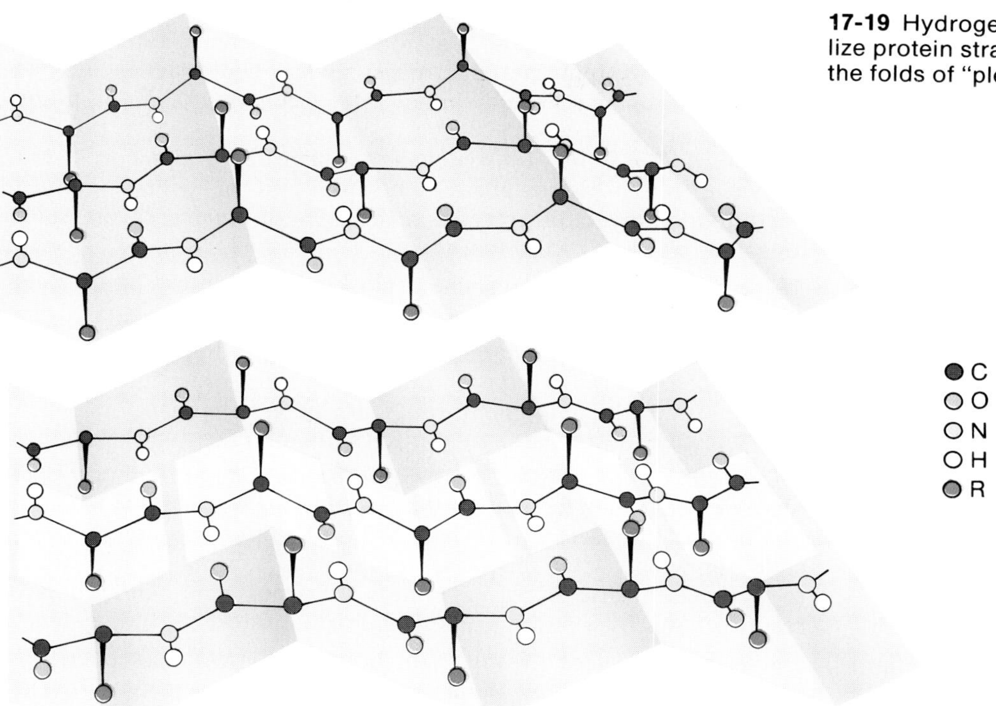

17-19 Hydrogen bonds stabilize protein strands across the folds of "pleated sheets."

Each protein's distinctive shape equips the protein to perform its own unique function. Hemoglobin, the protein that carries oxygen in the bloodstream, consists of four interwoven chains. The shape of the protein provides perfectly shaped crevices for oxygen molecules to nestle into.

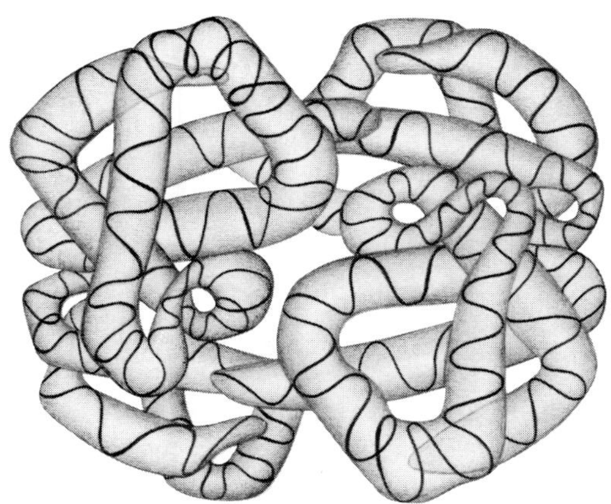

17-20 The three-dimensional shape of hemoglobin.

17–7 Functions of Proteins

"Structure determines function." This generalization helps explain how proteins manage to do such a wide variety of jobs in living organisms. Their shapes have been designed for many functions.

Structural Materials. Twisted helixes form fibers and cords that tie skin, hair, blood clots, tendons, and arteries together. Accumulated layers of proteins in the form of pleated sheets build up spider webs, silk, and feathers.

Motion. Muscles contract when two kinds of protein fibers slide over each other.

Transport. Hemoglobin carries oxygen in the blood stream because protein chains cradle oxygen molecules in an optimum position. Proteins embedded in membranes act as revolving doors when they selectively transfer some particles through the membrane.

Enzymatic Catalysis. Practically all the reactions in the body take place at rates much faster than they would outside the body because of proteins that act as catalysts. Without these organic catalysts, called enzymes, vital reactions would need searing temperatures to proceed at the necessary rates. Enzymes routinely increase reaction rates by a million times the normal rates.

Hormonal Messages. Many of the body's chemical messengers are proteins. Their unusual shapes allow them to be received by the cells that should receive the particular message.

Disease Protection. The human body's immunity system uses antibodies, which are proteins, to fight off bacteria and viruses.

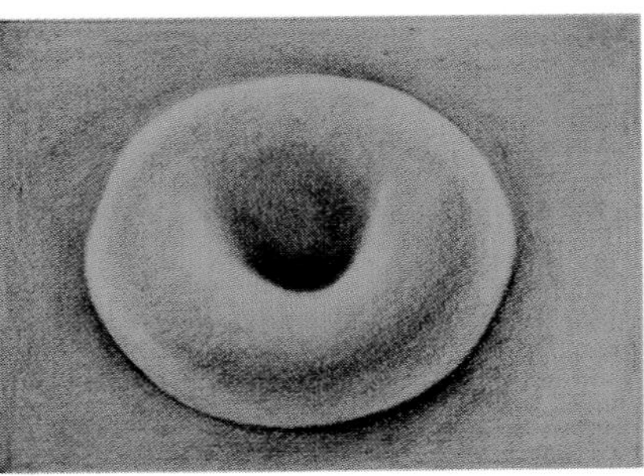

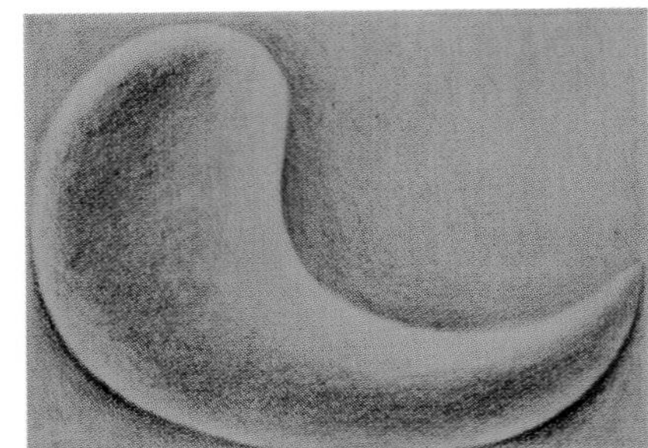

17-21 Sickle cell anemia results when a faulty pattern of amino acids changes hemoglobin's shape and function. Normal red blood cells **(left)** can carry oxygen much better than sickle cells can **(right)**.

Lipids

Although water is sometimes called the universal solvent, it does not mix with all the compounds in the human body. An entire class of compounds called **lipids** cannot dissolve in water. Fatty acids, fats, oils, waxes, and steroids are examples of vital lipids.

17–8 Fats and Oils: Unsaturated or Saturated?

Fats and oils are esters of glycerol and fatty acids. **Glycerol** is a three-carbon molecule that has three OH groups on separate carbons. Fatty acids are carboxylic acids with long hydrocarbon tails. Ester linkages join the COOH groups of acids to the OH groups in the glycerol to construct a fat or oil molecule.

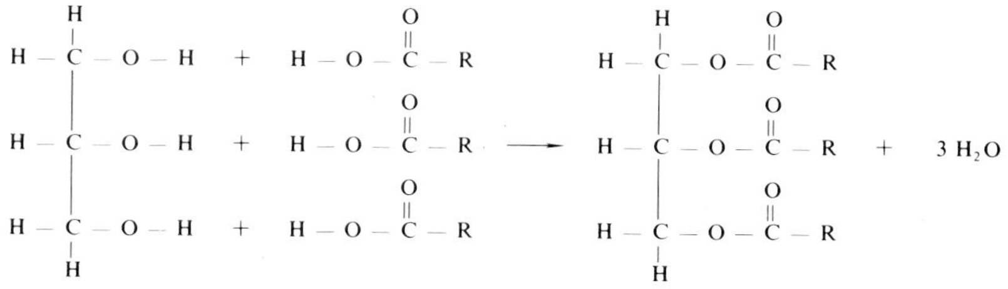

G
l
y
c
e
r
o
l

Fatty acid

Fatty acid

Fatty acid

$$
\begin{array}{l}
H-\overset{H}{\overset{|}{C}}-O-H \quad + \quad H-O-\overset{O}{\overset{\|}{C}}-R \qquad\qquad H-\overset{H}{\overset{|}{C}}-O-\overset{O}{\overset{\|}{C}}-R \\
H-C-O-H \quad + \quad H-O-\overset{O}{\overset{\|}{C}}-R \;\longrightarrow\; H-C-O-\overset{O}{\overset{\|}{C}}-R \quad + \quad 3\,H_2O \\
H-\underset{H}{\underset{|}{C}}-O-H \quad + \quad H-O-\overset{O}{\overset{\|}{C}}-R \qquad\qquad H-\underset{H}{\underset{|}{C}}-O-\overset{O}{\overset{\|}{C}}-R
\end{array}
$$

Glycerol + Three fatty acids ⟶ Fat (triglyceride) + Three molecules of water

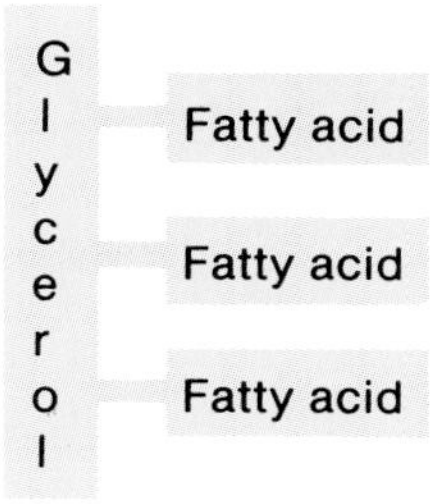

The acids that bond to the glycerol usually contain a large hydrocarbon chain (12 to 18 carbons are common), and they usually contain an even number of carbons (the chains are made in two-carbon units). Some chains contain all single carbon-carbon bonds, and some contain a few double bonds. This difference leads to the distinction between fats and oils.

Fats exist as solids at room temperature. Because most of their fatty acids have a large degree of saturation (single bonds), the chains tend to extend in straight lines from the glycerol backbone. They fit together well and have effective dispersion forces. As a result of these intermolecular attractions, fats such as lard are solid at room temperature.

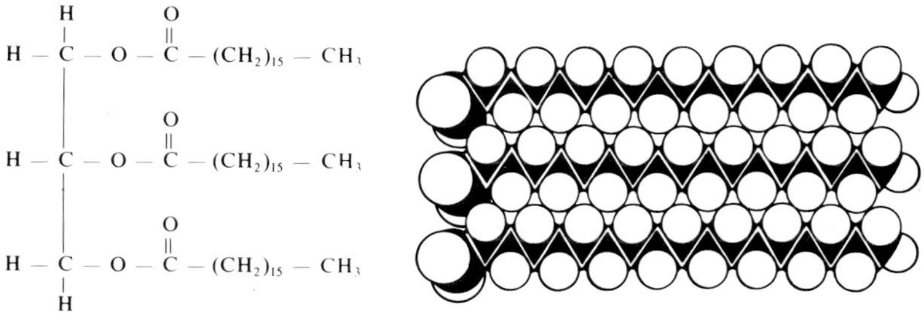

$$
\begin{array}{l}
H-\overset{H}{\overset{|}{C}}-O-\overset{O}{\overset{\|}{C}}-(CH_2)_{15}-CH_3 \\
H-C-O-\overset{O}{\overset{\|}{C}}-(CH_2)_{15}-CH_3 \\
H-\underset{H}{\underset{|}{C}}-O-\overset{O}{\overset{\|}{C}}-(CH_2)_{15}-CH_3
\end{array}
$$

17-22 Structural formula and space-filling model of a molecule of fat.

Oils are liquids at room temperature. As a rule, their fatty acids contain more double bonds than do the fats. Because of their double bonds, oils are considered to be unsaturated (recall that double bonds lessen the number of hydrogen atoms that are bonded). The double bonds in oils introduce bends in the chains. Because these irregularly shaped molecules do not fit together as

17-23 Structural formula and space-filling model of linseed oil.

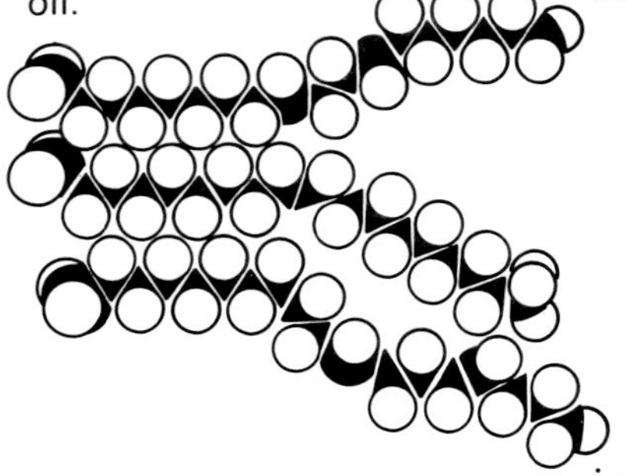

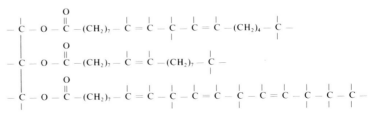

well as the molecules in fats do, their dispersion forces are not as effective. As a result, oil molecules do not experience strong intermolecular forces.

$$-\overset{|}{C}-O-\overset{O}{\overset{\|}{C}}-(CH_2)_7-\overset{|}{C}=\overset{|}{C}-\underset{|}{\overset{|}{C}}-\overset{|}{C}=\overset{|}{C}-(CH_2)_4-\underset{|}{\overset{|}{C}}-$$

$$-\overset{|}{C}-O-\overset{O}{\overset{\|}{C}}-(CH_2)_7-\overset{|}{C}=\overset{|}{C}-(CH_2)_7-\underset{|}{\overset{|}{C}}-$$

$$-\underset{|}{\overset{|}{C}}-O-\overset{O}{\overset{\|}{C}}-(CH_2)_7-\overset{|}{C}=\overset{|}{C}-\underset{|}{\overset{|}{C}}-\overset{|}{C}=\overset{|}{C}-\underset{|}{\overset{|}{C}}-\overset{|}{C}=\overset{|}{C}-\underset{|}{\overset{|}{C}}-\underset{|}{\overset{|}{C}}-\underset{|}{\overset{|}{C}}-$$

Today there is much talk about the virtues of "polyunsaturated" ingredients in foods. Polyunsaturation (many unsaturated oils) is an essentially new selling point. Thirty years ago most people preferred saturated fats. Although oils are abundant and relatively inexpensive, they are subject to oxidation when exposed to the air. The products of this oxidation taste and smell foul, so many housewives shied away from using oils when they cooked. Instead, they used chunks of animal fat. Manufacturers even developed ways to hydrogenate unsaturated oils into fats to meet the demand. Since those "good old days," medical researchers have discovered a correlation between eating fat and getting clogged arteries. Now saturation is out of vogue and unsaturation is "in." This is why so much is said about products that are "high in polyunsaturated fat."

17-24 Cooking oil **(top)** is a liquid because its fatty acids contain more double bonds than the fatty acids in vegetable shortening **(bottom)**.

Despite the fact that too much dietary fat can harm the arteries, fats are far from being bad substances. In fact, fats are good. They play many crucial roles in the human body. First of all, they provide excellent energy storehouses. A gram of fat can release 9 Calories of energy whereas a gram of carbohydrate or a gram of protein can release only 4 Calories. All the carbons in the chain eventually are converted to carbon dioxide when the molecule is used as fuel. Since fat molecules exclude water, they do not require an aqueous environment during storage. Consequently, they do not have the additional weight of water that is associated with carbohydrates or proteins. Hibernating animals utilize the excellent insulating qualities of fats and their energy-storing capabilities at the same time. Fats are also used to pad vital organs, and they serve as building blocks for fat-related compounds.

17–9 Steroids: Cholesterol and Company

Steroids are lipids, but their structures do not resemble triglyceride fats and oils in any way. They are the nonester lipids. The basic structure of a steroid is a combination of three six-membered rings and one five-membered ring. Functional groups attached to various points on the rings result in a wide variety of steroids. Cholesterol, vitamin D, cortisone, testosterone, and estrogen all use this common "chicken wire" frame.

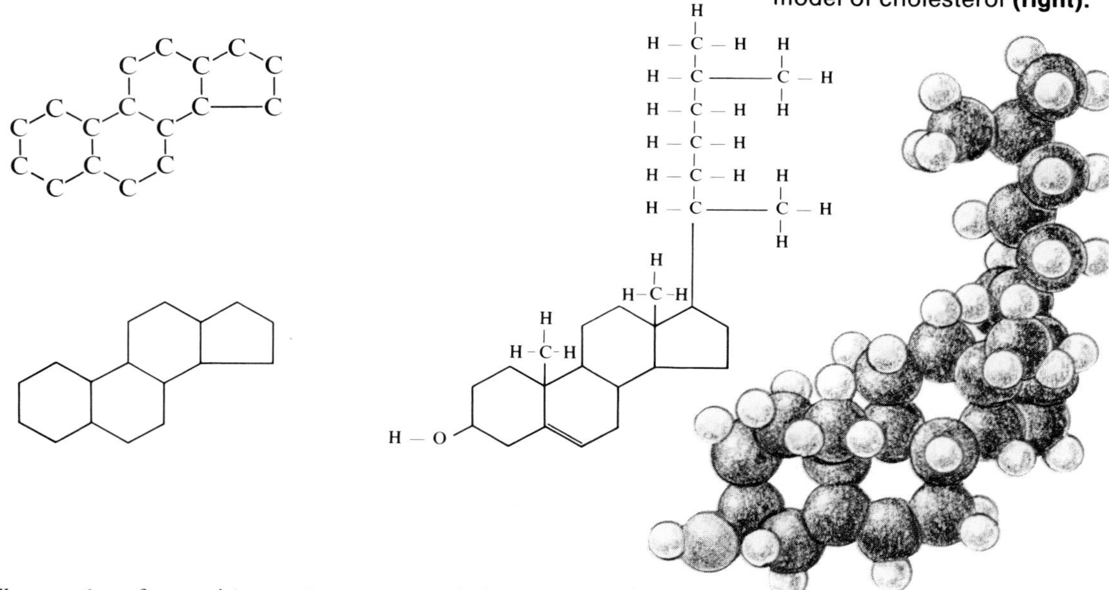

17-25 General structure of steroids **(left).** Structural formula and space-filling model of cholesterol **(right).**

The study of steroids ranks as one of the most active areas of chemical research. One steroid that has been studied much in recent years is cholesterol—a compound that contributes to the clogging of arteries. A correlation has been established between eating saturated fats and accumulating high cholesterol levels in the bloodstream. However, this does not prove that eating animal fats causes heart disease. No one knows for sure how (or if) saturated fats lead to high levels of cholesterol. Further evidence suggests that moderate amounts of fats and cholesterol are necessary for normal growth.

Cellular Processes: Carbohydrates, Proteins, and Lipids Work Together

An organism that contains carbohydrates, proteins, and lipids may be complete structurally, but it still does not have all the compounds it needs to carry on its cellular processes. Specialized proteins called *enzymes* facilitate almost every reaction that takes place in living organisms. *Vitamins* are small but indispensable nutrients that organisms cannot produce by themselves. *Hormones* serve as chemical messengers from one part of an organism to another. Finally, *nucleic acids* guide the construction of proteins and carry genetic information to offspring. These too are the molecules of life.

17–10 Enzymes: Organic Catalysts

Enzymes are protein molecules that act as catalysts. The fantastic speed at which enzymes work befuddles the mind. An equilibrium between carbon dioxide, water, and carbonic acid functions as the bloodstream picks up carbon dioxide from muscles, transports it, and then releases it in the lungs. An enzyme named carbonic anhydrase catalyzes both the forward and the reverse reactions. Without the enzyme, one molecule would react approximately every 100 seconds. With the enzyme, however, 100,000 molecules can react every second. In this reaction, the rate is multiplied by a factor of 10^7. Without that increase, there would be no way for the lungs to exchange enough gases to support respiration.

$$CO_2 + H_2O \underset{\text{anhydrase}}{\overset{\text{carbonic}}{\rightleftharpoons}} H_2CO_3$$

Enzymes act with amazing preciseness. They were designed with the uncanny ability to select just certain types of molecules to work on. An enzyme called trypsin catalyzes a reaction that breaks down protein chains. What is remarkable is that the enzyme splits protein chains only on a certain side of two amino acids; it ignores all other sites on the protein chain.

How can enzymes work so fast, in so many applications, and with such precision? Scientists do not know for sure, but several proposed theories can explain most of their observations. One widely accepted explanation is the **lock-and-key theory.** It holds that enzymes catalyze reactions by positioning reactants in ideal positions for reactions to occur. When an enzyme and the substance it works on combine, collisions with other reactants are more effective than without the enzyme.

A complete understanding of how enzymes work will probably involve a thorough knowledge of the shapes and sizes of the biological molecules—not an easy task, considering how complex large proteins can be. Like the study of steroids, enzyme research is currently one of the most exciting and active areas in biochemistry.

17–11 Vitamins: Micronutrients

As far as biochemistry is concerned, sailors had it rough in the old days. For British seamen long trips almost certainly meant bleeding gums, loose teeth, cuts that did not heal, and weight loss.

Japanese navigators faced stiff lower limbs and possible paralysis. The causes of these plights had nothing to do with the sea, but rather with the unbalanced diets of the seamen. These men had the vitamin deficiency diseases now known as scurvy and beri-beri.

Vitamins are micronutrients that are essential for normal nutrition. The British sailors lacked ascorbic acid, or vitamin C, in their on-board diets. A daily ration of lemon or lime juice provided the necessary nutrient, combatted the symptoms of scurvy, and earned the sailors the nickname "limeys." The Japanese navy combatted the disease of beri-beri in the late 1800s by introducing portions of wheat and barley and unpolished rice into the regular diets. The hulls of these grains contained the vitamin B_1 that relieved the sailors' suffering. The doctor who first isolated the organic substance that cured beri-beri found that it contained an amine (NH_2) group; he called it a "vital amine," or vitamin.

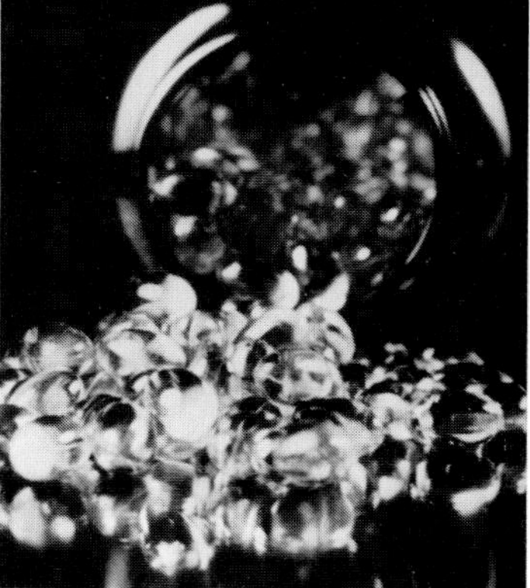

17-26 Vitamin E pills.

Vitamins are vital to the proper functioning of enzymes. Vitamin C is somehow connected with the formation of the intercellular "glue" in bones, teeth, and cartilage. The B vitamins help enzymes break down carbohydrates. Without them, pyruvic acid, a product of incomplete carbohydrate breakdown, accumulates in the muscles and causes the pain of beri-beri. Today scientists know of approximately twenty-one vitamins, but they suspect that several others exist. The ones they know about can be classified as either water soluble or fat soluble. Water-soluble vitamins can be excreted from the kidneys, so humans need a constant supply of them. Megadoses of these vitamins can be eliminated by the urinary system before they cause immediate damage. The functions of fat-soluble vitamins are not as well understood. If too many of them are ingested, dangerous concentrations accumulate in fatty tissues. Tables 17-27 and 17-28 list the common vitamins, their functions, and consequences of deficiencies.

Table 17-27

Fat-Soluble Vitamins

Vitamin	Function	Deficiency Symptoms
A	contributes to visual pigments in the eye	inflammation of eyes, night blindness, drying of mucous membranes
D	aids in absorption and deposition of calcium	rickets
E	protects blood cells, unsaturated fatty acids, and vitamin A from oxidation	anemia, bursting of red blood cells
K	aids clotting of blood	increased clotting time of blood at wounds

Table 17-28

Water-Soluble Vitamins		
Vitamin	**Functions**	**Deficiency Symptoms**
B_1 (thiamine)	helps carbohydrate metabolism	fatigue, beri-beri, accumulation of body fluids
Niacin	helps energy utilization	inflammation of nerves and mucous membranes, dermatitis
B_2 (riboflavin)	helps protein metabolism	dermatitis, inflammation of the tongue, anemia
B_6 (pyridoxine)	helps amino acid metabolism	convulsions in infants, inflammation of the tongue, susceptibility to infections
B_{12}	helps in the formation of nucleic acids	retarded growth, spinal cord degeneration
C (ascorbic acid)	helps in binding bones, teeth, cartilage, and blood vessels together	slow wound healing, scurvy, anemia
Pantothenic acid	helps respiration	gastrointestinal disturbances, depression, mental confusion
Folic acid	helps formation of heme groups and nucleotides	various types of anemia

17–12 Hormones: Chemical Messengers

Complex organisms have many specialized body parts that must constantly communicate with each other. The brain must know when the eyes see something as significant as a charging rhinoceros, the adrenal medulla gland must know when it is time to secrete adrenaline, and the muscles must know when to respond to the danger with increased activity. Nerves, which carry electrical messages, handle many of the body's communications, but they are not alone in this task. Chemicals called **hormones** produced in one part of the body often act on cells in remote parts of the body.

Hormones are a chemically diverse lot. They can be steroids, polypeptide chains, or proteins. These compounds, when released into the bloodstream or other body fluids, travel throughout the body. Despite the fact that they come into contact with many cells, they act only on their target cells. Research findings suggest that the "target" cells contain receptor molecules that recognize specific hormones by their shapes.

17–13 Nucleic Acids: Chemical Blueprints

When cells reproduce, they pass genetic information to one another in long-chain molecules called **chromosomes.** Human body cells contain forty-six of these long molecules in their nuclei. Segments of chromosomes, called **genes,** carry the coded information that "orders" the production of specific polypeptide chains. Genes are constructed of many **nucleotides,** which are the building blocks of **nucleic acids.**

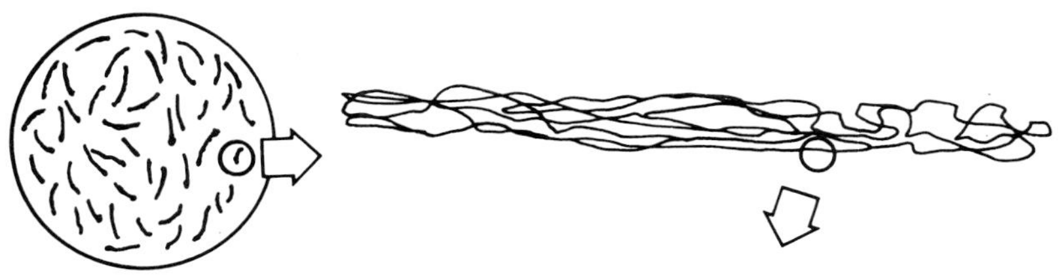

(a) Cell nucleus (b) One chromosome

(c) One DNA strand

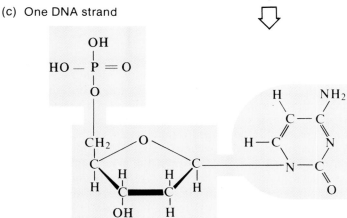

(d) One nucleotide

17-30 The nucleus **(a)** contains chromosomes **(b),** which are made of DNA strands **(c),** which are made of nucleotides **(d).**

Each nucleotide consists of three units: a pentose sugar, a phosphate group, and a ring-shaped nitrogenous base. The pentose sugar and the phosphate groups alternate to form a long chain that supports the nitrogenous bases. In RNA (ribonucleic acid), the pentose sugar is ribose, while in DNA (deoxyribonucleic acid) it is deoxyribose, which is a ribose with one less OH group than usual.

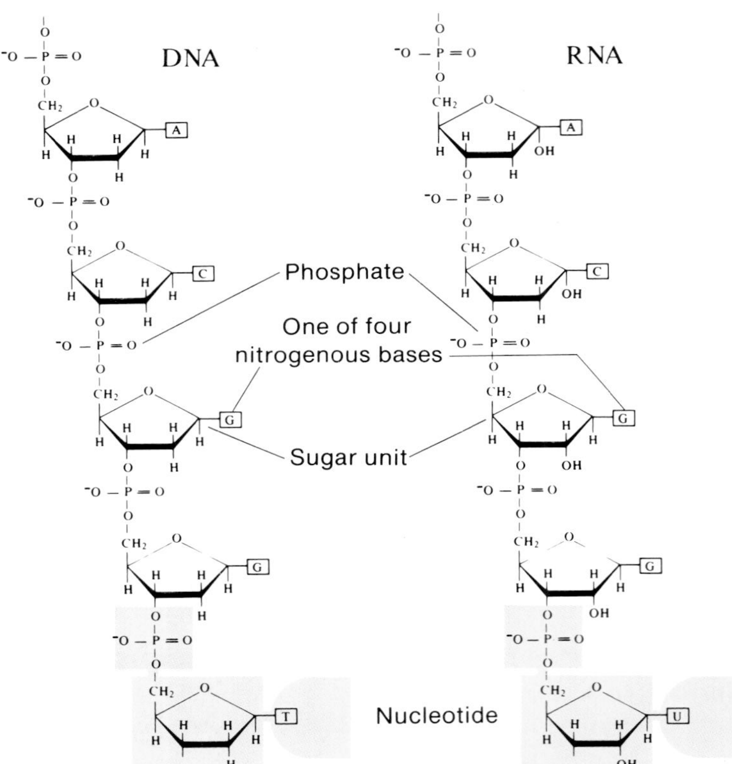

17-31 Single strands of DNA and RNA.

The nitrogenous bases attached to the sugar may be one of five possibilities: adenine, cytosine, guanine, thymine, or uracil (abbreviated A, C, G, T, and U). DNA strands contain only A, C, G, and T bases, and RNA strands have A, C, G, and U. Of these bases, C, T, and U are small, single-ringed structures, and A and G are larger, double-ringed structures.

DNA has been designed so that two strands coil around each other in a double helix. It looks somewhat like a ladder that has been twisted several times. The backbones circle around the outside, and the bases mesh together inside the coil. Large, double-ringed adenine bases pair with smaller thymine bases, while large guanine bases fit neatly next to smaller cytosine bases. Hydrogen bonds hold the complementing bases snugly in position.

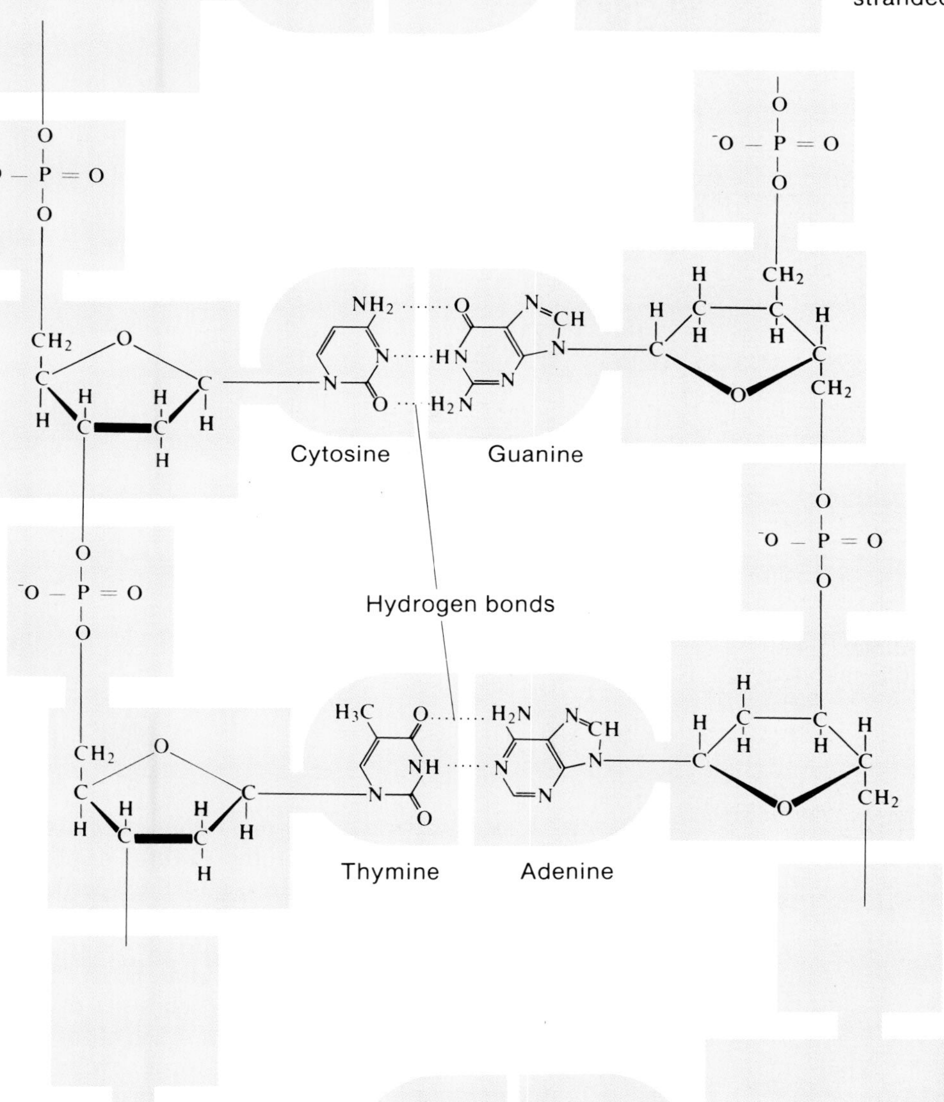

17-32 A two-nucleotide sequence of double-stranded DNA.

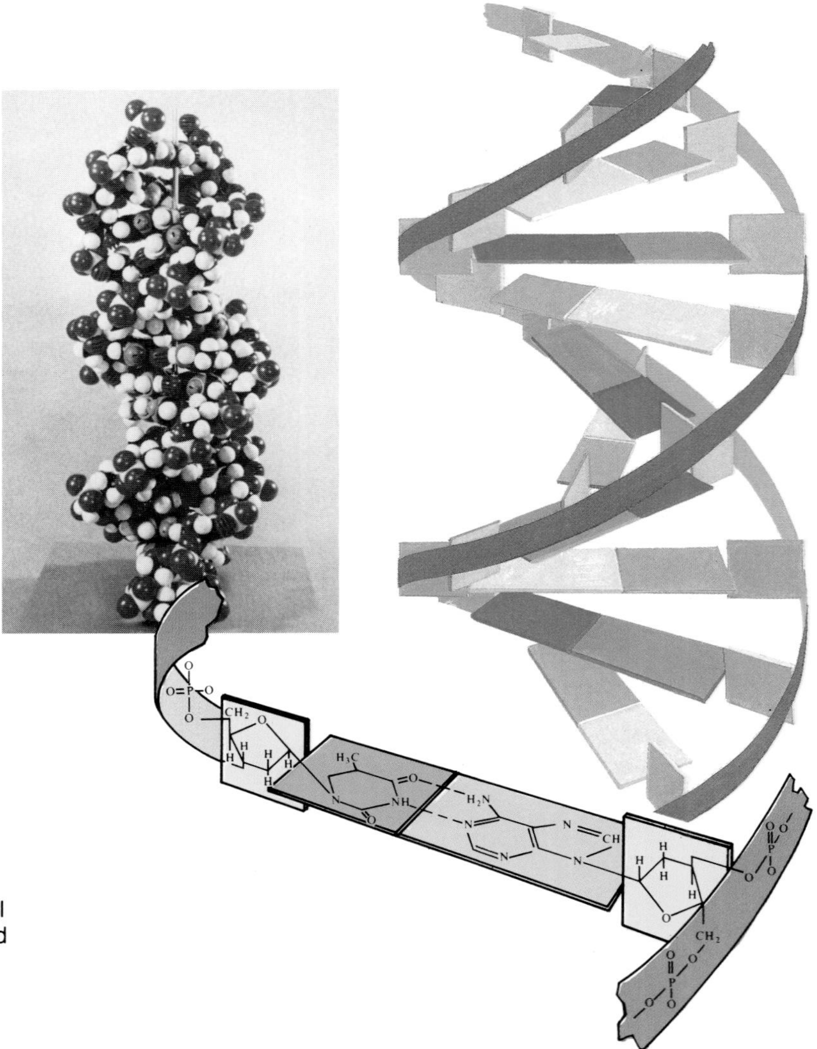

17-33 Three-dimensional shape of double-stranded DNA.

Nucleic acids function in a marvelous, almost miraculous manner. They are responsible for the faithful duplication of an organism's distinctive characteristics, and they perform this task with great precision and accuracy. In this regard God's creation is astonishingly complex. Man has been privileged to unravel some of its workings and to further verify that he is "fearfully and wonderfully made" (Psalm 139:14). When cells divide, a DNA strand reproduces by first unraveling itself. Each of the two resulting strands serves as a template, or pattern, for a new complementary chain. Complementing bases on the newly forming strand match the now-exposed bases of the old strand. When completed, two identical double-stranded DNA molecules result. One strand goes to each half of the dividing cell.

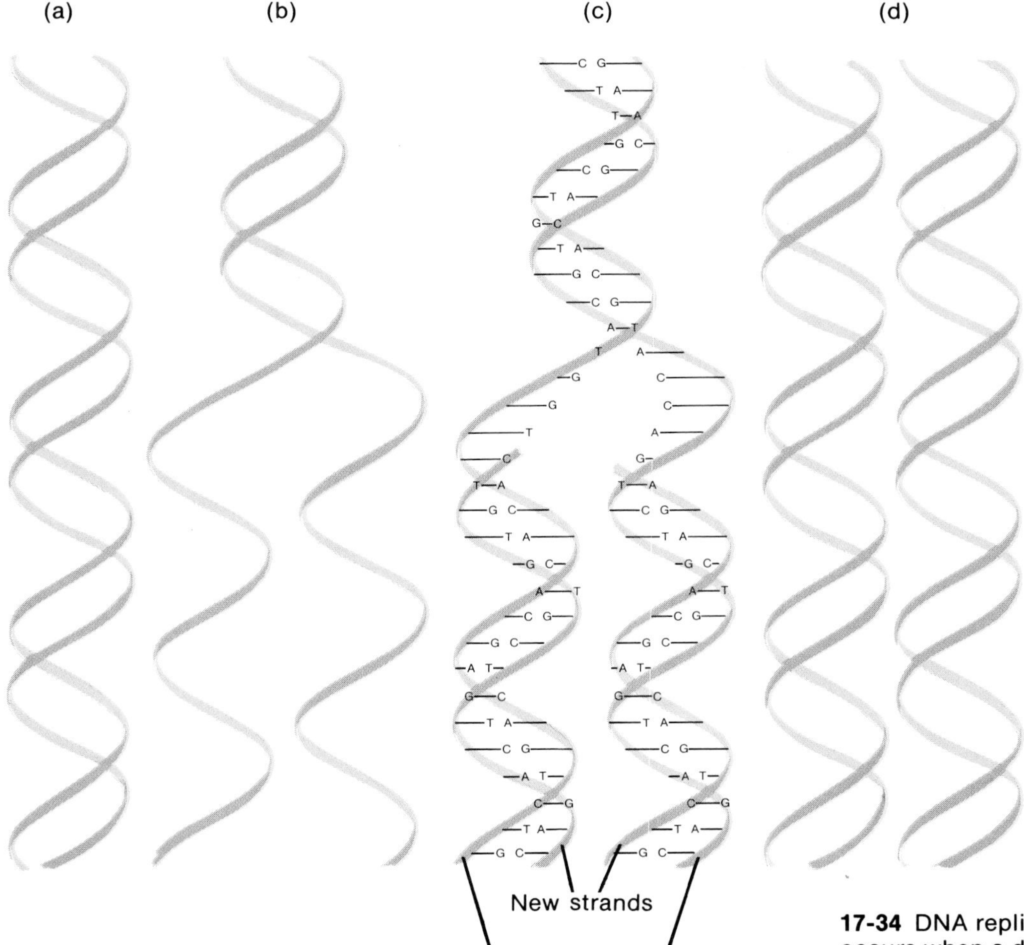

17-34 DNA replication occurs when a double strand of DNA **(a)** unravels **(b).** Complementary strands form and attach onto each of the unraveled DNA strands **(c),** producing two identical double-stranded DNA molecules **(d).**

DNA and RNA molecules provide sets of "blueprints" instructing cells on how to make proteins. Amazingly, scientists have discovered how to translate the genetic code in these blueprints. The order of nitrogenous bases along a DNA strand dictates which amino acids are to follow each other in a protein. For instance, the sequence guanine-guanine-adenine along a DNA strand calls for the amino acid *glycine*. Other sequences of three bases call for other amino acids until entire polypeptide chains have been constructed. Considering the length of the average protein and the number of different proteins that must be constructed to maintain even the simplest organism, one can begin to understand the awesome task of nucleic acids.

Coming to Terms

carbohydrate
monosaccharide
disaccharide
polysaccharide
starch
glycogen
amino acid
peptide bond
dipeptide
polypeptide
protein
lipid
glycerol
fat
oil
steroid
enzyme
lock-and-key theory
vitamin
hormone
chromosome
gene
nucleotide
nucleic acid

Review Questions

1. List three major functions of carbohydrates.
2. The melting point of glucose ($C_6H_{12}O_6$) is 146 °C. This seems quite high compared to the 6.5° C melting point of cyclohexane. What functional groups on the glucose are responsible for the difference? What do these functional groups do to raise the melting point?
3. Describe what is meant by each term, and give one example of each.
   a. monosaccharide
   b. disaccharide
   c. polysaccharide
4. How are cellulose and glycogen similar? How are they different? How does the difference between cellulose and glycogen affect their nutritional value to man?
5. Postulate a reason that termites can eat wood but people cannot.
6. Why are amino acids named *amino acids?* Draw the structural formula of an amino acid, and identify the functional groups.
7. Polysaccharides and polypeptides are both polymers. What is the difference between them?
8. Why is the three-dimensional shape of a protein important?
9. Can a protein consist of more than one polypeptide? Explain.
10. List three functions of proteins.
11. What is the difference between a fat molecule and an oil molecule?
12. What distinguishes steroids from other lipids?

13. What do enzymes do? In terms of energy, how do they do this? In terms of chemical structure, how do they do this?
14. What are the two general classes of vitamins?
15. Some people think that massive doses of vitamins can be beneficial. They routinely take large doses of vitamin C, yet these people do not take large doses of vitamin A. Why is this?
16. What are the functions of hormones in the human body?
17. What is a nucleotide? What are nucleotides composed of? How do the nucleotides of DNA and RNA differ?
18. What is the general shape of a DNA molecule? What is the function of DNA?
19. Match each of the following structural formulas to the general class of compound it represents.

amino acid	monosaccharide	fat	polysaccharide
disaccharide	polypeptide	oil	steroid

a.

CHO
— C — OH
HO — C —
— C — OH
— C — OH
CH_2OH

b.

C_8H_{17}
HO

c.

H
H — C — COOH
NH_2

d.

CH_2OH CH_2OH CH_2OH CH_2OH
etc. — O — [H, H, OH, H, H, OH] — O — [H, H, OH, H, H, OH] — O — [H, H, OH, H, H, OH] — O — [H, H, OH, H, H, OH] — O — etc.

e.

~ N(H) — C(H) — C(=O) — N(H) — C(H) — C(=O) — N(H) — C(H) — C(=O) ~
CH_2 — C = CH, $^+$HN, NH, C, H | CH_2 — C(=O) — NH_2 | CH_2 — SH

f.

H — C(H) — O — C(=O) — $C_{17}H_{35}$
H — C — O — C(=O) — $C_{15}H_{31}$
H — C(H) — O — C(=O) — $C_{15}H_{29}$

g.

CH_2OH CH_2OH
H, H, OH, H, OH, H, OH — O — H, H, OH, H, H, OH, OH, H

h.

H — C(H) — O — C(=O) — $(CH_2)_7$ — CH = CH — $(CH_2)_7$ — CH_3
H — C — O — C(=O) — $(CH_2)_7$ — CH = CH — $(CH_2)_7$ — CH_3
H — C(H) — O — C(=O) — $(CH_2)_7$ — CH = CH — $(CH_2)_7$ — CH_3

EIGHTEEN

NUCLEAR CHEMISTRY

GETTING TO THE HEART OF MATTER

ON August 6, 1945, the first nuclear weapon in the history of warfare was dropped by the United States Air Force on the Japanese city of Hiroshima. The results were horrifying. No one doubts that nuclear power can be destructive. However, this same energy source can offer numerous peaceful uses. Radioactive tracers, for instance, are used medically to diagnose diseases. Properly constructed nuclear power plants offer a clean, reliable source of electricity.

What causes radiation? How are nuclear reactions different from chemical reactions? Where does the awesome power come from? What makes a nuclear weapon different from a nuclear power plant? The answers to all these questions lie in the remarkable nature of the nucleus.

Natural Radioactivity

In normal chemical activity, an atom's valence electrons play the crucial role. But this is not so in nuclear chemistry. The reactions that occur in the nuclei of the atoms have nothing to do with the electrons in the atom's energy levels. The nuclei have a chemistry all their own.

18–1 The Discovery of Radiation: Becquerel's Mysterious Rays

Soon after the discovery of x-rays, a French physicist named Henri Becquerel set out to determine whether some "glow-in-the-dark" crystals he had could give off x-rays. Becquerel gathered crystals of potassium uranyl sulfate ($K_2UO_2[SO_4]_2$) that had been exposed to bright sunlight. These crystals have the strange ability to glow in the dark after they have been exposed to sunlight. To determine whether light from the crystals contained x-rays, he covered a photographic plate with black paper and exposed it to glowing crystals. He reasoned that only x-rays could pass through the paper to expose the film. As expected, the glowing crystals left marks on the plate. Becquerel correctly concluded that potassium uranyl sulfate emits some kind of penetrating rays. Yet Becquerel soon made an accidental discovery that caused him to wonder just what kind of rays were coming out of the crystals.

Toward the end of his study, Becquerel accidentally discovered that the crystals left marks on photographic plates even though the crystals had not been exposed to the sun. Further investigations showed that other uranium compounds also darkened photographic plates. The crystals constantly gave off energetic rays despite their being melted, dissolved, and recrystallized. No one knew where the energetic rays came from.

18-1 Marie and Pierre Curie.

In 1898 two scientists in France, Marie Sklodowska Curie and her husband Pierre, discovered another element that seemed to defy the law of energy conservation. They coined the word **radioactivity** to describe the spontaneous emission of the penetrating rays. The Curies correctly concluded that radioactivity is an atomic property that does not depend on how the atoms are chemically bonded. Becquerel's experimental results were then understood. It was the uranium atoms, not the potassium uranyl sulfate crystals, that were responsible for the radiation. While Becquerel had actually discovered radioactivity, the Curies correctly identified its source.

In time, scientists analyzed the rays from radioactive substances. They passed streams of radiation through powerful electrical and magnetic fields. By charting the deflections of the rays, they could determine the electrical charges of the different types of radiation.

They found that radiation had three components: one with a positive charge, one with a negative charge, and one with no charge at all.

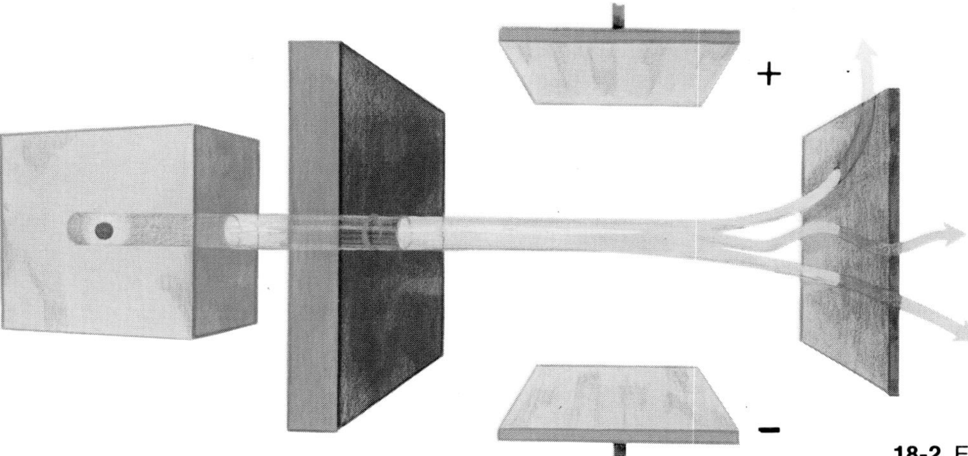

18-2 Experiment for separating and analyzing the components of radiation.

18–2 Alpha Particles: Helium Nuclei

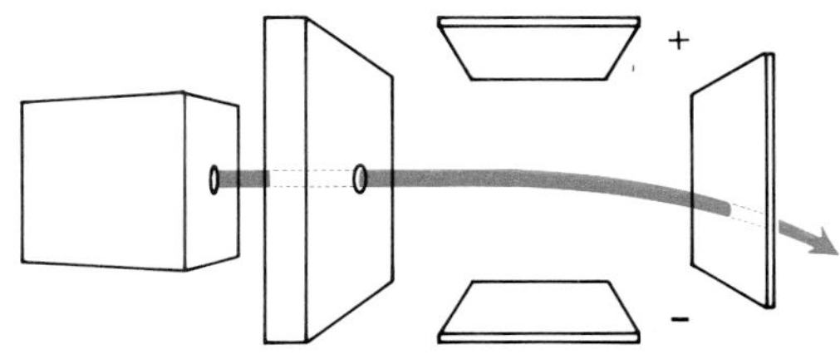

18-3 Alpha particles bend slightly toward the negative plate.

A stream of positively charged particles was deflected slightly toward the negative electrical plate. Because the particles swerved only slightly, scientists deduced that they must be more massive than the other types of radiation. They later found that these **alpha particles** contained two protons and two neutrons. Isotopic notation shows that alpha particles are actually $^{4}_{2}He$ nuclei. The superscripted number shows that the mass of the particles is approximately 4 amu, and the subscripted number gives the atomic number of the element. Another name for an alpha particle is the He^{2+} ion.

While alpha radiation penetrates matter, it can be stopped easily. The particles interact with matter quickly to produce helium atoms. For instance, alpha particles cannot go through this page. If He^{2+} ions hit the page, they would each immediately grab two electrons from the paper and turn into ordinary helium atoms. If ionizing radiation passes into an organism, it can cause biological damage as it ionizes molecules that are vital to biological processes. The damage may take the form of burns, sickness, and even death. Some of the superficial burns that resulted from the nuclear weapons dropped on Hiroshima and Nagasaki were caused by the enormous amounts of alpha particles released by the bombs.

18–3 Beta Particles: Electrons from the Nucleus

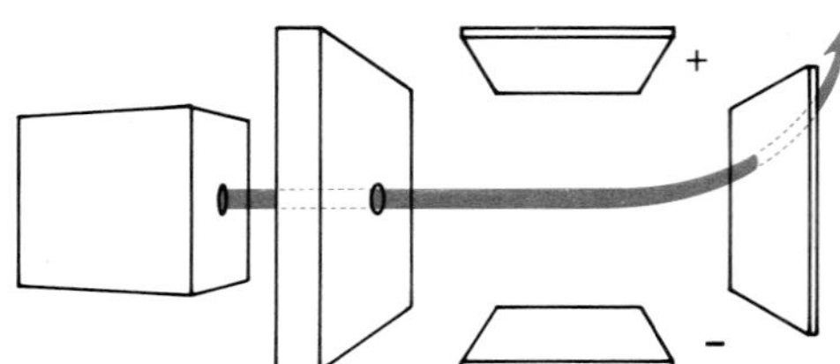

18-4 Beta particles bend sharply toward the positive plate.

Like alpha radiation, the second type of radiation is also composed of particles. **Beta particles** carry a negative charge and have very little mass. Scientists noted that beta particles acted much like electrons when they swerved sharply toward a positively charged plate. The direction of the swerve told the particle's charge, and the amount of the swerve indicated that the particle had hardly any mass. Further studies gave a surprisingly simple identity to beta particles: they are electrons. Beta particles are represented as $_{-1}^{0}e$ in isotopic notation. This convention shows both the negligible mass and the -1 charge of the particle.

Beta radiation penetrates into substances deeper than alpha radiation does. Beta particles can zip through sheets of paper, but they can be stopped by wood or metal. Like alpha particles, they ionize atoms and molecules in matter when they hit, but not as readily as alpha particles do. Because they do not ionize as readily, beta particles penetrate deeper and are more dangerous than alpha particles.

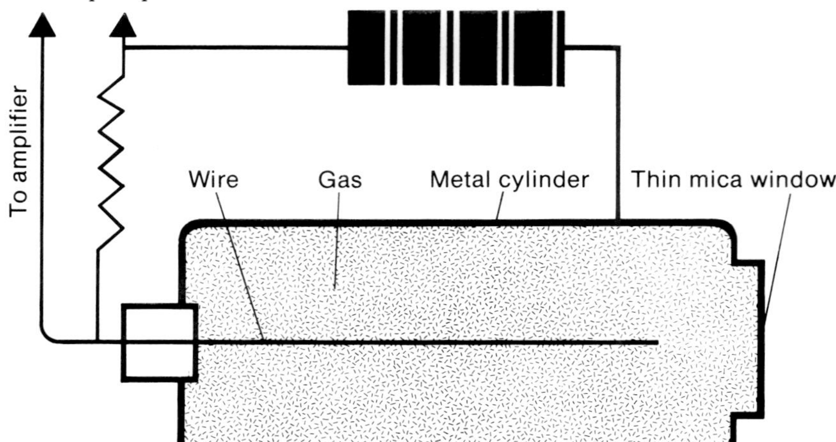

18-5 A Geiger counter can detect radiation passing through its chamber because gases ionize and allow an electrical current to flow. This current is amplified and converted into sound.

18–4 Gamma Rays: High Energy Waves

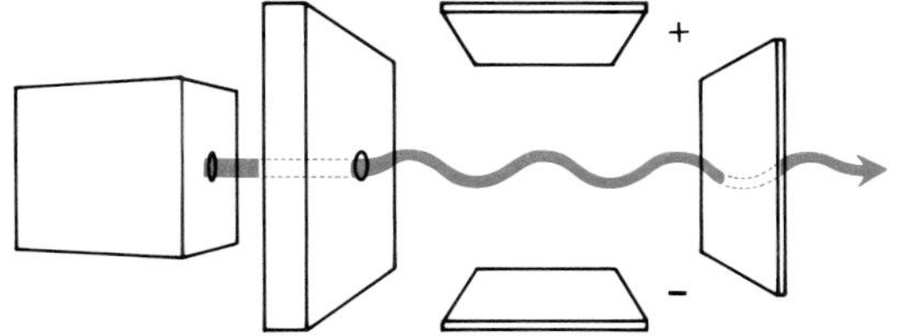

18-6 Gamma rays are not deflected by electrical charges.

Unlike alpha and beta radiation, gamma radiation is not composed of particles. It consists of electromagnetic waves similar to those of visible and ultraviolet light, but with more energy. **Gamma rays** are uncharged and, as can be seen in Figure 18-6, are undeflected in an electrical field.

If no particles are formed by gamma emission, why are gamma rays produced? Gamma rays are emitted by nuclei in excited states. An excited nucleus is nothing more than a normal nucleus with extra energy. Nuclei in excited states are sometimes produced as the result of alpha and beta emission. An excited nucleus returns to its ground state by releasing energy in the form of gamma rays.

Of the three types of radiation, gamma rays are the most harmful. Partly because they have no electrical charge and partly because they are not particles, gamma rays have a lower ionizing ability than alpha or beta particles. As a result, gamma rays penetrate more deeply than either alpha or beta particles. They are not stopped by ionization reactions near the surface of a body. They can be stopped by several feet of concrete or a sheet of lead.

Table 18-7

Three Types of Radiation

Name	Symbol	Identity	Charge	Mass	Penetration
Alpha	${}^{4}_{2}He$	helium nucleus	+2	4 amu	low
Beta	${}^{0}_{-1}e$	electron	-1	1/1836 amu	medium
Gamma	${}^{0}_{0}\gamma$	electromagnetic radiation	0	0	high

18–5 Nuclear Equations: Describing Nuclear Reactions

Chemical equations describe the reactants and products in a chemical reaction. **Nuclear equations** describe what goes on when nuclei split, fuse, or release radiation. These equations identify the nuclei that react and are produced. Where appropriate, they show whether alpha particles, beta particles, or gamma rays leave nuclei. For example, U-238 emits alpha particles. Because two protons in the alpha particle depart, the atomic number decreases by two, and the nucleus becomes a thorium nucleus (atomic number = 90). Because the departed alpha particle had a mass of 4 amu, the mass of the remaining nucleus is 234 instead of the original 238. A nuclear equation describes this process.

$$^{238}_{92}U \longrightarrow {}^{234}_{90}Th + {}^{4}_{2}He$$

Remember that $^{4}_{2}He$ is an alpha particle. Two things can be noted about the nuclear equation for an alpha-emitting process. First, the sum of the atomic numbers of the reactants equals the sum of the atomic numbers of the products (92 = 90 + 2). Second, the sum of the mass numbers on one side of the equation equals the sum of the mass numbers on the other (238 = 234 + 4).

Sample Problem. Write the nuclear equation that describes the alpha decay of U-234.

Solution.

$$^{234}_{92}U \longrightarrow {}^{230}_{90}Th + {}^{4}_{2}He$$

Scientists have concluded that beta particles emitted from nuclei are actually electrons. How can electrons be in the nucleus? Scientists think that neutrons produce beta radiation by breaking apart to form a proton and an electron. The proton stays in the nucleus, and the electron leaves as a beta particle. A carbon nucleus with six protons and eight neutrons is prone to this kind of reaction.

$$^{14}_{6}C \longrightarrow {}^{14}_{7}N + {}^{0}_{-1}e$$

The mass numbers of the reactant (C-14) and the product (N-14) are the same. The reacting nucleus does not lose nuclear particles when a neutron changes into a proton. The atomic number of the product nucleus is one greater than that of the reactant nucleus because of the extra proton.

Sample Problem. Write the nuclear equation for the beta decay of Al-28.

Solution.

$$^{28}_{13}Al \longrightarrow {}^{28}_{14}Si + {}^{0}_{-1}e$$

Gamma emission is not accompanied by any changes in mass number or atomic number. The only change that occurs in gamma emission is a change in energy. For instance, an excited technetium-99 nucleus decays to form an unexcited technetium-99 nucleus and a gamma ray.

$$\text{Excited } {}^{99}_{43}\text{Tc} \longrightarrow {}^{99}_{43}\text{Tc} + \text{Gamma ray}$$

18–6 Radioactive Decay Series: The Long Road to Stability

Unstable nuclei attain stable states by emitting various types of radioactivity. Some nuclei release alpha particles, and some release beta particles. Some highly radioactive nuclei, such as U-238, do not stop decaying after just one alpha emission. The Th-234 that is produced by alpha emission is also an unstable nucleus, and it decays by beta emission.

$${}^{234}_{90}\text{Th} \longrightarrow {}^{234}_{91}\text{Pa} + {}^{0}_{-1}e$$

The protactinium-234 produced by this reaction is unstable, and it decays by beta emission.

$${}^{234}_{91}\text{Pa} \longrightarrow {}^{234}_{92}\text{U} + {}^{0}_{-1}e$$

U-234 is also unstable, and it too decays by a radioactive decay process. Do these decay reactions ever stop? Yes, but not until a stable nucleus is formed. When the product of a nuclear decay is stable, the radiations cease. Sequential alpha and beta emissions often form long series of nuclear reactions called **radioactive decay series.** When U-238 decays, nuclear decay reactions proceed until Pb-206 is formed. Figure 18-8 shows the complete radioactive decay series of U-238.

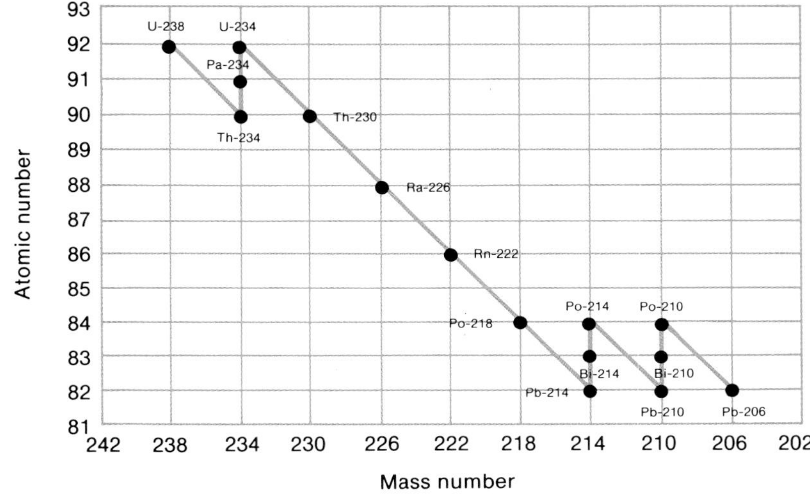

18-8 The radioactive decay series of U-238. On the graph, alpha decays angle downward and beta decays progress straight up.

All natural nuclei with more than eighty-two protons (bismuth) exhibit radioactivity. They all decay according to one of three natural radioactive decay series: the uranium series, the thorium series, or the actinium series. The uranium series begins with U-238 and ends with Pb-206. The actinium series begins with U-235 and ends with Pb-207. The thorium series begins with Th-232 and ends with Pb-208.

18–7 Half-Life: Two Do Not Make a Whole

How quickly do nuclear reactions occur? It might seem that individual decay steps occur instantaneously. But this is not necessarily so. While some radioactive nuclei release particles and waves quickly, others release them only occasionally.

Nuclear chemists and physicists use **radioactive decay constants** to describe how often radioactive decays take place. Radioactive substances with small decay constants decay more slowly than do substances with large decay constants.

How long will a sample of U-238 exist before it turns into thorium? Will C-14 spew out beta particles and quickly turn into N-14, or will it emit beta particles once in a while and remain as C-14 for centuries? Scientists use the concept of the half-life of an isotope to answer questions such as these. The **half-life** of a radioactive element is the amount of time that elapses when half of the nuclei in an element decay to form another element. Half-lives indicate how fast certain nuclei give off radioactivity. Short half-lives mean that the nuclei quickly decay into other kinds of nuclei. Long half-lives show that radioactive decays proceed more leisurely.

Table 18-9

Half-Lives

Nucleus	Half-Life
O-13	0.0087 second
Br-80	17.6 minutes
Mg-28	21 hours
Th-234	24.1 days
H-3	12.26 years
C-14	5730 years
U-238	4,510,000,000 years

The half-life of Th-234 is 24.1 days. Of 40 grams of Th-234, 20 grams will decay into other elements within 24.1 days. How much Th-234 will be left after two half-lives? It might seem logical to say "none," but that is not the correct answer. Half-lives do not work that way. Half of the *remaining* mass decays during each half-life. Twenty grams remain when the second half-life begins. During this half-life half of this amount, or 10 grams, will decay. After another 24.1 days, half of that, or 5 grams, will decay.

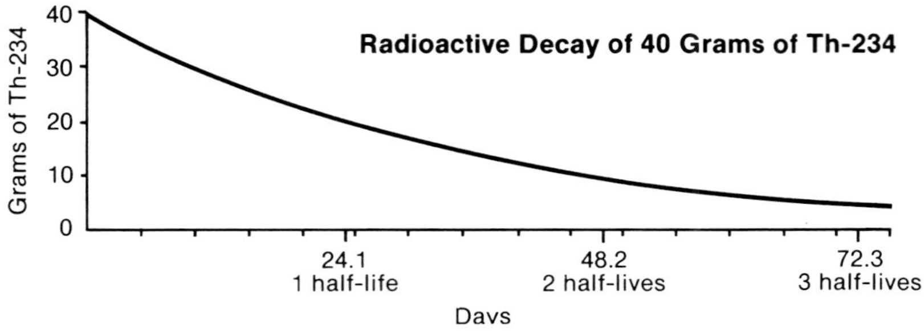

Radioactive Decay of 40 Grams of Th-234

Grams of Th-234: 0, 10, 20, 30, 40

Days: 24.1 (1 half-life), 48.2 (2 half-lives), 72.3 (3 half-lives)

18-10 The mass of a Th-234 sample decreases exponentially with time.

Sample Problem. A 192-gram sample of Th-234 decays for 96.4 days. At the end of this time, how much Th-234 is left?

Solution.

Since the half-life is 24.1 days, you know that four half-lives have passed. During each half-life the sample of Th-234 loses half its mass.

First half-life: 192 grams/2 = 96 grams

Second half-life: 96 grams/2 = 48 grams

Third half-life: 48 grams/2 = 24 grams

Fourth half-life: 24 grams/2 = 12 grams

18–8 Nuclear Stability: Why Nuclei Do Not Aways Fly Apart

"It requires a very unusual mind to undertake the analysis of the obvious."

Alfred North Whitehead, 1925

One obvious question that has been ignored so far is "What keeps nuclei together?" Nuclei contain many protons that are packed together. Since protons are positively charged, they should repel each other and immediately fly apart. Yet some nuclei are so stable that they exist for centuries without changing. Other nuclei are so unstable that their half-lives must be measured in units of seconds. Why are some nuclei stable (unradioactive) and others unstable (radioactive)?

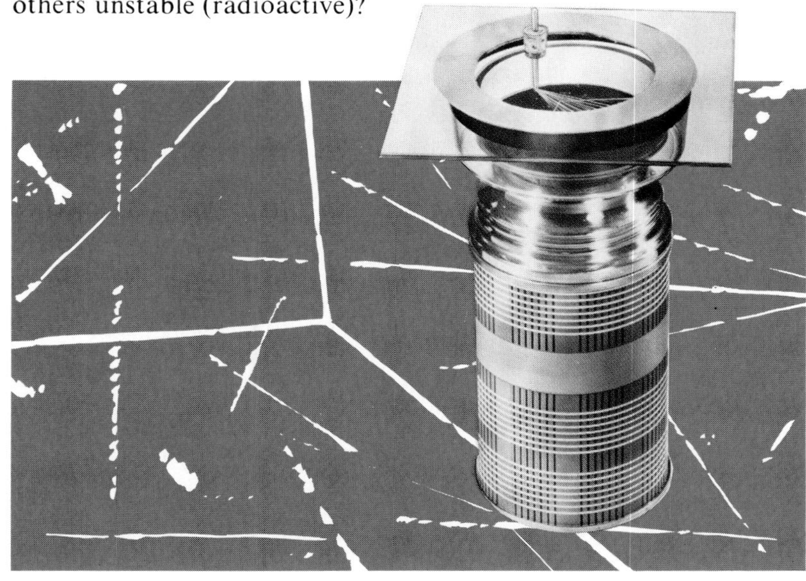

18-11 A cloud chamber marks the paths taken by fragments of nuclear decay as they pass through a vapor near condensation point. Liquid droplets condense on the paths of the fragments.

FACETS OF CHEMISTRY

IN THE CARBON DATING LAB, SCIENTISTS DISCOVERED THE WORLD'S OLDEST MAN... RALPH STEVENS, COAL MINER.

Radioactive Age-Dating Methods

Newspaper headline: "Three-Million-Year-Old Human Fossil Found in Kenya." Evolutionists often turn to radioactive age-dating methods to support their claims that fossils and rocks are millions or billions of years old. But these radioactive "clocks" usually do not tell time accurately.

A clock is a device or system in which some component changes at a constant rate of speed. To be useful, the change must be observable so that men can distinguish one moment in time from another. The clock must also be "set," or calibrated, with another clock; a clock that has not been set properly is worthless for telling time, even though it runs at a constant rate.

Radioactive dating techniques attempt to use radioactive reactions as clocks. A parent radioactive substance decays and forms a daughter product at a presumably constant rate. The quantities of each substance can be measured and compared. Problems arise because no one has calibrated the system. The amount of each material present at the beginning of the process cannot be known. In the absence of these needed measurements, the investigator is forced to guess at the original quantities. This guesswork is not based on observation and is therefore not science. Many of the "scientific" age-dating methods are actually very unscientific. The following two examples illustrate unscientific methods; the third example has scientific merit when properly used.

The uranium-lead method measures the radioactive decay of uranium into lead. It has been applied to both earth rocks and moon rocks that contain these elements. The greater the amount of lead is, compared to the amount of uranium in a sample, the older it is assumed to be. The major problem, of course, is that much of the lead could already have been present in the original rock. A revealing fact about this method is that widely differing results are often obtained on different portions of the same sample. Yet it is impossible for one rock to have several different ages.

The potassium-argon method has recently become popular because it produces large numbers—larger than those from the uranium-lead method. In this procedure the parent substance is potassium, and the daughter substance is argon. The major problem of this method is similar to that of the uranium-lead method—much of the observed argon could have been present in the original rock. There is strong experimental evidence against this method. When used on 170-year-old Hawaiian lava, potassium-argon dating gave results ranging from 22 million to 3 billion years. Yet the entire lava flow had been observed flowing and hardening in the years 1800 and 1801.

The radiocarbon method, based on carbon-14, differs from those discussed above because a calibration curve has been set up according to measurements of the radioactivity in several samples of known age.

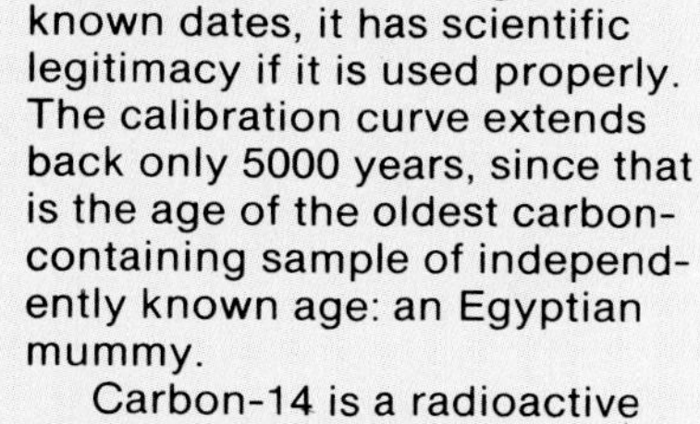

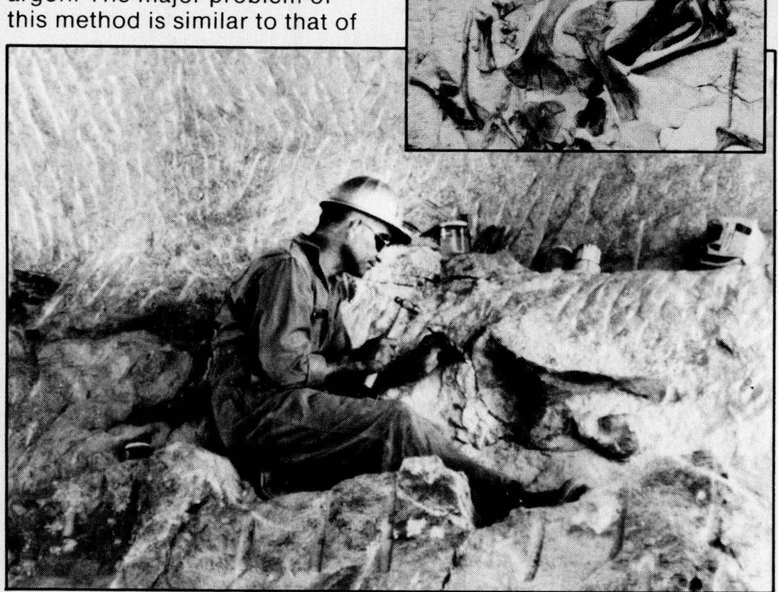

Since it is calibrated against known dates, it has scientific legitimacy if it is used properly. The calibration curve extends back only 5000 years, since that is the age of the oldest carbon-containing sample of independently known age: an Egyptian mummy.

Carbon-14 is a radioactive isotope of carbon produced when cosmic rays from the sun strike nitrogen in the upper atmosphere. The isotope has a half-life of 5730 years. Carbon-14 mixes with the other carbon in the world's supply and eventually finds its way into all living organisms. When an organism dies, no new carbon-14 is brought in from the outside. That which is present decays into nitrogen, and radioactivity continually decreases. The older the sample is, the less radioactivity there will be. Once the radioactivity level of a new sample has been determined, it can be compared to the calibrated curve. The radiocarbon method works acceptably when it is kept within the range of its calibration curve: the past 5000 years. Going beyond that involves an extrapolation (projecting a trend into an uncharted region of space or time), and the results are unreliable at best.

Scientists explain these facts by saying that **strong nuclear forces** hold the protons together. Nuclear forces are not well understood. In fact, they are merely labels for something that must exist but that has not yet been truly discovered. Scientists postulate that these forces work well only over small distances (less than 10^{-13} cm) to account for the fact that protons repel each other when they are not bound in nuclei. Scientists say that stable nuclei have effective nuclear forces, while unstable nuclei have insufficient forces to keep them together.

While unsaved scientists wonder what strong nuclear forces are, Christians have an authoritative source of information about this seeming mystery. Colossians 1:17 reveals that Jesus Christ "is before all things, and by him all things consist." God is ultimately responsible for holding all the protons in all the atoms of this world together.

A brief analysis of the stable nuclei of the elements reveals an interesting trend. Figure 18-12 represents the set of nuclei that scientists have observed to be stable. If the spot on the graph that corresponds to a particular nucleus is filled in, that nucleus is stable and not radioactive. Empty spots on the graph represent nuclei that are unstable. The curved band of points in this figure is called the **belt of stability** because it identifies the nuclei that do not undergo radioactive decay.

Sample Problem. Are ${}^{110}_{50}Sn$ atoms radioactive or stable?

Solution.

${}^{110}_{50}Sn$ atoms have fifty protons and sixty neutrons. The point on the graph corresponding to fifty protons and sixty neutrons is not filled in. This represents an unstable, radioactive nucleus.

The straight line represents nuclei that contain equal numbers of protons and neutrons. Note that only small nuclei in this group are stable. Larger nuclei need extra neutrons to be stable. In the absence of neutrons, even nuclear forces cannot keep the many protons from repelling each other. The more protons a nucleus contains, the more neutrons it needs to remain stable.

The graph of stable nuclei can also be used to predict *how* unstable nuclei will decay. Nuclei with atomic numbers less than eighty-three that fall above the belt of stability have more neutrons than their stable isotopes. It is reasonable, then, that they will transform one of these extra neutrons into a proton and will emit a beta particle. For instance, Tl-208 (81 protons) decays by beta emission to form Pb-208 (82 protons), which has a stable nuclear structure. Nuclei with eighty-three or more protons frequently demonstrate alpha decay. ${}^{222}_{86}Rn$ decays by alpha emission to form ${}^{218}_{84}Po$.

18-12 Stable Nuclei

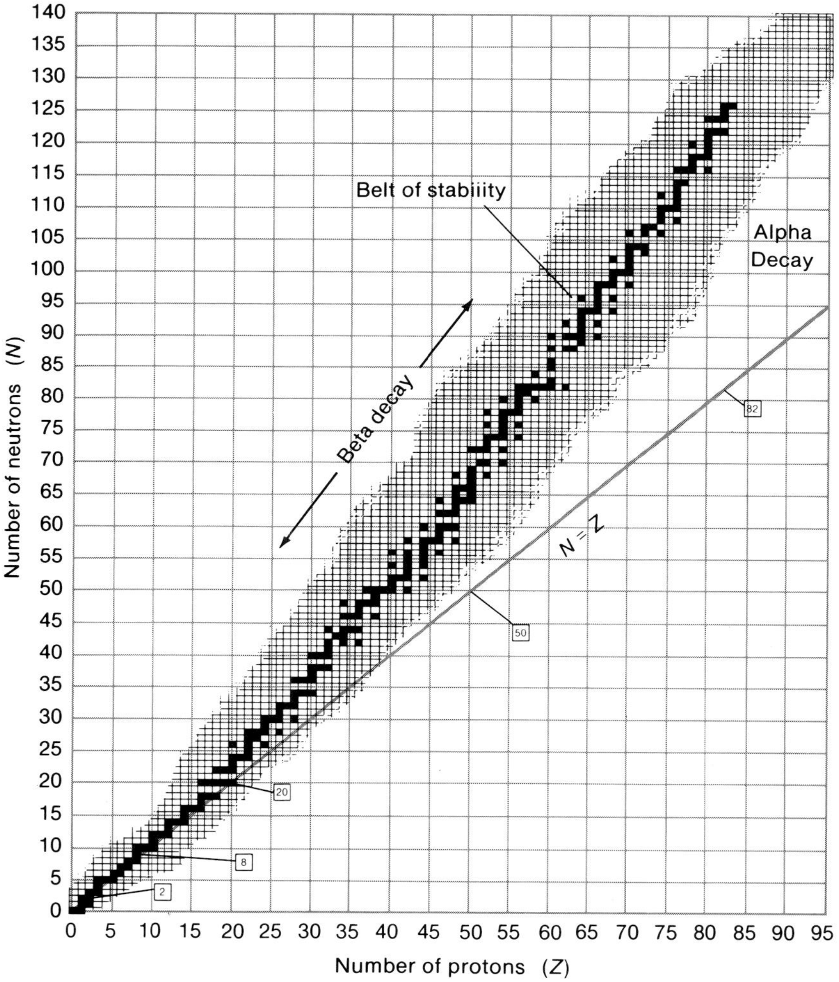

Sample Problem. What type of radioactive decay (if any) are the following nuclei most likely to undergo?

a. $^{23}_{11}Na$ b. $^{230}_{90}Th$ c. $^{29}_{13}Al$

Solution.

a. No radioactive decay occurs because this nucleus is one of those marked on the line of stability.

b. Alpha emission is most likely because the atomic number is greater than eighty-two.

c. Beta emission is most likely because the nucleus has less than eighty-two protons, and it falls above the line of stability.

Induced Reactions

The alchemists dreamed of the day that they could transform base metals into gold. Of course, they worked on that project before modern chemistry proved that transformations like this are impossible. Or are they? The transformation of lead into gold requires the removal of three protons and eight neutrons from a Pb-208 nucleus. Ordinary chemical reactions cannot alter the nucleus, but particle accelerators can. Lead can be changed into gold, but this nonspontaneous reaction can be forced to occur only with multimillion dollars' worth of equipment and massive inputs of energy. Nonspontaneous nuclear reactions that are forced to occur are called induced nuclear reactions.

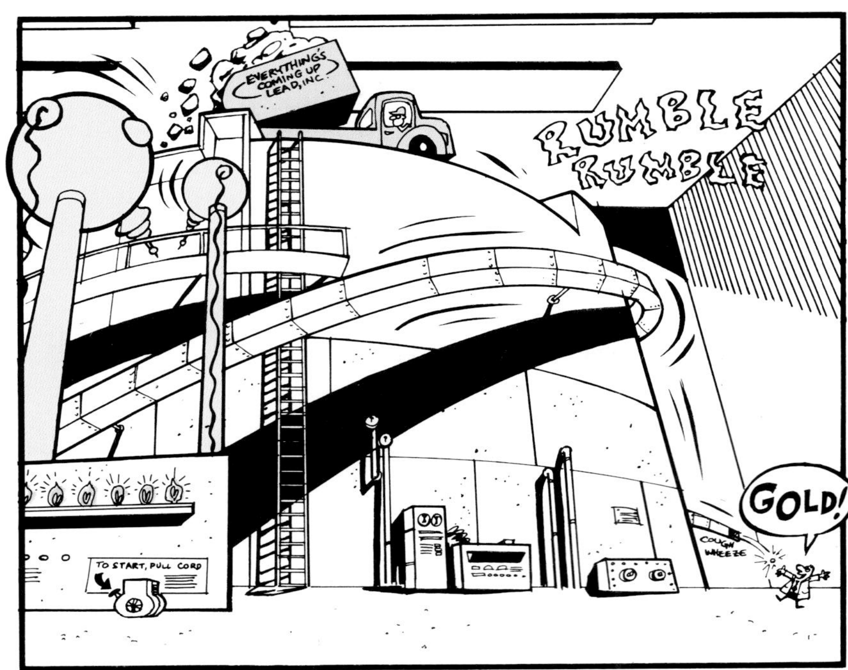

18-13 Magnetic and electrical fields in the main ring of the National Accelerator Laboratory in Batavia, Illinois, energize subatomic particles to speeds near that of light.

18–9 Fission: Splitting Nuclei

Extra neutrons induce some nuclei to split apart into smaller nuclei in a process called **nuclear fission.** For instance, U-235 can be bombarded with neutrons until its nucleus splits and releases various fragments, some liberated neutrons, and a tremendous amount of energy. There may be more than one way for the nucleus to split. Two of these ways are shown for U-235.

$$^{235}_{92}U + ^{1}_{0}n \longrightarrow ^{139}_{56}Ba + ^{94}_{36}Kr + 3\,^{1}_{0}n + \text{Heat}$$

$$^{235}_{92}U + ^{1}_{0}n \longrightarrow ^{144}_{55}Cs + ^{90}_{37}Rb + 2\,^{1}_{0}n + \text{Heat}$$

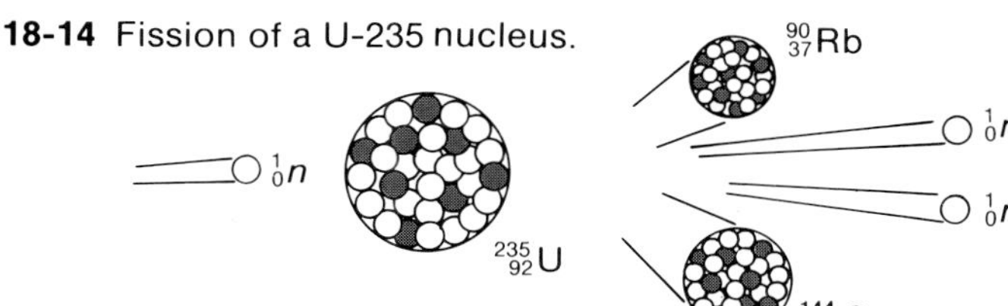

18-14 Fission of a U-235 nucleus.

18-15 One of these fuel pellets for a fission reactor can release energy equivalent to three tons of coal, twelve barrels of oil, or five hundred gallons of gasoline.

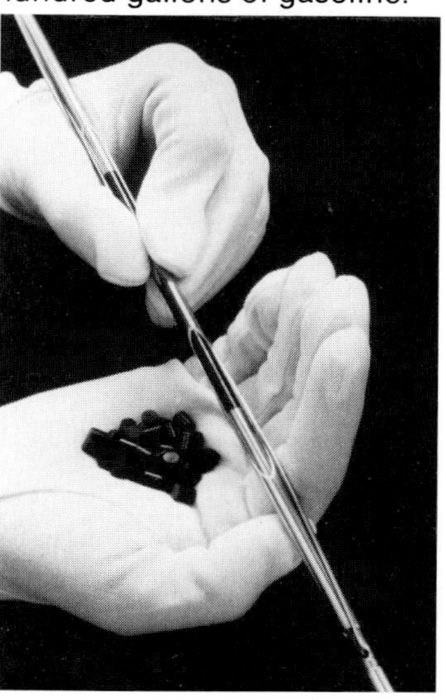

The energy released by nuclear fission is the result of the transformation of a small amount of nuclear mass into energy. According to Albert Einstein's theory of relativity, mass and energy are related by the equation $E = mc^2$, where E is energy, m is mass, and c is the speed of light. Since the speed of light is a fantastic 3×10^{10} centimeters per second, the energy released by the conversion of even a small amount of mass into energy is huge. A careful examination of the products and reactants of a fission process reveals that some matter is missing.

18–10 Chain Reactions: One Thing Leads to Another

The fission of U-235 produces, among other things, two neutrons. What happens to these neutrons? They can either escape from the sample of uranium or they can slam into other U-235 atoms. If the two neutrons hit and fuse into two other U-235 nuclei, the resulting nuclei will immediately undergo fission.

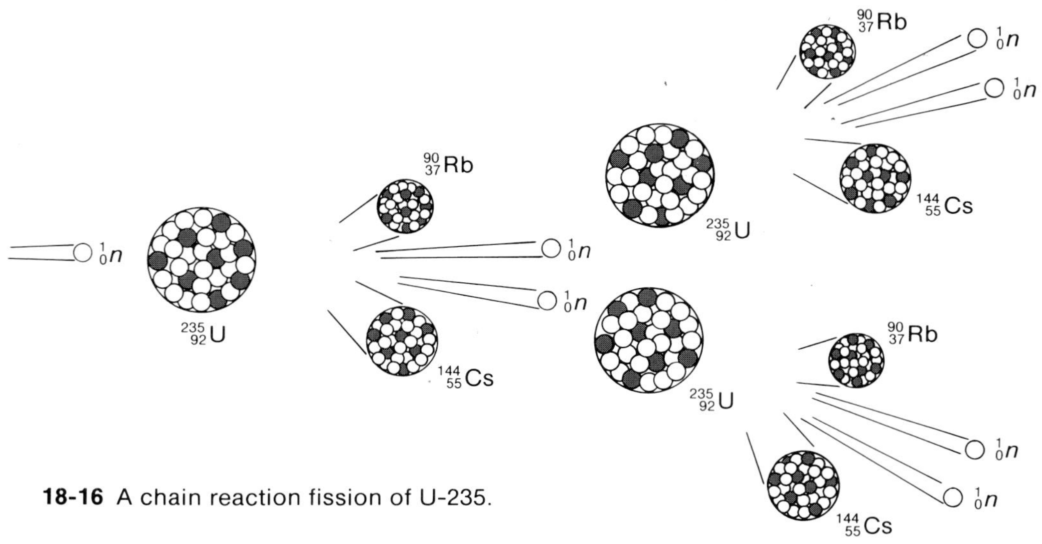

18-16 A chain reaction fission of U-235.

18-17 Nagasaki, Japan: the aftermath of an atomic bomb.

The neutrons produced by these two fissions can, in turn, initiate more nuclear fissions, and so on. The ongoing, self-sustaining fission process is called a **chain reaction.** For all this to happen, the sample of uranium must be large enough to intercept many of the released neutrons. If the mass of uranium is small, many neutrons escape without initiating more nuclear fissions, and a chain reaction does not occur. The smallest mass of a fissionable substance that can sustain a chain reaction is called the **critical mass** of the substance.

Chain reactions release large amounts of energy because many nuclei are split apart. Each split converts a minute amount of matter into energy. If technicians control the reaction in nuclear reactors, the heat may be harnessed and transformed into useful forms of energy (such as electricity). If the mass of fissionable material is larger than the critical mass, many neutrons are produced. The chain reaction proceeds quickly, even explosively, if it is not controlled. The amount of fissionable material that can support an explosion is called the supercritical mass. An atomic bomb uses a supercritical mass of a fissionable substance to achieve extraordinarily large energy releases and great destruction.

18–11 Synthetic Elements: Bigger, Yes, But Are They Better?

Before the atomic age began, scientists knew of no elements with atomic numbers greater than that of uranium. The elements following uranium on modern tables were synthesized with induced nuclear reactions. Scientists call elements with atomic numbers higher than ninety-two **transuranium elements.**

Transmutation is any process that converts one element into another. Ernest Rutherford, discoverer of the nucleus, discovered transmutation in 1919. He bombarded nitrogen with alpha particles and found that protons and an isotope of oxygen were produced.

$$^{14}_{7}N + ^{4}_{2}He \longrightarrow ^{17}_{8}O + ^{1}_{1}H$$

Transmutation can be performed on other light (low atomic number) elements, but (as with Rutherford's experiments) no new elements will be produced. If, however, heavier elements are bombarded, it is possible to produce an element with an atomic number greater than ninety-two.

Soon after discovering that beta decay increased the atomic number of an atom, scientists reasoned that this process could be the key to producing new elements. If uranium could be forced to emit an electron from one of its neutrons, the remaining part of the neutron would become a proton. The added proton would turn the uranium nucleus into element number ninety-three. To make a uranium atom emit a beta particle, scientists bombarded a sample of uranium with neutrons to produce U-239.

$$^{238}_{92}U + ^{1}_{0}n \longrightarrow ^{239}_{92}U$$

Neptunium was first synthesized in 1940 when U-239 atoms released beta particles.

$$^{239}_{92}U \longrightarrow ^{239}_{93}Np + ^{0}_{-1}e$$

A year later the same technique produced element number ninety-four. Larger elements resulted when alpha particles were used as projectiles. Einsteinium and fermium emerged from the fireball of an experimental hydrogen bomb in 1952. More sophisticated techniques and larger projectiles have since produced the newest transuranium elements. Scientists produced element 105 in 1970 when they bombarded californium-249 with nitrogen-15 nuclei.

18–12 Fusion: Ramming Nuclei Together

Nuclear fusion is the transmutation process of directly combining several light (low atomic number) nuclei to form different, heavier elements. Before nuclear fusion can occur, light nuclei must ram into each other with enough kinetic energy to overcome the natural repulsion between nuclei. Nuclei have enough energy for fusion when they have been heated to astronomical temperatures like those on the sun.

18-18 The exterior of a laser target chamber under construction. Scientists hope that the combined impact of many powerful lasers will create the conditions necessary for fusion to occur.

Scientists hope to control nuclear fusion reactions on earth and to convert their energy into electricity. The formation of helium by the fusion of two of hydrogen's isotopes ($^{2}_{1}H$ and $^{3}_{1}H$) offers particular promise.

$$^{2}_{1}H + ^{3}_{1}H \longrightarrow ^{4}_{2}He + ^{1}_{0}n$$

Temperatures close to 100 million°C are required for this reaction to proceed on its own. Needless to say, large amounts of energy must be expended to heat atoms to this temperature. Once the hot gases reach this temperature, additional energy must be expended to form strong magnetic fields to contain the ionized gases, plasma, and electrons that form.

Like fission, fusion processes convert matter into energy. The nuclei that form the larger nucleus have more mass than the product of the reaction. For example, the nuclear mass of helium is 4.0015 amu. If, however, the masses of two protons (1.0073 amu each) and the masses of two neutrons (1.0087 amu each) were added together, the result would be 4.0320 amu. When two protons and two neutrons form a helium nucleus, 0.0305 amu are converted into energy.

Will fusion solve all the earth's energy needs? Fusion requires no hard-to-find fuels, produces only low-level radioactive wastes, and offers great amounts of power. Although it has many selling points, many technological hurdles must be cleared before this question can be answered. Scientists have yet to devise a workable, let alone economical, way of controlling fusion reactions. Even if this is done, there is the possibility that the neutrons given off during the reaction could make entire power plants radioactive after ten to twenty years of operation.

18–13 Nuclear Binding Energy and Mass Defect: Transforming Matter into Energy

All nuclei have slightly less mass than their components. The idea that energy and mass are interconvertible explains this otherwise inexplicable physical phenomenon. The difference between the mass of an atom and the total mass of all its components is called the **mass defect** of the nucleus.

While scientists do not understand what holds a nucleus together, they do know that energy would be required to separate all the protons and neutrons in the nucleus. This energy is called the **nuclear binding energy** of the nucleus. For the purpose of comparing the elements, scientists determined the nuclear binding energies of various nuclei. They then divided this total by the number of particles in the nuclei to get the binding energy per nuclear particle. Figure 18-19 shows the binding energy per nuclear

FACETS OF CHEMISTRY

Solar Neutrinos

How does the sun generate its energy? Since the 1930s, scientists have believed that the sun derives its energy from thermonuclear reactions in its core. Unfortunately, they can see only the sun's surface, so they cannot look inside to see whether this is so. But there is a way, theoretically, that events in the core can be monitored indirectly. At least one of the hypothetical reactions in the fusion process generates subatomic particles called neutrinos. Neutrinos have no charge, almost no mass, and an uncanny ability to race through matter at high speeds without being absorbed. These properties should enable many neutrinos produced in the core to travel outward to the sun's surface and out into space. Billions of them should be racing away from the sun in all directions, some of them towards the earth. With a neutrino detector, scientists could verify the existence of solar neutrinos and lend support to the theory that fusion takes place in the core.

Such a detector has actually been built. It is an unusual piece of research equipment in at least two respects. The first is its location. It is situated in a gold mine in South Dakota, 1.5 kilometers beneath the surface of the earth. The purpose of this unusual placement is to shield the detector from extraneous radiation that might accidentally be misinterpreted as neutrinos. The second is its gigantic size. To trap the neutrinos, scientists must use a large quantity of dense chlorine-containing material. A huge tank of C_2Cl_4, a commercial cleaning solvent, is employed. The volume of the tank is 400,000 liters. Theoretically, there is a slight probability that an occasional chlorine nucleus will be struck by a neutrino and converted to an argon nucleus. Because the amount of argon produced can be accurately measured, the number of neutrinos entering the detector can be determined and compared with the theoretical number that should be arriving.

The detector has been in operation since 1970. The results, or rather, the lack of results, have created a major controversy. Not enough neutrinos have been detected to verify the fusion theory. Everything conceivable has been done to eliminate inaccuracies, both in the calculations and in the experimental setup. Still, the number of neutrinos detected is only one-third to one-fourth the predicted number.

Many different approaches have been used in an attempt to explain this discrepancy. Some theoreticians have speculated that the reactions in the core have slowed down or stopped. A small minority believe that there never were any thermonuclear reactions and that the sun gets all its energy by gravitational contraction. Creationists point out that a sun that is shrinking would have to be younger than the billion-year figures tossed about by evolutionists. A view that is growing in popularity is that since there are several kinds of neutrinos, and since it is now suspected that they can change from one kind to another in transit, perhaps the majority of them are in the wrong form to make their presence known as they come through the detector. This is an exceedingly difficult and complex experiment and one that will require much more time before a satisfactory understanding is achieved.

particle plotted as a function of mass number. It shows that nuclei with atomic masses near 50 amu have the most binding energy per nuclear particle.

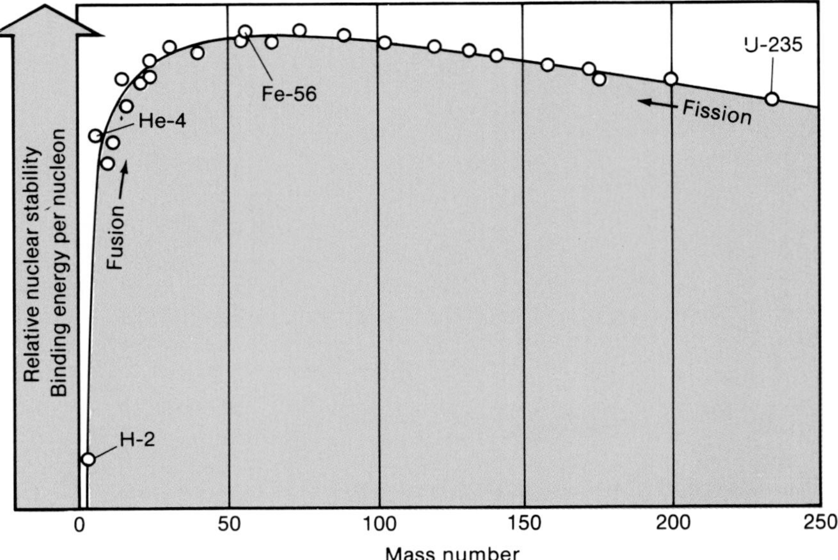

18-19 Graph of nuclear binding energy per nuclear particle versus mass number.

Nuclei with high binding energies per nuclear particle are more stable than those with low binding energies per nuclear particle. As it turns out, observed mass defects for the various elements match the observed binding energies. Nuclei with masses near 50 amu have the most mass defect per nuclear particle. It is reasonable to assume that the mass that has disappeared serves as the nuclear binding energy.

Sample Problem. Which of the following nuclei is the most stable: H-2, As-75, or U-235?

Solution.

From Figure 18-19 you can see that of the three nuclei mentioned, As-75 has the highest binding energy per nuclear particle. It is the most stable.

18-20 Hydrogen bombs release energy when small nuclei fuse together.

Both fission and fusion proceed in the direction that produces stable nuclei as end products. According to Figure 18-19, the most stable nuclei are those with mass numbers between about 60 and 80 amu. Accordingly, those elements with mass numbers less than 60 amu must increase in mass to produce more stable nuclei. The fusion reaction of hydrogen isotopes produces helium and a neutron. This reaction releases energy because it produces a more stable nucleus from a less stable nucleus. On the other hand, elements with mass numbers greater than 80 amu must undergo fission to produce more stable nuclei.

18–14 Responsible Citizenship: Chicken Little or Ostrich Big?

Once upon a time, in a barnyard far away, there lived a cowardly chicken named Chicken Little. One day an acorn fell on Chicken Little's head. "The sky is falling! The sky is falling!" he exclaimed. Chicken Little started a rumor to this end, and before long a delegation of barnyard animals left the farm to go and tell their king about the dangers of the falling sky.

Was Chicken Little's conclusion about the falling sky based on facts? Did he even make an effort to ascertain all the facts? Of course not. Today some nuclear activists are prophesying unavoidable annihilation for mankind if all nuclear weapons are not immediately destroyed. Nuclear power plants are said to be equally bad.

The other extreme is illustrated by a character called Ostrich Big. At the slightest sign of trouble, Ostrich Big sticks his head into the sand and hopes that the trouble will go away. Is Ostrich Big sensible? Do his actions resolve the trouble? The answer is obvious. People who see no need to be informed about nuclear weapons and the nuclear-power debate either believe that no real risks exist or that any problems that do exist will go away if they are ignored long enough. Neither the approach of Chicken Little nor the approach of Ostrich Big is responsible, reasonable, or scholarly.

The awesome power of the atom brings real risks. Nuclear weapons could spread large quantities of radioactive substances throughout the atmosphere. Nuclear fallout, as these airborne radioactive by-products are called, would spread throughout the earth. Water and food supplies would be contaminated. Since some of the radioactive substances have long half-lives, health problems from the fallout (birth defects and cancer) would continue for years.

The Bible makes it clear that life on earth will not be accidentally wiped out because of a nuclear accident or war (Rev. 20:7-9). God, not man, controls the destiny of the human race. While God will not allow man to completely destroy the earth, He has given man the responsibility to care for the earth. Ignoring this responsibility and misusing nuclear power could result in the deaths of many people and long-term damage to the environment.

Similar difficulties could result if a massive accident occurred at a nuclear power plant. A nuclear explosion at a nuclear power plant is unlikely because reliable methods are used to keep the masses of fissionable materials below the supercritical level. It is conceivable, however, that some radioactive waste could be spilled into the environment near a nuclear power plant.

Man has released radiation into the environment, but this is not the only source of radiation. Background radiation, or natural radiation as it is sometimes called, is always present in the environment. Cosmic rays coming to earth from the sun and other stars consist of alpha and beta radiation. Once cosmic rays reach the earth's atmosphere, they induce reactions in the atmosphere that release gamma radiation. These processes create a significant amount of radiation in the environment.

Science alone cannot supply the answers to the problems associated with nuclear power. Men need common sense, a code of ethics, and wisdom in order to apply science correctly. These things can be obtained in part from other men, but the best source of guidance is God's Word, the Bible. In it, Christians can find the truth and insight necessary to make difficult decisions.

Coming to Terms

radioactivity
alpha particle
beta particle
gamma ray
nuclear equation
radioactive decay series
radioactive decay constant
half-life
strong nuclear force
belt of stability
nuclear fission
chain reaction
critical mass
transuranium element
transmutation
nuclear fusion
mass defect
nuclear binding energy

Review Questions

1. Which types of radiation consist of particles and which type consists of waves?
2. What are the charges on the three types of radiation?
3. Rank the three types of radiation according to ionizing power and then according to penetrating power.
4. Explain why the different types of radiation have different ionizing capabilities.
5. Explain the relationship between ionizing power and penetrating power.
6. Gamma radiation, visible light, and radio waves are all forms of electromagnetic radiation. Why are gamma rays much more dangerous than visible light and radio waves?
7. Write the nuclear equation for the following.
   a. alpha decay of $^{217}_{86}Rn$
   b. alpha decay of $^{238}_{94}Pu$
   c. beta decay of $^{214}_{83}Bi$
   d. beta decay of $^{234}_{91}Pa$
   e. gamma decay of $^{152}_{63}Eu$
   f. gamma decay of $^{165}_{66}Dy$
8. Complete these nuclear reactions.
   a. $^{242}_{95}Am \longrightarrow ^{242}_{96}Cm + $ _____
   b. $^{220}_{87}Fr \longrightarrow ^{216}_{85}At + $ _____
   c. _____ $\longrightarrow ^{126}_{54}Xe + ^{0}_{-1}e$
   d. _____ $\longrightarrow ^{216}_{85}At + ^{4}_{2}He$
9. Identify each of the reactions in the previous question as alpha, beta, or gamma decay.
10. Why do the decay processes in a radioactive decay series not continue indefinitely?
11. Referring to Table 18-9, which nucleus decays more quickly, Br-80 or Mg-28?

12. The half-life of H-3 is 12.26 years. If 35.8 g of H-3 are allowed to decay for 36.78 years, what mass of H-3 will be left?
13. Scientific theories are based on observation. What observation led to the concept of strong nuclear forces?
14. Refer to Figure 18-12, and tell whether the following nuclei are stable or unstable. If they are unstable, predict whether the nucleus will undergo alpha or beta emission.
    a. $^{154}_{64}Gd$
    b. $^{59}_{26}Fe$
    c. $^{232}_{94}Pu$
    d. $^{200}_{80}Hg$
    e. $^{106}_{44}Ru$
15. Give two ways in which nuclear fission and nuclear fusion are similar and one way in which they are dissimilar.
16. Why do nuclear fission and nuclear fusion both release energy?
17. Why do some nuclei undergo fission but not fusion?
18. Determine which nucleus is the more stable by referring to Figure 18-19.
    a. Li-6 or Mg-24
    b. U-235 or Fe-56
    c. He-4 or U-235

APPENDIXES

Appendix A

The SI system of units is based on seven base units.

SI Base Units*

Quantity	Name	Symbol	Definition
Length	meter	m	"the length equal to 1,650,763.73 wavelengths in vacuum of the radiation corresponding to the transition between the levels $2p_{10}$ and $5d_5$ of the krypton-86 atom." (1960)
Mass	kilogram	kg	"this prototype (a certain platinum-iridium cylinder) shall henceforth be considered to be the unit of mass." (1889)
Time	second	s	"the duration of 9,192,631,770 periods of the radiation corresponding to the transition between the two hyperfine levels of the ground state of the cesium-133 atom." (1967)
Electric current	ampere	A	"that constant current which, if maintained in two straight parallel conductors of infinite length, of negligible circular cross section, and placed 1 meter apart in vacuum, would produce between these conductors a force equal to 2×10^{-7} newton per meter of length." (1946)
Thermodynamic temperature	kelvin	K	"the fraction 1/273.16 of the thermodynamic temperature of the triple point of water." (1967)
Amount of substance	mole	mol	"the amount of substance of a system which contains as many elementary entities as there are atoms in 0.012 kilogram of carbon-12." (1971)
Luminous intensity	candela	cd	"the luminous intensity, in the perpendicular direction, of a surface of 1/600,000 square meter of a blackbody at the temperature of freezing platinum under a pressure of 101,325 newton per square meter." (1967)

*Adapted from "The International System of Units (SI)," National Bureau of Standards Special Publication 330, 1972 edition.

Some SI Derived Units

Quantity	Name	Symbol	Expression in Terms of SI Base Units
Frequency	hertz	Hz	s^{-1}
Force	newton	N	$m \cdot kg/s^2$
Pressure	pascal	Pa	$kg/m \cdot s^2$
Energy	joule	J	$kg \cdot m^2/s^2$

Appendix B
Physical Constants

Quantity	Symbol	Traditional Units	SI Units
Atomic mass unit (1/12 the mass of C-12 atom)	amu	1.66×10^{-24} g	1.66×10^{-27} kg
Avogadro's number	N	6.023×10^{23} particles/mol	6.023×10^{23} particles/mol
Charge-to-mass ratio of electron	e/m	1.76×10^{8} coulomb/g	1.76×10^{11} C/kg
Electronic charge	e	1.60×10^{-19} coulomb	1.60×10^{-19} C
Electron rest mass	m_e	9.11×10^{-28} g 0.000549 amu	9.11×10^{-31} kg
Gas constant	R	0.08206 ℓ·atm/mol·K 62.36 ℓ·mm Hg/mol·K	8.3145 J/mol·K
Molar volume (STP)	V_m	22.4 ℓ/mol	
Neutron rest mass	m_n	1.67495×10^{-24} g 1.008669 amu	$1.67495\ 10^{-27}$ kg
Proton rest mass	m_p	1.6726×10^{-24} g 1.007277 amu	1.6726×10^{-27} kg
Velocity of light	c	2.9979×10^{10} cm/s (186,281 mi./s)	2.9979×10^{8} m/s

Appendix C
Unit Conversion Factors

The number that is used to convert one unit to another may be found in the box in which the columns containing the two units cross. The conversion factor can be used in unit analysis.

Example: The table shows that 1 centimeter = 6.214×10^{-6} mile. The conversion factor 1 cm/6.214×10^{-6} mile can be constructed from this equality.

Length

	cm	m	km	in.	ft.	mi.
1 centimeter =	1	10^{-2}	10^{-5}	0.3937	3.281×10^{-2}	6.214×10^{-6}
1 meter =	100	1	10^{-3}	39.3	3.281	6.214×10^{-4}
1 kilometer =	10^{5}	1000	1	3.937×10^{4}	3281	0.6214
1 inch =	2.540	2.540×10^{-2}	2.540×10^{-5}	1	8.333×10^{-2}	1.578×10^{-5}
1 foot =	30.48	0.3048	3.048×10^{-4}	12	1	1.894×10^{-4}
1 mile =	1.609×10^{5}	1609	1.609	6.336×10^{4}	5280	1

1 angstrom (Å) = 10^{-10} m

1 light-yr. = 9.4600×10^{12} km

Time

	s	min.	hr.	d.	yr.
1 second =	1	1.667×10^{-2}	2.778×10^{-4}	1.157×10^{-5}	3.169×10^{-8}
1 minute =	60	1	1.667×10^{-2}	6.944×10^{-4}	1.901×10^{-6}
1 hour =	3600	60	1	4.167×10^{-2}	1.141×10^{-4}
1 day =	8.640×10^{4}	1440	24	1	2.738×10^{-3}
1 year =	3.156×10^{7}	5.259×10^{5}	8.766×10^{3}	365.2	1

Density

	g/cm^3	kg/m^3	$lb./in.^3$	$lb./ft.^3$
1 gram per cubic centimeter =	1	1000	3.613×10^{-2}	62.43
1 kilogram per cubic meter =	0.001	1	3.613×10^{-5}	6.243×10^{-2}
1 pound per cubic inch =	27.68	2.768×10^{4}	1	1728
1 pound per cubic foot =	1.602×10^{-2}	16.02	5.787×10^{-4}	1

Volume

	cm^3	m^3	l	$in.^3$	$ft.^3$
1 cubic centimeter =	1	10^{-6}	1.000×10^{-3}	6.102×10^{-2}	3.531×10^{-5}
1 cubic meter =	10^6	1	1000	6.102×10^4	35.31
1 liter =	1000	1.000×10^{-3}	1	61.02	3.531×10^{-2}
1 cubic inch =	16.39	1.639×10^{-5}	1.639×10^{-2}	1	5.787×10^{-4}
1 cubic foot =	2.832×10^4	2.832×10^{-2}	28.32	1728	1

1 U.S. fl. gal. = 4 U.S. fl. qt. = 8 U.S. pt. = 128 U.S. fl. oz. = 231 $in.^3$
1 British imperial gal. = 277.4 $in.^3$ 1 liter = $10^{-3} m^3$

Pressure

	atm	in. of water	mm Hg	Pa	$lb./in.^2$
1 atmosphere =	1	406.8	760	1.013×10^5	14.70
1 inch of water at 4°C =	2.458×10^{-3}	1	1.868	249.1	3.613×10^{-2}
1 millimeter of mercury at 0°C =	1.316×10^3	0.5353	1	133.3	0.01934
1 pascal =	9.869×10^{-6}	4.015×10^{-3}	7.501×10^{-3}	1	1.450×10^{-4}
1 pound per square inch =	6.805×10^{-2}	27.68	51.71	6.895×10^3	1

Mass

	g	kg	amu	oz.	lb.	t.
1 gram =	1	0.001	6.024×10^{23}	3.527×10^{-2}	2.205×10^{-3}	1.102×10^{-6}
1 kilogram =	1000	1	6.024×10^{26}	35.27	2.205	1.102×10^{-3}
1 atomic mass unit =	1.660×10^{-24}	1.660×10^{-27}	1	5.855×10^{-26}	3.660×10^{-27}	1.829×10^{-30}
1 ounce =	28.35	2.835×10^{-2}	1.708×10^{25}	1	6.250×10^{-2}	3.125×10^{-5}
1 pound =	453.6	0.4536	2.732×10^{26}	16	1	0.0005
1 ton =	9.072×10^5	907.2	5.465×10^{29}	3.2×10^4	2000	1

Energy, Heat

	Btu	J	kcal	cal
1 British thermal unit =	1	1055	0.252	252.0
1 joule =	9.481×10^{-4}	1	2.389×10^{-4}	0.2389
1 kilocalorie =	3.968	4.186×10^3	1	1000
1 calorie =	3.98×10^{-3}	4.186	0.001	1

Appendix D

Electron Configurations of the Elements

Element	Atomic Number	1s	2s	2p	3s	3p	3d	4s	4p	4d	4f	5s
		Populations of Subshells										
H	1	1										
He	2	2										
Li	3	2	1									
Be	4	2	2									
B	5	2	2	1								
C	6	2	2	2								
N	7	2	2	3								
O	8	2	2	4								
F	9	2	2	5								
Ne	10	2	2	6								
Na	11				1							
Mg	12				2							
Al	13		Neon		2	1						
Si	14		core		2	2						
P	15				2	3						
S	16				2	4						
Cl	17				2	5						
Ar	18	2	2	6	2	6						
K	19							1				
Ca	20							2				
Sc	21						1	2				
Ti	22						2	2				
V	23						3	2				
Cr	24						5	1				
Mn	25						5	2				
Fe	26						6	2				
Co	27			Argon			7	2				
Ni	28			core			8	2				
Cu	29						10	1				
Zn	30						10	2				
Ga	31						10	2	1			
Ge	32						10	2	2			
As	33						10	2	3			
Se	34						10	2	4			
Br	35						10	2	5			
Kr	36	2	2	6	2	6	10	2	6			
Rb	37											1
Sr	38											2
Y	39									1		2
Zr	40									2		2
Nb	41									4		1
Mo	42				Krypton					5		1
Tc	43				core					6		1
Ru	44									7		1
Rh	45									8		1
Pd	46									10		
Ag	47									10		1
Cd	48									10		2

Element	Atomic Number		Populations of Subshells									
			4d	*4f*	*5s*	*5p*	*5d*	*5f*	*6s*	*6p*	*6d*	*7s*
In	49		10		2	1						
Sn	50		10		2	2						
Sb	51		10		2	3						
Te	52		10		2	4						
I	53		10		2	5						
Xe	54		10		2	6						
Cs	55		10		2	6			1			
Ba	56		10		2	6			2			
La	57		10		2	6	1		2			
Ce	58		10	2	2	6			2			
Pr	59		10	3	2	6			2			
Nd	60		10	4	2	6			2			
Pm	61		10	5	2	6			2			
Sm	62		10	6	2	6			2			
Eu	63		10	7	2	6			2			
Gd	64		10	7	2	6	1		2			
Tb	65		10	9	2	6			2			
Dy	66		10	10	2	6			2			
Ho	67		10	11	2	6			2			
Er	68		10	12	2	6			2			
Tm	69		10	13	2	6			2			
Yb	70		10	14	2	6			2			
Lu	71	Krypton core	10	14	2	6	1		2			
Hf	72		10	14	2	6	2		2			
Ta	73		10	14	2	6	3		2			
W	74		10	14	2	6	4		2			
Re	75		10	14	2	6	5		2			
Os	76		10	14	2	6	6		2			
Ir	77		10	14	2	6	9					
Pt	78		10	14	2	6	9		1			
Au	79		10	14	2	6	10		1			
Hg	80		10	14	2	6	10		2			
Tl	81		10	14	2	6	10		2	1		
Pb	82		10	14	2	6	10		2	2		
Bi	83		10	14	2	6	10		2	3		
Po	84		10	14	2	6	10		2	4		
At	85		10	14	2	6	10		2	5		
Rn	86		10	14	2	6	10		2	6		
Fr	87		10	14	2	6	10		2	6		1
Ra	88		10	14	2	6	10		2	6		2
Ac	89		10	14	2	6	10		2	6	1	2
Th	90		10	14	2	6	10		2	6	2	2
Pa	91		10	14	2	6	10	2	2	6	1	2
U	92		10	14	2	6	10	3	2	6	1	2
Np	93		10	14	2	6	10	5	2	6		2
Pu	94		10	14	2	6	10	6	2	6		2
Am	95		10	14	2	6	10	7	2	6		2
Cm	96		10	14	2	6	10	7	2	6	1	2
Bk	97		10	14	2	6	10	9	2	6		2
Cf	98		10	14	2	6	10	10	2	6		2
Es	99		10	14	2	6	10	11	2	6		2
Fm	100		10	14	2	6	10	12	2	6		2
Md	101		10	14	2	6	10	13	2	6		2

Appendix E

Logarithms

For the equation $n = b^l$, $\log_b n = l$ (read "the logarithm of n base b is l"). The logarithm of a number n is the power to which a base must be raised to equal n. A logarithm is thus an exponent. For example,

$$9 = 3^2;\ \log_3 9 = 2$$
$$100 = 10^2;\ \log_{10} 100 = 2$$
$$10000 = 10^4;\ \log_{10} 10000 = 4$$
$$0.01 = 10^{-2};\ \log_{10} 0.01 = -2$$

Any number may serve as the base, but 10 is the base used most often in basic chemistry. When no base is indicated, assume that base 10 is being used. A logarithm in the base 10 system is called the common logarithm and is denoted by the abbreviation *log*.

Unless a number is an exact power of 10, its log consists of an integer and a decimal. The integer part of the log is called the characteristic, and the decimal part of the log is called the mantissa. The characteristic of the log describes the location of the decimal point in the original number. Positive characteristics indicate that the original number is greater than 1. If a characteristic is negative, the original number is between 0 and 1.

log 100 = 2.0000; the characteristic is 2, the mantissa is 0000

log 0.01 = -2.0000; the characteristic is -2, the mantissa is 0000

log 59 = 1.7709; the characteristic is 1, the mantissa is 7709

The logs of numbers can be found with a calculator or with a printed table. A printed table gives the logs only for numbers between 1 and 10. To find the log of 3.24 on the table, scan down the column at the far left of the table until you find 3.2. Next, move across the row until you reach the column headed with a 4. The number in this square is the log of 3.24.

The logarithms of numbers less than 1 and greater than 10 can be determined through the mathematical principles that govern exponents. When confronted with a number that is not between 1 and 10, express it in scientific notation. The log of the first portion of the number will then be listed on the table. The log of the second portion of the number is simply the exponent of 10. To find the log of the entire number, add the two logs.

Examples:

$$\begin{aligned}\log 324 &= \log (3.24 \times 10^2)\\ &= \log 3.24 + \log 10^2\\ &= .5105 + 2\\ &= 2.5105\end{aligned}$$

$$\begin{aligned}\log 0.0056 &= \log (5.60 \times 10^{-3})\\ &= \log 5.60 + \log 10^{-3}\\ &= .7482 + (-3)\\ &= -2.2518\end{aligned}$$

An antilog is the number that corresponds to a given logarithm. The antilog of 2 is 100, and the antilog of -2 is 0.01. Antilogs can be found with calculators or with printed tables. For example, finding the antilog of 0.5105 requires searching the body of a log table for the mantissa 5105. This value falls in the row labeled 3.2 and the column headed 4. Thus the antilog of 0.5105 is 3.24. If the mantissa does not appear in the table, the mantissa that is closest to the one you are seeking should be used.

Antilogs of numbers that are not between 0 and 1 (corresponding to numbers less than 1 or greater than 10) can be found by the reverse process of that used to find logarithms. To find these antilogs, express the number as a sum of the mantissa and the characteristic, find the antilogs of each portion, and then multiply them.

Example:

$$\begin{aligned} \text{antilog } 2.5105 &= \text{antilog } (0.5105 + 2) \\ &= (\text{antilog } 0.5105)(\text{antilog } 2) \\ &= 3.24 \times 10^2 \end{aligned}$$

Finding the antilogs of negative numbers requires a similar procedure, but it is a bit more difficult. To find the antilog of a negative number, express the number as a positive decimal minus an integer. Then find the antilogs of the resulting numbers and multiply them.

$$\begin{aligned} \text{antilog } -4.4895 &= \text{antilog } (0.5105 - 5) \\ &= (\text{antilog } 0.5105)(\text{antilog } -5) \\ &= 3.24 \times 10^{-5} \end{aligned}$$

Logarithms are often used to simplify complex calculations. Because logarithms are exponents, the following theorems regulate the use of logarithms.

$$\begin{aligned} \log (m \times n) &= \log m + \log n \\ \log (m/n) &= \log m - \log n \\ \log (m^n) &= (\log m)n \\ \log (\sqrt[n]{m}) &= (\log m)/n \end{aligned}$$

These theorems allow problems involving multiplication, division, powers, or roots to be solved easily. To multiply two numbers, add their logs and find the antilog. To divide, subtract one log from the other and then find the antilog. To find a power of a number, multiply the number's log by the exponent. To find a root of a number, divide the number's log by the root.

Examples:

324 × 5340

$$\begin{aligned} \log (324 \times 5340) &= \log 324 + \log 5340 \\ &= 2.5105 + 3.7275 \\ &= 6.2380 \\ \text{antilog } 6.2380 &= 1.73 \times 10^6 \end{aligned}$$

5340/324

$$\begin{aligned} \log (5340/324) &= \log 5340 - \log 324 \\ &= 3.7275 - 2.5105 \\ &= 1.2170 \\ \text{antilog } 1.2170 &= 1.65 \times 10^1 \text{ or } 16.5 \end{aligned}$$

$\sqrt[3]{5340}$

$$\begin{aligned} \log (5340^3) &= (\log 5340) \times 3 \\ &= 3.7275 \times 3 \\ &= 11.1825 \\ \text{antilog } 11.1825 &= 1.52 \times 10^{11} \end{aligned}$$

5340

$$\begin{aligned} \log 5340 &= (\log 5340)/3 \\ &= 3.7275/3 \\ &= 1.2425 \\ \text{antilog } 1.2425 &= 1.75 \times 10^{1} \text{ or } 17.5 \end{aligned}$$

Table of Common Logarithms

N	0	1	2	3	4	5	6	7	8	9
1.0	0000	0043	0086	0128	0170	0212	0253	0294	0334	0374
1.1	0414	0453	0492	0531	0569	0607	0645	0682	0719	0755
1.2	0792	0828	0864	0899	0934	0969	1004	1038	1072	1106
1.3	1139	1173	1206	1239	1271	1303	1335	1367	1399	1430
1.4	1461	1492	1523	1553	1584	1614	1644	1673	1703	1732
1.5	1761	1790	1818	1847	1875	1903	1931	1959	1987	2014
1.6	2041	2068	2095	2122	2148	2175	2201	2227	2253	2279
1.7	2304	2330	2355	2380	2405	2430	2455	2480	2504	2529
1.8	2553	2577	2601	2625	2648	2672	2695	2718	2742	2765
1.9	2788	2810	2833	2856	2878	2900	2923	2945	2967	2989
2.0	3010	3032	3054	3075	3096	3118	3139	3160	3181	3201
2.1	3222	3243	3263	3284	3304	3324	3345	3365	3385	3404
2.2	3424	3444	3464	3483	3502	3522	3541	3560	3579	3598
2.3	3617	3636	3655	3674	3692	3711	3729	3747	3766	3784
2.4	3802	3820	3838	3856	3874	3892	3909	3927	3945	3962
2.5	3979	3997	4014	4031	4048	4065	4082	4099	4116	4133
2.6	4150	4166	4183	4200	4216	4232	4249	4265	4281	4298
2.7	4314	4330	4346	4362	4378	4393	4409	4425	4440	4456
2.8	4472	4487	4502	4518	4533	4548	4564	4579	4594	4609
2.9	4624	4639	4654	4669	4683	4698	4713	4728	4742	4757
3.0	4771	4786	4800	4814	4829	4843	4857	4871	4886	4900
3.1	4914	4928	4942	4955	4969	4983	4997	5011	5024	5038
3.2	5051	5065	5079	5092	5105	5119	5132	5145	5159	5172
3.3	5185	5198	5211	5224	5237	5250	5263	5276	5289	5302
3.4	5315	5328	5340	5353	5366	5378	5391	5403	5416	5428
3.5	5441	5453	5465	5478	5490	5502	5514	5527	5539	5551
3.6	5563	5575	5587	5599	5611	5623	5635	5647	5658	5670
3.7	5682	5694	5705	5717	5729	5740	5752	5763	5775	5786
3.8	5798	5809	5821	5832	5843	5855	5866	5877	5888	5899
3.9	5911	5922	5933	5944	5955	5966	5977	5988	5999	6010
4.0	6021	6031	6042	6053	6064	6075	6085	6096	6107	6117
4.1	6128	6138	6149	6160	6170	6180	6191	6201	6212	6222
4.2	6232	6243	6253	6263	6274	6284	6294	6304	6314	6325
4.3	6335	6345	6355	6365	6375	6385	6395	6405	6415	6425
4.4	6435	6444	6454	6464	6474	6484	6493	6503	6513	6522
4.5	6532	6542	6551	6561	6571	6580	6590	6599	6609	6618
4.6	6628	6637	6646	6656	6665	6675	6684	6693	6702	6712
4.7	6721	6730	6739	6749	6758	6767	6776	6785	6794	6803
4.8	6812	6821	6830	6839	6848	6857	6866	6875	6884	6893
4.9	6902	6911	6920	6928	6937	6946	6955	6964	6972	6981

Table of Common Logarithms

N	0	1	2	3	4	5	6	7	8	9
5.0	6990	6998	7007	7016	7024	7033	7042	7050	7059	7067
5.1	7076	7084	7093	7101	7110	7118	7126	7135	7143	7152
5.2	7160	7168	7177	7185	7193	7202	7210	7218	7226	7235
5.3	7243	7251	7259	7267	7275	7284	7292	7300	7308	7316
5.4	7324	7332	7340	7348	7356	7364	7372	7380	7388	7396
5.5	7404	7412	7419	7427	7435	7443	7451	7459	7466	7474
5.6	7482	7490	7497	7505	7513	7520	7528	7536	7543	7551
5.7	7559	7566	7574	7582	7589	7597	7604	7612	7619	7627
5.8	7634	7642	7649	7657	7664	7672	7679	7686	7694	7701
5.9	7709	7716	7723	7731	7738	7745	7752	7760	7767	7774
6.0	7782	7789	7796	7803	7810	7818	7825	7832	7839	7846
6.1	7853	7860	7868	7875	7882	7889	7896	7903	7910	7917
6.2	7924	7931	7938	7945	7952	7959	7966	7973	7980	7987
6.3	7993	8000	8007	8014	8021	8028	8035	8041	8048	8055
6.4	8062	8069	8075	8082	8089	8096	8102	8109	8116	8122
6.5	8129	8136	8142	8149	8156	8162	8169	8176	8182	8189
6.6	8195	8202	8209	8215	8222	8228	8235	8241	8248	8254
6.7	8261	8267	8274	8280	8287	8293	8299	8306	8312	8319
6.8	8325	8331	8338	8344	8351	8357	8363	8370	8376	8382
6.9	8388	8395	8401	8407	8414	8420	8426	8432	8439	8445
7.0	8451	8457	7463	8470	8476	8482	8488	8494	8500	8506
7.1	8513	8519	8525	8531	8537	8543	8549	8555	8561	8567
7.2	8573	8579	8585	8591	8597	8603	8609	8615	8621	8627
7.3	8633	8639	8645	8651	8657	8663	8669	8675	8681	8686
7.4	8692	8698	8704	8710	8716	8722	8727	8733	8739	8745
7.5	8751	8756	8762	8768	8774	8779	8785	8791	8797	8802
7.6	8808	8814	8820	8825	8831	8837	8842	8848	8854	8859
7.7	8865	8871	8876	8882	8887	8893	8899	8904	8910	8915
7.8	8921	8927	8932	8938	8943	8949	8954	8960	8965	8971
7.9	8976	8982	8987	8993	8998	9004	9009	9015	9020	9025
8.0	9031	9036	9042	9047	9053	9058	9063	9069	9074	9079
8.1	9085	9090	9096	9101	9106	9112	9117	9122	9128	9133
8.2	9138	9143	9149	9154	9159	9165	9170	9175	9180	9186
8.3	9191	9196	9201	9206	9212	9217	9222	9227	9232	9238
8.4	9243	9248	9253	9258	9263	9269	9274	9279	9284	9289
8.5	9294	9299	9304	9309	9315	9320	9325	9330	9335	9340
8.6	9345	9350	9355	9360	9365	9370	9375	9380	9385	9390
8.7	9395	9400	9405	9410	9415	9420	9425	9430	9435	9440
8.8	9445	9450	9455	9460	9465	9469	9474	9479	9484	9489
8.9	9494	9499	9504	9509	9513	9518	9523	9528	9533	9538
9.0	9542	9547	9552	9557	9562	9566	9571	9576	9581	9586
9.1	9590	9595	9600	9605	9609	9614	9619	9624	9628	9633
9.2	9638	9643	9647	9652	9657	9661	9666	9671	9675	9680
9.3	9685	9689	9694	9699	9703	9708	9713	9717	9722	9727
9.4	9731	9736	9741	9745	9750	9754	9759	9763	9768	9773
9.5	9777	9782	9786	9791	9795	9800	9805	9809	9814	9818
9.6	9823	9827	9832	9836	9841	9845	9850	9854	9859	9863
9.7	9868	9872	9877	9881	9886	9890	9894	9899	9903	9908
9.8	9912	9917	9921	9926	9930	9934	9939	9943	9948	9952
9.9	9956	9961	9965	9969	9974	9978	9983	9987	9991	9996

GLOSSARY

A

absolute zero 0 K; theoretically, the temperature at which all molecular motion would cease; the coldest temperature possible.

acidic anhydride A nonmetal oxide that forms an acid when added to water. Example: SO_3.

acid dissociation constant The special name given to the resulting constant of the equilibrium between an acid and its conjugate base.

acidic salt A salt formed from a partially neutralized polyprotic acid; its negative ion contains an ionizable hydrogen atom. Examples: $NaHSO_4$, $NaHCO_3$.

acidic solution A solution with more H_3O^+ ions than OH^- ions, resulting in a pH less than 7.

activated complex An unstable, energetic group of reactants that forms as a transitional structure during a chemical reaction.

activation energy The minimum amount of kinetic energy that must be possessed by reactants before they can have an effective collision.

activity series A table of metals or nonmetals arranged in order of descending activities.

addition reaction An organic reaction in which one reactant joins another reactant at the site of a double or triple bond.

adsorption The attachment of charged particles to the particles in a colloid.

alchemy The ancient study of transmutations between base metals and gold, sickness and health, age and youth, or even earthly and supernatural existence.

alcohol An organic compound of the general form R—OH, having a covalently bonded OH^- functional group attached to a nonaromatic group.

aldehyde Any organic compound of the general form $R-\overset{\overset{\displaystyle O}{\|}}{C}-H$ having an aldehyde group in its structure.

aliphatic compound An open-chain compound and any cyclic compound whose bonds resemble those of an open-chain compound.

alkali metal A family I A metal, which has only one valence electron.

alkaline earth metal A family II A metal, which has two valence electrons.

alkane An open-chain, aliphatic hydrocarbon that contains only single bonds.

alkene An open-chain, aliphatic hydrocarbon that contains at least one carbon-carbon double bond.

alkyl group (-R group) A group of bonded atoms that can be thought of as an alkane with one hydrogen atom missing.

alkyl halide An organic compound that contains an alkyl group and a halogen as a functional group.

alkyne An open-chain, aliphatic hydrocarbon containing triple bonds.

allotrope One of two or more forms of a polymorphic element that exist in the same physical state. Example: O_2 and O_3 are allotropic forms of oxygen.

allotropic A term describing elements that can exist in more than one form.

alpha particle The nucleus of the helium atom (two protons, two neutrons); represented by He^{2+} or He-4^{2+}.

amide An organic compound of the general form $R-\overset{\overset{\displaystyle O}{\|}}{C}-NH_2$, in which an amine is substituted for an OH group in a carboxylic acid.

amine An organic compound of the general form -N—H_2, which can be thought of as an ammonia molecule whose hydrogen atoms have been replaced by other atoms or groups of atoms.

amino acid The building block of a protein; a carboxylic acid containing the amino group.

amorphous solid A solid without any definite shape or crystalline structure.

amphiprotic A term describing a substance that can act as either an acid or a base by releasing or accepting a proton.

analytical chemistry The techniques by which chemists devise equipment and methods to discover what is in a sample of material and to quantify its constituents.

angstrom A unit of length equal to 10^{-10} m or 10^{-8} cm.

anhydride A compound that reacts with water in a composition reaction.

anion A negative ion.

anode The electrode at which oxidation occurs during an electrochemical reaction; the electrode that attracts anions because of its positive charge.

apothecary A person who prepares and sells medicines (a person similar to a modern pharmacist).

aromatic compound Benzene and any compound that has a structure resembling benzene's characteristic ring structure; aromatic compounds are all cyclic compounds with clouds of delocalized electrons.

Arrhenius acid A substance that releases hydrogen ions (H^+) into aqueous solutions.

Arrhenius base A substance that releases hydroxide ions (OH^-) into aqueous solutions.

aryl group (-Ar group) A group of bonded atoms that can be thought of as an aromatic compound with one hydrogen atom missing.

aryl halide An organic compound that contains an aryl group and a halogen as a functional group.

atmosphere A standard unit of pressure equal to the pressure exerted by a column of mercury exactly 760 mm high at 0°C; 14.7 lb./in.^{2} = 760 mm Hg = 760 torr = 1 atm.

atom A neutral particle with a centrally located nucleus consisting of protons and neutrons with electrons around it; the smallest representative unit in an element.

atomic mass The average mass of the isotopes of an element expressed in atomic mass units (amu).

atomic mass number The sum of the number of protons and neutrons in the nucleus of an atom.

atomic mass unit One-twelfth the mass of one atom of carbon-12; 1.6606×10^{-24} g (which is very close to the mass of one proton or one neutron).

atomic number The number of protons in the nucleus of an atom.

Aufbau principle The principle that the electron configuration of an atom may be obtained by building on the electron configuration of an atom of lower atomic number; the electrons fill the sublevels in the order given by the diagonal rule.

autoionization See **autoprotolysis constant of water.**

autoprotolysis A process in an acid-base reaction in which one molecule donates a proton to another molecule of the same substance.

autoprotolysis constant of water The special name given to the dissociation constant of water molecules at 25° C; $K_w = 1 \times 10^{-14}$.

Avogadro's number 6.023×10^{23}; the number of atoms in exactly 12.0 g of carbon-12.

Avogadro's principle The principle that equal volumes of gases at the same temperature and pressure contain equal numbers of molecules.

B

balanced chemical equation A chemical equation in which coefficients are arranged to show conservation of mass in a reaction.

barometer An apparatus that measures atmospheric pressure by allowing atmospheric pressure to support a column of liquid.

basic anhydride A metal oxide that forms a base when added to water. Example: Na_2O.

basic salt A salt containing OH^- ions. Example: $CuCO_3 \cdot Cu(OH)_2$.

basic solution A solution with fewer H_3O^+ ions than OH^- ions, resulting in a pH greater than 7.

battery One or more voltaic cells arranged to produce electricity.

belt of stability The group of stable nuclei represented on a graph of atomic numbers versus number of neutrons.

bent An arrangement in which two particles bonded to a central particle are nonlinear.

beta particle An electron that has been emitted from a nucleus.

binary compound A compound that contains only two kinds of elements.

biochemistry The study of the chemical processes in living things.

boiling A physical change from the liquid state to the gaseous state that occurs when the vapor pressure of a liquid equals the prevailing atmospheric pressure.

boiling point The temperature at which the vapor pressure of a liquid equals the applied atmospheric pressure.

boiling point elevation A raising of the boiling point of a solvent due to the presence of solute particles.

Boyle's law A law of gas behavior that states that the pressure of a dry gas is inversely proportional to its volume if the temperature is held constant ($PV = k$).

Brönsted-Lowry acid A substance that donates protons.

Brönsted-Lowry base A substance that accepts protons.

Brownian motion The random, chaotic movements of microscopic particles in a colloidal dispersion.

buffer A solution that can receive moderate amounts of either acid or base without a significant change in pH.

C

calorie The amount of energy required to raise the temperature of 1 g of water 1° C.

capillary rise The movement of a liquid up a narrow tube caused by the attraction of the molecules in the tube for the molecules of the liquid.

carbohydrate A polyhydroxy aldehyde or ketone; a compound that can be hydrolyzed to form a polyhydroxy aldehyde or ketone.

carbonyl group A carbon atom with a doubly bonded oxygen atom attached to it.

carboxyl group The COOH group.

carboxylic acid An organic compound of the general form R—CO—OH, having a carboxylic acid functional group in its structure.

catalyst A substance that changes a reaction rate without being permanently changed by the reaction.

cathode The electrode at which reduction occurs during an electrochemical reaction; the electrode that attracts cations because of its negative charge.

cathode rays The stream of electrons emitted from the cathode in a cathode-ray tube (CRT).

cation A positive ion.

Celsius scale A temperature scale, proposed by Anders Celsius, that divides the range from the freezing point of water (0° C) to the boiling point of water (100° C) into 100 increments and labels absolute zero as -273° C; the centigrade scale.

chain reaction A self-sustaining fission process in which neutrons from fissions cause more fissions.

characteristic The power to which 10 is raised in scientific notation expressions; the number that indicates how many places the decimal point must be moved to return to conventional decimal format. Example: 3 is the characteristic in 1.200×10^3.

Charles's law A law of gas behavior that states that the volume and absolute temperature of a gas are directly proportional to one another when the pressure is held constant ($V/T = k$).

chemical bond An electrostatic attraction that holds atoms together in compounds; an attraction produced by the transfer or sharing of electrons.

chemical change See **chemical reaction.**

chemical equation An expression that represents a chemical reaction by using chemical formulas, chemical symbols, and coefficients.

chemical equilibrium The state of balance attained in a reversible reaction in which the forward and reverse reactions proceed at the same rate.

chemical property A property of matter that describes how one substance reacts in the presence of other substances.

chemical reaction A change in which a substance loses its characteristics and becomes one or more new substances.

chemistry The study of the composition and properties of matter and the energy transformations accompanying changes in the fundamental structure of matter.

chromosome Strands of DNA combined with proteins; it is usually formed within the nucleus of the cell.

coefficient A number that appears in front of a chemical formula and indicates how many units of that substance are present. Examples: 2 O_2—two oxygen molecules; 4 K_2SO_4—four potassium sulfate compounds.

colligative property A property of solutions that depends only on the number of particles present, without regard to type.

collision theory The theory that states that molecules and atoms must undergo forceful, properly oriented collisions before they can react.

colloid A mixture of fine particles (between 1 and 1000 nanometers in size) that do not settle out of the mixture.

combined gas law A law of gas behavior that combines Boyle's law and Charles's law ($P_1V_1/T_1 = P_2V_2/T_2$).

common ion effect An equilibrium phenomenon in which two or more substances dissolve and release a common ion, thereby decreasing the ionization of the weaker electrolyte.

composition reaction A chemical reaction of the general form $A + B \longrightarrow AB$, in which two or more reactants combine into a single product.

compound A substance that consists of atoms of different elements chemically bonded together.

compressibility The property of a substance that allows its particles to be squeezed into smaller volumes.

concentrated solution A solution whose ratio of solute to solvent is relatively high.

condensation A physical change from the gaseous state to the liquid state.

condensation reaction An organic reaction in which two compounds combine with each other by losing water; the opposite of hydrolysis.

conductivity A physical property of matter indicating the ability to transfer heat or electrons between internal particles.

conjugate acid The structure formed when a base is protonated.

conjugate base The structure formed when an acid has donated a proton.

conjugate pair Two particles that differ from each other by only a hydrogen ion.

continuous spectrum A spectrum that has segments that blend into each other without distinct boundaries.

conversion factor A ratio that is constructed from the relationship between two units and is equal to 1. Example: 1 kg/1000 g.

coordinate covalent bond A linkage between atoms due to the sharing of electrons that originate from the same atom.

covalent bond The electrostatic attraction that two nuclei have for the same pair of shared electrons.

critical mass The smallest mass of a fissionable substance that can sustain a chain reaction.

critical pressure The pressure needed to liquefy a gas at its critical temperature.

critical temperature The temperature above which no amount of pressure will liquefy a gas.

crystal A solid in which the particles occur in a regular, repeating pattern.

crystal lattice A three-dimensional structure of points or objects that represents the regular alternating pattern of positive and negative ions.

crystalline solid See **crystal.**

cyclic aliphatic compound An aliphatic, organic compound whose carbon chains are bonded in ring shapes. Examples: cycloalkanes, cycloalkenes.

D

decomposition reaction A chemical reaction of the general form $AB \longrightarrow A + B$, in which a single reactant breaks down into two or more products.

deductive reasoning The process of beginning with a general conclusion and predicting specific facts.

deliquescence The action of a compound that absorbs enough water from the air to dissolve itself and form a solution.

delocalized electrons Electrons that can move between several different bonds; in benzene, delocalized electrons can move throughout circular spaces above and below the plane of bonded nuclei.

density A measure of the concentration of matter; it is expressed as a ratio of the object's mass to its volume.

deprotonation The process of losing a proton. Example: $H_2SO_4 \longrightarrow H^+ + HSO_4^-$.

descriptive chemistry The study of elements and compounds that stresses identification of properties rather than theoretical calculations.

desiccator An airtight container with a hygroscopic substance that removes moisture to protect the compound being stored.

diagonal rule A mnemonic device that gives the energy levels and sublevels in their order of filling.

diatomic element An element whose atoms bond into two-atom units. Examples: N_2, O_2, H_2, Cl_2, F_2, Br_2, F_2.

diffusion Spontaneous mixing due to particle motion.

dilute solution A solution whose ratio of solute to solvent is relatively low.

dipeptide Two amino acids joined by a peptide bond.

dipole moment The product of the distance between charges and the strength of the charges; a measure of the polarity of a molecule.

dipole-dipole interaction The attraction of the positive end of one polar molecule to the negative end of another polar molecule.

diprotic acid An acid that can donate two protons.

disaccharide A carbohydrate composed of two monosaccharide units. Example: sucrose.

dispersion force An electrostatic attraction that arises between atoms or molecules because of the presence of instantaneous and induced dipoles.

dissociation The process in which a solvent disrupts the attractive forces in a solute and pulls the solute apart.

distillation A laboratory technique by which chemists separate a mixture by evaporating its components at their boiling points and then condensing and collecting the vapors.

double covalent bond A covalent bond in which two atoms share two pairs of electrons. Example: SO.

double replacement reaction A chemical reaction of the general form $AX + CZ \longrightarrow AZ + BX$, in which the cation of one compound combines with the anion of another compound, and vice versa.

ductility A physical property of matter describing the ability of matter to be drawn into a wire.

dynamic equilibrium An equilibrium (chemical) in which there is a continuation of two or more opposing events occurring at the same rates but resulting in no net change.

E

efflorescence The action of a hydrate that loses part or all of its water of hydration when exposed to air.

electrochemical cell An apparatus consisting of two electrical contacts (electrodes) that are immersed in an electrolyte solution and joined by a wire.

electrode A conductor that allows an electrical current to enter or leave an electrolytic cell (or other apparatus).

electrolysis A process that uses electricity to force an otherwise nonspontaneous chemical reaction to occur; the separation of a compound into simpler substances by an electrical current.

electrolyte A substance that releases ions and conducts electricity when it dissolves in water.

electrolytic cell An electrochemical cell used to split compounds.

electron A particle with a -1 charge and a mass of 0.00055 amu found orbiting the nucleus in an atom.

electron affinity The amount of energy released when an electron is added to an atom to form a negative ion.

electron configuration A representation of how electrons are positioned in an atom: a number indicates the principal energy level, and a letter indicates the sublevel.

electron-dot structure A representation of the electronic structure of atoms and compounds: chemical symbols represent nuclei, and dots represent valence electrons. Examples: Na·, Na:C̤̈l:

electronegativity A measure of the tendency of bonded atoms to attract electrons.

electroplating The deposition of a metal on a surface by means of an electrical current.

electron-sea theory A theory that offers an explanation of how metals bond; the valence electrons of atoms are said to be freely shared between all atoms.

electrostatic attraction Forces between particles caused by their opposite electrical charges.

element A substance that cannot be broken down by ordinary chemical means into anything that is stable and simpler and whose atoms all have the same atomic number.

empirical formula A formula that tells the types of atoms that are present in a compound and the simplest whole-number ratio between the atoms. Example: The empirical formula of C_2H_4 is CH_2.

endothermic A term describing a process that absorbs heat energy.

energy The ability to do work.

enthalpy The heat content of a system at constant pressure; abbreviated *H*.

enthalpy of bond formation (bond enthalpy) The enthalpy change that occurs when 1 mole of bonds in a gaseous compound is broken.

enthalpy of formation The change in enthalpy that occurs when 1 mole of a compound is formed from its elements; abbreviated ΔH_f°.

entropy The measure of randomness or disorder in a specified portion of the universe.

enzyme A protein molecule that acts as a catalyst.

equilibrium constant A mathematical expression of the ratio between the concentrations of the products and reactants at equilibrium: each concentration in the expression is raised to the power that matches the substance's coefficient in the balanced chemical reaction.

equivalent For redox reactions, one equivalent is defined as the amount of substance that gains or loses a mole of electrons; for an acid-base reaction, it is the amount of substance that gains, loses, or neutralizes a mole of hydrogen ions.

ester An organic compound of the general form $R_1-\overset{\overset{\displaystyle O}{\|}}{C}-O-R_2$, having a carbonyl-oxygen-carbon system.

esterification The formation of an ester through the reaction of an acid with an alcohol.

ether An organic compound of the general form R_1-O-R_2, in which an oxygen atom links alkyl groups. Ethers differ from esters in that the carbons next to the oxygen link are not bonded to another oxygen atom.

evaporation A physical change from the liquid state to the gaseous state that occurs at the surface of a liquid.

exothermic A term describing a process that releases heat energy.

expansibility The property of a substance that allows its particles to spread out.

F

family A vertical column of elements in the periodic table with similar physical and chemical properties.

fat A molecule formed from glycerol and three carboxylic acids with mostly saturated carbon chains; a fat differs from an oil in that it is solid at room temperature, while an oil is liquid.

fatty acid A carboxylic acid with a long, aliphatic chain that can be obtained by the hydrolysis of animal fat or vegetable oils.

first law of thermodynamics The physical law that states that energy cannot be created nor destroyed but can be converted from one form into another (also called the law of conservation of energy).

flow chart A diagram showing the progress of work through a sequence of operations.

formula A combination of subscripts and chemical symbols that indicate the number and kinds of atoms that are present in a compound.

formula unit The simplest ratio between the different kinds of atoms in an ionic compound.

free energy (Gibbs free energy) A term that includes the enthalpy and entropy of a substance.

free energy change The driving force of a reaction and the indicator of spontaneity; $\Delta G = \Delta H - T\Delta S$. If ΔG is negative for a process, the process is energetically favorable.

freezing A physical change from the liquid state to the solid state.

freezing point depression A lowering of the freezing point of a solvent due to the presence of solute particles.

functional group An atom or group of atoms that is common to the members of a family of compounds and imparts characteristic chemical properties to that family.

G

gamma ray Electromagnetic waves of very high frequency and short wavelength.

gas A state of matter in which the particles have enough energy to overcome the attractive forces: a gas has no definite size or shape.

Gay-Lussac's law A law of gas behavior that states that the pressure of a confined gas is proportional to its absolute temperature, provided its volume is held constant ($P/T = k$).

gene A segment of DNA capable of producing a specific polypeptide that is responsible for a particular characteristic (hair color, for example).

glycerol A three-carbon molecule with three hydroxyl groups.

$$\begin{array}{ccccc} OH & & OH & & OH \\ | & & | & & | \\ -C & - & C & - & C- \\ | & & | & & | \end{array}$$

glycogen A branched polymer of glucose that serves to store energy for animals.

gram-atomic mass The mass in grams of a mole of atoms; a value numerically equivalent to the average atomic mass expressed in grams.

gram-equivalent mass The mass of one equivalent expressed in grams.

gram-formula mass The mass in grams of a mole of formula units; a value numerically equivalent to the average formula mass expressed in grams.

gram-molecular mass The mass in grams of a mole of molecular units; a value numerically equivalent to the average molecular mass expressed in grams.

Greek prefix system A system of prefixes used to indicate the number of atoms in a binary covalent compound or the number of water molecules in a hydrate. Examples: dinitrogen pentoxide, sodium carbonate monohydrate.

group See **family.**

H

Haber process The industrial preparation of ammonia from nitrogen and hydrogen gas that uses high temperatures, high pressures, and catalysts.

half-life The amount of time required for one-half of the nuclei in a radioactive sample to decay into another kind of nucleus.

half-reaction A hypothetical portion of a redox reaction that consists of either the substances involved in oxidation or the substances involved in reduction.

half-reaction method A method of balancing redox equations using half-reactions.

halogen A family VIIA element, which has seven valence electrons.

heat of condensation The amount of heat that must be removed from a vapor at its boiling point to condense it to a liquid at the same temperature.

heat of fusion The amount of heat required to change 1 g of a substance at its melting point from a solid to a liquid.

heat of vaporization The amount of heat required to change a liquid at its boiling point to a gas at the same temperature.

Heisenberg uncertainty principle The principle that states that it is impossible to know the energy (velocity) and exact position of an object at the same time.

Henry's law The law that states that the solubility of gases increases with pressure.

Hess's law The law that states that the enthalpy change of a reaction equals the sum of the enthalpy changes for each step of the reaction.

heterogeneous mixture A mixture composed of two or more distinctly separate regions that have their own properties. Example: a suspension.

homogeneous mixture A mixture existing in only one distinctly separate region with its own properties. Example: a solution.

hormone A steroid, polypeptide chain, or protein that serves as a chemical messenger and is transported by the blood stream.

Hund's rule The rule that states that when electrons fill a sublevel, all orbitals receive one electron before any receive two.

hybridization The process of forming new kinds of orbitals with equal energies from a combination of orbitals of different energies.

hydrate A compound that has water molecules in its crystalline structure. Example: $CaCO_3 \cdot H_2O$.

hydration The process by which water molecules surround and interact with solute particles (the type of solvation in which water molecules act as the solvent).

hydrocarbon An organic compound containing only hydrogen and carbon atoms.

hydrogen bond The electrostatic attraction between an unshared pair of electrons in a highly electronegative atom and a hydrogen atom that is bonded to a different highly electronegative atom.

hydrolysis A reaction in which one molecule is split by the addition of water.

hygroscopic compound Any substance that absorbs water from the air.

hypothesis An educated guess about the solution to a problem; when supported by scientific facts, it may become a theory.

I

ideal gas A hypothetical gas that behaves exactly according to the ideal gas law.

ideal gas law A law of gas behavior that relates pressure, volume, temperature, and amount for any gas at moderate conditions ($PV = nRT$).

immiscible A term describing two liquids that are not soluble in each other.

indicator A substance that changes color when the pH of a solution changes.

inductive reasoning In scientific context, the process of beginning with specific facts or assumptions and drawing a general conclusion.

inner transition metal A member of the lanthanide and actinide series.

inorganic chemistry The study of all elements and compounds other than covalent compounds containing carbon-carbon bonds.

intermolecular force An electrostatic attraction between molecules; it is much weaker than the electrostatic attractions (bonds) that form within molecules.

ion An atom or group of atoms that has acquired an electrical charge by losing or gaining one or more electrons.

ion product constant of water See **autoprotolysis constant of water.**

ionic bond The electrostatic attraction between two oppositely charged ions in a solid.

ionic compound A type of compound that consists of positive and negative ions whose electrical charges hold them together while neutralizing each other.

ionic equation An equation that represents all the substances present during a reaction, including the spectator ions, non-ionic products, and insoluble precipitates.

ionization energy The minimum amount of energy needed to remove an electron from an atom.

irreversible reaction A reaction that proceeds in only one direction: the reactants change into products but not vice versa.

isotope One of two or more atoms of the same element with the same number of protons (atomic number) but with different numbers of neutrons.

isotopic notation A convention that includes the symbol, atomic number, and atomic mass of an element: it specifies the exact composition of an atom.

K

Kelvin scale A temperature scale that divides the range from the freezing point of water (273 K) to the boiling point of water (373 K) into 100 increments and labels absolute zero (0 K) as its zero point; the absolute scale.

ketone Any organic compound of the general form $R_1 - \overset{\overset{\displaystyle O}{\|}}{C} - R_2$, in which an interior carbon double bonds to an oxygen atom.

kinetic energy Energy due to motion.

kinetic theory A theory that states that the particles of matter are in constant motion and that the properties of matter are consequences of that motion; usually used in reference to gases and their properties but sometimes applied to solids and liquids.

kinetics In chemistry, the study of reaction rates and the mechanisms by which reactions occur.

L

lattice energy The energy released when gaseous particles form a crystal.

law A description of the behavior of matter based on the results of many experiments.

law of combining volumes A law of gas behavior that states that gases at the same temperature and pressure react with one another in volume ratios of small whole numbers.

law of definite composition A law that states that every compound has a definite composition by weight.

law of mass conservation A corollary to the first law of thermodynamics: during ordinary physical and chemical processes, mass is neither created nor destroyed.

law of partial pressures A law that states that the total pressure of a mixture of gases equals the sum of the partial pressures.

Le Chatelier's principle The principle that when a system at equilibrium is subjected to stress, the equilibrium is shifted in the direction that relieves the stress.

Lewis acid Any substance that can accept a pair of electrons.

Lewis base Any substance that can donate a pair of electrons.

line spectrum A set of lines, either dark or bright, produced by an element when it is in the gaseous atomic state.

linear An arrangement in which particles are positioned in a straight line.

lipid A member of the large class of biological molecules that are not soluble in water. Examples: fat, oil, wax, steroid, fatty acid.

liquid A state of matter in which the particles have enough energy to partially overcome the attractive forces: the particles of a liquid have a limited "flowing" motion.

lock-and-key theory A theory that maintains that enzymes catalyze reactions by positioning reactants in ideal positions for reactions to occur.

M

main group One of the eight *A* groups in the periodic table that contain elements whose outermost electrons are in *s* or *p* sublevels.

malleability A physical property of matter indicating the capability of matter to be shaped by pounding.

mantissa The part of the scientific notation expression that is the actual measurement, with a decimal point following the first significant figure. Example: 1.200 is the mantissa in 1.200×10^3.

mass A measure of the amount of matter in a given substance.

mass defect The difference between the mass of a nucleus and the sum of the masses of the particles from which it was formed.

matter Anything that occupies space and has mass.

measurement A number that indicates quantity and is followed by a unit.

melting A physical change from the solid to the liquid state.

meniscus The curved upper surface of a column of liquid.

metal An element located to the left of, but not touching, the heavy, stair-step line in the periodic table; an element that is typically malleable, ductile, shiny, and conductive of electricity and that forms positive ions when it gives away its few valence electrons.

metallic hydride A compound in which the oxidation number of hydrogen is -1; formed when hydrogen reacts with an active metal. Examples: LiH, NaH, MgH_2

metalloid An element whose properties lie between those of metals and nonmetals; a compound found along the heavy, stair-step line in the periodic table.

metallurgy The process of extracting metals from their ores and adapting them for commercial use.

millimeters of mercury (mm Hg) A standard unit of pressure derived from the fact that normal atmospheric pressure can support 760 mm Hg in a column.

miscible A term describing two liquids that are soluble in each other.

mixture Two or more pure substances physically combined with no definite proportions.

model A working representation of experimental facts.

molal boiling point elevation constant A number that relates the change in boiling point of a particular solvent to the concentration of solute particles.

molal freezing point depression constant A number that relates the change in freezing point of a particular solvent to the concentration of solute particles.

molality A quantitative measure of concentration equal to the number of moles of solute per kilogram of solvent; m = moles solute/kg solvent.

molar volume of a gas The volume that a mole of gas occupies if it is at standard temperature and pressure: 22.4 ℓ.

molarity A quantitative measure of concentration equal to the number of moles of solute per liter of solution; M = moles solute/ ℓ solution.

mole The amount of substance contained in 6.023×10^{23} units.

molecular compound A compound made of separate, distinct, independent units (molecules).

molecular formula A formula that shows the types of atoms involved and the exact composition of each molecule. Example: C_2H_4.

molecule Two or more covalently bonded atoms found as a separate, distinct, independent unit.

monatomic element An element whose atoms exist independently. Example: noble gases.

monoprotic acid An acid that can donate only one proton.

monosaccharide A three- to six-carbon carbohydrate with attached hydroxyl groups and either an aldehyde or ketone group that cannot be hydrolyzed into simpler compounds. Example: glucose.

N

net ionic equation An equation that shows only the substances actually involved in a reaction and excludes spectator ions.

neutral salt A salt that causes no change in pH when dissolved in water.

neutral solution A solution with equal numbers of H_3O^+ and OH^- ions resulting in a pH of 7.

neutralization reaction The reaction of an acid and a base to produce a neutral (pH = 7) solution of water and a salt.

neutron A neutral particle with a mass of 1.0087 amu found in the nucleus of an atom.

noble gas A family VIII A element, which has a full outer energy level.

nomenclature A system or set of names used by a branch of learning, such as the system of names for compounds in chemistry.

nonelectrolyte A substance that will not conduct electricity when melted or dissolved, because it does not release ions.

nonmetal An element located to the right of, but not touching, the heavy, stair-step line in the periodic table; an element that is nonductile, nonmalleable, and nonconducting, and that usually forms negative ions because it has a strong attraction for its numerous valence electrons.

normality A quantitative measure of concentration equal to the number of equivalents of solute per ℓ of solution; $N = eq/\ell$.

nuclear binding energy The energy required to separate all the protons and neutrons in a specific nucleus from each other; the energy equivalent of the nucleus's mass defect.

nuclear chemistry The study of radioactivity, the nucleus, and the changes the nucleus undergoes.

nuclear equation An equation that identifies the nuclei that react and are produced when nuclei split, fuse, or release radiation.

nuclear fission The process of splitting a massive nucleus, usually with the release of great amounts of energy and two large fragments of comparable mass.

nuclear fusion The process of combining two or more smaller nuclei into one larger nucleus, releasing great amounts of energy.

nucleic acid A large molecule that stores and translates genetic information in living cells and consists of sugar units, nitrogenous bases, and phosphate groups.

nucleotide The "building block" of a DNA or RNA molecule: each block is made of a sugar unit, a phosphate group, and a nitrogenous base (adenine, guanine, cytosine, thymine, or uracil).

nucleus The dense central part of an atom made up of protons and neutrons; the nucleus contains virtually all of the atom's mass but only a small portion of the atomic volume.

O

octet rule The rule that states that an atom tends to gain, lose, or share electrons until its outer level *s* and *p* orbitals are filled with eight electrons: this gives the element the electron configuration of a noble gas.

oil A molecule formed from glycerol and three carboxylic acids in which the carbon chains have a high degree of unsaturation; it differs from a fat in that it is liquid at room temperature, while a fat is solid.

orbital A three-dimensional region of space in which as many as two electrons may exist; sections of the sublevels.

orbital notation A diagrammatic representation that uses dashes and arrows to show the principal energy levels and sublevels for all the electrons in an atom.

organic chemistry The study of compounds containing carbon-to-carbon covalent bonds.

osmosis Diffusion of pure solvent molecules, such as water, through a membrane.

osmotic pressure The pressure required to prevent a solution from gaining water by osmosis.

oxidation A chemical process in which electrons are lost and an oxidation number increases.

oxidation number A number that reflects the charge that an atom in a compound would have if all the bonding electrons were arbitrarily assigned to the most electronegative element.

oxidation-reduction reaction (redox reaction) Any chemical reaction in which electrons transfer or shift: the shift of electrons is shown by changes in oxidation numbers.

oxide A binary compound in which the oxidation number of oxygen is -2. Example: Li_2O.

oxidizing agent The atom or ion that receives electrons during a redox reaction; the substance that causes other substances to be oxidized; the substance that is reduced.

P

peptide bond The bond between an amino group of one amino acid and a carbonyl group of another.

per cent by mass A quantitative measure of concentration in which the mass of the solute is compared to the mass of the solution; per cent composition = mass solute/mass solution.

per cent composition A per cent that gives the relative amount (based on mass) of each element present. Example: There is 52.9% Al and 47.1% O by mass in Al_2O_2.

periodic law The law that states that the properties of elements are a periodic function of their atomic numbers.

periodic table A table in which elements are arranged in order of increasing atomic numbers so that the elements with similar properties fall into the same vertical columns, or families.

period A horizontal row of elements in the periodic table; also called a series.

permeability The property of a substance that allows other substance particles to spread or flow throughout it.

peroxide A compound that contains an oxygen-oxygen bond; the name of the O_2^{-2} ion.

pH A measure of the hydrogium ion (H_3O^+) concentration; the negative logarithm of the H_3O^+ ion concentration: $pH = -\log [H_3O^+]$.

phase diagram A graphic representation of the function of pressure versus temperature; a diagram showing conditions under which a pure substance exists as a solid, liquid, or gas.

physical change A change that alters the physical properties of a substance (state, size) but that does not change its identity.

physical chemistry The foundational theories of chemistry that examine interactions in substances, structure of matter, and energy changes accompanying transformations.

physical property A property of matter that results from the position and characteristics of its particles and that can be measured without causing a change in the identity of the material.

pOH A measure of OH^- ion concentration; the negative logarithm of the OH^- ion concentration: $pOH = -\log [OH^-]$.

polar Having unequally distributed electrical charges.

polar covalent bond A chemical bond that has partially positive and partially negative ends because of unevenly shared electrons. All bonds between nonidentical atoms are polar.

polyatomic compound A compound that contains at least three different elements. Examples: $NaNO_3$ and NH_4OH.

polyatomic element An element whose atoms bond in multiatom units. Example: S_8.

polyatomic ion A group of atoms that maintains a constant electrical charge while existing as a unit in a wide variety of chemical reactions. Example: SO_4^{-2}.

polymer A substance consisting of huge molecules that have repeating structural units.

polymorphous A term describing substances (either elements or compounds) that form more than one crystalline form.

polypeptide A series of many amino acids joined by peptide bonds.

polyprotic acid An acid that can donate more than one proton.

polysaccharide A carbohydrate composed of many monosaccharide units.

post-transition metal A metal found in families IIIA, IVA, or VA in the periodic table.

precipitate A solid that separates from a solution.

precipitation The separation of a solid from a solution.

pressure Average force per unit area.

principal energy level A region around the nucleus containing a specified group of electrons in sublevels and orbitals.

product An element or compound that is produced from a chemical change and is usually written to the right of the arrow in a chemical equation.

protein A complex structure of many amino acids that is joined by peptide bonds and has a molecular mass greater than 10,000 amu.

proton A particle with a +1 charge and a mass of 1.0073 amu in the nucleus of an atom.

protonation The process of gaining a proton. Example: $H_2O + H^+ \longrightarrow H_3O^+$.

pure substance A substance that is made up of only one kind of particle and has uniform composition.

pyramidal An arrangement in which three particles and an unshared electron pair surrounding a central particle are oriented toward the corners of a four-sided pyramid.

Q

quantized A term describing something that has only separate, discrete values.

quantum (pl. *quanta*) A discrete amount of energy.

quantum numbers Four numbers that describe the location of an electron in an atom: the first number identifies the relative size of the principal energy level, the second describes the type of sublevel, the third indicates the direction of the orbital in space, and the fourth describes the spin of an electron.

R

radioactive decay constant A special name for the rate constant that describes how often radioactive decays take place.

radioactive decay series A series of sequential reactions of alpha and beta emissions that changes a larger, unstable nucleus to a smaller, stable nucleus.

radioactivity The spontaneous emission of penetrating rays from nuclei.

Raoult's law The law that states that the lowering of a solvent's vapor pressure is directly proportional to the concentration of solute particles.

rate law A mathematical equation that describes how fast a reaction occurs.

reactant An element or compound that undergoes chemical change and is usually written to the left of the arrow in a chemical equation.

reaction mechanism The series of steps that make up a reaction.

reaction rate The speed at which reactants disappear or products appear in a chemical reaction.

redox reaction Short name for an oxidation-reduction reaction.

reducing agent The atom or ion that supplies electrons during a redox reaction; the substance that causes other substances to be reduced; the substance that is oxidized in a redox reaction.

reduction A chemical process in which electrons are gained and an oxidation number decreases.

reversible reaction A reaction in which the products can change back into the original reactants so that an equilibrium is reached.

Roman numeral system See **Stock system.**

S

salt A compound formed from the positive ions of a base and the negative ions of an acid.

saponification The reaction by which soaps are made from an ester and an aqueous hydroxide: an alcohol and the salt of a large carboxylic acid result.

saturated A term describing a solution that contains the maximum amount of solute possible at a given set of conditions; a term describing an organic compound that contains the maximum possible number of hydrogens; the compound has no double or triple bonds.

science A systematic study of the physical world based on observations.

scientific method A logical method of problem-solving that starts with observations and follows steps.

scientific notation A convenient way of expressing very large and very small numbers as a mantissa between 1 and 10, which is multiplied by 10 raised by some power. Example: 1,200 is 1.200×10^3.

second law of thermodynamics The physical law that states that during any energy transformation, some energy goes to an unusable form.

semipermeable membrane A barrier that allows small particles (ions and molecules) to pass through but that will stop large particles.

semiconductor A substance with an electrical conductivity intermediate between a conductor and an insulator.

significant figures The digits in the numerical value of a measurement that indicate how precise the techniques and devices allow that measurement to be.

single replacement reaction A chemical reaction of the general form $A + BZ \longrightarrow B + AZ$, in which an active element replaces a less active element in a compound.

solid A state of matter in which the particles have relatively little energy and cannot overcome the attractive forces: the particles of a solid remain in fixed positions with set distances between them.

solubility product constant The equilibrium constant for the dissolving of a slightly soluble salt.

solute One of the least abundant substances in a solution; the substance that is dissolved.

solution A homogeneous mixture of two or more substances.

solvation The process in which solvent particles surround and interact with solutes.

solvent The most abundant substance in a solution; the substance that does the dissolving.

specific heat The amount of heat required to raise the temperature of 1 g of a substance 1°C.

spectator ion An ion present on both sides of an ionic equation: it does not actually participate in the reaction.

standard molar enthalpy of formation The enthalpy change for the reaction that produces 1 mole of a compound in its standard state from its elements in their standard states; abbreviated ΔH_f°.

standard state An accepted set of conditions for a substance that specifies temperature, pressure, and concentration; for thermodynamics, the standard state is usually 298 K and 1 atm; for gas laws, it is usually 273 K and 1 atm.

standard temperature and pressure (STP) A set of agreed-upon conditions; for gas laws, standard temperature and pressure are 0°C (or 273 K) and 1 atm (or 760 mm Hg).

starch A mixture of straight and branched polymers of glucose that serves to store energy for plants.

steroid A member of the class of lipids that contains a characteristic set of three six-membered rings and one five-membered ring. Example: cholesterol.

Stock system A convention used to show the oxidation state of a metal ion. Example: The Stock system nomenclature for $CuCl_2$ is copper(II) chloride.

stoichiometry The measurement and calculation of the mass and molar relationships between reactants and products in chemical reactions.

strong acid A substance that gives up protons very easily and ionizes to a great extent in water.

strong base A substance that readily accepts protons.

strong nuclear forces A term used to describe the forces that hold a nucleus together.

structural formula A formula that shows the types of atoms involved, the exact composition of a molecule, and the location of chemical bonds. Example: The structural formula of C_2H_4 is $-\overset{|}{C}=\overset{|}{C}-$.

structural isomers Compounds that have the same molecular formula but different structural formulas.

sublevel A portion of a principal energy level made up of one or more orbitals. Examples: *s, p, d,* and *f* sublevels.

sublimation A physical change directly between the solid and gaseous states; usually refers to the change from solid to gas. Example: solid CO_2 (dry ice) changing to gaseous CO_2.

subscript A number written at the lower right of a chemical symbol in a formula to indicate the number of components immediately preceding it.

substitution reaction A reaction in which one atom or group replaces another atom or group in a molecule.

sulfide A binary compound in which the oxidation number of sulfur is -2. Example: H_2S.

surface tension The apparent "skin" effect on the surface of a liquid due to unbalanced forces on the surface particles.

symbol A one- or two-letter representation for an element.

Systéme Internationale An accepted system of units for physical measurements; the system is based on seven units: the meter, the kilogram, the second, the kelvin, the mole, the ampere (electrical current), and the candela (light intensity).

T

temperature A measure of the average kinetic energy of the atoms, molecules, or ions in matter (measured in degrees).

tetrahedral An arrangement in which four particles surrounding a central particle are oriented toward the corners of a four-sided pyramid.

theory A tested explanation of scientific observations.

thermal energy The measure of the total kinetic energy (motion) of the molecules or ions in matter (usually measured in calories).

thermodynamics The study of energy transformations in chemical and physical processes.

titration The procedure for measuring the capacity of a solution of unknown concentration to combine with one of known concentration.

titration curve A graph that plots the pH change of a solution versus the addition of acids and bases.

torr See **millimeters of mercury.**

transition metal One of the *B* families of metals in the periodic table.

transmutation Any process that converts one element into another. Example: the changing of lead into gold.

transuranium element An element with an atomic number higher than ninety-two.

trigonal planar An arrangement in which three particles surrounding a central particle are oriented toward the corners of a flat triangle.

triple covalent bond A covalent bond in which two atoms share three pairs of electrons. Example: N_2.

triple point The temperature and pressure at which the solid, liquid, and gaseous states of a substance exist in equilibrium.

triprotic acid An acid that can donate three protons.

Tyndall effect The scattering of light by particles in a colloidal dispersion.

U

unit A label, such as "inches" or "meters," used to specify the terms in which a measurement is being reported.

unit analysis A problem-solving tool in which the units of numbers are changed by being multiplied by a conversion factor equal to 1.

unit cell The simplest unit of repetition in a crystal lattice.

universal gas constant The constant R in the ideal gas law ($PV = nRT$) whose value and units depend on the units used for P, V, n, and T. Examples: $83.1\ cm^3 \cdot bar/mole \cdot K = 8.31\ J/mole \cdot K = 0.0821\ \ell \cdot atm/mole \cdot K$.

unsaturated A term describing a solution that contains less than the maximum amount of solute at a given set of conditions; a term describing organic compounds that contain less than the maximum possible number of hydrogen atoms because they have at least one double or triple bond between the carbon atoms.

V

valence bond theory The idea that covalent bonds are formed when orbitals of different atoms overlap.

valence electron The most loosely bound electron, which is usually found in the outermost energy level.

Valence Shell Electron Pair Repulsion theory A theory that states that because of electron-electron repulsion, the electron orbitals in molecules are arranged so that they are as far apart as possible.

vapor pressure The pressure exerted by a gaseous substance that is a liquid or a solid at room temperature.

viscosity The thickness of a liquid or the ability of a liquid to resist flowing.

vitamin A micronutrient that is required by the body for normal metabolism, growth, and development and is acquired through the diet.

voltaic cell An electrochemical cell in which a spontaneous redox reaction produces electricity.

W

water of hydration The water molecules held in some definite molar ratio to the rest of the substance; if the hydrate is a crystal, the water is often called the water of crystallization.

weak acid A substance that does not give up protons easily and does not ionize very much in water.

weak base A substance that is a poor proton acceptor.

INDEX

A

absolute zero, 28
acetaminophen, 153
acetic acid, 310, 324, 330, 335, 402-3
acetone, 401
  boiling point, 266
acetylene, 389
acid-base reactions
  equivalents, 263
  See also **titration, neutralization.**
acid dissociation constant, 337-41, 403
acidic anhydrides, 247
acid rain, 92, 336-37
acids, 162, 327-47
  carboxylic, 401-3
  definitions of, 327-30
  diprotic, 340
  monoprotic, 340
  nomenclature, 133, 135, 138-39
  polyprotic, 340
  properties of, 330
  strengths of, 338
  strong, 335
  weak, 335
acid salt, 344
activated complex, 293
activation energy, 293-94
activity series, 163-64, 330
  halogens, 164
  metals, 163-64
addition reaction, 407
adenine, 438-41
adsorption, 272
air, 190
  density of, 197
air pollution, 336-37
Alaskan pipeline, 372
alchemy, 7, 458
alcohol, 315-16, 397-99
aldehydes, 400, 405
aliphatic compounds, 382
alkali metals, 85
alkaline earth metals, 86
alkane, 383-88, 405
alkene, 388-89, 405
alkyl group, 396, 403
alkyl halide, 396
alkyne, 389-90, 405
allotrope, 217
alloy, 254, 372
alpha decay, 456-57
alpha particles, 47, 447-48, 450
aluminum, 88
  in soil, 336
  production, 368-69
  uses, 89
aluminum sulfate, 145, 147
amides, 404-5
amines, 404-5
amino acids, 424-27
  evolution, 357
ammonia, 144, 329, 339
  equilibrium, 309, 313-14, 316-17
  formation of, 195, 316-17
  molecular shape of, 112
  pH of, 333
  reaction, 290
ammonium chloride, 290
ammonium ion, 329
  electron-dot structure, 107-8
amorphous solids, 210-11, 213
amphiprotic substances, 340-42
analytical chemistry, 9-10, 141
anesthetic, 399
anhydrides, 246
  metal oxides, 246-47
  nonmetal oxides, 246-47
anion, 65, 367-74
  in salts, 343-44
anode, 367-74
antacid, 343-44
antilog, 334, 476
apothecaries, 5
apple juice
  pH of, 333
applied science, 12
argon, 94, 182, 191
aromatic compounds, 382
Arrhenius, Svante, 327
arsenic, 89, 140-41
aryl halide, 396
ascorbic acid, 435
aspirin, 153, 395
atmosphere, 179, 191
  early, 357-58
atmospheric pressure, 192
  effect on boiling, 225-26
atom, 22, 42-67
atomic bomb, 460
atomic mass, 63
atomic mass number, 61-62
atomic mass unit, 61-62, 142
atomic models, 43-54
atomic number, 62
atomic theory, 44-45
Aufbau principle, 58-60
autoprotolysis constant of water, 331
autoprotolysis of water, 331
Avogadro, Amedeo, 194-95
Avogadro's number, 139-44
Avogadro's principle, 194

B

Bacon, Francis, 7, 314
baking soda, 324
balancing chemical equations, 158-60
  half-reaction method, 359-63
  limitations, 160
barium sulfate, 325
barometer, 179
bases, 327-47
  definitions of, 327-30
  properties of, 330
  strengths of, 335, 338
basic anhydrides, 247
basic salt, 344
batteries, 369-73

bauxite, 368
Becquerel, Henri, 445
bee stings, 402
benzene, 392-95
formation of, 280
beri-beri, 435
beta particles, 448, 450, 456-57, 461
binary acids, 138
binary compounds, 134
biochemistry, 9-10, 415-41
bleach, 359
blood
pH of, 347
Bohr, Niels, 48
model of atom, 48-49, 53
boiling, 225-26
boiling point elevation, 265-66
Bonaparte, Napoleon, 140-41
bonds, 99-122, 277
coordinate covalent, 106
covalent, 104-6
double, 104
enthalpy, 284
ionic, 101-3
metallic, 108-9
polar covalent, 115-16
properties of, 122
quantum model of, 108-9
stability of, 284
triple covalent, 105
types of, 100-101, 122
boric acid, 330, 333, 338
boron, 88-89
Boyle, Robert, 7, 181, 315
Boyle's law, 181, 184-85
brass, 254
bright-line spectra, 49-50
bromine, 93
bond enthalpy, 284
properties of, 93
reaction of, 263
test for unsaturation, 408
Brönsted, J. N., 328
bronze, 4
Brownian movement, 271-72
Brown, Robert, 271
buffers, 346-47
buret, 345
butane, 383-85

C

calcium, 156, 246
calcium chloride, 267
formation of, 102
freezing point of solution, 268
calorie, 28, 229
calorimeter, 280
capillary rise, 221
carbohydrates, 416-24
carbon, 89-90, 209-10
bonding, 380-81
charcoal, 89-90
forms of, 89-90
hybridization of, 110-11
physical properties of, 90
uses, 90
carbon-14
radioactive dating, 455
carbonated drink, 162, 257
carbon dioxide, 182-83
empirical formula, 149
solutions of, 257
carbonic acid
in blood, 347
carbonic anhydrase, 434
carbon monoxide, 183, 324
carbon tetrachloride, 209, 396
electron-dot structure, 105
nonpolar bonds of, 116
carbonyl group, 400-401
carboxylic acid, 315-16, 401-3, 405, 425
catalyst, 158, 298, 316
See also **enzyme.**
catalytic converter, 298, 393
cathode, 367-74
cathode rays, 45-46
cation, 65, 367-74
in salts, 343-44
Cavendish, Henry, 84
cellulose, 416, 420-23
Celsius scale, 28
Chadwick, James, 48
chain reactions, 459-60
charcoal, 89
Charles's law, 185-87
chemical
bonds, 99-122
changes, 20
equations, 156-60
properties, 20
reactions, 20-21
symbols, 22-24
chemistry,
history of, 4-11
major branches of, 10
study of, 11
vocational application, 12-13
chitin, 416
chlorine, 92-94, 183
covalent bonding of, 104
in redox reactions, 354, 356
production of, 368-69
chloroacetophenone, 183
chloroform, 396
cholesterol, 433
chromosomes, 437
citric acid, 330, 420
classification
of matter, 20-26
of organic compounds, 382-83, 405
clone, 415
coal, 382
dust, 296-97
coefficients, 157, 166
coffee
pH of, 333
colligative properties, 264-70
boiling point elevation, 265-66
decreased vapor pressure, 264
freezing point depression, 267-68
osmotic pressure, 269-70
Raoult's law, 264
collisions
in gases, 177-78
collision theory
of reactions, 292-99, 434
colloids, 270-72
combined gas laws, 189-90
combustion, 406
spontaneous, 296-97
common ion effect, 321
composition reactions, 161
compounds, 24-25
number of, 380
compression
of gases, 227-28
concentration
effect on equilibrium, 311-12
effect on reaction rate, 295
condensation, 223, 226
condensation reactions, 408
conductivity, 20
conjugate acid, 328
conjugate base, 328
conservation, 278
See also **first law of thermodynamics.**
continuous spectrum, 49
conversion factor, 33
coordinate covalent bond, 106, 329
copper sulfate, 263
corrosion, 372-73
covalent bond, 104-6
of carbon, 381

Creation, 278, 373
critical mass, 460
critical pressure, 228
critical temperatures, 227-28
critical thought, 5-6
cryogenics, 228-29
cryosurgery, 228-29
crystal, 102, 210, 212-19
crystalline structures, 213-16
Curie, Marie and Pierre, 169, 446
cyclic aliphatic compounds, 391
cytosine, 438

D

Dalton, John, 23, 44-45
Dalton's law of partial pressures, 190-93
DDT, 395
Dead Sea, 261
decomposition reactions, 161-62
deductive reasoning, 2
deliquescence, 249-50
delocalized electrons, 394
Democritus, 44
denature, 399
density, 20
  of gases, 197-98
  of water, 240
descriptive chemistry, 82-95
desiccator, 249
diamond, 89, 218-19
  oxidation of, 290
diatomic elements, 22, 107
dimethyl ether, 380
dipeptide, 426
dipole-dipole interactions, 120
dipole moment, 117
disaccharides, 418-20
dispersion forces, 121, 431-32
displacement reactions, 162
dissociation, 254
dissolving
  and equilibria, 306
  mechanism, 254-55
distillation, 226
  fractional, 384, 393
DNA, 438-41
Dobereiner, Johann, 71-72
double bonds, 104
  in fats, 431
double replacement reaction, 164-65, 322
Downs cell, 368-69
dry cell, 371
dry ice, 213
drying agent, 249

E

ecology, 92, 337, 465
efflorescence, 249-50
Egypt, 5
Einstein, Albert, 459
electrochemical cell, 367
electrode, 367-74
electrolysis, 244-45, 367-69
electrolyte, 366-74
electron affinity, 80
electron configuration, 58-60
  from the periodic table, 77-78
electron-dot structure, 65, 105-6
  of polyatomic ions, 107
electronegativity, 81
  in bonding, 100-101
  in hydrogen bonds, 120
  of carbon, 381
electrons, 46-47
  as waves, 53-54
  electrostatic attraction, 78
  in quantum model, 54-61
  octet rule, 100
  oxidation numbers, 127-32
electron-sea theory, 108-9
electron spin, 61
electroplating, 374-75
element, 22
empirical formulas, 146-50
emulsion, 272
endothermic, 255, 279-84
energy, 26-30
  in bonds, 277, 284
  transformations, 278
energy diagrams, 291
engine
  automobile, 392-93
enthalpy, 279-84, 288-90
  of formation, 280-84
entropy, 285-90
enzyme, 423-24, 430, 434
  in honey, 420
Epsom salts, 132, 153
equations, 156-57
  ionic, 165
  special symbols, 157-58
equilibrium, 305-22
  autoprotolysis, 331
  forms of monosaccharides, 417-18
  vaporization, 223
equilibrium constant, 308-12
equivalents, 262-63
ester, 315-16, 403, 405
  formation of, 408
esterification, 408
ethane, 383-85
  combustion of, 160
ethanol, 380
ether, 399-400, 405
  formation of, 408
ethics, 228-29, 415
evaporation, 222-23
  equilibria, 306
evolution, 315, 358
exothermic, 255, 278
explosives, 316

F

faith
  of scientists, 314-15
Faraday, Michael, 393
fats, 409, 431-33
fatty acid, 402, 406, 431
ferrous sulfate, 153
fertilizer, 270, 316
film, 353-55
first law of thermodynamics, 26, 278
flavoring, 315-16, 400, 403
fluorine, 92-94
  dipole moment, 117
  reaction with water, 246
fog, 270-71
formaldehyde, 400
formic acid, 402
formula, 24, 145-50
  empirical, 146
  molecular, 145, 380
  per cent composition, 146
  structural, 145, 380
formula units, 103
fossil fuels, 336
  See also **coal.**
fractional distillation, 384
  of gasoline, 393
fragrance, 403
free energy, 288-90
free-energy change, 288-90
freezing, 29, 211-13
  of cells, 229
freezing point depression, 267-68
freon, 396
fructose, 417-18
functional groups, 396
fusion, 463

G

Galileo, 1
galvanization, 372-75
gamma emission, 451
gamma rays, 449
gases, 29-30, 177-204
and pressure, 178-80
and temperature, 179-80
and volume, 179-80
collection, 192
critical values of, 227-28
densities of, 197-98
from batteries, 373
ideal, 201
kinetic description of, 177-78, 201
mixtures of, 190, 192-93
molar volume, 195-97, 201
physical properties of, 178-79
stoichiometric conversions, 199-200
sublimation, 211
gas laws, 181, 184-90, 192-93
gasoline, 392-93
gastric juice
pH of, 333
Gay-Lussac, Joseph, 93, 193-94
Gay-Lussac's law, 187-88
Geiger counter, 448
genes, 437
genetic engineering, 415
Gibbs, J. Willard, 288
glass, 211
glucose, 417-18
glycerol, 398-99, 431
glycine, 441
glycogen, 423
gold, 7, 254, 458
grain dust, 297
gram-atomic mass, 144-45
gram-equivalent mass, 263, 345, 364
gram-formula mass, 144-45
gram-molecular mass, 144-45
of gases, 197-204
graphite, 89
Greek prefix system, 133
Greeks, 5-6
groups
alkali metals (IA), 85
alkaline earth metals (IIA), 86-87
halogens (VIIA), 92-94
hydrogen, 84-85
nitrogen and phosphorus (VA), 90-91
noble gases (VIIIA), 94-95
oxygen and sulfur (VIA), 91-92
post-transition metals, 88-89
transition metals, 87
guanine, 438
gunpowder, 277

H

Haber, Fritz, 316
Haber process, 316-17
half-life, 452
half-reaction, 360
balancing equations, 359-63
Hall-Heroult process, 368
halogens, 92-94
activity series, 163
diatomic molecules, 107
oxidation numbers, 128
reactions, 163, 246
hard water, 86
heartburn, 343
heat of condensation, 226
heat of fusion, 212
heat of reaction See **enthalpy.**
heat of vaporization, 223
Heisenberg uncertainty principle, 53
Heisenberg, Werner, 53
helium, 50, 94-95, 182, 197
See also **alpha particles.**
helix
DNA, 438
in starch, 420-21
protein, 427, 430
hemoglobin, 429
Henry's law, 258
Hess's law, 282
heterogeneous mixtures, 26
hexane, 386
Hindenburg, 84
Hiroshima, 445
homogeneous mixtures, 26
honey, 420
hormones, 436-37
Hund's rule, 59-60
hybridization, 110-11
hydrates, 137, 162, 248-49
hydration, 255
hydrocarbons, 382-83
hydrofluoric acid, 339
hydrogen, 84-85
bond, 120, 236-37, 427-28, 438
density of, 197
formation of, 330
liquid, 227
molecular velocity of, 180
oxidation number, 128
reactions, 163, 193-94, 294
hydrogen bomb, 461, 464
hydrogen bond See **hydrogen.**
hydrogen carbonate, 347
hydrogen cyanide, 183
hydrogen sulfide, 183
hydrolysis reaction, 409
hydronium ion, 328
hydroxide ions
in bases, 327-47
hydroxides, 161
hygroscopic compounds, 249
hypothesis, 2-4

I

ideal gases, 201
ideal gas law, 202-4
immiscible, 254
indicators, 341-43
inductive reasoning, 2
inert gases, 94
inner transition metals, 87
inorganic chemistry, 9-10
insecticide, 395
intermolecular forces, 120-22
dipole-dipole interactions, 120
in alkenes, 389
in fats, 431
International Union of Pure and Applied Chemistry (IUPAC), 132, 384
iodine, 93-94
reactions, 294
sublimation of, 213
iodine chloride, 294
ionic bonds, 101-3
ionic compounds, 102-3
nomenclature, 134-37
ionic equation, 165
ionization energy, 80
ions, 65, 327
nomenclature, 134-37
spectator, 165
iron, 372-73
isomers
structural, 387-88
isotopes, 62-64
isotopic notation, 62-63, 449-65

J

Jabir ibn-Hayyan (Geber), 7
jelly, 420
Joliot, Irene and Frederic, 169

K

Kekule, August, 394
Kelvin, Lord, 315
Kelvin scale, 28, 185
ketone, 401, 405
kilocalorie, 28
kinetic energy, 27
kinetics, 290-300, 305
kinetic theory, 28-29, 177-78, 201

L

lactic acid, 296, 330, 419
lactose, 296, 418-20, 424
laser, 461
lattice energy, 217
lattice structures, 214-15
laughing gas, 182, 324
Lavoisier, Antoine, 8-9, 168
Lavoisier, Marie Anne, 168
law of combining volumes, 194
law of definite proportion, 194
law of energy conservation, 26
law of mass conservation, 27
laws, 4
lead, 7, 211, 458
  oxidation number, 131
lead chromate, 165
leaded gasoline, 393
Le Chatelier, Henri, 311
Le Chatelier's principle, 311-17
lemon juice, 420
  pH of, 333
Lewis, Gilbert N., 329
light, 459
limestone, 87, 337
lime water, 333
line spectrum, 49-50
linseed oil, 432
lipids, 430-33
liquefaction, 29, 118, 227-28
  See also **condensation.**
liquid, 29-30, 220-30
  distillation, 226-27
  kinetic description, 220
lithium, 85
litmus, 330
lock-and-key model, 298, 434
logarithm, 332
Long, Crawford, 399
Lowry, T. M., 328

M

magnesium, 86
  reaction with acid, 163
  reaction with oxygen, 291-93
malleability, 20
maltose, 418-20
mantissa, 36
mass composition, 146-50
mass defect, 462-65
matter
  classification of, 19-29
  energy in, 26-30
  measurement of, 30-37
  states of, 28-30
mayonnaise, 272
measurements, 30
measure of concentrations, 259-64
  equivalents, 262-63
  molality, 260
  molarity, 260, 262
  normality, 262-64
melting, 29, 211-13
melting points, 212-13
Mendeleev, Dmitri, 72-73
meniscus, 221
mercury, 87
  in barometer, 179
  reaction with gold, 254
metal carbonates, 162
metal chlorates, 161
metal hydroxides, 162
  production of, 246
metallic bonding, 108-9
metallic hydrides, 85, 132
metallurgy, 4
metal oxides, 161, 246-47
metals, 76
  activity series of, 163
  in ionic bonds, 101
  in metallic bonding, 108-9
  purification of, 368-69
methane, 339, 383
  combustion, 283, 290
  molecular shape, 112
  physical states, 30
methanol, 324, 399
milk, 333, 419, 424
milk of magnesia, 333
Miller, Stanley, 358
miracles, 278
miscible, 254
mixtures, 21, 25-26
molal boiling point elevation constant, 265
molal freezing point depression constant, 267
molality, 262
  See also **colligative properties.**
molarity, 260
molar volume of a gas, 195-97, 201
mole, 139-50
  conversion factors, 143
  stoichiometric conversions, 166-67
molecular formula, 145, 380
molecular orbital theory, 118-19
molecular shapes, 111-16
molecule, 25, 116
monatomic elements, 22
monosaccharides, 417-18
mothballs, 395
muscles, 430

N

Nagasaki, 460
natural gas, 386
neon, 94-95
neptunium, 461
nerve gas, 183
net ionic equations, 165
neutralization reactions, 165
  acids and bases, 343-47
  See also **titration.**
neutral salt, 344
neutrinos, 463
neutrons, 48, 450
Newlands, John, 72
nitrogen, 90-91, 95, 182, 191
  liquid, 228-29
nitrogen oxide
  reaction with oxygen, 158-59
nitrous oxide, 182
noble gases, 94-95
Noddack, Ida and Walter, 169
nomenclature, 132-39
  flow chart of, 133
  of binary acids, 138
  of binary compounds, 134
  of hydrates, 137
  of organic compounds, 384, 405
  of polyatomic ions, 134-36
  of ternary acids, 138-39
nonelectrolyte, 366
nonmetal oxides
  acid anhydrides, 246-47
nonmetals, 76
  covalent bonding, 104-6
  ionic bonds, 101
  multiple oxidation states, 130

nonpolar molecules
intermolecular forces, 120-22
normality, 262, 345-46, 364
nuclear binding energy, 462-65
nuclear chemistry, 9-10
nuclear equations, 450-51
nuclear fallout, 465
nuclear fission, 458-60
nuclear fusion, 461-62
nuclear power, 337
safety, 465
nuclear weapons, 465
nucleic acids, 437-41
nucleotides, 437-41
nucleus, 48, 445, 453

O

oceans, 268-69
octane numbers, 392-93
octet rule, 100
oil, 384, 431-33
Oparin, A. I., 357
orange juice, 333
orbital notation, 58-60
orbitals, 53-58
organic chemistry, 9-10, 379-410
osmosis, 269
osmotic pressure, 269-70
oxidation, 353-65
oxidation number, 127-32
metallic hydrides, 132
multiple, 130, 136
peroxides, 132
polyatomic ions, 131
rules, 127-28, 131
oxidation-reduction reactions, 353-75, 406
oxides, 92, 161
oxidizing agent, 356
oxyacids, 161
oxyanions, 134-35
oxygen, 91-92, 182, 191
discovery of, 8, 91
in redox reactions, 354
in the blood stream, 430
origin of, 357-58
oxidation number of, 128
reaction with magnesium, 291-93
test for, 295
ozone, 91-92, 360

P

palladium, 3
Paracelsus, Philippus, 7
paraffin, 386
partial charges, 115
partial pressures, 190-93
particle accelerators, 458
Pauling, Linus, 81
pentane
isomers, 387
peptide bond, 426-30
perbromic acid, 139
per cent by mass, 259
per cent composition, 146-49
perfumes, 393, 395
periodic table, 71-95
chart, 74-75
history of, 71-73
parts of, 76-77
periodic trends, 78-82
atomic radii, 78-79
electron affinity, 80
electronegativity, 81
ionic radii, 78-79
ionization energy, 80
periods, 78
peroxides, 132
petroleum, 384, 391
pH meter, 333
pH scale, 332-35, 344-47
phase diagram, 239
Philistines, 5
philosophy, 1
Phoenicians, 5
phosphate
in DNA, 438-41
ion, 135
phosphoric acid, 165
phosphorus, 90-91
photography, 353-55, 446
photosynthesis, 279, 358
physical changes, 20-21
physical chemistry, 9-10
physical properties, 20
plastic, 397
pleated sheet, 428-30
plum-pudding model, 47
pOH scale, 332-35
polar bonds, 115-17
polar molecules, 116
intermolecular forces, 120-22
polarity, 384, 398
polonium, 168
polyatomic compounds, 136
polyatomic elements, 22
polyatomic ions, 107-8, 131, 134-36
polyester, 408
polymers, 408
polymorphs, 217
polypeptide, 426
polysaccharides, 420-23
polyunsaturated, 432
polyvinyl chloride, 397
post-transition metals, 88-89
potassium, 85
reaction with water, 246, 328
potassium hydroxide, 328
potassium permanganate, 365
potassium uranyl sulfate, 446
precipitate, 157, 322-23
pressure, 178-80
atmospheric, 192
Boyle's law, 181, 184-85
effect on equilibrium, 312-13
effect on solubility, 258
Gay-Lussac's law, 187-88
law of partial pressures, 190, 192-93
measurement of, 179
vapor, 192
pressure cooker, 225
Priestley, Joseph, 8, 91
principal energy levels, 49, 52-53
capacity of, 56
possible sublevels, 56
problem solving, 31
products, 157
propane, 383-86
proteins, 424-30
proton, 48
in acids, 327
protonation, 328
pure science, 12
pure substances, 21-22
pyramidal, 112

Q

qualitative analysis, 82
quantitative analysis, 83
quantized, 49
quantum model, 53-61
bonding, 109-22
valence bond theory, 109-10
Valence Shell Electron Pair Repulsion theory, 111
quantum numbers, 60-61

R

R, universal gas constant, 201
radioactive age-dating, 454
potassium-argon, 455
uranium-lead, 455
radioactive decay constants, 452

radioactive decay series, 451
radioactivity, 445-53
radium, 168
Raleigh, Lord, 94
Raoult's law, 264
rate law, 299-300, 308
rates of reactions, 294-300
reactants, 157
reaction mechanisms, 298-99
reactions, 161-65
  composition, 161
  decomposition, 161-62
  double replacement, 164-65
  oxidation-reduction, 353-75
  rates, 294-300
  single replacement, 162-64
  spontaneous, 277, 288-90
  See also **equilibrium.**
red blood cells, 430
redox reactions, 353-75
reducing agent, 356
reduction, 353-65
refining, 393
rhenium, 169
rhodium, 3
rickets, 435
RNA, 438-41
Roentgen, Wilhelm, 47
Roman numeral system, 136
rubbing alcohol, 254
Rutherford, Daniel, 90
Rutherford, Ernest, 47-48, 460
  model of atom, 47-48

S

saliva, 333
salt, 85, 161
  formation of, 343-44
  solubility product constants, 318-23
  types of, 344
salt bridge, 370
saponification, 409
sarin, 183
saturated, 257, 383, 431
science, 2-4
scientific law, 2-4
scientific method, 2-4
scientific notation, 36-37
scrubbers, 337
scurvy, 435
seawater, 333
second law of thermodynamics, 27
semiconductors, 88
shampoo, 332-33
SI, Système International, 32
sickle cell anemia, 430
significant figures, 34-35
silicon, 89
silver, 353-55
silver chloride, 320-21
silver nitrate, 322
single replacement reactions, 162-64
soap, 330, 333, 403, 409
soda ash, 132
sodium, 85
  freezing point of, 268
  production of, 368-69
  reactions, 163, 263
sodium carbonate, 132
sodium chloride
  crystal structure, 102-3
  dipole-dipole interaction, 120
  formation of, 101-2
  hydration of, 256
  unit cell, 216
sodium hydroxide, 246
sodium sulfate, 249
solidification, 29
solids, 28-30, 209-19
  amorphous, 210-11, 213
  crystalline, 210, 212-19
  freezing of, 211-13
  kinetic description of, 209-10
  melting of, 211-13
  properties of, 209-10
  sublimation of, 213
solubility, 255-57
  effect of pressure, 258
  effect of temperature, 258
  factors that affect, 257-58
  graph, 259
  Henry's law, 258
  of salts, 318-23
solutes, 253
  effects on solutions, 264-70
  polar, 255-56
solution, 253-72
  acidic, 333
  basic, 333
  concentrated, 259
  dilute, 259
  dissociation of, 254-55
  electrolytic, 366-69
  equilibria, 257
  measuring concentration of, 259-64
  molality, 262
  molarity, 260, 262
  normality, 262-64
  per cent by mass, 259
  rates of, 257-58
  saturated, 257
  solvation, 255
  types of, 253-54
  unsaturated, 257
  See also **acids** and **bases.**
solvation, 255
solvent, 253
  polar, 255-56
Sorensen, S. P. L., 332
specific heat, 229-30
spectator ions, 165
spectroscopy, 49-52
spontaneous reactions, 277, 288-90
standard conditions
  gas laws, 181
  thermodynamics, 280
standard molar enthalpy of formation, 280-83
starches, 419-22
sterling silver, 374
steroids, 432-33
stewardship, 337, 465
Stock system, 136
  flow chart, 171
  gas, 193
  stoichiometry, 165-71
STP, standard conditions, 181
strong nuclear forces, 456
structural formula, 145, 380
structural isomers, 387-88
sublevels, 54-58
  energies of, 57-58
  in periodic table, 77
  types of, 55-56
sublimation, 29, 213
subscripts, 24
substituted hydrocarbons, 396-405
substitution reaction, 162, 406
sucrose, 418-20
sugar, 419
  hydration of, 255
sulfate ion
  nomenclature, 135-37
  oxidation number of, 131
sulfides, 92
sulfur, 91-92
  allotropic forms, 217
  oxides, 336-37
sulfur dioxide, 183
sulfuric acid, 330
  in batteries, 371
Sumerians, 4
sun, 461

supercritical mass, 460
surface area
effect on reaction rate, 296
surface tension, 220-22
symbols, 157
synthesis reactions
composition reactions, 161
Système International, 32

T

tear gas, 183
technecium, 169
Teflon, 397
temperature, 27, 179-80
calorie, 229
Charles's law, 185-87
critical, 227-28
effect on equilibrium, 313-14
effect on reaction rate, 295
effect on solubility, 258
Gay-Lussac's law, 187-88
Kelvin scale, 185
specific heat, 229-30
ternary acids, 138-39
tetrahedral, 112
theory, 2-3
theory of relativity, 459
thermal energy, 27
thermodynamics, 26-27, 277-91, 305
Thomson, J. J., 45
model of atom, 45-47
thymine, 438
tin can, 372-73
titration, 337
acid-base, 344-46
redox, 363-65
titration curve, 345
TNT, 278, 395
tomato juice, 333
torr, 179
Torricelli, Evangelista, 179
transition metals, 87
transmutation, 460
transuranium elements, 460
trigonal planar, 113
triple covalent bonds, 105
triple point
of water, 239
Tyndall effect, 271
Tyndall, John, 271

U

ultraviolet radiation, 358
unit analysis, 33
unit cell, 215-16
units, 30
universal gas constant, 202
unsaturated, 257, 388
uracil, 438
uranium, 450
urine, 333

V

valence bond theory, 109-10
valence electrons, 64-65
in bonding, 99-109
Valence Shell Electron Pair Repulsion theory (VSEPR), 111
value judgments, 3
vanillin, 395
vapor pressure, 192, 223-34
of water, 192
vinegar, 259, 333, 402
viscosity, 222
vitamin C, 435
vitamins, 434-36
volcanos, 358
Volta, Alessandro, 369
voltaic cell, 369
volume, 179-80
Boyle's law, 181, 184-85
Charles's law, 185-87
water, 240

W

warming curve, 212-13
specific heat, 230
water, 162, 235-50, 339
acid-base reactions, 244
amphiprotic, 340
anhydrides, 246-47
autoprotolysis, 331
boiling points of, 237-38
combustion, 244
covalent bonding of, 104
crystal structure of ice, 241
electrolysis, 244-45
enthalpy of formation, 279-80
hydrates, 137, 248-49
hydration, 255
hydrogen bonding, 237
in compounds, 247-49
melting point, 237-38
molecular shape, 113, 235
per cent composition, 146
properties of, 237-41
purification, 242-43
reactions, 244, 246-47
stability of, 244
surface tension, 241
triple point, 239
vapor, 182
warming curve, 212
water of hydration, 249
wetness, 221
wheat, 420
Whitehead, Alfred North, 453
Wohler, Friedrich, 9, 382
Wollaston, William, 3
wood, 416, 420-24
See also **cellulose.**

X

x-rays, 47, 325, 445-46

Z

zinc, 163, 263
galvanization, 374
zinc hydroxide, 320

Photo Credits

Cover: Unusual Films
Title Page: John Wolsieffer; Eastman Chemicals Division (insets)
Alcoa: 88, 368
American Chemical Society: 48
APV Crepaco, Incorporated: 225
Australian Creation Research Society: 109, 416 (right)
Bethlehem Steel: 20, 87, 297
Billings Energy Corporation: 244
Brinkman Instruments Corporation, Division of Sybron Corporation: 260
Roger Bruckner: 306 (bottom)
Stephen Christopher: 42, 304, 420 (bottom)
George Collins: 9, 12 (b), 13 (c), 18, 126, 176, 208, 242 (top), 352, 414
Consulate General of Israel: 261 (bottom)
Cryogenic Technology, Incorporated: 227
Department of Energy: 371, 374, 464
Diamond Information Center: 90 (inset)
Duracell, Incorporated: 193 (bottom), 373 (right)
The Ealing Corporation: 440
Eastman Chemicals Division: 11, 70, 82-83, 93, 98, 148, 243, 252, 271, 276, 311, 326, 378, 382, 397, 435, 459
Eastman Kodak Company: 354 (bottom)
E.M. Laboratories: 343 (top)
Fisher Scientific Company: 7 (top), 8
Ford Motor Company: 392 (bottom)
Robert Franklin: 154
General Electric Company: 95
W.R. Grace & Company: 316
Grumman Aerospace Corporation: 86 (b)
Steve Hicklin: 90 (top), 221 (a), 229, 254, 306 (top), 336, 386 (a), 393
Jones & Laughlin Steel Corporation: 375
Photo Courtesy Lawrence Livermore National Laboratory: x, 444, 461
Arthur P. Little, Incorporated: 118
Luray Caverns, Va.: 86 (a)
Morton-Norwich Products, Incorporated: 343 (bottom)
Morton Salt, Division of Morton Thickol: 103
NASA: 26, 191, 201, 228, 241, 269
National Accelerator Laboratory: 458
National Archives: 84, 337 (bottom)
National Institute of Health: 12 (a)
National Park Service—
Photo by Cecil Stoughton: 29
Photo by Richard Frear: 416 (left), 455
Naval Photographic Center: 94, 178, 240 (right), 242 (bottom)
Naval Research Laboratory: 333
Parke-Davis Division of Warner-Lambert Company: 5, 7 (bottom), 168
PPG Industries: 369
Redwood Empire Association: 92
Royal Swedish Academy: 328 (top)
Sergeant Welch Scientific Company: 453
The Smithsonian Institution: 446
South African Tourism Board: 218-19
The Standard Oil Company: 392 (top)
Union Carbide Corporation: 337 (top), 389
United States Geological Survey: 194
Unusual Films: 13 (a, b), 36, 85, 90 (bottom), 107-8, 132, 142, 155 (a, b, d, e), 161-62, 165, 181, 187, 192, 193 (top), 211, 213, 217, 220, 221 (b, c), 222, 226, 240 (left), 246-50, 257, 259, 261 (top), 263, 265, 267, 278, 285, 287, 290, 295, 321, 328 (bottom), 329-30, 345, 354 (top), 359, 365-66, 372, 373 (left), 386 (b, c), 396, 398, 406, 408, 420 (top), 424, 432
U.S. Atomic Commission: 460
USDA: 155 (c), 296
Vermont Travel Division: 423
John Wolsieffer: 15, 234
Zion National Park, Utah—
Photo by Allen Hagood: 360